CHESTERTON FICTION COLLECTION

*The Napoleon of Notting Hill, The Man Who Was Thursday,
The Ball and the Cross, Manalive, The Man Who Knew
Too Much*

G.K. CHESTERTON

Dear Dad,

Chesterton's fiction is delightful,
funny, dry, and engaging — the
perfect thing to celebrate your
80th. We love you and we're
so happy to get to spend this
time with you. Love, Ka & Bay

⚜

CONTENTS

THE NAPOLEON OF
NOTTING HILL

TO HILAIRE BELLOC

For every tiny town or place
God made the stars especially;
Babies look up with owlish face
And see them tangled in a tree:
You saw a moon from Sussex Downs,
A Sussex moon, untravelled still,
I saw a moon that was the town's,
The largest lamp on Campden Hill.

Yea; Heaven is everywhere at home
The big blue cap that always fits,
And so it is (be calm; they come
To goal at last, my wandering wits),
So is it with the heroic thing;
This shall not end for the world's end,
And though the sullen engines swing,
Be you not much afraid, my friend.

This did not end by Nelson's urn
Where an immortal England sits—
Nor where your tall young men in turn
Drank death like wine at Austerlitz.
And when the pedants bade us mark
What cold mechanic happenings
Must come; our souls said in the dark,
"Belike; but there are likelier things."

Likelier across these flats afar
These sulky levels smooth and free
The drums shall crash a waltz of war
And Death shall dance with Liberty;
Likelier the barricades shall blare
Slaughter below and smoke above,
And death and hate and hell declare
That men have found a thing to love.

Far from your sunny uplands set
I saw the dream; the streets I trod
The lit straight streets shot out and met
The starry streets that point to God.
This legend of an epic hour
A child I dreamed, and dream it still,
Under the great grey water-tower
That strikes the stars on Campden Hill.
G. K. C.

BOOK I

1. INTRODUCTORY REMARKS ON THE ART OF PROPHECY

The human race, to which so many of my readers belong, has been playing at children's games from the beginning, and will probably do it till the end, which is a nuisance for the few people who grow up. And one of the games to which it is most attached is called "Keep to-morrow dark," and which is also named (by the rustics in Shropshire, I have no doubt) "Cheat the Prophet." The players listen very carefully and respectfully to all that the clever men have to say about what is to happen in the next generation. The players then wait until all the clever men are dead, and bury them nicely. They then go and do something else. That is all. For a race of simple tastes, however, it is great fun.

For human beings, being children, have the childish wilfulness and the childish secrecy. And they never have from the beginning of the world done what the wise men have seen to be inevitable. They stoned the false prophets, it is said; but they could have stoned true prophets with a greater and juster enjoyment. Individually, men may present a more or less rational appearance, eating, sleeping, and scheming. But humanity as a whole is changeful, mystical, fickle, delightful. Men are men, but Man is a woman.

But in the beginning of the twentieth century the game of Cheat the Prophet was made far more difficult than it had ever been before. The reason was, that there were so many prophets and so many prophecies, that it was difficult to elude all their ingenuities. When a man did something free and frantic and entirely his own, a horrible thought struck him afterwards; it might have been predicted. Whenever a duke climbed a lamp-post, when a dean got drunk, he could not be really happy, he could not be certain that he was not fulfilling some prophecy. In the beginning of the twentieth century you could not see the ground for clever men. They were so common that a stupid man was quite exceptional, and when they found him, they followed him in crowds down the street and treasured him up and gave him some high post in the State.

5

And all these clever men were at work giving accounts of what would happen in the next age, all quite clear, all quite keen-sighted and ruthless, and all quite different. And it seemed that the good old game of hoodwinking your ancestors could not really be managed this time, because the ancestors neglected meat and sleep and practical politics, so that they might meditate day and night on what their descendants would be likely to do.

But the way the prophets of the twentieth century went to work was this. They took something or other that was certainly going on in their time, and then said that it would go on more and more until something extraordinary happened. And very often they added that in some odd place that extraordinary thing had happened, and that it showed the signs of the times.

Thus, for instance, there were Mr. H. G. Wells and others, who thought that science would take charge of the future; and just as the motor-car was quicker than the coach, so some lovely thing would be quicker than the motor-car; and so on for ever. And there arose from their ashes Dr. Quilp, who said that a man could be sent on his machine so fast round the world that he could keep up a long, chatty conversation in some old-world village by saying a word of a sentence each time he came round. And it was said that the experiment had been tried on an apoplectic old major, who was sent round the world so fast that there seemed to be (to the inhabitants of some other star) a continuous band round the earth of white whiskers, red complexion and tweeds—a thing like the ring of Saturn.

Then there was the opposite school. There was Mr. Edward Carpenter, who thought we should in a very short time return to Nature, and live simply and slowly as the animals do. And Edward Carpenter was followed by James Pickie, D.D. (of Pocohontas College), who said that men were immensely improved by grazing, or taking their food slowly and continuously, after the manner of cows. And he said that he had, with the most encouraging results, turned city men out on all fours in a field covered with veal cutlets. Then Tolstoy and the Humanitarians said that the world was growing more merciful, and therefore no one would ever desire to kill. And Mr. Mick not only became a vegetarian, but at length declared vegetarianism doomed ("shedding," as he called it finely, "the green blood of the silent animals"), and predicted that men in a better age would live on nothing but salt. And then came the pamphlet from Oregon (where the thing was tried), the pamphlet called "Why should Salt suffer?" and there was more trouble.

And on the other hand, some people were predicting that the lines of kinship would become narrower and sterner. There was Mr. Cecil Rhodes, who thought that the one thing of the future was the British Empire, and that there would be a gulf between those who were of the Empire and those who were not, between the Chinaman in Hong Kong and the Chinaman outside, between the Spaniard on the Rock of Gibraltar and the Spaniard off it, similar to the gulf between man and the lower animals. And in the same way his impetuous friend, Dr. Zoppi ("the Paul of Anglo-Saxonism"), carried it yet further, and held that, as a result of this view, cannibalism should be held to mean eating a member of the Empire, not eating one of the subject peoples, who should, he said, be killed without needless pain. His horror at the idea of eating a man in British Guiana showed how they misunderstood his stoicism who thought him devoid of feeling. He was, however, in a hard position; as it was said that he had attempted the

6

experiment, and, living in London, had to subsist entirely on Italian organ-grinders. And his end was terrible, for just when he had begun, Sir Paul Swiller read his great paper at the Royal Society, proving that the savages were not only quite right in eating their enemies, but right on moral and hygienic grounds, since it was true that the qualities of the enemy, when eaten, passed into the eater. The notion that the nature of an Italian organ-man was irrevocably growing and burgeoning inside him was almost more than the kindly old professor could bear.

There was Mr. Benjamin Kidd, who said that the growing note of our race would be the care for and knowledge of the future. His idea was developed more powerfully by William Borker, who wrote that passage which every schoolboy knows by heart, about men in future ages weeping by the graves of their descendants, and tourists being shown over the scene of the historic battle which was to take place some centuries afterwards.

And Mr. Stead, too, was prominent, who thought that England would in the twentieth century be united to America; and his young lieutenant, Graham Podge, who included the states of France, Germany, and Russia in the American Union, the State of Russia being abbreviated to Ra.

There was Mr. Sidney Webb, also, who said that the future would see a continuously increasing order and neatness in the life of the people, and his poor friend Fipps, who went mad and ran about the country with an axe, hacking branches off the trees whenever there were not the same number on both sides.

All these clever men were prophesying with every variety of ingenuity what would happen soon, and they all did it in the same way, by taking something they saw "going strong," as the saying is, and carrying it as far as ever their imagination could stretch. This, they said, was the true and simple way of anticipating the future. "Just as," said Dr. Pellkins, in a fine passage,—"just as when we see a pig in a litter larger than the other pigs, we know that by an unalterable law of the Inscrutable it will some day be larger than an elephant,—just as we know, when we see weeds and dandelions growing more and more thickly in a garden, that they must, in spite of all our efforts, grow taller than the chimney-pots and swallow the house from sight, so we know and reverently acknowledge, that when any power in human politics has shown for any period of time any considerable activity, it will go on until it reaches to the sky."

And it did certainly appear that the prophets had put the people (engaged in the old game of Cheat the Prophet) in a quite unprecedented difficulty. It seemed really hard to do anything without fulfilling some of their prophecies.

But there was, nevertheless, in the eyes of labourers in the streets, of peasants in the fields, of sailors and children, and especially women, a strange look that kept the wise men in a perfect fever of doubt. They could not fathom the motionless mirth in their eyes. They still had something up their sleeve; they were still playing the game of Cheat the Prophet.

Then the wise men grew like wild things, and swayed hither and thither, crying, "What can it be? What can it be? What will London be like a century hence? Is there anything we have not thought of? Houses upside down—more hygienic, perhaps? Men walking on hands—make feet flexible, don't you know? Moon ... motor-cars ... no heads...." And so they swayed and wondered until they died and were buried nicely.

Then the people went and did what they liked. Let me no longer conceal the painful truth. The people had cheated the prophets of the twentieth century. When the curtain goes up on this story, eighty years after the present date, London is almost exactly like what it is now.

2. THE MAN IN GREEN

Very few words are needed to explain why London, a hundred years hence, will be very like it is now, or rather, since I must slip into a prophetic past, why London, when my story opens, was very like it was in those enviable days when I was still alive.

The reason can be stated in one sentence. The people had absolutely lost faith in revolutions. All revolutions are doctrinal—such as the French one, or the one that introduced Christianity. For it stands to common sense that you cannot upset all existing things, customs, and compromises, unless you believe in something outside them, something positive and divine. Now, England, during this century, lost all belief in this. It believed in a thing called Evolution. And it said, "All theoretic changes have ended in blood and ennui. If we change, we must change slowly and safely, as the animals do. Nature's revolutions are the only successful ones. There has been no conservative reaction in favour of tails."

And some things did change. Things that were not much thought of dropped out of sight. Things that had not often happened did not happen at all. Thus, for instance, the actual physical force ruling the country, the soldiers and police, grew smaller and smaller, and at last vanished almost to a point. The people combined could have swept the few policemen away in ten minutes: they did not, because they did not believe it would do them the least good. They had lost faith in revolutions.

Democracy was dead; for no one minded the governing class governing. England was now practically a despotism, but not an hereditary one. Some one in the official class was made King. No one cared how: no one cared who. He was merely an universal secretary.

In this manner it happened that everything in London was very quiet. That vague and somewhat depressed reliance upon things happening as they have always happened, which is with all Londoners a mood, had become an assumed condition. There was really no reason for any man doing anything but the thing he had done the day before.

There was therefore no reason whatever why the three young men who had always walked up to their Government office together should not walk up to it together on this particular wintry and cloudy morning. Everything in that age had become mechanical, and Government clerks especially. All those clerks assembled regularly at their posts. Three of those clerks always walked into town together. All the neighbourhood knew them: two of them were tall and one short. And on this particular morning the short clerk was only a few seconds late to join the other two as they passed his gate: he could have overtaken them in three strides; he could have called after them easily. But he did not.

For some reason that will never be understood until all souls are judged (if they are ever judged; the idea was at this time classed with fetish worship) he did not join his two companions, but walked steadily behind them. The day was dull, their dress was dull, everything was dull; but in some odd impulse he walked through street after street, through district after district, looking at the backs of the two men, who would have swung round at the sound of his voice. Now, there is a law written in the darkest of the Books of Life, and it is this: If you look at a thing nine hundred and ninety-nine times, you are perfectly safe; if you look at it the thousandth time, you are in frightful danger of seeing it for the first time.

So the short Government official looked at the coat-tails of the tall Government officials, and through street after street, and round corner after corner, saw only coat-tails, coat-tails, and again coat-tails—when, he did not in the least know why, something happened to his eyes.

Two black dragons were walking backwards in front of him. Two black dragons were looking at him with evil eyes. The dragons were walking backwards it was true, but they kept their eyes fixed on him none the less. The eyes which he saw were, in truth, only the two buttons at the back of a frock-coat: perhaps some traditional memory of their meaningless character gave this half-witted prominence to their gaze. The slit between the tails was the nose-line of the monster: whenever the tails flapped in the winter wind the dragons licked their lips. It was only a momentary fancy, but the small clerk found it imbedded in his soul ever afterwards. He never could again think of men in frock-coats except as dragons walking backwards. He explained afterwards, quite tactfully and nicely, to his two official friends, that (while feeling an inexpressible regard for each of them) he could not seriously regard the face of either of them as anything but a kind of tail. It was, he admitted, a handsome tail—a tail elevated in the air. But if, he said, any true friend of theirs wished to see their faces, to look into the eyes of their soul, that friend must be allowed to walk reverently round behind them, so as to see them from the rear. There he would see the two black dragons with the blind eyes.

But when first the two black dragons sprang out of the fog upon the small clerk, they had merely the effect of all miracles—they changed the universe. He discovered the fact that all romantics know—that adventures happen on dull days, and not on sunny ones. When the chord of monotony is stretched most tight, then it breaks with a sound like song. He had scarcely noticed the weather before, but with the four dead eyes glaring at him he looked round and realised the strange dead day.

The morning was wintry and dim, not misty, but darkened with that shadow of cloud or snow which steeps everything in a green or copper twilight. The light there is on such a day seems not so much to come from the clear heavens as to be a phosphorescence clinging to the shapes themselves. The load of heaven and the clouds is like a load of waters, and the men move like fishes, feeling that they are on the floor of a sea. Everything in a London street completes the fantasy; the carriages and cabs themselves resemble deep-sea creatures with eyes of flame. He had been startled at first to meet two dragons. Now he found he was among deep-sea dragons possessing the deep sea.

The two young men in front were like the small young man himself, well-dressed. The lines of their frock-coats and silk hats had that luxuriant severity which makes the modern fop, hideous as he is, a favourite exercise of the modern draughtsman; that element which Mr. Max Beerbohm has admirably expressed in speaking of "certain congruities of dark cloth and the rigid perfection of linen."

They walked with the gait of an affected snail, and they spoke at the longest intervals, dropping a sentence at about every sixth lamp-post.

They crawled on past the lamp-posts; their mien was so immovable that a fanciful description might almost say, that the lamp-posts crawled past the men, as in a dream. Then the small man suddenly ran after them and said—

"I want to get my hair cut. I say, do you know a little shop anywhere where they cut your hair properly? I keep on having my hair cut, but it keeps on growing again."

One of the tall men looked at him with the air of a pained naturalist.

"Why, here is a little place," cried the small man, with a sort of imbecile cheerfulness, as the bright bulging window of a fashionable toilet-saloon glowed abruptly out of the foggy twilight. "Do you know, I often find hair-dressers when I walk about London. I'll lunch with you at Cicconani's. You know, I'm awfully fond of hair-dressers' shops. They're miles better than those nasty butchers'." And he disappeared into the doorway.

The man called James continued to gaze after him, a monocle screwed into his eye.

"What the devil do you make of that fellow?" he asked his companion, a pale young man with a high nose.

The pale young man reflected conscientiously for some minutes, and then said—

"Had a knock on his head when he was a kid, I should think."

"No, I don't think it's that," replied the Honourable James Barker. "I've sometimes fancied he was a sort of artist, Lambert."

"Bosh!" cried Mr. Lambert, briefly.

"I admit I can't make him out," resumed Barker, abstractedly; "he never opens his mouth without saying something so indescribably half-witted that to call him a fool seems the very feeblest attempt at characterisation. But there's another thing about him that's rather funny. Do you know that he has the one collection of Japanese lacquer in Europe? Have you ever seen his books? All Greek poets and mediæval French and that sort of thing. Have you ever been in his rooms? It's like being inside an amethyst. And he moves about in all that and talks like—like a turnip."

"Well, damn all books. Your blue books as well," said the ingenuous Mr. Lambert, with a friendly simplicity. "You ought to understand such things. What do you make of him?"

"He's beyond me," returned Barker. "But if you asked me for my opinion, I should say he was a man with a taste for nonsense, as they call it—artistic fooling, and all that kind of thing. And I seriously believe that he has talked nonsense so much that he has half bewildered his own mind and doesn't know the difference between sanity and insanity. He has gone round the mental world, so to speak, and found the place where the East and the West are one, and extreme idiocy is as good as sense. But I can't explain these psychological games."

"You can't explain them to me," replied Mr. Wilfrid Lambert, with candour.

As they passed up the long streets towards their restaurant the copper twilight cleared slowly to a pale yellow, and by the time they reached it they stood discernible in a tolerable winter daylight. The Honourable James Barker, one of the most powerful officials in the English Government (by this time a rigidly official one), was a lean and elegant young man, with a blank handsome face and bleak blue eyes. He had a great amount of intellectual capacity, of that peculiar kind which raises a man from throne to throne and lets him die loaded with honours without having either amused or enlightened the mind of a single man. Wilfrid Lambert, the youth with the nose which appeared to impoverish the rest of his face, had also contributed little to the enlargement of the human spirit, but he had the honourable excuse of being a fool.

Lambert would have been called a silly man; Barker, with all his cleverness, might have been called a stupid man. But mere silliness and stupidity sank into insignificance in the presence of the awful and mysterious treasures of foolishness apparently stored up in the small figure that stood waiting for them outside Cicconani's. The little man, whose name was Auberon Quin, had an appearance compounded of a baby and an owl. His round head, round eyes, seemed to have been designed by nature playfully with a pair of compasses. His flat dark hair and preposterously long frock-coat gave him something of the look of a child's "Noah." When he entered a room of strangers, they mistook him for a small boy, and wanted to take him on their knees, until he spoke, when they perceived that a boy would have been more intelligent.

"I have been waiting quite a long time," said Quin, mildly. "It's awfully funny I should see you coming up the street at last."

"Why?" asked Lambert, staring. "You told us to come here yourself."

"My mother used to tell people to come to places," said the sage.

They were about to turn into the restaurant with a resigned air, when their eyes were caught by something in the street. The weather, though cold and blank, was now quite clear, and across the dull brown of the wood pavement and between the dull grey terraces was moving something not to be seen for miles round—not to be seen perhaps at that time in England—a man dressed in bright colours. A small crowd hung on the man's heels.

He was a tall stately man, clad in a military uniform of brilliant green, splashed with great silver facings. From the shoulder swung a short green furred cloak, somewhat like that of a Hussar, the lining of which gleamed every now and then with a kind of tawny crimson. His breast glittered with medals; round his neck was the red ribbon and star of some foreign order; and a long straight sword, with a blazing hilt, trailed and clattered along the pavement. At this time the pacific and utilitarian development of Europe had relegated all such customs to the Museums. The only remaining force, the small but well-organised police, were attired in a sombre and hygienic manner. But even those who remembered the last Life Guards and Lancers who disappeared in 1912 must have known at a glance that this was not, and never had been, an English uniform; and this conviction would have been heightened by the yellow aquiline face, like Dante carved in bronze, which rose, crowned with white hair, out of the green military collar, a keen and distinguished, but not an English face.

The magnificence with which the green-clad gentleman walked down the centre of the road would be something difficult to express in human language. For it was an ingrained simplicity and arrogance, something in the mere carriage of the head and body, which made ordinary moderns in the street stare after him; but it had comparatively little to do with actual conscious gestures or expression. In the matter of these merely temporary movements, the man appeared to be rather worried and inquisitive, but he was inquisitive with the inquisitiveness of a despot and worried as with the responsibilities of a god. The men who lounged and wondered behind him followed partly with an astonishment at his brilliant uniform, that is to say, partly because of that instinct which makes us all follow one who looks like a madman, but far more because of that instinct which makes all men follow (and worship) any one who chooses to behave like a king. He had to so sublime an extent that great quality of royalty—an almost imbecile unconsciousness of everybody, that people went after him as they do after kings—to see what would be the first thing or person he would take notice of. And all the time, as we have said, in spite of his quiet splendour, there was an air about him as if he were looking for somebody; an expression of inquiry.

Suddenly that expression of inquiry vanished, none could tell why, and was replaced by an expression of contentment. Amid the rapt attention of the mob of idlers, the magnificent green gentleman deflected himself from his direct course down the centre of the road and walked to one side of it. He came to a halt opposite to a large poster of Colman's Mustard erected on a wooden hoarding. His spectators almost held their breath.

He took from a small pocket in his uniform a little penknife; with this he made a slash at the stretched paper. Completing the rest of the operation with his fingers, he tore off a strip or rag of paper, yellow in colour and wholly irregular in outline. Then for the first time the great being addressed his adoring onlookers—

"Can any one," he said, with a pleasing foreign accent, "lend me a pin?"

Mr. Lambert, who happened to be nearest, and who carried innumerable pins for the purpose of attaching innumerable buttonholes, lent him one, which was received with extravagant but dignified bows, and hyperboles of thanks.

The gentleman in green, then, with every appearance of being gratified, and even puffed up, pinned the piece of yellow paper to the green silk and silver-lace adornments of his breast. Then he turned his eyes round again, searching and unsatisfied.

"Anything else I can do, sir?" asked Lambert, with the absurd politeness of the Englishman when once embarrassed.

"Red," said the stranger, vaguely, "red."

"I beg your pardon?"

"I beg yours also, Señor," said the stranger, bowing. "I was wondering whether any of you had any red about you."

"Any red about us?—well really—no, I don't think I have—I used to carry a red bandanna once, but—"

"Barker," asked Auberon Quin, suddenly, "where's your red cockatoo? Where's your red cockatoo?"

"What do you mean?" asked Barker, desperately. "What cockatoo? You've never seen me with any cockatoo!"

"I know," said Auberon, vaguely mollified. "Where's it been all the time?"

Barker swung round, not without resentment.

"I am sorry, sir," he said, shortly but civilly, "none of us seem to have anything red to lend you. But why, if one may ask—"

"I thank you, Señor, it is nothing. I can, since there is nothing else, fulfil my own requirements."

And standing for a second of thought with the penknife in his hand, he stabbed his left palm. The blood fell with so full a stream that it struck the stones without dripping. The foreigner pulled out his handkerchief and tore a piece from it with his teeth. The rag was immediately soaked in scarlet.

"Since you are so generous, Señor," he said, "another pin, perhaps."

Lambert held one out, with eyes protruding like a frog's.

The red linen was pinned beside the yellow paper, and the foreigner took off his hat.

"I have to thank you all, gentlemen," he said; and wrapping the remainder of the handkerchief round his bleeding hand, he resumed his walk with an overwhelming stateliness.

While all the rest paused, in some disorder, little Mr. Auberon Quin ran after the stranger and stopped him, with hat in hand. Considerably to everybody's astonishment, he addressed him in the purest Spanish—

"Señor," he said in that language, "pardon a hospitality, perhaps indiscreet, towards one who appears to be a distinguished, but a solitary guest in London. Will you do me and my friends, with whom you have held some conversation, the honour of lunching with us at the adjoining restaurant?"

The man in the green uniform had turned a fiery colour of pleasure at the mere sound of his own language, and he accepted the invitation with that profusion of bows which so often shows, in the case of the Southern races, the falsehood of the notion that ceremony has nothing to do with feeling.

"Señor," he said, "your language is my own; but all my love for my people shall not lead me to deny to yours the possession of so chivalrous an entertainer. Let me say that the tongue is Spanish but the heart English." And he passed with the rest into Cicconani's.

"Now, perhaps," said Barker, over the fish and sherry, intensely polite, but burning with curiosity, "perhaps it would be rude of me to ask why you did that?"

"Did what, Señor?" asked the guest, who spoke English quite well, though in a manner indefinably American.

"Well," said the Englishman, in some confusion, "I mean tore a strip off a hoarding and ... er ... cut yourself ... and...."

"To tell you that, Señor," answered the other, with a certain sad pride, "involves merely telling you who I am. I am Juan del Fuego, President of Nicaragua."

The manner with which the President of Nicaragua leant back and drank his sherry showed that to him this explanation covered all the facts observed and a great deal more. Barker's brow, however, was still a little clouded.

"And the yellow paper," he began, with anxious friendliness, "and the red rag...."

"The yellow paper and the red rag," said Fuego, with indescribable grandeur, "are the colours of Nicaragua."

"But Nicaragua ..." began Barker, with great hesitation, "Nicaragua is no longer a...."

"Nicaragua has been conquered like Athens. Nicaragua has been annexed like Jerusalem," cried the old man, with amazing fire. "The Yankee and the German and the brute powers of modernity have trampled it with the hoofs of oxen. But Nicaragua is not dead. Nicaragua is an idea."

Auberon Quin suggested timidly, "A brilliant idea."

"Yes," said the foreigner, snatching at the word. "You are right, generous

13

Englishman. An idea *brilliant*, a burning thought. Señor, you asked me why, in my desire to see the colours of my country, I snatched at paper and blood. Can you not understand the ancient sanctity of colours? The Church has her symbolic colours. And think of what colours mean to us—think of the position of one like myself, who can see nothing but those two colours, nothing but the red and the yellow. To me all shapes are equal, all common and noble things are in a democracy of combination. Wherever there is a field of marigolds and the red cloak of an old woman, there is Nicaragua. Wherever there is a field of poppies and a yellow patch of sand, there is Nicaragua. Wherever there is a lemon and a red sunset, there is my country. Wherever I see a red pillar-box and a yellow sunset, there my heart beats. Blood and a splash of mustard can be my heraldry. If there be yellow mud and red mud in the same ditch, it is better to me than white stars."

"And if," said Quin, with equal enthusiasm, "there should happen to be yellow wine and red wine at the same lunch, you could not confine yourself to sherry. Let me order some Burgundy, and complete, as it were, a sort of Nicaraguan heraldry in your inside."

Barker was fiddling with his knife, and was evidently making up his mind to say something, with the intense nervousness of the amiable Englishman.

"I am to understand, then," he said at last, with a cough, "that you, ahem, were the President of Nicaragua when it made its—er—one must, of course, agree—its quite heroic resistance to—er—"

The ex-President of Nicaragua waved his hand.

"You need not hesitate in speaking to me," he said. "I'm quite fully aware that the whole tendency of the world of to-day is against Nicaragua and against me. I shall not consider it any diminution of your evident courtesy if you say what you think of the misfortunes that have laid my republic in ruins."

Barker looked immeasurably relieved and gratified.

"You are most generous, President," he said, with some hesitation over the title, "and I will take advantage of your generosity to express the doubts which, I must confess, we moderns have about such things as—er—the Nicaraguan independence."

"So your sympathies are," said Del Fuego, quite calmly, "with the big nation which—"

"Pardon me, pardon me, President," said Barker, warmly; "my sympathies are with no nation. You misunderstand, I think, the modern intellect. We do not disapprove of the fire and extravagance of such commonwealths as yours only to become more extravagant on a larger scale. We do not condemn Nicaragua because we think Britain ought to be more Nicaraguan. We do not discourage small nationalities because we wish large nationalities to have all their smallness, all their uniformity of outlook, all their exaggeration of spirit. If I differ with the greatest respect from your Nicaraguan enthusiasm, it is not because a nation or ten nations were against you; it is because civilisation was against you. We moderns believe in a great cosmopolitan civilisation, one which shall include all the talents of all the absorbed peoples—"

"The Señor will forgive me," said the President. "May I ask the Señor how, under ordinary circumstances, he catches a wild horse?"

"I never catch a wild horse," replied Barker, with dignity.

"Precisely," said the other; "and there ends your absorption of the talents. That is what I complain of your cosmopolitanism. When you say you want all peoples to unite, you really mean that you want all peoples to unite to learn the tricks of your people. If the Bedouin Arab does not know how to read, some English missionary or schoolmaster must be sent to teach him to read, but no one ever says, 'This schoolmaster does not know how to ride on a camel; let us pay a Bedouin to teach him.' You say your civilisation will include all talents. Will it? Do you really mean to say that at the moment when the Esquimaux has learnt to vote for a County Council, you will have learnt to spear a walrus? I recur to the example I gave. In Nicaragua we had a way of catching wild horses—by lassoing the fore feet—which was supposed to be the best in South America. If you are going to include all the talents, go and do it. If not, permit me to say what I have always said, that something went from the world when Nicaragua was civilised."

"Something, perhaps," replied Barker, "but that something a mere barbarian dexterity. I do not know that I could chip flints as well as a primeval man, but I know that civilisation can make these knives which are better, and I trust to civilisation."

"You have good authority," answered the Nicaraguan. "Many clever men like you have trusted to civilisation. Many clever Babylonians, many clever Egyptians, many clever men at the end of Rome. Can you tell me, in a world that is flagrant with the failures of civilisation, what there is particularly immortal about yours?"

"I think you do not quite understand, President, what ours is," answered Barker. "You judge it rather as if England was still a poor and pugnacious island; you have been long out of Europe. Many things have happened."

"And what," asked the other, "would you call the summary of those things?"

"The summary of those things," answered Barker, with great animation, "is that we are rid of the superstitions, and in becoming so we have not merely become rid of the superstitions which have been most frequently and most enthusiastically so described. The superstition of big nationalities is bad, but the superstition of small nationalities is worse. The superstition of reverencing our own country is bad, but the superstition of reverencing other people's countries is worse. It is so everywhere, and in a hundred ways. The superstition of monarchy is bad, and the superstition of aristocracy is bad, but the superstition of democracy is the worst of all."

The old gentleman opened his eyes with some surprise.

"Are you, then," he said, "no longer a democracy in England?"

Barker laughed.

"The situation invites paradox," he said. "We are, in a sense, the purest democracy. We have become a despotism. Have you not noticed how continually in history democracy becomes despotism? People call it the decay of democracy. It is simply its fulfilment. Why take the trouble to number and register and enfranchise all the innumerable John Robinsons, when you can take one John Robinson with the same intellect or lack of intellect as all the rest, and have done with it? The old idealistic republicans used to found democracy on the idea that all men were equally intelligent. Believe me, the sane and enduring democracy is founded on the fact that all men are equally idiotic. Why should we not choose out of them one as much as another. All that we want for Government is a man not criminal and insane, who can rapidly look over some petitions and sign some proclamations. To think what time was wasted in arguing about the House of Lords, Tories saying it ought to be preserved because it was clever, and Radicals saying it ought to be destroyed because it was stupid, and all the time no one saw that it was right because it was stupid, because that chance mob of ordinary men thrown there by accident of blood, were a great democratic protest against the Lower House, against the eternal insolence of the aristocracy of talents. We have established now in England, the thing towards which all systems have dimly groped, the dull popular despotism without illusions. We want one man at the head of our State, not because he is brilliant or virtuous, but because he is one man and not a chattering crowd. To avoid the possible chance of hereditary diseases or such things, we have abandoned hereditary monarchy. The King of England is chosen like a juryman upon an official rotation list. Beyond that the whole system is quietly despotic, and we have not found it raise a murmur."

"Do you really mean," asked the President, incredulously, "that you choose any ordinary man that comes to hand and make him despot—that you trust to the chance of some alphabetical list...."

"And why not?" cried Barker. "Did not half the historical nations trust to the chance of the eldest sons of eldest sons, and did not half of them get on tolerably well? To have a perfect system is impossible; to have a system is indispensable. All hereditary monarchies were a matter of luck: so are alphabetical monarchies. Can you find a deep philosophical meaning in the difference between the Stuarts and the Hanoverians? Believe me, I will undertake to find a deep philosophical meaning in the contrast between the dark tragedy of the A's, and the solid success of the B's."

"And you risk it?" asked the other. "Though the man may be a tyrant or a cynic or a criminal."

"We risk it," answered Barker, with a perfect placidity. "Suppose he is a tyrant—he is still a check on a hundred tyrants. Suppose he is a cynic, it is to his interest to govern well. Suppose he is a criminal—by removing poverty and substituting power, we put a check on his criminality. In short, by substituting despotism we have put a total check on one criminal and a partial check on all the rest."

The Nicaraguan old gentleman leaned over with a queer expression in his eyes.

"My church, sir," he said, "has taught me to respect faith. I do not wish to speak with any disrespect of yours, however fantastic. But do you really mean that you will trust to the ordinary man, the man who may happen to come next, as a good despot?"

"I do," said Barker, simply. "He may not be a good man. But he will be a good despot. For when he comes to a mere business routine of government he will endeavour to do ordinary justice. Do we not assume the same thing in a jury?"

The old President smiled.

"I don't know," he said, "that I have any particular objection in detail to your excellent scheme of Government. My only objection is a quite personal one. It is, that if I were asked whether I would belong to it, I should ask first of all, if I was not permitted, as an alternative, to be a toad in a ditch. That is all. You cannot argue with the choice of the soul."

"Of the soul," said Barker, knitting his brows, "I cannot pretend to say anything, but speaking in the interests of the public—"

Mr. Auberon Quin rose suddenly to his feet.

"If you'll excuse me, gentlemen," he said, "I will step out for a moment into the air."

"I'm so sorry, Auberon," said Lambert, good-naturedly; "do you feel bad?"

"Not bad exactly," said Auberon, with self-restraint; "rather good, if anything. Strangely and richly good. The fact is, I want to reflect a little on those beautiful words that have just been uttered. 'Speaking,' yes, that was the phrase, 'speaking in the interests of the public.' One cannot get the honey from such things without being alone for a little."

"Is he really off his chump, do you think?" asked Lambert.

The old President looked after him with queerly vigilant eyes.

"He is a man, I think," he said, "who cares for nothing but a joke. He is a dangerous man."

Lambert laughed in the act of lifting some macaroni to his mouth.

"Dangerous!" he said. "You don't know little Quin, sir!"

"Every man is dangerous," said the old man without moving, "who cares only for one thing. I was once dangerous myself."

And with a pleasant smile he finished his coffee and rose, bowing profoundly, passed out into the fog, which had again grown dense and sombre. Three days afterwards they heard that he had died quietly in lodgings in Soho.

Drowned somewhere else in the dark sea of fog was a little figure shaking and quaking, with what might at first sight have seemed terror or ague: but which was really that strange malady, a lonely laughter. He was repeating over and over to himself with a rich accent—"But speaking in the interests of the public...."

3. THE HILL OF HUMOUR

"In a little square garden of yellow roses, beside the sea," said Auberon Quin, "there was a Nonconformist minister who had never been to Wimbledon. His family did not understand his sorrow or the strange look in his eyes. But one day they repented their neglect, for they heard that a body had been found on the shore, battered, but wearing patent leather boots. As it happened, it turned out not to be the minister at all. But in the dead man's pocket there was a return ticket to Maidstone."

There was a short pause as Quin and his friends Barker and Lambert went swinging on through the slushy grass of Kensington Gardens. Then Auberon resumed.

"That story," he said reverently, "is the test of humour."

They walked on further and faster, wading through higher grass as they began to climb a slope.

"I perceive," continued Auberon, "that you have passed the test, and consider the anecdote excruciatingly funny; since you say nothing. Only coarse humour is received with pot-house applause. The great anecdote is received in silence, like a benediction. You felt pretty benedicted, didn't you, Barker?"

"I saw the point," said Barker, somewhat loftily.

"Do you know," said Quin, with a sort of idiot gaiety, "I have lots of stories as good as that. Listen to this one."

And he slightly cleared his throat.

"Dr. Polycarp was, as you all know, an unusually sallow bimetallist. 'There,' people of wide experience would say, 'There goes the sallowest bimetallist in Cheshire.' Once this was said so that he overheard it: it was said by an actuary, under a sunset of mauve and grey. Polycarp turned upon him. 'Sallow!' he cried fiercely, 'sallow! *Quis tulerit Gracchos de seditione querentes.*' It was said that no actuary ever made game of Dr. Polycarp again."

Barker nodded with a simple sagacity. Lambert only grunted.

"Here is another," continued the insatiable Quin. "In a hollow of the grey-green hills of rainy Ireland, lived an old, old woman, whose uncle was always Cambridge at the Boat Race. But in her grey-green hollows, she knew nothing of this: she didn't know that there was a Boat Race. Also she did not know that she had an uncle. She had heard of nobody at all, except of George the First, of whom she had heard (I know not why), and in whose historical memory she put her simple trust. And by and by in God's good time, it was discovered that this uncle of hers was not really her uncle, and they came and told her so. She smiled through her tears, and said only, 'Virtue is its own reward.'"

Again there was a silence, and then Lambert said—

"It seems a bit mysterious."

"Mysterious!" cried the other. "The true humour is mysterious. Do you not realise the chief incident of the nineteenth and twentieth centuries?"

"And what's that?" asked Lambert, shortly.

"It is very simple," replied the other. "Hitherto it was the ruin of a joke that people did not see it. Now it is the sublime victory of a joke that people do not see it. Humour, my friends, is the one sanctity remaining to mankind. It is the one thing you are thoroughly afraid of. Look at that tree."

His interlocutors looked vaguely towards a beech that leant out towards them from the ridge of the hill.

"If," said Mr. Quin, "I were to say that you did not see the great truths of science exhibited by that tree, though they stared any man of intellect in the face, what would you think or say? You would merely regard me as a pedant with some unimportant theory about vegetable cells. If I were to say that you did not see in that tree the vile mismanagement of local politics, you would dismiss me as a Socialist crank with some particular fad about public parks. If I were to say that you were guilty of the supreme blasphemy of looking at that tree and not seeing in it a new religion, a special revelation of God, you would simply say I was a mystic, and think no more about me. But if"—and he lifted a pontifical hand—"if I say that you cannot see the humour of that tree, and that I see the humour of it—my God! you will roll about at my feet."

He paused a moment, and then resumed.

"Yes; a sense of humour, a weird and delicate sense of humour, is the new religion of mankind! It is towards that men will strain themselves with the asceticism of saints. Exercises, spiritual exercises, will be set in it. It will be asked, 'Can you see the humour of this iron railing?' or 'Can you see the humour of this field of corn? Can you see the humour of the stars? Can you see the humour of the sunsets?' How often I have laughed myself to sleep over a violet sunset."

"Quite so," said Mr. Barker, with an intelligent embarrassment.

"Let me tell you another story. How often it happens that the M.P.'s for Essex are less punctual than one would suppose. The least punctual Essex M.P., perhaps, was James Wilson, who said, in the very act of plucking a poppy—"

Lambert suddenly faced round and struck his stick into the ground in a defiant attitude.

"Auberon," he said, "chuck it. I won't stand it. It's all bosh."

Both men stared at him, for there was something very explosive about the words, as if they had been corked up painfully for a long time.

"You have," began Quin, "no—"

"I don't care a curse," said Lambert, violently, "whether I have 'a delicate sense of humour' or not. I won't stand it. It's all a confounded fraud. There's no joke in those infernal tales at all. You know there isn't as well as I do."

"Well," replied Quin, slowly, "it is true that I, with my rather gradual mental processes, did not see any joke in them. But the finer sense of Barker perceived it."

Barker turned a fierce red, but continued to stare at the horizon.

"You ass," said Lambert; "why can't you be like other people? Why can't you say something really funny, or hold your tongue? The man who sits on his hat in a pantomime is a long sight funnier than you are."

Quin regarded him steadily. They had reached the top of the ridge and the wind struck their faces.

"Lambert," said Auberon, "you are a great and good man, though I'm hanged if you look it. You are more. You are a great revolutionist or deliverer of the world, and I look forward to seeing you carved in marble between Luther and Danton, if possible in your present attitude, the hat slightly on one side. I said as I came up the hill that the new humour was the last of the religions. You have made it the last of the superstitions. But let me give you a very serious warning. Be careful how you ask me to do anything *outré*, to imitate the man in the pantomime, and to sit on my hat. Because I am a man whose soul has been emptied of all pleasures but folly. And for twopence I'd do it."

"Do it, then," said Lambert, swinging his stick impatiently. "It would be funnier than the bosh you and Barker talk."

Quin, standing on the top of the hill, stretched his hand out towards the main avenue of Kensington Gardens.

"Two hundred yards away," he said, "are all your fashionable acquaintances with nothing on earth to do but to stare at each other and at us. We are standing upon an elevation under the open sky, a peak as it were of fantasy, a Sinai of humour. We are in a great pulpit or platform, lit up with sunlight, and half London can see us. Be careful how you suggest things to me. For there is in me a madness which goes beyond martyrdom, the madness of an utterly idle man."

"I don't know what you are talking about," said Lambert, contemptuously. "I only know I'd rather you stood on your silly head, than talked so much."

"Auberon! for goodness' sake...." cried Barker, springing forward; but he was too late. Faces from all the benches and avenues were turned in their direction. Groups stopped and small crowds collected; and the sharp sunlight picked out the whole scene in blue, green and black, like a picture in a child's toy-book. And on the top of the small hill Mr. Auberon Quin stood with considerable athletic neatness upon his head, and waved his patent-leather boots in the air.

"For God's sake, Quin, get up, and don't be an idiot," cried Barker, wringing his hands; "we shall have the whole town here."

"Yes, get up, get up, man," said Lambert, amused and annoyed. "I was only fooling; get up."

Auberon did so with a bound, and flinging his hat higher than the trees, proceeded to hop about on one leg with a serious expression. Barker stamped wildly.

"Oh, let's get home, Barker, and leave him," said Lambert; "some of your proper and correct police will look after him. Here they come!"

Two grave-looking men in quiet uniforms came up the hill towards them. One held a paper in his hand.

"There he is, officer," said Lambert, cheerfully; "we ain't responsible for him."

The officer looked at the capering Mr. Quin with a quiet eye.

"We have not come, gentlemen," he said, "about what I think you are alluding to. We have come from head-quarters to announce the selection of His Majesty the King. It is the rule, inherited from the old *régime*, that the news should be brought to the new Sovereign immediately, wherever he is; so we have followed you across Kensington Gardens."

Barker's eyes were blazing in his pale face. He was consumed with ambition throughout his life. With a certain dull magnanimity of the intellect he had really believed in the chance method of selecting despots. But this sudden suggestion, that the selection might have fallen upon him, unnerved him with pleasure.

"Which of us," he began, and the respectful official interrupted him.

"Not you, sir, I am sorry to say. If I may be permitted to say so, we know your services to the Government, and should be very thankful if it were. The choice has fallen...."

"God bless my soul!" said Lambert, jumping back two paces. "Not me. Don't say I'm autocrat of all the Russias."

"No, sir," said the officer, with a slight cough and a glance towards Auberon, who was at that moment putting his head between his legs and making a noise like a cow; "the gentleman whom we have to congratulate seems at the moment—er—er —occupied."

"Not Quin!" shrieked Barker, rushing up to him; "it can't be. Auberon, for God's sake pull yourself together. You've been made King!"

With his head still upside down between his legs, Mr. Quin answered modestly—

"I am not worthy. I cannot reasonably claim to equal the great men who have previously swayed the sceptre of Britain. Perhaps the only peculiarity that I can claim is that I am probably the first monarch that ever spoke out his soul to the people of England with his head and body in this position. This may in some sense give me, to quote a poem that I wrote in my youth—

A nobler office on the earth

Than valour, power of brain, or birth
Could give the warrior kings of old.
The intellect clarified by this posture—"

Lambert and Barker made a kind of rush at him.

"Don't you understand?" cried Lambert. "It's not a joke. They've really made you King. By gosh! they must have rum taste."

"The great Bishops of the Middle Ages," said Quin, kicking his legs in the air, as he was dragged up more or less upside down, "were in the habit of refusing the honour of election three times and then accepting it. A mere matter of detail separates me from those great men. I will accept the post three times and refuse it afterwards. Oh! I will toil for you, my faithful people! You shall have a banquet of humour."

By this time he had been landed the right way up, and the two men were still trying in vain to impress him with the gravity of the situation.

"Did you not tell me, Wilfrid Lambert," he said, "that I should be of more public value if I adopted a more popular form of humour? And when should a popular form of humour be more firmly riveted upon me than now, when I have become the darling of a whole people? Officer," he continued, addressing the startled messenger, "are there no ceremonies to celebrate my entry into the city?"

"Ceremonies," began the official, with embarrassment, "have been more or less neglected for some little time, and—"

Auberon Quin began gradually to take off his coat.

"All ceremony," he said, "consists in the reversal of the obvious. Thus men, when they wish to be priests or judges, dress up like women. Kindly help me on with this coat." And he held it out.

"But, your Majesty," said the officer, after a moment's bewilderment and manipulation, "you're putting it on with the tails in front."

"The reversal of the obvious," said the King, calmly, "is as near as we can come to ritual with our imperfect apparatus. Lead on."

The rest of that afternoon and evening was to Barker and Lambert a nightmare, which they could not properly realise or recall. The King, with his coat on the wrong way, went towards the streets that were awaiting him, and the old Kensington Palace which was the Royal residence. As he passed small groups of men, the groups turned into crowds, and gave forth sounds which seemed strange in welcoming an autocrat. Barker walked behind, his brain reeling, and, as the crowds grew thicker and thicker, the sounds became more and more unusual. And when he had reached the great market-place opposite the church, Barker knew that he had reached it, though he was roods behind, because a cry went up such as had never before greeted any of the kings of the earth.

BOOK II

1. THE CHARTER OF THE CITIES

Lambert was standing bewildered outside the door of the King's apartments amid the scurry of astonishment and ridicule. He was just passing out into the street, in a dazed manner, when James Barker dashed by him.

"Where are you going?" he asked.

"To stop all this foolery, of course," replied Barker; and he disappeared into the room.

He entered it headlong, slamming the door, and slapping his incomparable silk hat on the table. His mouth opened, but before he could speak, the King said—

"Your hat, if you please."

Fidgeting with his fingers, and scarcely knowing what he was doing, the young politician held it out.

The King placed it on his own chair, and sat on it.

"A quaint old custom," he explained, smiling above the ruins. "When the King receives the representatives of the House of Barker, the hat of the latter is immediately destroyed in this manner. It represents the absolute finality of the act of homage expressed in the removal of it. It declares that never until that hat shall once more appear upon your head (a contingency which I firmly believe to be remote) shall the House of Barker rebel against the Crown of England."

Barker stood with clenched fist, and shaking lip.

"Your jokes," he began, "and my property—" and then exploded with an oath, and stopped again.

"Continue, continue," said the King, waving his hands.

"What does it all mean?" cried the other, with a gesture of passionate rationality. "Are you mad?"

"Not in the least," replied the King, pleasantly. "Madmen are always serious; they go mad from lack of humour. You are looking serious yourself, James."

"Why can't you keep it to your own private life?" expostulated the other. "You've got plenty of money, and plenty of houses now to play the fool in, but in the interests of the public—"

"Epigrammatic," said the King, shaking his finger sadly at him. "None of your daring scintillations here. As to why I don't do it in private, I rather fail to understand your question. The answer is of comparative limpidity. I don't do it in private, because it is funnier to do it in public. You appear to think that it would be amusing to be dignified in the banquet hall and in the street, and at my own fireside (I could procure a fireside) to keep the company in a roar. But that is what every one does. Every one is grave in public, and funny in private. My sense of humour suggests the reversal of this; it suggests that one should be funny in public, and solemn in private. I desire to make the State functions, parliaments, coronations, and so on, one roaring old-fashioned pantomime. But, on the other hand, I shut myself up alone in a small store-room for two hours a day, where I am so dignified that I come out quite ill."

By this time Barker was walking up and down the room, his frock coat flapping like the black wings of a bird.

"Well, you will ruin the country, that's all," he said shortly.

"It seems to me," said Auberon, "that the tradition of ten centuries is being broken, and the House of Barker is rebelling against the Crown of England. It would be with regret (for I admire your appearance) that I should be obliged forcibly to decorate your head with the remains of this hat, but—"

"What I can't understand," said Barker flinging up his fingers with a feverish American movement, "is why you don't care about anything else but your games."

The King stopped sharply in the act of lifting the silken remnants, dropped them, and walked up to Barker, looking at him steadily.

"I made a kind of vow," he said, "that I would not talk seriously, which always means answering silly questions. But the strong man will always be gentle with politicians.

> 'The shape my scornful looks deride
> Required a God to form;'

if I may so theologically express myself. And for some reason I cannot in the least understand, I feel impelled to answer that question of yours, and to answer it as if there were really such a thing in the world as a serious subject. You ask me why I don't care for anything else. Can you tell me, in the name of all the gods you don't believe in, why I should care for anything else?"

"Don't you realise common public necessities?" cried Barker. "Is it possible that a man of your intelligence does not know that it is every one's interest—"

"Don't you believe in Zoroaster? Is it possible that you neglect Mumbo-Jumbo?" returned the King, with startling animation. "Does a man of your intelligence come to me with these damned early Victorian ethics? If, on studying my features and manner, you detect any particular resemblance to the Prince Consort, I assure you you are

G.K. CHESTERTON

mistaken. Did Herbert Spencer ever convince you—did he ever convince anybody—did he ever for one mad moment convince himself—that it must be to the interest of the individual to feel a public spirit? Do you believe that, if you rule your department badly, you stand any more chance, or one half of the chance, of being guillotined, that an angler stands of being pulled into the river by a strong pike? Herbert Spencer refrained from theft for the same reason that he refrained from wearing feathers in his hair, because he was an English gentleman with different tastes. I am an English gentleman with different tastes. He liked philosophy. I like art. He liked writing ten books on the nature of human society. I like to see the Lord Chamberlain walking in front of me with a piece of paper pinned to his coat-tails. It is my humour. Are you answered? At any rate, I have said my last serious word to-day, and my last serious word I trust for the remainder of my life in this Paradise of Fools. The remainder of my conversation with you to-day, which I trust will be long and stimulating, I propose to conduct in a new language of my own by means of rapid and symbolic movements of the left leg." And he began to pirouette slowly round the room with a preoccupied expression.

Barker ran round the room after him, bombarding him with demands and entreaties. But he received no response except in the new language. He came out banging the door again, and sick like a man coming on shore. As he strode along the streets he found himself suddenly opposite Cicconani's restaurant, and for some reason there rose up before him the green fantastic figure of the Spanish General, standing, as he had seen him last, at the door, with the words on his lips, "You cannot argue with the choice of the soul."

The King came out from his dancing with the air of a man of business legitimately tired. He put on an overcoat, lit a cigar, and went out into the purple night.

"I will go," he said, "and mingle with the people."

He passed swiftly up a street in the neighbourhood of Notting Hill, when suddenly he felt a hard object driven into his waistcoat. He paused, put up his single eye-glass, and beheld a boy with a wooden sword and a paper cocked hat, wearing that expression of awed satisfaction with which a child contemplates his work when he has hit some one very hard. The King gazed thoughtfully for some time at his assailant, and slowly took a note-book from his breast-pocket.

"I have a few notes," he said, "for my dying speech;" and he turned over the leaves. "Dying speech for political assassination; ditto, if by former friend—h'm, h'm. Dying speech for death at hands of injured husband (repentant). Dying speech for same (cynical). I am not quite sure which meets the present...."

"I'm the King of the Castle," said the boy, truculently, and very pleased with nothing in particular.

The King was a kind-hearted man, and very fond of children, like all people who are fond of the ridiculous.

"Infant," he said, "I'm glad you are so stalwart a defender of your old inviolate Notting Hill. Look up nightly to that peak, my child, where it lifts itself among the stars so ancient, so lonely, so unutterably Notting. So long as you are ready to die for the sacred mountain, even if it were ringed with all the armies of Bayswater—"

The King stopped suddenly, and his eyes shone.

"Perhaps," he said, "perhaps the noblest of all my conceptions. A revival of the arrogance of the old mediæval cities applied to our glorious suburbs. Clapham with a city guard. Wimbledon with a city wall. Surbiton tolling a bell to raise its citizens. West Hampstead going into battle with its own banner. It shall be done. I, the King, have said it." And, hastily presenting the boy with half a crown, remarking, "For the war-chest of Notting Hill," he ran violently home at such a rate of speed that crowds followed him for miles. On reaching his study, he ordered a cup of coffee, and plunged into profound meditation upon the project. At length he called his favourite Equerry, Captain Bowler, for whom he had a deep affection, founded principally upon the shape of his whiskers.

"Bowler," he said, "isn't there some society of historical research, or something of which I am an honorary member?"

"Yes, sir," said Captain Bowler, rubbing his nose, "you are a member of 'The Encouragers of Egyptian Renaissance,' and 'The Teutonic Tombs Club,' and 'The Society for the Recovery of London Antiquities,' and—"

"That is admirable," said the King. "The London Antiquities does my trick. Go to the Society for the Recovery of London Antiquities and speak to their secretary, and their sub-secretary, and their president, and their vice-president, saying, 'The King of England is proud, but the honorary member of the Society for the Recovery of London Antiquities is prouder than kings. I should like to tell you of certain discoveries I have made touching the neglected traditions of the London boroughs. The revelations may cause some excitement, stirring burning memories and touching old wounds in Shepherd's Bush and Bayswater, in Pimlico and South Kensington. The King hesitates, but the honorary member is firm. I approach you invoking the vows of my initiation, the Sacred Seven Cats, the Poker of Perfection, and the Ordeal of the Indescribable Instant (forgive me if I mix you up with the Clan-na-Gael or some other club I belong to), and ask you to permit me to read a paper at your next meeting on the "Wars of the London Boroughs."' Say all this to the Society, Bowler. Remember it very carefully, for it is most important, and I have forgotten it altogether, and send me another cup of coffee and some of the cigars that we keep for vulgar and successful people. I am going to write my paper."

The Society for the Recovery of London Antiquities met a month after in a corrugated iron hall on the outskirts of one of the southern suburbs of London. A large number of people had collected there under the coarse and flaring gas-jets when the King arrived, perspiring and genial. On taking off his great-coat, he was perceived to be in evening dress, wearing the Garter. His appearance at the small table, adorned only with a glass of water, was received with respectful cheering.

The chairman (Mr. Huggins) said that he was sure that they had all been pleased to listen to such distinguished lecturers as they had heard for some time past (hear, hear). Mr. Burton (hear, hear), Mr. Cambridge, Professor King (loud and continued cheers), our old friend Peter Jessop, Sir William White (loud laughter), and other eminent men, had done honour to their little venture (cheers). But there were other circumstances which lent a certain unique quality to the present occasion (hear, hear). So far as his recollection went, and in connection with the Society for the Recovery of London Antiquities it went very far (loud cheers), he did not remember that any of their lecturers had borne the title of King. He would therefore call upon King Auberon briefly to address the meeting.

The King began by saying that this speech might be regarded as the first declaration of his new policy for the nation. "At this supreme hour of my life I feel that to no one but the members of the Society for the Recovery of London Antiquities can I open my heart (cheers). If the world turns upon my policy, and the storms of popular hostility begin to rise (no, no), I feel that it is here, with my brave Recoverers around me, that I can best meet them, sword in hand" (loud cheers).

His Majesty then went on to explain that, now old age was creeping upon him, he proposed to devote his remaining strength to bringing about a keener sense of local patriotism in the various municipalities of London. How few of them knew the legends of their own boroughs! How many there were who had never heard of the true origin of the Wink of Wandsworth! What a large proportion of the younger generation in Chelsea neglected to perform the old Chelsea Chuff! Pimlico no longer pumped the Pimlies. Battersea had forgotten the name of Blick.

There was a short silence, and then a voice said "Shame!"

The King continued: "Being called, however unworthily, to this high estate, I have resolved that, so far as possible, this neglect shall cease. I desire no military glory. I lay claim to no constitutional equality with Justinian or Alfred. If I can go down to history as the man who saved from extinction a few old English customs, if our descendants can say it was through this man, humble as he was, that the Ten Turnips are still eaten in Fulham, and the Putney parish councillor still shaves one half of his head, I shall look my great fathers reverently but not fearfully in the face when I go down to the last house of Kings."

The King paused, visibly affected, but collecting himself, resumed once more.

"I trust that to very few of you, at least, I need dwell on the sublime origins of these legends. The very names of your boroughs bear witness to them. So long as Hammersmith is called Hammersmith, its people will live in the shadow of that primal hero, the Blacksmith, who led the democracy of the Broadway into battle till he drove the chivalry of Kensington before him and overthrew them at that place which in honour of the best blood of the defeated aristocracy is still called Kensington Gore. Men of Hammersmith will not fail to remember that the very name of Kensington originated from the lips of their hero. For at the great banquet of reconciliation held after the war, when the disdainful oligarchs declined to join in the songs of the men of the Broadway (which are to this day of a rude and popular character), the great Republican leader, with his rough humour, said the words which are written in gold upon his monument, 'Little birds that can sing and won't sing, must be made to sing.' So that the Eastern Knights were called Cansings or Kensings ever afterwards. But you also have great memories, O men of Kensington! You showed that you could sing, and sing great war-songs. Even after the dark day of Kensington Gore, history will not forget those three Knights who guarded your disordered retreat from Hyde Park (so called from your hiding there), those three Knights after whom Knightsbridge is named. Nor will it forget the day of your re-emergence, purged in the fire of calamity, cleansed of your oligarchic corruptions, when, sword in hand, you drove the Empire of Hammersmith back mile by mile, swept it past its own Broadway, and broke it at last in a battle so long and bloody that the birds of prey have left their name upon it. Men have called it, with austere irony, the Ravenscourt. I shall not, I trust, wound the patriotism of Bayswater, or the lonelier pride of Brompton, or that of any other historic township, by taking these two special examples. I select them, not because they are more glorious than the rest, but partly from personal association (I am myself descended from one of the three heroes of Knightsbridge), and partly from the consciousness that I am an amateur antiquarian, and cannot presume to deal with times and places more remote and more mysterious. It is not for me to settle the question between two such men as Professor Hugg and Sir William Whisky as to whether Notting Hill means Nutting Hill (in allusion to the rich woods which no longer cover it), or whether it is a corruption of Nothing-ill, referring to its reputation among the ancients as an Earthly Paradise. When a Podkins and a Jossy confess themselves doubtful about the boundaries of West Kensington (said to have been traced in the blood of Oxen), I need not be ashamed to confess a similar doubt. I will ask you to excuse me from further history, and to assist me with your encouragement in dealing with the problem which faces us to-day. Is this ancient spirit of the London townships to die out? Are our omnibus conductors and policemen to lose altogether that light which we see so often in their eyes, the dreamy light of

> 'Old unhappy far-off things
> And battles long ago'

—to quote the words of a little-known poet who was a friend of my youth? I have resolved, as I have said, so far as possible, to preserve the eyes of policemen and omnibus conductors in their present dreamy state. For what is a state without dreams? And the remedy I propose is as follows:—

"To-morrow morning at twenty-five minutes past ten, if Heaven spares my life, I purpose to issue a Proclamation. It has been the work of my life, and is about half finished. With the assistance of a whisky and soda, I shall conclude the other half to-night, and my people will receive it to-morrow. All these boroughs where you were born, and hope to lay your bones, shall be reinstated in their ancient magnificence,— Hammersmith, Kensington, Bayswater, Chelsea, Battersea, Clapham, Balham, and a hundred others. Each shall immediately build a city wall with gates to be closed at sunset. Each shall have a city guard, armed to the teeth. Each shall have a banner, a coat-of-arms, and, if convenient, a gathering cry. I will not enter into the details now, my heart is too full. They will be found in the proclamation itself. You will all, however, be subject to enrolment in the local city guards, to be summoned together by a thing called the Tocsin, the meaning of which I am studying in my researches into history. Personally, I believe a tocsin to be some kind of highly paid official. If, therefore, any of you happen to have such a thing as a halberd in the house, I should advise you to practise with it in the garden."

Here the King buried his face in his handkerchief and hurriedly left the platform, overcome by emotions.

The members of the Society for the Recovery of London Antiquities rose in an indescribable state of vagueness. Some were purple with indignation; an intellectual few were purple with laughter; the great majority found their minds a blank. There remains a tradition that one pale face with burning blue eyes remained fixed upon the lecturer, and after the lecture a red-haired boy ran out of the room.

2. THE COUNCIL OF THE PROVOSTS

The King got up early next morning and came down three steps at a time like a schoolboy. Having eaten his breakfast hurriedly, but with an appetite, he summoned one of the highest officials of the Palace, and presented him with a shilling. "Go and buy me," he said, "a shilling paint-box, which you will get, unless the mists of time mislead me, in a shop at the corner of the second and dirtier street that leads out of Rochester Row. I have already requested the Master of the Buckhounds to provide me with cardboard. It seemed to me (I know not why) that it fell within his department."

The King was happy all that morning with his cardboard and his paint-box. He was engaged in designing the uniforms and coats-of-arms for the various municipalities of London. They gave him deep and no inconsiderable thought. He felt the responsibility.

"I cannot think," he said, "why people should think the names of places in the country more poetical than those in London. Shallow romanticists go away in trains and stop in places called Hugmy-in-the-Hole, or Bumps-on-the-Puddle. And all the time they could, if they liked, go and live at a place with the dim, divine name of St. John's Wood. I have never been to St. John's Wood. I dare not. I should be afraid of the innumerable night of fir trees, afraid to come upon a blood-red cup and the beating of the wings of the Eagle. But all these things can be imagined by remaining reverently in the Harrow train."

And he thoughtfully retouched his design for the head-dress of the halberdier of St. John's Wood, a design in black and red, compounded of a pine tree and the plumage of an eagle. Then he turned to another card. "Let us think of milder matters," he said. "Lavender Hill! Could any of your glebes and combes and all the rest of it produce so fragrant an idea? Think of a mountain of lavender lifting itself in purple poignancy into the silver skies and filling men's nostrils with a new breath of life—a purple hill of incense. It is true that upon my few excursions of discovery on a halfpenny tram I have failed to hit the precise spot. But it must be there; some poet called it by its name. There is at least warrant enough for the solemn purple plumes (following the botanical formation of lavender) which I have required people to wear in the neighbourhood of Clapham Junction. It is so everywhere, after all. I have never been actually to Southfields, but I suppose a scheme of lemons and olives represent their austral instincts. I have never visited Parson's Green, or seen either the Green or the Parson, but surely the pale-green shovel-hats I have designed must be more or less in the spirit. I must work in the dark and let my instincts guide me. The great love I bear to my people will certainly save me from distressing their noble spirit or violating their great traditions."

As he was reflecting in this vein, the door was flung open, and an official announced Mr. Barker and Mr. Lambert.

Mr. Barker and Mr. Lambert were not particularly surprised to find the King sitting on the floor amid a litter of water-colour sketches. They were not particularly surprised because the last time they had called on him they had found him sitting on the floor, surrounded by a litter of children's bricks, and the time before surrounded by a litter of wholly unsuccessful attempts to make paper darts. But the trend of the royal infant's remarks, uttered from amid this infantile chaos, was not quite the same affair.

For some time they let him babble on, conscious that his remarks meant nothing.

And then a horrible thought began to steal over the mind of James Barker. He began to think that the King's remarks did not mean nothing.

"In God's name, Auberon," he suddenly volleyed out, startling the quiet hall, "you don't mean that you are really going to have these city guards and city walls and things?"

"I am, indeed," said the infant, in a quiet voice. "Why shouldn't I have them? I have modelled them precisely on your political principles. Do you know what I've done, Barker? I've behaved like a true Barkerian. I've ... but perhaps it won't interest you, the account of my Barkerian conduct."

"Oh, go on, go on," cried Barker.

"The account of my Barkerian conduct," said Auberon, calmly, "seems not only to interest, but to alarm you. Yet it is very simple. It merely consists in choosing all the provosts under any new scheme by the same principle by which you have caused the central despot to be appointed. Each provost, of each city, under my charter, is to be appointed by rotation. Sleep, therefore, my Barker, a rosy sleep."

Barker's wild eyes flared.

"But, in God's name, don't you see, Quin, that the thing is quite different? In the centre it doesn't matter so much, just because the whole object of despotism is to get some sort of unity. But if any damned parish can go to any damned man—"

"I see your difficulty," said King Auberon, calmly. "You feel that your talents may be neglected. Listen!" And he rose with immense magnificence. "I solemnly give to my liege subject, James Barker, my special and splendid favour, the right to override the obvious text of the Charter of the Cities, and to be, in his own right, Lord High Provost of South Kensington. And now, my dear James, you are all right. Good day."

"But—" began Barker.

"The audience is at an end, Provost," said the King, smiling.

How far his confidence was justified, it would require a somewhat complicated description to explain. "The Great Proclamation of the Charter of the Free Cities" appeared in due course that morning, and was posted by bill-stickers all over the front of the Palace, the King assisting them with animated directions, and standing in the middle of the road, with his head on one side, contemplating the result. It was also carried up and down the main thoroughfares by sandwichmen, and the King was, with difficulty, restrained from going out in that capacity himself, being, in fact, found by the Groom of the Stole and Captain Bowler, struggling between two boards. His excitement had positively to be quieted like that of a child.

The reception which the Charter of the Cities met at the hands of the public may mildly be described as mixed. In one sense it was popular enough. In many happy homes that remarkable legal document was read aloud on winter evenings amid uproarious appreciation, when everything had been learnt by heart from that quaint but immortal old classic, Mr. W. W. Jacobs. But when it was discovered that the King had every intention of seriously requiring the provisions to be carried out, of insisting that the grotesque cities, with their tocsins and city guards, should really come into existence, things were thrown into a far angrier confusion. Londoners had no particular objection to the King making a fool of himself, but they became indignant when it became evident that he wished to make fools of them; and protests began to come in.

The Lord High Provost of the Good and Valiant City of West Kensington wrote a respectful letter to the King, explaining that upon State occasions it would, of course, be his duty to observe what formalities the King thought proper, but that it was really awkward for a decent householder not to be allowed to go out and put a post-card in a pillar-box without being escorted by five heralds, who announced, with formal cries and blasts of a trumpet, that the Lord High Provost desired to catch the post.

The Lord High Provost of North Kensington, who was a prosperous draper, wrote a curt business note, like a man complaining of a railway company, stating that definite inconvenience had been caused him by the presence of the halberdiers, whom he had to take with him everywhere. When attempting to catch an omnibus to the City, he had found that while room could have been found for himself, the halberdiers had a difficulty in getting in to the vehicle—believe him, theirs faithfully.

The Lord High Provost of Shepherd's Bush said his wife did not like men hanging round the kitchen.

The King was always delighted to listen to these grievances, delivering lenient and kingly answers, but as he always insisted, as the absolute *sine qua non*, that verbal complaints should be presented to him with the fullest pomp of trumpets, plumes, and halberds, only a few resolute spirits were prepared to run the gauntlet of the little boys in the street.

Among these, however, was prominent the abrupt and business-like gentleman who ruled North Kensington. And he had before long, occasion to interview the King about a matter wider and even more urgent than the problem of the halberdiers and the omnibus. This was the great question which then and for long afterwards brought a stir to the blood and a flush to the cheek of all the speculative builders and house agents from Shepherd's Bush to the Marble Arch, and from Westbourne Grove to High Street, Kensington. I refer to the great affair of the improvements in Notting Hill. The scheme was conducted chiefly by Mr. Buck, the abrupt North Kensington magnate, and by Mr. Wilson, the Provost of Bayswater. A great thoroughfare was to be driven through three boroughs, through West Kensington, North Kensington and Notting Hill, opening at one end into Hammersmith Broadway, and at the other into Westbourne Grove. The negotiations, buyings, sellings, bullying and bribing took ten years, and by the end of it Buck, who had conducted them almost single-handed, had proved himself a man of the strongest type of material energy and material diplomacy. And just as his splendid patience and more splendid impatience had finally brought him victory, when workmen were already demolishing houses and walls along the great line from Hammersmith, a sudden obstacle appeared that had neither been reckoned with nor dreamed of, a small and strange obstacle, which, like a speck of grit in a great machine, jarred the whole vast scheme and brought it to a stand-still, and Mr. Buck, the draper, getting with great impatience into his robes of office and summoning with indescribable disgust his halberdiers, hurried over to speak to the King.

Ten years had not tired the King of his joke. There were still new faces to be seen looking out from the symbolic head-gears he had designed, gazing at him from amid the pastoral ribbons of Shepherd's Bush or from under the sombre hoods of the Blackfriars Road. And the interview which was promised him with the Provost of North

Kensington he anticipated with a particular pleasure, for "he never really enjoyed," he said, "the full richness of the mediæval garments unless the people compelled to wear them were very angry and business-like."

Mr. Buck was both. At the King's command the door of the audience-chamber was thrown open and a herald appeared in the purple colours of Mr. Buck's commonwealth emblazoned with the Great Eagle which the King had attributed to North Kensington, in vague reminiscence of Russia, for he always insisted on regarding North Kensington as some kind of semi-arctic neighbourhood. The herald announced that the Provost of that city desired audience of the King.

"From North Kensington?" said the King, rising graciously. "What news does he bring from that land of high hills and fair women? He is welcome."

The herald advanced into the room, and was immediately followed by twelve guards clad in purple, who were followed by an attendant bearing the banner of the Eagle, who was followed by another attendant bearing the keys of the city upon a cushion, who was followed by Mr. Buck in a great hurry. When the King saw his strong animal face and steady eyes, he knew that he was in the presence of a great man of business, and consciously braced himself.

"Well, well," he said, cheerily coming down two or three steps from a daïs, and striking his hands lightly together, "I am glad to see you. Never mind, never mind. Ceremony is not everything."

"I don't understand your Majesty," said the Provost, stolidly.

"Never mind, never mind," said the King, gaily. "A knowledge of Courts is by no means an unmixed merit; you will do it next time, no doubt."

The man of business looked at him sulkily from under his black brows and said again without show of civility—

"I don't follow you."

"Well, well," replied the King, good-naturedly, "if you ask me I don't mind telling you, not because I myself attach any importance to these forms in comparison with the Honest Heart. But it is usual—it is usual—that is all, for a man when entering the presence of Royalty to lie down on his back on the floor and elevating his feet towards heaven (as the source of Royal power) to say three times 'Monarchical institutions improve the manners.' But there, there—such pomp is far less truly dignified than your simple kindliness."

The Provost's face was red with anger, and he maintained silence.

"And now," said the King, lightly, and with the exasperating air of a man softening a snub; "what delightful weather we are having! You must find your official robes warm, my Lord. I designed them for your own snow-bound land."

"They're as hot as hell," said Buck, briefly. "I came here on business."

"Right," said the King, nodding a great number of times with quite unmeaning solemnity; "right, right, right. Business, as the sad glad old Persian said, is business. Be punctual. Rise early. Point the pen to the shoulder. Point the pen to the shoulder, for you know not whence you come nor why. Point the pen to the shoulder, for you know not when you go nor where."

The Provost pulled a number of papers from his pocket and savagely flapped them open.

· · ·

31

"Your Majesty may have heard," he began, sarcastically, "of Hammersmith and a thing called a road. We have been at work ten years buying property and getting compulsory powers and fixing compensation and squaring vested interests, and now at the very end, the thing is stopped by a fool. Old Prout, who was Provost of Notting Hill, was a business man, and we dealt with him quite satisfactorily. But he's dead, and the cursed lot has fallen on a young man named Wayne, who's up to some game that's perfectly incomprehensible to me. We offer him a better price than any one ever dreamt of, but he won't let the road go through. And his Council seems to be backing him up. It's midsummer madness."

The King, who was rather inattentively engaged in drawing the Provost's nose with his finger on the window-pane, heard the last two words.

"What a perfect phrase that is!" he said. "'Midsummer madness'!"

"The chief point is," continued Buck, doggedly, "that the only part that is really in question is one dirty little street—Pump Street—a street with nothing in it but a public-house and a penny toy-shop, and that sort of thing. All the respectable people of Notting Hill have accepted our compensation. But the ineffable Wayne sticks out over Pump Street. Says he's Provost of Notting Hill. He's only Provost of Pump Street."

"A good thought," replied Auberon. "I like the idea of a Provost of Pump Street. Why not let him alone?"

"And drop the whole scheme!" cried out Buck, with a burst of brutal spirit. "I'll be damned if we do. No. I'm for sending in workmen to pull down without more ado."

"Strike for the purple Eagle!" cried the King, hot with historical associations.

"I'll tell you what it is," said Buck, losing his temper altogether. "If your Majesty would spend less time in insulting respectable people with your silly coats-of-arms, and more time over the business of the nation—"

The King's brow wrinkled thoughtfully.

"The situation is not bad," he said; "the haughty burgher defying the King in his own Palace. The burgher's head should be thrown back and the right arm extended; the left may be lifted towards Heaven, but that I leave to your private religious sentiment. I have sunk back in this chair, stricken with baffled fury. Now again, please."

Buck's mouth opened like a dog's, but before he could speak another herald appeared at the door.

"The Lord High Provost of Bayswater," he said, "desires an audience."

"Admit him," said Auberon. "This *is* a jolly day."

The halberdiers of Bayswater wore a prevailing uniform of green, and the banner which was borne after them was emblazoned with a green bay-wreath on a silver ground, which the King, in the course of his researches into a bottle of champagne, had discovered to be the quaint old punning cognisance of the city of Bayswater.

"It is a fit symbol," said the King, "your immortal bay-wreath. Fulham may seek for wealth, and Kensington for art, but when did the men of Bayswater care for anything but glory?"

Immediately behind the banner, and almost completely hidden by it, came the Provost of the city, clad in splendid robes of green and silver with white fur and crowned with bay. He was an anxious little man with red whiskers, originally the owner of a small sweet-stuff shop.

· · ·

"Our cousin of Bayswater," said the King, with delight; "what can we get for you?" The King was heard also distinctly to mutter, "Cold beef, cold 'am, cold chicken," his voice dying into silence.

"I came to see your Majesty," said the Provost of Bayswater, whose name was Wilson, "about that Pump Street affair."

"I have just been explaining the situation to his Majesty," said Buck, curtly, but recovering his civility. "I am not sure, however, whether his Majesty knows how much the matter affects you also."

"It affects both of us, yer see, yer Majesty, as this scheme was started for the benefit of the 'ole neighbourhood. So Mr. Buck and me we put our 'eads together—"

The King clasped his hands.

"Perfect!" he cried in ecstacy. "Your heads together! I can see it! Can't you do it now? Oh, do do it now!"

A smothered sound of amusement appeared to come from the halberdiers, but Mr. Wilson looked merely bewildered, and Mr. Buck merely diabolical.

"I suppose," he began bitterly, but the King stopped him with a gesture of listening.

"Hush," he said, "I think I hear some one else coming. I seem to hear another herald, a herald whose boots creak."

As he spoke another voice cried from the doorway—

"The Lord High Provost of South Kensington desires an audience."

"The Lord High Provost of South Kensington!" cried the King. "Why, that is my old friend James Barker! What does he want, I wonder? If the tender memories of friendship have not grown misty, I fancy he wants something for himself, probably money. How are you, James?"

Mr. James Barker, whose guard was attired in a splendid blue, and whose blue banner bore three gold birds singing, rushed, in his blue and gold robes, into the room. Despite the absurdity of all the dresses, it was worth noticing that he carried his better than the rest, though he loathed it as much as any of them. He was a gentleman, and a very handsome man, and could not help unconsciously wearing even his preposterous robe as it should be worn. He spoke quickly, but with the slight initial hesitation he always showed in addressing the King, due to suppressing an impulse to address his old acquaintance in the old way.

"Your Majesty—pray forgive my intrusion. It is about this man in Pump Street. I see you have Buck here, so you have probably heard what is necessary. I—"

The King swept his eyes anxiously round the room, which now blazed with the trappings of three cities.

"There is one thing necessary," he said.

"Yes, your Majesty," said Mr. Wilson of Bayswater, a little eagerly. "What does yer Majesty think necessary?"

"A little yellow," said the King, firmly. "Send for the Provost of West Kensington."

Amid some materialistic protests he was sent for, and arrived with his yellow halberdiers in his saffron robes, wiping his forehead with a handkerchief. After all, placed as he was, he had a good deal to say on the matter.

"Welcome, West Kensington," said the King. "I have long wished to see you touching that matter of the Hammersmith land to the south of the Rowton House. Will you hold it feudally from the Provost of Hammersmith? You have only to do him homage by putting his left arm in his overcoat and then marching home in state."

"No, your Majesty; I'd rather not," said the Provost of West Kensington, who was a pale young man with a fair moustache and whiskers, who kept a successful dairy.

The King struck him heartily on the shoulder.

"The fierce old West Kensington blood," he said; "they are not wise who ask it to do homage."

Then he glanced again round the room. It was full of a roaring sunset of colour, and he enjoyed the sight, possible to so few artists—the sight of his own dreams moving and blazing before him. In the foreground the yellow of the West Kensington liveries outlined itself against the dark blue draperies of South Kensington. The crests of these again brightened suddenly into green as the almost woodland colours of Bayswater rose behind them. And over and behind all, the great purple plumes of North Kensington showed almost funereal and black.

"There is something lacking," said the King—"something lacking. What can—Ah, there it is! there it is!"

In the doorway had appeared a new figure, a herald in flaming red. He cried in a loud but unemotional voice—

"The Lord High Provost of Notting Hill desires an audience."

3. ENTER A LUNATIC

The King of the Fairies, who was, it is to be presumed, the godfather of King Auberon, must have been very favourable on this particular day to his fantastic godchild, for with the entrance of the guard of the Provost of Notting Hill there was a certain more or less inexplicable addition to his delight. The wretched navvies and sandwich-men who carried the colours of Bayswater or South Kensington, engaged merely for the day to satisfy the Royal hobby, slouched into the room with a comparatively hang-dog air, and a great part of the King's intellectual pleasure consisted in the contrast between the arrogance of their swords and feathers and the meek misery of their faces. But these Notting Hill halberdiers in their red tunics belted with gold had the air rather of an absurd gravity. They seemed, so to speak, to be taking part in the joke. They marched and wheeled into position with an almost startling dignity and discipline.

They carried a yellow banner with a great red lion, named by the King as the Notting Hill emblem, after a small public-house in the neighbourhood, which he once frequented.

Between the two lines of his followers there advanced towards the King a tall, red-haired young man, with high features and bold blue eyes. He would have been called handsome, but that a certain indefinable air of his nose being too big for his face, and his feet for his legs, gave him a look of awkwardness and extreme youth. His robes were red, according to the King's heraldry, and, alone among the Provosts, he was girt with a great sword. This was Adam Wayne, the intractable Provost of Notting Hill.

The King flung himself back in his chair, and rubbed his hands.

"What a day, what a day!" he said to himself. "Now there'll be a row. I'd no idea it would be such fun as it is. These Provosts are so very indignant, so very reasonable, so very right. This fellow, by the look in his eyes, is even more indignant than the rest. No sign in those large blue eyes, at any rate, of ever having heard of a joke. He'll remonstrate with the others, and they'll remonstrate with him, and they'll all make themselves sumptuously happy remonstrating with me."

"Welcome, my Lord," he said aloud. "What news from the Hill of a Hundred Legends? What have you for the ear of your King? I know that troubles have arisen between you and these others, our cousins, but these troubles it shall be our pride to compose. And I doubt not, and cannot doubt, that your love for me is not less tender, no less ardent, than theirs."

Mr. Buck made a bitter face, and James Barker's nostrils curled; Wilson began to giggle faintly, and the Provost of West Kensington followed in a smothered way. But the big blue eyes of Adam Wayne never changed, and he called out in an odd, boyish voice down the hall—

"I bring homage to my King. I bring him the only thing I have—my sword."

And with a great gesture he flung it down on the ground, and knelt on one knee behind it.

There was a dead silence.

"I beg your pardon," said the King, blankly.

"You speak well, sire," said Adam Wayne, "as you ever speak, when you say that my love is not less than the love of these. Small would it be if it were not more. For I am the heir of your scheme—the child of the great Charter. I stand here for the rights the Charter gave me, and I swear, by your sacred crown, that where I stand, I stand fast."

The eyes of all five men stood out of their heads.

Then Buck said, in his jolly, jarring voice: "Is the whole world mad?"

The King sprang to his feet, and his eyes blazed.

"Yes," he cried, in a voice of exultation, "the whole world is mad, but Adam Wayne and me. It is true as death what I told you long ago, James Barker, seriousness sends men mad. You are mad, because you care for politics, as mad as a man who collects tram tickets. Buck is mad, because he cares for money, as mad as a man who lives on opium. Wilson is mad, because he thinks himself right, as mad as a man who thinks himself God Almighty. The Provost of West Kensington is mad, because he thinks he is respectable, as mad as a man who thinks he is a chicken. All men are mad but the humorist, who cares for nothing and possesses everything. I thought that there was only one humorist in England. Fools!—dolts!—open your cows' eyes; there are two! In Notting Hill—in that unpromising elevation—there has been born an artist! You thought to spoil my joke, and bully me out of it, by becoming more and more modern, more and more practical, more and more bustling and rational. Oh, what a feast it was to answer you by becoming more and more august, more and more gracious, more and more ancient and mellow! But this lad has seen how to bowl me out. He has answered me back, vaunt for vaunt, rhetoric for rhetoric. He has lifted the only shield I cannot break, the shield of an impenetrable pomposity. Listen to him. You have come, my Lord, about Pump Street?"

"About the city of Notting Hill," answered Wayne, proudly, "of which Pump Street is a living and rejoicing part."

"Not a very large part," said Barker, contemptuously.

"That which is large enough for the rich to covet," said Wayne, drawing up his head, "is large enough for the poor to defend."

The King slapped both his legs, and waved his feet for a second in the air.

"Every respectable person in Notting Hill," cut in Buck, with his cold, coarse voice, "is for us and against you. I have plenty of friends in Notting Hill."

"Your friends are those who have taken your gold for other men's hearthstones, my Lord Buck," said Provost Wayne. "I can well believe they are your friends."

"They've never sold dirty toys, anyhow," said Buck, laughing shortly.

"They've sold dirtier things," said Wayne, calmly: "they have sold themselves."

"It's no good, my Buckling," said the King, rolling about on his chair. "You can't cope with this chivalrous eloquence. You can't cope with an artist. You can't cope with the humorist of Notting Hill. Oh, *Nunc dimittis*—that I have lived to see this day! Provost Wayne, you stand firm?"

"Let them wait and see," said Wayne. "If I stood firm before, do you think I shall weaken now that I have seen the face of the King? For I fight for something greater, if greater there can be, than the hearthstones of my people and the Lordship of the Lion. I fight for your royal vision, for the great dream you dreamt of the League of the Free Cities. You have given me this liberty. If I had been a beggar and you had flung me a coin, if I had been a peasant in a dance and you had flung me a favour, do you think I would have let it be taken by any ruffians on the road? This leadership and liberty of Notting Hill is a gift from your Majesty, and if it is taken from me, by God! it shall be taken in battle, and the noise of that battle shall be heard in the flats of Chelsea and in the studios of St. John's Wood."

"It is too much—it is too much," said the King. "Nature is weak. I must speak to you, brother artist, without further disguise. Let me ask you a solemn question. Adam Wayne, Lord High Provost of Notting Hill, don't you think it splendid?"

"Splendid!" cried Adam Wayne. "It has the splendour of God."

"Bowled out again," said the King. "You will keep up the pose. Funnily, of course, it is serious. But seriously, isn't it funny?"

"What?" asked Wayne, with the eyes of a baby.

"Hang it all, don't play any more. The whole business—the Charter of the Cities. Isn't it immense?"

"Immense is no unworthy word for that glorious design."

"Oh, hang you! But, of course, I see. You want me to clear the room of these reasonable sows. You want the two humorists alone together. Leave us, gentlemen."

Buck threw a sour look at Barker, and at a sullen signal the whole pageant of blue and green, of red, gold, and purple, rolled out of the room, leaving only two in the great hall, the King sitting in his seat on the daïs, and the red-clad figure still kneeling on the floor before his fallen sword.

The King bounded down the steps and smacked Provost Wayne on the back.

"Before the stars were made," he cried, "we were made for each other. It is too beautiful. Think of the valiant independence of Pump Street. That is the real thing. It is the deification of the ludicrous."

The kneeling figure sprang to his feet with a fierce stagger.

"Ludicrous!" he cried, with a fiery face.

"Oh, come, come," said the King, impatiently, "you needn't keep it up with me. The augurs must wink sometimes from sheer fatigue of the eyelids. Let us enjoy this for half an hour, not as actors, but as dramatic critics. Isn't it a joke?"

Adam Wayne looked down like a boy, and answered in a constrained voice—

"I do not understand your Majesty. I cannot believe that while I fight for your royal charter your Majesty deserts me for these dogs of the gold hunt."

"Oh, damn your—But what's this? What the devil's this?"

The King stared into the young Provost's face, and in the twilight of the room began to see that his face was quite white and his lip shaking.

"What in God's name is the matter?" cried Auberon, holding his wrist.

Wayne flung back his face, and the tears were shining on it.

"I am only a boy," he said, "but it's true. I would paint the Red Lion on my shield if I had only my blood."

King Auberon dropped the hand and stood without stirring, thunderstruck.

"My God in Heaven!" he said; "is it possible that there is within the four seas of Britain a man who takes Notting Hill seriously?"

"And my God in Heaven!" said Wayne passionately; "is it possible that there is within the four seas of Britain a man who does not take it seriously?"

The King said nothing, but merely went back up the steps of the daïs, like a man dazed. He fell back in his chair again and kicked his heels.

"If this sort of thing is to go on," he said weakly, "I shall begin to doubt the superiority of art to life. In Heaven's name, do not play with me. Do you really mean that you are—God help me!—a Notting Hill patriot; that you are—?"

Wayne made a violent gesture, and the King soothed him wildly.

"All right—all right—I see you are; but let me take it in. You do really propose to fight these modern improvers with their boards and inspectors and surveyors and all the rest of it?"

"Are they so terrible?" asked Wayne, scornfully.

The King continued to stare at him as if he were a human curiosity.

"And I suppose," he said, "that you think that the dentists and small tradesmen and maiden ladies who inhabit Notting Hill, will rally with war-hymns to your standard?"

"If they have blood they will," said the Provost.

"And I suppose," said the King, with his head back among the cushions, "that it never crossed your mind that"—his voice seemed to lose itself luxuriantly—"never crossed your mind that any one ever thought that the idea of a Notting Hill idealism was—er—slightly—slightly ridiculous?"

"Of course they think so," said Wayne. "What was the meaning of mocking the prophets?"

"Where," asked the King, leaning forward—"where in Heaven's name did you get this miraculously inane idea?"

"You have been my tutor, Sire," said the Provost, "in all that is high and honourable."

37

"Eh?" said the King.

"It was your Majesty who first stirred my dim patriotism into flame. Ten years ago, when I was a boy (I am only nineteen), I was playing on the slope of Pump Street, with a wooden sword and a paper helmet, dreaming of great wars. In an angry trance I struck out with my sword, and stood petrified, for I saw that I had struck you, Sire, my King, as you wandered in a noble secrecy, watching over your people's welfare. But I need have had no fear. Then was I taught to understand Kingliness. You neither shrank nor frowned. You summoned no guards. You invoked no punishments. But in august and burning words, which are written in my soul, never to be erased, you told me ever to turn my sword against the enemies of my inviolate city. Like a priest pointing to the altar, you pointed to the hill of Notting. 'So long,' you said, 'as you are ready to die for the sacred mountain, even if it were ringed with all the armies of Bayswater.' I have not forgotten the words, and I have reason now to remember them, for the hour is come and the crown of your prophecy. The sacred hill is ringed with the armies of Bayswater, and I am ready to die."

The King was lying back in his chair, a kind of wreck.

"Oh, Lord, Lord, Lord," he murmured, "what a life! what a life! All my work! I seem to have done it all. So you're the red-haired boy that hit me in the waistcoat. What have I done? God, what have I done? I thought I would have a joke, and I have created a passion. I tried to compose a burlesque, and it seems to be turning halfway through into an epic. What is to be done with such a world? In the Lord's name, wasn't the joke broad and bold enough? I abandoned my subtle humour to amuse you, and I seem to have brought tears to your eyes. What's to be done with people when you write a pantomime for them—call the sausages classic festoons, and the policeman cut in two a tragedy of public duty? But why am I talking? Why am I asking questions of a nice young gentleman who is totally mad? What is the good of it? What is the good of anything? Oh, Lord! Oh, Lord!"

Suddenly he pulled himself upright.

"Don't you really think the sacred Notting Hill at all absurd?"

"Absurd?" asked Wayne, blankly. "Why should I?"

The King stared back equally blankly.

"I beg your pardon," he said.

"Notting Hill," said the Provost, simply, "is a rise or high ground of the common earth, on which men have built houses to live, in which they are born, fall in love, pray, marry, and die. Why should I think it absurd?"

The King smiled.

"Because, my Leonidas—" he began, then suddenly, he knew not how, found his mind was a total blank. After all, why was it absurd? Why was it absurd? He felt as if the floor of his mind had given way. He felt as all men feel when their first principles are hit hard with a question. Barker always felt so when the King said, "Why trouble about politics?"

The King's thoughts were in a kind of rout; he could not collect them.

"It is generally felt to be a little funny," he said vaguely.

· · ·

"I suppose," said Adam, turning on him with a fierce suddenness—"I suppose you fancy crucifixion was a serious affair?"

"Well, I—" began Auberon—"I admit I have generally thought it had its graver side."

"Then you are wrong," said Wayne, with incredible violence. "Crucifixion is comic. It is exquisitely diverting. It was an absurd and obscene kind of impaling reserved for people who were made to be laughed at—for slaves and provincials, for dentists and small tradesmen, as you would say. I have seen the grotesque gallows-shape, which the little Roman gutter-boys scribbled on walls as a vulgar joke, blazing on the pinnacles of the temples of the world. And shall I turn back?"

The King made no answer.

Adam went on, his voice ringing in the roof.

"This laughter with which men tyrannise is not the great power you think it. Peter was crucified, and crucified head downwards. What could be funnier than the idea of a respectable old Apostle upside down? What could be more in the style of your modern humour? But what was the good of it? Upside down or right side up, Peter was Peter to mankind. Upside down he stills hangs over Europe, and millions move and breathe only in the life of his Church."

King Auberon got up absently.

"There is something in what you say," he said. "You seem to have been thinking, young man."

"Only feeling, sire," answered the Provost. "I was born, like other men, in a spot of the earth which I loved because I had played boys' games there, and fallen in love, and talked with my friends through nights that were nights of the gods. And I feel the riddle. These little gardens where we told our loves. These streets where we brought out our dead. Why should they be commonplace? Why should they be absurd? Why should it be grotesque to say that a pillar-box is poetic when for a year I could not see a red pillar-box against the yellow evening in a certain street without being wracked with something of which God keeps the secret, but which is stronger than sorrow or joy? Why should any one be able to raise a laugh by saying 'the Cause of Notting Hill'?—Notting Hill where thousands of immortal spirits blaze with alternate hope and fear."

Auberon was flicking dust off his sleeve with quite a new seriousness on his face, distinct from the owlish solemnity which was the pose of his humour.

"It is very difficult," he said at last. "It is a damned difficult thing. I see what you mean; I agree with you even up to a point—or I should like to agree with you, if I were young enough to be a prophet and poet. I feel a truth in everything you say until you come to the words 'Notting Hill.' And then I regret to say that the old Adam awakes roaring with laughter and makes short work of the new Adam, whose name is Wayne."

For the first time Provost Wayne was silent, and stood gazing dreamily at the floor. Evening was closing in, and the room had grown darker.

"I know," he said, in a strange, almost sleepy voice, "there is truth in what you say, too. It is hard not to laugh at the common names—I only say we should not. I have thought of a remedy; but such thoughts are rather terrible."

"What thoughts?" asked Auberon.

The Provost of Notting Hill seemed to have fallen into a kind of trance; in his eyes was an elvish light.

. . .

"I know of a magic wand, but it is a wand that only one or two may rightly use, and only seldom. It is a fairy wand of great fear, stronger than those who use it—often frightful, often wicked to use. But whatever is touched with it is never again wholly common; whatever is touched with it takes a magic from outside the world. If I touch, with this fairy wand, the railways and the roads of Notting Hill, men will love them, and be afraid of them for ever."

"What the devil are you talking about?" asked the King.

"It has made mean landscapes magnificent, and hovels outlast cathedrals," went on the madman. "Why should it not make lamp-posts fairer than Greek lamps; and an omnibus-ride like a painted ship? The touch of it is the finger of a strange perfection."

"What is your wand?" cried the King, impatiently.

"There it is," said Wayne; and pointed to the floor, where his sword lay flat and shining.

"The sword!" cried the King; and sprang up straight on the daïs.

"Yes, yes," cried Wayne, hoarsely. "The things touched by that are not vulgar; the things touched by that—"

King Auberon made a gesture of horror.

"You will shed blood for that!" he cried. "For a cursed point of view—"

"Oh, you kings, you kings!" cried out Adam, in a burst of scorn. "How humane you are, how tender, how considerate! You will make war for a frontier, or the imports of a foreign harbour; you will shed blood for the precise duty on lace, or the salute to an admiral. But for the things that make life itself worthy or miserable—how humane you are! I say here, and I know well what I speak of, there were never any necessary wars but the religious wars. There were never any just wars but the religious wars. There were never any humane wars but the religious wars. For these men were fighting for something that claimed, at least, to be the happiness of a man, the virtue of a man. A Crusader thought, at least, that Islam hurt the soul of every man, king or tinker, that it could really capture. I think Buck and Barker and these rich vultures hurt the soul of every man, hurt every inch of the ground, hurt every brick of the houses, that they can really capture. Do you think I have no right to fight for Notting Hill, you whose English Government has so often fought for tomfooleries? If, as your rich friends say, there are no gods, and the skies are dark above us, what should a man fight for, but the place where he had the Eden of childhood and the short heaven of first love? If no temples and no scriptures are sacred, what is sacred if a man's own youth is not sacred?"

The King walked a little restlessly up and down the daïs.

"It is hard," he said, biting his lips, "to assent to a view so desperate—so responsible...."

As he spoke, the door of the audience chamber fell ajar, and through the aperture came, like the sudden chatter of a bird, the high, nasal, but well-bred voice of Barker.

"I said to him quite plainly—the public interests—"

Auberon turned on Wayne with violence.

"What the devil is all this? What am I saying? What are you saying? Have you hypnotised me? Curse your uncanny blue eyes! Let me go. Give me back my sense of humour. Give it me back—give it me back, I say!"

"I solemnly assure you," said Wayne, uneasily, with a gesture, as if feeling all over himself, "that I haven't got it."

The King fell back in his chair, and went into a roar of Rabelaisian laughter.

"I don't think you have," he cried.

BOOK III

1. THE MENTAL CONDITION OF ADAM WAYNE

A little while after the King's accession a small book of poems appeared, called "Hymns on the Hill." They were not good poems, nor was the book successful, but it attracted a certain amount of attention from one particular school of critics. The King himself, who was a member of the school, reviewed it in his capacity of literary critic to "Straight from the Stables," a sporting journal. They were known as the Hammock School, because it had been calculated malignantly by an enemy that no less than thirteen of their delicate criticisms had begun with the words, "I read this book in a hammock: half asleep in the sleepy sunlight, I ..."; after that there were important differences. Under these conditions they liked everything, but especially everything silly. "Next to authentic goodness in a book," they said—"next to authentic goodness in a book (and that, alas! we never find) we desire a rich badness." Thus it happened that their praise (as indicating the presence of a rich badness) was not universally sought after, and authors became a little disquieted when they found the eye of the Hammock School fixed upon them with peculiar favour.

The peculiarity of "Hymns on the Hill" was the celebration of the poetry of London as distinct from the poetry of the country. This sentiment or affectation was, of course, not uncommon in the twentieth century, nor was it, although sometimes exaggerated, and sometimes artificial, by any means without a great truth at its root, for there is one respect in which a town must be more poetical than the country, since it is closer to the spirit of man; for London, if it be not one of the masterpieces of man, is at least one of his sins. A street is really more poetical than a meadow, because a street has a secret. A street is going somewhere, and a meadow nowhere. But, in the case of the book called "Hymns on the Hill," there was another peculiarity, which the King pointed out with great acumen in his review. He was naturally interested in the matter, for he had himself

42

published a volume of lyrics about London under his pseudonym of "Daisy Daydream."

This difference, as the King pointed out, consisted in the fact that, while mere artificers like "Daisy Daydream" (on whose elaborate style the King, over his signature of "Thunderbolt," was perhaps somewhat too severe) thought to praise London by comparing it to the country—using nature, that is, as a background from which all poetical images had to be drawn—the more robust author of "Hymns on the Hill" praised the country, or nature, by comparing it to the town, and used the town itself as a background. "Take," said the critic, "the typically feminine lines, 'To the Inventor of The Hansom Cab'—

'Poet, whose cunning carved this amorous shell,
Where twain may dwell.'"

"Surely," wrote the King, "no one but a woman could have written those lines. A woman has always a weakness for nature; with her art is only beautiful as an echo or shadow of it. She is praising the hansom cab by theme and theory, but her soul is still a child by the sea, picking up shells. She can never be utterly of the town, as a man can; indeed, do we not speak (with sacred propriety) of 'a man about town'? Who ever spoke of a woman about town? However much, physically, 'about town' a woman may be, she still models herself on nature; she tries to carry nature with her; she bids grasses to grow on her head, and furry beasts to bite her about the throat. In the heart of a dim city, she models her hat on a flaring cottage garden of flowers. We, with our nobler civic sentiment, model ours on a chimney pot; the ensign of civilisation. And rather than be without birds, she will commit massacre, that she may turn her head into a tree, with dead birds to sing on it."

This kind of thing went on for several pages, and then the critic remembered his subject, and returned to it.

"Poet, whose cunning carved this amorous shell,
Where twain may dwell."

"The peculiarity of these fine though feminine lines," continued "Thunderbolt," "is, as we have said, that they praise the hansom cab by comparing it to the shell, to a natural thing. Now, hear the author of 'Hymns on the Hill,' and how he deals with the same subject. In his fine nocturne, entitled 'The Last Omnibus' he relieves the rich and poignant melancholy of the theme by a sudden sense of rushing at the end—

'The wind round the old street corner
Swung sudden and quick as a cab.'

"Here the distinction is obvious. 'Daisy Daydream' thinks it a great compliment to a hansom cab to be compared to one of the spiral chambers of the sea. And the author of 'Hymns on the Hill' thinks it a great compliment to the immortal whirlwind to be compared to a hackney coach. He surely is the real admirer of London. We have no space to speak of all his perfect applications of the idea; of the poem in which, for instance, a lady's eyes are compared, not to stars, but to two perfect street-lamps guiding the wanderer. We have no space to speak of the fine lyric, recalling the Elizabethan spirit, in which the poet, instead of saying that the rose and the lily contend in her complexion, says, with a purer modernism, that the red omnibus of Hammersmith and the white omnibus of Fulham fight there for the mastery. How perfect the image of two contending omnibuses!"

Here, somewhat abruptly, the review concluded, probably because the King had to send off his copy at that moment, as he was in some want of money. But the King was a very good critic, whatever he may have been as King, and he had, to a considerable extent, hit the right nail on the head. "Hymns on the Hill" was not at all like the poems originally published in praise of the poetry of London. And the reason was that it was really written by a man who had seen nothing else but London, and who regarded it, therefore, as the universe. It was written by a raw, red-headed lad of seventeen, named Adam Wayne, who had been born in Notting Hill. An accident in his seventh year prevented his being taken away to the seaside, and thus his whole life had been passed in his own Pump Street, and in its neighbourhood. And the consequence was, that he saw the street-lamps as things quite as eternal as the stars; the two fires were mingled. He saw the houses as things enduring, like the mountains, and so he wrote about them as one would write about mountains. Nature puts on a disguise when she speaks to every man; to this man she put on the disguise of Notting Hill. Nature would mean to a poet born in the Cumberland hills, a stormy sky-line and sudden rocks. Nature would mean to a poet born in the Essex flats, a waste of splendid waters and splendid sunsets. So nature meant to this man Wayne a line of violet roofs and lemon lamps, the chiaroscuro of the town. He did not think it clever or funny to praise the shadows and colours of the town; he had seen no other shadows or colours, and so he praised them— because they were shadows and colours. He saw all this because he was a poet, though in practice a bad poet. It is too often forgotten that just as a bad man is nevertheless a man, so a bad poet is nevertheless a poet.

Mr. Wayne's little volume of verse was a complete failure; and he submitted to the decision of fate with a quite rational humility, went back to his work, which was that of a draper's assistant, and wrote no more. He still retained his feeling about the town of Notting Hill, because he could not possibly have any other feeling, because it was the back and base of his brain. But he does not seem to have made any particular attempt to express it or insist upon it.

He was a genuine natural mystic, one of those who live on the border of fairyland. But he was perhaps the first to realise how often the boundary of fairyland runs through a crowded city. Twenty feet from him (for he was very short-sighted) the red and white and yellow suns of the gas-lights thronged and melted into each other like an orchard of fiery trees, the beginning of the woods of elf-land.

But, oddly enough, it was because he was a small poet that he came to his strange and isolated triumph. It was because he was a failure in literature that he became a portent in English history. He was one of those to whom nature has given the desire without the power of artistic expression. He had been a dumb poet from his cradle. He might have been so to his grave, and carried unuttered into the darkness a treasure of new and sensational song. But he was born under the lucky star of a single coincidence. He happened to be at the head of his dingy municipality at the time of the King's jest, at the time when all municipalities were suddenly commanded to break out into banners and flowers. Out of the long procession of the silent poets, who have been passing since the beginning of the world, this one man found himself in the midst of an heraldic vision, in which he could act and speak and live lyrically. While the author and the victims alike treated the whole matter as a silly public charade, this one man, by taking it seriously, sprang suddenly into a throne of artistic omnipotence. Armour, music, standards, watch-fires, the noise of drums, all the theatrical properties were thrown before him. This one poor rhymster, having burnt his own rhymes, began to live that life of open air and acted poetry of which all the poets of the earth have dreamed in vain; the life for which the Iliad is only a cheap substitute.

Upwards from his abstracted childhood, Adam Wayne had grown strongly and silently in a certain quality or capacity which is in modern cities almost entirely artificial, but which can be natural, and was primarily almost brutally natural in him, the quality or capacity of patriotism. It exists, like other virtues and vices, in a certain undiluted reality. It is not confused with all kinds of other things. A child speaking of his country or his village may make every mistake in Mandeville or tell every lie in Munchausen, but in his statement there will be no psychological lies any more than there can be in a good song. Adam Wayne, as a boy, had for his dull streets in Notting Hill the ultimate and ancient sentiment that went out to Athens or Jerusalem. He knew the secret of the passion, those secrets which make real old national songs sound so strange to our civilisation. He knew that real patriotism tends to sing about sorrows and forlorn hopes much more than about victory. He knew that in proper names themselves is half the poetry of all national poems. Above all, he knew the supreme psychological fact about patriotism, as certain in connection with it as that a fine shame comes to all lovers, the fact that the patriot never under any circumstances boasts of the largeness of his country, but always, and of necessity, boasts of the smallness of it.

All this he knew, not because he was a philosopher or a genius, but because he was a child. Any one who cares to walk up a side slum like Pump Street, can see a little Adam claiming to be king of a paving-stone. And he will always be proudest if the stone is almost too narrow for him to keep his feet inside it.

It was while he was in such a dream of defensive battle, marking out some strip of street or fortress of steps as the limit of his haughty claim, that the King had met him, and, with a few words flung in mockery, ratified for ever the strange boundaries of his soul. Thenceforward the fanciful idea of the defence of Notting Hill in war became to him a thing as solid as eating or drinking or lighting a pipe. He disposed his meals for it, altered his plans for it, lay awake in the night and went over it again. Two or three shops were to him an arsenal; an area was to him a moat; corners of balconies and turns of stone steps were points for the location of a culverin or an archer. It is almost impossible to convey to any ordinary imagination the degree to which he had transmitted the leaden London landscape to a romantic gold. The process began almost in babyhood, and became habitual like a literal madness. It was felt most keenly at night, when London is really herself, when her lights shine in the dark like the eyes of innumerable cats, and the outline of the dark houses has the bold simplicity of blue hills. But for him the night revealed instead of concealing, and he read all the blank hours of morning and afternoon, by a contradictory phrase, in the light of that darkness. To this man, at any rate, the inconceivable had happened. The artificial city had become to him nature, and he felt the curbstones and gas-lamps as things as ancient as the sky.

One instance may suffice. Walking along Pump Street with a friend, he said, as he gazed dreamily at the iron fence of a little front garden, "How those railings stir one's blood!"

His friend, who was also a great intellectual admirer, looked at them painfully, but without any particular emotion. He was so troubled about it that he went back quite a large number of times on quiet evenings and stared at the railings, waiting for something to happen to his blood, but without success. At last he took refuge in asking Wayne himself. He discovered that the ecstacy lay in the one point he had never noticed about the railings even after his six visits—the fact that they were, like the great majority of others—in London, shaped at the top after the manner of a spear. As a child, Wayne had half unconsciously compared them with the spears in pictures of Lancelot and St. George, and had grown up under the shadow of the graphic association. Now, whenever he looked at them, they were simply the serried weapons that made a hedge of steel round the sacred homes of Notting Hill. He could not have cleansed his mind of that meaning even if he tried. It was not a fanciful comparison, or anything like it. It would not have been true to say that the familiar railings reminded him of spears; it would have been far truer to say that the familiar spears occasionally reminded him of railings.

A couple of days after his interview with the King, Adam Wayne was pacing like a caged lion in front of five shops that occupied the upper end of the disputed street. They were a grocer's, a chemist's, a barber's, an old curiosity shop and a toy-shop that sold also newspapers. It was these five shops which his childish fastidiousness had first selected as the essentials of the Notting Hill campaign, the citadel of the city. If Notting Hill was the heart of the universe, and Pump Street was the heart of Notting Hill, this was the heart of Pump Street. The fact that they were all small and side by side realised that feeling for a formidable comfort and compactness which, as we have said, was the heart of his patriotism, and of all patriotism. The grocer (who had a wine and spirit licence) was included because he could provision the garrison; the old curiosity shop because it contained enough swords, pistols, partisans, cross-bows, and blunderbusses to arm a whole irregular regiment; the toy and paper shop because Wayne thought a free press an essential centre for the soul of Pump Street; the chemist's to cope with outbreaks of disease among the besieged; and the barber's because it was in the middle of all the rest, and the barber's son was an intimate friend and spiritual affinity.

It was a cloudless October evening settling down through purple into pure silver around the roofs and chimneys of the steep little street, which looked black and sharp and dramatic. In the deep shadows the gas-lit shop fronts gleamed like five fires in a row, and before them, darkly outlined like a ghost against some purgatorial furnaces, passed to and fro the tall bird-like figure and eagle nose of Adam Wayne.

He swung his stick restlessly, and seemed fitfully talking to himself.

"There are, after all, enigmas," he said "even to the man who has faith. There are doubts that remain even after the true philosophy is completed in every rung and rivet. And here is one of them. Is the normal human need, the normal human condition, higher or lower than those special states of the soul which call out a doubtful and dangerous glory? those special powers of knowledge or sacrifice which are made possible only by the existence of evil? Which should come first to our affections, the enduring sanities of peace or the half-maniacal virtues of battle? Which should come first, the man great in the daily round or the man great in emergency? Which should come first, to return to the enigma before me, the grocer or the chemist? Which is more certainly the stay of the city, the swift chivalrous chemist or the benignant all-providing grocer? In such ultimate spiritual doubts it is only possible to choose a side by the higher instincts, and to abide the issue. In any case, I have made my choice. May I be pardoned if I choose wrongly, but I choose the grocer."

"Good morning, sir," said the grocer, who was a middle-aged man, partially bald, with harsh red whiskers and beard, and forehead lined with all the cares of the small tradesman. "What can I do for you, sir?"

Wayne removed his hat on entering the shop, with a ceremonious gesture, which, slight as it was, made the tradesman eye him with the beginnings of wonder.

"I come, sir," he said soberly, "to appeal to your patriotism."

"Why, sir," said the grocer, "that sounds like the times when I was a boy and we used to have elections."

"You will have them again," said Wayne, firmly, "and far greater things. Listen, Mr. Mead. I know the temptations which a grocer has to a too cosmopolitan philosophy. I can imagine what it must be to sit all day as you do surrounded with wares from all the ends of the earth, from strange seas that we have never sailed and strange forests that we could not even picture. No Eastern king ever had such argosies or such cargoes coming from the sunrise and the sunset, and Solomon in all his glory was not enriched like one of you. India is at your elbow," he cried, lifting his voice and pointing his stick at a drawer of rice, the grocer making a movement of some alarm, "China is before you, Demerara is behind you, America is above your head, and at this very moment, like some old Spanish admiral, you hold Tunis in your hands."

Mr. Mead dropped the box of dates which he was just lifting, and then picked it up again vaguely.

Wayne went on with a heightened colour, but a lowered voice,

"I know, I say, the temptations of so international, so universal a vision of wealth. I know that it must be your danger not to fall like many tradesmen into too dusty and mechanical a narrowness, but rather to be too broad, to be too general, too liberal. If a narrow nationalism be the danger of the pastry-cook, who makes his own wares under his own heavens, no less is cosmopolitanism the danger of the grocer. But I come to you in the name of that patriotism which no wanderings or enlightenments should ever wholly extinguish, and I ask you to remember Notting Hill. For, after all, in this cosmopolitan magnificence, she has played no small part. Your dates may come from the tall palms of Barbary, your sugar from the strange islands of the tropics, your tea from the secret villages of the Empire of the Dragon. That this room might be furnished, forests may have been spoiled under the Southern Cross, and leviathans speared under the Polar Star. But you yourself—surely no inconsiderable treasure—you yourself, the brain that wields these vast interests—you yourself, at least, have grown to strength and wisdom between these grey houses and under this rainy sky. This city which made you, and thus made your fortunes, is threatened with war. Come forth and tell to the ends of the earth this lesson. Oil is from the North and fruits from the South; rices are from

India and spices from Ceylon; sheep are from New Zealand and men from Notting Hill."

The grocer sat for some little while, with dim eyes and his mouth open, looking rather like a fish. Then he scratched the back of his head, and said nothing. Then he said—

"Anything out of the shop, sir?"

Wayne looked round in a dazed way. Seeing a pile of tins of pine-apple chunks, he waved his stick generally towards them.

"Yes," he said; "I'll take those."

"All those, sir?" said the grocer, with greatly increased interest.

"Yes, yes; all those," replied Wayne, still a little bewildered, like a man splashed with cold water.

"Very good, sir; thank you, sir," said the grocer with animation. "You may count upon my patriotism, sir."

"I count upon it already," said Wayne, and passed out into the gathering night.

The grocer put the box of dates back in its place.

"What a nice fellow he is!" he said. "It's odd how often they are nice. Much nicer than those as are all right."

Meanwhile Adam Wayne stood outside the glowing chemist's shop, unmistakably wavering.

"What a weakness it is!" he muttered. "I have never got rid of it from childhood— the fear of this magic shop. The grocer is rich, he is romantic, he is poetical in the truest sense, but he is not—no, he is not supernatural. But the chemist! All the other shops stand in Notting Hill, but this stands in Elf-land. Look at those great burning bowls of colour. It must be from them that God paints the sunsets. It is superhuman, and the superhuman is all the more uncanny when it is beneficent. That is the root of the fear of God. I am afraid. But I must be a man and enter."

He was a man, and entered. A short, dark young man was behind the counter with spectacles, and greeted him with a bright but entirely business-like smile.

"A fine evening, sir," he said.

"Fine indeed, strange Father," said Adam, stretching his hands somewhat forward. "It is on such clear and mellow nights that your shop is most itself. Then they appear most perfect, those moons of green and gold and crimson, which from afar oft guide the pilgrim of pain and sickness to this house of merciful witchcraft."

"Can I get you anything?" asked the chemist.

"Let me see," said Wayne, in a friendly but vague manner. "Let me have some sal volatile."

"Eightpence, tenpence, or one and sixpence a bottle?" said the young man, genially.

"One and six—one and six," replied Wayne, with a wild submissiveness. "I come to ask you, Mr. Bowles, a terrible question."

He paused and collected himself.

. . .

"It is necessary," he muttered—"it is necessary to be tactful, and to suit the appeal to each profession in turn."

"I come," he resumed aloud, "to ask you a question which goes to the roots of your miraculous toils. Mr. Bowles, shall all this witchery cease?" And he waved his stick around the shop.

Meeting with no answer, he continued with animation—

"In Notting Hill we have felt to its core the elfish mystery of your profession. And now Notting Hill itself is threatened."

"Anything more, sir?" asked the chemist.

"Oh," said Wayne, somewhat disturbed—"oh, what is it chemists sell? Quinine, I think. Thank you. Shall it be destroyed? I have met these men of Bayswater and North Kensington—Mr. Bowles, they are materialists. They see no witchery in your work, even when it is wrought within their own borders. They think the chemist is commonplace. They think him human."

The chemist appeared to pause, only a moment, to take in the insult, and immediately said—

"And the next article, please?"

"Alum," said the Provost, wildly. "I resume. It is in this sacred town alone that your priesthood is reverenced. Therefore, when you fight for us you fight not only for yourself, but for everything you typify. You fight not only for Notting Hill, but for Fairyland, for as surely as Buck and Barker and such men hold sway, the sense of Fairyland in some strange manner diminishes."

"Anything more, sir?" asked Mr. Bowles, with unbroken cheerfulness.

"Oh yes, jujubes—Gregory powder—magnesia. The danger is imminent. In all this matter I have felt that I fought not merely for my own city (though to that I owe all my blood), but for all places in which these great ideas could prevail. I am fighting not merely for Notting Hill, but for Bayswater itself; for North Kensington itself. For if the gold-hunters prevail, these also will lose all their ancient sentiments and all the mystery of their national soul. I know I can count upon you."

"Oh yes, sir," said the chemist, with great animation; "we are always glad to oblige a good customer."

Adam Wayne went out of the shop with a deep sense of fulfilment of soul.

"It is so fortunate," he said, "to have tact, to be able to play upon the peculiar talents and specialities, the cosmopolitanism of the grocer and the world-old necromancy of the chemist. Where should I be without tact?"

2. THE REMARKABLE MR. TURNBULL

After two more interviews with shopmen, however, the patriot's confidence in his own psychological diplomacy began vaguely to wane. Despite the care with which he considered the peculiar rationale and the peculiar glory of each separate shop, there seemed to be something unresponsive about the shopmen. Whether it was a dark resentment against the uninitiate for peeping into their masonic magnificence, he could not quite conjecture.

His conversation with the man who kept the shop of curiosities had begun encouragingly. The man who kept the shop of curiosities had, indeed, enchanted him with a phrase. He was standing drearily at the door of his shop, a wrinkled man with a grey pointed beard, evidently a gentleman who had come down in the world.

"And how does your commerce go, you strange guardian of the past?" said Wayne, affably.

"Well, sir, not very well," replied the man, with that patient voice of his class which is one of the most heart-breaking things in the world. "Things are terribly quiet."

Wayne's eyes shone suddenly.

"A great saying," he said, "worthy of a man whose merchandise is human history. Terribly quiet; that is in two words the spirit of this age, as I have felt it from my cradle. I sometimes wondered how many other people felt the oppression of this union between quietude and terror. I see blank well-ordered streets and men in black moving about inoffensively, sullenly. It goes on day after day, day after day, and nothing happens; but to me it is like a dream from which I might wake screaming. To me the straightness of our life is the straightness of a thin cord stretched tight. Its stillness is terrible. It might snap with a noise like thunder. And you who sit, amid the *debris* of the great wars, you who sit, as it were, upon a battlefield, you know that war was less terrible than this evil peace; you know that the idle lads who carried those swords under Francis or Elizabeth, the rude Squire or Baron who swung that mace about in Picardy or Northumberland battles, may have been terribly noisy, but were not like us, terribly quiet."

Whether it was a faint embarrassment of conscience as to the original source and date of the weapons referred to, or merely an engrained depression, the guardian of the past looked, if anything, a little more worried.

"But I do not think," continued Wayne, "that this horrible silence of modernity will last, though I think for the present it will increase. What a farce is this modern liberality! Freedom of speech means practically, in our modern civilisation, that we must only talk about unimportant things. We must not talk about religion, for that is illiberal; we must not talk about bread and cheese, for that is talking shop; we must not talk about death, for that is depressing; we must not talk about birth, for that is indelicate. It cannot last. Something must break this strange indifference, this strange dreamy egoism, this strange loneliness of millions in a crowd. Something must break it. Why should it not be you and I? Can you do nothing else but guard relics?"

The shopman wore a gradually clearing expression, which would have led those unsympathetic with the cause of the Red Lion to think that the last sentence was the only one to which he had attached any meaning.

"I am rather old to go into a new business," he said, "and I don't quite know what to be, either."

"Why not," said Wayne, gently having reached the crisis of his delicate persuasion —"why not be a colonel?"

It was at this point, in all probability, that the interview began to yield more disappointing results. The man appeared inclined at first to regard the suggestion of becoming a colonel as outside the sphere of immediate and relevant discussion. A long exposition of the inevitable war of independence, coupled with the purchase of a doubtful sixteenth-century sword for an exaggerated price, seemed to resettle matters. Wayne left the shop, however, somewhat infected with the melancholy of its owner.

That melancholy was completed at the barber's.

"Shaving, sir?" inquired that artist from inside his shop.

"War!" replied Wayne, standing on the threshold.

"I beg your pardon," said the other, sharply.

"War!" said Wayne, warmly. "But not for anything inconsistent with the beautiful and the civilised arts. War for beauty. War for society. War for peace. A great chance is offered you of repelling that slander which, in defiance of the lives of so many artists, attributes poltroonery to those who beautify and polish the surface of our lives. Why should not hairdressers be heroes? Why should not—"

"Now, you get out," said the barber, irascibly. "We don't want any of your sort here. You get out."

And he came forward with the desperate annoyance of a mild person when enraged.

Adam Wayne laid his hand for a moment on the sword, then dropped it.

"Notting Hill," he said, "will need her bolder sons;" and he turned gloomily to the toy-shop.

It was one of those queer little shops so constantly seen in the side streets of London, which must be called toy-shops only because toys upon the whole predominate; for the remainder of goods seem to consist of almost everything else in the world—tobacco, exercise-books, sweet-stuff, novelettes, halfpenny paper clips, halfpenny pencil sharpeners, bootlaces, and cheap fireworks. It also sold newspapers, and a row of dirty-looking posters hung along the front of it.

"I am afraid," said Wayne, as he entered, "that I am not getting on with these tradesmen as I should. Is it that I have neglected to rise to the full meaning of their work? Is there some secret buried in each of these shops which no mere poet can discover?"

He stepped to the counter with a depression which he rapidly conquered as he addressed the man on the other side of it,—a man of short stature, and hair prematurely white, and the look of a large baby.

"Sir," said Wayne, "I am going from house to house in this street of ours, seeking to stir up some sense of the danger which now threatens our city. Nowhere have I felt my duty so difficult as here. For the toy-shop keeper has to do with all that remains to us of Eden before the first wars began. You sit here meditating continually upon the wants of that wonderful time when every staircase leads to the stars, and every garden-path to the other end of nowhere. Is it thoughtlessly, do you think, that I strike the dark old drum of peril in the paradise of children? But consider a moment; do not condemn me hastily. Even that paradise itself contains the rumour or beginning of that danger, just as the Eden that was made for perfection contained the terrible tree. For judge childhood, even by your own arsenal of its pleasures. You keep bricks; you make yourself thus, doubtless, the witness of the constructive instinct older than the destructive. You keep dolls; you make yourself the priest of that divine idolatry. You keep Noah's Arks; you perpetuate the memory of the salvation of all life as a precious, an irreplaceable thing. But do you keep only, sir, the symbols of this prehistoric sanity, this childish rationality of the earth? Do you not keep more terrible things? What are those boxes, seemingly of lead soldiers, that I see in that glass case? Are they not witnesses to that terror and beauty, that desire for a lovely death, which could not be excluded even from the immortality of Eden? Do not despise the lead soldiers, Mr. Turnbull."

"I don't," said Mr. Turnbull, of the toy-shop, shortly, but with great emphasis.

"I am glad to hear it," replied Wayne. "I confess that I feared for my military schemes the awful innocence of your profession. How, I thought to myself, will this man, used only to the wooden swords that give pleasure, think of the steel swords that give pain? But I am at least partly reassured. Your tone suggests to me that I have at least the entry of a gate of your fairyland—the gate through which the soldiers enter, for it cannot be denied—I ought, sir, no longer to deny, that it is of soldiers that I come to speak. Let your gentle employment make you merciful towards the troubles of the world. Let your own silvery experience tone down our sanguine sorrows. For there is war in Notting Hill."

The little toy-shop keeper sprang up suddenly, slapping his fat hands like two fans on the counter.

"War?" he cried. "Not really, sir? Is it true? Oh, what a joke! Oh, what a sight for sore eyes!"

Wayne was almost taken aback by this outburst.

"I am delighted," he stammered. "I had no notion—"

He sprang out of the way just in time to avoid Mr. Turnbull, who took a flying leap over the counter and dashed to the front of the shop.

"You look here, sir," he said; "you just look here."

He came back with two of the torn posters in his hand which were flapping outside his shop.

"Look at those, sir," he said, and flung them down on the counter.

Wayne bent over them, and read on one—

> "LAST FIGHTING.
> REDUCTION OF THE CENTRAL DERVISH CITY.
> REMARKABLE, ETC."

On the other he read—

> "LAST SMALL REPUBLIC ANNEXED.
> NICARAGUAN CAPITAL SURRENDERS AFTER A MONTH'S FIGHTING.
> GREAT SLAUGHTER."

Wayne bent over them again, evidently puzzled; then he looked at the dates. They were both dated in August fifteen years before.

"Why do you keep these old things?" he said, startled entirely out of his absurd tact of mysticism. "Why do you hang them outside your shop?"

"Because," said the other, simply, "they are the records of the last war. You mentioned war just now. It happens to be my hobby."

Wayne lifted his large blue eyes with an infantile wonder.

"Come with me," said Turnbull, shortly, and led him into a parlour at the back of the shop.

. . .

In the centre of the parlour stood a large deal table. On it were set rows and rows of the tin and lead soldiers which were part of the shopkeeper's stock. The visitor would have thought nothing of it if it had not been for a certain odd grouping of them, which did not seem either entirely commercial or entirely haphazard.

"You are acquainted, no doubt," said Turnbull, turning his big eyes upon Wayne —"you are acquainted, no doubt, with the arrangement of the American and Nicaraguan troops in the last battle;" and he waved his hand towards the table.

"I am afraid not," said Wayne. "I—"

"Ah! you were at that time occupied too much, perhaps, with the Dervish affair. You will find it in this corner." And he pointed to a part of the floor where there was another arrangement of children's soldiers grouped here and there.

"You seem," said Wayne, "to be interested in military matters."

"I am interested in nothing else," answered the toy-shop keeper, simply.

Wayne appeared convulsed with a singular, suppressed excitement.

"In that case," he said, "I may approach you with an unusual degree of confidence. Touching the matter of the defence of Notting Hill, I—"

"Defence of Notting Hill? Yes, sir. This way, sir," said Turnbull, with great perturbation. "Just step into this side room;" and he led Wayne into another apartment, in which the table was entirely covered with an arrangement of children's bricks. A second glance at it told Wayne that the bricks were arranged in the form of a precise and perfect plan of Notting Hill. "Sir," said Turnbull, impressively, "you have, by a kind of accident, hit upon the whole secret of my life. As a boy, I grew up among the last wars of the world, when Nicaragua was taken and the dervishes wiped out. And I adopted it as a hobby, sir, as you might adopt astronomy or bird-stuffing. I had no ill-will to any one, but I was interested in war as a science, as a game. And suddenly I was bowled out. The big Powers of the world, having swallowed up all the small ones, came to that confounded agreement, and there was no more war. There was nothing more for me to do but to do what I do now—to read the old campaigns in dirty old newspapers, and to work them out with tin soldiers. One other thing had occurred to me. I thought it an amusing fancy to make a plan of how this district or ours ought to be defended if it were ever attacked. It seems to interest you too."

"If it were ever attacked," repeated Wayne, awed into an almost mechanical enunciation. "Mr. Turnbull, it is attacked. Thank Heaven, I am bringing to at least one human being the news that is at bottom the only good news to any son of Adam. Your life has not been useless. Your work has not been play. Now, when the hair is already grey on your head, Turnbull, you shall have your youth. God has not destroyed, He has only deferred it. Let us sit down here, and you shall explain to me this military map of Notting Hill. For you and I have to defend Notting Hill together."

Mr. Turnbull looked at the other for a moment, then hesitated, and then sat down beside the bricks and the stranger. He did not rise again for seven hours, when the dawn broke.

The headquarters of Provost Adam Wayne and his Commander-in-Chief consisted of a small and somewhat unsuccessful milk-shop at the corner of Pump Street. The blank white morning had only just begun to break over the blank London buildings when

Wayne and Turnbull were to be found seated in the cheerless and unswept shop. Wayne had something feminine in his character; he belonged to that class of persons who forget their meals when anything interesting is in hand. He had had nothing for sixteen hours but hurried glasses of milk, and, with a glass standing empty beside him, he was writing and sketching and dotting and crossing out with inconceivable rapidity with a pencil and a piece of paper. Turnbull was of that more masculine type in which a sense of responsibility increases the appetite, and with his sketch-map beside him he was dealing strenuously with a pile of sandwiches in a paper packet, and a tankard of ale from the tavern opposite, whose shutters had just been taken down. Neither of them spoke, and there was no sound in the living stillness except the scratching of Wayne's pencil and the squealing of an aimless-looking cat. At length Wayne broke the silence by saying—

"Seventeen pounds eight shillings and ninepence."

Turnbull nodded and put his head in the tankard.

"That," said Wayne, "is not counting the five pounds you took yesterday. What did you do with it?"

"Ah, that is rather interesting!" replied Turnbull, with his mouth full. "I used that five pounds in a kindly and philanthropic act."

Wayne was gazing with mystification in his queer and innocent eyes.

"I used that five pounds," continued the other, "in giving no less than forty little London boys rides in hansom cabs."

"Are you insane?" asked the Provost.

"It is only my light touch," returned Turnbull. "These hansom-cab rides will raise the tone—raise the tone, my dear fellow—of our London youths, widen their horizon, brace their nervous system, make them acquainted with the various public monuments of our great city. Education, Wayne, education. How many excellent thinkers have pointed out that political reform is useless until we produce a cultured populace. So that twenty years hence, when these boys are grown up—"

"Mad!" said Wayne, laying down his pencil; "and five pounds gone!"

"You are in error," explained Turnbull. "You grave creatures can never be brought to understand how much quicker work really goes with the assistance of nonsense and good meals. Stripped of its decorative beauties, my statement was strictly accurate. Last night I gave forty half-crowns to forty little boys, and sent them all over London to take hansom cabs. I told them in every case to tell the cabman to bring them to this spot. In half an hour from now the declaration of war will be posted up. At the same time the cabs will have begun to come in, you will have ordered out the guard, the little boys will drive up in state, we shall commandeer the horses for cavalry, use the cabs for barricade, and give the men the choice between serving in our ranks and detention in our basements and cellars. The little boys we can use as scouts. The main thing is that we start the war with an advantage unknown in all the other armies—horses. And now," he said, finishing his beer, "I will go and drill the troops."

And he walked out of the milk-shop, leaving the Provost staring.

A minute or two afterwards, the Provost laughed. He only laughed once or twice in his life, and then he did it in a queer way as if it were an art he had not mastered. Even he saw something funny in the preposterous coup of the half-crowns and the little boys. He did not see the monstrous absurdity of the whole policy and the whole war. He enjoyed it seriously as a crusade, that is, he enjoyed it far more than any joke can be enjoyed. Turnbull enjoyed it partly as a joke, even more perhaps as a reversion from the things he hated—modernity and monotony and civilisation. To break up the vast machinery of modern life and use the fragments as engines of war, to make the barricade of omnibuses and points of vantage of chimney-pots, was to him a game worth infinite risk and trouble. He had that rational and deliberate preference which will always to the end trouble the peace of the world, the rational and deliberate preference for a short life and a merry one.

3. THE EXPERIMENT OF MR. BUCK

An earnest and eloquent petition was sent up to the King signed with the names of Wilson, Barker, Buck, Swindon, and others. It urged that at the forthcoming conference to be held in his Majesty's presence touching the final disposition of the property in Pump Street, it might be held not inconsistent with political decorum and with the unutterable respect they entertained for his Majesty if they appeared in ordinary morning dress, without the costume decreed for them as Provosts. So it happened that the company appeared at that council in frock-coats and that the King himself limited his love of ceremony to appearing (after his not unusual manner), in evening dress with one order—in this case not the Garter, but the button of the Club of Old Clipper's Best Pals, a decoration obtained (with difficulty) from a halfpenny boy's paper. Thus also it happened that the only spot of colour in the room was Adam Wayne, who entered in great dignity with the great red robes and the great sword.

"We have met," said Auberon, "to decide the most arduous of modern problems. May we be successful." And he sat down gravely.

Buck turned his chair a little, and flung one leg over the other.

"Your Majesty," he said, quite good-humouredly, "there is only one thing I can't understand, and that is why this affair is not settled in five minutes. Here's a small property which is worth a thousand to us and is not worth a hundred to any one else. We offer the thousand. It's not business-like, I know, for we ought to get it for less, and it's not reasonable and it's not fair on us, but I'm damned if I can see why it's difficult."

"The difficulty may be very simply stated," said Wayne. "You may offer a million and it will be very difficult for you to get Pump Street."

"But look here, Mr. Wayne," cried Barker, striking in with a kind of cold excitement. "Just look here. You've no right to take up a position like that. You've a right to stand out for a bigger price, but you aren't doing that. You're refusing what you and every sane man knows to be a splendid offer simply from malice or spite—it must be malice or spite. And that kind of thing is really criminal; it's against the public good. The King's Government would be justified in forcing you."

With his lean fingers spread on the table, he stared anxiously at Wayne's face, which did not move.

"In forcing you ... it would," he repeated.

"It shall," said Buck, shortly, turning to the table with a jerk. "We have done our best to be decent."

Wayne lifted his large eyes slowly.

"Was it my Lord Buck," he inquired, "who said that the King of England 'shall' do something?"

Buck flushed and said testily—

"I mean it must—it ought to. As I say, we've done our best to be generous; I defy any one to deny it. As it is, Mr. Wayne, I don't want to say a word that's uncivil. I hope it's not uncivil to say that you can be, and ought to be, in gaol. It is criminal to stop public works for a whim. A man might as well burn ten thousand onions in his front garden or bring up his children to run naked in the street, as do what you say you have a right to do. People have been compelled to sell before now. The King could compel you, and I hope he will."

"Until he does," said Wayne, calmly, "the power and government of this great nation is on my side and not yours, and I defy you to defy it."

"In what sense," cried Barker, with his feverish eyes and hands, "is the Government on your side?"

With one ringing movement Wayne unrolled a great parchment on the table. It was decorated down the sides with wild water-colour sketches of vestrymen in crowns and wreaths.

"The Charter of the Cities," he began.

Buck exploded in a brutal oath and laughed.

"That tomfool's joke. Haven't we had enough—"

"And there you sit," cried Wayne, springing erect and with a voice like a trumpet, "with no argument but to insult the King before his face."

Buck rose also with blazing eyes.

"I am hard to bully," he began—and the slow tones of the King struck in with incomparable gravity—

"My Lord Buck, I must ask you to remember that your King is present. It is not often that he needs to protect himself among his subjects."

Barker turned to him with frantic gestures.

"For God's sake don't back up the madman now," he implored. "Have your joke another time. Oh, for Heaven's sake—"

"My Lord Provost of South Kensington," said King Auberon, steadily, "I do not follow your remarks, which are uttered with a rapidity unusual at Court. Nor do your well-meant efforts to convey the rest with your fingers materially assist me. I say that my Lord Provost of North Kensington, to whom I spoke, ought not in the presence of his Sovereign to speak disrespectfully of his Sovereign's ordinances. Do you disagree?"

Barker turned restlessly in his chair, and Buck cursed without speaking. The King went on in a comfortable voice—

"My Lord Provost of Notting Hill, proceed."

Wayne turned his blue eyes on the King, and to every one's surprise there was a look in them not of triumph, but of a certain childish distress.

"I am sorry, your Majesty," he said; "I fear I was more than equally to blame with the Lord Provost of North Kensington. We were debating somewhat eagerly, and we both rose to our feet. I did so first, I am ashamed to say. The Provost of North Kensington is, therefore, comparatively innocent. I beseech your Majesty to address your rebuke chiefly, at least, to me. Mr. Buck is not innocent, for he did no doubt, in the heat of the moment, speak disrespectfully. But the rest of the discussion he seems to me to have conducted with great good temper."

Buck looked genuinely pleased, for business men are all simple-minded, and have therefore that degree of communion with fanatics. The King, for some reason, looked, for the first time in his life, ashamed.

"This very kind speech of the Provost of Notting Hill," began Buck, pleasantly, "seems to me to show that we have at least got on to a friendly footing. Now come, Mr. Wayne. Five hundred pounds have been offered to you for a property you admit not to be worth a hundred. Well, I am a rich man and I won't be outdone in generosity. Let us say fifteen hundred pounds, and have done with it. And let us shake hands;" and he rose, glowing and laughing.

"Fifteen hundred pounds," whispered Mr. Wilson of Bayswater; "can we do fifteen hundred pounds?"

"I'll stand the racket," said Buck, heartily. "Mr. Wayne is a gentleman and has spoken up for me. So I suppose the negotiations are at an end."

Wayne bowed.

"They are indeed at an end. I am sorry I cannot sell you the property."

"What?" cried Mr. Barker, starting to his feet.

"Mr. Buck has spoken correctly," said the King.

"I have, I have," cried Buck, springing up also; "I said—"

"Mr. Buck has spoken correctly," said the King; "the negotiations are at an end."

All the men at the table rose to their feet; Wayne alone rose without excitement.

"Have I, then," he said, "your Majesty's permission to depart? I have given my last answer."

"You have it," said Auberon, smiling, but not lifting his eyes from the table. And amid a dead silence the Provost of Notting Hill passed out of the room.

"Well?" said Wilson, turning round to Barker—"well?"

Barker shook his head desperately.

"The man ought to be in an asylum," he said. "But one thing is clear—we need not bother further about him. The man can be treated as mad."

"Of course," said Buck, turning to him with sombre decisiveness. "You're perfectly right, Barker. He is a good enough fellow, but he can be treated as mad. Let's put it in simple form. Go and tell any twelve men in any town, go and tell any doctor in any town, that there is a man offered fifteen hundred pounds for a thing he could sell commonly for four hundred, and that when asked for a reason for not accepting it he pleads the inviolate sanctity of Notting Hill and calls it the Holy Mountain. What would they say? What more can we have on our side than the common sense of everybody? On what else do all laws rest? I'll tell you, Barker, what's better than any further discussion. Let's send in workmen on the spot to pull down Pump Street. And if old Wayne says a word, arrest him as a lunatic. That's all."

Barker's eyes kindled.

"I always regarded you, Buck, if you don't mind my saying so, as a very strong man. I'll follow you."

"So, of course, will I," said Wilson.

Buck rose again impulsively.

"Your Majesty," he said, glowing with popularity, "I beseech your Majesty to consider favourably the proposal to which we have committed ourselves. Your Majesty's leniency, our own offers, have fallen in vain on that extraordinary man. He may be right. He may be God. He may be the devil. But we think it, for practical purposes, more probable that he is off his head. Unless that assumption were acted on, all human affairs would go to pieces. We act on it, and we propose to start operations in Notting Hill at once."

The King leaned back in his chair.

"The Charter of the Cities ...," he said with a rich intonation.

But Buck, being finally serious, was also cautious, and did not again make the mistake of disrespect.

"Your Majesty," he said, bowing, "I am not here to say a word against anything your Majesty has said or done. You are a far better educated man than I, and no doubt there were reasons, upon intellectual grounds, for those proceedings. But may I ask you and appeal to your common good-nature for a sincere answer? When you drew up the Charter of the Cities, did you contemplate the rise of a man like Adam Wayne? Did you expect that the Charter—whether it was an experiment, or a scheme of decoration, or a joke—could ever really come to this—to stopping a vast scheme of ordinary business, to shutting up a road, to spoiling the chances of cabs, omnibuses, railway stations, to disorganising half a city, to risking a kind of civil war? Whatever were your objects, were they that?"

Barker and Wilson looked at him admiringly; the King more admiringly still.

"Provost Buck," said Auberon, "you speak in public uncommonly well. I give you your point with the magnanimity of an artist. My scheme did not include the appearance of Mr. Wayne. Alas! would that my poetic power had been great enough."

"I thank your Majesty," said Buck, courteously, but quickly. "Your Majesty's statements are always clear and studied; therefore I may draw a deduction. As the scheme, whatever it was, on which you set your heart did not include the appearance of Mr. Wayne, it will survive his removal. Why not let us clear away this particular Pump Street, which does interfere with our plans, and which does not, by your Majesty's own statement, interfere with yours."

"Caught out!" said the King, enthusiastically and quite impersonally, as if he were watching a cricket match.

"This man Wayne," continued Buck, "would be shut up by any doctors in England. But we only ask to have it put before them. Meanwhile no one's interests, not even in all probability his own, can be really damaged by going on with the improvements in Notting Hill. Not our interests, of course, for it has been the hard and quiet work of ten years. Not the interests of Notting Hill, for nearly all its educated inhabitants desire the change. Not the interests of your Majesty, for you say, with characteristic sense, that you never contemplated the rise of the lunatic at all. Not, as I say, his own interests, for the man has a kind heart and many talents, and a couple of good doctors would probably put him righter than all the free cities and sacred mountains in creation. I therefore assume, if I may use so bold a word, that your Majesty will not offer any obstacle to our proceeding with the improvements."

And Mr. Buck sat down amid subdued but excited applause among the allies.

"Mr. Buck," said the King, "I beg your pardon, for a number of beautiful and sacred thoughts, in which you were generally classified as a fool. But there is another thing to be considered. Suppose you send in your workmen, and Mr. Wayne does a thing regrettable indeed, but of which, I am sorry to say, I think him quite capable—knocks their teeth out?"

"I have thought of that, your Majesty," said Mr. Buck, easily, "and I think it can simply be guarded against. Let us send in a strong guard of, say, a hundred men—a hundred of the North Kensington Halberdiers" (he smiled grimly), "of whom your Majesty is so fond. Or say a hundred and fifty. The whole population of Pump Street, I fancy, is only about a hundred."

"Still they might stand together and lick you," said the King, dubiously.

"Then say two hundred," said Buck, gaily.

"It might happen," said the King, restlessly, "that one Notting Hiller fought better than two North Kensingtons."

"It might," said Buck, coolly; "then say two hundred and fifty."

The King bit his lip.

"And if they are beaten too?" he said viciously.

"Your Majesty," said Buck, and leaned back easily in his chair, "suppose they are. If anything be clear, it is clear that all fighting matters are mere matters of arithmetic. Here we have a hundred and fifty, say, of Notting Hill soldiers. Or say two hundred. If one of them can fight two of us—we can send in, not four hundred, but six hundred, and smash him. That is all. It is out of all immediate probability that one of them could fight four of us. So what I say is this. Run no risks. Finish it at once. Send in eight hundred men and smash him—smash him almost without seeing him. And go on with the improvements."

And Mr. Buck pulled out a bandanna and blew his nose.

"Do you know, Mr. Buck," said the King, staring gloomily at the table, "the admirable clearness of your reason produces in my mind a sentiment which I trust I shall not offend you by describing as an aspiration to punch your head. You irritate me sublimely. What can it be in me? Is it the relic of a moral sense?"

"But your Majesty," said Barker, eagerly and suavely, "does not refuse our proposals?"

"My dear Barker, your proposals are as damnable as your manners. I want to have nothing to do with them. Suppose I stopped them altogether. What would happen?"

Barker answered in a very low voice—

"Revolution."

The King glanced quickly at the men round the table. They were all looking down silently: their brows were red.

He rose with a startling suddenness, and an unusual pallor.

"Gentlemen," he said, "you have overruled me. Therefore I can speak plainly. I think Adam Wayne, who is as mad as a hatter, worth more than a million of you. But you have the force, and, I admit, the common sense, and he is lost. Take your eight hundred halberdiers and smash him. It would be more sportsmanlike to take two hundred."

"More sportsmanlike," said Buck, grimly, "but a great deal less humane. We are not artists, and streets purple with gore do not catch our eye in the right way."

"It is pitiful," said Auberon. "With five or six times their number, there will be no fight at all."

"I hope not," said Buck, rising and adjusting his gloves. "We desire no fight, your Majesty. We are peaceable business men."

"Well," said the King, wearily, "the conference is at an end at last."

And he went out of the room before any one else could stir.

Forty workmen, a hundred Bayswater Halberdiers, two hundred from South, and three from North Kensington, assembled at the foot of Holland Walk and marched up it, under the general direction of Barker, who looked flushed and happy in full dress. At the end of the procession a small and sulky figure lingered like an urchin. It was the King.

"Barker," he said at length, appealingly, "you are an old friend of mine—you understand my hobbies as I understand yours. Why can't you let it alone? I hoped that such fun might come out of this Wayne business. Why can't you let it alone? It doesn't really so much matter to you—what's a road or so? For me it's the one joke that may save me from pessimism. Take fewer men and give me an hour's fun. Really and truly, James, if you collected coins or humming-birds, and I could buy one with the price of your road, I would buy it. I collect incidents—those rare, those precious things. Let me have one. Pay a few pounds for it. Give these Notting Hillers a chance. Let them alone."

"Auberon," said Barker, kindly, forgetting all royal titles in a rare moment of sincerity, "I do feel what you mean. I have had moments when these hobbies have hit me. I have had moments when I have sympathised with your humours. I have had moments, though you may not easily believe it, when I have sympathised with the madness of Adam Wayne. But the world, Auberon, the real world, is not run on these hobbies. It goes on great brutal wheels of facts—wheels on which you are the butterfly; and Wayne is the fly on the wheel."

Auberon's eyes looked frankly at the other's.

"Thank you, James; what you say is true. It is only a parenthetical consolation to me to compare the intelligence of flies somewhat favourably with the intelligence of wheels. But it is the nature of flies to die soon, and the nature of wheels to go on for ever. Go on with the wheel. Good-bye, old man."

And James Barker went on, laughing, with a high colour, slapping his bamboo on his leg.

The King watched the tail of the retreating regiment with a look of genuine depression, which made him seem more like a baby than ever. Then he swung round and struck his hands together.

"In a world without humour," he said, "the only thing to do is to eat. And how perfect an exception! How can these people strike dignified attitudes, and pretend that things matter, when the total ludicrousness of life is proved by the very method by which it is supported? A man strikes the lyre, and says, 'Life is real, life is earnest,' and then goes into a room and stuffs alien substances into a hole in his head. I think Nature was indeed a little broad in her humour in these matters. But we all fall back on the pantomime, as I have in this municipal affair. Nature has her farces, like the act of eating or the shape of the kangaroo, for the more brutal appetite. She keeps her stars and mountains for those who can appreciate something more subtly ridiculous." He turned to his equerry. "But, as I said 'eating,' let us have a picnic like two nice little children. Just run and bring me a table and a dozen courses or so, and plenty of champagne, and under these swinging boughs, Bowler, we will return to Nature."

It took about an hour to erect in Holland Lane the monarch's simple repast, during which time he walked up and down and whistled, but still with an unaffected air of gloom. He had really been done out of a pleasure he had promised himself, and had that empty and sickened feeling which a child has when disappointed of a pantomime. When he and the equerry had sat down, however, and consumed a fair amount of dry champagne, his spirits began mildly to revive.

"Things take too long in this world," he said. "I detest all this Barkerian business about evolution and the gradual modification of things. I wish the world had been made in six days, and knocked to pieces again in six more. And I wish I had done it. The joke's good enough in a broad way, sun and moon and the image of God, and all that, but they keep it up so damnably long. Did you ever long for a miracle, Bowler?"

"No, sir," said Bowler, who was an evolutionist, and had been carefully brought up.

"Then I have," answered the King. "I have walked along a street with the best cigar in the cosmos in my mouth, and more Burgundy inside me than you ever saw in your life, and longed that the lamp-post would turn into an elephant to save me from the hell of blank existence. Take my word for it, my evolutionary Bowler, don't you believe people when they tell you that people sought for a sign, and believed in miracles because they were ignorant. They did it because they were wise, filthily, vilely wise— too wise to eat or sleep or put on their boots with patience. This seems delightfully like a new theory of the origin of Christianity, which would itself be a thing of no mean absurdity. Take some more wine."

The wind blew round them as they sat at their little table, with its white cloth and bright wine-cups, and flung the tree-tops of Holland Park against each other, but the sun was in that strong temper which turns green into gold. The King pushed away his plate, lit a cigar slowly, and went on—

"Yesterday I thought that something next door to a really entertaining miracle might happen to me before I went to amuse the worms. To see that red-haired maniac waving a great sword, and making speeches to his incomparable followers, would have been a glimpse of that Land of Youth from which the Fates shut us out. I had planned some quite delightful things. A Congress of Knightsbridge with a treaty, and myself in the chair, and perhaps a Roman triumph, with jolly old Barker led in chains. And now these wretched prigs have gone and stamped out the exquisite Mr. Wayne altogether, and I suppose they will put him in a private asylum somewhere in their damned humane way. Think of the treasures daily poured out to his unappreciative keeper! I wonder whether they would let me be his keeper. But life is a vale. Never forget at any moment of your existence to regard it in the light of a vale. This graceful habit, if not acquired in youth—"

The King stopped, with his cigar lifted, for there had slid into his eyes the startled look of a man listening. He did not move for a few moments; then he turned his head sharply towards the high, thin, and lath-like paling which fenced certain long gardens and similar spaces from the lane. From behind it there was coming a curious scrambling and scraping noise, as of a desperate thing imprisoned in this box of thin wood. The King threw away his cigar, and jumped on to the table. From this position he saw a pair of hands hanging with a hungry clutch on the top of the fence. Then the hands quivered with a convulsive effort, and a head shot up between them—the head of one of the Bayswater Town Council, his eyes and whiskers wild with fear. He swung himself over, and fell on the other side on his face, and groaned openly and without ceasing. The next moment the thin, taut wood of the fence was struck as by a bullet, so that it reverberated like a drum, and over it came tearing and cursing, with torn clothes and broken nails and bleeding faces, twenty men at one rush. The King sprang five feet clear off the table on to the ground. The moment after the table was flung over, sending bottles and glasses flying, and the *debris* was literally swept along the ground by that stream of men pouring past, and Bowler was borne along with them, as the King said in his famous newspaper article, "like a captured bride." The great fence swung and split under the load of climbers that still scaled and cleared it. Tremendous gaps were torn in it by this living artillery; and through them the King could see more and more frantic faces, as in a dream, and more and more men running. They were as miscellaneous as if some one had taken the lid off a human dustbin. Some were untouched, some were slashed and battered and bloody, some were splendidly dressed, some tattered and half naked, some were in the fantastic garb of the burlesque cities, some in the dullest modern dress. The King stared at all of them, but none of them looked at the King. Suddenly he stepped forward.

"Barker," he said, "what is all this?"

"Beaten," said the politician—"beaten all to hell!" And he plunged past with nostrils shaking like a horse's, and more and more men plunged after him.

Almost as he spoke, the last standing strip of fence bowed and snapped, flinging, as from a catapult, a new figure upon the road. He wore the flaming red of the halberdiers of Notting Hill, and on his weapon there was blood, and in his face victory. In another moment masses of red glowed through the gaps of the fence, and the pursuers, with their halberds, came pouring down the lane. Pursued and pursuers alike swept by the little figure with the owlish eyes, who had not taken his hands out of his pockets.

The King had still little beyond the confused sense of a man caught in a torrent—the feeling of men eddying by. Then something happened which he was never able afterwards to describe, and which we cannot describe for him. Suddenly in the dark entrance, between the broken gates of a garden, there appeared framed a flaming figure.

Adam Wayne, the conqueror, with his face flung back, and his mane like a lion's, stood with his great sword point upwards, the red raiment of his office flapping round him like the red wings of an archangel. And the King saw, he knew not how, something new and overwhelming. The great green trees and the great red robes swung together in the wind. The sword seemed made for the sunlight. The preposterous masquerade, born of his own mockery, towered over him and embraced the world. This was the normal, this was sanity, this was nature; and he himself, with his rationality and his detachment and his black frock-coat, he was the exception and the accident—a blot of black upon a world of crimson and gold.

BOOK IV

1. THE BATTLE OF THE LAMPS

Mr. Buck, who, though retired, frequently went down to his big drapery stores in Kensington High Street, was locking up those premises, being the last to leave. It was a wonderful evening of green and gold, but that did not trouble him very much. If you had pointed it out, he would have agreed seriously, for the rich always desire to be artistic.

He stepped out into the cool air, buttoning up his light yellow coat, and blowing great clouds from his cigar, when a figure dashed up to him in another yellow overcoat, but unbuttoned and flying behind him.

"Hullo, Barker!" said the draper. "Any of our summer articles? You're too late. Factory Acts, Barker. Humanity and progress, my boy."

"Oh, don't chatter," cried Barker, stamping. "We've been beaten."

"Beaten—by what?" asked Buck, mystified.

"By Wayne."

Buck looked at Barker's fierce white face for the first time, as it gleamed in the lamplight.

"Come and have a drink," he said.

They adjourned to a cushioned and glaring buffet, and Buck established himself slowly and lazily in a seat, and pulled out his cigar-case.

"Have a smoke," he said.

Barker was still standing, and on the fret, but after a moment's hesitation, he sat down as if he might spring up again the next minute. They ordered drinks in silence.

"How did it happen?" asked Buck, turning his big bold eyes on him.

"How the devil do I know?" cried Barker. "It happened like—like a dream. How can two hundred men beat six hundred? How can they?"

"Well," said Buck, coolly, "how did they? You ought to know."

"I don't know; I can't describe," said the other, drumming on the table. "It seemed like this. We were six hundred, and marched with those damned poleaxes of Auberon's —the only weapons we've got. We marched two abreast. We went up Holland Walk, between the high palings which seemed to me to go straight as an arrow for Pump Street. I was near the tail of the line, and it was a long one. When the end of it was still between the high palings, the head of the line was already crossing Holland Park Avenue. Then the head plunged into the network of narrow streets on the other side, and the tail and myself came out on the great crossing. When we also had reached the northern side and turned up a small street that points, crookedly as it were, towards Pump Street, the whole thing felt different. The streets dodged and bent so much that the head of our line seemed lost altogether: it might as well have been in North America. And all this time we hadn't seen a soul."

Buck, who was idly dabbing the ash of his cigar on the ash-tray, began to move it deliberately over the table, making feathery grey lines, a kind of map.

"But though the little streets were all deserted (which got a trifle on my nerves), as we got deeper and deeper into them, a thing began to happen that I couldn't understand. Sometimes a long way ahead—three turns or corners ahead, as it were— there broke suddenly a sort of noise, clattering, and confused cries, and then stopped. Then, when it happened, something, I can't describe it—a kind of shake or stagger went down the line, as if the line were a live thing, whose head had been struck, or had been an electric cord. None of us knew why we were moving, but we moved and jostled. Then we recovered, and went on through the little dirty streets, round corners, and up twisted ways. The little crooked streets began to give me a feeling I can't explain—as if it were a dream. I felt as if things had lost their reason, and we should never get out of the maze. Odd to hear me talk like that, isn't it? The streets were quite well-known streets, all down on the map. But the fact remains. I wasn't afraid of something happening. I was afraid of nothing ever happening—nothing ever happening for all God's eternity."

He drained his glass and called for more whisky. He drank it, and went on.

"And then something did happen. Buck, it's the solemn truth, that nothing has ever happened to you in your life. Nothing had ever happened to me in my life."

"Nothing ever happened!" said Buck, staring. "What do you mean?"

"Nothing has ever happened," repeated Barker, with a morbid obstinacy. "You don't know what a thing happening means? You sit in your office expecting customers, and customers come; you walk in the street expecting friends, and friends meet you; you want a drink, and get it; you feel inclined for a bet, and make it. You expect either to win or lose, and you do either one or the other. But things happening!" and he shuddered ungovernably.

"Go on," said Buck, shortly. "Get on."

"As we walked wearily round the corners, something happened. When something happens, it happens first, and you see it afterwards. It happens of itself, and you have nothing to do with it. It proves a dreadful thing—that there are other things besides one's self. I can only put it in this way. We went round one turning, two turnings, three turnings, four turnings, five. Then I lifted myself slowly up from the gutter where I had been shot half senseless, and was beaten down again by living men crashing on top of me, and the world was full of roaring, and big men rolling about like nine-pins."

Buck looked at his map with knitted brows.

"Was that Portobello Road?" he asked.

"Yes," said Barker—"yes; Portobello Road. I saw it afterwards; but, my God, what a place it was! Buck, have you ever stood and let a six foot of man lash and lash at your head with six feet of pole with six pounds of steel at the end? Because, when you have had that experience, as Walt Whitman says, 'you re-examine philosophies and religions.'"

"I have no doubt," said Buck. "If that was Portobello Road, don't you see what happened?"

"I know what happened exceedingly well. I was knocked down four times; an experience which, as I say, has an effect on the mental attitude. And another thing happened, too. I knocked down two men. After the fourth fall (there was not much bloodshed—more brutal rushing and throwing—for nobody could use their weapons), after the fourth fall, I say, I got up like a devil, and I tore a poleaxe out of a man's hand and struck where I saw the scarlet of Wayne's fellows, struck again and again. Two of them went over, bleeding on the stones, thank God; and I laughed and found myself sprawling in the gutter again, and got up again, and struck again, and broke my halberd to pieces. I hurt a man's head, though."

Buck set down his glass with a bang, and spat out curses through his thick moustache.

"What is the matter?" asked Barker, stopping, for the man had been calm up to now, and now his agitation was far more violent than his own.

"The matter?" said Buck, bitterly; "don't you see how these maniacs have got us? Why should two idiots, one a clown and the other a screaming lunatic, make sane men so different from themselves? Look here, Barker; I will give you a picture. A very well-bred young man of this century is dancing about in a frock-coat. He has in his hands a nonsensical seventeenth-century halberd, with which he is trying to kill men in a street in Notting Hill. Damn it! don't you see how they've got us? Never mind how you felt—that is how you looked. The King would put his cursed head on one side and call it exquisite. The Provost of Notting Hill would put his cursed nose in the air and call it heroic. But in Heaven's name what would you have called it—two days before?"

Barker bit his lip.

"You haven't been through it, Buck," he said. "You don't understand fighting—the atmosphere."

"I don't deny the atmosphere," said Buck, striking the table. "I only say it's their atmosphere. It's Adam Wayne's atmosphere. It's the atmosphere which you and I thought had vanished from an educated world for ever."

"Well, it hasn't," said Barker; "and if you have any lingering doubts, lend me a poleaxe, and I'll show you."

. . .

There was a long silence, and then Buck turned to his neighbour and spoke in that good-tempered tone that comes of a power of looking facts in the face—the tone in which he concluded great bargains.

"Barker," he said, "you are right. This old thing—this fighting, has come back. It has come back suddenly and taken us by surprise. So it is first blood to Adam Wayne. But, unless reason and arithmetic and everything else have gone crazy, it must be next and last blood to us. But when an issue has really arisen, there is only one thing to do—to study that issue as such and win in it. Barker, since it is fighting, we must understand fighting. I must understand fighting as coolly and completely as I understand drapery; you must understand fighting as coolly and completely as you understand politics. Now, look at the facts. I stick without hesitation to my original formula. Fighting, when we have the stronger force, is only a matter of arithmetic. It must be. You asked me just now how two hundred men could defeat six hundred. I can tell you. Two hundred men can defeat six hundred when the six hundred behave like fools. When they forget the very conditions they are fighting in; when they fight in a swamp as if it were a mountain; when they fight in a forest as if it were a plain; when they fight in streets without remembering the object of streets."

"What is the object of streets?" asked Barker.

"What is the object of supper?" cried Buck, furiously. "Isn't it obvious? This military science is mere common sense. The object of a street is to lead from one place to another; therefore all streets join; therefore street fighting is quite a peculiar thing. You advanced into that hive of streets as if you were advancing into an open plain where you could see everything. Instead of that, you were advancing into the bowels of a fortress, with streets pointing at you, streets turning on you, streets jumping out at you, and all in the hands of the enemy. Do you know what Portobello Road is? It is the only point on your journey where two side streets run up opposite each other. Wayne massed his men on the two sides, and when he had let enough of your line go past, cut it in two like a worm. Don't you see what would have saved you?"

Barker shook his head.

"Can't your 'atmosphere' help you?" asked Buck, bitterly. "Must I attempt explanations in the romantic manner? Suppose that, as you were fighting blindly with the red Notting Hillers who imprisoned you on both sides, you had heard a shout from behind them. Suppose, oh, romantic Barker! that behind the red tunics you had seen the blue and gold of South Kensington taking them in the rear, surrounding them in their turn and hurling them on to your halberds."

"If the thing had been possible," began Barker, cursing.

"The thing would have been as possible," said Buck, simply, "as simple as arithmetic. There are a certain number of street entries that lead to Pump Street. There are not nine hundred; there are not nine million. They do not grow in the night. They do not increase like mushrooms. It must be possible, with such an overwhelming force as we have, to advance by all of them at once. In every one of the arteries, or approaches, we can put almost as many men as Wayne can put into the field altogether. Once do that, and we have him to demonstration. It is like a proposition of Euclid."

"You think that is certain?" said Barker, anxious, but dominated delightfully.

"I'll tell you what I think," said Buck, getting up jovially. "I think Adam Wayne made an uncommonly spirited little fight; and I think I am confoundedly sorry for him."

"Buck, you are a great man!" cried Barker, rising also. "You've knocked me sensible again. I am ashamed to say it, but I was getting romantic. Of course, what you say is adamantine sense. Fighting, being physical, must be mathematical. We were beaten because we were neither mathematical nor physical nor anything else—because we deserved to be beaten. Hold all the approaches, and with our force we must have him. When shall we open the next campaign?"

"Now," said Buck, and walked out of the bar.

"Now!" cried Barker, following him eagerly. "Do you mean now? It is so late."

Buck turned on him, stamping.

"Do you think fighting is under the Factory Acts?" he said; and he called a cab. "Notting Hill Gate Station," he said; and the two drove off.

A genuine reputation can sometimes be made in an hour. Buck, in the next sixty or eighty minutes, showed himself a really great man of action. His cab carried him like a thunderbolt from the King to Wilson, from Wilson to Swindon, from Swindon to Barker again; if his course was jagged, it had the jaggedness of the lightning. Only two things he carried with him—his inevitable cigar and the map of North Kensington and Notting Hill. There were, as he again and again pointed out, with every variety of persuasion and violence, only nine possible ways of approaching Pump Street within a quarter of a mile round it; three out of Westbourne Grove, two out of Ladbroke Grove, and four out of Notting Hill High Street. And he had detachments of two hundred each, stationed at every one of the entrances before the last green of that strange sunset had sunk out of the black sky.

The sky was particularly black, and on this alone was one false protest raised against the triumphant optimism of the Provost of North Kensington. He overruled it with his infectious common sense.

"There is no such thing," he said, "as night in London. You have only to follow the line of street lamps. Look, here is the map. Two hundred purple North Kensington soldiers under myself march up Ossington Street, two hundred more under Captain Bruce, of the North Kensington Guard, up Clanricarde Gardens.[1] Two hundred yellow West Kensingtons under Provost Swindon attack from Pembridge Road. Two hundred more of my men from the eastern streets, leading away from Queen's Road. Two detachments of yellows enter by two roads from Westbourne Grove. Lastly, two hundred green Bayswaters come down from the North through Chepstow Place, and two hundred more under Provost Wilson himself, through the upper part of Pembridge Road. Gentlemen, it is mate in two moves. The enemy must either mass in Pump Street and be cut to pieces; or they must retreat past the Gaslight & Coke Co., and rush on my four hundred; or they must retreat past St. Luke's Church, and rush on the six hundred from the West. Unless we are all mad, it's plain. Come on. To your quarters and await Captain Brace's signal to advance. Then you have only to walk up a line of gas-lamps and smash this nonsense by pure mathematics. To-morrow we shall all be civilians again."

[1] Clanricarde Gardens at this time was no longer a *cul-de-sac*, but was connected by Pump Street to Pembridge Square. See map.

His optimism glowed like a great fire in the night, and ran round the terrible ring in which Wayne was now held helpless. The fight was already over. One man's energy for one hour had saved the city from war.

For the next ten minutes Buck walked up and down silently beside the motionless clump of his two hundred. He had not changed his appearance in any way, except to sling across his yellow overcoat a case with a revolver in it. So that his light-clad modern figure showed up oddly beside the pompous purple uniforms of his halberdiers, which darkly but richly coloured the black night.

At length a shrill trumpet rang from some way up the street; it was the signal of advance. Buck briefly gave the word, and the whole purple line, with its dimly shining steel, moved up the side alley. Before it was a slope of street, long, straight, and shining in the dark. It was a sword pointed at Pump Street, the heart at which nine other swords were pointed that night.

A quarter of an hour's silent marching brought them almost within earshot of any tumult in the doomed citadel. But still there was no sound and no sign of the enemy. This time, at any rate, they knew that they were closing in on it mechanically, and they marched on under the lamplight and the dark without any of that eerie sense of ignorance which Barker had felt when entering the hostile country by one avenue alone.

"Halt—point arms!" cried Buck, suddenly, and as he spoke there came a clatter of feet tumbling along the stones. But the halberds were levelled in vain. The figure that rushed up was a messenger from the contingent of the North.

"Victory, Mr. Buck!" he cried, panting; "they are ousted. Provost Wilson of Bayswater has taken Pump Street."

Buck ran forward in his excitement.

"Then, which way are they retreating? It must be either by St. Luke's to meet Swindon, or by the Gas Company to meet us. Run like mad to Swindon, and see that the yellows are holding the St. Luke's Road. We will hold this, never fear. We have them in an iron trap. Run!"

As the messenger dashed away into the darkness, the great guard of North Kensington swung on with the certainty of a machine. Yet scarcely a hundred yards further their halberd-points again fell in line gleaming in the gaslight; for again a clatter of feet was heard on the stones, and again it proved to be only the messenger.

"Mr. Provost," he said, "the yellow West Kensingtons have been holding the road by St. Luke's for twenty minutes since the capture of Pump Street. Pump Street is not two hundred yards away; they cannot be retreating down that road."

"Then they are retreating down this," said Provost Buck, with a final cheerfulness, "and by good fortune down a well-lighted road, though it twists about. Forward!"

As they moved along the last three hundred yards of their journey, Buck fell, for the first time in his life, perhaps, into a kind of philosophical reverie, for men of his type are always made kindly, and as it were melancholy, by success.

"I am sorry for poor old Wayne, I really am," he thought. "He spoke up splendidly for me at that Council. And he blacked old Barker's eye with considerable spirit. But I don't see what a man can expect when he fights against arithmetic, to say nothing of civilisation. And what a wonderful hoax all this military genius is! I suspect I've just discovered what Cromwell discovered, that a sensible tradesman is the best general, and that a man who can buy men and sell men can lead and kill them. The thing's simply like adding up a column in a ledger. If Wayne has two hundred men, he can't put two hundred men in nine places at once. If they're ousted from Pump Street they're flying somewhere. If they're not flying past the church they're flying past the Works. And so we have them. We business men should have no chance at all except that cleverer people than we get bees in their bonnets that prevent them from reasoning properly—so we reason alone. And so I, who am comparatively stupid, see things as God sees them, as a vast machine. My God, what's this?" and he clapped his hands to his eyes and staggered back.

Then through the darkness he cried in a dreadful voice—

"Did I blaspheme God? I am struck blind."

"What?" wailed another voice behind him, the voice of a certain Wilfred Jarvis of North Kensington.

"Blind!" cried Buck; "blind!"

"I'm blind too!" cried Jarvis, in an agony.

"Fools, all of you," said a gross voice behind them; "we're all blind. The lamps have gone out."

"The lamps! But why? where?" cried Buck, turning furiously in the darkness. "How are we to get on? How are we to chase the enemy? Where have they gone?"

"The enemy went—" said the rough voice behind, and then stopped doubtfully.

"Where?" shouted Buck, stamping like a madman.

"They went," said the gruff voice, "past the Gas Works, and they've used their chance."

"Great God!" thundered Buck, and snatched at his revolver; "do you mean they've turned out—"

But almost before he had spoken the words, he was hurled like a stone from catapult into the midst of his own men.

"Notting Hill! Notting Hill!" cried frightful voices out of the darkness, and they seemed to come from all sides, for the men of North Kensington, unacquainted with the road, had lost all their bearings in the black world of blindness.

"Notting Hill! Notting Hill!" cried the invisible people, and the invaders were hewn down horribly with black steel, with steel that gave no glint against any light.

Buck, though badly maimed with the blow of a halberd, kept an angry but splendid sanity. He groped madly for the wall and found it. Struggling with crawling fingers along it, he found a side opening and retreated into it with the remnants of his men. Their adventures during that prodigious night are not to be described. They did not know whether they were going towards or away from the enemy. Not knowing where they themselves were, or where their opponents were, it was mere irony to ask where was the rest of their army. For a thing had descended upon them which London does not know—darkness, which was before the stars were made, and they were as much lost in it as if they had been made before the stars. Every now and then, as those frightful hours wore on, they buffeted in the darkness against living men, who struck at them and at whom they struck, with an idiot fury. When at last the grey dawn came, they found they had wandered back to the edge of the Uxbridge Road. They found that in those horrible eyeless encounters, the North Kensingtons and the Bayswaters and the West Kensingtons had again and again met and butchered each other, and they heard that Adam Wayne was barricaded in Pump Street.

2. THE CORRESPONDENT OF THE COURT JOURNAL

Journalism had become, like most other such things in England under the cautious government and philosophy represented by James Barker, somewhat sleepy and much diminished in importance. This was partly due to the disappearance of party government and public speaking, partly to the compromise or dead-lock which had made foreign wars impossible, but mostly, of course, to the temper of the whole nation which was that of a people in a kind of back-water. Perhaps the most well known of the remaining newspapers was the *Court Journal*, which was published in a dusty but genteel-looking office just out of Kensington High Street. For when all the papers of a people have been for years growing more and more dim and decorous and optimistic, the dimmest and most decorous and most optimistic is very likely to win. In the journalistic competition which was still going on at the beginning of the twentieth century, the final victor was the *Court Journal*.

For some mysterious reason the King had a great affection for hanging about in the *Court Journal* office, smoking a morning cigarette and looking over files. Like all ingrainedly idle men, he was very fond of lounging and chatting in places where other people were doing work. But one would have thought that, even in the prosaic England of his day, he might have found a more bustling centre.

On this particular morning, however, he came out of Kensington Palace with a more alert step and a busier air than usual. He wore an extravagantly long frock-coat, a pale-green waistcoat, a very full and *dégagé* black tie, and curious yellow gloves. This was his uniform as Colonel of a regiment of his own creation, the 1st Decadents Green. It was a beautiful sight to see him drilling them. He walked quickly across the Park and the High Street, lighting his cigarette as he went, and flung open the door of the *Court Journal* office.

"You've heard the news, Pally—you've heard the news?" he said.

The Editor's name was Hoskins, but the King called him Pally, which was an abbreviation of Paladium of our Liberties.

"Well, your Majesty," said Hoskins, slowly (he was a worried, gentlemanly looking person, with a wandering brown beard)—"well, your Majesty, I have heard rather curious things, but I—"

"You'll hear more of them," said the King, dancing a few steps of a kind of negro shuffle. "You'll hear more of them, my blood-and-thunder tribune. Do you know what I am going to do for you?"

"No, your Majesty," replied the Paladium, vaguely.

"I'm going to put your paper on strong, dashing, enterprising lines," said the King. "Now, where are your posters of last night's defeat?"

"I did not propose, your Majesty," said the Editor, "to have any posters exactly—"

"Paper, paper!" cried the King, wildly; "bring me paper as big as a house. I'll do you posters. Stop, I must take my coat off." He began removing that garment with an air of set intensity, flung it playfully at Mr. Hoskins' head, entirely enveloping him, and looked at himself in the glass. "The coat off," he said, "and the hat on. That looks like a sub-editor. It is indeed the very essence of sub-editing. Well," he continued, turning round abruptly, "come along with that paper."

The Paladium had only just extricated himself reverently from the folds of the King's frock-coat, and said bewildered—

"I am afraid, your Majesty—"

"Oh, you've got no enterprise," said Auberon. "What's that roll in the corner? Wall-paper? Decorations for your private residence? Art in the home, Pally? Fling it over here, and I'll paint such posters on the back of it that when you put it up in your drawing-room you'll paste the original pattern against the wall." And the King unrolled the wall-paper, spreading it over the whole floor. "Now give me the scissors," he cried, and took them himself before the other could stir.

He slit the paper into about five pieces, each nearly as big as a door. Then he took a big blue pencil, and went down on his knees on the dusty oil-cloth and began to write on them, in huge letters—

"FROM THE FRONT.
GENERAL BUCK DEFEATED.
DARKNESS, DANGER, AND DEATH.
WAYNE SAID TO BE IN PUMP STREET.
FEELING IN THE CITY."

He contemplated it for some time, with his head on one side, and got up, with a sigh.

"Not quite intense enough," he said—"not alarming. I want the *Court Journal* to be feared as well as loved. Let's try something more hard-hitting." And he went down on his knees again. After sucking the blue pencil for some time, he began writing again busily. "How will this do?" he said—

WAYNE'S WONDERFUL VICTORY."

"I suppose," he said, looking up appealingly, and sucking the pencil—"I suppose we couldn't say 'wictory'—'Wayne's wonderful wictory'? No, no. Refinement, Pally, refinement. I have it."

"WAYNE WINS.
ASTOUNDING FIGHT IN THE DARK.
The gas-lamps in their courses fought against Buck."

"(Nothing like our fine old English translation.) What else can we say? Well, anything to annoy old Buck;" and he added, thoughtfully, in smaller letters—

"Rumoured Court-martial on General Buck."

"Those will do for the present," he said, and turned them both face downwards. "Paste, please."

The Paladium, with an air of great terror, brought the paste out of an inner room.

The King slabbed it on with the enjoyment of a child messing with treacle. Then taking one of his huge compositions fluttering in each hand, he ran outside, and began pasting them up in prominent positions over the front of the office.

"And now," said Auberon, entering again with undiminished vivacity—"now for the leading article."

He picked up another of the large strips of wall-paper, and, laying it across a desk, pulled out a fountain-pen and began writing with feverish intensity, reading clauses and fragments aloud to himself, and rolling them on his tongue like wine, to see if they had the pure journalistic flavour.

"The news of the disaster to our forces in Notting Hill, awful as it is—awful as it is— (no, distressing as it is), may do some good if it draws attention to the what's-his-name inefficiency (scandalous inefficiency, of course) of the Government's preparations. In our present state of information, it would be premature (what a jolly word!)—it would be premature to cast any reflections upon the conduct of General Buck, whose services upon so many stricken fields (ha, ha!), and whose honourable scars and laurels, give him a right to have judgment upon him at least suspended. But there is one matter on which we must speak plainly. We have been silent on it too long, from feelings, perhaps of mistaken caution, perhaps of mistaken loyalty. This situation would never have arisen but for what we can only call the indefensible conduct of the King. It pains us to say such things, but, speaking as we do in the public interests (I plagiarise from Barker's famous epigram), we shall not shrink because of the distress we may cause to any individual, even the most exalted. At this crucial moment of our country, the voice of the People demands with a single tongue, 'Where is the King?' What is he doing while his subjects tear each other in pieces in the streets of a great city? Are his amusements and his dissipations (of which we cannot pretend to be ignorant) so engrossing that he can spare no thought for a perishing nation? It is with a deep sense of our responsibility that we warn that exalted person that neither his great position nor his incomparable talents will save him in the hour of delirium from the fate of all those who, in the madness of luxury or tyranny, have met the English people in the rare day of its wrath."

"I am now," said the King, "going to write an account of the battle by an eye-witness." And he picked up a fourth sheet of wall-paper. Almost at the same moment Buck strode quickly into the office. He had a bandage round his head.

"I was told," he said, with his usual gruff civility, "that your Majesty was here."

"And of all things on earth," cried the King, with delight, "here is an eye-witness! An eye-witness who, I regret to observe, has at present only one eye to witness with. Can you write us the special article, Buck? Have you a rich style?"

Buck, with a self-restraint which almost approached politeness, took no notice whatever of the King's maddening geniality.

"I took the liberty, your Majesty," he said shortly, "of asking Mr. Barker to come here also."

As he spoke, indeed, Barker came swinging into the office, with his usual air of hurry.

"What is happening now?" asked Buck, turning to him with a kind of relief.

"Fighting still going on," said Barker. "The four hundred from West Kensington were hardly touched last night. They hardly got near the place. Poor Wilson's Bayswater men got cut about, though. They fought confoundedly well. They took Pump Street once. What mad things do happen in the world. To think that of all of us it should be little Wilson with the red whiskers who came out best."

The King made a note on his paper—

"Romantic Conduct of Mr. Wilson."

"Yes," said Buck; "it makes one a bit less proud of one's *h's*."

The King suddenly folded or crumpled up the paper, and put it in his pocket.

"I have an idea," he said. "I will be an eye-witness. I will write you such letters from the Front as will be more gorgeous than the real thing. Give me my coat, Paladium. I entered this room a mere King of England. I leave it, Special War Correspondent of the *Court Journal*. It is useless to stop me, Pally; it is vain to cling to my knees, Buck; it is hopeless, Barker, to weep upon my neck. 'When duty calls'—the remainder of the sentiment escapes me. You will receive my first article this evening by the eight-o'clock post."

And, running out of the office, he jumped upon a blue Bayswater omnibus that went swinging by.

"Well," said Barker, gloomily, "well."

"Barker," said Buck, "business may be lower than politics, but war is, as I discovered last night, a long sight more like business. You politicians are such ingrained demagogues that even when you have a despotism you think of nothing but public opinion. So you learn to tack and run, and are afraid of the first breeze. Now we stick to a thing and get it. And our mistakes help us. Look here! at this moment we've beaten Wayne."

"Beaten Wayne," repeated Barker.

"Why the dickens not?" cried the other, flinging out his hands. "Look here. I said last night that we had them by holding the nine entrances. Well, I was wrong. We should have had them but for a singular event—the lamps went out. But for that it was certain. Has it occurred to you, my brilliant Barker, that another singular event has happened since that singular event of the lamps going out?"

"What event?" asked Barker.

"By an astounding coincidence, the sun has risen," cried out Buck, with a savage air of patience. "Why the hell aren't we holding all those approaches now, and passing in on them again? It should have been done at sunrise. The confounded doctor wouldn't let me go out. You were in command."

Barker smiled grimly.

"It is a gratification to me, my dear Buck, to be able to say that we anticipated your suggestions precisely. We went as early as possible to reconnoitre the nine entrances. Unfortunately, while we were fighting each other in the dark, like a lot of drunken navvies, Mr. Wayne's friends were working very hard indeed. Three hundred yards from Pump Street, at every one of those entrances, there is a barricade nearly as high as the houses. They were finishing the last, in Pembridge Road, when we arrived. Our mistakes," he cried bitterly, and flung his cigarette on the ground. "It is not we who learn from them."

There was a silence for a few moments, and Barker lay back wearily in a chair. The office clock ticked exactly in the stillness.

At length Barker said suddenly—

"Buck, does it ever cross your mind what this is all about? The Hammersmith to Maida Vale thoroughfare was an uncommonly good speculation. You and I hoped a great deal from it. But is it worth it? It will cost us thousands to crush this ridiculous riot. Suppose we let it alone?"

"And be thrashed in public by a red-haired madman whom any two doctors would lock up?" cried out Buck, starting to his feet. "What do you propose to do, Mr. Barker? To apologise to the admirable Mr. Wayne? To kneel to the Charter of the Cities? To clasp to your bosom the flag of the Red Lion? To kiss in succession every sacred lamp-post that saved Notting Hill? No, by God! My men fought jolly well—they were beaten by a trick. And they'll fight again."

"Buck," said Barker, "I always admired you. And you were quite right in what you said the other day."

"In what?"

"In saying," said Barker, rising quietly, "that we had all got into Adam Wayne's atmosphere and out of our own. My friend, the whole territorial kingdom of Adam Wayne extends to about nine streets, with barricades at the end of them. But the spiritual kingdom of Adam Wayne extends, God knows where—it extends to this office, at any rate. The red-haired madman whom any two doctors would lock up is filling this room with his roaring, unreasonable soul. And it was the red-haired madman who said the last word you spoke."

Buck walked to the window without replying. "You understand, of course," he said at last, "I do not dream of giving in."

The King, meanwhile, was rattling along on the top of his blue omnibus. The traffic of London as a whole had not, of course, been greatly disturbed by these events, for the affair was treated as a Notting Hill riot, and that area was marked off as if it had been in the hands of a gang of recognised rioters. The blue omnibuses simply went round as they would have done if a road were being mended, and the omnibus on which the correspondent of the *Court Journal* was sitting swept round the corner of Queen's Road, Bayswater.

The King was alone on the top of the vehicle, and was enjoying the speed at which it was going.

"Forward, my beauty, my Arab," he said, patting the omnibus encouragingly, "fleetest of all thy bounding tribe. Are thy relations with thy driver, I wonder, those of the Bedouin and his steed? Does he sleep side by side with thee—"

His meditations were broken by a sudden and jarring stoppage. Looking over the edge, he saw that the heads of the horses were being held by men in the uniform of Wayne's army, and heard the voice of an officer calling out orders.

King Auberon descended from the omnibus with dignity. The guard or picket of red halberdiers who had stopped the vehicle did not number more than twenty, and they were under the command of a short, dark, clever-looking young man, conspicuous among the rest as being clad in an ordinary frock-coat, but girt round the waist with a red sash and a long seventeenth-century sword. A shiny silk hat and spectacles completed the outfit in a pleasing manner.

"To whom have I the honour of speaking?" said the King, endeavouring to look like Charles I., in spite of personal difficulties.

The dark man in spectacles lifted his hat with equal gravity.

"My name is Bowles," he said. "I am a chemist. I am also a captain of O company of the army of Notting Hill. I am distressed at having to incommode you by stopping the omnibus, but this area is covered by our proclamation, and we intercept all traffic. May I ask to whom I have the honour—Why, good gracious, I beg your Majesty's pardon. I am quite overwhelmed at finding myself concerned with the King."

Auberon put up his hand with indescribable grandeur.

"Not with the King," he said; "with the special war correspondent of the *Court Journal*."

"I beg your Majesty's pardon," began Mr. Bowles, doubtfully.

"Do you call me Majesty? I repeat," said Auberon, firmly, "I am a representative of the press. I have chosen, with a deep sense of responsibility, the name of Pinker. I should desire a veil to be drawn over the past."

"Very well, sir," said Mr. Bowles, with an air of submission, "in our eyes the sanctity of the press is at least as great as that of the throne. We desire nothing better than that our wrongs and our glories should be widely known. May I ask, Mr. Pinker, if you have any objection to being presented to the Provost and to General Turnbull?"

"The Provost I have had the honour of meeting," said Auberon, easily. "We old journalists, you know, meet everybody. I should be most delighted to have the same honour again. General Turnbull, also, it would be a gratification to know. The younger men are so interesting. We of the old Fleet Street gang lose touch with them."

"Will you be so good as to step this way?" said the leader of O company.

"I am always good," said Mr. Pinker. "Lead on."

3. THE GREAT ARMY OF SOUTH KENSINGTON

The article from the special correspondent of the *Court Journal* arrived in due course, written on very coarse copy-paper in the King's arabesque of handwriting, in which three words filled a page, and yet were illegible. Moreover, the contribution was the more perplexing at first, as it opened with a succession of erased paragraphs. The writer appeared to have attempted the article once or twice in several journalistic styles. At the side of one experiment was written, "Try American style," and the fragment began—

"The King must go. We want gritty men. Flapdoodle is all very ...;" and then broke off, followed by the note, "Good sound journalism safer. Try it."

The experiment in good sound journalism appeared to begin—

"The greatest of English poets has said that a rose by any ..."

This also stopped abruptly. The next annotation at the side was almost undecipherable, but seemed to be something like—

"How about old Steevens and the *mot juste*? E.g...."

"Morning winked a little wearily at me over the curt edge of Campden Hill and its houses with their sharp shadows. Under the abrupt black cardboard of the outline, it took some little time to detect colours; but at length I saw a brownish yellow shifting in the obscurity, and I knew that it was the guard of Swindon's West Kensington army. They are being held as a reserve, and lining the whole ridge above the Bayswater Road. Their camp and their main force is under the great Waterworks Tower on Campden Hill. I forgot to say that the Waterworks Tower looked swart.

"As I passed them and came over the curve of Silver Street, I saw the blue cloudy masses of Barker's men blocking the entrance to the high-road like a sapphire smoke (good). The disposition of the allied troops, under the general management of Mr. Wilson, appears to be as follows: The Yellow army (if I may so describe the West Kensingtonians) lies, as I have said, in a strip along the ridge, its furthest point westward being the west side of Campden Hill Road, its furthest point eastward the beginning of Kensington Gardens. The Green army of Wilson lines the Notting Hill High Road itself from Queen's Road to the corner of Pembridge Road, curving round the latter, and extending some three hundred yards up towards Westbourne Grove. Westbourne Grove itself is occupied by Barker of South Kensington. The fourth side of this rough square, the Queen's Road side, is held by some of Buck's Purple warriors.

"The whole resembles some ancient and dainty Dutch flower-bed. Along the crest of Campden Hill lie the golden crocuses of West Kensington. They are, as it were, the first fiery fringe of the whole. Northward lies our hyacinth Barker, with all his blue hyacinths. Round to the south-west run the green rushes of Wilson of Bayswater, and a line of violet irises (aptly symbolised by Mr. Buck) complete the whole. The argent exterior ... (I am losing the style. I should have said 'Curving with a whisk' instead of merely 'Curving.' Also I should have called the hyacinths 'sudden.' I cannot keep this up. War is too rapid for this style of writing. Please ask office-boy to insert *mots justes*.)

"The truth is that there is nothing to report. That commonplace element which is always ready to devour all beautiful things (as the Black Pig in the Irish Mythology will finally devour the stars and gods); that commonplace element, as I say, has in its Black

Piggish way devoured finally the chances of any romance in this affair; that which once consisted of absurd but thrilling combats in the streets, has degenerated into something which is the very prose of warfare—it has degenerated into a siege. A siege may be defined as a peace plus the inconvenience of war. Of course Wayne cannot hold out. There is no more chance of help from anywhere else than of ships from the moon. And if old Wayne had stocked his street with tinned meats till all his garrison had to sit on them, he couldn't hold out for more than a month or two. As a matter of melancholy fact, he has done something rather like this. He has stocked his street with food until there must be uncommonly little room to turn round. But what is the good? To hold out for all that time and then to give in of necessity, what does it mean? It means waiting until your victories are forgotten, and then taking the trouble to be defeated. I cannot understand how Wayne can be so inartistic.

"And how odd it is that one views a thing quite differently when one knows it is defeated! I always thought Wayne was rather fine. But now, when I know that he is done for, there seem to be nothing else but Wayne. All the streets seem to point at him, all the chimneys seem to lean towards him. I suppose it is a morbid feeling; but Pump Street seems to be the only part of London that I feel physically. I suppose, I say, that it is morbid. I suppose it is exactly how a man feels about his heart when his heart is weak. 'Pump Street'—the heart is a pump. And I am drivelling.

"Our finest leader at the front is, beyond all question, General Wilson. He has adopted alone among the other Provosts the uniform of his own halberdiers, although that fine old sixteenth-century garb was not originally intended to go with red side-whiskers. It was he who, against a most admirable and desperate defence, broke last night into Pump Street and held it for at least half an hour. He was afterwards expelled from it by General Turnbull, of Notting Hill, but only after desperate fighting and the sudden descent of that terrible darkness which proved so much more fatal to the forces of General Buck and General Swindon.

"Provost Wayne himself, with whom I had, with great good fortune, a most interesting interview, bore the most eloquent testimony to the conduct of General Wilson and his men. His precise words are as follows: 'I have bought sweets at his funny little shop when I was four years old, and ever since. I never noticed anything, I am ashamed to say, except that he talked through his nose, and didn't wash himself particularly. And he came over our barricade like a devil from hell.' I repeated this speech to General Wilson himself, with some delicate improvements, and he seemed pleased with it. He does not, however, seem pleased with anything so much just now as he is with the wearing of a sword. I have it from the front on the best authority that General Wilson was not completely shaved yesterday. It is believed in military circles that he is growing a moustache....

"As I have said, there is nothing to report. I walk wearily to the pillar-box at the corner of Pembridge Road to post my copy. Nothing whatever has happened, except the preparations for a particularly long and feeble siege, during which I trust I shall not be required to be at the Front. As I glance up Pembridge Road in the growing dusk, the aspect of that road reminds me that there is one note worth adding. General Buck has suggested, with characteristic acumen, to General Wilson that, in order to obviate the possibility of such a catastrophe as overwhelmed the allied forces in the last advance on Notting Hill (the catastrophe, I mean, of the extinguished lamps), each soldier should have a lighted lantern round his neck. This is one of the things which I really admire about General Buck. He possesses what people used to mean by 'the humility of the man of science,' that is, he learns steadily from his mistakes. Wayne may score off him in some other way, but not in that way. The lanterns look like fairy lights as they curve round the end of Pembridge Road.

"*Later.*—I write with some difficulty, because the blood will run down my face and make patterns on the paper. Blood is a very beautiful thing; that is why it is concealed. If you ask why blood runs down my face, I can only reply that I was kicked by a horse. If you ask me what horse, I can reply with some pride that it was a war-horse. If you ask me how a war-horse came on the scene in our simple pedestrian warfare, I am reduced to the necessity, so painful to a special correspondent, of recounting my experiences.

"I was, as I have said, in the very act of posting my copy at the pillar-box, and of glancing as I did so up the glittering curve of Pembridge Road, studded with the lights of Wilson's men. I don't know what made me pause to examine the matter, but I had a fancy that the line of lights, where it melted into the indistinct brown twilight, was more indistinct than usual. I was almost certain that in a certain stretch of the road where there had been five lights there were now only four. I strained my eyes; I counted them again, and there were only three. A moment after there were only two; an instant after only one; and an instant after that the lanterns near to me swung like jangled bells, as if struck suddenly. They flared and fell; and for the moment the fall of them was like the fall of the sun and stars out of heaven. It left everything in a primal blindness. As a matter of fact, the road was not yet legitimately dark. There were still red rays of a sunset in the sky, and the brown gloaming was still warmed, as it were, with a feeling as of firelight. But for three seconds after the lanterns swung and sank, I saw in front of me a blackness blocking the sky. And with the fourth second I knew that this blackness which blocked the sky was a man on a great horse; and I was trampled and tossed aside as a swirl of horsemen swept round the corner. As they turned I saw that they were not black, but scarlet; they were a sortie of the besieged, Wayne riding ahead.

"I lifted myself from the gutter, blinded with blood from a very slight skin-wound, and, queerly enough, not caring either for the blindness or for the slightness of the wound. For one mortal minute after that amazing cavalcade had spun past, there was dead stillness on the empty road. And then came Barker and all his halberdiers running like devils in the track of them. It had been their business to guard the gate by which the sortie had broken out; but they had not reckoned, and small blame to them, on cavalry. As it was, Barker and his men made a perfectly splendid run after them, almost catching Wayne's horses by the tails.

"Nobody can understand the sortie. It consists only of a small number of Wayne's garrison. Turnbull himself, with the vast mass of it, is undoubtedly still barricaded in Pump Street. Sorties of this kind are natural enough in the majority of historical sieges, such as the siege of Paris in 1870, because in such cases the besieged are certain of some support outside. But what can be the object of it in this case? Wayne knows (or if he is too mad to know anything, at least Turnbull knows) that there is not, and never has been, the smallest chance of support for him outside; that the mass of the sane modern inhabitants of London regard his farcical patriotism with as much contempt as they do the original idiotcy that gave it birth—the folly of our miserable King. What Wayne and his horsemen are doing nobody can even conjecture. The general theory round here is that he is simply a traitor, and has abandoned the besieged. But all such larger but yet more soluble riddles are as nothing compared to the one small but unanswerable riddle: Where did they get the horses?

"*Later.*—I have heard a most extraordinary account of the origin of the appearance of the horses. It appears that that amazing person, General Turnbull, who is now ruling Pump Street in the absence of Wayne, sent out, on the morning of the declaration of war, a vast number of little boys (or cherubs of the gutter, as we pressmen say), with half-crowns in their pockets, to take cabs all over London. No less than a hundred and sixty cabs met at Pump Street; were commandeered by the garrison. The men were set free, the cabs used to make barricades, and the horses kept in Pump Street, where they were fed and exercised for several days, until they were sufficiently rapid and efficient to be used for this wild ride out of the town. If this is so, and I have it on the best possible authority, the method of the sortie is explained. But we have no explanation of its object. Just as Barker's Blues were swinging round the corner after them, they were stopped, but not by an enemy; only by the voice of one man, and he a friend. Red Wilson of Bayswater ran alone along the main road like a madman, waving them back with a halberd snatched from a sentinel. He was in supreme command, and Barker stopped at the corner, staring and bewildered. We could hear Wilson's voice loud and distinct out of the dusk, so that it seemed strange that the great voice should come out of the little body. 'Halt, South Kensington! Guard this entry, and prevent them returning. I will pursue. Forward, the Green Guards!'

"A wall of dark blue uniforms and a wood of pole-axes was between me and Wilson, for Barker's men blocked the mouth of the road in two rigid lines. But through them and through the dusk I could hear the clear orders and the clank of arms, and see the green army of Wilson marching by towards the west. They were our great fighting-men. Wilson had filled them with his own fire; in a few days they had become veterans. Each of them wore a silver medal of a pump, to boast that they alone of all the allied armies had stood victorious in Pump Street.

"I managed to slip past the detachment of Barker's Blues, who are guarding the end of Pembridge Road, and a sharp spell of running brought me to the tail of Wilson's green army as it swung down the road in pursuit of the flying Wayne. The dusk had deepened into almost total darkness; for some time I only heard the throb of the marching pace. Then suddenly there was a cry, and the tall fighting men were flung back on me, almost crushing me, and again the lanterns swung and jingled, and the cold nozzles of great horses pushed into the press of us. They had turned and charged us.

"'You fools!' came the voice of Wilson, cleaving our panic with a splendid cold anger. 'Don't you see? the horses have no riders!'

"It was true. We were being plunged at by a stampede of horses with empty saddles. What could it mean? Had Wayne met some of our men and been defeated? Or had he flung these horses at us as some kind of ruse or mad new mode of warfare, such as he seemed bent on inventing? Or did he and his men want to get away in disguise? Or did they want to hide in houses somewhere?

"Never did I admire any man's intellect (even my own) so much as I did Wilson's at that moment. Without a word, he simply pointed the halberd (which he still grasped) to the southern side of the road. As you know, the streets running up to the ridge of Campden Hill from the main road are peculiarly steep, they are more like sudden flights of stairs. We were just opposite Aubrey Road, the steepest of all; up that it would have been far more difficult to urge half-trained horses than to run up on one's feet.

"'Left wheel!' hallooed Wilson. 'They have gone up here,' he added to me, who happened to be at his elbow.

"'Why?' I ventured to ask.

"'Can't say for certain,' replied the Bayswater General. 'They've gone up here in a great hurry, anyhow. They've simply turned their horses loose, because they couldn't take them up. I fancy I know. I fancy they're trying to get over the ridge to Kensingston or Hammersmith, or somewhere, and are striking up here because it's just beyond the end of our line. Damned fools, not to have gone further along the road, though. They've only just shaved our last outpost. Lambert is hardly four hundred yards from here. And I've sent him word.'

"'Lambert!' I said. 'Not young Wilfrid Lambert—my old friend.'

"'Wilfrid Lambert's his name,' said the General; 'used to be a "man about town;" silly fellow with a big nose. That kind of man always volunteers for some war or other; and what's funnier, he generally isn't half bad at it. Lambert is distinctly good. The yellow West Kensingtons I always reckoned the weakest part of the army; but he has pulled them together uncommonly well, though he's subordinate to Swindon, who's a donkey. In the attack from Pembridge Road the other night he showed great pluck.'

"'He has shown greater pluck than that,' I said. 'He has criticised my sense of humour. That was his first engagement.'

"This remark was, I am sorry to say, lost on the admirable commander of the allied forces. We were in the act of climbing the last half of Aubrey Road, which is so abrupt a slope that it looks like an old-fashioned map leaning up against the wall. There are lines of little trees, one above the other, as in the old-fashioned map.

"We reached the top of it, panting somewhat, and were just about to turn the corner by a place called (in chivalrous anticipation of our wars of sword and axe) Tower Creçy, when we were suddenly knocked in the stomach (I can use no other term) by a horde of men hurled back upon us. They wore the red uniform of Wayne; their halberds were broken; their foreheads bleeding; but the mere impetus of their retreat staggered us as we stood at the last ridge of the slope.

"'Good old Lambert!' yelled out suddenly the stolid Mr. Wilson of Bayswater, in an uncontrollable excitement. 'Damned jolly old Lambert! He's got there already! He's driving them back on us! Hurrah! hurrah! Forward, the Green Guards!'

"We swung round the corner eastwards, Wilson running first, brandishing the halberd—

"Will you pardon a little egotism? Every one likes a little egotism, when it takes the form, as mine does in this case, of a disgraceful confession. The thing is really a little interesting, because it shows how the merely artistic habit has bitten into men like me. It was the most intensely exciting occurrence that had ever come to me in my life; and I was really intensely excited about it. And yet, as we turned that corner, the first impression I had was of something that had nothing to do with the fight at all. I was stricken from the sky as by a thunderbolt, by the height of the Waterworks Tower on Campden Hill. I don't know whether Londoners generally realise how high it looks when one comes out, in this way, almost immediately under it. For the second it seemed to me that at the foot of it even human war was a triviality. For the second I felt as if I had been drunk with some trivial orgie, and that I had been sobered by the shock of that shadow. A moment afterwards, I realised that under it was going on something more enduring than stone, and something wilder than the dizziest height—the agony of man. And I knew that, compared to that, this overwhelming tower was itself a triviality; it was a mere stalk of stone which humanity could snap like a stick.

"I don't know why I have talked so much about this silly old Waterworks Tower, which at the very best was only a tremendous background. It was that, certainly, a sombre and awful landscape, against which our figures were relieved. But I think the real reason was, that there was in my own mind so sharp a transition from the tower of stone to the man of flesh. For what I saw first when I had shaken off, as it were, the shadow of the tower, was a man, and a man I knew.

"Lambert stood at the further corner of the street that curved round the tower, his figure outlined in some degree by the beginning of moonrise. He looked magnificent, a hero; but he looked something much more interesting than that. He was, as it happened, in almost precisely the same swaggering attitude in which he had stood nearly fifteen years ago, when he swung his walking-stick and struck it into the ground, and told me that all my subtlety was drivel. And, upon my soul, I think he required more courage to say that than to fight as he does now. For then he was fighting against something that was in the ascendant, fashionable, and victorious. And now he is fighting (at the risk of his life, no doubt) merely against something which is already dead, which is impossible, futile; of which nothing has been more impossible and futile than this very sortie which has brought him into contact with it. People nowadays allow infinitely too little for the psychological sense of victory as a factor in affairs. Then he was attacking the degraded but undoubtedly victorious Quin; now he is attacking the interesting but totally extinguished Wayne.

"His name recalls me to the details of the scene. The facts were these. A line of red halberdiers, headed by Wayne, were marching up the street, close under the northern wall, which is, in fact, the bottom of a sort of dyke or fortification of the Waterworks. Lambert and his yellow West Kensingtons had that instant swept round the corner and had shaken the Waynites heavily, hurling back a few of the more timid, as I have just described, into our very arms. When our force struck the tail of Wayne's, every one knew that all was up with him. His favourite military barber was struck down. His grocer was stunned. He himself was hurt in the thigh, and reeled back against the wall. We had him in a trap with two jaws. 'Is that you?' shouted Lambert, genially, to Wilson, across the hemmed-in host of Notting Hill. 'That's about the ticket,' replied General Wilson; 'keep them under the wall.'

"The men of Notting Hill were falling fast. Adam Wayne threw up his long arms to the wall above him, and with a spring stood upon it; a gigantic figure against the moon. He tore the banner out of the hands of the standard-bearer below him, and shook it out suddenly above our heads, so that it was like thunder in the heavens.

"'Round the Red Lion!' he cried. 'Swords round the Red Lion! Halberds round the Red Lion! They are the thorns round rose.'

"His voice and the crack of the banner made a momentary rally, and Lambert, whose idiotic face was almost beautiful with battle, felt it as by an instinct, and cried—

"'Drop your public-house flag, you footler! Drop it!'

"'The banner of the Red Lion seldom stoops,' said Wayne, proudly, letting it out luxuriantly on the night wind.

"The next moment I knew that poor Adam's sentimental theatricality had cost him much. Lambert was on the wall at a bound, his sword in his teeth, and had slashed at Wayne's head before he had time to draw his sword, his hands being busy with the enormous flag. He stepped back only just in time to avoid the first cut, and let the flag-staff fall, so that the spear-blade at the end of it pointed to Lambert.

"'The banner stoops,' cried Wayne, in a voice that must have startled streets. 'The banner of Notting Hill stoops to a hero.' And with the words he drove the spear-point and half the flag-staff through Lambert's body and dropped him dead upon the road below, a stone upon the stones of the street.

"'Notting Hill! Notting Hill!' cried Wayne, in a sort of divine rage. 'Her banner is all the holier for the blood of a brave enemy! Up on the wall, patriots! Up on the wall! Notting Hill!'

"With his long strong arm he actually dragged a man up on to the wall to be silhouetted against the moon, and more and more men climbed up there, pulled themselves and were pulled, till clusters and crowds of the half-massacred men of Pump Street massed upon the wall above us.

"'Notting Hill! Notting Hill!' cried Wayne, unceasingly.

"'Well, what about Bayswater?' said a worthy working-man in Wilson's army, irritably. 'Bayswater for ever!'

"'We have won!' cried Wayne, striking his flag-staff in the ground. 'Bayswater for ever! We have taught our enemies patriotism!'

"'Oh, cut these fellows up and have done with it!' cried one of Lambert's lieutenants, who was reduced to something bordering on madness by the responsibility of succeeding to the command.

"'Let us by all means try,' said Wilson, grimly; and the two armies closed round the third.

"I simply cannot describe what followed. I am sorry, but there is such a thing as physical fatigue, as physical nausea, and, I may add, as physical terror. Suffice it to say that the above paragraph was written about 11 p.m., and that it is now about 2 a.m., and that the battle is not finished, and is not likely to be. Suffice it further to say that down the steep streets which lead from the Waterworks Tower to the Notting Hill High Road, blood has been running, and is running, in great red serpents, that curl out into the main thoroughfare and shine in the moon.

· · ·

"*Later.*—The final touch has been given to all this terrible futility. Hours have passed; morning has broken; men are still swaying and fighting at the foot of the tower and round the corner of Aubrey Road; the fight has not finished. But I know it is a farce.

"News has just come to show that Wayne's amazing sortie, followed by the amazing resistance through a whole night on the wall of the Waterworks, is as if it had not been. What was the object of that strange exodus we shall probably never know, for the simple reason that every one who knew will probably be cut to pieces in the course of the next two or three hours.

"I have heard, about three minutes ago, that Buck and Buck's methods have won after all. He was perfectly right, of course, when one comes to think of it, in holding that it was physically impossible for a street to defeat a city. While we thought he was patrolling the eastern gates with his Purple army; while we were rushing about the streets and waving halberds and lanterns; while poor old Wilson was scheming like Moltke and fighting like Achilles to entrap the wild Provost of Notting Hill—Mr. Buck, retired draper, has simply driven down in a hansom cab and done something about as plain as butter and about as useful and nasty. He has gone down to South Kensington, Brompton, and Fulham, and by spending about four thousand pounds of his private means, has raised an army of nearly as many men; that is to say, an army big enough to beat, not only Wayne, but Wayne and all his present enemies put together. The army, I understand, is encamped along High Street, Kensington, and fills it from the Church to Addison Road Bridge. It is to advance by ten different roads uphill to the north.

"I cannot endure to remain here. Everything makes it worse than it need be. The dawn, for instance, has broken round Campden Hill; splendid spaces of silver, edged with gold, are torn out of the sky. Worse still, Wayne and his men feel the dawn; their faces, though bloody and pale, are strangely hopeful ... insupportably pathetic. Worst of all, for the moment they are winning. If it were not for Buck and the new army they might just, and only just, win.

"I repeat, I cannot stand it. It is like watching that wonderful play of old Maeterlinck's (you know my partiality for the healthy, jolly old authors of the nineteenth century), in which one has to watch the quiet conduct of people inside a parlour, while knowing that the very men are outside the door whose word can blast it all with tragedy. And this is worse, for the men are not talking, but writhing and bleeding and dropping dead for a thing that is already settled—and settled against them. The great grey masses of men still toil and tug and sway hither and thither around the great grey tower; and the tower is still motionless, as it will always be motionless. These men will be crushed before the sun is set; and new men will arise and be crushed, and new wrongs done, and tyranny will always rise again like the sun, and injustice will always be as fresh as the flowers of spring. And the stone tower will always look down on it. Matter, in its brutal beauty, will always look down on those who are mad enough to consent to die, and yet more mad, since they consent to live."

Thus ended abruptly the first and last contribution of the Special Correspondent of the *Court Journal* to that valued periodical.

The Correspondent himself, as has been said, was simply sick and gloomy at the last news of the triumph of Buck. He slouched sadly down the steep Aubrey Road, up which he had the night before run in so unusual an excitement, and strolled out into the empty dawn-lit main road, looking vaguely for a cab. He saw nothing in the vacant space except a blue-and-gold glittering thing, running very fast, which looked at first like a very tall beetle, but turned out, to his great astonishment, to be Barker.

"Have you heard the good news?" asked that gentleman.

"Yes," said Quin, with a measured voice. "I have heard the glad tidings of great joy. Shall we take a hansom down to Kensington? I see one over there."

They took the cab, and were, in four minutes, fronting the ranks of the multitudinous and invincible army. Quin had not spoken a word all the way, and something about him had prevented the essentially impressionable Barker from speaking either.

The great army, as it moved up Kensington High Street, calling many heads to the numberless windows, for it was long indeed—longer than the lives of most of the tolerably young—since such an army had been seen in London. Compared with the vast organisation which was now swallowing up the miles, with Buck at its head as leader, and the King hanging at its tail as journalist, the whole story of our problem was insignificant. In the presence of that army the red Notting Hills and the green Bayswaters were alike tiny and straggling groups. In its presence the whole struggle round Pump Street was like an ant-hill under the hoof of an ox. Every man who felt or looked at that infinity of men knew that it was the triumph of Buck's brutal arithmetic. Whether Wayne was right or wrong, wise or foolish, was quite a fair matter for discussion. But it was a matter of history. At the foot of Church Street, opposite Kensington Church, they paused in their glowing good humour.

"Let us send some kind of messenger or herald up to them," said Buck, turning to Barker and the King. "Let us send and ask them to cave in without more muddle."

"What shall we say to them?" said Barker, doubtfully.

"The facts of the case are quite sufficient," rejoined Buck. "It is the facts of the case that make an army surrender. Let us simply say that our army that is fighting their army, and their army that is fighting our army, amount altogether to about a thousand men. Say that we have four thousand. It is very simple. Of the thousand fighting, they have at the very most, three hundred, so that, with those three hundred, they have now to fight four thousand seven hundred men. Let them do it if it amuses them."

And the Provost of North Kensington laughed.

The herald who was despatched up Church Street in all the pomp of the South Kensington blue and gold, with the Three Birds on his tabard, was attended by two trumpeters.

"What will they do when they consent?" asked Barker, for the sake of saying something in the sudden stillness of that immense army.

"I know my Wayne very well," said Buck, laughing. "When he submits he will send a red herald flaming with the Lion of Notting Hill. Even defeat will be delightful to him, since it is formal and romantic."

The King, who had strolled up to the head of the line, broke silence for the first time.

"I shouldn't wonder," he said, "if he defied you, and didn't send the herald after all. I don't think you do know your Wayne quite so well as you think."

"All right, your Majesty," said Buck, easily; "if it isn't disrespectful, I'll put my political calculations in a very simple form. I'll lay you ten pounds to a shilling the herald comes with the surrender."

"All right," said Auberon. "I may be wrong, but it's my notion of Adam Wayne that he'll die in his city, and that, till he is dead, it will not be a safe property."

"The bet's made, your Majesty," said Buck.

Another long silence ensued, in the course of which Barker alone, amid the motionless army, strolled and stamped in his restless way.

Then Buck suddenly leant forward.

"It's taking your money, your Majesty," he said. "I knew it was. There comes the herald from Adam Wayne."

"It's not," cried the King, peering forward also. "You brute, it's a red omnibus."

"It's not," said Buck, calmly; and the King did not answer, for down the centre of the spacious and silent Church Street was walking, beyond question, the herald of the Red Lion, with two trumpeters.

Buck had something in him which taught him how to be magnanimous. In his hour of success he felt magnanimous towards Wayne, whom he really admired; magnanimous towards the King, off whom he had scored so publicly; and, above all, magnanimous towards Barker, who was the titular leader of this vast South Kensington army, which his own talent had evoked.

"General Barker," he said, bowing, "do you propose now to receive the message from the besieged?"

Barker bowed also, and advanced towards the herald.

"Has your master, Mr. Adam Wayne, received our request for surrender?" he asked.

The herald conveyed a solemn and respectful affirmative.

Barker resumed, coughing slightly, but encouraged.

"What answer does your master send?"

The herald again inclined himself submissively, and answered in a kind of monotone.

"My message is this. Adam Wayne, Lord High Provost of Notting Hill, under the charter of King Auberon and the laws of God and all mankind, free and of a free city, greets James Barker, Lord High Provost of South Kensington, by the same rights free and honourable, leader of the army of the South. With all friendly reverence, and with all constitutional consideration, he desires James Barker to lay down his arms, and the whole army under his command to lay down their arms also."

Before the words were ended the King had run forward into the open space with shining eyes. The rest of the staff and the forefront of the army were literally struck breathless. When they recovered they began to laugh beyond restraint; the revulsion was too sudden.

"The Lord High Provost of Notting Hill," continued the herald, "does not propose, in the event of your surrender, to use his victory for any of those repressive purposes which others have entertained against him. He will leave you your free laws and your free cities, your flags and your governments. He will not destroy the religion of South Kensington, or crush the old customs of Bayswater."

An irrepressible explosion of laughter went up from the forefront of the great army.

"The King must have had something to do with this humour," said Buck, slapping his thigh. "It's too deliciously insolent. Barker, have a glass of wine."

And in his conviviality he actually sent a soldier across to the restaurant opposite the church and brought out two glasses for a toast.

When the laughter had died down, the herald continued quite monotonously—

"In the event of your surrendering your arms and dispersing under the superintendence of our forces, these local rights of yours shall be carefully observed. In the event of your not doing so, the Lord High Provost of Notting Hill desires to announce that he has just captured the Waterworks Tower, just above you, on Campden Hill, and that within ten minutes from now, that is, on the reception through me of your refusal, he will open the great reservoir and flood the whole valley where you stand in thirty feet of water. God save King Auberon!"

Buck had dropped his glass and sent a great splash of wine over the road.

"But—but—" he said; and then by a last and splendid effort of his great sanity, looked the facts in the face.

"We must surrender," he said. "You could do nothing against fifty thousand tons of water coming down a steep hill, ten minutes hence. We must surrender. Our four thousand men might as well be four. *Vicisti Galilæe!* Perkins, you may as well get me another glass of wine."

In this way the vast army of South Kensington surrendered and the Empire of Notting Hill began. One further fact in this connection is perhaps worth mentioning— the fact that, after his victory, Adam Wayne caused the great tower on Campden Hill to be plated with gold and inscribed with a great epitaph, saying that it was the monument of Wilfrid Lambert, the heroic defender of the place, and surmounted with a statue, in which his large nose was done something less than justice to.

BOOK V

1. THE EMPIRE OF NOTTING HILL

On the evening of the third of October, twenty years after the great victory of Notting Hill, which gave it the dominion of London, King Auberon came, as of old, out of Kensington Palace.

He had changed little, save for a streak or two of grey in his hair, for his face had always been old, and his step slow, and, as it were, decrepit.

If he looked old, it was not because of anything physical or mental. It was because he still wore, with a quaint conservatism, the frock-coat and high hat of the days before the great war. "I have survived the Deluge," he said. "I am a pyramid, and must behave as such."

As he passed up the street the Kensingtonians, in their picturesque blue smocks, saluted him as a King, and then looked after him as a curiosity. It seemed odd to them that men had once worn so elvish an attire.

The King, cultivating the walk attributed to the oldest inhabitant ("Gaffer Auberon" his friends were now confidentially desired to call him), went toddling northward. He paused, with reminiscence in his eye, at the Southern Gate of Notting Hill, one of those nine great gates of bronze and steel, wrought with reliefs of the old battles, by the hand of Chiffy himself.

"Ah!" he said, shaking his head and assuming an unnecessary air of age, and a provincialism of accent—"Ah! I mind when there warn't none of this here."

He passed through the Ossington Gate, surmounted by a great lion, wrought in red copper on yellow brass, with the motto, "Nothing Ill." The guard in red and gold saluted him with his halberd.

It was about sunset, and the lamps were being lit. Auberon paused to look at them, for they were Chiffy's finest work, and his artistic eye never failed to feast on them. In memory of the Great Battle of the Lamps, each great iron lamp was surmounted by a

88

veiled figure, sword in hand, holding over the flame an iron hood or extinguisher, as if ready to let it fall if the armies of the South and West should again show their flags in the city. Thus no child in Notting Hill could play about the streets without the very lamp-posts reminding him of the salvation of his country in the dreadful year.

"Old Wayne was right in a way," commented the King. "The sword does make things beautiful. It has made the whole world romantic by now. And to think people once thought me a buffoon for suggesting a romantic Notting Hill. Deary me, deary me! (I think that is the expression)—it seems like a previous existence."

Turning a corner, he found himself in Pump Street, opposite the four shops which Adam Wayne had studied twenty years before. He entered idly the shop of Mr. Mead, the grocer. Mr. Mead was somewhat older, like the rest of the world, and his red beard, which he now wore with a moustache, and long and full, was partly blanched and discoloured. He was dressed in a long and richly embroidered robe of blue, brown, and crimson, interwoven with an Eastern complexity of pattern, and covered with obscure symbols and pictures, representing his wares passing from hand to hand and from nation to nation. Round his neck was the chain with the Blue Argosy cut in turquoise, which he wore as Grand Master of the Grocers. The whole shop had the sombre and sumptuous look of its owner. The wares were displayed as prominently as in the old days, but they were now blended and arranged with a sense of tint and grouping, too often neglected by the dim grocers of those forgotten days. The wares were shown plainly, but shown not so much as an old grocer would have shown his stock, but rather as an educated virtuoso would have shown his treasures. The tea was stored in great blue and green vases, inscribed with the nine indispensable sayings of the wise men of China. Other vases of a confused orange and purple, less rigid and dominant, more humble and dreamy, stored symbolically the tea of India. A row of caskets of a simple silvery metal contained tinned meats. Each was wrought with some rude but rhythmic form, as a shell, a horn, a fish, or an apple, to indicate what material had been canned in it.

"Your Majesty," said Mr. Mead, sweeping an Oriental reverence. "This is an honour to me, but yet more an honour to the city."

Auberon took off his hat.

"Mr. Mead," he said, "Notting Hill, whether in giving or taking, can deal in nothing but honour. Do you happen to sell liquorice?"

"Liquorice, sire," said Mr. Mead, "is not the least important of our benefits out of the dark heart of Arabia."

And going reverently towards a green and silver canister, made in the form of an Arabian mosque, he proceeded to serve his customer.

"I was just thinking, Mr. Mead," said the King, reflectively, "I don't know why I should think about it just now, but I was just thinking of twenty years ago. Do you remember the times before the war?"

The grocer, having wrapped up the liquorice sticks in a piece of paper (inscribed with some appropriate sentiment), lifted his large grey eyes dreamily, and looked at the darkening sky outside.

"Oh yes, your Majesty," he said. "I remember these streets before the Lord Provost began to rule us. I can't remember how we felt very well. All the great songs and the fighting change one so; and I don't think we can really estimate all we owe to the

Provost; but I can remember his coming into this very shop twenty-two years ago, and I remember the things he said. The singular thing is that, as far as I remember, I thought the things he said odd at that time. Now it's the things that I said, as far as I can recall them, that seem to me odd—as odd as a madman's antics."

"Ah!" said the King; and looked at him with an unfathomable quietness.

"I thought nothing of being a grocer then," he said. "Isn't that odd enough for anybody? I thought nothing of all the wonderful places that my goods come from, and wonderful ways that they are made. I did not know that I was for all practical purposes a king with slaves spearing fishes near the secret pool, and gathering fruits in the islands under the world. My mind was a blank on the thing. I was as mad as a hatter."

The King turned also, and stared out into the dark, where the great lamps that commemorated the battle were already flaming.

"And is this the end of poor old Wayne?" he said, half to himself. "To inflame every one so much that he is lost himself in the blaze. Is this his victory that he, my incomparable Wayne, is now only one in a world of Waynes? Has he conquered and become by conquest commonplace? Must Mr. Mead, the grocer, talk as high as he? Lord! what a strange world in which a man cannot remain unique even by taking the trouble to go mad!"

And he went dreamily out of the shop.

He paused outside the next one almost precisely as the Provost had done two decades before.

"How uncommonly creepy this shop looks!" he said. "But yet somehow encouragingly creepy, invitingly creepy. It looks like something in a jolly old nursery story in which you are frightened out of your skin, and yet know that things always end well. The way those low sharp gables are carved like great black bat's wings folded down, and the way those queer-coloured bowls underneath are made to shine like giants eye-balls. It looks like a benevolent warlock's hut. It is apparently a chemist's."

Almost as he spoke, Mr. Bowles, the chemist, came to his shop door in a long black velvet gown and hood, monastic as it were, but yet with a touch of the diabolic. His hair was still quite black, and his face even paler than of old. The only spot of colour he carried was a red star cut in some precious stone of strong tint, hung on his breast. He belonged to the Society of the Red Star of Charity, founded on the lamps displayed by doctors and chemists.

"A fine evening, sir," said the chemist. "Why, I can scarcely be mistaken in supposing it to be your Majesty. Pray step inside and share a bottle of sal-volatile, or anything that may take your fancy. As it happens, there is an old acquaintance of your Majesty's in my shop carousing (if I may be permitted the term) upon that beverage at this moment."

The King entered the shop, which was an Aladdin's garden of shades and hues, for as the chemist's scheme of colour was more brilliant than the grocer's scheme, so it was arranged with even more delicacy and fancy. Never, if the phrase may be employed, had such a nosegay of medicines been presented to the artistic eye.

But even the solemn rainbow of that evening interior was rivalled or even eclipsed by the figure standing in the centre of the shop. His form, which was a large and stately one, was clad in a brilliant blue velvet, cut in the richest Renaissance fashion, and slashed so as to show gleams and gaps of a wonderful lemon or pale yellow. He had several chains round his neck, and his plumes, which were of several tints of bronze and gold, hung down to the great gold hilt of his long sword. He was drinking a dose of sal-volatile, and admiring its opal tint. The King advanced with a slight mystification towards the tall figure, whose face was in shadow; then he said—

"By the Great Lord of Luck, Barker!"

The figure removed his plumed cap, showing the same dark head and long, almost equine face which the King had so often seen rising out of the high collar of Bond Street. Except for a grey patch on each temple, it was totally unchanged.

"Your Majesty," said Barker, "this is a meeting nobly retrospective, a meeting that has about it a certain October gold. I drink to old days;" and he finished his sal-volatile with simple feeling.

"I am delighted to see you again, Barker," said the King. "It is indeed long since we met. What with my travels in Asia Minor, and my book having to be written (you have read my 'Life of Prince Albert for Children,' of course?), we have scarcely met twice since the Great War. That is twenty years ago."

"I wonder," said Barker, thoughtfully, "if I might speak freely to your Majesty?"

"Well," said Auberon, "it's rather late in the day to start speaking respectfully. Flap away, my bird of freedom."

"Well, your Majesty," replied Barker, lowering his voice, "I don't think it will be so long to the next war."

"What do you mean?" asked Auberon.

"We will stand this insolence no longer," burst out Barker, fiercely. "We are not slaves because Adam Wayne twenty years ago cheated us with a water-pipe. Notting Hill is Notting Hill; it is not the world. We in South Kensington, we also have memories —ay, and hopes. If they fought for these trumpery shops and a few lamp-posts, shall we not fight for the great High Street and the sacred Natural History Museum?"

"Great Heavens!" said the astounded Auberon. "Will wonders never cease? Have the two greatest marvels been achieved? Have you turned altruistic, and has Wayne turned selfish? Are you the patriot, and he the tyrant?"

"It is not from Wayne himself altogether that the evil comes," answered Barker. "He, indeed, is now mostly wrapped in dreams, and sits with his old sword beside the fire. But Notting Hill is the tyrant, your Majesty. Its Council and its crowds have been so intoxicated by the spreading over the whole city of Wayne's old ways and visions, that they try to meddle with every one, and rule every one, and civilise every one, and tell every one what is good for him. I do not deny the great impulse which his old war, wild as it seemed, gave to the civic life of our time. It came when I was still a young man, and I admit it enlarged my career. But we are not going to see our own cities flouted and thwarted from day to day because of something Wayne did for us all nearly a quarter of a century ago. I am just waiting here for news upon this very matter. It is rumoured that Notting Hill has vetoed the statue of General Wilson they are putting up opposite Chepstow Place. If that is so, it is a black and white shameless breach of the terms on which we surrendered to Turnbull after the battle of the Tower. We were to keep our own customs and self-government. If that is so—"

"It is so," said a deep voice; and both men turned round.

A burly figure in purple robes, with a silver eagle hung round his neck and moustaches almost as florid as his plumes, stood in the doorway.

"Yes," he said, acknowledging the King's start, "I am Provost Buck, and the news is true. These men of the Hill have forgotten that we fought round the Tower as well as they, and that it is sometimes foolish, as well as base, to despise the conquered."

"Let us step outside," said Barker, with a grim composure.

Buck did so, and stood rolling his eyes up and down the lamp-lit street.

"I would like to have a go at smashing all this," he muttered, "though I am over sixty. I would like—"

His voice ended in a cry, and he reeled back a step, with his hands to his eyes, as he had done in those streets twenty years before.

"Darkness!" he cried—"darkness again! What does it mean?"

For in truth every lamp in the street had gone out, so that they could not see even each other's outline, except faintly. The voice of the chemist came with startling cheerfulness out of the density.

"Oh, don't you know?" he said. "Did they never tell you this is the Feast of the Lamps, the anniversary of the great battle that almost lost and just saved Notting Hill? Don't you know, your Majesty, that on this night twenty-one years ago we saw Wilson's green uniforms charging down this street, and driving Wayne and Turnbull back upon the gas-works, fighting with their handful like fiends from hell? And that then, in that great hour, Wayne sprang through a window of the gas-works, with one blow of his hand brought darkness on the whole city, and then with a cry like a lion's, that was heard through four streets, flew at Wilson's men, sword in hand, and swept them, bewildered as they were, and ignorant of the map, clear out of the sacred street again? And don't you know that upon that night every year all lights are turned out for half an hour while we sing the Notting Hill anthem in the darkness? Hark! there it begins."

Through the night came a crash of drums, and then a strong swell of human voices—

> "When the world was in the balance, there was night on Notting
>   Hill,
> (There was night on Notting Hill): it was nobler than the day;
> On the cities where the lights are and the firesides glow,
> From the seas and from the deserts came the thing we did not
>   know,
> Came the darkness, came the darkness, came the darkness on
>   the foe,
> And the old guard of God turned to bay.
> For the old guard of God turns to bay, turns to bay,
> And the stars fall down before it ere its banners fall to-day:
> For when armies were around us as a howling and a horde,
> When falling was the citadel and broken was the sword,
> The darkness came upon them like the Dragon of the Lord,
> When the old guard of God turned to bay."

The voices were just uplifting themselves in a second verse when they were stopped by a scurry and a yell. Barker had bounded into the street with a cry of "South Kensington!" and a drawn dagger. In less time than a man could blink, the whole packed street was full of curses and struggling. Barker was flung back against the shop-front, but used the second only to draw his sword as well as his dagger, and calling out, "This is not the first time I've come through the thick of you," flung himself again into the press. It was evident that he had drawn blood at last, for a more violent outcry arose, and many other knives and swords were discernible in the faint light. Barker, after having wounded more than one man, seemed on the point of being flung back again, when Buck suddenly stepped out into the street. He had no weapon, for he affected rather the peaceful magnificence of the great burgher, than the pugnacious dandyism which had replaced the old sombre dandyism in Barker. But with a blow of his clenched fist he broke the pane of the next shop, which was the old curiosity shop, and, plunging in his hand, snatched a kind of Japanese scimitar, and calling out, "Kensington! Kensington!" rushed to Barker's assistance.

Barker's sword was broken, but he was laying about him with his dagger. Just as Buck ran up, a man of Notting Hill struck Barker down, but Buck struck the man down on top of him, and Barker sprang up again, the blood running down his face.

Suddenly all these cries were cloven by a great voice, that seemed to fall out of heaven. It was terrible to Buck and Barker and the King, from its seeming to come out the empty skies; but it was more terrible because it was a familiar voice, and one which at the same time they had not heard for so long.

"Turn up the lights," said the voice from above them, and for a moment there was no reply, but only a tumult.

"In the name of Notting Hill and of the great Council of the City, turn up the lights."

There was again a tumult and a vagueness for a moment, then the whole street and every object in it sprang suddenly out of the darkness, as every lamp sprang into life. And looking up they saw, standing upon a balcony near the roof of one of the highest houses, the figure and the face of Adam Wayne, his red hair blowing behind him, a little streaked with grey.

"What is this, my people?" he said. "Is it altogether impossible to make a thing good without it immediately insisting on being wicked? The glory of Notting Hill in having achieved its independence, has been enough for me to dream of for many years, as I sat beside the fire. Is it really not enough for you, who have had so many other affairs to excite and distract you? Notting Hill is a nation. Why should it condescend to be a mere Empire? You wish to pull down the statue of General Wilson, which the men of Bayswater have so rightly erected in Westbourne Grove. Fools! Who erected that statue? Did Bayswater erect it? No. Notting Hill erected it. Do you not see that it is the glory of our achievement that we have infected the other cities with the idealism of Notting Hill? It is we who have created not only our own side, but both sides of this controversy. O too humble fools, why should you wish to destroy your enemies? You have done something more to them. You have created your enemies. You wish to pull down that gigantic silver hammer, which stands, like an obelisk, in the centre of the Broadway of Hammersmith. Fools! Before Notting Hill arose, did any person passing through Hammersmith Broadway expect to see there a gigantic silver hammer? You wish to abolish the great bronze figure of a knight standing upon the artificial bridge at Knightsbridge. Fools! Who would have thought of it before Notting Hill arose? I have even heard, and with

93

deep pain I have heard it, that the evil eye of our imperial envy has been cast towards the remote horizon of the west, and that we have objected to the great black monument of a crowned raven, which commemorates the skirmish of Ravenscourt Park. Who created all these things? Were they there before we came? Cannot you be content with that destiny which was enough for Athens, which was enough for Nazareth? the destiny, the humble purpose, of creating a new world. Is Athens angry because Romans and Florentines have adopted her phraseology for expressing their own patriotism? Is Nazareth angry because as a little village it has become the type of all little villages out of which, as the Snobs say, no good can come? Has Athens asked every one to wear the chlamys? Are all followers of the Nazarene compelled to wear turbans. No! but the soul of Athens went forth and made men drink hemlock, and the soul of Nazareth went forth and made men consent to be crucified. So has the soul of Notting Hill gone forth and made men realise what it is to live in a city. Just as we inaugurated our symbols and ceremonies, so they have inaugurated theirs; and are you so mad as to contend against them? Notting Hill is right; it has always been right. It has moulded itself on its own necessities, its own *sine quâ non*; it has accepted its own ultimatum. Because it is a nation it has created itself; and because it is a nation it can destroy itself. Notting Hill shall always be the judge. If it is your will because of this matter of General Wilson's statue to make war upon Bayswater—"

A roar of cheers broke in upon his words, and further speech was impossible. Pale to the lips, the great patriot tried again and again to speak; but even his authority could not keep down the dark and roaring masses in the street below him. He said something further, but it was not audible. He descended at last sadly from the garret in which he lived, and mingled with the crowd at the foot of the houses. Finding General Turnbull, he put his hand on his shoulder with a queer affection and gravity, and said—

"To-morrow, old man, we shall have a new experience, as fresh as the flowers of spring. We shall be defeated. You and I have been through three battles together, and have somehow or other missed this peculiar delight. It is unfortunate that we shall not probably be able to exchange our experiences, because, as it most annoyingly happens, we shall probably both be dead."

Turnbull looked dimly surprised.

"I don't mind so much about being dead," he said, "but why should you say that we shall be defeated?"

"The answer is very simple," replied Wayne, calmly. "It is because we ought to be defeated. We have been in the most horrible holes before now; but in all those I was perfectly certain that the stars were on our side, and that we ought to get out. Now I know that we ought not to get out; and that takes away from me everything with which I won."

As Wayne spoke he started a little, for both men became aware that a third figure was listening to them—a small figure with wondering eyes.

"Is it really true, my dear Wayne," said the King, interrupting, "that you think you will be beaten to-morrow?"

"There can be no doubt about it whatever," replied Adam Wayne; "the real reason is the one of which I have just spoken. But as a concession to your materialism, I will add that they have an organised army of a hundred allied cities against our one. That in itself, however, would be unimportant."

Quin, with his round eyes, seemed strangely insistent.

"You are quite sure," he said, "that you must be beaten?"

"I am afraid," said Turnbull, gloomily, "that there can be no doubt about it."

"Then," cried the King, flinging out his arms, "give me a halberd! Give me a halberd, somebody! I desire all men to witness that I, Auberon, King of England, do here and now abdicate, and implore the Provost of Notting Hill to permit me to enlist in his army. Give me a halberd!"

He seized one from some passing guard, and, shouldering it, stamped solemnly after the shouting columns of halberdiers which were, by this time, parading the streets. He had, however, nothing to do with the wrecking of the statue of General Wilson, which took place before morning.

2. THE LAST BATTLE

The day was cloudy when Wayne went down to die with all his army in Kensington Gardens; it was cloudy again when that army had been swallowed up by the vast armies of a new world. There had been an almost uncanny interval of sunshine, in which the Provost of Notting Hill, with all the placidity of an onlooker, had gazed across to the hostile armies on the great spaces of verdure opposite; the long strips of green and blue and gold lay across the park in squares and oblongs like a proposition in Euclid wrought in a rich embroidery. But the sunlight was a weak and, as it were, a wet sunlight, and was soon swallowed up. Wayne spoke to the King, with a queer sort of coldness and languor, as to the military operations. It was as he had said the night before—that being deprived of his sense of an impracticable rectitude, he was, in effect, being deprived of everything. He was out of date, and at sea in a mere world of compromise and competition, of Empire against Empire, of the tolerably right and the tolerably wrong. When his eye fell on the King, however, who was marching very gravely with a top hat and a halberd, it brightened slightly.

"Well, your Majesty," he said, "you at least ought to be proud to-day. If your children are fighting each other, at least those who win are your children. Other kings have distributed justice, you have distributed life. Other kings have ruled a nation, you have created nations. Others have made kingdoms, you have begotten them. Look at your children, father!" and he stretched his hand out towards the enemy.

Auberon did not raise his eyes.

"See how splendidly," cried Wayne, "the new cities come on—the new cities from across the river. See where Battersea advances over there—under the flag of the Lost Dog; and Putney—don't you see the Man on the White Boar shining on their standard as the sun catches it? It is the coming of a new age, your Majesty. Notting Hill is not a common empire; it is a thing like Athens, the mother of a mode of life, of a manner of living, which shall renew the youth of the world—a thing like Nazareth. When I was young I remember, in the old dreary days, wiseacres used to write books about how trains would get faster, and all the world be one empire, and tram-cars go to the moon. And even as a child I used to say to myself, 'Far more likely that we shall go on the crusades again, or worship the gods of the city.' And so it has been. And I am glad, though this is my last battle."

Even as he spoke there came a crash of steel from the left, and he turned his head.

"Wilson!" he cried, with a kind of joy. "Red Wilson has charged our left. No one can hold him in; he eats swords. He is as keen a soldier as Turnbull, but less patient—less really great. Ha! and Barker is moving. How Barker has improved; how handsome he looks! It is not all having plumes; it is also having a soul in one's daily life. Ha!"

And another crash of steel on the right showed that Barker had closed with Notting Hill on the other side.

"Turnbull is there!" cried Wayne. "See him hurl them back! Barker is checked! Turnbull charges—wins! But our left is broken. Wilson has smashed Bowles and Mead, and may turn our flank. Forward, the Provost's Guard!"

And the whole centre moved forward, Wayne's face and hair and sword flaming in the van.

The King ran suddenly forward.

The next instant a great jar that went through it told that it had met the enemy. And right over against them through the wood of their own weapons Auberon saw the Purple Eagle of Buck of North Kensington.

On the left Red Wilson was storming the broken ranks, his little green figure conspicuous even in the tangle of men and weapons, with the flaming red moustaches and the crown of laurel. Bowles slashed at his head and tore away some of the wreath, leaving the rest bloody, and, with a roar like a bull's, Wilson sprang at him, and, after a rattle of fencing, plunged his point into the chemist, who fell, crying, "Notting Hill!" Then the Notting Hillers wavered, and Bayswater swept them back in confusion. Wilson had carried everything before him.

On the right, however, Turnbull had carried the Red Lion banner with a rush against Barker's men, and the banner of the Golden Birds bore up with difficulty against it. Barker's men fell fast. In the centre Wayne and Buck were engaged, stubborn and confused. So far as the fighting went, it was precisely equal. But the fighting was a farce. For behind the three small armies with which Wayne's small army was engaged lay the great sea of the allied armies, which looked on as yet as scornful spectators, but could have broken all four armies by moving a finger.

Suddenly they did move. Some of the front contingents, the pastoral chiefs from Shepherd's Bush, with their spears and fleeces, were seen advancing, and the rude clans from Paddington Green. They were advancing for a very good reason. Buck, of North Kensington, was signalling wildly; he was surrounded, and totally cut off. His regiments were a struggling mass of people, islanded in a red sea of Notting Hill.

The allies had been too careless and confident. They had allowed Barker's force to be broken to pieces by Turnbull, and the moment that was done, the astute old leader of Notting Hill swung his men round and attacked Buck behind and on both sides. At the same moment Wayne cried, "Charge!" and struck him in front like a thunderbolt.

Two-thirds of Buck's men were cut to pieces before their allies could reach them. Then the sea of cities came on with their banners like breakers, and swallowed Notting Hill for ever. The battle was not over, for not one of Wayne's men would surrender, and it lasted till sundown, and long after. But it was decided; the story of Notting Hill was ended.

When Turnbull saw it, he ceased a moment from fighting, and looked round him. The evening sunlight struck his face; it looked like a child's.

"I have had my youth," he said. Then, snatching an axe from a man, he dashed into the thick of the spears of Shepherd's Bush, and died somewhere far in the depths of their reeling ranks. Then the battle roared on; every man of Notting Hill was slain before night.

Wayne was standing by a tree alone after the battle. Several men approached him with axes. One struck at him. His foot seemed partly to slip; but he flung his hand out, and steadied himself against the tree.

Barker sprang after him, sword in hand, and shaking with excitement.

"How large now, my lord," he cried, "is the Empire of Notting Hill?"

Wayne smiled in the gathering dark.

"Always as large as this," he said, and swept his sword round in a semicircle of silver.

Barker dropped, wounded in the neck; and Wilson sprang over his body like a tiger-cat, rushing at Wayne. At the same moment there came behind the Lord of the Red Lion a cry and a flare of yellow, and a mass of the West Kensington halberdiers ploughed up the slope, knee-deep in grass, bearing the yellow banner of the city before them, and shouting aloud.

At the same second Wilson went down under Wayne's sword, seemingly smashed like a fly. The great sword rose again like a bird, but Wilson seemed to rise with it, and, his sword being broken, sprang at Wayne's throat like a dog. The foremost of the yellow halberdiers had reached the tree and swung his axe above the struggling Wayne. With a curse the King whirled up his own halberd, and dashed the blade in the man's face. He reeled and rolled down the slope, just as the furious Wilson was flung on his back again. And again he was on his feet, and again at Wayne's throat. Then he was flung again, but this time laughing triumphantly. Grasped in his hand was the red and yellow favour that Wayne wore as Provost of Notting Hill. He had torn it from the place where it had been carried for twenty-five years.

With a shout the West Kensington men closed round Wayne, the great yellow banner flapping over his head.

"Where is your favour now, Provost?" cried the West Kensington leader.

And a laugh went up.

Adam struck at the standard-bearer and brought him reeling forward. As the banner stooped, he grasped the yellow folds and tore off a shred. A halberdier struck him on the shoulder, wounding bloodily.

"Here is one colour!" he cried, pushing the yellow into his belt; "and here!" he cried, pointing to his own blood—"here is the other."

At the same instant the shock of a sudden and heavy halberd laid the King stunned or dead. In the wild visions of vanishing consciousness, he saw again something that belonged to an utterly forgotten time, something that he had seen somewhere long ago in a restaurant. He saw, with his swimming eyes, red and yellow, the colours of Nicaragua.

Quin did not see the end. Wilson, wild with joy, sprang again at Adam Wayne, and the great sword of Notting Hill was whirled above once more. Then men ducked instinctively at the rushing noise of the sword coming down out of the sky, and Wilson of Bayswater was smashed and wiped down upon the floor like a fly. Nothing was left of him but a wreck; but the blade that had broken him was broken. In dying he had snapped the great sword and the spell of it; the sword of Wayne was broken at the hilt. One rush of the enemy carried Wayne by force against the tree. They were too close to use halberd or even sword; they were breast to breast, even nostrils to nostrils. But Buck got his dagger free.

"Kill him!" he cried, in a strange stifled voice. "Kill him! Good or bad, he is none of us! Do not be blinded by the face!... God! have we not been blinded all along!" and he drew his arm back for a stab, and seemed to close his eyes.

Wayne did not drop the hand that hung on to the tree-branch. But a mighty heave went over his breast and his whole huge figure, like an earthquake over great hills. And with that convulsion of effort he rent the branch out of the tree, with tongues of torn wood; and, swaying it once only, he let the splintered club fall on Buck, breaking his neck. The planner of the Great Road fell face foremost dead, with his dagger in a grip of steel.

"For you and me, and for all brave men, my brother," said Wayne, in his strange chant, "there is good wine poured in the inn at the end of the world."

The packed men made another lurch or heave towards him; it was almost too dark to fight clearly. He caught hold of the oak again, this time getting his hand into a wide crevice and grasping, as it were, the bowels of the tree. The whole crowd, numbering some thirty men, made a rush to tear him away from it; they hung on with all their weight and numbers, and nothing stirred. A solitude could not have been stiller than that group of straining men. Then there was a faint sound.

"His hand is slipping," cried two men in exultation.

"You don't know much of him," said another, grimly (a man of the old war). "More likely his bone cracks."

"It is neither—by God, it is neither!" said one of the first two.

"What is it, then?" asked the second.

"The tree is falling," he replied.

"As the tree falleth, so shall it lie," said Wayne's voice out of the darkness, and it had the same sweet and yet horrible air that it had had throughout, of coming from a great distance, from before or after the event. Even when he was struggling like an eel or battering like a madman, he spoke like a spectator. "As the tree falleth, so shall it lie," he said. "Men have called that a gloomy text. It is the essence of all exultation. I am doing now what I have done all my life, what is the only happiness, what is the only universality. I am clinging to something. Let it fall, and there let it lie. Fools, you go about and see the kingdoms of the earth, and are liberal and wise and cosmopolitan, which is all that the devil can give you—all that he could offer to Christ, only to be spurned away. I am doing what the truly wise do. When a child goes out into the garden and takes hold of a tree, saying, 'Let this tree be all I have,' that moment its roots take hold on hell and its branches on the stars. The joy I have is what the lover knows when a woman is everything. It is what a savage knows when his idol is everything. It is what I know when Notting Hill is everything. I have a city. Let it stand or fall."

As he spoke, the turf lifted itself like a living thing, and out of it rose slowly, like crested serpents, the roots of the oak. Then the great head of the tree, that seemed a green cloud among grey ones, swept the sky suddenly like a broom, and the whole tree heeled over like a ship, smashing every one in its fall.

3. TWO VOICES

In a place in which there was total darkness for hours, there was also for hours total silence. Then a voice spoke out of the darkness, no one could have told from where, and said aloud—

"So ends the Empire of Notting Hill. As it began in blood, so it ended in blood, and all things are always the same."

And there was silence again, and then again there was a voice, but it had not the same tone; it seemed that it was not the same voice.

"If all things are always the same, it is because they are always heroic. If all things are always the same, it is because they are always new. To each man one soul only is given; to each soul only is given a little power—the power at some moments to outgrow and swallow up the stars. If age after age that power comes upon men, whatever gives it to them is great. Whatever makes men feel old is mean—an empire or a skin-flint shop. Whatever makes men feel young is great—a great war or a love-story. And in the darkest of the books of God there is written a truth that is also a riddle. It is of the new things that men tire—of fashions and proposals and improvements and change. It is the old things that startle and intoxicate. It is the old things that are young. There is no sceptic who does not feel that many have doubted before. There is no rich and fickle man who does not feel that all his novelties are ancient. There is no worshipper of change who does not feel upon his neck the vast weight of the weariness of the universe. But we who do the old things are fed by nature with a perpetual infancy. No man who is in love thinks that any one has been in love before. No woman who has a child thinks that there have been such things as children. No people that fight for their own city are haunted with the burden of the broken empires. Yes, O dark voice, the world is always the same, for it is always unexpected."

A little gust of wind blew through the night, and then the first voice answered—

"But in this world there are some, be they wise or foolish, whom nothing intoxicates. There are some who see all your disturbances like a cloud of flies. They know that while men will laugh at your Notting Hill, and will study and rehearse and sing of Athens and Jerusalem, Athens and Jerusalem were silly suburbs like your Notting Hill. They know that the earth itself is a suburb, and can feel only drearily and respectably amused as they move upon it."

"They are philosophers or they are fools," said the other voice. "They are not men. Men live, as I say, rejoicing from age to age in something fresher than progress—in the fact that with every baby a new sun and a new moon are made. If our ancient humanity were a single man, it might perhaps be that he would break down under the memory of so many loyalties, under the burden of so many diverse heroisms, under the load and terror of all the goodness of men. But it has pleased God so to isolate the individual soul that it can only learn of all other souls by hearsay, and to each one goodness and happiness come with the youth and violence of lightning, as momentary and as pure. And the doom of failure that lies on all human systems does not in real fact affect them any more than the worms of the inevitable grave affect a children's game in a meadow. Notting Hill has fallen; Notting Hill has died. But that is not the tremendous issue. Notting Hill has lived."

"But if," answered the other voice, "if what is achieved by all these efforts be only the common contentment of humanity, why do men so extravagantly toil and die in them? Has nothing been done by Notting Hill than any chance clump of farmers or clan of savages would not have done without it? What might have been done to Notting Hill if the world had been different may be a deep question; but there is a deeper. What could have happened to the world if Notting Hill had never been?"

The other voice replied—

"The same that would have happened to the world and all the starry systems if an apple-tree grew six apples instead of seven; something would have been eternally lost. There has never been anything in the world absolutely like Notting Hill. There will never be anything quite like it to the crack of doom. I cannot believe anything but that God loved it as He must surely love anything that is itself and unreplaceable. But even for that I do not care. If God, with all His thunders, hated it, I loved it."

And with the voice a tall, strange figure lifted itself out of the *debris* in the half-darkness.

The other voice came after a long pause, and as it were hoarsely.

"But suppose the whole matter were really a hocus-pocus. Suppose that whatever meaning you may choose in your fancy to give to it, the real meaning of the whole was mockery. Suppose it was all folly. Suppose—"

"I have been in it," answered the voice from the tall and strange figure, "and I know it was not."

A smaller figure seemed half to rise in the dark.

"Suppose I am God," said the voice, "and suppose I made the world in idleness. Suppose the stars, that you think eternal, are only the idiot fireworks of an everlasting schoolboy. Suppose the sun and the moon, to which you sing alternately, are only the two eyes of one vast and sneering giant, opened alternately in a never-ending wink. Suppose the trees, in my eyes, are as foolish as enormous toad-stools. Suppose Socrates and Charlemagne are to me only beasts, made funnier by walking on their hind legs. Suppose I am God, and having made things, laugh at them."

"And suppose I am man," answered the other. "And suppose that I give the answer that shatters even a laugh. Suppose I do not laugh back at you, do not blaspheme you, do not curse you. But suppose, standing up straight under the sky, with every power of my being, I thank you for the fools' paradise you have made. Suppose I praise you, with a literal pain of ecstasy, for the jest that has brought me so terrible a joy. If we have taken the child's games, and given them the seriousness of a Crusade, if we have drenched your grotesque Dutch garden with the blood of martyrs, we have turned a nursery into a temple. I ask you, in the name of Heaven, who wins?"

The sky close about the crests of the hills and trees was beginning to turn from black to grey, with a random suggestion of the morning. The slight figure seemed to crawl towards the larger one, and the voice was more human.

"But suppose, friend," it said, "suppose that, in a bitterer and more real sense, it was all a mockery. Suppose that there had been, from the beginning of these great wars, one who watched them with a sense that is beyond expression, a sense of detachment, of responsibility, of irony, of agony. Suppose that there were one who knew it was all a joke."

The tall figure answered—

"He could not know it. For it was not all a joke."

And a gust of wind blew away some clouds that sealed the sky-line, and showed a strip of silver behind his great dark legs. Then the other voice came, having crept nearer still.

"Adam Wayne," it said, "there are men who confess only in *articulo mortis*; there are people who blame themselves only when they can no longer help others. I am one of them. Here, upon the field of the bloody end of it all, I come to tell you plainly what you would never understand before. Do you know who I am?"

"I know you, Auberon Quin," answered the tall figure, "and I shall be glad to unburden your spirit of anything that lies upon it."

"Adam Wayne," said the other voice, "of what I have to say you cannot in common reason be glad to unburden me. Wayne, it was all a joke. When I made these cities, I cared no more for them than I care for a centaur, or a merman, or a fish with legs, or a pig with feathers, or any other absurdity. When I spoke to you solemnly and encouragingly about the flag of your freedom and the peace of your city, I was playing a vulgar practical joke on an honest gentleman, a vulgar practical joke that has lasted for twenty years. Though no one could believe it of me, perhaps, it is the truth that I am a man both timid and tender-hearted. I never dared in the early days of your hope, or the central days of your supremacy, to tell you this; I never dared to break the colossal calm of your face. God knows why I should do it now, when my farce has ended in tragedy and the ruin of all your people! But I say it now. Wayne, it was done as a joke."

There was silence, and the freshening breeze blew the sky clearer and clearer, leaving great spaces of the white dawn.

At last Wayne said, very slowly—

"You did it all only as a joke?"

"Yes," said Quin, briefly.

"When you conceived the idea," went on Wayne, dreamily, "of an army for Bayswater and a flag for Notting Hill, there was no gleam, no suggestion in your mind that such things might be real and passionate?"

"No," answered Auberon, turning his round white face to the morning with a dull and splendid sincerity; "I had none at all."

Wayne sprang down from the height above him and held out his hand.

"I will not stop to thank you," he said, with a curious joy in his voice, "for the great good for the world you have actually wrought. All that I think of that I have said to you a moment ago, even when I thought that your voice was the voice of a derisive omnipotence, its laughter older than the winds of heaven. But let me say what is immediate and true. You and I, Auberon Quin, have both of us throughout our lives been again and again called mad. And we are mad. We are mad, because we are not two men, but one man. We are mad, because we are two lobes of the same brain, and that brain has been cloven in two. And if you ask for the proof of it, it is not hard to find. It is not merely that you, the humorist, have been in these dark days stripped of the joy of gravity. It is not merely that I, the fanatic, have had to grope without humour. It is that, though we seem to be opposite in everything, we have been opposite like man and woman, aiming at the same moment at the same practical thing. We are the father and the mother of the Charter of the Cities."

Quin looked down at the *debris* of leaves and timber, the relics of the battle and stampede, now glistening in the growing daylight, and finally said—

"Yet nothing can alter the antagonism—the fact that I laughed at these things and you adored them."

Wayne's wild face flamed with something god-like, as he turned it to be struck by the sunrise.

"I know of something that will alter that antagonism, something that is outside us, something that you and I have all our lives perhaps taken too little account of. The equal and eternal human being will alter that antagonism, for the human being sees no real antagonism between laughter and respect, the human being, the common man, whom mere geniuses like you and me can only worship like a god. When dark and dreary days come, you and I are necessary, the pure fanatic, the pure satirist. We have between us remedied a great wrong. We have lifted the modern cities into that poetry which every one who knows mankind knows to be immeasurably more common than the commonplace. But in healthy people there is no war between us. We are but the two lobes of the brain of a ploughman. Laughter and love are everywhere. The cathedrals, built in the ages that loved God, are full of blasphemous grotesques. The mother laughs continually at the child, the lover laughs continually at the lover, the wife at the husband, the friend at the friend. Auberon Quin, we have been too long separated; let us go out together. You have a halberd and I a sword, let us start our wanderings over the world. For we are its two essentials. Come, it is already day."

In the blank white light Auberon hesitated a moment. Then he made the formal salute with his halberd, and they went away together into the unknown world.

THE MAN WHO WAS THURSDAY

A Nightmare

TO EDMUND CLERIHEW BENTLEY

A cloud was on the mind of men, and wailing went the weather,
Yea, a sick cloud upon the soul when we were boys together.
Science announced nonentity and art admired decay;
The world was old and ended: but you and I were gay;
Round us in antic order their crippled vices came —
Lust that had lost its laughter, fear that had lost its shame.
Like the white lock of Whistler, that lit our aimless gloom,
Men showed their own white feather as proudly as a plume.
Life was a fly that faded, and death a drone that stung;
The world was very old indeed when you and I were young.
They twisted even decent sin to shapes not to be named:
Men were ashamed of honour; but we were not ashamed.
Weak if we were and foolish, not thus we failed, not thus;
When that black Baal blocked the heavens he had no hymns from us
Children we were — our forts of sand were even as weak as we,
High as they went we piled them up to break that bitter sea.
Fools as we were in motley, all jangling and absurd,
When all church bells were silent our cap and bells were heard.

Not all unhelped we held the fort, our tiny flags unfurled;
Some giants laboured in that cloud to lift it from the world.
I find again the book we found, I feel the hour that flings
Far out of fish-shaped Paumanok some cry of cleaner things;
And the Green Carnation withered, as in forest fires that pass,
Roared in the wind of all the world ten million leaves of grass;
Or sane and sweet and sudden as a bird sings in the rain —
Truth out of Tusitala spoke and pleasure out of pain.

Yea, cool and clear and sudden as a bird sings in the grey,
Dunedin to Samoa spoke, and darkness unto day.
But we were young; we lived to see God break their bitter charms.
God and the good Republic come riding back in arms:
We have seen the City of Mansoul, even as it rocked, relieved —
Blessed are they who did not see, but being blind, believed.

This is a tale of those old fears, even of those emptied hells,
And none but you shall understand the true thing that it tells —
Of what colossal gods of shame could cow men and yet crash,
Of what huge devils hid the stars, yet fell at a pistol flash.
The doubts that were so plain to chase, so dreadful to withstand —
Oh, who shall understand but you; yea, who shall understand?
The doubts that drove us through the night as we two talked amain,
And day had broken on the streets e'er it broke upon the brain.
Between us, by the peace of God, such truth can now be told;
Yea, there is strength in striking root and good in growing old.
We have found common things at last and marriage and a creed,
And I may safely write it now, and you may safely read.

— G.K.C.

THE MAN WHO WAS THURSDAY

A NIGHTMARE

I. THE TWO POETS OF SAFFRON PARK

THE suburb of Saffron Park lay on the sunset side of London, as red and ragged as a cloud of sunset. It was built of a bright brick throughout; its sky-line was fantastic, and even its ground plan was wild. It had been the outburst of a speculative builder, faintly tinged with art, who called its architecture sometimes Elizabethan and sometimes Queen Anne, apparently under the impression that the two sovereigns were identical. It was described with some justice as an artistic colony, though it never in any definable way produced any art. But although its pretensions to be an intellectual centre were a little vague, its pretensions to be a pleasant place were quite indisputable. The stranger who looked for the first time at the quaint red houses could only think how very oddly shaped the people must be who could fit in to them. Nor when he met the people was he disappointed in this respect. The place was not only pleasant, but perfect, if once he could regard it not as a deception but rather as a dream. Even if the people were not "artists," the whole was nevertheless artistic. That young man with the long, auburn hair and the impudent face—that young man was not really a poet; but surely he was a poem. That old gentleman with the wild, white beard and the wild, white hat—that venerable humbug was not really a philosopher; but at least he was the cause of philosophy in others. That scientific gentleman with the bald, egg-like head and the bare, bird-like neck had no real right to the airs of science that he assumed. He had not discovered anything new in biology; but what biological creature could he have discovered more singular than himself? Thus, and thus only, the whole place had properly to be regarded; it had to be considered not so much as a workshop for artists, but as a frail but finished work of art. A man who stepped into its social atmosphere felt as if he had stepped into a written comedy.

More especially this attractive unreality fell upon it about nightfall, when the extravagant roofs were dark against the afterglow and the whole insane village seemed as separate as a drifting cloud. This again was more strongly true of the many nights of local festivity, when the little gardens were often illuminated, and the big Chinese lanterns glowed in the dwarfish trees like some fierce and monstrous fruit. And this was strongest of all on one particular evening, still vaguely remembered in the locality, of which the auburn-haired poet was the hero. It was not by any means the only evening of which he was the hero. On many nights those passing by his little back garden might hear his high, didactic voice laying down the law to men and particularly to women. The attitude of women in such cases was indeed one of the paradoxes of the place. Most of the women were of the kind vaguely called emancipated, and professed some protest against male supremacy. Yet these new women would always pay to a man the extravagant compliment which no ordinary woman ever pays to him, that of listening while he is talking. And Mr. Lucian Gregory, the red-haired poet, was really (in some sense) a man worth listening to, even if one only laughed at the end of it. He put the old cant of the lawlessness of art and the art of lawlessness with a certain impudent freshness which gave at least a momentary pleasure. He was helped in some degree by the arresting oddity of his appearance, which he worked, as the phrase goes, for all it was worth. His dark red hair parted in the middle was literally like a woman's, and curved into the slow curls of a virgin in a pre-Raphaelite picture. From within this almost saintly oval, however, his face projected suddenly broad and brutal, the chin carried forward with a look of cockney contempt. This combination at once tickled and terrified the nerves of a neurotic population. He seemed like a walking blasphemy, a blend of the angel and the ape.

This particular evening, if it is remembered for nothing else, will be remembered in that place for its strange sunset. It looked like the end of the world. All the heaven seemed covered with a quite vivid and palpable plumage; you could only say that the sky was full of feathers, and of feathers that almost brushed the face. Across the great part of the dome they were grey, with the strangest tints of violet and mauve and an unnatural pink or pale green; but towards the west the whole grew past description, transparent and passionate, and the last red-hot plumes of it covered up the sun like something too good to be seen. The whole was so close about the earth, as to express nothing but a violent secrecy. The very empyrean seemed to be a secret. It expressed that splendid smallness which is the soul of local patriotism. The very sky seemed small.

I say that there are some inhabitants who may remember the evening if only by that oppressive sky. There are others who may remember it because it marked the first appearance in the place of the second poet of Saffron Park. For a long time the red-haired revolutionary had reigned without a rival; it was upon the night of the sunset that his solitude suddenly ended. The new poet, who introduced himself by the name of Gabriel Syme was a very mild-looking mortal, with a fair, pointed beard and faint, yellow hair. But an impression grew that he was less meek than he looked. He signalised his entrance by differing with the established poet, Gregory, upon the whole nature of poetry. He said that he (Syme) was poet of law, a poet of order; nay, he said he was a poet of respectability. So all the Saffron Parkers looked at him as if he had that moment fallen out of that impossible sky.

In fact, Mr. Lucian Gregory, the anarchic poet, connected the two events.

"It may well be," he said, in his sudden lyrical manner, "it may well be on such a night of clouds and cruel colours that there is brought forth upon the earth such a portent as a respectable poet. You say you are a poet of law; I say you are a contradiction in terms. I only wonder there were not comets and earthquakes on the night you appeared in this garden."

The man with the meek blue eyes and the pale, pointed beard endured these thunders with a certain submissive solemnity. The third party of the group, Gregory's sister Rosamond, who had her brother's braids of red hair, but a kindlier face underneath them, laughed with such mixture of admiration and disapproval as she gave commonly to the family oracle.

Gregory resumed in high oratorical good humour.

"An artist is identical with an anarchist," he cried. "You might transpose the words anywhere. An anarchist is an artist. The man who throws a bomb is an artist, because he prefers a great moment to everything. He sees how much more valuable is one burst of blazing light, one peal of perfect thunder, than the mere common bodies of a few shapeless policemen. An artist disregards all governments, abolishes all conventions. The poet delights in disorder only. If it were not so, the most poetical thing in the world would be the Underground Railway."

"So it is," said Mr. Syme.

"Nonsense!" said Gregory, who was very rational when anyone else attempted paradox. "Why do all the clerks and navvies in the railway trains look so sad and tired, so very sad and tired? I will tell you. It is because they know that the train is going right. It is because they know that whatever place they have taken a ticket for that place they will reach. It is because after they have passed Sloane Square they know that the next station must be Victoria, and nothing but Victoria. Oh, their wild rapture! oh, their eyes like stars and their souls again in Eden, if the next station were unaccountably Baker Street!"

"It is you who are unpoetical," replied the poet Syme. "If what you say of clerks is true, they can only be as prosaic as your poetry. The rare, strange thing is to hit the mark; the gross, obvious thing is to miss it. We feel it is epical when man with one wild arrow strikes a distant bird. Is it not also epical when man with one wild engine strikes a distant station? Chaos is dull; because in chaos the train might indeed go anywhere, to Baker Street or to Bagdad. But man is a magician, and his whole magic is in this, that he does say Victoria, and lo! it is Victoria. No, take your books of mere poetry and prose; let me read a time table, with tears of pride. Take your Byron, who commemorates the defeats of man; give me Bradshaw, who commemorates his victories. Give me Bradshaw, I say!"

"Must you go?" inquired Gregory sarcastically.

"I tell you," went on Syme with passion, "that every time a train comes in I feel that it has broken past batteries of besiegers, and that man has won a battle against chaos. You say contemptuously that when one has left Sloane Square one must come to Victoria. I say that one might do a thousand things instead, and that whenever I really come there I have the sense of hairbreadth escape. And when I hear the guard shout out the word 'Victoria,' it is not an unmeaning word. It is to me the cry of a herald announcing conquest. It is to me indeed 'Victoria'; it is the victory of Adam."

Gregory wagged his heavy, red head with a slow and sad smile.

"And even then," he said, "we poets always ask the question, 'And what is Victoria now that you have got there?' You think Victoria is like the New Jerusalem. We know that the New Jerusalem will only be like Victoria. Yes, the poet will be discontented even in the streets of heaven. The poet is always in revolt."

"There again," said Syme irritably, "what is there poetical about being in revolt? You might as well say that it is poetical to be sea-sick. Being sick is a revolt. Both being sick and being rebellious may be the wholesome thing on certain desperate occasions; but I'm hanged if I can see why they are poetical. Revolt in the abstract is—revolting. It's mere vomiting."

The girl winced for a flash at the unpleasant word, but Syme was too hot to heed her.

"It is things going right," he cried, "that is poetical! Our digestions, for instance, going sacredly and silently right, that is the foundation of all poetry. Yes, the most poetical thing, more poetical than the flowers, more poetical than the stars—the most poetical thing in the world is not being sick."

"Really," said Gregory superciliously, "the examples you choose—"

"I beg your pardon," said Syme grimly, "I forgot we had abolished all conventions."

For the first time a red patch appeared on Gregory's forehead.

"You don't expect me," he said, "to revolutionise society on this lawn?"

Syme looked straight into his eyes and smiled sweetly.

"No, I don't," he said; "but I suppose that if you were serious about your anarchism, that is exactly what you would do."

Gregory's big bull's eyes blinked suddenly like those of an angry lion, and one could almost fancy that his red mane rose.

"Don't you think, then," he said in a dangerous voice, "that I am serious about my anarchism?"

"I beg your pardon?" said Syme.

"Am I not serious about my anarchism?" cried Gregory, with knotted fists.

"My dear fellow!" said Syme, and strolled away.

With surprise, but with a curious pleasure, he found Rosamond Gregory still in his company.

"Mr. Syme," she said, "do the people who talk like you and my brother often mean what they say? Do you mean what you say now?"

Syme smiled.

"Do you?" he asked.

"What do you mean?" asked the girl, with grave eyes.

"My dear Miss Gregory," said Syme gently, "there are many kinds of sincerity and insincerity. When you say 'thank you' for the salt, do you mean what you say? No. When you say 'the world is round,' do you mean what you say? No. It is true, but you don't mean it. Now, sometimes a man like your brother really finds a thing he does mean. It may be only a half-truth, quarter-truth, tenth-truth; but then he says more than he means—from sheer force of meaning it."

She was looking at him from under level brows; her face was grave and open, and there had fallen upon it the shadow of that unreasoning responsibility which is at the bottom of the most frivolous woman, the maternal watch which is as old as the world.

"Is he really an anarchist, then?" she asked.

"Only in that sense I speak of," replied Syme; "or if you prefer it, in that nonsense."

She drew her broad brows together and said abruptly—

"He wouldn't really use—bombs or that sort of thing?"

Syme broke into a great laugh, that seemed too large for his slight and somewhat dandified figure.

"Good Lord, no!" he said, "that has to be done anonymously."

And at that the corners of her own mouth broke into a smile, and she thought with a simultaneous pleasure of Gregory's absurdity and of his safety.

Syme strolled with her to a seat in the corner of the garden, and continued to pour out his opinions. For he was a sincere man, and in spite of his superficial airs and graces, at root a humble one. And it is always the humble man who talks too much; the proud man watches himself too closely. He defended respectability with violence and exaggeration. He grew passionate in his praise of tidiness and propriety. All the time there was a smell of lilac all round him. Once he heard very faintly in some distant street a barrel-organ begin to play, and it seemed to him that his heroic words were moving to a tiny tune from under or beyond the world.

He stared and talked at the girl's red hair and amused face for what seemed to be a few minutes; and then, feeling that the groups in such a place should mix, rose to his feet. To his astonishment, he discovered the whole garden empty. Everyone had gone long ago, and he went himself with a rather hurried apology. He left with a sense of champagne in his head, which he could not afterwards explain. In the wild events which were to follow this girl had no part at all; he never saw her again until all his tale was over. And yet, in some indescribable way, she kept recurring like a motive in music through all his mad adventures afterwards, and the glory of her strange hair ran like a red thread through those dark and ill-drawn tapestries of the night. For what followed was so improbable, that it might well have been a dream.

When Syme went out into the starlit street, he found it for the moment empty. Then he realised (in some odd way) that the silence was rather a living silence than a dead one. Directly outside the door stood a street lamp, whose gleam gilded the leaves of the tree that bent out over the fence behind him. About a foot from the lamp-post stood a figure almost as rigid and motionless as the lamp-post itself. The tall hat and long frock coat were black; the face, in an abrupt shadow, was almost as dark. Only a fringe of fiery hair against the light, and also something aggressive in the attitude, proclaimed that it was the poet Gregory. He had something of the look of a masked bravo waiting sword in hand for his foe.

He made a sort of doubtful salute, which Syme somewhat more formally returned.

"I was waiting for you," said Gregory. "Might I have a moment's conversation?"

"Certainly. About what?" asked Syme in a sort of weak wonder.

Gregory struck out with his stick at the lamp-post, and then at the tree. "About this and this," he cried; "about order and anarchy. There is your precious order, that lean, iron lamp, ugly and barren; and there is anarchy, rich, living, reproducing itself—there is anarchy, splendid in green and gold."

"All the same," replied Syme patiently, "just at present you only see the tree by the light of the lamp. I wonder when you would ever see the lamp by the light of the tree." Then after a pause he said, "But may I ask if you have been standing out here in the dark only to resume our little argument?"

G.K. CHESTERTON

"No," cried out Gregory, in a voice that rang down the street, "I did not stand here to resume our argument, but to end it for ever."

The silence fell again, and Syme, though he understood nothing, listened instinctively for something serious. Gregory began in a smooth voice and with a rather bewildering smile.

"Mr. Syme," he said, "this evening you succeeded in doing something rather remarkable. You did something to me that no man born of woman has ever succeeded in doing before."

"Indeed!"

"Now I remember," resumed Gregory reflectively, "one other person succeeded in doing it. The captain of a penny steamer (if I remember correctly) at Southend. You have irritated me."

"I am very sorry," replied Syme with gravity.

"I am afraid my fury and your insult are too shocking to be wiped out even with an apology," said Gregory very calmly. "No duel could wipe it out. If I struck you dead I could not wipe it out. There is only one way by which that insult can be erased, and that way I choose. I am going, at the possible sacrifice of my life and honour, to prove to you that you were wrong in what you said."

"In what I said?"

"You said I was not serious about being an anarchist."

"There are degrees of seriousness," replied Syme. "I have never doubted that you were perfectly sincere in this sense, that you thought what you said well worth saying, that you thought a paradox might wake men up to a neglected truth."

Gregory stared at him steadily and painfully.

"And in no other sense," he asked, "you think me serious? You think me a flaneur who lets fall occasional truths. You do not think that in a deeper, a more deadly sense, I am serious."

Syme struck his stick violently on the stones of the road.

"Serious!" he cried. "Good Lord! is this street serious? Are these damned Chinese lanterns serious? Is the whole caboodle serious? One comes here and talks a pack of bosh, and perhaps some sense as well, but I should think very little of a man who didn't keep something in the background of his life that was more serious than all this talking —something more serious, whether it was religion or only drink."

"Very well," said Gregory, his face darkening, "you shall see something more serious than either drink or religion."

Syme stood waiting with his usual air of mildness until Gregory again opened his lips.

"You spoke just now of having a religion. Is it really true that you have one?"

"Oh," said Syme with a beaming smile, "we are all Catholics now."

"Then may I ask you to swear by whatever gods or saints your religion involves that you will not reveal what I am now going to tell you to any son of Adam, and especially not to the police? Will you swear that! If you will take upon yourself this awful abnegation if you will consent to burden your soul with a vow that you should never make and a knowledge you should never dream about, I will promise you in return—"

"You will promise me in return?" inquired Syme, as the other paused.

"I will promise you a very entertaining evening." Syme suddenly took off his hat.

"Your offer," he said, "is far too idiotic to be declined. You say that a poet is always an anarchist. I disagree; but I hope at least that he is always a sportsman. Permit me, here and now, to swear as a Christian, and promise as a good comrade and a fellow-artist, that I will not report anything of this, whatever it is, to the police. And now, in the name of Colney Hatch, what is it?"

"I think," said Gregory, with placid irrelevancy, "that we will call a cab."

He gave two long whistles, and a hansom came rattling down the road. The two got into it in silence. Gregory gave through the trap the address of an obscure public-house on the Chiswick bank of the river. The cab whisked itself away again, and in it these two fantastics quitted their fantastic town.

2. THE SECRET OF GABRIEL SYME

THE cab pulled up before a particularly dreary and greasy beershop, into which Gregory rapidly conducted his companion. They seated themselves in a close and dim sort of bar-parlour, at a stained wooden table with one wooden leg. The room was so small and dark, that very little could be seen of the attendant who was summoned, beyond a vague and dark impression of something bulky and bearded.

"Will you take a little supper?" asked Gregory politely. "The pate de foie gras is not good here, but I can recommend the game."

Syme received the remark with stolidity, imagining it to be a joke. Accepting the vein of humour, he said, with a well-bred indifference—

"Oh, bring me some lobster mayonnaise."

To his indescribable astonishment, the man only said "Certainly, sir!" and went away apparently to get it.

"What will you drink?" resumed Gregory, with the same careless yet apologetic air. "I shall only have a creme de menthe myself; I have dined. But the champagne can really be trusted. Do let me start you with a half-bottle of Pommery at least?"

"Thank you!" said the motionless Syme. "You are very good."

His further attempts at conversation, somewhat disorganised in themselves, were cut short finally as by a thunderbolt by the actual appearance of the lobster. Syme tasted it, and found it particularly good. Then he suddenly began to eat with great rapidity and appetite.

"Excuse me if I enjoy myself rather obviously!" he said to Gregory, smiling. "I don't often have the luck to have a dream like this. It is new to me for a nightmare to lead to a lobster. It is commonly the other way."

"You are not asleep, I assure you," said Gregory. "You are, on the contrary, close to the most actual and rousing moment of your existence. Ah, here comes your champagne! I admit that there may be a slight disproportion, let us say, between the inner arrangements of this excellent hotel and its simple and unpretentious exterior. But that is all our modesty. We are the most modest men that ever lived on earth."

"And who are we?" asked Syme, emptying his champagne glass.

"It is quite simple," replied Gregory. "We are the serious anarchists, in whom you do not believe."

"Oh!" said Syme shortly. "You do yourselves well in drinks."

"Yes, we are serious about everything," answered Gregory.

Then after a pause he added—

"If in a few moments this table begins to turn round a little, don't put it down to your inroads into the champagne. I don't wish you to do yourself an injustice."

"Well, if I am not drunk, I am mad," replied Syme with perfect calm; "but I trust I can behave like a gentleman in either condition. May I smoke?"

"Certainly!" said Gregory, producing a cigar-case. "Try one of mine."

Syme took the cigar, clipped the end off with a cigar-cutter out of his waistcoat pocket, put it in his mouth, lit it slowly, and let out a long cloud of smoke. It is not a little to his credit that he performed these rites with so much composure, for almost before he had begun them the table at which he sat had begun to revolve, first slowly, and then rapidly, as if at an insane seance.

"You must not mind it," said Gregory; "it's a kind of screw."

"Quite so," said Syme placidly, "a kind of screw. How simple that is!"

The next moment the smoke of his cigar, which had been wavering across the room in snaky twists, went straight up as if from a factory chimney, and the two, with their chairs and table, shot down through the floor as if the earth had swallowed them. They went rattling down a kind of roaring chimney as rapidly as a lift cut loose, and they came with an abrupt bump to the bottom. But when Gregory threw open a pair of doors and let in a red subterranean light, Syme was still smoking with one leg thrown over the other, and had not turned a yellow hair.

Gregory led him down a low, vaulted passage, at the end of which was the red light. It was an enormous crimson lantern, nearly as big as a fireplace, fixed over a small but heavy iron door. In the door there was a sort of hatchway or grating, and on this Gregory struck five times. A heavy voice with a foreign accent asked him who he was. To this he gave the more or less unexpected reply, "Mr. Joseph Chamberlain." The heavy hinges began to move; it was obviously some kind of password.

Inside the doorway the passage gleamed as if it were lined with a network of steel. On a second glance, Syme saw that the glittering pattern was really made up of ranks and ranks of rifles and revolvers, closely packed or interlocked.

"I must ask you to forgive me all these formalities," said Gregory; "we have to be very strict here."

"Oh, don't apologise," said Syme. "I know your passion for law and order," and he stepped into the passage lined with the steel weapons. With his long, fair hair and rather foppish frock-coat, he looked a singularly frail and fanciful figure as he walked down that shining avenue of death.

They passed through several such passages, and came out at last into a queer steel chamber with curved walls, almost spherical in shape, but presenting, with its tiers of benches, something of the appearance of a scientific lecture-theatre. There were no rifles or pistols in this apartment, but round the walls of it were hung more dubious and dreadful shapes, things that looked like the bulbs of iron plants, or the eggs of iron birds. They were bombs, and the very room itself seemed like the inside of a bomb. Syme knocked his cigar ash off against the wall, and went in.

"And now, my dear Mr. Syme," said Gregory, throwing himself in an expansive manner on the bench under the largest bomb, "now we are quite cosy, so let us talk properly. Now no human words can give you any notion of why I brought you here. It was one of those quite arbitrary emotions, like jumping off a cliff or falling in love.

Suffice it to say that you were an inexpressibly irritating fellow, and, to do you justice, you are still. I would break twenty oaths of secrecy for the pleasure of taking you down a peg. That way you have of lighting a cigar would make a priest break the seal of confession. Well, you said that you were quite certain I was not a serious anarchist. Does this place strike you as being serious?"

"It does seem to have a moral under all its gaiety," assented Syme; "but may I ask you two questions? You need not fear to give me information, because, as you remember, you very wisely extorted from me a promise not to tell the police, a promise I shall certainly keep. So it is in mere curiosity that I make my queries. First of all, what is it really all about? What is it you object to? You want to abolish Government?"

"To abolish God!" said Gregory, opening the eyes of a fanatic. "We do not only want to upset a few despotisms and police regulations; that sort of anarchism does exist, but it is a mere branch of the Nonconformists. We dig deeper and we blow you higher. We wish to deny all those arbitrary distinctions of vice and virtue, honour and treachery, upon which mere rebels base themselves. The silly sentimentalists of the French Revolution talked of the Rights of Man! We hate Rights as we hate Wrongs. We have abolished Right and Wrong."

"And Right and Left," said Syme with a simple eagerness, "I hope you will abolish them too. They are much more troublesome to me."

"You spoke of a second question," snapped Gregory.

"With pleasure," resumed Syme. "In all your present acts and surroundings there is a scientific attempt at secrecy. I have an aunt who lived over a shop, but this is the first time I have found people living from preference under a public-house. You have a heavy iron door. You cannot pass it without submitting to the humiliation of calling yourself Mr. Chamberlain. You surround yourself with steel instruments which make the place, if I may say so, more impressive than homelike. May I ask why, after taking all this trouble to barricade yourselves in the bowels of the earth, you then parade your whole secret by talking about anarchism to every silly woman in Saffron Park?"

Gregory smiled.

"The answer is simple," he said. "I told you I was a serious anarchist, and you did not believe me. Nor do they believe me. Unless I took them into this infernal room they would not believe me."

Syme smoked thoughtfully, and looked at him with interest. Gregory went on.

"The history of the thing might amuse you," he said. "When first I became one of the New Anarchists I tried all kinds of respectable disguises. I dressed up as a bishop. I read up all about bishops in our anarchist pamphlets, in Superstition the Vampire and Priests of Prey. I certainly understood from them that bishops are strange and terrible old men keeping a cruel secret from mankind. I was misinformed. When on my first appearing in episcopal gaiters in a drawing-room I cried out in a voice of thunder, 'Down! down! presumptuous human reason!' they found out in some way that I was not a bishop at all. I was nabbed at once. Then I made up as a millionaire; but I defended Capital with so much intelligence that a fool could see that I was quite poor. Then I tried being a major. Now I am a humanitarian myself, but I have, I hope, enough intellectual breadth to understand the position of those who, like Nietzsche, admire violence—the proud, mad war of Nature and all that, you know. I threw myself into the major. I drew my sword and waved it constantly. I called out 'Blood!' abstractedly, like a man calling for wine. I often said, 'Let the weak perish; it is the Law.' Well, well, it seems majors don't do this. I was nabbed again. At last I went in despair to the President of the Central Anarchist Council, who is the greatest man in Europe."

"What is his name?" asked Syme.

"You would not know it," answered Gregory. "That is his greatness. Caesar and Napoleon put all their genius into being heard of, and they were heard of. He puts all his genius into not being heard of, and he is not heard of. But you cannot be for five minutes in the room with him without feeling that Caesar and Napoleon would have been children in his hands."

He was silent and even pale for a moment, and then resumed—

"But whenever he gives advice it is always something as startling as an epigram, and yet as practical as the Bank of England. I said to him, 'What disguise will hide me from the world? What can I find more respectable than bishops and majors?' He looked at me with his large but indecipherable face. 'You want a safe disguise, do you? You want a dress which will guarantee you harmless; a dress in which no one would ever look for a bomb?' I nodded. He suddenly lifted his lion's voice. 'Why, then, dress up as an anarchist, you fool!' he roared so that the room shook. 'Nobody will ever expect you to do anything dangerous then.' And he turned his broad back on me without another word. I took his advice, and have never regretted it. I preached blood and murder to those women day and night, and—by God!—they would let me wheel their perambulators."

Syme sat watching him with some respect in his large, blue eyes.

"You took me in," he said. "It is really a smart dodge."

Then after a pause he added—

"What do you call this tremendous President of yours?"

"We generally call him Sunday," replied Gregory with simplicity. "You see, there are seven members of the Central Anarchist Council, and they are named after days of the week. He is called Sunday, by some of his admirers Bloody Sunday. It is curious you should mention the matter, because the very night you have dropped in (if I may so express it) is the night on which our London branch, which assembles in this room, has to elect its own deputy to fill a vacancy in the Council. The gentleman who has for some time past played, with propriety and general applause, the difficult part of Thursday, has died quite suddenly. Consequently, we have called a meeting this very evening to elect a successor."

He got to his feet and strolled across the room with a sort of smiling embarrassment.

"I feel somehow as if you were my mother, Syme," he continued casually. "I feel that I can confide anything to you, as you have promised to tell nobody. In fact, I will confide to you something that I would not say in so many words to the anarchists who will be coming to the room in about ten minutes. We shall, of course, go through a form of election; but I don't mind telling you that it is practically certain what the result will be." He looked down for a moment modestly. "It is almost a settled thing that I am to be Thursday."

"My dear fellow." said Syme heartily, "I congratulate you. A great career!"

Gregory smiled in deprecation, and walked across the room, talking rapidly.

"As a matter of fact, everything is ready for me on this table," he said, "and the ceremony will probably be the shortest possible."

Syme also strolled across to the table, and found lying across it a walking-stick, which turned out on examination to be a sword-stick, a large Colt's revolver, a sandwich case, and a formidable flask of brandy. Over the chair, beside the table, was thrown a heavy-looking cape or cloak.

"I have only to get the form of election finished," continued Gregory with animation, "then I snatch up this cloak and stick, stuff these other things into my pocket, step out of a door in this cavern, which opens on the river, where there is a steam-tug already waiting for me, and then—then—oh, the wild joy of being Thursday!" And he clasped his hands.

Syme, who had sat down once more with his usual insolent languor, got to his feet with an unusual air of hesitation.

"Why is it," he asked vaguely, "that I think you are quite a decent fellow? Why do I positively like you, Gregory?" He paused a moment, and then added with a sort of fresh curiosity, "Is it because you are such an ass?"

There was a thoughtful silence again, and then he cried out—

"Well, damn it all! this is the funniest situation I have ever been in in my life, and I am going to act accordingly. Gregory, I gave you a promise before I came into this place. That promise I would keep under red-hot pincers. Would you give me, for my own safety, a little promise of the same kind?"

"A promise?" asked Gregory, wondering.

"Yes," said Syme very seriously, "a promise. I swore before God that I would not tell your secret to the police. Will you swear by Humanity, or whatever beastly thing you believe in, that you will not tell my secret to the anarchists?"

"Your secret?" asked the staring Gregory. "Have you got a secret?"

"Yes," said Syme, "I have a secret." Then after a pause, "Will you swear?"

Gregory glared at him gravely for a few moments, and then said abruptly—

"You must have bewitched me, but I feel a furious curiosity about you. Yes, I will swear not to tell the anarchists anything you tell me. But look sharp, for they will be here in a couple of minutes."

Syme rose slowly to his feet and thrust his long, white hands into his long, grey trousers' pockets. Almost as he did so there came five knocks on the outer grating, proclaiming the arrival of the first of the conspirators.

"Well," said Syme slowly, "I don't know how to tell you the truth more shortly than by saying that your expedient of dressing up as an aimless poet is not confined to you or your President. We have known the dodge for some time at Scotland Yard."

Gregory tried to spring up straight, but he swayed thrice.

"What do you say?" he asked in an inhuman voice.

"Yes," said Syme simply, "I am a police detective. But I think I hear your friends coming."

From the doorway there came a murmur of "Mr. Joseph Chamberlain." It was repeated twice and thrice, and then thirty times, and the crowd of Joseph Chamberlains (a solemn thought) could be heard trampling down the corridor.

3. THE MAN WHO WAS THURSDAY

BEFORE one of the fresh faces could appear at the doorway, Gregory's stunned surprise had fallen from him. He was beside the table with a bound, and a noise in his throat like a wild beast. He caught up the Colt's revolver and took aim at Syme. Syme did not flinch, but he put up a pale and polite hand.

"Don't be such a silly man," he said, with the effeminate dignity of a curate. "Don't you see it's not necessary? Don't you see that we're both in the same boat? Yes, and jolly sea-sick."

Gregory could not speak, but he could not fire either, and he looked his question.

"Don't you see we've checkmated each other?" cried Syme. "I can't tell the police you are an anarchist. You can't tell the anarchists I'm a policeman. I can only watch you, knowing what you are; you can only watch me, knowing what I am. In short, it's a lonely, intellectual duel, my head against yours. I'm a policeman deprived of the help of the police. You, my poor fellow, are an anarchist deprived of the help of that law and organisation which is so essential to anarchy. The one solitary difference is in your favour. You are not surrounded by inquisitive policemen; I am surrounded by inquisitive anarchists. I cannot betray you, but I might betray myself. Come, come! wait and see me betray myself. I shall do it so nicely."

Gregory put the pistol slowly down, still staring at Syme as if he were a sea-monster.

"I don't believe in immortality," he said at last, "but if, after all this, you were to break your word, God would make a hell only for you, to howl in for ever."

"I shall not break my word," said Syme sternly, "nor will you break yours. Here are your friends."

The mass of the anarchists entered the room heavily, with a slouching and somewhat weary gait; but one little man, with a black beard and glasses—a man somewhat of the type of Mr. Tim Healy—detached himself, and bustled forward with some papers in his hand.

"Comrade Gregory," he said, "I suppose this man is a delegate?"

Gregory, taken by surprise, looked down and muttered the name of Syme; but Syme replied almost pertly—

"I am glad to see that your gate is well enough guarded to make it hard for anyone to be here who was not a delegate."

The brow of the little man with the black beard was, however, still contracted with something like suspicion.

"What branch do you represent?" he asked sharply.

"I should hardly call it a branch," said Syme, laughing; "I should call it at the very least a root."

"What do you mean?"

"The fact is," said Syme serenely, "the truth is I am a Sabbatarian. I have been specially sent here to see that you show a due observance of Sunday."

The little man dropped one of his papers, and a flicker of fear went over all the faces of the group. Evidently the awful President, whose name was Sunday, did sometimes send down such irregular ambassadors to such branch meetings.

"Well, comrade," said the man with the papers after a pause, "I suppose we'd better give you a seat in the meeting?"

"If you ask my advice as a friend," said Syme with severe benevolence, "I think you'd better."

When Gregory heard the dangerous dialogue end, with a sudden safety for his rival, he rose abruptly and paced the floor in painful thought. He was, indeed, in an agony of diplomacy. It was clear that Syme's inspired impudence was likely to bring him out of all merely accidental dilemmas. Little was to be hoped from them. He could not himself betray Syme, partly from honour, but partly also because, if he betrayed him and for some reason failed to destroy him, the Syme who escaped would be a Syme freed from all obligation of secrecy, a Syme who would simply walk to the nearest police station. After all, it was only one night's discussion, and only one detective who would know of it. He would let out as little as possible of their plans that night, and then let Syme go, and chance it.

He strode across to the group of anarchists, which was already distributing itself along the benches.

"I think it is time we began," he said; "the steam-tug is waiting on the river already. I move that Comrade Buttons takes the chair."

This being approved by a show of hands, the little man with the papers slipped into the presidential seat.

"Comrades," he began, as sharp as a pistol-shot, "our meeting tonight is important, though it need not be long. This branch has always had the honour of electing Thursdays for the Central European Council. We have elected many and splendid Thursdays. We all lament the sad decease of the heroic worker who occupied the post until last week. As you know, his services to the cause were considerable. He organised the great dynamite coup of Brighton which, under happier circumstances, ought to have killed everybody on the pier. As you also know, his death was as self-denying as his life, for he died through his faith in a hygienic mixture of chalk and water as a substitute for milk, which beverage he regarded as barbaric, and as involving cruelty to the cow. Cruelty, or anything approaching to cruelty, revolted him always. But it is not to acclaim his virtues that we are met, but for a harder task. It is difficult properly to praise his qualities, but it is more difficult to replace them. Upon you, comrades, it devolves this evening to choose out of the company present the man who shall be Thursday. If any comrade suggests a name I will put it to the vote. If no comrade suggests a name, I can only tell myself that that dear dynamiter, who is gone from us, has carried into the unknowable abysses the last secret of his virtue and his innocence."

There was a stir of almost inaudible applause, such as is sometimes heard in church. Then a large old man, with a long and venerable white beard, perhaps the only real working-man present, rose lumberingly and said—

"I move that Comrade Gregory be elected Thursday," and sat lumberingly down again.

"Does anyone second?" asked the chairman.

A little man with a velvet coat and pointed beard seconded.

"Before I put the matter to the vote," said the chairman, "I will call on Comrade Gregory to make a statement."

Gregory rose amid a great rumble of applause. His face was deadly pale, so that by contrast his queer red hair looked almost scarlet. But he was smiling and altogether at ease. He had made up his mind, and he saw his best policy quite plain in front of him like a white road. His best chance was to make a softened and ambiguous speech, such as would leave on the detective's mind the impression that the anarchist brotherhood was a very mild affair after all. He believed in his own literary power, his capacity for suggesting fine shades and picking perfect words. He thought that with care he could succeed, in spite of all the people around him, in conveying an impression of the institution, subtly and delicately false. Syme had once thought that anarchists, under all their bravado, were only playing the fool. Could he not now, in the hour of peril, make Syme think so again?

"Comrades," began Gregory, in a low but penetrating voice, "it is not necessary for me to tell you what is my policy, for it is your policy also. Our belief has been slandered, it has been disfigured, it has been utterly confused and concealed, but it has never been altered. Those who talk about anarchism and its dangers go everywhere and anywhere to get their information, except to us, except to the fountain head. They learn about anarchists from sixpenny novels; they learn about anarchists from tradesmen's newspapers; they learn about anarchists from Ally Sloper's Half-Holiday and the Sporting Times. They never learn about anarchists from anarchists. We have no chance of denying the mountainous slanders which are heaped upon our heads from one end of Europe to another. The man who has always heard that we are walking plagues has never heard our reply. I know that he will not hear it tonight, though my passion were to rend the roof. For it is deep, deep under the earth that the persecuted are permitted to assemble, as the Christians assembled in the Catacombs. But if, by some incredible accident, there were here tonight a man who all his life had thus immensely misunderstood us, I would put this question to him: 'When those Christians met in those Catacombs, what sort of moral reputation had they in the streets above? What tales were told of their atrocities by one educated Roman to another? Suppose' (I would say to him), 'suppose that we are only repeating that still mysterious paradox of history. Suppose we seem as shocking as the Christians because we are really as harmless as the Christians. Suppose we seem as mad as the Christians because we are really as meek.'"

The applause that had greeted the opening sentences had been gradually growing fainter, and at the last word it stopped suddenly. In the abrupt silence, the man with the velvet jacket said, in a high, squeaky voice—

"I'm not meek!"

"Comrade Witherspoon tells us," resumed Gregory, "that he is not meek. Ah, how little he knows himself! His words are, indeed, extravagant; his appearance is ferocious, and even (to an ordinary taste) unattractive. But only the eye of a friendship as deep and delicate as mine can perceive the deep foundation of solid meekness which lies at the base of him, too deep even for himself to see. I repeat, we are the true early Christians, only that we come too late. We are simple, as they revere simple—look at Comrade Witherspoon. We are modest, as they were modest—look at me. We are merciful—"

"No, no!" called out Mr. Witherspoon with the velvet jacket.

"I say we are merciful," repeated Gregory furiously, "as the early Christians were merciful. Yet this did not prevent their being accused of eating human flesh. We do not eat human flesh—"

"Shame!" cried Witherspoon. "Why not?"

"Comrade Witherspoon," said Gregory, with a feverish gaiety, "is anxious to know why nobody eats him (laughter). In our society, at any rate, which loves him sincerely, which is founded upon love—"

"No, no!" said Witherspoon, "down with love."

"Which is founded upon love," repeated Gregory, grinding his teeth, "there will be no difficulty about the aims which we shall pursue as a body, or which I should pursue were I chosen as the representative of that body. Superbly careless of the slanders that represent us as assassins and enemies of human society, we shall pursue with moral courage and quiet intellectual pressure, the permanent ideals of brotherhood and simplicity."

Gregory resumed his seat and passed his hand across his forehead. The silence was sudden and awkward, but the chairman rose like an automaton, and said in a colourless voice—

"Does anyone oppose the election of Comrade Gregory?"

The assembly seemed vague and sub-consciously disappointed, and Comrade Witherspoon moved restlessly on his seat and muttered in his thick beard. By the sheer rush of routine, however, the motion would have been put and carried. But as the chairman was opening his mouth to put it, Syme sprang to his feet and said in a small and quiet voice—

"Yes, Mr. Chairman, I oppose."

The most effective fact in oratory is an unexpected change in the voice. Mr. Gabriel Syme evidently understood oratory. Having said these first formal words in a moderated tone and with a brief simplicity, he made his next word ring and volley in the vault as if one of the guns had gone off.

"Comrades!" he cried, in a voice that made every man jump out of his boots, "have we come here for this? Do we live underground like rats in order to listen to talk like this? This is talk we might listen to while eating buns at a Sunday School treat. Do we line these walls with weapons and bar that door with death lest anyone should come and hear Comrade Gregory saying to us, 'Be good, and you will be happy,' 'Honesty is the best policy,' and 'Virtue is its own reward'? There was not a word in Comrade Gregory's address to which a curate could not have listened with pleasure (hear, hear). But I am not a curate (loud cheers), and I did not listen to it with pleasure (renewed cheers). The man who is fitted to make a good curate is not fitted to make a resolute, forcible, and efficient Thursday (hear, hear)."

"Comrade Gregory has told us, in only too apologetic a tone, that we are not the enemies of society. But I say that we are the enemies of society, and so much the worse for society. We are the enemies of society, for society is the enemy of humanity, its oldest and its most pitiless enemy (hear, hear). Comrade Gregory has told us (apologetically again) that we are not murderers. There I agree. We are not murderers, we are executioners (cheers)."

Ever since Syme had risen Gregory had sat staring at him, his face idiotic with astonishment. Now in the pause his lips of clay parted, and he said, with an automatic and lifeless distinctness—

"You damnable hypocrite!"

Syme looked straight into those frightful eyes with his own pale blue ones, and said with dignity—

"Comrade Gregory accuses me of hypocrisy. He knows as well as I do that I am keeping all my engagements and doing nothing but my duty. I do not mince words. I do not pretend to. I say that Comrade Gregory is unfit to be Thursday for all his amiable qualities. He is unfit to be Thursday because of his amiable qualities. We do not want the Supreme Council of Anarchy infected with a maudlin mercy (hear, hear). This is no time for ceremonial politeness, neither is it a time for ceremonial modesty. I set myself against Comrade Gregory as I would set myself against all the Governments of Europe, because the anarchist who has given himself to anarchy has forgotten modesty as much as he has forgotten pride (cheers). I am not a man at all. I am a cause (renewed cheers). I set myself against Comrade Gregory as impersonally and as calmly as I should choose one pistol rather than another out of that rack upon the wall; and I say that rather than have Gregory and his milk-and-water methods on the Supreme Council, I would offer myself for election—"

His sentence was drowned in a deafening cataract of applause. The faces, that had grown fiercer and fiercer with approval as his tirade grew more and more uncompromising, were now distorted with grins of anticipation or cloven with delighted cries. At the moment when he announced himself as ready to stand for the post of Thursday, a roar of excitement and assent broke forth, and became uncontrollable, and at the same moment Gregory sprang to his feet, with foam upon his mouth, and shouted against the shouting.

"Stop, you blasted madmen!" he cried, at the top of a voice that tore his throat. "Stop, you—"

But louder than Gregory's shouting and louder than the roar of the room came the voice of Syme, still speaking in a peal of pitiless thunder—

"I do not go to the Council to rebut that slander that calls us murderers; I go to earn it (loud and prolonged cheering). To the priest who says these men are the enemies of religion, to the judge who says these men are the enemies of law, to the fat parliamentarian who says these men are the enemies of order and public decency, to all these I will reply, 'You are false kings, but you are true prophets. I am come to destroy you, and to fulfil your prophecies.'"

The heavy clamour gradually died away, but before it had ceased Witherspoon had jumped to his feet, his hair and beard all on end, and had said—

"I move, as an amendment, that Comrade Syme be appointed to the post."

"Stop all this, I tell you!" cried Gregory, with frantic face and hands. "Stop it, it is all—"

The voice of the chairman clove his speech with a cold accent.

"Does anyone second this amendment?" he said. A tall, tired man, with melancholy eyes and an American chin beard, was observed on the back bench to be slowly rising to his feet. Gregory had been screaming for some time past; now there was a change in his accent, more shocking than any scream. "I end all this!" he said, in a voice as heavy as stone.

"This man cannot be elected. He is a—"

"Yes," said Syme, quite motionless, "what is he?" Gregory's mouth worked twice without sound; then slowly the blood began to crawl back into his dead face. "He is a man quite inexperienced in our work," he said, and sat down abruptly.

Before he had done so, the long, lean man with the American beard was again upon his feet, and was repeating in a high American monotone—

"I beg to second the election of Comrade Syme."

"The amendment will, as usual, be put first," said Mr. Buttons, the chairman, with mechanical rapidity.

"The question is that Comrade Syme—"

Gregory had again sprung to his feet, panting and passionate.

"Comrades," he cried out, "I am not a madman."

"Oh, oh!" said Mr. Witherspoon.

"I am not a madman," reiterated Gregory, with a frightful sincerity which for a moment staggered the room, "but I give you a counsel which you can call mad if you like. No, I will not call it a counsel, for I can give you no reason for it. I will call it a command. Call it a mad command, but act upon it. Strike, but hear me! Kill me, but obey me! Do not elect this man." Truth is so terrible, even in fetters, that for a moment Syme's slender and insane victory swayed like a reed. But you could not have guessed it from Syme's bleak blue eyes. He merely began—

"Comrade Gregory commands—"

Then the spell was snapped, and one anarchist called out to Gregory—

"Who are you? You are not Sunday;" and another anarchist added in a heavier voice, "And you are not Thursday."

"Comrades," cried Gregory, in a voice like that of a martyr who in an ecstacy of pain has passed beyond pain, "it is nothing to me whether you detest me as a tyrant or detest me as a slave. If you will not take my command, accept my degradation. I kneel to you. I throw myself at your feet. I implore you. Do not elect this man."

"Comrade Gregory," said the chairman after a painful pause, "this is really not quite dignified."

For the first time in the proceedings there was for a few seconds a real silence. Then Gregory fell back in his seat, a pale wreck of a man, and the chairman repeated, like a piece of clock-work suddenly started again—

"The question is that Comrade Syme be elected to the post of Thursday on the General Council."

The roar rose like the sea, the hands rose like a forest, and three minutes afterwards Mr. Gabriel Syme, of the Secret Police Service, was elected to the post of Thursday on the General Council of the Anarchists of Europe.

Everyone in the room seemed to feel the tug waiting on the river, the sword-stick and the revolver, waiting on the table. The instant the election was ended and irrevocable, and Syme had received the paper proving his election, they all sprang to their feet, and the fiery groups moved and mixed in the room. Syme found himself, somehow or other, face to face with Gregory, who still regarded him with a stare of stunned hatred. They were silent for many minutes.

"You are a devil!" said Gregory at last.

"And you are a gentleman," said Syme with gravity.

"It was you that entrapped me," began Gregory, shaking from head to foot, "entrapped me into—"

"Talk sense," said Syme shortly. "Into what sort of devils' parliament have you entrapped me, if it comes to that? You made me swear before I made you. Perhaps we are both doing what we think right. But what we think right is so damned different that there can be nothing between us in the way of concession. There is nothing possible between us but honour and death," and he pulled the great cloak about his shoulders and picked up the flask from the table.

"The boat is quite ready," said Mr. Buttons, bustling up. "Be good enough to step this way."

With a gesture that revealed the shop-walker, he led Syme down a short, iron-bound passage, the still agonised Gregory following feverishly at their heels. At the end of the passage was a door, which Buttons opened sharply, showing a sudden blue and silver picture of the moonlit river, that looked like a scene in a theatre. Close to the opening lay a dark, dwarfish steam-launch, like a baby dragon with one red eye.

Almost in the act of stepping on board, Gabriel Syme turned to the gaping Gregory.

"You have kept your word," he said gently, with his face in shadow. "You are a man of honour, and I thank you. You have kept it even down to a small particular. There was one special thing you promised me at the beginning of the affair, and which you have certainly given me by the end of it."

"What do you mean?" cried the chaotic Gregory. "What did I promise you?"

"A very entertaining evening," said Syme, and he made a military salute with the sword-stick as the steamboat slid away.

4. THE TALE OF A DETECTIVE

GABRIEL SYME was not merely a detective who pretended to be a poet; he was really a poet who had become a detective. Nor was his hatred of anarchy hypocritical. He was one of those who are driven early in life into too conservative an attitude by the bewildering folly of most revolutionists. He had not attained it by any tame tradition. His respectability was spontaneous and sudden, a rebellion against rebellion. He came of a family of cranks, in which all the oldest people had all the newest notions. One of his uncles always walked about without a hat, and another had made an unsuccessful attempt to walk about with a hat and nothing else. His father cultivated art and self-realisation; his mother went in for simplicity and hygiene. Hence the child, during his tenderer years, was wholly unacquainted with any drink between the extremes of absinth and cocoa, of both of which he had a healthy dislike. The more his mother preached a more than Puritan abstinence the more did his father expand into a more than pagan latitude; and by the time the former had come to enforcing vegetarianism, the latter had pretty well reached the point of defending cannibalism.

Being surrounded with every conceivable kind of revolt from infancy, Gabriel had to revolt into something, so he revolted into the only thing left—sanity. But there was just enough in him of the blood of these fanatics to make even his protest for common sense a little too fierce to be sensible. His hatred of modern lawlessness had been crowned also by an accident. It happened that he was walking in a side street at the instant of a dynamite outrage. He had been blind and deaf for a moment, and then seen, the smoke clearing, the broken windows and the bleeding faces. After that he went about as usual—quiet, courteous, rather gentle; but there was a spot on his mind that was not sane. He did not regard anarchists, as most of us do, as a handful of morbid men, combining ignorance with intellectualism. He regarded them as a huge and pitiless peril, like a Chinese invasion.

He poured perpetually into newspapers and their waste-paper baskets a torrent of tales, verses and violent articles, warning men of this deluge of barbaric denial. But he seemed to be getting no nearer his enemy, and, what was worse, no nearer a living. As he paced the Thames embankment, bitterly biting a cheap cigar and brooding on the advance of Anarchy, there was no anarchist with a bomb in his pocket so savage or so solitary as he. Indeed, he always felt that Government stood alone and desperate, with its back to the wall. He was too quixotic to have cared for it otherwise.

He walked on the Embankment once under a dark red sunset. The red river reflected the red sky, and they both reflected his anger. The sky, indeed, was so swarthy, and the light on the river relatively so lurid, that the water almost seemed of fiercer flame than the sunset it mirrored. It looked like a stream of literal fire winding under the vast caverns of a subterranean country.

Syme was shabby in those days. He wore an old-fashioned black chimney-pot hat; he was wrapped in a yet more old-fashioned cloak, black and ragged; and the combination gave him the look of the early villains in Dickens and Bulwer Lytton. Also his yellow beard and hair were more unkempt and leonine than when they appeared long afterwards, cut and pointed, on the lawns of Saffron Park. A long, lean, black cigar, bought in Soho for twopence, stood out from between his tightened teeth, and altogether he looked a very satisfactory specimen of the anarchists upon whom he had vowed a holy war. Perhaps this was why a policeman on the Embankment spoke to him, and said "Good evening."

Syme, at a crisis of his morbid fears for humanity, seemed stung by the mere stolidity of the automatic official, a mere bulk of blue in the twilight.

"A good evening is it?" he said sharply. "You fellows would call the end of the world a good evening. Look at that bloody red sun and that bloody river! I tell you that if that were literally human blood, spilt and shining, you would still be standing here as solid as ever, looking out for some poor harmless tramp whom you could move on. You policemen are cruel to the poor, but I could forgive you even your cruelty if it were not for your calm."

"If we are calm," replied the policeman, "it is the calm of organised resistance."

"Eh?" said Syme, staring.

"The soldier must be calm in the thick of the battle," pursued the policeman. "The composure of an army is the anger of a nation."

"Good God, the Board Schools!" said Syme. "Is this undenominational education?"

"No," said the policeman sadly, "I never had any of those advantages. The Board Schools came after my time. What education I had was very rough and old-fashioned, I am afraid."

"Where did you have it?" asked Syme, wondering.

"Oh, at Harrow," said the policeman

The class sympathies which, false as they are, are the truest things in so many men, broke out of Syme before he could control them.

"But, good Lord, man," he said, "you oughtn't to be a policeman!"

The policeman sighed and shook his head.

"I know," he said solemnly, "I know I am not worthy."

"But why did you join the police?" asked Syme with rude curiosity.

"For much the same reason that you abused the police," replied the other. "I found that there was a special opening in the service for those whose fears for humanity were concerned rather with the aberrations of the scientific intellect than with the normal and excusable, though excessive, outbreaks of the human will. I trust I make myself clear."

"If you mean that you make your opinion clear," said Syme, "I suppose you do. But as for making yourself clear, it is the last thing you do. How comes a man like you to be talking philosophy in a blue helmet on the Thames embankment?"

"You have evidently not heard of the latest development in our police system," replied the other. "I am not surprised at it. We are keeping it rather dark from the educated class, because that class contains most of our enemies. But you seem to be exactly in the right frame of mind. I think you might almost join us."

"Join you in what?" asked Syme.

"I will tell you," said the policeman slowly. "This is the situation: The head of one of our departments, one of the most celebrated detectives in Europe, has long been of opinion that a purely intellectual conspiracy would soon threaten the very existence of civilisation. He is certain that the scientific and artistic worlds are silently bound in a crusade against the Family and the State. He has, therefore, formed a special corps of policemen, policemen who are also philosophers. It is their business to watch the beginnings of this conspiracy, not merely in a criminal but in a controversial sense. I am a democrat myself, and I am fully aware of the value of the ordinary man in matters of ordinary valour or virtue. But it would obviously be undesirable to employ the common policeman in an investigation which is also a heresy hunt."

Syme's eyes were bright with a sympathetic curiosity.

"What do you do, then?" he said.

"The work of the philosophical policeman," replied the man in blue, "is at once bolder and more subtle than that of the ordinary detective. The ordinary detective goes to pot-houses to arrest thieves; we go to artistic tea-parties to detect pessimists. The ordinary detective discovers from a ledger or a diary that a crime has been committed. We discover from a book of sonnets that a crime will be committed. We have to trace the origin of those dreadful thoughts that drive men on at last to intellectual fanaticism and intellectual crime. We were only just in time to prevent the assassination at Hartlepool, and that was entirely due to the fact that our Mr. Wilks (a smart young fellow) thoroughly understood a triolet."

"Do you mean," asked Syme, "that there is really as much connection between crime and the modern intellect as all that?"

"You are not sufficiently democratic," answered the policeman, "but you were right when you said just now that our ordinary treatment of the poor criminal was a pretty brutal business. I tell you I am sometimes sick of my trade when I see how perpetually it means merely a war upon the ignorant and the desperate. But this new movement of ours is a very different affair. We deny the snobbish English assumption that the uneducated are the dangerous criminals. We remember the Roman Emperors. We remember the great poisoning princes of the Renaissance. We say that the dangerous criminal is the educated criminal. We say that the most dangerous criminal now is the entirely lawless modern philosopher. Compared to him, burglars and bigamists are essentially moral men; my heart goes out to them. They accept the essential ideal of man; they merely seek it wrongly. Thieves respect property. They merely wish the property to become their property that they may more perfectly respect it. But philosophers dislike property as property; they wish to destroy the very idea of personal possession. Bigamists respect marriage, or they would not go through the highly ceremonial and even ritualistic formality of bigamy. But philosophers despise marriage as marriage. Murderers respect human life; they merely wish to attain a greater fulness of human life in themselves by the sacrifice of what seems to them to be lesser lives. But philosophers hate life itself, their own as much as other people's."

Syme struck his hands together.

"How true that is," he cried. "I have felt it from my boyhood, but never could state the verbal antithesis. The common criminal is a bad man, but at least he is, as it were, a conditional good man. He says that if only a certain obstacle be removed—say a wealthy uncle—he is then prepared to accept the universe and to praise God. He is a reformer, but not an anarchist. He wishes to cleanse the edifice, but not to destroy it. But the evil philosopher is not trying to alter things, but to annihilate them. Yes, the modern world has retained all those parts of police work which are really oppressive and ignominious, the harrying of the poor, the spying upon the unfortunate. It has given up its more dignified work, the punishment of powerful traitors in the State and powerful heresiarchs in the Church. The moderns say we must not punish heretics. My only doubt is whether we have a right to punish anybody else."

"But this is absurd!" cried the policeman, clasping his hands with an excitement uncommon in persons of his figure and costume, "but it is intolerable! I don't know what you're doing, but you're wasting your life. You must, you shall, join our special army against anarchy. Their armies are on our frontiers. Their bolt is ready to fall. A moment more, and you may lose the glory of working with us, perhaps the glory of dying with the last heroes of the world."

"It is a chance not to be missed, certainly," assented Syme, "but still I do not quite understand. I know as well as anybody that the modern world is full of lawless little men and mad little movements. But, beastly as they are, they generally have the one merit of disagreeing with each other. How can you talk of their leading one army or hurling one bolt. What is this anarchy?"

"Do not confuse it," replied the constable, "with those chance dynamite outbreaks from Russia or from Ireland, which are really the outbreaks of oppressed, if mistaken, men. This is a vast philosophic movement, consisting of an outer and an inner ring. You might even call the outer ring the laity and the inner ring the priesthood. I prefer to call the outer ring the innocent section, the inner ring the supremely guilty section. The outer ring—the main mass of their supporters—are merely anarchists; that is, men who believe that rules and formulas have destroyed human happiness. They believe that all the evil results of human crime are the results of the system that has called it crime. They do not believe that the crime creates the punishment. They believe that the punishment has created the crime. They believe that if a man seduced seven women he would naturally walk away as blameless as the flowers of spring. They believe that if a man picked a pocket he would naturally feel exquisitely good. These I call the innocent section."

"Oh!" said Syme.

"Naturally, therefore, these people talk about 'a happy time coming'; 'the paradise of the future'; 'mankind freed from the bondage of vice and the bondage of virtue,' and so on. And so also the men of the inner circle speak—the sacred priesthood. They also speak to applauding crowds of the happiness of the future, and of mankind freed at last. But in their mouths"—and the policeman lowered his voice—"in their mouths these happy phrases have a horrible meaning. They are under no illusions; they are too intellectual to think that man upon this earth can ever be quite free of original sin and the struggle. And they mean death. When they say that mankind shall be free at last, they mean that mankind shall commit suicide. When they talk of a paradise without right or wrong, they mean the grave.

"They have but two objects, to destroy first humanity and then themselves. That is why they throw bombs instead of firing pistols. The innocent rank and file are disappointed because the bomb has not killed the king; but the high-priesthood are happy because it has killed somebody."

"How can I join you?" asked Syme, with a sort of passion.

"I know for a fact that there is a vacancy at the moment," said the policeman, "as I have the honour to be somewhat in the confidence of the chief of whom I have spoken. You should really come and see him. Or rather, I should not say see him, nobody ever sees him; but you can talk to him if you like."

"Telephone?" inquired Syme, with interest.

"No," said the policeman placidly, "he has a fancy for always sitting in a pitch-dark room. He says it makes his thoughts brighter. Do come along."

Somewhat dazed and considerably excited, Syme allowed himself to be led to a side-door in the long row of buildings of Scotland Yard. Almost before he knew what he was doing, he had been passed through the hands of about four intermediate officials, and was suddenly shown into a room, the abrupt blackness of which startled him like a blaze of light. It was not the ordinary darkness, in which forms can be faintly traced; it was like going suddenly stone-blind.

"Are you the new recruit?" asked a heavy voice.

And in some strange way, though there was not the shadow of a shape in the gloom, Syme knew two things: first, that it came from a man of massive stature; and second, that the man had his back to him.

"Are you the new recruit?" said the invisible chief, who seemed to have heard all about it. "All right. You are engaged."

Syme, quite swept off his feet, made a feeble fight against this irrevocable phrase.

"I really have no experience," he began.

"No one has any experience," said the other, "of the Battle of Armageddon."

"But I am really unfit—"

"You are willing, that is enough," said the unknown.

"Well, really," said Syme, "I don't know any profession of which mere willingness is the final test."

"I do," said the other—"martyrs. I am condemning you to death. Good day."

Thus it was that when Gabriel Syme came out again into the crimson light of evening, in his shabby black hat and shabby, lawless cloak, he came out a member of the New Detective Corps for the frustration of the great conspiracy. Acting under the advice of his friend the policeman (who was professionally inclined to neatness), he trimmed his hair and beard, bought a good hat, clad himself in an exquisite summer suit of light blue-grey, with a pale yellow flower in the button-hole, and, in short, became that elegant and rather insupportable person whom Gregory had first encountered in the little garden of Saffron Park. Before he finally left the police premises his friend provided him with a small blue card, on which was written, "The Last Crusade," and a number, the sign of his official authority. He put this carefully in his upper waistcoat pocket, lit a cigarette, and went forth to track and fight the enemy in all the drawing-rooms of London. Where his adventure ultimately led him we have already seen. At about half-past one on a February night he found himself steaming in a small tug up the silent Thames, armed with swordstick and revolver, the duly elected Thursday of the Central Council of Anarchists.

When Syme stepped out on to the steam-tug he had a singular sensation of stepping out into something entirely new; not merely into the landscape of a new land, but even into the landscape of a new planet. This was mainly due to the insane yet solid decision of that evening, though partly also to an entire change in the weather and the sky since he entered the little tavern some two hours before. Every trace of the passionate plumage of the cloudy sunset had been swept away, and a naked moon stood in a naked sky. The moon was so strong and full that (by a paradox often to be noticed) it seemed like a weaker sun. It gave, not the sense of bright moonshine, but rather of a dead daylight.

Over the whole landscape lay a luminous and unnatural discoloration, as of that disastrous twilight which Milton spoke of as shed by the sun in eclipse; so that Syme fell easily into his first thought, that he was actually on some other and emptier planet, which circled round some sadder star. But the more he felt this glittering desolation in the moonlit land, the more his own chivalric folly glowed in the night like a great fire. Even the common things he carried with him—the food and the brandy and the loaded pistol—took on exactly that concrete and material poetry which a child feels when he takes a gun upon a journey or a bun with him to bed. The sword-stick and the brandy-flask, though in themselves only the tools of morbid conspirators, became the expressions of his own more healthy romance. The sword-stick became almost the sword of chivalry, and the brandy the wine of the stirrup-cup. For even the most dehumanised modern fantasies depend on some older and simpler figure; the adventures may be mad, but the adventurer must be sane. The dragon without St. George would not even be grotesque. So this inhuman landscape was only imaginative by the presence of a man really human. To Syme's exaggerative mind the bright, bleak houses and terraces by the Thames looked as empty as the mountains of the moon. But even the moon is only poetical because there is a man in the moon.

The tug was worked by two men, and with much toil went comparatively slowly. The clear moon that had lit up Chiswick had gone down by the time that they passed Battersea, and when they came under the enormous bulk of Westminster day had already begun to break. It broke like the splitting of great bars of lead, showing bars of silver; and these had brightened like white fire when the tug, changing its onward course, turned inward to a large landing stage rather beyond Charing Cross.

The great stones of the Embankment seemed equally dark and gigantic as Syme looked up at them. They were big and black against the huge white dawn. They made him feel that he was landing on the colossal steps of some Egyptian palace; and, indeed, the thing suited his mood, for he was, in his own mind, mounting to attack the solid thrones of horrible and heathen kings. He leapt out of the boat on to one slimy step, and stood, a dark and slender figure, amid the enormous masonry. The two men in the tug put her off again and turned up stream. They had never spoken a word.

5. THE FEAST OF FEAR

AT first the large stone stair seemed to Syme as deserted as a pyramid; but before he reached the top he had realised that there was a man leaning over the parapet of the Embankment and looking out across the river. As a figure he was quite conventional, clad in a silk hat and frock-coat of the more formal type of fashion; he had a red flower in his buttonhole. As Syme drew nearer to him step by step, he did not even move a hair; and Syme could come close enough to notice even in the dim, pale morning light that his face was long, pale and intellectual, and ended in a small triangular tuft of dark beard at the very point of the chin, all else being clean-shaven. This scrap of hair almost seemed a mere oversight; the rest of the face was of the type that is best shaven—clear-cut, ascetic, and in its way noble. Syme drew closer and closer, noting all this, and still the figure did not stir.

At first an instinct had told Syme that this was the man whom he was meant to meet. Then, seeing that the man made no sign, he had concluded that he was not. And now again he had come back to a certainty that the man had something to do with his mad adventure. For the man remained more still than would have been natural if a stranger had come so close. He was as motionless as a wax-work, and got on the nerves somewhat in the same way. Syme looked again and again at the pale, dignified and delicate face, and the face still looked blankly across the river. Then he took out of his pocket the note from Buttons proving his election, and put it before that sad and beautiful face. Then the man smiled, and his smile was a shock, for it was all on one side, going up in the right cheek and down in the left.

There was nothing, rationally speaking, to scare anyone about this. Many people have this nervous trick of a crooked smile, and in many it is even attractive. But in all Syme's circumstances, with the dark dawn and the deadly errand and the loneliness on the great dripping stones, there was something unnerving in it.

There was the silent river and the silent man, a man of even classic face. And there was the last nightmare touch that his smile suddenly went wrong.

The spasm of smile was instantaneous, and the man's face dropped at once into its harmonious melancholy. He spoke without further explanation or inquiry, like a man speaking to an old colleague.

"If we walk up towards Leicester Square," he said, "we shall just be in time for breakfast. Sunday always insists on an early breakfast. Have you had any sleep?"

"No," said Syme.

"Nor have I," answered the man in an ordinary tone. "I shall try to get to bed after breakfast."

He spoke with casual civility, but in an utterly dead voice that contradicted the fanaticism of his face. It seemed almost as if all friendly words were to him lifeless conveniences, and that his only life was hate. After a pause the man spoke again.

"Of course, the Secretary of the branch told you everything that can be told. But the one thing that can never be told is the last notion of the President, for his notions grow like a tropical forest. So in case you don't know, I'd better tell you that he is carrying out his notion of concealing ourselves by not concealing ourselves to the most extraordinary lengths just now. Originally, of course, we met in a cell underground, just as your branch does. Then Sunday made us take a private room at an ordinary restaurant. He said that if you didn't seem to be hiding nobody hunted you out. Well, he is the only man on earth, I know; but sometimes I really think that his huge brain is going a little mad in its old age. For now we flaunt ourselves before the public. We have our breakfast on a balcony—on a balcony, if you please—overlooking Leicester Square."

"And what do the people say?" asked Syme.

"It's quite simple what they say," answered his guide. "They say we are a lot of jolly gentlemen who pretend they are anarchists."

"It seems to me a very clever idea," said Syme.

"Clever! God blast your impudence! Clever!" cried out the other in a sudden, shrill voice which was as startling and discordant as his crooked smile. "When you've seen Sunday for a split second you'll leave off calling him clever."

With this they emerged out of a narrow street, and saw the early sunlight filling Leicester Square. It will never be known, I suppose, why this square itself should look so alien and in some ways so continental. It will never be known whether it was the foreign look that attracted the foreigners or the foreigners who gave it the foreign look. But on this particular morning the effect seemed singularly bright and clear. Between the open square and the sunlit leaves and the statue and the Saracenic outlines of the Alhambra, it looked the replica of some French or even Spanish public place. And this effect increased in Syme the sensation, which in many shapes he had had through the whole adventure, the eerie sensation of having strayed into a new world. As a fact, he had bought bad cigars round Leicester Square ever since he was a boy. But as he turned that corner, and saw the trees and the Moorish cupolas, he could have sworn that he was turning into an unknown Place de something or other in some foreign town.

At one corner of the square there projected a kind of angle of a prosperous but quiet hotel, the bulk of which belonged to a street behind. In the wall there was one large French window, probably the window of a large coffee-room; and outside this window, almost literally overhanging the square, was a formidably buttressed balcony, big enough to contain a dining-table. In fact, it did contain a dining-table, or more strictly a breakfast-table; and round the breakfast-table, glowing in the sunlight and evident to the street, were a group of noisy and talkative men, all dressed in the insolence of fashion, with white waistcoats and expensive button-holes. Some of their jokes could almost be heard across the square. Then the grave Secretary gave his unnatural smile, and Syme knew that this boisterous breakfast party was the secret conclave of the European Dynamiters.

Then, as Syme continued to stare at them, he saw something that he had not seen before. He had not seen it literally because it was too large to see. At the nearest end of the balcony, blocking up a great part of the perspective, was the back of a great mountain of a man. When Syme had seen him, his first thought was that the weight of him must break down the balcony of stone. His vastness did not lie only in the fact that he was abnormally tall and quite incredibly fat. This man was planned enormously in his original proportions, like a statue carved deliberately as colossal. His head, crowned with white hair, as seen from behind looked bigger than a head ought to be. The ears that stood out from it looked larger than human ears. He was enlarged terribly to scale; and this sense of size was so staggering, that when Syme saw him all the other figures seemed quite suddenly to dwindle and become dwarfish. They were still sitting there as before with their flowers and frock-coats, but now it looked as if the big man was entertaining five children to tea.

As Syme and the guide approached the side door of the hotel, a waiter came out smiling with every tooth in his head.

"The gentlemen are up there, sare," he said. "They do talk and they do laugh at what they talk. They do say they will throw bombs at ze king."

And the waiter hurried away with a napkin over his arm, much pleased with the singular frivolity of the gentlemen upstairs.

The two men mounted the stairs in silence.

Syme had never thought of asking whether the monstrous man who almost filled and broke the balcony was the great President of whom the others stood in awe. He knew it was so, with an unaccountable but instantaneous certainty. Syme, indeed, was one of those men who are open to all the more nameless psychological influences in a degree a little dangerous to mental health. Utterly devoid of fear in physical dangers, he was a great deal too sensitive to the smell of spiritual evil. Twice already that night little unmeaning things had peeped out at him almost pruriently, and given him a sense of drawing nearer and nearer to the head-quarters of hell. And this sense became overpowering as he drew nearer to the great President.

The form it took was a childish and yet hateful fancy. As he walked across the inner room towards the balcony, the large face of Sunday grew larger and larger; and Syme was gripped with a fear that when he was quite close the face would be too big to be possible, and that he would scream aloud. He remembered that as a child he would not look at the mask of Memnon in the British Museum, because it was a face, and so large.

By an effort, braver than that of leaping over a cliff, he went to an empty seat at the breakfast-table and sat down. The men greeted him with good-humoured raillery as if they had always known him. He sobered himself a little by looking at their conventional coats and solid, shining coffee-pot; then he looked again at Sunday. His face was very large, but it was still possible to humanity.

In the presence of the President the whole company looked sufficiently commonplace; nothing about them caught the eye at first, except that by the President's caprice they had been dressed up with a festive respectability, which gave the meal the look of a wedding breakfast. One man indeed stood out at even a superficial glance. He at least was the common or garden Dynamiter. He wore, indeed, the high white collar and satin tie that were the uniform of the occasion; but out of this collar there sprang a head quite unmanageable and quite unmistakable, a bewildering bush of brown hair and beard that almost obscured the eyes like those of a Skye terrier. But the eyes did look out of the tangle, and they were the sad eyes of some Russian serf. The effect of this figure was not terrible like that of the President, but it had every diablerie that can come from the utterly grotesque. If out of that stiff tie and collar there had come abruptly the head of a cat or a dog, it could not have been a more idiotic contrast.

The man's name, it seemed, was Gogol; he was a Pole, and in this circle of days he was called Tuesday. His soul and speech were incurably tragic; he could not force himself to play the prosperous and frivolous part demanded of him by President Sunday. And, indeed, when Syme came in the President, with that daring disregard of public suspicion which was his policy, was actually chaffing Gogol upon his inability to assume conventional graces.

"Our friend Tuesday," said the President in a deep voice at once of quietude and volume, "our friend Tuesday doesn't seem to grasp the idea. He dresses up like a gentleman, but he seems to be too great a soul to behave like one. He insists on the ways of the stage conspirator. Now if a gentleman goes about London in a top hat and a frock-coat, no one need know that he is an anarchist. But if a gentleman puts on a top hat and a frock-coat, and then goes about on his hands and knees—well, he may attract attention. That's what Brother Gogol does. He goes about on his hands and knees with such inexhaustible diplomacy, that by this time he finds it quite difficult to walk upright."

"I am not good at concealment," said Gogol sulkily, with a thick foreign accent; "I am not ashamed of the cause."

"Yes you are, my boy, and so is the cause of you," said the President good-naturedly. "You hide as much as anybody; but you can't do it, you see, you're such an ass! You try to combine two inconsistent methods. When a householder finds a man under his bed, he will probably pause to note the circumstance. But if he finds a man under his bed in a top hat, you will agree with me, my dear Tuesday, that he is not likely even to forget it. Now when you were found under Admiral Biffin's bed—"

"I am not good at deception," said Tuesday gloomily, flushing.

"Right, my boy, right," said the President with a ponderous heartiness, "you aren't good at anything."

While this stream of conversation continued, Syme was looking more steadily at the men around him. As he did so, he gradually felt all his sense of something spiritually queer return.

He had thought at first that they were all of common stature and costume, with the evident exception of the hairy Gogol. But as he looked at the others, he began to see in each of them exactly what he had seen in the man by the river, a demoniac detail somewhere. That lop-sided laugh, which would suddenly disfigure the fine face of his original guide, was typical of all these types. Each man had something about him, perceived perhaps at the tenth or twentieth glance, which was not normal, and which seemed hardly human. The only metaphor he could think of was this, that they all looked as men of fashion and presence would look, with the additional twist given in a false and curved mirror.

Only the individual examples will express this half-concealed eccentricity. Syme's original cicerone bore the title of Monday; he was the Secretary of the Council, and his twisted smile was regarded with more terror than anything, except the President's horrible, happy laughter. But now that Syme had more space and light to observe him, there were other touches. His fine face was so emaciated, that Syme thought it must be wasted with some disease; yet somehow the very distress of his dark eyes denied this. It was no physical ill that troubled him. His eyes were alive with intellectual torture, as if pure thought was pain.

He was typical of each of the tribe; each man was subtly and differently wrong. Next to him sat Tuesday, the tousle-headed Gogol, a man more obviously mad. Next was Wednesday, a certain Marquis de St. Eustache, a sufficiently characteristic figure. The first few glances found nothing unusual about him, except that he was the only man at table who wore the fashionable clothes as if they were really his own. He had a black French beard cut square and a black English frock-coat cut even squarer. But Syme, sensitive to such things, felt somehow that the man carried a rich atmosphere with him, a rich atmosphere that suffocated. It reminded one irrationally of drowsy odours and of dying lamps in the darker poems of Byron and Poe. With this went a sense of his being clad, not in lighter colours, but in softer materials; his black seemed richer and warmer than the black shades about him, as if it were compounded of profound colour. His black coat looked as if it were only black by being too dense a purple. His black beard looked as if it were only black by being too deep a blue. And in the gloom and thickness of the beard his dark red mouth showed sensual and scornful. Whatever he was he was not a Frenchman; he might be a Jew; he might be something deeper yet in the dark heart of the East. In the bright coloured Persian tiles and pictures showing tyrants hunting, you may see just those almond eyes, those blue-black beards, those cruel, crimson lips.

Then came Syme, and next a very old man, Professor de Worms, who still kept the chair of Friday, though every day it was expected that his death would leave it empty. Save for his intellect, he was in the last dissolution of senile decay. His face was as grey as his long grey beard, his forehead was lifted and fixed finally in a furrow of mild despair. In no other case, not even that of Gogol, did the bridegroom brilliancy of the morning dress express a more painful contrast. For the red flower in his button-hole showed up against a face that was literally discoloured like lead; the whole hideous effect was as if some drunken dandies had put their clothes upon a corpse. When he rose or sat down, which was with long labour and peril, something worse was expressed than mere weakness, something indefinably connected with the horror of the whole scene. It did not express decrepitude merely, but corruption. Another hateful fancy crossed Syme's quivering mind. He could not help thinking that whenever the man moved a leg or arm might fall off.

Right at the end sat the man called Saturday, the simplest and the most baffling of all. He was a short, square man with a dark, square face clean-shaven, a medical practitioner going by the name of Bull. He had that combination of savoir-faire with a sort of well-groomed coarseness which is not uncommon in young doctors. He carried his fine clothes with confidence rather than ease, and he mostly wore a set smile. There was nothing whatever odd about him, except that he wore a pair of dark, almost opaque spectacles. It may have been merely a crescendo of nervous fancy that had gone before, but those black discs were dreadful to Syme; they reminded him of half-remembered ugly tales, of some story about pennies being put on the eyes of the dead. Syme's eye always caught the black glasses and the blind grin. Had the dying Professor worn them, or even the pale Secretary, they would have been appropriate. But on the younger and grosser man they seemed only an enigma. They took away the key of the face. You could not tell what his smile or his gravity meant. Partly from this, and partly because he had a vulgar virility wanting in most of the others it seemed to Syme that he might be the wickedest of all those wicked men. Syme even had the thought that his eyes might be covered up because they were too frightful to see.

6. THE EXPOSURE

SUCH were the six men who had sworn to destroy the world. Again and again Syme strove to pull together his common sense in their presence. Sometimes he saw for an instant that these notions were subjective, that he was only looking at ordinary men, one of whom was old, another nervous, another short-sighted. The sense of an unnatural symbolism always settled back on him again. Each figure seemed to be, somehow, on the borderland of things, just as their theory was on the borderland of thought. He knew that each one of these men stood at the extreme end, so to speak, of some wild road of reasoning. He could only fancy, as in some old-world fable, that if a man went westward to the end of the world he would find something—say a tree—that was more or less than a tree, a tree possessed by a spirit; and that if he went east to the end of the world he would find something else that was not wholly itself—a tower, perhaps, of which the very shape was wicked. So these figures seemed to stand up, violent and unaccountable, against an ultimate horizon, visions from the verge. The ends of the earth were closing in.

Talk had been going on steadily as he took in the scene; and not the least of the contrasts of that bewildering breakfast-table was the contrast between the easy and unobtrusive tone of talk and its terrible purport. They were deep in the discussion of an actual and immediate plot. The waiter downstairs had spoken quite correctly when he said that they were talking about bombs and kings. Only three days afterwards the Czar was to meet the President of the French Republic in Paris, and over their bacon and eggs upon their sunny balcony these beaming gentlemen had decided how both should die. Even the instrument was chosen; the black-bearded Marquis, it appeared, was to carry the bomb.

Ordinarily speaking, the proximity of this positive and objective crime would have sobered Syme, and cured him of all his merely mystical tremors. He would have thought of nothing but the need of saving at least two human bodies from being ripped in pieces with iron and roaring gas. But the truth was that by this time he had begun to feel a third kind of fear, more piercing and practical than either his moral revulsion or his social responsibility. Very simply, he had no fear to spare for the French President or the Czar; he had begun to fear for himself. Most of the talkers took little heed of him, debating now with their faces closer together, and almost uniformly grave, save when for an instant the smile of the Secretary ran aslant across his face as the jagged lightning runs aslant across the sky. But there was one persistent thing which first troubled Syme and at last terrified him. The President was always looking at him, steadily, and with a great and baffling interest. The enormous man was quite quiet, but his blue eyes stood out of his head. And they were always fixed on Syme.

Syme felt moved to spring up and leap over the balcony. When the President's eyes were on him he felt as if he were made of glass. He had hardly the shred of a doubt that in some silent and extraordinary way Sunday had found out that he was a spy. He looked over the edge of the balcony, and saw a policeman, standing abstractedly just beneath, staring at the bright railings and the sunlit trees.

Then there fell upon him the great temptation that was to torment him for many days. In the presence of these powerful and repulsive men, who were the princes of anarchy, he had almost forgotten the frail and fanciful figure of the poet Gregory, the mere aesthete of anarchism. He even thought of him now with an old kindness, as if they had played together when children. But he remembered that he was still tied to Gregory by a great promise. He had promised never to do the very thing that he now felt himself almost in the act of doing. He had promised not to jump over that balcony and speak to that policeman. He took his cold hand off the cold stone balustrade. His soul swayed in a vertigo of moral indecision. He had only to snap the thread of a rash vow made to a villainous society, and all his life could be as open and sunny as the square beneath him. He had, on the other hand, only to keep his antiquated honour, and be delivered inch by inch into the power of this great enemy of mankind, whose very intellect was a torture-chamber. Whenever he looked down into the square he saw the comfortable policeman, a pillar of common sense and common order. Whenever he looked back at the breakfast-table he saw the President still quietly studying him with big, unbearable eyes.

In all the torrent of his thought there were two thoughts that never crossed his mind. First, it never occurred to him to doubt that the President and his Council could crush him if he continued to stand alone. The place might be public, the project might seem impossible. But Sunday was not the man who would carry himself thus easily without having, somehow or somewhere, set open his iron trap. Either by anonymous poison or sudden street accident, by hypnotism or by fire from hell, Sunday could certainly strike him. If he defied the man he was probably dead, either struck stiff there in his chair or long afterwards as by an innocent ailment. If he called in the police promptly, arrested everyone, told all, and set against them the whole energy of England, he would probably escape; certainly not otherwise. They were a balconyful of gentlemen overlooking a bright and busy square; but he felt no more safe with them than if they had been a boatful of armed pirates overlooking an empty sea.

There was a second thought that never came to him. It never occurred to him to be spiritually won over to the enemy. Many moderns, inured to a weak worship of intellect and force, might have wavered in their allegiance under this oppression of a great personality. They might have called Sunday the super-man. If any such creature be conceivable, he looked, indeed, somewhat like it, with his earth-shaking abstraction, as of a stone statue walking. He might have been called something above man, with his large plans, which were too obvious to be detected, with his large face, which was too frank to be understood. But this was a kind of modern meanness to which Syme could not sink even in his extreme morbidity. Like any man, he was coward enough to fear great force; but he was not quite coward enough to admire it.

The men were eating as they talked, and even in this they were typical. Dr. Bull and the Marquis ate casually and conventionally of the best things on the table—cold pheasant or Strasbourg pie. But the Secretary was a vegetarian, and he spoke earnestly of the projected murder over half a raw tomato and three quarters of a glass of tepid water. The old Professor had such slops as suggested a sickening second childhood. And even in this President Sunday preserved his curious predominance of mere mass. For he ate like twenty men; he ate incredibly, with a frightful freshness of appetite, so that it was like watching a sausage factory. Yet continually, when he had swallowed a dozen crumpets or drunk a quart of coffee, he would be found with his great head on one side staring at Syme.

"I have often wondered," said the Marquis, taking a great bite out of a slice of bread and jam, "whether it wouldn't be better for me to do it with a knife. Most of the best things have been brought off with a knife. And it would be a new emotion to get a knife into a French President and wriggle it round."

"You are wrong," said the Secretary, drawing his black brows together. "The knife was merely the expression of the old personal quarrel with a personal tyrant. Dynamite is not only our best tool, but our best symbol. It is as perfect a symbol of us as is incense of the prayers of the Christians. It expands; it only destroys because it broadens; even so, thought only destroys because it broadens. A man's brain is a bomb," he cried out, loosening suddenly his strange passion and striking his own skull with violence. "My brain feels like a bomb, night and day. It must expand! It must expand! A man's brain must expand, if it breaks up the universe."

"I don't want the universe broken up just yet," drawled the Marquis. "I want to do a lot of beastly things before I die. I thought of one yesterday in bed."

"No, if the only end of the thing is nothing," said Dr. Bull with his sphinx-like smile, "it hardly seems worth doing."

The old Professor was staring at the ceiling with dull eyes.

"Every man knows in his heart," he said, "that nothing is worth doing."

There was a singular silence, and then the Secretary said—

"We are wandering, however, from the point. The only question is how Wednesday is to strike the blow. I take it we should all agree with the original notion of a bomb. As to the actual arrangements, I should suggest that tomorrow morning he should go first of all to—"

The speech was broken off short under a vast shadow. President Sunday had risen to his feet, seeming to fill the sky above them.

"Before we discuss that," he said in a small, quiet voice, "let us go into a private room. I have something very particular to say."

Syme stood up before any of the others. The instant of choice had come at last, the pistol was at his head. On the pavement before he could hear the policeman idly stir and stamp, for the morning, though bright, was cold.

A barrel-organ in the street suddenly sprang with a jerk into a jovial tune. Syme stood up taut, as if it had been a bugle before the battle. He found himself filled with a supernatural courage that came from nowhere. That jingling music seemed full of the vivacity, the vulgarity, and the irrational valour of the poor, who in all those unclean streets were all clinging to the decencies and the charities of Christendom. His youthful prank of being a policeman had faded from his mind; he did not think of himself as the representative of the corps of gentlemen turned into fancy constables, or of the old eccentric who lived in the dark room. But he did feel himself as the ambassador of all these common and kindly people in the street, who every day marched into battle to the music of the barrel-organ. And this high pride in being human had lifted him unaccountably to an infinite height above the monstrous men around him. For an instant, at least, he looked down upon all their sprawling eccentricities from the starry pinnacle of the commonplace. He felt towards them all that unconscious and elementary superiority that a brave man feels over powerful beasts or a wise man over powerful errors. He knew that he had neither the intellectual nor the physical strength of President Sunday; but in that moment he minded it no more than the fact that he had not the muscles of a tiger or a horn on his nose like a rhinoceros. All was swallowed up in an ultimate certainty that the President was wrong and that the barrel-organ was right. There clanged in his mind that unanswerable and terrible truism in the song of Roland—

"Pagens ont tort et Chretiens ont droit."

which in the old nasal French has the clang and groan of great iron. This liberation of his spirit from the load of his weakness went with a quite clear decision to embrace death. If the people of the barrel-organ could keep their old-world obligations, so could he. This very pride in keeping his word was that he was keeping it to miscreants. It was his last triumph over these lunatics to go down into their dark room and die for something that they could not even understand. The barrel-organ seemed to give the marching tune with the energy and the mingled noises of a whole orchestra; and he could hear deep and rolling, under all the trumpets of the pride of life, the drums of the pride of death.

The conspirators were already filing through the open window and into the rooms behind. Syme went last, outwardly calm, but with all his brain and body throbbing with romantic rhythm. The President led them down an irregular side stair, such as might be used by servants, and into a dim, cold, empty room, with a table and benches, like an abandoned boardroom. When they were all in, he closed and locked the door.

The first to speak was Gogol, the irreconcilable, who seemed bursting with inarticulate grievance.

"Zso! Zso!" he cried, with an obscure excitement, his heavy Polish accent becoming almost impenetrable. "You zay you nod 'ide. You zay you show himselves. It is all nuzzinks. Ven you vant talk importance you run yourselves in a dark box!"

The President seemed to take the foreigner's incoherent satire with entire good humour.

"You can't get hold of it yet, Gogol," he said in a fatherly way. "When once they have heard us talking nonsense on that balcony they will not care where we go afterwards. If we had come here first, we should have had the whole staff at the keyhole. You don't seem to know anything about mankind."

"I die for zem," cried the Pole in thick excitement, "and I slay zare oppressors. I care not for these games of gonzealment. I would zmite ze tyrant in ze open square."

"I see, I see," said the President, nodding kindly as he seated himself at the top of a long table. "You die for mankind first, and then you get up and smite their oppressors. So that's all right. And now may I ask you to control your beautiful sentiments, and sit down with the other gentlemen at this table. For the first time this morning something intelligent is going to be said."

Syme, with the perturbed promptitude he had shown since the original summons, sat down first. Gogol sat down last, grumbling in his brown beard about gombromise. No one except Syme seemed to have any notion of the blow that was about to fall. As for him, he had merely the feeling of a man mounting the scaffold with the intention, at any rate, of making a good speech.

"Comrades," said the President, suddenly rising, "we have spun out this farce long enough. I have called you down here to tell you something so simple and shocking that even the waiters upstairs (long inured to our levities) might hear some new seriousness in my voice. Comrades, we were discussing plans and naming places. I propose, before saying anything else, that those plans and places should not be voted by this meeting, but should be left wholly in the control of some one reliable member. I suggest Comrade Saturday, Dr. Bull."

They all stared at him; then they all started in their seats, for the next words, though not loud, had a living and sensational emphasis. Sunday struck the table.

"Not one word more about the plans and places must be said at this meeting. Not one tiny detail more about what we mean to do must be mentioned in this company."

Sunday had spent his life in astonishing his followers; but it seemed as if he had never really astonished them until now. They all moved feverishly in their seats, except Syme. He sat stiff in his, with his hand in his pocket, and on the handle of his loaded revolver. When the attack on him came he would sell his life dear. He would find out at least if the President was mortal.

Sunday went on smoothly—

"You will probably understand that there is only one possible motive for forbidding free speech at this festival of freedom. Strangers overhearing us matters nothing. They assume that we are joking. But what would matter, even unto death, is this, that there should be one actually among us who is not of us, who knows our grave purpose, but does not share it, who—"

The Secretary screamed out suddenly like a woman.

"It can't be!" he cried, leaping. "There can't—"

The President flapped his large flat hand on the table like the fin of some huge fish.

"Yes," he said slowly, "there is a spy in this room. There is a traitor at this table. I will waste no more words. His name—"

Syme half rose from his seat, his finger firm on the trigger.

"His name is Gogol," said the President. "He is that hairy humbug over there who pretends to be a Pole."

Gogol sprang to his feet, a pistol in each hand. With the same flash three men sprang at his throat. Even the Professor made an effort to rise. But Syme saw little of the scene, for he was blinded with a beneficent darkness; he had sunk down into his seat shuddering, in a palsy of passionate relief.

7. THE UNACCOUNTABLE CONDUCT OF PROFESSOR DE WORMS

"SIT down!" said Sunday in a voice that he used once or twice in his life, a voice that made men drop drawn swords.

The three who had risen fell away from Gogol, and that equivocal person himself resumed his seat.

"Well, my man," said the President briskly, addressing him as one addresses a total stranger, "will you oblige me by putting your hand in your upper waistcoat pocket and showing me what you have there?"

The alleged Pole was a little pale under his tangle of dark hair, but he put two fingers into the pocket with apparent coolness and pulled out a blue strip of card. When Syme saw it lying on the table, he woke up again to the world outside him. For although the card lay at the other extreme of the table, and he could read nothing of the inscription on it, it bore a startling resemblance to the blue card in his own pocket, the card which had been given to him when he joined the anti-anarchist constabulary.

"Pathetic Slav," said the President, "tragic child of Poland, are you prepared in the presence of that card to deny that you are in this company—shall we say de trop?"

"Right oh!" said the late Gogol. It made everyone jump to hear a clear, commercial and somewhat cockney voice coming out of that forest of foreign hair. It was irrational, as if a Chinaman had suddenly spoken with a Scotch accent.

"I gather that you fully understand your position," said Sunday.

"You bet," answered the Pole. "I see it's a fair cop. All I say is, I don't believe any Pole could have imitated my accent like I did his."

"I concede the point," said Sunday. "I believe your own accent to be inimitable, though I shall practise it in my bath. Do you mind leaving your beard with your card?"

"Not a bit," answered Gogol; and with one finger he ripped off the whole of his shaggy head-covering, emerging with thin red hair and a pale, pert face. "It was hot," he added.

"I will do you the justice to say," said Sunday, not without a sort of brutal admiration, "that you seem to have kept pretty cool under it. Now listen to me. I like you. The consequence is that it would annoy me for just about two and a half minutes if I heard that you had died in torments. Well, if you ever tell the police or any human soul about us, I shall have that two and a half minutes of discomfort. On your discomfort I will not dwell. Good day. Mind the step."

The red-haired detective who had masqueraded as Gogol rose to his feet without a word, and walked out of the room with an air of perfect nonchalance. Yet the astonished Syme was able to realise that this ease was suddenly assumed; for there was a slight stumble outside the door, which showed that the departing detective had not minded the step.

"Time is flying," said the President in his gayest manner, after glancing at his watch, which like everything about him seemed bigger than it ought to be. "I must go off at once; I have to take the chair at a Humanitarian meeting."

The Secretary turned to him with working eyebrows.

"Would it not be better," he said a little sharply, "to discuss further the details of our project, now that the spy has left us?"

"No, I think not," said the President with a yawn like an unobtrusive earthquake. "Leave it as it is. Let Saturday settle it. I must be off. Breakfast here next Sunday."

But the late loud scenes had whipped up the almost naked nerves of the Secretary. He was one of those men who are conscientious even in crime.

"I must protest, President, that the thing is irregular," he said. "It is a fundamental rule of our society that all plans shall be debated in full council. Of course, I fully appreciate your forethought when in the actual presence of a traitor—"

"Secretary," said the President seriously, "if you'd take your head home and boil it for a turnip it might be useful. I can't say. But it might."

The Secretary reared back in a kind of equine anger.

"I really fail to understand—" he began in high offense.

"That's it, that's it," said the President, nodding a great many times. "That's where you fail right enough. You fail to understand. Why, you dancing donkey," he roared, rising, "you didn't want to be overheard by a spy, didn't you? How do you know you aren't overheard now?"

And with these words he shouldered his way out of the room, shaking with incomprehensible scorn.

Four of the men left behind gaped after him without any apparent glimmering of his meaning. Syme alone had even a glimmering, and such as it was it froze him to the bone. If the last words of the President meant anything, they meant that he had not after all passed unsuspected. They meant that while Sunday could not denounce him like Gogol, he still could not trust him like the others.

The other four got to their feet grumbling more or less, and betook themselves elsewhere to find lunch, for it was already well past midday. The Professor went last, very slowly and painfully. Syme sat long after the rest had gone, revolving his strange position. He had escaped a thunderbolt, but he was still under a cloud. At last he rose and made his way out of the hotel into Leicester Square. The bright, cold day had grown increasingly colder, and when he came out into the street he was surprised by a few flakes of snow. While he still carried the sword-stick and the rest of Gregory's portable luggage, he had thrown the cloak down and left it somewhere, perhaps on the steam-tug, perhaps on the balcony. Hoping, therefore, that the snow-shower might be slight, he stepped back out of the street for a moment and stood up under the doorway of a small and greasy hair-dresser's shop, the front window of which was empty, except for a sickly wax lady in evening dress.

Snow, however, began to thicken and fall fast; and Syme, having found one glance at the wax lady quite sufficient to depress his spirits, stared out instead into the white and empty street. He was considerably astonished to see, standing quite still outside the shop and staring into the window, a man. His top hat was loaded with snow like the hat of Father Christmas, the white drift was rising round his boots and ankles; but it seemed as if nothing could tear him away from the contemplation of the colourless wax doll in dirty evening dress. That any human being should stand in such weather looking into such a shop was a matter of sufficient wonder to Syme; but his idle wonder turned suddenly into a personal shock; for he realised that the man standing there was the paralytic old Professor de Worms. It scarcely seemed the place for a person of his years and infirmities.

Syme was ready to believe anything about the perversions of this dehumanized brotherhood; but even he could not believe that the Professor had fallen in love with that particular wax lady. He could only suppose that the man's malady (whatever it was) involved some momentary fits of rigidity or trance. He was not inclined, however, to feel in this case any very compassionate concern. On the contrary, he rather congratulated himself that the Professor's stroke and his elaborate and limping walk would make it easy to escape from him and leave him miles behind. For Syme thirsted first and last to get clear of the whole poisonous atmosphere, if only for an hour. Then he could collect his thoughts, formulate his policy, and decide finally whether he should or should not keep faith with Gregory.

He strolled away through the dancing snow, turned up two or three streets, down through two or three others, and entered a small Soho restaurant for lunch. He partook reflectively of four small and quaint courses, drank half a bottle of red wine, and ended up over black coffee and a black cigar, still thinking. He had taken his seat in the upper room of the restaurant, which was full of the chink of knives and the chatter of foreigners. He remembered that in old days he had imagined that all these harmless and kindly aliens were anarchists. He shuddered, remembering the real thing. But even the shudder had the delightful shame of escape. The wine, the common food, the familiar place, the faces of natural and talkative men, made him almost feel as if the Council of the Seven Days had been a bad dream; and although he knew it was nevertheless an objective reality, it was at least a distant one. Tall houses and populous streets lay between him and his last sight of the shameful seven; he was free in free London, and drinking wine among the free. With a somewhat easier action, he took his hat and stick and strolled down the stair into the shop below.

When he entered that lower room he stood stricken and rooted to the spot. At a small table, close up to the blank window and the white street of snow, sat the old anarchist Professor over a glass of milk, with his lifted livid face and pendent eyelids. For an instant Syme stood as rigid as the stick he leant upon. Then with a gesture as of blind hurry, he brushed past the Professor, dashing open the door and slamming it behind him, and stood outside in the snow.

"Can that old corpse be following me?" he asked himself, biting his yellow moustache. "I stopped too long up in that room, so that even such leaden feet could catch me up. One comfort is, with a little brisk walking I can put a man like that as far away as Timbuctoo. Or am I too fanciful? Was he really following me? Surely Sunday would not be such a fool as to send a lame man?"

He set off at a smart pace, twisting and whirling his stick, in the direction of Covent Garden. As he crossed the great market the snow increased, growing blinding and bewildering as the afternoon began to darken. The snow-flakes tormented him like a swarm of silver bees. Getting into his eyes and beard, they added their unremitting futility to his already irritated nerves; and by the time that he had come at a swinging pace to the beginning of Fleet Street, he lost patience, and finding a Sunday teashop, turned into it to take shelter. He ordered another cup of black coffee as an excuse. Scarcely had he done so, when Professor de Worms hobbled heavily into the shop, sat down with difficulty and ordered a glass of milk.

Syme's walking-stick had fallen from his hand with a great clang, which confessed the concealed steel. But the Professor did not look round. Syme, who was commonly a cool character, was literally gaping as a rustic gapes at a conjuring trick. He had seen no cab following; he had heard no wheels outside the shop; to all mortal appearances the man had come on foot. But the old man could only walk like a snail, and Syme had walked like the wind. He started up and snatched his stick, half crazy with the contradiction in mere arithmetic, and swung out of the swinging doors, leaving his coffee untasted. An omnibus going to the Bank went rattling by with an unusual rapidity. He had a violent run of a hundred yards to reach it; but he managed to spring, swaying upon the splash-board and, pausing for an instant to pant, he climbed on to the top. When he had been seated for about half a minute, he heard behind him a sort of heavy and asthmatic breathing.

Turning sharply, he saw rising gradually higher and higher up the omnibus steps a top hat soiled and dripping with snow, and under the shadow of its brim the short-sighted face and shaky shoulders of Professor de Worms. He let himself into a seat with characteristic care, and wrapped himself up to the chin in the mackintosh rug.

Every movement of the old man's tottering figure and vague hands, every uncertain gesture and panic-stricken pause, seemed to put it beyond question that he was helpless, that he was in the last imbecility of the body. He moved by inches, he let himself down with little gasps of caution. And yet, unless the philosophical entities called time and space have no vestige even of a practical existence, it appeared quite unquestionable that he had run after the omnibus.

Syme sprang erect upon the rocking car, and after staring wildly at the wintry sky, that grew gloomier every moment, he ran down the steps. He had repressed an elemental impulse to leap over the side.

Too bewildered to look back or to reason, he rushed into one of the little courts at the side of Fleet Street as a rabbit rushes into a hole. He had a vague idea, if this incomprehensible old Jack-in-the-box was really pursuing him, that in that labyrinth of little streets he could soon throw him off the scent. He dived in and out of those crooked lanes, which were more like cracks than thoroughfares; and by the time that he had completed about twenty alternate angles and described an unthinkable polygon, he paused to listen for any sound of pursuit. There was none; there could not in any case have been much, for the little streets were thick with the soundless snow. Somewhere behind Red Lion Court, however, he noticed a place where some energetic citizen had cleared away the snow for a space of about twenty yards, leaving the wet, glistening cobble-stones. He thought little of this as he passed it, only plunging into yet another arm of the maze. But when a few hundred yards farther on he stood still again to listen, his heart stood still also, for he heard from that space of rugged stones the clinking crutch and labouring feet of the infernal cripple.

The sky above was loaded with the clouds of snow, leaving London in a darkness and oppression premature for that hour of the evening. On each side of Syme the walls of the alley were blind and featureless; there was no little window or any kind of eye. He felt a new impulse to break out of this hive of houses, and to get once more into the open and lamp-lit street. Yet he rambled and dodged for a long time before he struck the main thoroughfare. When he did so, he struck it much farther up than he had fancied. He came out into what seemed the vast and void of Ludgate Circus, and saw St. Paul's Cathedral sitting in the sky.

At first he was startled to find these great roads so empty, as if a pestilence had swept through the city. Then he told himself that some degree of emptiness was natural; first because the snow-storm was even dangerously deep, and secondly because it was Sunday. And at the very word Sunday he bit his lip; the word was henceforth for hire like some indecent pun. Under the white fog of snow high up in the heaven the whole atmosphere of the city was turned to a very queer kind of green twilight, as of men under the sea. The sealed and sullen sunset behind the dark dome of St. Paul's had in it smoky and sinister colours—colours of sickly green, dead red or decaying bronze, that were just bright enough to emphasise the solid whiteness of the snow. But right up against these dreary colours rose the black bulk of the cathedral; and upon the top of the cathedral was a random splash and great stain of snow, still clinging as to an Alpine peak. It had fallen accidentally, but just so fallen as to half drape the dome from its very topmost point, and to pick out in perfect silver the great orb and the cross. When Syme saw it he suddenly straightened himself, and made with his sword-stick an involuntary salute.

He knew that that evil figure, his shadow, was creeping quickly or slowly behind him, and he did not care.

It seemed a symbol of human faith and valour that while the skies were darkening that high place of the earth was bright. The devils might have captured heaven, but they had not yet captured the cross. He had a new impulse to tear out the secret of this dancing, jumping and pursuing paralytic; and at the entrance of the court as it opened upon the Circus he turned, stick in hand, to face his pursuer.

Professor de Worms came slowly round the corner of the irregular alley behind him, his unnatural form outlined against a lonely gas-lamp, irresistibly recalling that very imaginative figure in the nursery rhymes, "the crooked man who went a crooked mile." He really looked as if he had been twisted out of shape by the tortuous streets he had been threading. He came nearer and nearer, the lamplight shining on his lifted spectacles, his lifted, patient face. Syme waited for him as St. George waited for the dragon, as a man waits for a final explanation or for death. And the old Professor came right up to him and passed him like a total stranger, without even a blink of his mournful eyelids.

There was something in this silent and unexpected innocence that left Syme in a final fury. The man's colourless face and manner seemed to assert that the whole following had been an accident. Syme was galvanised with an energy that was something between bitterness and a burst of boyish derision. He made a wild gesture as if to knock the old man's hat off, called out something like "Catch me if you can," and went racing away across the white, open Circus. Concealment was impossible now; and looking back over his shoulder, he could see the black figure of the old gentleman coming after him with long, swinging strides like a man winning a mile race. But the head upon that bounding body was still pale, grave and professional, like the head of a lecturer upon the body of a harlequin.

This outrageous chase sped across Ludgate Circus, up Ludgate Hill, round St. Paul's Cathedral, along Cheapside, Syme remembering all the nightmares he had ever known. Then Syme broke away towards the river, and ended almost down by the docks. He saw the yellow panes of a low, lighted public-house, flung himself into it and ordered beer. It was a foul tavern, sprinkled with foreign sailors, a place where opium might be smoked or knives drawn.

A moment later Professor de Worms entered the place, sat down carefully, and asked for a glass of milk.

8. THE PROFESSOR EXPLAINS

WHEN Gabriel Syme found himself finally established in a chair, and opposite to him, fixed and final also, the lifted eyebrows and leaden eyelids of the Professor, his fears fully returned. This incomprehensible man from the fierce council, after all, had certainly pursued him. If the man had one character as a paralytic and another character as a pursuer, the antithesis might make him more interesting, but scarcely more soothing. It would be a very small comfort that he could not find the Professor out, if by some serious accident the Professor should find him out. He emptied a whole pewter pot of ale before the professor had touched his milk.

One possibility, however, kept him hopeful and yet helpless. It was just possible that this escapade signified something other than even a slight suspicion of him. Perhaps it was some regular form or sign. Perhaps the foolish scamper was some sort of friendly signal that he ought to have understood. Perhaps it was a ritual. Perhaps the new Thursday was always chased along Cheapside, as the new Lord Mayor is always escorted along it. He was just selecting a tentative inquiry, when the old Professor opposite suddenly and simply cut him short. Before Syme could ask the first diplomatic question, the old anarchist had asked suddenly, without any sort of preparation—

"Are you a policeman?"

Whatever else Syme had expected, he had never expected anything so brutal and actual as this. Even his great presence of mind could only manage a reply with an air of rather blundering jocularity.

"A policeman?" he said, laughing vaguely. "Whatever made you think of a policeman in connection with me?"

"The process was simple enough," answered the Professor patiently. "I thought you looked like a policeman. I think so now."

"Did I take a policeman's hat by mistake out of the restaurant?" asked Syme, smiling wildly. "Have I by any chance got a number stuck on to me somewhere? Have my boots got that watchful look? Why must I be a policeman? Do, do let me be a postman."

The old Professor shook his head with a gravity that gave no hope, but Syme ran on with a feverish irony.

"But perhaps I misunderstood the delicacies of your German philosophy. Perhaps policeman is a relative term. In an evolutionary sense, sir, the ape fades so gradually into the policeman, that I myself can never detect the shade. The monkey is only the policeman that may be. Perhaps a maiden lady on Clapham Common is only the policeman that might have been. I don't mind being the policeman that might have been. I don't mind being anything in German thought."

"Are you in the police service?" said the old man, ignoring all Syme's improvised and desperate raillery. "Are you a detective?"

Syme's heart turned to stone, but his face never changed.

"Your suggestion is ridiculous," he began. "Why on earth—"

The old man struck his palsied hand passionately on the rickety table, nearly breaking it.

"Did you hear me ask a plain question, you pattering spy?" he shrieked in a high, crazy voice. "Are you, or are you not, a police detective?"

"No!" answered Syme, like a man standing on the hangman's drop.

"You swear it," said the old man, leaning across to him, his dead face becoming as it were loathsomely alive. "You swear it! You swear it! If you swear falsely, will you be damned? Will you be sure that the devil dances at your funeral? Will you see that the nightmare sits on your grave? Will there really be no mistake? You are an anarchist, you are a dynamiter! Above all, you are not in any sense a detective? You are not in the British police?"

He leant his angular elbow far across the table, and put up his large loose hand like a flap to his ear.

"I am not in the British police," said Syme with insane calm.

Professor de Worms fell back in his chair with a curious air of kindly collapse.

"That's a pity," he said, "because I am."

Syme sprang up straight, sending back the bench behind him with a crash.

"Because you are what?" he said thickly. "You are what?"

"I am a policeman," said the Professor with his first broad smile, and beaming through his spectacles. "But as you think policeman only a relative term, of course I have nothing to do with you. I am in the British police force; but as you tell me you are not in the British police force, I can only say that I met you in a dynamiters' club. I suppose I ought to arrest you." And with these words he laid on the table before Syme an exact facsimile of the blue card which Syme had in his own waistcoat pocket, the symbol of his power from the police.

Syme had for a flash the sensation that the cosmos had turned exactly upside down, that all trees were growing downwards and that all stars were under his feet. Then came slowly the opposite conviction. For the last twenty-four hours the cosmos had really been upside down, but now the capsized universe had come right side up again. This devil from whom he had been fleeing all day was only an elder brother of his own house, who on the other side of the table lay back and laughed at him. He did not for the moment ask any questions of detail; he only knew the happy and silly fact that this shadow, which had pursued him with an intolerable oppression of peril, was only the shadow of a friend trying to catch him up. He knew simultaneously that he was a fool and a free man. For with any recovery from morbidity there must go a certain healthy humiliation. There comes a certain point in such conditions when only three things are possible: first a perpetuation of Satanic pride, secondly tears, and third laughter. Syme's egotism held hard to the first course for a few seconds, and then suddenly adopted the third. Taking his own blue police ticket from his own waist coat pocket, he tossed it on to the table; then he flung his head back until his spike of yellow beard almost pointed at the ceiling, and shouted with a barbaric laughter.

Even in that close den, perpetually filled with the din of knives, plates, cans, clamorous voices, sudden struggles and stampedes, there was something Homeric in Syme's mirth which made many half-drunken men look round.

"What yer laughing at, guv'nor?" asked one wondering labourer from the docks.

"At myself," answered Syme, and went off again into the agony of his ecstatic reaction.

"Pull yourself together," said the Professor, "or you'll get hysterical. Have some more beer. I'll join you."

"You haven't drunk your milk," said Syme.

"My milk!" said the other, in tones of withering and unfathomable contempt, "my milk! Do you think I'd look at the beastly stuff when I'm out of sight of the bloody anarchists? We're all Christians in this room, though perhaps," he added, glancing around at the reeling crowd, "not strict ones. Finish my milk? Great blazes! yes, I'll finish it right enough!" and he knocked the tumbler off the table, making a crash of glass and a splash of silver fluid.

Syme was staring at him with a happy curiosity.

"I understand now," he cried; "of course, you're not an old man at all."

"I can't take my face off here," replied Professor de Worms. "It's rather an elaborate make-up. As to whether I'm an old man, that's not for me to say. I was thirty-eight last birthday."

"Yes, but I mean," said Syme impatiently, "there's nothing the matter with you."

"Yes," answered the other dispassionately. "I am subject to colds."

Syme's laughter at all this had about it a wild weakness of relief. He laughed at the idea of the paralytic Professor being really a young actor dressed up as if for the foot-lights. But he felt that he would have laughed as loudly if a pepperpot had fallen over.

The false Professor drank and wiped his false beard.

"Did you know," he asked, "that that man Gogol was one of us?"

"I? No, I didn't know it," answered Syme in some surprise. "But didn't you?"

"I knew no more than the dead," replied the man who called himself de Worms. "I thought the President was talking about me, and I rattled in my boots."

"And I thought he was talking about me," said Syme, with his rather reckless laughter. "I had my hand on my revolver all the time."

"So had I," said the Professor grimly; "so had Gogol evidently."

Syme struck the table with an exclamation.

"Why, there were three of us there!" he cried. "Three out of seven is a fighting number. If we had only known that we were three!"

The face of Professor de Worms darkened, and he did not look up.

"We were three," he said. "If we had been three hundred we could still have done nothing."

"Not if we were three hundred against four?" asked Syme, jeering rather boisterously.

"No," said the Professor with sobriety, "not if we were three hundred against Sunday."

And the mere name struck Syme cold and serious; his laughter had died in his heart before it could die on his lips. The face of the unforgettable President sprang into his mind as startling as a coloured photograph, and he remarked this difference between Sunday and all his satellites, that their faces, however fierce or sinister, became gradually blurred by memory like other human faces, whereas Sunday's seemed almost to grow more actual during absence, as if a man's painted portrait should slowly come alive.

They were both silent for a measure of moments, and then Syme's speech came with a rush, like the sudden foaming of champagne.

"Professor," he cried, "it is intolerable. Are you afraid of this man?"

The Professor lifted his heavy lids, and gazed at Syme with large, wide-open, blue eyes of an almost ethereal honesty.

"Yes, I am," he said mildly. "So are you."

Syme was dumb for an instant. Then he rose to his feet erect, like an insulted man, and thrust the chair away from him.

"Yes," he said in a voice indescribable, "you are right. I am afraid of him. Therefore I swear by God that I will seek out this man whom I fear until I find him, and strike him on the mouth. If heaven were his throne and the earth his footstool, I swear that I would pull him down."

"How?" asked the staring Professor. "Why?"

"Because I am afraid of him," said Syme; "and no man should leave in the universe anything of which he is afraid."

De Worms blinked at him with a sort of blind wonder. He made an effort to speak, but Syme went on in a low voice, but with an undercurrent of inhuman exaltation—

"Who would condescend to strike down the mere things that he does not fear? Who would debase himself to be merely brave, like any common prizefighter? Who would stoop to be fearless—like a tree? Fight the thing that you fear. You remember the old tale of the English clergyman who gave the last rites to the brigand of Sicily, and how on his death-bed the great robber said, 'I can give you no money, but I can give you advice for a lifetime: your thumb on the blade, and strike upwards.' So I say to you, strike upwards, if you strike at the stars."

The other looked at the ceiling, one of the tricks of his pose.

"Sunday is a fixed star," he said.

"You shall see him a falling star," said Syme, and put on his hat.

The decision of his gesture drew the Professor vaguely to his feet.

"Have you any idea," he asked, with a sort of benevolent bewilderment, "exactly where you are going?"

"Yes," replied Syme shortly, "I am going to prevent this bomb being thrown in Paris."

"Have you any conception how?" inquired the other.

"No," said Syme with equal decision.

"You remember, of course," resumed the soi-disant de Worms, pulling his beard and looking out of the window, "that when we broke up rather hurriedly the whole arrangements for the atrocity were left in the private hands of the Marquis and Dr. Bull. The Marquis is by this time probably crossing the Channel. But where he will go and what he will do it is doubtful whether even the President knows; certainly we don't know. The only man who does know is Dr. Bull."

"Confound it!" cried Syme. "And we don't know where he is."

"Yes," said the other in his curious, absent-minded way, "I know where he is myself."

"Will you tell me?" asked Syme with eager eyes.

"I will take you there," said the Professor, and took down his own hat from a peg.

Syme stood looking at him with a sort of rigid excitement.

"What do you mean?" he asked sharply. "Will you join me? Will you take the risk?"

"Young man," said the Professor pleasantly, "I am amused to observe that you think I am a coward. As to that I will say only one word, and that shall be entirely in the manner of your own philosophical rhetoric. You think that it is possible to pull down the President. I know that it is impossible, and I am going to try it," and opening the tavern door, which let in a blast of bitter air, they went out together into the dark streets by the docks.

Most of the snow was melted or trampled to mud, but here and there a clot of it still showed grey rather than white in the gloom. The small streets were sloppy and full of pools, which reflected the flaming lamps irregularly, and by accident, like fragments of some other and fallen world. Syme felt almost dazed as he stepped through this growing confusion of lights and shadows; but his companion walked on with a certain briskness, towards where, at the end of the street, an inch or two of the lamplit river looked like a bar of flame.

"Where are you going?" Syme inquired.

"Just now," answered the Professor, "I am going just round the corner to see whether Dr. Bull has gone to bed. He is hygienic, and retires early."

"Dr. Bull!" exclaimed Syme. "Does he live round the corner?"

"No," answered his friend. "As a matter of fact he lives some way off, on the other side of the river, but we can tell from here whether he has gone to bed."

Turning the corner as he spoke, and facing the dim river, flecked with flame, he pointed with his stick to the other bank. On the Surrey side at this point there ran out into the Thames, seeming almost to overhang it, a bulk and cluster of those tall tenements, dotted with lighted windows, and rising like factory chimneys to an almost insane height. Their special poise and position made one block of buildings especially look like a Tower of Babel with a hundred eyes. Syme had never seen any of the sky-scraping buildings in America, so he could only think of the buildings in a dream.

Even as he stared, the highest light in this innumerably lighted turret abruptly went out, as if this black Argus had winked at him with one of his innumerable eyes.

Professor de Worms swung round on his heel, and struck his stick against his boot.

"We are too late," he said, "the hygienic Doctor has gone to bed."

"What do you mean?" asked Syme. "Does he live over there, then?"

"Yes," said de Worms, "behind that particular window which you can't see. Come along and get some dinner. We must call on him tomorrow morning."

Without further parley, he led the way through several by-ways until they came out into the flare and clamour of the East India Dock Road. The Professor, who seemed to know his way about the neighbourhood, proceeded to a place where the line of lighted shops fell back into a sort of abrupt twilight and quiet, in which an old white inn, all out of repair, stood back some twenty feet from the road.

"You can find good English inns left by accident everywhere, like fossils," explained the Professor. "I once found a decent place in the West End."

"I suppose," said Syme, smiling, "that this is the corresponding decent place in the East End?"

"It is," said the Professor reverently, and went in.

In that place they dined and slept, both very thoroughly. The beans and bacon, which these unaccountable people cooked well, the astonishing emergence of Burgundy from their cellars, crowned Syme's sense of a new comradeship and comfort. Through all this ordeal his root horror had been isolation, and there are no words to express the abyss between isolation and having one ally. It may be conceded to the mathematicians that four is twice two. But two is not twice one; two is two thousand times one. That is why, in spite of a hundred disadvantages, the world will always return to monogamy.

Syme was able to pour out for the first time the whole of his outrageous tale, from the time when Gregory had taken him to the little tavern by the river. He did it idly and amply, in a luxuriant monologue, as a man speaks with very old friends. On his side, also, the man who had impersonated Professor de Worms was not less communicative. His own story was almost as silly as Syme's.

"That's a good get-up of yours," said Syme, draining a glass of Macon; "a lot better than old Gogol's. Even at the start I thought he was a bit too hairy."

"A difference of artistic theory," replied the Professor pensively. "Gogol was an idealist. He made up as the abstract or platonic ideal of an anarchist. But I am a realist. I am a portrait painter. But, indeed, to say that I am a portrait painter is an inadequate expression. I am a portrait."

"I don't understand you," said Syme.

"I am a portrait," repeated the Professor. "I am a portrait of the celebrated Professor de Worms, who is, I believe, in Naples."

"You mean you are made up like him," said Syme. "But doesn't he know that you are taking his nose in vain?"

"He knows it right enough," replied his friend cheerfully.

"Then why doesn't he denounce you?"

"I have denounced him," answered the Professor.

"Do explain yourself," said Syme.

"With pleasure, if you don't mind hearing my story," replied the eminent foreign philosopher. "I am by profession an actor, and my name is Wilks. When I was on the stage I mixed with all sorts of Bohemian and blackguard company. Sometimes I touched the edge of the turf, sometimes the riff-raff of the arts, and occasionally the political refugee. In some den of exiled dreamers I was introduced to the great German Nihilist philosopher, Professor de Worms. I did not gather much about him beyond his appearance, which was very disgusting, and which I studied carefully. I understood that he had proved that the destructive principle in the universe was God; hence he insisted on the need for a furious and incessant energy, rending all things in pieces. Energy, he said, was the All. He was lame, shortsighted, and partially paralytic. When I met him I was in a frivolous mood, and I disliked him so much that I resolved to imitate him. If I had been a draughtsman I would have drawn a caricature. I was only an actor, I could only act a caricature. I made myself up into what was meant for a wild exaggeration of the old Professor's dirty old self. When I went into the room full of his supporters I expected to be received with a roar of laughter, or (if they were too far gone) with a roar of indignation at the insult. I cannot describe the surprise I felt when my entrance was received with a respectful silence, followed (when I had first opened my lips) with a murmur of admiration. The curse of the perfect artist had fallen upon me. I had been too subtle, I had been too true. They thought I really was the great Nihilist Professor. I was a healthy-minded young man at the time, and I confess that it was a blow. Before I could fully recover, however, two or three of these admirers ran up to me radiating indignation, and told me that a public insult had been put upon me in the next room. I inquired its nature. It seemed that an impertinent fellow had dressed himself up as a preposterous parody of myself. I had drunk more champagne than was good for me, and in a flash of folly I decided to see the situation through. Consequently it was to meet the glare of the company and my own lifted eyebrows and freezing eyes that the real Professor came into the room.

"I need hardly say there was a collision. The pessimists all round me looked anxiously from one Professor to the other Professor to see which was really the more feeble. But I won. An old man in poor health, like my rival, could not be expected to be so impressively feeble as a young actor in the prime of life. You see, he really had paralysis, and working within this definite limitation, he couldn't be so jolly paralytic as I was. Then he tried to blast my claims intellectually. I countered that by a very simple dodge. Whenever he said something that nobody but he could understand, I replied with something which I could not even understand myself. 'I don't fancy,' he said, 'that you could have worked out the principle that evolution is only negation, since there inheres in it the introduction of lacuna, which are an essential of differentiation.' I replied quite scornfully, 'You read all that up in Pinckwerts; the notion that involution functioned eugenically was exposed long ago by Glumpe.' It is unnecessary for me to say that there never were such people as Pinckwerts and Glumpe. But the people all round (rather to my surprise) seemed to remember them quite well, and the Professor, finding that the learned and mysterious method left him rather at the mercy of an enemy slightly deficient in scruples, fell back upon a more popular form of wit. 'I see,' he sneered, 'you prevail like the false pig in Aesop.' 'And you fail,' I answered, smiling, 'like the hedgehog in Montaigne.' Need I say that there is no hedgehog in Montaigne?

'Your claptrap comes off,' he said; 'so would your beard.' I had no intelligent answer to this, which was quite true and rather witty. But I laughed heartily, answered, 'Like the Pantheist's boots,' at random, and turned on my heel with all the honours of victory. The real Professor was thrown out, but not with violence, though one man tried very patiently to pull off his nose. He is now, I believe, received everywhere in Europe as a delightful impostor. His apparent earnestness and anger, you see, make him all the more entertaining."

"Well," said Syme, "I can understand your putting on his dirty old beard for a night's practical joke, but I don't understand your never taking it off again."

"That is the rest of the story," said the impersonator. "When I myself left the company, followed by reverent applause, I went limping down the dark street, hoping that I should soon be far enough away to be able to walk like a human being. To my astonishment, as I was turning the corner, I felt a touch on the shoulder, and turning, found myself under the shadow of an enormous policeman. He told me I was wanted. I struck a sort of paralytic attitude, and cried in a high German accent, 'Yes, I am wanted —by the oppressed of the world. You are arresting me on the charge of being the great anarchist, Professor de Worms.' The policeman impassively consulted a paper in his hand, 'No, sir,' he said civilly, 'at least, not exactly, sir. I am arresting you on the charge of not being the celebrated anarchist, Professor de Worms.' This charge, if it was criminal at all, was certainly the lighter of the two, and I went along with the man, doubtful, but not greatly dismayed. I was shown into a number of rooms, and eventually into the presence of a police officer, who explained that a serious campaign had been opened against the centres of anarchy, and that this, my successful masquerade, might be of considerable value to the public safety. He offered me a good salary and this little blue card. Though our conversation was short, he struck me as a man of very massive common sense and humour; but I cannot tell you much about him personally, because—"

Syme laid down his knife and fork.

"I know," he said, "because you talked to him in a dark room."

Professor de Worms nodded and drained his glass.

9. THE MAN IN SPECTACLES

"BURGUNDY is a jolly thing," said the Professor sadly, as he set his glass down.

"You don't look as if it were," said Syme; "you drink it as if it were medicine."

"You must excuse my manner," said the Professor dismally, "my position is rather a curious one. Inside I am really bursting with boyish merriment; but I acted the paralytic Professor so well, that now I can't leave off. So that when I am among friends, and have no need at all to disguise myself, I still can't help speaking slow and wrinkling my forehead—just as if it were my forehead. I can be quite happy, you understand, but only in a paralytic sort of way. The most buoyant exclamations leap up in my heart, but they come out of my mouth quite different. You should hear me say, 'Buck up, old cock!' It would bring tears to your eyes."

"It does," said Syme; "but I cannot help thinking that apart from all that you are really a bit worried."

The Professor started a little and looked at him steadily.

"You are a very clever fellow," he said, "it is a pleasure to work with you. Yes, I have rather a heavy cloud in my head. There is a great problem to face," and he sank his bald brow in his two hands.

Then he said in a low voice—

"Can you play the piano?"

"Yes," said Syme in simple wonder, "I'm supposed to have a good touch."

Then, as the other did not speak, he added—

"I trust the great cloud is lifted."

After a long silence, the Professor said out of the cavernous shadow of his hands—

"It would have done just as well if you could work a typewriter."

"Thank you," said Syme, "you flatter me."

"Listen to me," said the other, "and remember whom we have to see tomorrow. You and I are going tomorrow to attempt something which is very much more dangerous than trying to steal the Crown Jewels out of the Tower. We are trying to steal a secret from a very sharp, very strong, and very wicked man. I believe there is no man, except the President, of course, who is so seriously startling and formidable as that little grinning fellow in goggles. He has not perhaps the white-hot enthusiasm unto death, the mad martyrdom for anarchy, which marks the Secretary. But then that very fanaticism in the Secretary has a human pathos, and is almost a redeeming trait. But the little Doctor has a brutal sanity that is more shocking than the Secretary's disease. Don't you notice his detestable virility and vitality. He bounces like an india-rubber ball. Depend on it, Sunday was not asleep (I wonder if he ever sleeps?) when he locked up all the plans of this outrage in the round, black head of Dr. Bull."

"And you think," said Syme, "that this unique monster will be soothed if I play the piano to him?"

"Don't be an ass," said his mentor. "I mentioned the piano because it gives one quick and independent fingers. Syme, if we are to go through this interview and come out sane or alive, we must have some code of signals between us that this brute will not see. I have made a rough alphabetical cypher corresponding to the five fingers—like this, see," and he rippled with his fingers on the wooden table—"B A D, bad, a word we may frequently require."

Syme poured himself out another glass of wine, and began to study the scheme. He was abnormally quick with his brains at puzzles, and with his hands at conjuring, and it did not take him long to learn how he might convey simple messages by what would seem to be idle taps upon a table or knee. But wine and companionship had always the effect of inspiring him to a farcical ingenuity, and the Professor soon found himself struggling with the too vast energy of the new language, as it passed through the heated brain of Syme.

"We must have several word-signs," said Syme seriously—"words that we are likely to want, fine shades of meaning. My favourite word is 'coeval'. What's yours?"

"Do stop playing the goat," said the Professor plaintively. "You don't know how serious this is."

"'Lush' too," said Syme, shaking his head sagaciously, "we must have 'lush'—word applied to grass, don't you know?"

"Do you imagine," asked the Professor furiously, "that we are going to talk to Dr. Bull about grass?"

"There are several ways in which the subject could be approached," said Syme reflectively, "and the word introduced without appearing forced. We might say, 'Dr. Bull, as a revolutionist, you remember that a tyrant once advised us to eat grass; and indeed many of us, looking on the fresh lush grass of summer...'"

"Do you understand," said the other, "that this is a tragedy?"

"Perfectly," replied Syme; "always be comic in a tragedy. What the deuce else can you do? I wish this language of yours had a wider scope. I suppose we could not extend it from the fingers to the toes? That would involve pulling off our boots and socks during the conversation, which however unobtrusively performed—"

"Syme," said his friend with a stern simplicity, "go to bed!"

Syme, however, sat up in bed for a considerable time mastering the new code. He was awakened next morning while the east was still sealed with darkness, and found his grey-bearded ally standing like a ghost beside his bed.

Syme sat up in bed blinking; then slowly collected his thoughts, threw off the bed-clothes, and stood up. It seemed to him in some curious way that all the safety and sociability of the night before fell with the bedclothes off him, and he stood up in an air of cold danger. He still felt an entire trust and loyalty towards his companion; but it was the trust between two men going to the scaffold.

"Well," said Syme with a forced cheerfulness as he pulled on his trousers, "I dreamt of that alphabet of yours. Did it take you long to make it up?"

The Professor made no answer, but gazed in front of him with eyes the colour of a wintry sea; so Syme repeated his question.

"I say, did it take you long to invent all this? I'm considered good at these things, and it was a good hour's grind. Did you learn it all on the spot?"

The Professor was silent; his eyes were wide open, and he wore a fixed but very small smile.

"How long did it take you?"

The Professor did not move.

"Confound you, can't you answer?" called out Syme, in a sudden anger that had something like fear underneath. Whether or no the Professor could answer, he did not.

Syme stood staring back at the stiff face like parchment and the blank, blue eyes. His first thought was that the Professor had gone mad, but his second thought was more frightful. After all, what did he know about this queer creature whom he had heedlessly accepted as a friend? What did he know, except that the man had been at the anarchist breakfast and had told him a ridiculous tale? How improbable it was that there should be another friend there beside Gogol! Was this man's silence a sensational way of declaring war? Was this adamantine stare after all only the awful sneer of some threefold traitor, who had turned for the last time? He stood and strained his ears in this heartless silence. He almost fancied he could hear dynamiters come to capture him shifting softly in the corridor outside.

Then his eye strayed downwards, and he burst out laughing. Though the Professor himself stood there as voiceless as a statue, his five dumb fingers were dancing alive upon the dead table. Syme watched the twinkling movements of the talking hand, and read clearly the message—

"I will only talk like this. We must get used to it."

He rapped out the answer with the impatience of relief—

"All right. Let's get out to breakfast."

They took their hats and sticks in silence; but as Syme took his sword-stick, he held it hard.

They paused for a few minutes only to stuff down coffee and coarse thick sandwiches at a coffee stall, and then made their way across the river, which under the grey and growing light looked as desolate as Acheron. They reached the bottom of the huge block of buildings which they had seen from across the river, and began in silence to mount the naked and numberless stone steps, only pausing now and then to make short remarks on the rail of the banisters. At about every other flight they passed a window; each window showed them a pale and tragic dawn lifting itself laboriously over London. From each the innumerable roofs of slate looked like the leaden surges of a grey, troubled sea after rain. Syme was increasingly conscious that his new adventure had somehow a quality of cold sanity worse than the wild adventures of the past. Last night, for instance, the tall tenements had seemed to him like a tower in a dream. As he now went up the weary and perpetual steps, he was daunted and bewildered by their almost infinite series. But it was not the hot horror of a dream or of anything that might be exaggeration or delusion. Their infinity was more like the empty infinity of arithmetic, something unthinkable, yet necessary to thought. Or it was like the stunning statements of astronomy about the distance of the fixed stars. He was ascending the house of reason, a thing more hideous than unreason itself.

By the time they reached Dr. Bull's landing, a last window showed them a harsh, white dawn edged with banks of a kind of coarse red, more like red clay than red cloud. And when they entered Dr. Bull's bare garret it was full of light.

Syme had been haunted by a half historic memory in connection with these empty rooms and that austere daybreak. The moment he saw the garret and Dr. Bull sitting writing at a table, he remembered what the memory was—the French Revolution. There should have been the black outline of a guillotine against that heavy red and white of the morning. Dr. Bull was in his white shirt and black breeches only; his cropped, dark head might well have just come out of its wig; he might have been Marat or a more slipshod Robespierre.

Yet when he was seen properly, the French fancy fell away. The Jacobins were idealists; there was about this man a murderous materialism. His position gave him a somewhat new appearance. The strong, white light of morning coming from one side creating sharp shadows, made him seem both more pale and more angular than he had looked at the breakfast on the balcony. Thus the two black glasses that encased his eyes might really have been black cavities in his skull, making him look like a death's-head. And, indeed, if ever Death himself sat writing at a wooden table, it might have been he.

He looked up and smiled brightly enough as the men came in, and rose with the resilient rapidity of which the Professor had spoken. He set chairs for both of them, and going to a peg behind the door, proceeded to put on a coat and waistcoat of rough, dark tweed; he buttoned it up neatly, and came back to sit down at his table.

The quiet good humour of his manner left his two opponents helpless. It was with some momentary difficulty that the Professor broke silence and began, "I'm sorry to disturb you so early, comrade," said he, with a careful resumption of the slow de Worms manner. "You have no doubt made all the arrangements for the Paris affair?"

Then he added with infinite slowness, "We have information which renders intolerable anything in the nature of a moment's delay."

Dr. Bull smiled again, but continued to gaze on them without speaking. The Professor resumed, a pause before each weary word—

"Please do not think me excessively abrupt; but I advise you to alter those plans, or if it is too late for that, to follow your agent with all the support you can get for him. Comrade Syme and I have had an experience which it would take more time to recount than we can afford, if we are to act on it. I will, however, relate the occurrence in detail, even at the risk of losing time, if you really feel that it is essential to the understanding of the problem we have to discuss."

He was spinning out his sentences, making them intolerably long and lingering, in the hope of maddening the practical little Doctor into an explosion of impatience which might show his hand. But the little Doctor continued only to stare and smile, and the monologue was uphill work. Syme began to feel a new sickness and despair. The Doctor's smile and silence were not at all like the cataleptic stare and horrible silence which he had confronted in the Professor half an hour before. About the Professor's makeup and all his antics there was always something merely grotesque, like a gollywog. Syme remembered those wild woes of yesterday as one remembers being afraid of Bogy in childhood. But here was daylight; here was a healthy, square-shouldered man in tweeds, not odd save for the accident of his ugly spectacles, not glaring or grinning at all, but smiling steadily and not saying a word. The whole had a sense of unbearable reality. Under the increasing sunlight the colours of the Doctor's complexion, the pattern of his tweeds, grew and expanded outrageously, as such things grow too important in a realistic novel. But his smile was quite slight, the pose of his head polite; the only uncanny thing was his silence.

"As I say," resumed the Professor, like a man toiling through heavy sand, "the incident that has occurred to us and has led us to ask for information about the Marquis, is one which you may think it better to have narrated; but as it came in the way of Comrade Syme rather than me—"

His words he seemed to be dragging out like words in an anthem; but Syme, who was watching, saw his long fingers rattle quickly on the edge of the crazy table. He read the message, "You must go on. This devil has sucked me dry!"

Syme plunged into the breach with that bravado of improvisation which always came to him when he was alarmed.

"Yes, the thing really happened to me," he said hastily. "I had the good fortune to fall into conversation with a detective who took me, thanks to my hat, for a respectable person. Wishing to clinch my reputation for respectability, I took him and made him very drunk at the Savoy. Under this influence he became friendly, and told me in so many words that within a day or two they hope to arrest the Marquis in France.

"So unless you or I can get on his track—"

The Doctor was still smiling in the most friendly way, and his protected eyes were still impenetrable. The Professor signalled to Syme that he would resume his explanation, and he began again with the same elaborate calm.

"Syme immediately brought this information to me, and we came here together to see what use you would be inclined to make of it. It seems to me unquestionably urgent that—"

All this time Syme had been staring at the Doctor almost as steadily as the Doctor stared at the Professor, but quite without the smile. The nerves of both comrades-in-arms were near snapping under that strain of motionless amiability, when Syme suddenly leant forward and idly tapped the edge of the table. His message to his ally ran, "I have an intuition."

The Professor, with scarcely a pause in his monologue, signalled back, "Then sit on it."

Syme telegraphed, "It is quite extraordinary."

The other answered, "Extraordinary rot!"

Syme said, "I am a poet."

The other retorted, "You are a dead man."

Syme had gone quite red up to his yellow hair, and his eyes were burning feverishly. As he said he had an intuition, and it had risen to a sort of lightheaded certainty. Resuming his symbolic taps, he signalled to his friend, "You scarcely realise how poetic my intuition is. It has that sudden quality we sometimes feel in the coming of spring."

He then studied the answer on his friend's fingers. The answer was, "Go to hell!"

The Professor then resumed his merely verbal monologue addressed to the Doctor.

"Perhaps I should rather say," said Syme on his fingers, "that it resembles that sudden smell of the sea which may be found in the heart of lush woods."

His companion disdained to reply.

"Or yet again," tapped Syme, "it is positive, as is the passionate red hair of a beautiful woman."

The Professor was continuing his speech, but in the middle of it Syme decided to act. He leant across the table, and said in a voice that could not be neglected—

"Dr. Bull!"

The Doctor's sleek and smiling head did not move, but they could have sworn that under his dark glasses his eyes darted towards Syme.

"Dr. Bull," said Syme, in a voice peculiarly precise and courteous, "would you do me a small favour? Would you be so kind as to take off your spectacles?"

The Professor swung round on his seat, and stared at Syme with a sort of frozen fury of astonishment. Syme, like a man who has thrown his life and fortune on the table, leaned forward with a fiery face. The Doctor did not move.

For a few seconds there was a silence in which one could hear a pin drop, split once by the single hoot of a distant steamer on the Thames. Then Dr. Bull rose slowly, still smiling, and took off his spectacles.

Syme sprang to his feet, stepping backwards a little, like a chemical lecturer from a successful explosion. His eyes were like stars, and for an instant he could only point without speaking.

The Professor had also started to his feet, forgetful of his supposed paralysis. He leant on the back of the chair and stared doubtfully at Dr. Bull, as if the Doctor had been turned into a toad before his eyes. And indeed it was almost as great a transformation scene.

The two detectives saw sitting in the chair before them a very boyish-looking young man, with very frank and happy hazel eyes, an open expression, cockney clothes like those of a city clerk, and an unquestionable breath about him of being very good and rather commonplace. The smile was still there, but it might have been the first smile of a baby.

"I knew I was a poet," cried Syme in a sort of ecstasy. "I knew my intuition was as infallible as the Pope. It was the spectacles that did it! It was all the spectacles. Given those beastly black eyes, and all the rest of him his health and his jolly looks, made him a live devil among dead ones."

"It certainly does make a queer difference," said the Professor shakily. "But as regards the project of Dr. Bull—"

"Project be damned!" roared Syme, beside himself. "Look at him! Look at his face, look at his collar, look at his blessed boots! You don't suppose, do you, that that thing's an anarchist?"

"Syme!" cried the other in an apprehensive agony.

"Why, by God," said Syme, "I'll take the risk of that myself! Dr. Bull, I am a police officer. There's my card," and he flung down the blue card upon the table.

The Professor still feared that all was lost; but he was loyal. He pulled out his own official card and put it beside his friend's. Then the third man burst out laughing, and for the first time that morning they heard his voice.

"I'm awfully glad you chaps have come so early," he said, with a sort of schoolboy flippancy, "for we can all start for France together. Yes, I'm in the force right enough," and he flicked a blue card towards them lightly as a matter of form.

Clapping a brisk bowler on his head and resuming his goblin glasses, the Doctor moved so quickly towards the door, that the others instinctively followed him. Syme seemed a little distrait, and as he passed under the doorway he suddenly struck his stick on the stone passage so that it rang.

"But Lord God Almighty," he cried out, "if this is all right, there were more damned detectives than there were damned dynamiters at the damned Council!"

"We might have fought easily," said Bull; "we were four against three."

The Professor was descending the stairs, but his voice came up from below.

"No," said the voice, "we were not four against three—we were not so lucky. We were four against One."

The others went down the stairs in silence.

The young man called Bull, with an innocent courtesy characteristic of him, insisted on going last until they reached the street; but there his own robust rapidity asserted itself unconsciously, and he walked quickly on ahead towards a railway inquiry office, talking to the others over his shoulder.

"It is jolly to get some pals," he said. "I've been half dead with the jumps, being quite alone. I nearly flung my arms round Gogol and embraced him, which would have been imprudent. I hope you won't despise me for having been in a blue funk."

"All the blue devils in blue hell," said Syme, "contributed to my blue funk! But the worst devil was you and your infernal goggles."

The young man laughed delightedly.

"Wasn't it a rag?" he said. "Such a simple idea—not my own. I haven't got the brains. You see, I wanted to go into the detective service, especially the anti-dynamite business. But for that purpose they wanted someone to dress up as a dynamiter; and they all swore by blazes that I could never look like a dynamiter. They said my very walk was respectable, and that seen from behind I looked like the British Constitution.

They said I looked too healthy and too optimistic, and too reliable and benevolent; they called me all sorts of names at Scotland Yard. They said that if I had been a criminal, I might have made my fortune by looking so like an honest man; but as I had the misfortune to be an honest man, there was not even the remotest chance of my assisting them by ever looking like a criminal. But at last I was brought before some old josser who was high up in the force, and who seemed to have no end of a head on his shoulders. And there the others all talked hopelessly. One asked whether a bushy beard would hide my nice smile; another said that if they blacked my face I might look like a negro anarchist; but this old chap chipped in with a most extraordinary remark. 'A pair of smoked spectacles will do it,' he said positively. 'Look at him now; he looks like an angelic office boy. Put him on a pair of smoked spectacles, and children will scream at the sight of him.' And so it was, by George! When once my eyes were covered, all the rest, smile and big shoulders and short hair, made me look a perfect little devil. As I say, it was simple enough when it was done, like miracles; but that wasn't the really miraculous part of it. There was one really staggering thing about the business, and my head still turns at it."

"What was that?" asked Syme.

"I'll tell you," answered the man in spectacles. "This big pot in the police who sized me up so that he knew how the goggles would go with my hair and socks—by God, he never saw me at all!"

Syme's eyes suddenly flashed on him.

"How was that?" he asked. "I thought you talked to him."

"So I did," said Bull brightly; "but we talked in a pitch-dark room like a coalcellar. There, you would never have guessed that."

"I could not have conceived it," said Syme gravely.

"It is indeed a new idea," said the Professor.

Their new ally was in practical matters a whirlwind. At the inquiry office he asked with businesslike brevity about the trains for Dover. Having got his information, he bundled the company into a cab, and put them and himself inside a railway carriage before they had properly realised the breathless process. They were already on the Calais boat before conversation flowed freely.

"I had already arranged," he explained, "to go to France for my lunch; but I am delighted to have someone to lunch with me. You see, I had to send that beast, the Marquis, over with his bomb, because the President had his eye on me, though God knows how. I'll tell you the story some day. It was perfectly choking. Whenever I tried to slip out of it I saw the President somewhere, smiling out of the bow-window of a club, or taking off his hat to me from the top of an omnibus. I tell you, you can say what you like, that fellow sold himself to the devil; he can be in six places at once."

"So you sent the Marquis off, I understand," asked the Professor. "Was it long ago? Shall we be in time to catch him?"

"Yes," answered the new guide, "I've timed it all. He'll still be at Calais when we arrive."

"But when we do catch him at Calais," said the Professor, "what are we going to do?"

At this question the countenance of Dr. Bull fell for the first time. He reflected a little, and then said—

"Theoretically, I suppose, we ought to call the police."

"Not I," said Syme. "Theoretically I ought to drown myself first. I promised a poor fellow, who was a real modern pessimist, on my word of honour not to tell the police. I'm no hand at casuistry, but I can't break my word to a modern pessimist. It's like breaking one's word to a child."

"I'm in the same boat," said the Professor. "I tried to tell the police and I couldn't, because of some silly oath I took. You see, when I was an actor I was a sort of all-round beast. Perjury or treason is the only crime I haven't committed. If I did that I shouldn't know the difference between right and wrong."

"I've been through all that," said Dr. Bull, "and I've made up my mind. I gave my promise to the Secretary—you know him, man who smiles upside down. My friends, that man is the most utterly unhappy man that was ever human. It may be his digestion, or his conscience, or his nerves, or his philosophy of the universe, but he's damned, he's in hell! Well, I can't turn on a man like that, and hunt him down. It's like whipping a leper. I may be mad, but that's how I feel; and there's jolly well the end of it."

"I don't think you're mad," said Syme. "I knew you would decide like that when first you—"

"Eh?" said Dr. Bull.

"When first you took off your spectacles."

Dr. Bull smiled a little, and strolled across the deck to look at the sunlit sea. Then he strolled back again, kicking his heels carelessly, and a companionable silence fell between the three men.

"Well," said Syme, "it seems that we have all the same kind of morality or immorality, so we had better face the fact that comes of it."

"Yes," assented the Professor, "you're quite right; and we must hurry up, for I can see the Grey Nose standing out from France."

"The fact that comes of it," said Syme seriously, "is this, that we three are alone on this planet. Gogol has gone, God knows where; perhaps the President has smashed him like a fly. On the Council we are three men against three, like the Romans who held the bridge. But we are worse off than that, first because they can appeal to their organization and we cannot appeal to ours, and second because—"

"Because one of those other three men," said the Professor, "is not a man."

Syme nodded and was silent for a second or two, then he said—

"My idea is this. We must do something to keep the Marquis in Calais till tomorrow midday. I have turned over twenty schemes in my head. We cannot denounce him as a dynamiter; that is agreed. We cannot get him detained on some trivial charge, for we should have to appear; he knows us, and he would smell a rat. We cannot pretend to keep him on anarchist business; he might swallow much in that way, but not the notion of stopping in Calais while the Czar went safely through Paris. We might try to kidnap him, and lock him up ourselves; but he is a well-known man here. He has a whole bodyguard of friends; he is very strong and brave, and the event is doubtful. The only thing I can see to do is actually to take advantage of the very things that are in the Marquis's favour. I am going to profit by the fact that he is a highly respected nobleman. I am going to profit by the fact that he has many friends and moves in the best society."

"What the devil are you talking about?" asked the Professor.

"The Symes are first mentioned in the fourteenth century," said Syme; "but there is a tradition that one of them rode behind Bruce at Bannockburn. Since 1350 the tree is quite clear."

"He's gone off his head," said the little Doctor, staring.

"Our bearings," continued Syme calmly, "are 'argent a chevron gules charged with three cross crosslets of the field.' The motto varies."

The Professor seized Syme roughly by the waistcoat.

"We are just inshore," he said. "Are you seasick or joking in the wrong place?"

"My remarks are almost painfully practical," answered Syme, in an unhurried manner. "The house of St. Eustache also is very ancient. The Marquis cannot deny that he is a gentleman. He cannot deny that I am a gentleman. And in order to put the matter of my social position quite beyond a doubt, I propose at the earliest opportunity to knock his hat off. But here we are in the harbour."

They went on shore under the strong sun in a sort of daze. Syme, who had now taken the lead as Bull had taken it in London, led them along a kind of marine parade until he came to some cafes, embowered in a bulk of greenery and overlooking the sea. As he went before them his step was slightly swaggering, and he swung his stick like a sword. He was making apparently for the extreme end of the line of cafes, but he stopped abruptly. With a sharp gesture he motioned them to silence, but he pointed with one gloved finger to a cafe table under a bank of flowering foliage at which sat the Marquis de St. Eustache, his teeth shining in his thick, black beard, and his bold, brown face shadowed by a light yellow straw hat and outlined against the violet sea.

10. THE DUEL

SYME sat down at a cafe table with his companions, his blue eyes sparkling like the bright sea below, and ordered a bottle of Saumur with a pleased impatience. He was for some reason in a condition of curious hilarity. His spirits were already unnaturally high; they rose as the Saumur sank, and in half an hour his talk was a torrent of nonsense. He professed to be making out a plan of the conversation which was going to ensue between himself and the deadly Marquis. He jotted it down wildly with a pencil. It was arranged like a printed catechism, with questions and answers, and was delivered with an extraordinary rapidity of utterance.

"I shall approach. Before taking off his hat, I shall take off my own. I shall say, 'The Marquis de Saint Eustache, I believe.' He will say, 'The celebrated Mr. Syme, I presume.' He will say in the most exquisite French, 'How are you?' I shall reply in the most exquisite Cockney, 'Oh, just the Syme—'"

"Oh, shut it," said the man in spectacles. "Pull yourself together, and chuck away that bit of paper. What are you really going to do?"

"But it was a lovely catechism," said Syme pathetically. "Do let me read it you. It has only forty-three questions and answers, and some of the Marquis's answers are wonderfully witty. I like to be just to my enemy."

"But what's the good of it all?" asked Dr. Bull in exasperation.

"It leads up to my challenge, don't you see," said Syme, beaming. "When the Marquis has given the thirty-ninth reply, which runs—"

"Has it by any chance occurred to you," asked the Professor, with a ponderous simplicity, "that the Marquis may not say all the forty-three things you have put down for him? In that case, I understand, your own epigrams may appear somewhat more forced."

Syme struck the table with a radiant face.

"Why, how true that is," he said, "and I never thought of it. Sir, you have an intellect beyond the common. You will make a name."

"Oh, you're as drunk as an owl!" said the Doctor.

"It only remains," continued Syme quite unperturbed, "to adopt some other method of breaking the ice (if I may so express it) between myself and the man I wish to kill. And since the course of a dialogue cannot be predicted by one of its parties alone (as you have pointed out with such recondite acumen), the only thing to be done, I suppose, is for the one party, as far as possible, to do all the dialogue by himself. And so I will, by George!" And he stood up suddenly, his yellow hair blowing in the slight sea breeze.

A band was playing in a cafe chantant hidden somewhere among the trees, and a woman had just stopped singing. On Syme's heated head the bray of the brass band seemed like the jar and jingle of that barrel-organ in Leicester Square, to the tune of which he had once stood up to die. He looked across to the little table where the Marquis sat. The man had two companions now, solemn Frenchmen in frock-coats and silk hats, one of them with the red rosette of the Legion of Honour, evidently people of a solid social position. Besides these black, cylindrical costumes, the Marquis, in his loose straw hat and light spring clothes, looked Bohemian and even barbaric; but he looked the Marquis. Indeed, one might say that he looked the king, with his animal elegance, his scornful eyes, and his proud head lifted against the purple sea. But he was no Christian king, at any rate; he was, rather, some swarthy despot, half Greek, half Asiatic, who in the days when slavery seemed natural looked down on the Mediterranean, on his galley and his groaning slaves. Just so, Syme thought, would the brown-gold face of such a tyrant have shown against the dark green olives and the burning blue.

"Are you going to address the meeting?" asked the Professor peevishly, seeing that Syme still stood up without moving.

Syme drained his last glass of sparkling wine.

"I am," he said, pointing across to the Marquis and his companions, "that meeting. That meeting displeases me. I am going to pull that meeting's great ugly, mahogany-coloured nose."

He stepped across swiftly, if not quite steadily. The Marquis, seeing him, arched his black Assyrian eyebrows in surprise, but smiled politely.

"You are Mr. Syme, I think," he said.

Syme bowed.

"And you are the Marquis de Saint Eustache," he said gracefully. "Permit me to pull your nose."

He leant over to do so, but the Marquis started backwards, upsetting his chair, and the two men in top hats held Syme back by the shoulders.

"This man has insulted me!" said Syme, with gestures of explanation.

"Insulted you?" cried the gentleman with the red rosette, "when?"

"Oh, just now," said Syme recklessly. "He insulted my mother."

"Insulted your mother!" exclaimed the gentleman incredulously.

"Well, anyhow," said Syme, conceding a point, "my aunt."

"But how can the Marquis have insulted your aunt just now?" said the second gentleman with some legitimate wonder. "He has been sitting here all the time."

"Ah, it was what he said!" said Syme darkly.

"I said nothing at all," said the Marquis, "except something about the band. I only said that I liked Wagner played well."

"It was an allusion to my family," said Syme firmly. "My aunt played Wagner badly. It was a painful subject. We are always being insulted about it."

"This seems most extraordinary," said the gentleman who was decore, looking doubtfully at the Marquis.

"Oh, I assure you," said Syme earnestly, "the whole of your conversation was simply packed with sinister allusions to my aunt's weaknesses."

"This is nonsense!" said the second gentleman. "I for one have said nothing for half an hour except that I liked the singing of that girl with black hair."

"Well, there you are again!" said Syme indignantly. "My aunt's was red."

"It seems to me," said the other, "that you are simply seeking a pretext to insult the Marquis."

"By George!" said Syme, facing round and looking at him, "what a clever chap you are!"

The Marquis started up with eyes flaming like a tiger's.

"Seeking a quarrel with me!" he cried. "Seeking a fight with me! By God! there was never a man who had to seek long. These gentlemen will perhaps act for me. There are still four hours of daylight. Let us fight this evening."

Syme bowed with a quite beautiful graciousness.

"Marquis," he said, "your action is worthy of your fame and blood. Permit me to consult for a moment with the gentlemen in whose hands I shall place myself."

In three long strides he rejoined his companions, and they, who had seen his champagne-inspired attack and listened to his idiotic explanations, were quite startled at the look of him. For now that he came back to them he was quite sober, a little pale, and he spoke in a low voice of passionate practicality.

"I have done it," he said hoarsely. "I have fixed a fight on the beast. But look here, and listen carefully. There is no time for talk. You are my seconds, and everything must come from you. Now you must insist, and insist absolutely, on the duel coming off after seven tomorrow, so as to give me the chance of preventing him from catching the 7.45 for Paris. If he misses that he misses his crime. He can't refuse to meet you on such a small point of time and place. But this is what he will do. He will choose a field somewhere near a wayside station, where he can pick up the train. He is a very good swordsman, and he will trust to killing me in time to catch it. But I can fence well too, and I think I can keep him in play, at any rate, until the train is lost. Then perhaps he may kill me to console his feelings. You understand? Very well then, let me introduce you to some charming friends of mine," and leading them quickly across the parade, he presented them to the Marquis's seconds by two very aristocratic names of which they had not previously heard.

Syme was subject to spasms of singular common sense, not otherwise a part of his character. They were (as he said of his impulse about the spectacles) poetic intuitions, and they sometimes rose to the exaltation of prophecy.

He had correctly calculated in this case the policy of his opponent. When the Marquis was informed by his seconds that Syme could only fight in the morning, he must fully have realised that an obstacle had suddenly arisen between him and his bomb-throwing business in the capital. Naturally he could not explain this objection to his friends, so he chose the course which Syme had predicted. He induced his seconds to settle on a small meadow not far from the railway, and he trusted to the fatality of the first engagement.

When he came down very coolly to the field of honour, no one could have guessed that he had any anxiety about a journey; his hands were in his pockets, his straw hat on the back of his head, his handsome face brazen in the sun. But it might have struck a stranger as odd that there appeared in his train, not only his seconds carrying the sword-case, but two of his servants carrying a portmanteau and a luncheon basket.

Early as was the hour, the sun soaked everything in warmth, and Syme was vaguely surprised to see so many spring flowers burning gold and silver in the tall grass in which the whole company stood almost knee-deep.

With the exception of the Marquis, all the men were in sombre and solemn morning-dress, with hats like black chimney-pots; the little Doctor especially, with the addition of his black spectacles, looked like an undertaker in a farce. Syme could not help feeling a comic contrast between this funereal church parade of apparel and the rich and glistening meadow, growing wild flowers everywhere. But, indeed, this comic contrast between the yellow blossoms and the black hats was but a symbol of the tragic contrast between the yellow blossoms and the black business. On his right was a little wood; far away to his left lay the long curve of the railway line, which he was, so to speak, guarding from the Marquis, whose goal and escape it was. In front of him, behind the black group of his opponents, he could see, like a tinted cloud, a small almond bush in flower against the faint line of the sea.

The member of the Legion of Honour, whose name it seemed was Colonel Ducroix, approached the Professor and Dr. Bull with great politeness, and suggested that the play should terminate with the first considerable hurt.

Dr. Bull, however, having been carefully coached by Syme upon this point of policy, insisted, with great dignity and in very bad French, that it should continue until one of the combatants was disabled. Syme had made up his mind that he could avoid disabling the Marquis and prevent the Marquis from disabling him for at least twenty minutes. In twenty minutes the Paris train would have gone by.

"To a man of the well-known skill and valour of Monsieur de St. Eustache," said the Professor solemnly, "it must be a matter of indifference which method is adopted, and our principal has strong reasons for demanding the longer encounter, reasons the delicacy of which prevent me from being explicit, but for the just and honourable nature of which I can—"

"Peste!" broke from the Marquis behind, whose face had suddenly darkened, "let us stop talking and begin," and he slashed off the head of a tall flower with his stick.

Syme understood his rude impatience and instinctively looked over his shoulder to see whether the train was coming in sight. But there was no smoke on the horizon.

Colonel Ducroix knelt down and unlocked the case, taking out a pair of twin swords, which took the sunlight and turned to two streaks of white fire. He offered one to the Marquis, who snatched it without ceremony, and another to Syme, who took it, bent it, and poised it with as much delay as was consistent with dignity.

Then the Colonel took out another pair of blades, and taking one himself and giving another to Dr. Bull, proceeded to place the men.

Both combatants had thrown off their coats and waistcoats, and stood sword in hand. The seconds stood on each side of the line of fight with drawn swords also, but still sombre in their dark frock-coats and hats. The principals saluted. The Colonel said quietly, "Engage!" and the two blades touched and tingled.

When the jar of the joined iron ran up Syme's arm, all the fantastic fears that have been the subject of this story fell from him like dreams from a man waking up in bed. He remembered them clearly and in order as mere delusions of the nerves—how the fear of the Professor had been the fear of the tyrannic accidents of nightmare, and how the fear of the Doctor had been the fear of the airless vacuum of science. The first was the old fear that any miracle might happen, the second the more hopeless modern fear that no miracle can ever happen. But he saw that these fears were fancies, for he found himself in the presence of the great fact of the fear of death, with its coarse and pitiless common sense. He felt like a man who had dreamed all night of falling over precipices, and had woke up on the morning when he was to be hanged. For as soon as he had seen the sunlight run down the channel of his foe's foreshortened blade, and as soon as he had felt the two tongues of steel touch, vibrating like two living things, he knew that his enemy was a terrible fighter, and that probably his last hour had come.

He felt a strange and vivid value in all the earth around him, in the grass under his feet; he felt the love of life in all living things. He could almost fancy that he heard the grass growing; he could almost fancy that even as he stood fresh flowers were springing up and breaking into blossom in the meadow—flowers blood red and burning gold and blue, fulfilling the whole pageant of the spring. And whenever his eyes strayed for a flash from the calm, staring, hypnotic eyes of the Marquis, they saw the little tuft of almond tree against the sky-line. He had the feeling that if by some miracle he escaped he would be ready to sit for ever before that almond tree, desiring nothing else in the world.

But while earth and sky and everything had the living beauty of a thing lost, the other half of his head was as clear as glass, and he was parrying his enemy's point with a kind of clockwork skill of which he had hardly supposed himself capable. Once his enemy's point ran along his wrist, leaving a slight streak of blood, but it either was not noticed or was tacitly ignored. Every now and then he riposted, and once or twice he could almost fancy that he felt his point go home, but as there was no blood on blade or shirt he supposed he was mistaken. Then came an interruption and a change.

At the risk of losing all, the Marquis, interrupting his quiet stare, flashed one glance over his shoulder at the line of railway on his right. Then he turned on Syme a face transfigured to that of a fiend, and began to fight as if with twenty weapons. The attack came so fast and furious, that the one shining sword seemed a shower of shining arrows. Syme had no chance to look at the railway; but also he had no need. He could guess the reason of the Marquis's sudden madness of battle—the Paris train was in sight.

But the Marquis's morbid energy over-reached itself. Twice Syme, parrying, knocked his opponent's point far out of the fighting circle; and the third time his riposte was so rapid, that there was no doubt about the hit this time. Syme's sword actually bent under the weight of the Marquis's body, which it had pierced.

Syme was as certain that he had stuck his blade into his enemy as a gardener that he has stuck his spade into the ground. Yet the Marquis sprang back from the stroke without a stagger, and Syme stood staring at his own sword-point like an idiot. There was no blood on it at all.

There was an instant of rigid silence, and then Syme in his turn fell furiously on the other, filled with a flaming curiosity. The Marquis was probably, in a general sense, a better fencer than he, as he had surmised at the beginning, but at the moment the Marquis seemed distraught and at a disadvantage. He fought wildly and even weakly, and he constantly looked away at the railway line, almost as if he feared the train more than the pointed steel. Syme, on the other hand, fought fiercely but still carefully, in an intellectual fury, eager to solve the riddle of his own bloodless sword. For this purpose, he aimed less at the Marquis's body, and more at his throat and head. A minute and a half afterwards he felt his point enter the man's neck below the jaw. It came out clean. Half mad, he thrust again, and made what should have been a bloody scar on the Marquis's cheek. But there was no scar.

For one moment the heaven of Syme again grew black with supernatural terrors. Surely the man had a charmed life. But this new spiritual dread was a more awful thing than had been the mere spiritual topsy-turvydom symbolised by the paralytic who pursued him. The Professor was only a goblin; this man was a devil—perhaps he was the Devil! Anyhow, this was certain, that three times had a human sword been driven into him and made no mark. When Syme had that thought he drew himself up, and all that was good in him sang high up in the air as a high wind sings in the trees. He thought of all the human things in his story—of the Chinese lanterns in Saffron Park, of the girl's red hair in the garden, of the honest, beer-swilling sailors down by the dock, of his loyal companions standing by. Perhaps he had been chosen as a champion of all these fresh and kindly things to cross swords with the enemy of all creation. "After all," he said to himself, "I am more than a devil; I am a man. I can do the one thing which Satan himself cannot do—I can die," and as the word went through his head, he heard a faint and far-off hoot, which would soon be the roar of the Paris train.

He fell to fighting again with a supernatural levity, like a Mohammedan panting for Paradise. As the train came nearer and nearer he fancied he could see people putting up the floral arches in Paris; he joined in the growing noise and the glory of the great Republic whose gate he was guarding against Hell. His thoughts rose higher and higher with the rising roar of the train, which ended, as if proudly, in a long and piercing whistle. The train stopped.

Suddenly, to the astonishment of everyone the Marquis sprang back quite out of sword reach and threw down his sword. The leap was wonderful, and not the less wonderful because Syme had plunged his sword a moment before into the man's thigh.

"Stop!" said the Marquis in a voice that compelled a momentary obedience. "I want to say something."

"What is the matter?" asked Colonel Ducroix, staring. "Has there been foul play?"

"There has been foul play somewhere," said Dr. Bull, who was a little pale. "Our principal has wounded the Marquis four times at least, and he is none the worse."

The Marquis put up his hand with a curious air of ghastly patience.

"Please let me speak," he said. "It is rather important. Mr. Syme," he continued, turning to his opponent, "we are fighting today, if I remember right, because you expressed a wish (which I thought irrational) to pull my nose. Would you oblige me by pulling my nose now as quickly as possible? I have to catch a train."

"I protest that this is most irregular," said Dr. Bull indignantly.

"It is certainly somewhat opposed to precedent," said Colonel Ducroix, looking wistfully at his principal. "There is, I think, one case on record (Captain Bellegarde and the Baron Zumpt) in which the weapons were changed in the middle of the encounter at the request of one of the combatants. But one can hardly call one's nose a weapon."

"Will you or will you not pull my nose?" said the Marquis in exasperation. "Come, come, Mr. Syme! You wanted to do it, do it! You can have no conception of how important it is to me. Don't be so selfish! Pull my nose at once, when I ask you!" and he bent slightly forward with a fascinating smile. The Paris train, panting and groaning, had grated into a little station behind the neighbouring hill.

Syme had the feeling he had more than once had in these adventures—the sense that a horrible and sublime wave lifted to heaven was just toppling over. Walking in a world he half understood, he took two paces forward and seized the Roman nose of this remarkable nobleman. He pulled it hard, and it came off in his hand.

He stood for some seconds with a foolish solemnity, with the pasteboard proboscis still between his fingers, looking at it, while the sun and the clouds and the wooded hills looked down upon this imbecile scene.

The Marquis broke the silence in a loud and cheerful voice.

"If anyone has any use for my left eyebrow," he said, "he can have it. Colonel Ducroix, do accept my left eyebrow! It's the kind of thing that might come in useful any day," and he gravely tore off one of his swarthy Assyrian brows, bringing about half his brown forehead with it, and politely offered it to the Colonel, who stood crimson and speechless with rage.

"If I had known," he spluttered, "that I was acting for a poltroon who pads himself to fight—"

"Oh, I know, I know!" said the Marquis, recklessly throwing various parts of himself right and left about the field. "You are making a mistake; but it can't be explained just now. I tell you the train has come into the station!"

"Yes," said Dr. Bull fiercely, "and the train shall go out of the station. It shall go out without you. We know well enough for what devil's work—"

The mysterious Marquis lifted his hands with a desperate gesture. He was a strange scarecrow standing there in the sun with half his old face peeled off, and half another face glaring and grinning from underneath.

"Will you drive me mad?" he cried. "The train—"

"You shall not go by the train," said Syme firmly, and grasped his sword.

The wild figure turned towards Syme, and seemed to be gathering itself for a sublime effort before speaking.

"You great fat, blasted, blear-eyed, blundering, thundering, brainless, Godforsaken, doddering, damned fool!" he said without taking breath. "You great silly, pink-faced, towheaded turnip! You—"

"You shall not go by this train," repeated Syme.

"And why the infernal blazes," roared the other, "should I want to go by the train?"

"We know all," said the Professor sternly. "You are going to Paris to throw a bomb!"

"Going to Jericho to throw a Jabberwock!" cried the other, tearing his hair, which came off easily.

"Have you all got softening of the brain, that you don't realise what I am? Did you really think I wanted to catch that train? Twenty Paris trains might go by for me. Damn Paris trains!"

"Then what did you care about?" began the Professor.

"What did I care about? I didn't care about catching the train; I cared about whether the train caught me, and now, by God! it has caught me."

"I regret to inform you," said Syme with restraint, "that your remarks convey no impression to my mind. Perhaps if you were to remove the remains of your original forehead and some portion of what was once your chin, your meaning would become clearer. Mental lucidity fulfils itself in many ways. What do you mean by saying that the train has caught you? It may be my literary fancy, but somehow I feel that it ought to mean something."

"It means everything," said the other, "and the end of everything. Sunday has us now in the hollow of his hand."

"Us!" repeated the Professor, as if stupefied. "What do you mean by 'us'?"

"The police, of course!" said the Marquis, and tore off his scalp and half his face.

The head which emerged was the blonde, well brushed, smooth-haired head which is common in the English constabulary, but the face was terribly pale.

"I am Inspector Ratcliffe," he said, with a sort of haste that verged on harshness. "My name is pretty well known to the police, and I can see well enough that you belong to them. But if there is any doubt about my position, I have a card," and he began to pull a blue card from his pocket.

The Professor gave a tired gesture.

"Oh, don't show it us," he said wearily; "we've got enough of them to equip a paper-chase."

The little man named Bull, had, like many men who seem to be of a mere vivacious vulgarity, sudden movements of good taste. Here he certainly saved the situation. In the midst of this staggering transformation scene he stepped forward with all the gravity and responsibility of a second, and addressed the two seconds of the Marquis.

"Gentlemen," he said, "we all owe you a serious apology; but I assure you that you have not been made the victims of such a low joke as you imagine, or indeed of anything undignified in a man of honour. You have not wasted your time; you have helped to save the world. We are not buffoons, but very desperate men at war with a vast conspiracy. A secret society of anarchists is hunting us like hares; not such unfortunate madmen as may here or there throw a bomb through starvation or German philosophy, but a rich and powerful and fanatical church, a church of eastern pessimism, which holds it holy to destroy mankind like vermin. How hard they hunt us you can gather from the fact that we are driven to such disguises as those for which I apologise, and to such pranks as this one by which you suffer."

The younger second of the Marquis, a short man with a black moustache, bowed politely, and said—

"Of course, I accept the apology; but you will in your turn forgive me if I decline to follow you further into your difficulties, and permit myself to say good morning! The sight of an acquaintance and distinguished fellow-townsman coming to pieces in the open air is unusual, and, upon the whole, sufficient for one day. Colonel Ducroix, I would in no way influence your actions, but if you feel with me that our present society is a little abnormal, I am now going to walk back to the town."

Colonel Ducroix moved mechanically, but then tugged abruptly at his white moustache and broke out—

"No, by George! I won't. If these gentlemen are really in a mess with a lot of low wreckers like that, I'll see them through it. I have fought for France, and it is hard if I can't fight for civilization."

Dr. Bull took off his hat and waved it, cheering as at a public meeting.

"Don't make too much noise," said Inspector Ratcliffe, "Sunday may hear you."

"Sunday!" cried Bull, and dropped his hat.

"Yes," retorted Ratcliffe, "he may be with them."

"With whom?" asked Syme.

"With the people out of that train," said the other.

"What you say seems utterly wild," began Syme. "Why, as a matter of fact—But, my God," he cried out suddenly, like a man who sees an explosion a long way off, "by God! if this is true the whole bally lot of us on the Anarchist Council were against anarchy! Every born man was a detective except the President and his personal secretary. What can it mean?"

"Mean!" said the new policeman with incredible violence. "It means that we are struck dead! Don't you know Sunday? Don't you know that his jokes are always so big and simple that one has never thought of them? Can you think of anything more like Sunday than this, that he should put all his powerful enemies on the Supreme Council, and then take care that it was not supreme? I tell you he has bought every trust, he has captured every cable, he has control of every railway line—especially of that railway line!" and he pointed a shaking finger towards the small wayside station. "The whole movement was controlled by him; half the world was ready to rise for him. But there were just five people, perhaps, who would have resisted him... and the old devil put them on the Supreme Council, to waste their time in watching each other. Idiots that we are, he planned the whole of our idiocies! Sunday knew that the Professor would chase Syme through London, and that Syme would fight me in France. And he was combining great masses of capital, and seizing great lines of telegraphy, while we five idiots were running after each other like a lot of confounded babies playing blind man's buff."

"Well?" asked Syme with a sort of steadiness.

"Well," replied the other with sudden serenity, "he has found us playing blind man's buff today in a field of great rustic beauty and extreme solitude. He has probably captured the world; it only remains to him to capture this field and all the fools in it. And since you really want to know what was my objection to the arrival of that train, I will tell you. My objection was that Sunday or his Secretary has just this moment got out of it."

Syme uttered an involuntary cry, and they all turned their eyes towards the far-off station. It was quite true that a considerable bulk of people seemed to be moving in their direction. But they were too distant to be distinguished in any way.

"It was a habit of the late Marquis de St. Eustache," said the new policeman, producing a leather case, "always to carry a pair of opera glasses. Either the President or the Secretary is coming after us with that mob. They have caught us in a nice quiet place where we are under no temptations to break our oaths by calling the police. Dr. Bull, I have a suspicion that you will see better through these than through your own highly decorative spectacles."

He handed the field-glasses to the Doctor, who immediately took off his spectacles and put the apparatus to his eyes.

"It cannot be as bad as you say," said the Professor, somewhat shaken. "There are a good number of them certainly, but they may easily be ordinary tourists."

"Do ordinary tourists," asked Bull, with the fieldglasses to his eyes, "wear black masks half-way down the face?"

Syme almost tore the glasses out of his hand, and looked through them. Most men in the advancing mob really looked ordinary enough; but it was quite true that two or three of the leaders in front wore black half-masks almost down to their mouths. This disguise is very complete, especially at such a distance, and Syme found it impossible to conclude anything from the clean-shaven jaws and chins of the men talking in the front. But presently as they talked they all smiled and one of them smiled on one side.

11. THE CRIMINALS CHASE THE POLICE

SYME put the field-glasses from his eyes with an almost ghastly relief.

"The President is not with them, anyhow," he said, and wiped his forehead.

"But surely they are right away on the horizon," said the bewildered Colonel, blinking and but half recovered from Bull's hasty though polite explanation. "Could you possibly know your President among all those people?"

"Could I know a white elephant among all those people!" answered Syme somewhat irritably. "As you very truly say, they are on the horizon; but if he were walking with them... by God! I believe this ground would shake."

After an instant's pause the new man called Ratcliffe said with gloomy decision—

"Of course the President isn't with them. I wish to Gemini he were. Much more likely the President is riding in triumph through Paris, or sitting on the ruins of St. Paul's Cathedral."

"This is absurd!" said Syme. "Something may have happened in our absence; but he cannot have carried the world with a rush like that. It is quite true," he added, frowning dubiously at the distant fields that lay towards the little station, "it is certainly true that there seems to be a crowd coming this way; but they are not all the army that you make out."

"Oh, they," said the new detective contemptuously; "no they are not a very valuable force. But let me tell you frankly that they are precisely calculated to our value—we are not much, my boy, in Sunday's universe. He has got hold of all the cables and telegraphs himself. But to kill the Supreme Council he regards as a trivial matter, like a post card; it may be left to his private secretary," and he spat on the grass.

Then he turned to the others and said somewhat austerely—

"There is a great deal to be said for death; but if anyone has any preference for the other alternative, I strongly advise him to walk after me."

With these words, he turned his broad back and strode with silent energy towards the wood. The others gave one glance over their shoulders, and saw that the dark cloud of men had detached itself from the station and was moving with a mysterious discipline across the plain. They saw already, even with the naked eye, black blots on the foremost faces, which marked the masks they wore. They turned and followed their leader, who had already struck the wood, and disappeared among the twinkling trees.

The sun on the grass was dry and hot. So in plunging into the wood they had a cool shock of shadow, as of divers who plunge into a dim pool. The inside of the wood was full of shattered sunlight and shaken shadows. They made a sort of shuddering veil, almost recalling the dizziness of a cinematograph. Even the solid figures walking with him Syme could hardly see for the patterns of sun and shade that danced upon them. Now a man's head was lit as with a light of Rembrandt, leaving all else obliterated; now again he had strong and staring white hands with the face of a negro. The ex-Marquis had pulled the old straw hat over his eyes, and the black shade of the brim cut his face so squarely in two that it seemed to be wearing one of the black half-masks of their pursuers. The fancy tinted Syme's overwhelming sense of wonder. Was he wearing a mask? Was anyone wearing a mask? Was anyone anything? This wood of witchery, in which men's faces turned black and white by turns, in which their figures first swelled into sunlight and then faded into formless night, this mere chaos of chiaroscuro (after the clear daylight outside), seemed to Syme a perfect symbol of the world in which he had been moving for three days, this world where men took off their beards and their spectacles and their noses, and turned into other people. That tragic self-confidence which he had felt when he believed that the Marquis was a devil had strangely disappeared now that he knew that the Marquis was a friend. He felt almost inclined to ask after all these bewilderments what was a friend and what an enemy. Was there anything that was apart from what it seemed? The Marquis had taken off his nose and turned out to be a detective. Might he not just as well take off his head and turn out to be a hobgoblin? Was not everything, after all, like this bewildering woodland, this dance of dark and light? Everything only a glimpse, the glimpse always unforeseen, and always forgotten. For Gabriel Syme had found in the heart of that sun-splashed wood what many modern painters had found there. He had found the thing which the modern people call Impressionism, which is another name for that final scepticism which can find no floor to the universe.

As a man in an evil dream strains himself to scream and wake, Syme strove with a sudden effort to fling off this last and worst of his fancies. With two impatient strides he overtook the man in the Marquis's straw hat, the man whom he had come to address as Ratcliffe. In a voice exaggeratively loud and cheerful, he broke the bottomless silence and made conversation.

"May I ask," he said, "where on earth we are all going to?"

So genuine had been the doubts of his soul, that he was quite glad to hear his companion speak in an easy, human voice.

"We must get down through the town of Lancy to the sea," he said. "I think that part of the country is least likely to be with them."

"What can you mean by all this?" cried Syme. "They can't be running the real world in that way. Surely not many working men are anarchists, and surely if they were, mere mobs could not beat modern armies and police."

"Mere mobs!" repeated his new friend with a snort of scorn. "So you talk about mobs and the working classes as if they were the question. You've got that eternal idiotic idea that if anarchy came it would come from the poor. Why should it? The poor have been rebels, but they have never been anarchists; they have more interest than anyone else in there being some decent government. The poor man really has a stake in the country. The rich man hasn't; he can go away to New Guinea in a yacht. The poor have sometimes objected to being governed badly; the rich have always objected to being governed at all. Aristocrats were always anarchists, as you can see from the barons' wars."

"As a lecture on English history for the little ones," said Syme, "this is all very nice; but I have not yet grasped its application."

"Its application is," said his informant, "that most of old Sunday's right-hand men are South African and American millionaires. That is why he has got hold of all the communications; and that is why the last four champions of the anti-anarchist police force are running through a wood like rabbits."

"Millionaires I can understand," said Syme thoughtfully, "they are nearly all mad. But getting hold of a few wicked old gentlemen with hobbies is one thing; getting hold of great Christian nations is another. I would bet the nose off my face (forgive the allusion) that Sunday would stand perfectly helpless before the task of converting any ordinary healthy person anywhere."

"Well," said the other, "it rather depends what sort of person you mean."

"Well, for instance," said Syme, "he could never convert that person," and he pointed straight in front of him.

They had come to an open space of sunlight, which seemed to express to Syme the final return of his own good sense; and in the middle of this forest clearing was a figure that might well stand for that common sense in an almost awful actuality. Burnt by the sun and stained with perspiration, and grave with the bottomless gravity of small necessary toils, a heavy French peasant was cutting wood with a hatchet. His cart stood a few yards off, already half full of timber; and the horse that cropped the grass was, like his master, valorous but not desperate; like his master, he was even prosperous, but yet was almost sad. The man was a Norman, taller than the average of the French and very angular; and his swarthy figure stood dark against a square of sunlight, almost like some allegoric figure of labour frescoed on a ground of gold.

"Mr. Syme is saying," called out Ratcliffe to the French Colonel, "that this man, at least, will never be an anarchist."

"Mr. Syme is right enough there," answered Colonel Ducroix, laughing, "if only for the reason that he has plenty of property to defend. But I forgot that in your country you are not used to peasants being wealthy."

"He looks poor," said Dr. Bull doubtfully.

"Quite so," said the Colonel; "that is why he is rich."

"I have an idea," called out Dr. Bull suddenly; "how much would he take to give us a lift in his cart? Those dogs are all on foot, and we could soon leave them behind."

"Oh, give him anything!" said Syme eagerly. "I have piles of money on me."

"That will never do," said the Colonel; "he will never have any respect for you unless you drive a bargain."

"Oh, if he haggles!" began Bull impatiently.

"He haggles because he is a free man," said the other. "You do not understand; he would not see the meaning of generosity. He is not being tipped."

And even while they seemed to hear the heavy feet of their strange pursuers behind them, they had to stand and stamp while the French Colonel talked to the French wood-cutter with all the leisurely badinage and bickering of market-day. At the end of the four minutes, however, they saw that the Colonel was right, for the wood-cutter entered into their plans, not with the vague servility of a tout too-well paid, but with the seriousness of a solicitor who had been paid the proper fee. He told them that the best thing they could do was to make their way down to the little inn on the hills above Lancy, where the innkeeper, an old soldier who had become devout in his latter years, would be certain to sympathise with them, and even to take risks in their support. The whole company, therefore, piled themselves on top of the stacks of wood, and went rocking in the rude cart down the other and steeper side of the woodland. Heavy and ramshackle as was the vehicle, it was driven quickly enough, and they soon had the exhilarating impression of distancing altogether those, whoever they were, who were hunting them. For, after all, the riddle as to where the anarchists had got all these followers was still unsolved. One man's presence had sufficed for them; they had fled at the first sight of the deformed smile of the Secretary. Syme every now and then looked back over his shoulder at the army on their track.

As the wood grew first thinner and then smaller with distance, he could see the sunlit slopes beyond it and above it; and across these was still moving the square black mob like one monstrous beetle. In the very strong sunlight and with his own very strong eyes, which were almost telescopic, Syme could see this mass of men quite plainly. He could see them as separate human figures; but he was increasingly surprised by the way in which they moved as one man. They seemed to be dressed in dark clothes and plain hats, like any common crowd out of the streets; but they did not spread and sprawl and trail by various lines to the attack, as would be natural in an ordinary mob. They moved with a sort of dreadful and wicked woodenness, like a staring army of automatons.

Syme pointed this out to Ratcliffe.

"Yes," replied the policeman, "that's discipline. That's Sunday. He is perhaps five hundred miles off, but the fear of him is on all of them, like the finger of God. Yes, they are walking regularly; and you bet your boots that they are talking regularly, yes, and thinking regularly. But the one important thing for us is that they are disappearing regularly."

Syme nodded. It was true that the black patch of the pursuing men was growing smaller and smaller as the peasant belaboured his horse.

The level of the sunlit landscape, though flat as a whole, fell away on the farther side of the wood in billows of heavy slope towards the sea, in a way not unlike the lower slopes of the Sussex downs. The only difference was that in Sussex the road would have been broken and angular like a little brook, but here the white French road fell sheer in front of them like a waterfall. Down this direct descent the cart clattered at a considerable angle, and in a few minutes, the road growing yet steeper, they saw below them the little harbour of Lancy and a great blue arc of the sea. The travelling cloud of their enemies had wholly disappeared from the horizon.

The horse and cart took a sharp turn round a clump of elms, and the horse's nose nearly struck the face of an old gentleman who was sitting on the benches outside the little cafe of "Le Soleil d'Or." The peasant grunted an apology, and got down from his seat. The others also descended one by one, and spoke to the old gentleman with fragmentary phrases of courtesy, for it was quite evident from his expansive manner that he was the owner of the little tavern.

He was a white-haired, apple-faced old boy, with sleepy eyes and a grey moustache; stout, sedentary, and very innocent, of a type that may often be found in France, but is still commoner in Catholic Germany. Everything about him, his pipe, his pot of beer, his flowers, and his beehive, suggested an ancestral peace; only when his visitors looked up as they entered the inn-parlour, they saw the sword upon the wall.

The Colonel, who greeted the innkeeper as an old friend, passed rapidly into the inn-parlour, and sat down ordering some ritual refreshment. The military decision of his action interested Syme, who sat next to him, and he took the opportunity when the old innkeeper had gone out of satisfying his curiosity.

"May I ask you, Colonel," he said in a low voice, "why we have come here?"

Colonel Ducroix smiled behind his bristly white moustache.

"For two reasons, sir," he said; "and I will give first, not the most important, but the most utilitarian. We came here because this is the only place within twenty miles in which we can get horses."

"Horses!" repeated Syme, looking up quickly.

"Yes," replied the other; "if you people are really to distance your enemies it is horses or nothing for you, unless of course you have bicycles and motor-cars in your pocket."

"And where do you advise us to make for?" asked Syme doubtfully.

"Beyond question," replied the Colonel, "you had better make all haste to the police station beyond the town. My friend, whom I seconded under somewhat deceptive circumstances, seems to me to exaggerate very much the possibilities of a general rising; but even he would hardly maintain, I suppose, that you were not safe with the gendarmes."

Syme nodded gravely; then he said abruptly—

"And your other reason for coming here?"

"My other reason for coming here," said Ducroix soberly, "is that it is just as well to see a good man or two when one is possibly near to death."

Syme looked up at the wall, and saw a crudely-painted and pathetic religious picture. Then he said—

"You are right," and then almost immediately afterwards, "Has anyone seen about the horses?"

"Yes," answered Ducroix, "you may be quite certain that I gave orders the moment I came in. Those enemies of yours gave no impression of hurry, but they were really moving wonderfully fast, like a well-trained army. I had no idea that the anarchists had so much discipline. You have not a moment to waste."

Almost as he spoke, the old innkeeper with the blue eyes and white hair came ambling into the room, and announced that six horses were saddled outside.

By Ducroix's advice the five others equipped themselves with some portable form of food and wine, and keeping their duelling swords as the only weapons available, they clattered away down the steep, white road. The two servants, who had carried the

Marquis's luggage when he was a marquis, were left behind to drink at the cafe by common consent, and not at all against their own inclination.

By this time the afternoon sun was slanting westward, and by its rays Syme could see the sturdy figure of the old innkeeper growing smaller and smaller, but still standing and looking after them quite silently, the sunshine in his silver hair. Syme had a fixed, superstitious fancy, left in his mind by the chance phrase of the Colonel, that this was indeed, perhaps, the last honest stranger whom he should ever see upon the earth.

He was still looking at this dwindling figure, which stood as a mere grey blot touched with a white flame against the great green wall of the steep down behind him. And as he stared over the top of the down behind the innkeeper, there appeared an army of black-clad and marching men. They seemed to hang above the good man and his house like a black cloud of locusts. The horses had been saddled none too soon.

12. THE EARTH IN ANARCHY

URGING the horses to a gallop, without respect to the rather rugged descent of the road, the horsemen soon regained their advantage over the men on the march, and at last the bulk of the first buildings of Lancy cut off the sight of their pursuers. Nevertheless, the ride had been a long one, and by the time they reached the real town the west was warming with the colour and quality of sunset. The Colonel suggested that, before making finally for the police station, they should make the effort, in passing, to attach to themselves one more individual who might be useful.

"Four out of the five rich men in this town," he said, "are common swindlers. I suppose the proportion is pretty equal all over the world. The fifth is a friend of mine, and a very fine fellow; and what is even more important from our point of view, he owns a motor-car."

"I am afraid," said the Professor in his mirthful way, looking back along the white road on which the black, crawling patch might appear at any moment, "I am afraid we have hardly time for afternoon calls."

"Doctor Renard's house is only three minutes off," said the Colonel.

"Our danger," said Dr. Bull, "is not two minutes off."

"Yes," said Syme, "if we ride on fast we must leave them behind, for they are on foot."

"He has a motor-car," said the Colonel.

"But we may not get it," said Bull.

"Yes, he is quite on your side."

"But he might be out."

"Hold your tongue," said Syme suddenly. "What is that noise?"

For a second they all sat as still as equestrian statues, and for a second—for two or three or four seconds—heaven and earth seemed equally still. Then all their ears, in an agony of attention, heard along the road that indescribable thrill and throb that means only one thing—horses!

The Colonel's face had an instantaneous change, as if lightning had struck it, and yet left it scatheless.

"They have done us," he said, with brief military irony. "Prepare to receive cavalry!"

"Where can they have got the horses?" asked Syme, as he mechanically urged his steed to a canter.

The Colonel was silent for a little, then he said in a strained voice—

"I was speaking with strict accuracy when I said that the 'Soleil d'Or' was the only place where one can get horses within twenty miles."

"No!" said Syme violently, "I don't believe he'd do it. Not with all that white hair."

"He may have been forced," said the Colonel gently. "They must be at least a hundred strong, for which reason we are all going to see my friend Renard, who has a motor-car."

With these words he swung his horse suddenly round a street corner, and went down the street with such thundering speed, that the others, though already well at the gallop, had difficulty in following the flying tail of his horse.

Dr. Renard inhabited a high and comfortable house at the top of a steep street, so that when the riders alighted at his door they could once more see the solid green ridge of the hill, with the white road across it, standing up above all the roofs of the town. They breathed again to see that the road as yet was clear, and they rang the bell.

Dr. Renard was a beaming, brown-bearded man, a good example of that silent but very busy professional class which France has preserved even more perfectly than England. When the matter was explained to him he pooh-poohed the panic of the ex-Marquis altogether; he said, with the solid French scepticism, that there was no conceivable probability of a general anarchist rising. "Anarchy," he said, shrugging his shoulders, "it is childishness!"

"Et ca," cried out the Colonel suddenly, pointing over the other's shoulder, "and that is childishness, isn't it?"

They all looked round, and saw a curve of black cavalry come sweeping over the top of the hill with all the energy of Attila. Swiftly as they rode, however, the whole rank still kept well together, and they could see the black vizards of the first line as level as a line of uniforms. But although the main black square was the same, though travelling faster, there was now one sensational difference which they could see clearly upon the slope of the hill, as if upon a slanted map. The bulk of the riders were in one block; but one rider flew far ahead of the column, and with frantic movements of hand and heel urged his horse faster and faster, so that one might have fancied that he was not the pursuer but the pursued. But even at that great distance they could see something so fanatical, so unquestionable in his figure, that they knew it was the Secretary himself. "I am sorry to cut short a cultured discussion," said the Colonel, "but can you lend me your motor-car now, in two minutes?"

"I have a suspicion that you are all mad," said Dr. Renard, smiling sociably; "but God forbid that madness should in any way interrupt friendship. Let us go round to the garage."

Dr. Renard was a mild man with monstrous wealth; his rooms were like the Musee de Cluny, and he had three motor-cars. These, however, he seemed to use very sparingly, having the simple tastes of the French middle class, and when his impatient friends came to examine them, it took them some time to assure themselves that one of them even could be made to work. This with some difficulty they brought round into the street before the Doctor's house. When they came out of the dim garage they were startled to find that twilight had already fallen with the abruptness of night in the tropics. Either they had been longer in the place than they imagined, or some unusual canopy of cloud had gathered over the town. They looked down the steep streets, and seemed to see a slight mist coming up from the sea.

"It is now or never," said Dr. Bull. "I hear horses."

"No," corrected the Professor, "a horse."

And as they listened, it was evident that the noise, rapidly coming nearer on the rattling stones, was not the noise of the whole cavalcade but that of the one horseman, who had left it far behind—the insane Secretary.

Syme's family, like most of those who end in the simple life, had once owned a motor, and he knew all about them. He had leapt at once into the chauffeur's seat, and with flushed face was wrenching and tugging at the disused machinery. He bent his strength upon one handle, and then said quite quietly—

"I am afraid it's no go."

As he spoke, there swept round the corner a man rigid on his rushing horse, with the rush and rigidity of an arrow. He had a smile that thrust out his chin as if it were dislocated. He swept alongside of the stationary car, into which its company had crowded, and laid his hand on the front. It was the Secretary, and his mouth went quite straight in the solemnity of triumph.

Syme was leaning hard upon the steering wheel, and there was no sound but the rumble of the other pursuers riding into the town. Then there came quite suddenly a scream of scraping iron, and the car leapt forward. It plucked the Secretary clean out of his saddle, as a knife is whipped out of its sheath, trailed him kicking terribly for twenty yards, and left him flung flat upon the road far in front of his frightened horse. As the car took the corner of the street with a splendid curve, they could just see the other anarchists filling the street and raising their fallen leader.

"I can't understand why it has grown so dark," said the Professor at last in a low voice.

"Going to be a storm, I think," said Dr. Bull. "I say, it's a pity we haven't got a light on this car, if only to see by."

"We have," said the Colonel, and from the floor of the car he fished up a heavy, old-fashioned, carved iron lantern with a light inside it. It was obviously an antique, and it would seem as if its original use had been in some way semi-religious, for there was a rude moulding of a cross upon one of its sides.

"Where on earth did you get that?" asked the Professor.

"I got it where I got the car," answered the Colonel, chuckling, "from my best friend. While our friend here was fighting with the steering wheel, I ran up the front steps of the house and spoke to Renard, who was standing in his own porch, you will remember. 'I suppose,' I said, 'there's no time to get a lamp.' He looked up, blinking amiably at the beautiful arched ceiling of his own front hall. From this was suspended, by chains of exquisite ironwork, this lantern, one of the hundred treasures of his treasure house. By sheer force he tore the lamp out of his own ceiling, shattering the painted panels, and bringing down two blue vases with his violence. Then he handed me the iron lantern, and I put it in the car. Was I not right when I said that Dr. Renard was worth knowing?"

"You were," said Syme seriously, and hung the heavy lantern over the front. There was a certain allegory of their whole position in the contrast between the modern automobile and its strange ecclesiastical lamp. Hitherto they had passed through the quietest part of the town, meeting at most one or two pedestrians, who could give them no hint of the peace or the hostility of the place. Now, however, the windows in the houses began one by one to be lit up, giving a greater sense of habitation and humanity. Dr. Bull turned to the new detective who had led their flight, and permitted himself one of his natural and friendly smiles.

"These lights make one feel more cheerful."

Inspector Ratcliffe drew his brows together.

"There is only one set of lights that make me more cheerful," he said, "and they are those lights of the police station which I can see beyond the town. Please God we may be there in ten minutes."

Then all Bull's boiling good sense and optimism broke suddenly out of him.

"Oh, this is all raving nonsense!" he cried. "If you really think that ordinary people in ordinary houses are anarchists, you must be madder than an anarchist yourself. If we turned and fought these fellows, the whole town would fight for us."

"No," said the other with an immovable simplicity, "the whole town would fight for them. We shall see."

While they were speaking the Professor had leant forward with sudden excitement.

"What is that noise?" he said.

"Oh, the horses behind us, I suppose," said the Colonel. "I thought we had got clear of them."

"The horses behind us! No," said the Professor, "it is not horses, and it is not behind us."

Almost as he spoke, across the end of the street before them two shining and rattling shapes shot past. They were gone almost in a flash, but everyone could see that they were motor-cars, and the Professor stood up with a pale face and swore that they were the other two motor-cars from Dr. Renard's garage.

"I tell you they were his," he repeated, with wild eyes, "and they were full of men in masks!"

"Absurd!" said the Colonel angrily. "Dr. Renard would never give them his cars."

"He may have been forced," said Ratcliffe quietly. "The whole town is on their side."

"You still believe that," asked the Colonel incredulously.

"You will all believe it soon," said the other with a hopeless calm.

There was a puzzled pause for some little time, and then the Colonel began again abruptly—

"No, I can't believe it. The thing is nonsense. The plain people of a peaceable French town—"

He was cut short by a bang and a blaze of light, which seemed close to his eyes. As the car sped on it left a floating patch of white smoke behind it, and Syme had heard a shot shriek past his ear.

"My God!" said the Colonel, "someone has shot at us."

"It need not interrupt conversation," said the gloomy Ratcliffe. "Pray resume your remarks, Colonel. You were talking, I think, about the plain people of a peaceable French town."

The staring Colonel was long past minding satire. He rolled his eyes all round the street.

"It is extraordinary," he said, "most extraordinary."

"A fastidious person," said Syme, "might even call it unpleasant. However, I suppose those lights out in the field beyond this street are the Gendarmerie. We shall soon get there."

"No," said Inspector Ratcliffe, "we shall never get there."

He had been standing up and looking keenly ahead of him. Now he sat down and smoothed his sleek hair with a weary gesture.

"What do you mean?" asked Bull sharply.

"I mean that we shall never get there," said the pessimist placidly. "They have two rows of armed men across the road already; I can see them from here. The town is in arms, as I said it was. I can only wallow in the exquisite comfort of my own exactitude."

And Ratcliffe sat down comfortably in the car and lit a cigarette, but the others rose excitedly and stared down the road. Syme had slowed down the car as their plans became doubtful, and he brought it finally to a standstill just at the corner of a side street that ran down very steeply to the sea.

The town was mostly in shadow, but the sun had not sunk; wherever its level light could break through, it painted everything a burning gold. Up this side street the last sunset light shone as sharp and narrow as the shaft of artificial light at the theatre. It struck the car of the five friends, and lit it like a burning chariot. But the rest of the street, especially the two ends of it, was in the deepest twilight, and for some seconds they could see nothing. Then Syme, whose eyes were the keenest, broke into a little bitter whistle, and said,

"It is quite true. There is a crowd or an army or some such thing across the end of that street."

"Well, if there is," said Bull impatiently, "it must be something else—a sham fight or the mayor's birthday or something. I cannot and will not believe that plain, jolly people in a place like this walk about with dynamite in their pockets. Get on a bit, Syme, and let us look at them."

The car crawled about a hundred yards farther, and then they were all startled by Dr. Bull breaking into a high crow of laughter.

"Why, you silly mugs!" he cried, "what did I tell you. That crowd's as law-abiding as a cow, and if it weren't, it's on our side."

"How do you know?" asked the professor, staring.

"You blind bat," cried Bull, "don't you see who is leading them?"

They peered again, and then the Colonel, with a catch in his voice, cried out—

"Why, it's Renard!"

There was, indeed, a rank of dim figures running across the road, and they could not be clearly seen; but far enough in front to catch the accident of the evening light was stalking up and down the unmistakable Dr. Renard, in a white hat, stroking his long brown beard, and holding a revolver in his left hand.

"What a fool I've been!" exclaimed the Colonel. "Of course, the dear old boy has turned out to help us."

Dr. Bull was bubbling over with laughter, swinging the sword in his hand as carelessly as a cane. He jumped out of the car and ran across the intervening space, calling out—

"Dr. Renard! Dr. Renard!"

An instant after Syme thought his own eyes had gone mad in his head. For the philanthropic Dr. Renard had deliberately raised his revolver and fired twice at Bull, so that the shots rang down the road.

Almost at the same second as the puff of white cloud went up from this atrocious explosion a long puff of white cloud went up also from the cigarette of the cynical Ratcliffe. Like all the rest he turned a little pale, but he smiled. Dr. Bull, at whom the bullets had been fired, just missing his scalp, stood quite still in the middle of the road without a sign of fear, and then turned very slowly and crawled back to the car, and climbed in with two holes through his hat.

"Well," said the cigarette smoker slowly, "what do you think now?"

"I think," said Dr. Bull with precision, "that I am lying in bed at No. 217 Peabody Buildings, and that I shall soon wake up with a jump; or, if that's not it, I think that I am sitting in a small cushioned cell in Hanwell, and that the doctor can't make much of my case. But if you want to know what I don't think, I'll tell you. I don't think what you think. I don't think, and I never shall think, that the mass of ordinary men are a pack of dirty modern thinkers. No, sir, I'm a democrat, and I still don't believe that Sunday could convert one average navvy or counter-jumper. No, I may be mad, but humanity isn't."

Syme turned his bright blue eyes on Bull with an earnestness which he did not commonly make clear.

"You are a very fine fellow," he said. "You can believe in a sanity which is not merely your sanity. And you're right enough about humanity, about peasants and people like that jolly old innkeeper. But you're not right about Renard. I suspected him from the first. He's rationalistic, and, what's worse, he's rich. When duty and religion are really destroyed, it will be by the rich."

"They are really destroyed now," said the man with a cigarette, and rose with his hands in his pockets. "The devils are coming on!"

The men in the motor-car looked anxiously in the direction of his dreamy gaze, and they saw that the whole regiment at the end of the road was advancing upon them, Dr. Renard marching furiously in front, his beard flying in the breeze.

The Colonel sprang out of the car with an intolerant exclamation.

"Gentlemen," he cried, "the thing is incredible. It must be a practical joke. If you knew Renard as I do—it's like calling Queen Victoria a dynamiter. If you had got the man's character into your head—"

"Dr. Bull," said Syme sardonically, "has at least got it into his hat."

"I tell you it can't be!" cried the Colonel, stamping.

"Renard shall explain it. He shall explain it to me," and he strode forward.

"Don't be in such a hurry," drawled the smoker. "He will very soon explain it to all of us."

But the impatient Colonel was already out of earshot, advancing towards the advancing enemy. The excited Dr. Renard lifted his pistol again, but perceiving his opponent, hesitated, and the Colonel came face to face with him with frantic gestures of remonstrance.

"It is no good," said Syme. "He will never get anything out of that old heathen. I vote we drive bang through the thick of them, bang as the bullets went through Bull's hat. We may all be killed, but we must kill a tidy number of them."

"I won't 'ave it," said Dr. Bull, growing more vulgar in the sincerity of his virtue. "The poor chaps may be making a mistake. Give the Colonel a chance."

"Shall we go back, then?" asked the Professor.

"No," said Ratcliffe in a cold voice, "the street behind us is held too. In fact, I seem to see there another friend of yours, Syme."

Syme spun round smartly, and stared backwards at the track which they had travelled. He saw an irregular body of horsemen gathering and galloping towards them in the gloom. He saw above the foremost saddle the silver gleam of a sword, and then as it grew nearer the silver gleam of an old man's hair. The next moment, with shattering violence, he had swung the motor round and sent it dashing down the steep side street to the sea, like a man that desired only to die.

"What the devil is up?" cried the Professor, seizing his arm.

"The morning star has fallen!" said Syme, as his own car went down the darkness like a falling star.

The others did not understand his words, but when they looked back at the street above they saw the hostile cavalry coming round the corner and down the slopes after them; and foremost of all rode the good innkeeper, flushed with the fiery innocence of the evening light.

"The world is insane!" said the Professor, and buried his face in his hands.

"No," said Dr. Bull in adamantine humility, "it is I."

"What are we going to do?" asked the Professor.

"At this moment," said Syme, with a scientific detachment, "I think we are going to smash into a lamppost."

The next instant the automobile had come with a catastrophic jar against an iron object. The instant after that four men had crawled out from under a chaos of metal, and a tall lean lamp-post that had stood up straight on the edge of the marine parade stood out, bent and twisted, like the branch of a broken tree.

"Well, we smashed something," said the Professor, with a faint smile. "That's some comfort."

"You're becoming an anarchist," said Syme, dusting his clothes with his instinct of daintiness.

"Everyone is," said Ratcliffe.

As they spoke, the white-haired horseman and his followers came thundering from above, and almost at the same moment a dark string of men ran shouting along the sea-front. Syme snatched a sword, and took it in his teeth; he stuck two others under his arm-pits, took a fourth in his left hand and the lantern in his right, and leapt off the high parade on to the beach below.

The others leapt after him, with a common acceptance of such decisive action, leaving the debris and the gathering mob above them.

"We have one more chance," said Syme, taking the steel out of his mouth. "Whatever all this pandemonium means, I suppose the police station will help us. We can't get there, for they hold the way. But there's a pier or breakwater runs out into the sea just here, which we could defend longer than anything else, like Horatius and his bridge. We must defend it till the Gendarmerie turn out. Keep after me."

They followed him as he went crunching down the beach, and in a second or two their boots broke not on the sea gravel, but on broad, flat stones. They marched down a long, low jetty, running out in one arm into the dim, boiling sea, and when they came to the end of it they felt that they had come to the end of their story. They turned and faced the town.

That town was transfigured with uproar. All along the high parade from which they had just descended was a dark and roaring stream of humanity, with tossing arms and fiery faces, groping and glaring towards them. The long dark line was dotted with torches and lanterns; but even where no flame lit up a furious face, they could see in the farthest figure, in the most shadowy gesture, an organised hate. It was clear that they were the accursed of all men, and they knew not why.

Two or three men, looking little and black like monkeys, leapt over the edge as they had done and dropped on to the beach. These came ploughing down the deep sand, shouting horribly, and strove to wade into the sea at random. The example was followed, and the whole black mass of men began to run and drip over the edge like black treacle.

Foremost among the men on the beach Syme saw the peasant who had driven their cart. He splashed into the surf on a huge cart-horse, and shook his axe at them.

"The peasant!" cried Syme. "They have not risen since the Middle Ages."

"Even if the police do come now," said the Professor mournfully, "they can do nothing with this mob."

"Nonsense!" said Bull desperately; "there must be some people left in the town who are human."

"No," said the hopeless Inspector, "the human being will soon be extinct. We are the last of mankind."

"It may be," said the Professor absently. Then he added in his dreamy voice, "What is all that at the end of the 'Dunciad'?

> 'Nor public flame; nor private, dares to shine;
> Nor human light is left, nor glimpse divine!
> Lo! thy dread Empire, Chaos, is restored;
> Light dies before thine uncreating word:
> Thy hand, great Anarch, lets the curtain fall;
> And universal darkness buries all.'"

"Stop!" cried Bull suddenly, "the gendarmes are out."

The low lights of the police station were indeed blotted and broken with hurrying figures, and they heard through the darkness the clash and jingle of a disciplined cavalry.

"They are charging the mob!" cried Bull in ecstacy or alarm.

"No," said Syme, "they are formed along the parade."

"They have unslung their carbines," cried Bull dancing with excitement.

"Yes," said Ratcliffe, "and they are going to fire on us."

As he spoke there came a long crackle of musketry, and bullets seemed to hop like hailstones on the stones in front of them.

"The gendarmes have joined them!" cried the Professor, and struck his forehead.

"I am in the padded cell," said Bull solidly.

There was a long silence, and then Ratcliffe said, looking out over the swollen sea, all a sort of grey purple—

"What does it matter who is mad or who is sane? We shall all be dead soon."

Syme turned to him and said—

"You are quite hopeless, then?"

Mr. Ratcliffe kept a stony silence; then at last he said quietly—

"No; oddly enough I am not quite hopeless. There is one insane little hope that I cannot get out of my mind. The power of this whole planet is against us, yet I cannot help wondering whether this one silly little hope is hopeless yet."

"In what or whom is your hope?" asked Syme with curiosity.

"In a man I never saw," said the other, looking at the leaden sea.

"I know what you mean," said Syme in a low voice, "the man in the dark room. But Sunday must have killed him by now."

"Perhaps," said the other steadily; "but if so, he was the only man whom Sunday found it hard to kill."

"I heard what you said," said the Professor, with his back turned. "I also am holding hard on to the thing I never saw."

All of a sudden Syme, who was standing as if blind with introspective thought, swung round and cried out, like a man waking from sleep—

"Where is the Colonel? I thought he was with us!"

"The Colonel! Yes," cried Bull, "where on earth is the Colonel?"

"He went to speak to Renard," said the Professor.

"We cannot leave him among all those beasts," cried Syme. "Let us die like gentlemen if—"

"Do not pity the Colonel," said Ratcliffe, with a pale sneer. "He is extremely comfortable. He is—"

"No! no! no!" cried Syme in a kind of frenzy, "not the Colonel too! I will never believe it!"

"Will you believe your eyes?" asked the other, and pointed to the beach.

Many of their pursuers had waded into the water shaking their fists, but the sea was rough, and they could not reach the pier. Two or three figures, however, stood on the beginning of the stone footway, and seemed to be cautiously advancing down it. The glare of a chance lantern lit up the faces of the two foremost. One face wore a black half-mask, and under it the mouth was twisting about in such a madness of nerves that the black tuft of beard wriggled round and round like a restless, living thing. The other was the red face and white moustache of Colonel Ducroix. They were in earnest consultation.

"Yes, he is gone too," said the Professor, and sat down on a stone. "Everything's gone. I'm gone! I can't trust my own bodily machinery. I feel as if my own hand might fly up and strike me."

"When my hand flies up," said Syme, "it will strike somebody else," and he strode along the pier towards the Colonel, the sword in one hand and the lantern in the other.

As if to destroy the last hope or doubt, the Colonel, who saw him coming, pointed his revolver at him and fired. The shot missed Syme, but struck his sword, breaking it short at the hilt. Syme rushed on, and swung the iron lantern above his head.

"Judas before Herod!" he said, and struck the Colonel down upon the stones. Then he turned to the Secretary, whose frightful mouth was almost foaming now, and held the lamp high with so rigid and arresting a gesture, that the man was, as it were, frozen for a moment, and forced to hear.

"Do you see this lantern?" cried Syme in a terrible voice. "Do you see the cross carved on it, and the flame inside? You did not make it. You did not light it. Better men than you, men who could believe and obey, twisted the entrails of iron and preserved the legend of fire. There is not a street you walk on, there is not a thread you wear, that was not made as this lantern was, by denying your philosophy of dirt and rats. You can make nothing. You can only destroy. You will destroy mankind; you will destroy the world. Let that suffice you. Yet this one old Christian lantern you shall not destroy. It shall go where your empire of apes will never have the wit to find it."

He struck the Secretary once with the lantern so that he staggered; and then, whirling it twice round his head, sent it flying far out to sea, where it flared like a roaring rocket and fell.

"Swords!" shouted Syme, turning his flaming face to the three behind him. "Let us charge these dogs, for our time has come to die."

His three companions came after him sword in hand. Syme's sword was broken, but he rent a bludgeon from the fist of a fisherman, flinging him down. In a moment they would have flung themselves upon the face of the mob and perished, when an interruption came. The Secretary, ever since Syme's speech, had stood with his hand to his stricken head as if dazed; now he suddenly pulled off his black mask.

The pale face thus peeled in the lamplight revealed not so much rage as astonishment. He put up his hand with an anxious authority.

"There is some mistake," he said. "Mr. Syme, I hardly think you understand your position. I arrest you in the name of the law."

"Of the law?" said Syme, and dropped his stick.

"Certainly!" said the Secretary. "I am a detective from Scotland Yard," and he took a small blue card from his pocket.

"And what do you suppose we are?" asked the Professor, and threw up his arms.

"You," said the Secretary stiffly, "are, as I know for a fact, members of the Supreme Anarchist Council. Disguised as one of you, I—"

Dr. Bull tossed his sword into the sea.

"There never was any Supreme Anarchist Council," he said. "We were all a lot of silly policemen looking at each other. And all these nice people who have been peppering us with shot thought we were the dynamiters. I knew I couldn't be wrong about the mob," he said, beaming over the enormous multitude, which stretched away to the distance on both sides. "Vulgar people are never mad. I'm vulgar myself, and I know. I am now going on shore to stand a drink to everybody here."

13. THE PURSUIT OF THE PRESIDENT

NEXT morning five bewildered but hilarious people took the boat for Dover. The poor old Colonel might have had some cause to complain, having been first forced to fight for two factions that didn't exist, and then knocked down with an iron lantern. But he was a magnanimous old gentleman, and being much relieved that neither party had anything to do with dynamite, he saw them off on the pier with great geniality.

The five reconciled detectives had a hundred details to explain to each other. The Secretary had to tell Syme how they had come to wear masks originally in order to approach the supposed enemy as fellow-conspirators.

Syme had to explain how they had fled with such swiftness through a civilised country. But above all these matters of detail which could be explained, rose the central mountain of the matter that they could not explain. What did it all mean? If they were all harmless officers, what was Sunday? If he had not seized the world, what on earth had he been up to? Inspector Ratcliffe was still gloomy about this.

"I can't make head or tail of old Sunday's little game any more than you can," he said. "But whatever else Sunday is, he isn't a blameless citizen. Damn it! do you remember his face?"

"I grant you," answered Syme, "that I have never been able to forget it."

"Well," said the Secretary, "I suppose we can find out soon, for tomorrow we have our next general meeting. You will excuse me," he said, with a rather ghastly smile, "for being well acquainted with my secretarial duties."

"I suppose you are right," said the Professor reflectively. "I suppose we might find it out from him; but I confess that I should feel a bit afraid of asking Sunday who he really is."

"Why," asked the Secretary, "for fear of bombs?"

"No," said the Professor, "for fear he might tell me."

"Let us have some drinks," said Dr. Bull, after a silence.

Throughout their whole journey by boat and train they were highly convivial, but they instinctively kept together. Dr. Bull, who had always been the optimist of the party, endeavoured to persuade the other four that the whole company could take the same hansom cab from Victoria; but this was over-ruled, and they went in a four-wheeler, with Dr. Bull on the box, singing. They finished their journey at an hotel in Piccadilly Circus, so as to be close to the early breakfast next morning in Leicester Square. Yet even then the adventures of the day were not entirely over. Dr. Bull, discontented with the general proposal to go to bed, had strolled out of the hotel at about eleven to see and taste some of the beauties of London. Twenty minutes afterwards, however, he came back and made quite a clamour in the hall. Syme, who tried at first to soothe him, was forced at last to listen to his communication with quite new attention.

"I tell you I've seen him!" said Dr. Bull, with thick emphasis.

"Whom?" asked Syme quickly. "Not the President?"

"Not so bad as that," said Dr. Bull, with unnecessary laughter, "not so bad as that. I've got him here."

"Got whom here?" asked Syme impatiently.

"Hairy man," said the other lucidly, "man that used to be hairy man—Gogol. Here he is," and he pulled forward by a reluctant elbow the identical young man who five days before had marched out of the Council with thin red hair and a pale face, the first of all the sham anarchists who had been exposed.

"Why do you worry with me?" he cried. "You have expelled me as a spy."

"We are all spies!" whispered Syme.

"We're all spies!" shouted Dr. Bull. "Come and have a drink."

Next morning the battalion of the reunited six marched stolidly towards the hotel in Leicester Square.

"This is more cheerful," said Dr. Bull; "we are six men going to ask one man what he means."

"I think it is a bit queerer than that," said Syme. "I think it is six men going to ask one man what they mean."

They turned in silence into the Square, and though the hotel was in the opposite corner, they saw at once the little balcony and a figure that looked too big for it. He was sitting alone with bent head, poring over a newspaper. But all his councillors, who had come to vote him down, crossed that Square as if they were watched out of heaven by a hundred eyes.

They had disputed much upon their policy, about whether they should leave the unmasked Gogol without and begin diplomatically, or whether they should bring him in and blow up the gunpowder at once. The influence of Syme and Bull prevailed for the latter course, though the Secretary to the last asked them why they attacked Sunday so rashly.

"My reason is quite simple," said Syme. "I attack him rashly because I am afraid of him."

They followed Syme up the dark stair in silence, and they all came out simultaneously into the broad sunlight of the morning and the broad sunlight of Sunday's smile.

"Delightful!" he said. "So pleased to see you all. What an exquisite day it is. Is the Czar dead?"

The Secretary, who happened to be foremost, drew himself together for a dignified outburst.

"No, sir," he said sternly "there has been no massacre. I bring you news of no such disgusting spectacles."

"Disgusting spectacles?" repeated the President, with a bright, inquiring smile. "You mean Dr. Bull's spectacles?"

The Secretary choked for a moment, and the President went on with a sort of smooth appeal—

"Of course, we all have our opinions and even our eyes, but really to call them disgusting before the man himself—"

Dr. Bull tore off his spectacles and broke them on the table.

"My spectacles are blackguardly," he said, "but I'm not. Look at my face."

"I dare say it's the sort of face that grows on one," said the President, "in fact, it grows on you; and who am I to quarrel with the wild fruits upon the Tree of Life? I dare say it will grow on me some day."

"We have no time for tomfoolery," said the Secretary, breaking in savagely. "We have come to know what all this means. Who are you? What are you? Why did you get us all here? Do you know who and what we are? Are you a half-witted man playing the conspirator, or are you a clever man playing the fool? Answer me, I tell you."

"Candidates," murmured Sunday, "are only required to answer eight out of the seventeen questions on the paper. As far as I can make out, you want me to tell you what I am, and what you are, and what this table is, and what this Council is, and what this world is for all I know. Well, I will go so far as to rend the veil of one mystery. If you want to know what you are, you are a set of highly well-intentioned young jackasses."

"And you," said Syme, leaning forward, "what are you?"

"I? What am I?" roared the President, and he rose slowly to an incredible height, like some enormous wave about to arch above them and break. "You want to know what I am, do you? Bull, you are a man of science. Grub in the roots of those trees and find out the truth about them. Syme, you are a poet. Stare at those morning clouds. But I tell you this, that you will have found out the truth of the last tree and the top-most cloud before the truth about me. You will understand the sea, and I shall be still a riddle; you shall know what the stars are, and not know what I am. Since the beginning of the world all men have hunted me like a wolf—kings and sages, and poets and lawgivers, all the churches, and all the philosophies. But I have never been caught yet, and the skies will fall in the time I turn to bay. I have given them a good run for their money, and I will now."

Before one of them could move, the monstrous man had swung himself like some huge ourang-outang over the balustrade of the balcony. Yet before he dropped he pulled himself up again as on a horizontal bar, and thrusting his great chin over the edge of the balcony, said solemnly—

"There's one thing I'll tell you though about who I am. I am the man in the dark room, who made you all policemen."

With that he fell from the balcony, bouncing on the stones below like a great ball of india-rubber, and went bounding off towards the corner of the Alhambra, where he hailed a hansom-cab and sprang inside it. The six detectives had been standing thunderstruck and livid in the light of his last assertion; but when he disappeared into the cab, Syme's practical senses returned to him, and leaping over the balcony so recklessly as almost to break his legs, he called another cab.

He and Bull sprang into the cab together, the Professor and the Inspector into another, while the Secretary and the late Gogol scrambled into a third just in time to pursue the flying Syme, who was pursuing the flying President. Sunday led them a wild chase towards the north-west, his cabman, evidently under the influence of more than common inducements, urging the horse at breakneck speed. But Syme was in no mood for delicacies, and he stood up in his own cab shouting, "Stop thief!" until crowds ran along beside his cab, and policemen began to stop and ask questions. All this had its influence upon the President's cabman, who began to look dubious, and to slow down to a trot. He opened the trap to talk reasonably to his fare, and in so doing let the long whip droop over the front of the cab. Sunday leant forward, seized it, and jerked it violently out of the man's hand. Then standing up in front of the cab himself, he lashed the horse and roared aloud, so that they went down the streets like a flying storm. Through street after street and square after square went whirling this preposterous vehicle, in which the fare was urging the horse and the driver trying desperately to stop it. The other three cabs came after it (if the phrase be permissible of a cab) like panting hounds. Shops and streets shot by like rattling arrows.

At the highest ecstacy of speed, Sunday turned round on the splashboard where he stood, and sticking his great grinning head out of the cab, with white hair whistling in the wind, he made a horrible face at his pursuers, like some colossal urchin. Then raising his right hand swiftly, he flung a ball of paper in Syme's face and vanished. Syme caught the thing while instinctively warding it off, and discovered that it consisted of two crumpled papers. One was addressed to himself, and the other to Dr. Bull, with a very long, and it is to be feared partly ironical, string of letters after his name. Dr. Bull's address was, at any rate, considerably longer than his communication, for the communication consisted entirely of the words:—

"What about Martin Tupper now?"

"What does the old maniac mean?" asked Bull, staring at the words. "What does yours say, Syme?"

Syme's message was, at any rate, longer, and ran as follows:—

"No one would regret anything in the nature of an interference by the Archdeacon more than I. I trust it will not come to that. But, for the last time, where are your goloshes? The thing is too bad, especially after what uncle said."

The President's cabman seemed to be regaining some control over his horse, and the pursuers gained a little as they swept round into the Edgware Road. And here there occurred what seemed to the allies a providential stoppage. Traffic of every kind was swerving to right or left or stopping, for down the long road was coming the unmistakable roar announcing the fire-engine, which in a few seconds went by like a brazen thunderbolt. But quick as it went by, Sunday had bounded out of his cab, sprung at the fire-engine, caught it, slung himself on to it, and was seen as he disappeared in the noisy distance talking to the astonished fireman with explanatory gestures.

"After him!" howled Syme. "He can't go astray now. There's no mistaking a fire-engine."

The three cabmen, who had been stunned for a moment, whipped up their horses and slightly decreased the distance between themselves and their disappearing prey. The President acknowledged this proximity by coming to the back of the car, bowing repeatedly, kissing his hand, and finally flinging a neatly-folded note into the bosom of Inspector Ratcliffe. When that gentleman opened it, not without impatience, he found it contained the words:—

"Fly at once. The truth about your trouser-stretchers is known.
—A FRIEND."

The fire-engine had struck still farther to the north, into a region that they did not recognise; and as it ran by a line of high railings shadowed with trees, the six friends were startled, but somewhat relieved, to see the President leap from the fire-engine, though whether through another whim or the increasing protest of his entertainers they could not see. Before the three cabs, however, could reach up to the spot, he had gone up the high railings like a huge grey cat, tossed himself over, and vanished in a darkness of leaves.

Syme with a furious gesture stopped his cab, jumped out, and sprang also to the escalade. When he had one leg over the fence and his friends were following, he turned a face on them which shone quite pale in the shadow.

"What place can this be?" he asked. "Can it be the old devil's house? I've heard he has a house in North London."

"All the better," said the Secretary grimly, planting a foot in a foothold, "we shall find him at home."

"No, but it isn't that," said Syme, knitting his brows. "I hear the most horrible noises, like devils laughing and sneezing and blowing their devilish noses!"

"His dogs barking, of course," said the Secretary.

"Why not say his black-beetles barking!" said Syme furiously, "snails barking! geraniums barking! Did you ever hear a dog bark like that?"

He held up his hand, and there came out of the thicket a long growling roar that seemed to get under the skin and freeze the flesh—a low thrilling roar that made a throbbing in the air all about them.

"The dogs of Sunday would be no ordinary dogs," said Gogol, and shuddered.

Syme had jumped down on the other side, but he still stood listening impatiently.

"Well, listen to that," he said, "is that a dog—anybody's dog?"

There broke upon their ear a hoarse screaming as of things protesting and clamouring in sudden pain; and then, far off like an echo, what sounded like a long nasal trumpet.

"Well, his house ought to be hell!" said the Secretary; "and if it is hell, I'm going in!" and he sprang over the tall railings almost with one swing.

The others followed. They broke through a tangle of plants and shrubs, and came out on an open path. Nothing was in sight, but Dr. Bull suddenly struck his hands together.

"Why, you asses," he cried, "it's the Zoo!"

As they were looking round wildly for any trace of their wild quarry, a keeper in uniform came running along the path with a man in plain clothes.

"Has it come this way?" gasped the keeper.

"Has what?" asked Syme.

"The elephant!" cried the keeper. "An elephant has gone mad and run away!"

"He has run away with an old gentleman," said the other stranger breathlessly, "a poor old gentleman with white hair!"

"What sort of old gentleman?" asked Syme, with great curiosity.

"A very large and fat old gentleman in light grey clothes," said the keeper eagerly.

"Well," said Syme, "if he's that particular kind of old gentleman, if you're quite sure that he's a large and fat old gentleman in grey clothes, you may take my word for it that the elephant has not run away with him. He has run away with the elephant. The elephant is not made by God that could run away with him if he did not consent to the elopement. And, by thunder, there he is!"

There was no doubt about it this time. Clean across the space of grass, about two hundred yards away, with a crowd screaming and scampering vainly at his heels, went a huge grey elephant at an awful stride, with his trunk thrown out as rigid as a ship's bowsprit, and trumpeting like the trumpet of doom. On the back of the bellowing and plunging animal sat President Sunday with all the placidity of a sultan, but goading the animal to a furious speed with some sharp object in his hand.

"Stop him!" screamed the populace. "He'll be out of the gate!"

"Stop a landslide!" said the keeper. "He is out of the gate!"

And even as he spoke, a final crash and roar of terror announced that the great grey elephant had broken out of the gates of the Zoological Gardens, and was careening down Albany Street like a new and swift sort of omnibus.

"Great Lord!" cried Bull, "I never knew an elephant could go so fast. Well, it must be hansom-cabs again if we are to keep him in sight."

As they raced along to the gate out of which the elephant had vanished, Syme felt a glaring panorama of the strange animals in the cages which they passed. Afterwards he thought it queer that he should have seen them so clearly. He remembered especially seeing pelicans, with their preposterous, pendant throats. He wondered why the pelican was the symbol of charity, except it was that it wanted a good deal of charity to admire a pelican. He remembered a hornbill, which was simply a huge yellow beak with a small bird tied on behind it. The whole gave him a sensation, the vividness of which he could not explain, that Nature was always making quite mysterious jokes. Sunday had told them that they would understand him when they had understood the stars. He wondered whether even the archangels understood the hornbill.

The six unhappy detectives flung themselves into cabs and followed the elephant sharing the terror which he spread through the long stretch of the streets. This time Sunday did not turn round, but offered them the solid stretch of his unconscious back, which maddened them, if possible, more than his previous mockeries. Just before they came to Baker Street, however, he was seen to throw something far up into the air, as a boy does a ball meaning to catch it again. But at their rate of racing it fell far behind, just by the cab containing Gogol; and in faint hope of a clue or for some impulse unexplainable, he stopped his cab so as to pick it up. It was addressed to himself, and was quite a bulky parcel. On examination, however, its bulk was found to consist of thirty-three pieces of paper of no value wrapped one round the other. When the last covering was torn away it reduced itself to a small slip of paper, on which was written:

—

"The word, I fancy, should be 'pink'."

The man once known as Gogol said nothing, but the movements of his hands and feet were like those of a man urging a horse to renewed efforts.

Through street after street, through district after district, went the prodigy of the flying elephant, calling crowds to every window, and driving the traffic left and right. And still through all this insane publicity the three cabs toiled after it, until they came to be regarded as part of a procession, and perhaps the advertisement of a circus. They went at such a rate that distances were shortened beyond belief, and Syme saw the Albert Hall in Kensington when he thought that he was still in Paddington. The animal's pace was even more fast and free through the empty, aristocratic streets of South Kensington, and he finally headed towards that part of the sky-line where the enormous Wheel of Earl's Court stood up in the sky. The wheel grew larger and larger, till it filled heaven like the wheel of stars.

The beast outstripped the cabs. They lost him round several corners, and when they came to one of the gates of the Earl's Court Exhibition they found themselves finally blocked. In front of them was an enormous crowd; in the midst of it was an enormous elephant, heaving and shuddering as such shapeless creatures do. But the President had disappeared.

"Where has he gone to?" asked Syme, slipping to the ground.

"Gentleman rushed into the Exhibition, sir!" said an official in a dazed manner. Then he added in an injured voice: "Funny gentleman, sir. Asked me to hold his horse, and gave me this."

He held out with distaste a piece of folded paper, addressed: "To the Secretary of the Central Anarchist Council."

The Secretary, raging, rent it open, and found written inside it:—

G.K. CHESTERTON

"When the herring runs a mile,
   Let the Secretary smile;
   When the herring tries to fly,
   Let the Secretary die."

— *RUSTIC PROVERB*

"Why the eternal crikey," began the Secretary, "did you let the man in? Do people commonly come to your Exhibition riding on mad elephants? Do—"

"Look!" shouted Syme suddenly. "Look over there!"

"Look at what?" asked the Secretary savagely.

"Look at the captive balloon!" said Syme, and pointed in a frenzy.

"Why the blazes should I look at a captive balloon?" demanded the Secretary. "What is there queer about a captive balloon?"

"Nothing," said Syme, "except that it isn't captive!"

They all turned their eyes to where the balloon swung and swelled above the Exhibition on a string, like a child's balloon. A second afterwards the string came in two just under the car, and the balloon, broken loose, floated away with the freedom of a soap bubble.

"Ten thousand devils!" shrieked the Secretary. "He's got into it!" and he shook his fists at the sky.

The balloon, borne by some chance wind, came right above them, and they could see the great white head of the President peering over the side and looking benevolently down on them.

"God bless my soul!" said the Professor with the elderly manner that he could never disconnect from his bleached beard and parchment face. "God bless my soul! I seemed to fancy that something fell on the top of my hat!"

He put up a trembling hand and took from that shelf a piece of twisted paper, which he opened absently only to find it inscribed with a true lover's knot and, the words:—

"Your beauty has not left me indifferent.—From LITTLE SNOWDROP."

There was a short silence, and then Syme said, biting his beard—

"I'm not beaten yet. The blasted thing must come down somewhere. Let's follow it!"

14. THE SIX PHILOSOPHERS

ACROSS green fields, and breaking through blooming hedges, toiled six draggled detectives, about five miles out of London. The optimist of the party had at first proposed that they should follow the balloon across South England in hansom-cabs. But he was ultimately convinced of the persistent refusal of the balloon to follow the roads, and the still more persistent refusal of the cabmen to follow the balloon. Consequently the tireless though exasperated travellers broke through black thickets and ploughed through ploughed fields till each was turned into a figure too outrageous to be mistaken for a tramp. Those green hills of Surrey saw the final collapse and tragedy of the admirable light grey suit in which Syme had set out from Saffron Park. His silk hat was broken over his nose by a swinging bough, his coat-tails were torn to the shoulder by arresting thorns, the clay of England was splashed up to his collar; but he still carried his yellow beard forward with a silent and furious determination, and his eyes were still fixed on that floating ball of gas, which in the full flush of sunset seemed coloured like a sunset cloud.

"After all," he said, "it is very beautiful!"

"It is singularly and strangely beautiful!" said the Professor. "I wish the beastly gas-bag would burst!"

"No," said Dr. Bull, "I hope it won't. It might hurt the old boy."

"Hurt him!" said the vindictive Professor, "hurt him! Not as much as I'd hurt him if I could get up with him. Little Snowdrop!"

"I don't want him hurt, somehow," said Dr. Bull.

"What!" cried the Secretary bitterly. "Do you believe all that tale about his being our man in the dark room? Sunday would say he was anybody."

"I don't know whether I believe it or not," said Dr. Bull. "But it isn't that that I mean. I can't wish old Sunday's balloon to burst because—"

"Well," said Syme impatiently, "because?"

"Well, because he's so jolly like a balloon himself," said Dr. Bull desperately. "I don't understand a word of all that idea of his being the same man who gave us all our blue cards. It seems to make everything nonsense. But I don't care who knows it, I always had a sympathy for old Sunday himself, wicked as he was. Just as if he was a great bouncing baby. How can I explain what my queer sympathy was? It didn't prevent my fighting him like hell! Shall I make it clear if I say that I liked him because he was so fat?"

"You will not," said the Secretary.

"I've got it now," cried Bull, "it was because he was so fat and so light. Just like a balloon. We always think of fat people as heavy, but he could have danced against a sylph. I see now what I mean. Moderate strength is shown in violence, supreme strength is shown in levity. It was like the old speculations—what would happen if an elephant could leap up in the sky like a grasshopper?"

"Our elephant," said Syme, looking upwards, "has leapt into the sky like a grasshopper."

"And somehow," concluded Bull, "that's why I can't help liking old Sunday. No, it's not an admiration of force, or any silly thing like that. There is a kind of gaiety in the thing, as if he were bursting with some good news. Haven't you sometimes felt it on a spring day? You know Nature plays tricks, but somehow that day proves they are good-natured tricks. I never read the Bible myself, but that part they laugh at is literal truth, 'Why leap ye, ye high hills?' The hills do leap—at least, they try to.... Why do I like Sunday?... how can I tell you?... because he's such a Bounder."

There was a long silence, and then the Secretary said in a curious, strained voice—

"You do not know Sunday at all. Perhaps it is because you are better than I, and do not know hell. I was a fierce fellow, and a trifle morbid from the first. The man who sits in darkness, and who chose us all, chose me because I had all the crazy look of a conspirator—because my smile went crooked, and my eyes were gloomy, even when I smiled. But there must have been something in me that answered to the nerves in all these anarchic men. For when I first saw Sunday he expressed to me, not your airy vitality, but something both gross and sad in the Nature of Things. I found him smoking in a twilight room, a room with brown blind down, infinitely more depressing than the genial darkness in which our master lives. He sat there on a bench, a huge heap of a man, dark and out of shape. He listened to all my words without speaking or even stirring. I poured out my most passionate appeals, and asked my most eloquent questions. Then, after a long silence, the Thing began to shake, and I thought it was shaken by some secret malady. It shook like a loathsome and living jelly. It reminded me of everything I had ever read about the base bodies that are the origin of life—the deep sea lumps and protoplasm. It seemed like the final form of matter, the most shapeless and the most shameful. I could only tell myself, from its shudderings, that it was something at least that such a monster could be miserable. And then it broke upon me that the bestial mountain was shaking with a lonely laughter, and the laughter was at me. Do you ask me to forgive him that? It is no small thing to be laughed at by something at once lower and stronger than oneself."

"Surely you fellows are exaggerating wildly," cut in the clear voice of Inspector Ratcliffe. "President Sunday is a terrible fellow for one's intellect, but he is not such a Barnum's freak physically as you make out. He received me in an ordinary office, in a grey check coat, in broad daylight. He talked to me in an ordinary way. But I'll tell you what is a trifle creepy about Sunday. His room is neat, his clothes are neat, everything seems in order; but he's absent-minded. Sometimes his great bright eyes go quite blind. For hours he forgets that you are there. Now absent-mindedness is just a bit too awful in a bad man. We think of a wicked man as vigilant. We can't think of a wicked man who is honestly and sincerely dreamy, because we daren't think of a wicked man alone with himself. An absentminded man means a good-natured man. It means a man who, if he happens to see you, will apologise. But how will you bear an absentminded man who, if he happens to see you, will kill you? That is what tries the nerves, abstraction combined with cruelty. Men have felt it sometimes when they went through wild forests, and felt that the animals there were at once innocent and pitiless. They might ignore or slay. How would you like to pass ten mortal hours in a parlour with an absent-minded tiger?"

"And what do you think of Sunday, Gogol?" asked Syme.

"I don't think of Sunday on principle," said Gogol simply, "any more than I stare at the sun at noonday."

"Well, that is a point of view," said Syme thoughtfully. "What do you say, Professor?"

The Professor was walking with bent head and trailing stick, and he did not answer at all.

"Wake up, Professor!" said Syme genially. "Tell us what you think of Sunday."

The Professor spoke at last very slowly.

"I think something," he said, "that I cannot say clearly. Or, rather, I think something that I cannot even think clearly. But it is something like this. My early life, as you know, was a bit too large and loose.

"Well, when I saw Sunday's face I thought it was too large—everybody does, but I also thought it was too loose. The face was so big, that one couldn't focus it or make it a face at all. The eye was so far away from the nose, that it wasn't an eye. The mouth was so much by itself, that one had to think of it by itself. The whole thing is too hard to explain."

He paused for a little, still trailing his stick, and then went on—

"But put it this way. Walking up a road at night, I have seen a lamp and a lighted window and a cloud make together a most complete and unmistakable face. If anyone in heaven has that face I shall know him again. Yet when I walked a little farther I found that there was no face, that the window was ten yards away, the lamp ten hundred yards, the cloud beyond the world. Well, Sunday's face escaped me; it ran away to right and left, as such chance pictures run away. And so his face has made me, somehow, doubt whether there are any faces. I don't know whether your face, Bull, is a face or a combination in perspective. Perhaps one black disc of your beastly glasses is quite close and another fifty miles away. Oh, the doubts of a materialist are not worth a dump. Sunday has taught me the last and the worst doubts, the doubts of a spiritualist. I am a Buddhist, I suppose; and Buddhism is not a creed, it is a doubt. My poor dear Bull, I do not believe that you really have a face. I have not faith enough to believe in matter."

Syme's eyes were still fixed upon the errant orb, which, reddened in the evening light, looked like some rosier and more innocent world.

"Have you noticed an odd thing," he said, "about all your descriptions? Each man of you finds Sunday quite different, yet each man of you can only find one thing to compare him to—the universe itself. Bull finds him like the earth in spring, Gogol like the sun at noonday. The Secretary is reminded of the shapeless protoplasm, and the Inspector of the carelessness of virgin forests. The Professor says he is like a changing landscape. This is queer, but it is queerer still that I also have had my odd notion about the President, and I also find that I think of Sunday as I think of the whole world."

"Get on a little faster, Syme," said Bull; "never mind the balloon."

"When I first saw Sunday," said Syme slowly, "I only saw his back; and when I saw his back, I knew he was the worst man in the world. His neck and shoulders were brutal, like those of some apish god. His head had a stoop that was hardly human, like the stoop of an ox. In fact, I had at once the revolting fancy that this was not a man at all, but a beast dressed up in men's clothes."

"Get on," said Dr. Bull.

"And then the queer thing happened. I had seen his back from the street, as he sat in the balcony. Then I entered the hotel, and coming round the other side of him, saw his face in the sunlight. His face frightened me, as it did everyone; but not because it was brutal, not because it was evil. On the contrary, it frightened me because it was so beautiful, because it was so good."

"Syme," exclaimed the Secretary, "are you ill?"

"It was like the face of some ancient archangel, judging justly after heroic wars. There was laughter in the eyes, and in the mouth honour and sorrow. There was the same white hair, the same great, grey-clad shoulders that I had seen from behind. But when I saw him from behind I was certain he was an animal, and when I saw him in front I knew he was a god."

"Pan," said the Professor dreamily, "was a god and an animal."

"Then, and again and always," went on Syme like a man talking to himself, "that has been for me the mystery of Sunday, and it is also the mystery of the world. When I see the horrible back, I am sure the noble face is but a mask. When I see the face but for an instant, I know the back is only a jest. Bad is so bad, that we cannot but think good an accident; good is so good, that we feel certain that evil could be explained. But the

193

whole came to a kind of crest yesterday when I raced Sunday for the cab, and was just behind him all the way."

"Had you time for thinking then?" asked Ratcliffe.

"Time," replied Syme, "for one outrageous thought. I was suddenly possessed with the idea that the blind, blank back of his head really was his face—an awful, eyeless face staring at me! And I fancied that the figure running in front of me was really a figure running backwards, and dancing as he ran."

"Horrible!" said Dr. Bull, and shuddered.

"Horrible is not the word," said Syme. "It was exactly the worst instant of my life. And yet ten minutes afterwards, when he put his head out of the cab and made a grimace like a gargoyle, I knew that he was only like a father playing hide-and-seek with his children."

"It is a long game," said the Secretary, and frowned at his broken boots.

"Listen to me," cried Syme with extraordinary emphasis. "Shall I tell you the secret of the whole world? It is that we have only known the back of the world. We see everything from behind, and it looks brutal. That is not a tree, but the back of a tree. That is not a cloud, but the back of a cloud. Cannot you see that everything is stooping and hiding a face? If we could only get round in front—"

"Look!" cried out Bull clamorously, "the balloon is coming down!"

There was no need to cry out to Syme, who had never taken his eyes off it. He saw the great luminous globe suddenly stagger in the sky, right itself, and then sink slowly behind the trees like a setting sun.

The man called Gogol, who had hardly spoken through all their weary travels, suddenly threw up his hands like a lost spirit.

"He is dead!" he cried. "And now I know he was my friend—my friend in the dark!"

"Dead!" snorted the Secretary. "You will not find him dead easily. If he has been tipped out of the car, we shall find him rolling as a colt rolls in a field, kicking his legs for fun."

"Clashing his hoofs," said the Professor. "The colts do, and so did Pan."

"Pan again!" said Dr. Bull irritably. "You seem to think Pan is everything."

"So he is," said the Professor, "in Greek. He means everything."

"Don't forget," said the Secretary, looking down, "that he also means Panic."

Syme had stood without hearing any of the exclamations.

"It fell over there," he said shortly. "Let us follow it!"

Then he added with an indescribable gesture—

"Oh, if he has cheated us all by getting killed! It would be like one of his larks."

He strode off towards the distant trees with a new energy, his rags and ribbons fluttering in the wind. The others followed him in a more footsore and dubious manner. And almost at the same moment all six men realised that they were not alone in the little field.

Across the square of turf a tall man was advancing towards them, leaning on a strange long staff like a sceptre. He was clad in a fine but old-fashioned suit with knee-breeches; its colour was that shade between blue, violet and grey which can be seen in certain shadows of the woodland. His hair was whitish grey, and at the first glance, taken along with his knee-breeches, looked as if it was powdered. His advance was very quiet; but for the silver frost upon his head, he might have been one to the shadows of the wood.

"Gentlemen," he said, "my master has a carriage waiting for you in the road just by."

"Who is your master?" asked Syme, standing quite still.

"I was told you knew his name," said the man respectfully.

There was a silence, and then the Secretary said—

"Where is this carriage?"

"It has been waiting only a few moments," said the stranger. "My master has only just come home."

Syme looked left and right upon the patch of green field in which he found himself. The hedges were ordinary hedges, the trees seemed ordinary trees; yet he felt like a man entrapped in fairyland.

He looked the mysterious ambassador up and down, but he could discover nothing except that the man's coat was the exact colour of the purple shadows, and that the man's face was the exact colour of the red and brown and golden sky.

"Show us the place," Syme said briefly, and without a word the man in the violet coat turned his back and walked towards a gap in the hedge, which let in suddenly the light of a white road.

As the six wanderers broke out upon this thoroughfare, they saw the white road blocked by what looked like a long row of carriages, such a row of carriages as might close the approach to some house in Park Lane. Along the side of these carriages stood a rank of splendid servants, all dressed in the grey-blue uniform, and all having a certain quality of stateliness and freedom which would not commonly belong to the servants of a gentleman, but rather to the officials and ambassadors of a great king. There were no less than six carriages waiting, one for each of the tattered and miserable band. All the attendants (as if in court-dress) wore swords, and as each man crawled into his carriage they drew them, and saluted with a sudden blaze of steel.

"What can it all mean?" asked Bull of Syme as they separated. "Is this another joke of Sunday's?"

"I don't know," said Syme as he sank wearily back in the cushions of his carriage; "but if it is, it's one of the jokes you talk about. It's a good-natured one."

The six adventurers had passed through many adventures, but not one had carried them so utterly off their feet as this last adventure of comfort. They had all become inured to things going roughly; but things suddenly going smoothly swamped them. They could not even feebly imagine what the carriages were; it was enough for them to know that they were carriages, and carriages with cushions. They could not conceive who the old man was who had led them; but it was quite enough that he had certainly led them to the carriages.

Syme drove through a drifting darkness of trees in utter abandonment. It was typical of him that while he had carried his bearded chin forward fiercely so long as anything could be done, when the whole business was taken out of his hands he fell back on the cushions in a frank collapse.

Very gradually and very vaguely he realised into what rich roads the carriage was carrying him. He saw that they passed the stone gates of what might have been a park, that they began gradually to climb a hill which, while wooded on both sides, was somewhat more orderly than a forest. Then there began to grow upon him, as upon a man slowly waking from a healthy sleep, a pleasure in everything. He felt that the hedges were what hedges should be, living walls; that a hedge is like a human army, disciplined, but all the more alive. He saw high elms behind the hedges, and vaguely thought how happy boys would be climbing there. Then his carriage took a turn of the path, and he saw suddenly and quietly, like a long, low, sunset cloud, a long, low house, mellow in the mild light of sunset. All the six friends compared notes afterwards and quarrelled; but they all agreed that in some unaccountable way the place reminded them of their boyhood. It was either this elm-top or that crooked path, it was either this scrap of orchard or that shape of a window; but each man of them declared that he could remember this place before he could remember his mother.

When the carriages eventually rolled up to a large, low, cavernous gateway, another man in the same uniform, but wearing a silver star on the grey breast of his coat, came out to meet them. This impressive person said to the bewildered Syme—

"Refreshments are provided for you in your room."

Syme, under the influence of the same mesmeric sleep of amazement, went up the large oaken stairs after the respectful attendant. He entered a splendid suite of apartments that seemed to be designed specially for him. He walked up to a long mirror with the ordinary instinct of his class, to pull his tie straight or to smooth his hair; and there he saw the frightful figure that he was—blood running down his face from where the bough had struck him, his hair standing out like yellow rags of rank grass, his clothes torn into long, wavering tatters. At once the whole enigma sprang up, simply as the question of how he had got there, and how he was to get out again. Exactly at the same moment a man in blue, who had been appointed as his valet, said very solemnly—

"I have put out your clothes, sir."

"Clothes!" said Syme sardonically. "I have no clothes except these," and he lifted two long strips of his frock-coat in fascinating festoons, and made a movement as if to twirl like a ballet girl.

"My master asks me to say," said the attendant, "that there is a fancy dress ball tonight, and that he desires you to put on the costume that I have laid out. Meanwhile, sir, there is a bottle of Burgundy and some cold pheasant, which he hopes you will not refuse, as it is some hours before supper."

"Cold pheasant is a good thing," said Syme reflectively, "and Burgundy is a spanking good thing. But really I do not want either of them so much as I want to know what the devil all this means, and what sort of costume you have got laid out for me. Where is it?"

The servant lifted off a kind of ottoman a long peacock-blue drapery, rather of the nature of a domino, on the front of which was emblazoned a large golden sun, and which was splashed here and there with flaming stars and crescents.

"You're to be dressed as Thursday, sir," said the valet somewhat affably.

"Dressed as Thursday!" said Syme in meditation. "It doesn't sound a warm costume."

"Oh, yes, sir," said the other eagerly, "the Thursday costume is quite warm, sir. It fastens up to the chin."

"Well, I don't understand anything," said Syme, sighing. "I have been used so long to uncomfortable adventures that comfortable adventures knock me out. Still, I may be allowed to ask why I should be particularly like Thursday in a green frock spotted all over with the sun and moon. Those orbs, I think, shine on other days. I once saw the moon on Tuesday, I remember."

"Beg pardon, sir," said the valet, "Bible also provided for you," and with a respectful and rigid finger he pointed out a passage in the first chapter of Genesis. Syme read it wondering. It was that in which the fourth day of the week is associated with the creation of the sun and moon. Here, however, they reckoned from a Christian Sunday.

"This is getting wilder and wilder," said Syme, as he sat down in a chair. "Who are these people who provide cold pheasant and Burgundy, and green clothes and Bibles? Do they provide everything?"

"Yes, sir, everything," said the attendant gravely. "Shall I help you on with your costume?"

"Oh, hitch the bally thing on!" said Syme impatiently.

But though he affected to despise the mummery, he felt a curious freedom and naturalness in his movements as the blue and gold garment fell about him; and when he found that he had to wear a sword, it stirred a boyish dream. As he passed out of the room he flung the folds across his shoulder with a gesture, his sword stood out at an angle, and he had all the swagger of a troubadour. For these disguises did not disguise, but reveal.

15. THE ACCUSER

AS Syme strode along the corridor he saw the Secretary standing at the top of a great flight of stairs. The man had never looked so noble. He was draped in a long robe of starless black, down the centre of which fell a band or broad stripe of pure white, like a single shaft of light. The whole looked like some very severe ecclesiastical vestment. There was no need for Syme to search his memory or the Bible in order to remember that the first day of creation marked the mere creation of light out of darkness. The vestment itself would alone have suggested the symbol; and Syme felt also how perfectly this pattern of pure white and black expressed the soul of the pale and austere Secretary, with his inhuman veracity and his cold frenzy, which made him so easily make war on the anarchists, and yet so easily pass for one of them. Syme was scarcely surprised to notice that, amid all the ease and hospitality of their new surroundings, this man's eyes were still stern. No smell of ale or orchards could make the Secretary cease to ask a reasonable question.

If Syme had been able to see himself, he would have realised that he, too, seemed to be for the first time himself and no one else. For if the Secretary stood for that philosopher who loves the original and formless light, Syme was a type of the poet who seeks always to make the light in special shapes, to split it up into sun and star. The philosopher may sometimes love the infinite; the poet always loves the finite. For him the great moment is not the creation of light, but the creation of the sun and moon.

As they descended the broad stairs together they overtook Ratcliffe, who was clad in spring green like a huntsman, and the pattern upon whose garment was a green tangle of trees. For he stood for that third day on which the earth and green things were made, and his square, sensible face, with its not unfriendly cynicism, seemed appropriate enough to it.

They were led out of another broad and low gateway into a very large old English garden, full of torches and bonfires, by the broken light of which a vast carnival of people were dancing in motley dress. Syme seemed to see every shape in Nature imitated in some crazy costume. There was a man dressed as a windmill with enormous sails, a man dressed as an elephant, a man dressed as a balloon; the two last, together, seemed to keep the thread of their farcical adventures. Syme even saw, with a queer thrill, one dancer dressed like an enormous hornbill, with a beak twice as big as himself —the queer bird which had fixed itself on his fancy like a living question while he was rushing down the long road at the Zoological Gardens. There were a thousand other such objects, however. There was a dancing lamp-post, a dancing apple tree, a dancing ship. One would have thought that the untamable tune of some mad musician had set all the common objects of field and street dancing an eternal jig. And long afterwards, when Syme was middle-aged and at rest, he could never see one of those particular objects—a lamppost, or an apple tree, or a windmill—without thinking that it was a strayed reveller from that revel of masquerade.

On one side of this lawn, alive with dancers, was a sort of green bank, like the terrace in such old-fashioned gardens.

Along this, in a kind of crescent, stood seven great chairs, the thrones of the seven days. Gogol and Dr. Bull were already in their seats; the Professor was just mounting to his. Gogol, or Tuesday, had his simplicity well symbolised by a dress designed upon the division of the waters, a dress that separated upon his forehead and fell to his feet, grey and silver, like a sheet of rain. The Professor, whose day was that on which the birds and fishes—the ruder forms of life—were created, had a dress of dim purple, over which sprawled goggle-eyed fishes and outrageous tropical birds, the union in him of unfathomable fancy and of doubt. Dr. Bull, the last day of Creation, wore a coat covered with heraldic animals in red and gold, and on his crest a man rampant. He lay back in his chair with a broad smile, the picture of an optimist in his element.

One by one the wanderers ascended the bank and sat in their strange seats. As each of them sat down a roar of enthusiasm rose from the carnival, such as that with which crowds receive kings. Cups were clashed and torches shaken, and feathered hats flung in the air. The men for whom these thrones were reserved were men crowned with some extraordinary laurels. But the central chair was empty.

Syme was on the left hand of it and the Secretary on the right. The Secretary looked across the empty throne at Syme, and said, compressing his lips—

"We do not know yet that he is not dead in a field."

Almost as Syme heard the words, he saw on the sea of human faces in front of him a frightful and beautiful alteration, as if heaven had opened behind his head. But Sunday had only passed silently along the front like a shadow, and had sat in the central seat. He was draped plainly, in a pure and terrible white, and his hair was like a silver flame on his forehead.

For a long time—it seemed for hours—that huge masquerade of mankind swayed and stamped in front of them to marching and exultant music. Every couple dancing seemed a separate romance; it might be a fairy dancing with a pillar-box, or a peasant girl dancing with the moon; but in each case it was, somehow, as absurd as Alice in

Wonderland, yet as grave and kind as a love story. At last, however, the thick crowd began to thin itself. Couples strolled away into the garden-walks, or began to drift towards that end of the building where stood smoking, in huge pots like fish-kettles, some hot and scented mixtures of old ale or wine. Above all these, upon a sort of black framework on the roof of the house, roared in its iron basket a gigantic bonfire, which lit up the land for miles. It flung the homely effect of firelight over the face of vast forests of grey or brown, and it seemed to fill with warmth even the emptiness of upper night. Yet this also, after a time, was allowed to grow fainter; the dim groups gathered more and more round the great cauldrons, or passed, laughing and clattering, into the inner passages of that ancient house. Soon there were only some ten loiterers in the garden; soon only four. Finally the last stray merry-maker ran into the house whooping to his companions. The fire faded, and the slow, strong stars came out. And the seven strange men were left alone, like seven stone statues on their chairs of stone. Not one of them had spoken a word.

They seemed in no haste to do so, but heard in silence the hum of insects and the distant song of one bird. Then Sunday spoke, but so dreamily that he might have been continuing a conversation rather than beginning one.

"We will eat and drink later," he said. "Let us remain together a little, we who have loved each other so sadly, and have fought so long. I seem to remember only centuries of heroic war, in which you were always heroes—epic on epic, iliad on iliad, and you always brothers in arms. Whether it was but recently (for time is nothing), or at the beginning of the world, I sent you out to war. I sat in the darkness, where there is not any created thing, and to you I was only a voice commanding valour and an unnatural virtue. You heard the voice in the dark, and you never heard it again. The sun in heaven denied it, the earth and sky denied it, all human wisdom denied it. And when I met you in the daylight I denied it myself."

Syme stirred sharply in his seat, but otherwise there was silence, and the incomprehensible went on.

"But you were men. You did not forget your secret honour, though the whole cosmos turned an engine of torture to tear it out of you. I knew how near you were to hell. I know how you, Thursday, crossed swords with King Satan, and how you, Wednesday, named me in the hour without hope."

There was complete silence in the starlit garden, and then the black-browed Secretary, implacable, turned in his chair towards Sunday, and said in a harsh voice—

"Who and what are you?"

"I am the Sabbath," said the other without moving. "I am the peace of God."

The Secretary started up, and stood crushing his costly robe in his hand.

"I know what you mean," he cried, "and it is exactly that that I cannot forgive you. I know you are contentment, optimism, what do they call the thing, an ultimate reconciliation. Well, I am not reconciled. If you were the man in the dark room, why were you also Sunday, an offense to the sunlight? If you were from the first our father and our friend, why were you also our greatest enemy? We wept, we fled in terror; the iron entered into our souls—and you are the peace of God! Oh, I can forgive God His anger, though it destroyed nations; but I cannot forgive Him His peace."

Sunday answered not a word, but very slowly he turned his face of stone upon Syme as if asking a question.

"No," said Syme, "I do not feel fierce like that. I am grateful to you, not only for wine and hospitality here, but for many a fine scamper and free fight. But I should like to know. My soul and heart are as happy and quiet here as this old garden, but my reason is still crying out. I should like to know."

Sunday looked at Ratcliffe, whose clear voice said—

"It seems so silly that you should have been on both sides and fought yourself."

Bull said—

"I understand nothing, but I am happy. In fact, I am going to sleep."

"I am not happy," said the Professor with his head in his hands, "because I do not understand. You let me stray a little too near to hell."

And then Gogol said, with the absolute simplicity of a child—

"I wish I knew why I was hurt so much."

Still Sunday said nothing, but only sat with his mighty chin upon his hand, and gazed at the distance. Then at last he said—

"I have heard your complaints in order. And here, I think, comes another to complain, and we will hear him also."

The falling fire in the great cresset threw a last long gleam, like a bar of burning gold, across the dim grass. Against this fiery band was outlined in utter black the advancing legs of a black-clad figure. He seemed to have a fine close suit with knee-breeches such as that which was worn by the servants of the house, only that it was not blue, but of this absolute sable. He had, like the servants, a kind of sword by his side. It was only when he had come quite close to the crescent of the seven and flung up his face to look at them, that Syme saw, with thunder-struck clearness, that the face was the broad, almost ape-like face of his old friend Gregory, with its rank red hair and its insulting smile.

"Gregory!" gasped Syme, half-rising from his seat. "Why, this is the real anarchist!"

"Yes," said Gregory, with a great and dangerous restraint, "I am the real anarchist."

"'Now there was a day,'" murmured Bull, who seemed really to have fallen asleep, "'when the sons of God came to present themselves before the Lord, and Satan came also among them.'"

"You are right," said Gregory, and gazed all round. "I am a destroyer. I would destroy the world if I could."

A sense of a pathos far under the earth stirred up in Syme, and he spoke brokenly and without sequence.

"Oh, most unhappy man," he cried, "try to be happy! You have red hair like your sister."

"My red hair, like red flames, shall burn up the world," said Gregory. "I thought I hated everything more than common men can hate anything; but I find that I do not hate everything so much as I hate you!"

"I never hated you," said Syme very sadly.

Then out of this unintelligible creature the last thunders broke.

"You!" he cried. "You never hated because you never lived. I know what you are all of you, from first to last—you are the people in power! You are the police—the great fat, smiling men in blue and buttons! You are the Law, and you have never been broken. But is there a free soul alive that does not long to break you, only because you have never been broken? We in revolt talk all kind of nonsense doubtless about this crime or that crime of the Government. It is all folly! The only crime of the Government is that it governs. The unpardonable sin of the supreme power is that it is supreme. I do not curse you for being cruel. I do not curse you (though I might) for being kind. I curse you for being safe! You sit in your chairs of stone, and have never come down from them. You are the seven angels of heaven, and you have had no troubles. Oh, I could forgive you everything, you that rule all mankind, if I could feel for once that you had suffered for one hour a real agony such as I—"

Syme sprang to his feet, shaking from head to foot.

"I see everything," he cried, "everything that there is. Why does each thing on the earth war against each other thing? Why does each small thing in the world have to fight against the world itself? Why does a fly have to fight the whole universe? Why does a dandelion have to fight the whole universe? For the same reason that I had to be alone in the dreadful Council of the Days. So that each thing that obeys law may have the glory and isolation of the anarchist. So that each man fighting for order may be as brave and good a man as the dynamiter. So that the real lie of Satan may be flung back in the face of this blasphemer, so that by tears and torture we may earn the right to say to this man, 'You lie!' No agonies can be too great to buy the right to say to this accuser, 'We also have suffered.'

"It is not true that we have never been broken. We have been broken upon the wheel. It is not true that we have never descended from these thrones. We have descended into hell. We were complaining of unforgettable miseries even at the very moment when this man entered insolently to accuse us of happiness. I repel the slander; we have not been happy. I can answer for every one of the great guards of Law whom he has accused. At least—"

He had turned his eyes so as to see suddenly the great face of Sunday, which wore a strange smile.

"Have you," he cried in a dreadful voice, "have you ever suffered?"

As he gazed, the great face grew to an awful size, grew larger than the colossal mask of Memnon, which had made him scream as a child. It grew larger and larger, filling the whole sky; then everything went black. Only in the blackness before it entirely destroyed his brain he seemed to hear a distant voice saying a commonplace text that he had heard somewhere, "Can ye drink of the cup that I drink of?"

When men in books awake from a vision, they commonly find themselves in some place in which they might have fallen asleep; they yawn in a chair, or lift themselves with bruised limbs from a field. Syme's experience was something much more psychologically strange if there was indeed anything unreal, in the earthly sense, about the things he had gone through. For while he could always remember afterwards that he had swooned before the face of Sunday, he could not remember having ever come to at all. He could only remember that gradually and naturally he knew that he was and had been walking along a country lane with an easy and conversational companion. That companion had been a part of his recent drama; it was the red-haired poet Gregory. They were walking like old friends, and were in the middle of a conversation about some triviality. But Syme could only feel an unnatural buoyancy in his body and a crystal simplicity in his mind that seemed to be superior to everything that he said or did. He felt he was in possession of some impossible good news, which made every other thing a triviality, but an adorable triviality.

Dawn was breaking over everything in colours at once clear and timid; as if Nature made a first attempt at yellow and a first attempt at rose. A breeze blew so clean and sweet, that one could not think that it blew from the sky; it blew rather through some hole in the sky. Syme felt a simple surprise when he saw rising all round him on both sides of the road the red, irregular buildings of Saffron Park. He had no idea that he had walked so near London. He walked by instinct along one white road, on which early birds hopped and sang, and found himself outside a fenced garden. There he saw the sister of Gregory, the girl with the gold-red hair, cutting lilac before breakfast, with the great unconscious gravity of a girl.

THE BALL AND THE CROSS

THE BALL AND THE CROSS

I. A DISCUSSION SOMEWHAT IN THE AIR

The flying ship of Professor Lucifer sang through the skies like a silver arrow; the bleak white steel of it, gleaming in the bleak blue emptiness of the evening. That it was far above the earth was no expression for it; to the two men in it, it seemed to be far above the stars. The professor had himself invented the flying machine, and had also invented nearly everything in it. Every sort of tool or apparatus had, in consequence, to the full, that fantastic and distorted look which belongs to the miracles of science. For the world of science and evolution is far more nameless and elusive and like a dream than the world of poetry and religion; since in the latter images and ideas remain themselves eternally, while it is the whole idea of evolution that identities melt into each other as they do in a nightmare.

All the tools of Professor Lucifer were the ancient human tools gone mad, grown into unrecognizable shapes, forgetful of their origin, forgetful of their names. That thing which looked like an enormous key with three wheels was really a patent and very deadly revolver. That object which seemed to be created by the entanglement of two corkscrews was really the key. The thing which might have been mistaken for a tricycle turned upside-down was the inexpressibly important instrument to which the corkscrew was the key. All these things, as I say, the professor had invented; he had invented everything in the flying ship, with the exception, perhaps, of himself. This he had been born too late actually to inaugurate, but he believed at least, that he had considerably improved it.

There was, however, another man on board, so to speak, at the time. Him, also, by a curious coincidence, the professor had not invented, and him he had not even very greatly improved, though he had fished him up with a lasso out of his own back garden, in Western Bulgaria, with the pure object of improving him. He was an exceedingly holy man, almost entirely covered with white hair. You could see nothing

205

but his eyes, and he seemed to talk with them. A monk of immense learning and acute intellect he had made himself happy in a little stone hut and a little stony garden in the Balkans, chiefly by writing the most crushing refutations of exposures of certain heresies, the last professors of which had been burnt (generally by each other) precisely 1,119 years previously. They were really very plausible and thoughtful heresies, and it was really a creditable or even glorious circumstance, that the old monk had been intellectual enough to detect their fallacy; the only misfortune was that nobody in the modern world was intellectual enough even to understand their argument. The old monk, one of whose names was Michael, and the other a name quite impossible to remember or repeat in our Western civilization, had, however, as I have said, made himself quite happy while he was in a mountain hermitage in the society of wild animals. And now that his luck had lifted him above all the mountains in the society of a wild physicist, he made himself happy still.

"I have no intention, my good Michael," said Professor Lucifer, "of endeavouring to convert you by argument. The imbecility of your traditions can be quite finally exhibited to anybody with mere ordinary knowledge of the world, the same kind of knowledge which teaches us not to sit in draughts or not to encourage friendliness in impecunious people. It is folly to talk of this or that demonstrating the rationalist philosophy. Everything demonstrates it. Rubbing shoulders with men of all kinds——"

"You will forgive me," said the monk, meekly from under loads of white beard, "but I fear I do not understand; was it in order that I might rub my shoulder against men of all kinds that you put me inside this thing?"

"An entertaining retort, in the narrow and deductive manner of the Middle Ages," replied the Professor, calmly, "but even upon your own basis I will illustrate my point. We are up in the sky. In your religion and all the religions, as far as I know (and I know everything), the sky is made the symbol of everything that is sacred and merciful. Well, now you are in the sky, you know better. Phrase it how you like, twist it how you like, you know that you know better. You know what are a man's real feelings about the heavens, when he finds himself alone in the heavens, surrounded by the heavens. You know the truth, and the truth is this. The heavens are evil, the sky is evil, the stars are evil. This mere space, this mere quantity, terrifies a man more than tigers or the terrible plague. You know that since our science has spoken, the bottom has fallen out of the Universe. Now, heaven is the hopeless thing, more hopeless than any hell. Now, if there be any comfort for all your miserable progeny of morbid apes, it must be in the earth, underneath you, under the roots of the grass, in the place where hell was of old. The fiery crypts, the lurid cellars of the underworld, to which you once condemned the wicked, are hideous enough, but at least they are more homely than the heaven in which we ride. And the time will come when you will all hide in them, to escape the horror of the stars."

"I hope you will excuse my interrupting you," said Michael, with a slight cough, "but I have always noticed——"

"Go on, pray go on," said Professor Lucifer, radiantly, "I really like to draw out your simple ideas."

"Well, the fact is," said the other, "that much as I admire your rhetoric and the rhetoric of your school, from a purely verbal point of view, such little study of you and your school in human history as I have been enabled to make has led me to—er—rather singular conclusion, which I find great difficulty in expressing, especially in a foreign language."

"Come, come," said the Professor, encouragingly, "I'll help you out. How did my view strike you?"

"Well, the truth is, I know I don't express it properly, but somehow it seemed to me that you always convey ideas of that kind with most eloquence, when—er—when——"

"Oh! get on," cried Lucifer, boisterously.

"Well, in point of fact when your flying ship is just going to run into something. I thought you wouldn't mind my mentioning it, but it's running into something now."

Lucifer exploded with an oath and leapt erect, leaning hard upon the handle that acted as a helm to the vessel. For the last ten minutes they had been shooting downwards into great cracks and caverns of cloud. Now, through a sort of purple haze, could be seen comparatively near to them what seemed to be the upper part of a huge, dark orb or sphere, islanded in a sea of cloud. The Professor's eyes were blazing like a maniac's.

"It is a new world," he cried, with a dreadful mirth. "It is a new planet and it shall bear my name. This star and not that other vulgar one shall be 'Lucifer, sun of the morning.' Here we will have no chartered lunacies, here we will have no gods. Here man shall be as innocent as the daisies, as innocent and as cruel—here the intellect——"

"There seems," said Michael, timidly, "to be something sticking up in the middle of it."

"So there is," said the Professor, leaning over the side of the ship, his spectacles shining with intellectual excitement. "What can it be? It might of course be merely a——"

Then a shriek indescribable broke out of him of a sudden, and he flung up his arms like a lost spirit. The monk took the helm in a tired way; he did not seem much astonished for he came from an ignorant part of the world in which it is not uncommon for lost spirits to shriek when they see the curious shape which the Professor had just seen on the top of the mysterious ball, but he took the helm only just in time, and by driving it hard to the left he prevented the flying ship from smashing into St. Paul's Cathedral.

A plain of sad-coloured cloud lay along the level of the top of the Cathedral dome, so that the ball and the cross looked like a buoy riding on a leaden sea. As the flying ship swept towards it, this plain of cloud looked as dry and definite and rocky as any grey desert. Hence it gave to the mind and body a sharp and unearthly sensation when the ship cut and sank into the cloud as into any common mist, a thing without resistance. There was, as it were, a deadly shock in the fact that there was no shock. It was as if they had cloven into ancient cliffs like so much butter. But sensations awaited them which were much stranger than those of sinking through the solid earth. For a moment their eyes and nostrils were stopped with darkness and opaque cloud; then the darkness warmed into a kind of brown fog. And far, far below them the brown fog fell until it warmed into fire. Through the dense London atmosphere they could see below them the flaming London lights; lights which lay beneath them in squares and oblongs of fire. The fog and fire were mixed in a passionate vapour; you might say that the fog was drowning the flames; or you might say that the flames had set the fog on fire. Beside the ship and beneath it (for it swung just under the ball), the immeasurable dome itself shot out and down into the dark like a combination of voiceless cataracts. Or it was like some cyclopean sea-beast sitting above London and letting down its tentacles bewilderingly on every side, a monstrosity in that starless heaven. For the clouds that belonged to London had closed over the heads of the voyagers sealing up the entrance of the upper air. They had broken through a roof and come into a temple of twilight.

They were so near to the ball that Lucifer leaned his hand against it, holding the vessel away, as men push a boat off from a bank. Above it the cross already draped in the dark mists of the borderland was shadowy and more awful in shape and size.

Professor Lucifer slapped his hand twice upon the surface of the great orb as if he were caressing some enormous animal. "This is the fellow," he said, "this is the one for my money."

"May I with all respect inquire," asked the old monk, "what on earth you are talking about?"

"Why this," cried Lucifer, smiting the ball again, "here is the only symbol, my boy. So fat. So satisfied. Not like that scraggy individual, stretching his arms in stark weariness." And he pointed up to the cross, his face dark with a grin. "I was telling you just now, Michael, that I can prove the best part of the rationalist case and the Christian humbug from any symbol you liked to give me, from any instance I came across. Here is an instance with a vengeance. What could possibly express your philosophy and my philosophy better than the shape of that cross and the shape of this ball? This globe is reasonable; that cross is unreasonable. It is a four-legged animal, with one leg longer than the others. The globe is inevitable. The cross is arbitrary. Above all the globe is at unity with itself; the cross is primarily and above all things at enmity with itself. The cross is the conflict of two hostile lines, of irreconcilable direction. That silent thing up there is essentially a collision, a crash, a struggle in stone. Pah! that sacred symbol of yours has actually given its name to a description of desperation and muddle. When we speak of men at once ignorant of each other and frustrated by each other, we say they are at cross-purposes. Away with the thing! The very shape of it is a contradiction in terms."

"What you say is perfectly true," said Michael, with serenity. "But we like contradictions in terms. Man is a contradiction in terms; he is a beast whose superiority to other beasts consists in having fallen. That cross is, as you say, an eternal collision; so am I. That is a struggle in stone. Every form of life is a struggle in flesh. The shape of the cross is irrational, just as the shape of the human animal is irrational. You say the cross is a quadruped with one limb longer than the rest. I say man is a quadruped who only uses two of his legs."

The Professor frowned thoughtfully for an instant, and said: "Of course everything is relative, and I would not deny that the element of struggle and self-contradiction, represented by that cross, has a necessary place at a certain evolutionary stage. But surely the cross is the lower development and the sphere the higher. After all it is easy enough to see what is really wrong with Wren's architectural arrangement."

"And what is that, pray?" inquired Michael, meekly.

"The cross is on top of the ball," said Professor Lucifer, simply. "That is surely wrong. The ball should be on top of the cross. The cross is a mere barbaric prop; the ball is perfection. The cross at its best is but the bitter tree of man's history; the ball is the rounded, the ripe and final fruit. And the fruit should be at the top of the tree, not at the bottom of it."

"Oh!" said the monk, a wrinkle coming into his forehead, "so you think that in a rationalistic scheme of symbolism the ball should be on top of the cross?"

"It sums up my whole allegory," said the professor.

"Well, that is really very interesting," resumed Michael slowly, "because I think in that case you would see a most singular effect, an effect that has generally been achieved by all those able and powerful systems which rationalism, or the religion of the ball, has produced to lead or teach mankind. You would see, I think, that thing happen which is always the ultimate embodiment and logical outcome of your logical scheme."

"What are you talking about?" asked Lucifer. "What would happen?"

"I mean it would fall down," said the monk, looking wistfully into the void.

Lucifer made an angry movement and opened his mouth to speak, but Michael, with all his air of deliberation, was proceeding before he could bring out a word.

"I once knew a man like you, Lucifer," he said, with a maddening monotony and slowness of articulation. "He took this——"

"There is no man like me," cried Lucifer, with a violence that shook the ship.

"As I was observing," continued Michael, "this man also took the view that the symbol of Christianity was a symbol of savagery and all unreason. His history is rather amusing. It is also a perfect allegory of what happens to rationalists like yourself. He began, of course, by refusing to allow a crucifix in his house, or round his wife's neck, or even in a picture. He said, as you say, that it was an arbitrary and fantastic shape, that it was a monstrosity, loved because it was paradoxical. Then he began to grow fiercer and more eccentric; he would batter the crosses by the roadside; for he lived in a Roman Catholic country. Finally in a height of frenzy he climbed the steeple of the Parish Church and tore down the cross, waving it in the air, and uttering wild soliloquies up there under the stars. Then one still summer evening as he was wending his way homewards, along a lane, the devil of his madness came upon him with a violence and transfiguration which changes the world. He was standing smoking, for a moment, in the front of an interminable line of palings, when his eyes were opened. Not a light shifted, not a leaf stirred, but he saw as if by a sudden change in the eyesight that this paling was an army of innumerable crosses linked together over hill and dale. And he whirled up his heavy stick and went at it as if at an army. Mile after mile along his homeward path he broke it down and tore it up. For he hated the cross and every paling is a wall of crosses. When he returned to his house he was a literal madman. He sat upon a chair and then started up from it for the cross-bars of the carpentry repeated the intolerable image. He flung himself upon a bed only to remember that this, too, like all workmanlike things, was constructed on the accursed plan. He broke his furniture because it was made of crosses. He burnt his house because it was made of crosses. He was found in the river."

Lucifer was looking at him with a bitten lip.

"Is that story really true?" he asked.

"Oh, no," said Michael, airily. "It is a parable. It is a parable of you and all your rationalists. You begin by breaking up the Cross; but you end by breaking up the habitable world. We leave you saying that nobody ought to join the Church against his will. When we meet you again you are saying that no one has any will to join it with. We leave you saying that there is no such place as Eden. We find you saying that there is no such place as Ireland. You start by hating the irrational and you come to hate everything, for everything is irrational and so——"

Lucifer leapt upon him with a cry like a wild beast's. "Ah," he screamed, "to every man his madness. You are mad on the cross. Let it save you."

And with a herculean energy he forced the monk backwards out of the reeling car on to the upper part of the stone ball. Michael, with as abrupt an agility, caught one of the beams of the cross and saved himself from falling. At the same instant Lucifer drove down a lever and the ship shot up with him in it alone.

"Ha! ha!" he yelled, "what sort of a support do you find it, old fellow?"

"For practical purposes of support," replied Michael grimly, "it is at any rate a great deal better than the ball. May I ask if you are going to leave me here?"

"Yes, yes. I mount! I mount!" cried the professor in ungovernable excitement. "*Altiora peto*. My path is upward."

"How often have you told me, Professor, that there is really no up or down in space?" said the monk. "I shall mount up as much as you will."

"Indeed," said Lucifer, leering over the side of the flying ship. "May I ask what you are going to do?"

The monk pointed downward at Ludgate Hill. "I am going," he said, "to climb up into a star."

Those who look at the matter most superficially regard paradox as something which belongs to jesting and light journalism. Paradox of this kind is to be found in the saying of the dandy, in the decadent comedy, "Life is much too important to be taken seriously." Those who look at the matter a little more deeply or delicately see that paradox is a thing which especially belongs to all religions. Paradox of this kind is to be found in such a saying as "The meek shall inherit the earth." But those who see and feel the fundamental fact of the matter know that paradox is a thing which belongs not to religion only, but to all vivid and violent practical crises of human living. This kind of paradox may be clearly perceived by anybody who happens to be hanging in mid-space, clinging to one arm of the Cross of St. Paul's.

Father Michael in spite of his years, and in spite of his asceticism (or because of it, for all I know), was a very healthy and happy old gentleman. And as he swung on a bar above the sickening emptiness of air, he realized, with that sort of dead detachment which belongs to the brains of those in peril, the deathless and hopeless contradiction which is involved in the mere idea of courage. He was a happy and healthy old gentleman and therefore he was quite careless about it. And he felt as every man feels in the taut moment of such terror that his chief danger was terror itself; his only possible strength would be a coolness amounting to carelessness, a carelessness amounting almost to a suicidal swagger. His one wild chance of coming out safely would be in not too desperately desiring to be safe. There might be footholds down that awful facade, if only he could not care whether they were footholds or no. If he were foolhardy he might escape; if he were wise he would stop where he was till he dropped from the cross like a stone. And this antinomy kept on repeating itself in his mind, a contradiction as large and staring as the immense contradiction of the Cross; he remembered having often heard the words, "Whosoever shall lose his life the same shall save it." He remembered with a sort of strange pity that this had always been made to mean that whoever lost his physical life should save his spiritual life. Now he knew the truth that is known to all fighters, and hunters, and climbers of cliffs. He knew that even his animal life could only be saved by a considerable readiness to lose it.

Some will think it improbable that a human soul swinging desperately in mid-air should think about philosophical inconsistencies. But such extreme states are dangerous things to dogmatize about. Frequently they produce a certain useless and joyless activity of the mere intellect, thought not only divorced from hope but even from desire. And if it is impossible to dogmatize about such states, it is still more impossible to describe them. To this spasm of sanity and clarity in Michael's mind succeeded a spasm of the elemental terror; the terror of the animal in us which regards the whole universe as its enemy; which, when it is victorious, has no pity, and so, when it is defeated has no imaginable hope. Of that ten minutes of terror it is not possible to speak in human words. But then again in that damnable darkness there began to grow a strange dawn as of grey and pale silver. And of this ultimate resignation or certainty it is even less possible to write; it is something stranger than hell itself; it is perhaps the last of the secrets of God. At the highest crisis of some incurable anguish there will suddenly fall upon the man the stillness of an insane contentment. It is not hope, for hope is broken and romantic and concerned with the future; this is complete and of the present. It is not faith, for faith by its very nature is fierce, and as it were at once doubtful and defiant; but this is simply a satisfaction. It is not knowledge, for the intellect seems to have no particular part in it. Nor is it (as the modern idiots would certainly say it is) a mere numbness or negative paralysis of the powers of grief. It is not negative in the least; it is as positive as good news. In some sense, indeed, it is good news. It seems almost as if there were some equality among things, some balance in all possible contingencies which we are not permitted to know lest we should learn indifference to good and evil, but which is sometimes shown to us for an instant as a last aid in our last agony.

Michael certainly could not have given any sort of rational account of this vast unmeaning satisfaction which soaked through him and filled him to the brim. He felt with a sort of half-witted lucidity that the cross was there, and the ball was there, and the dome was there, that he was going to climb down from them, and that he did not mind in the least whether he was killed or not. This mysterious mood lasted long enough to start him on his dreadful descent and to force him to continue it. But six times before he reached the highest of the outer galleries terror had returned on him like a flying storm of darkness and thunder. By the time he had reached that place of safety he almost felt (as in some impossible fit of drunkenness) that he had two heads; one was calm, careless, and efficient; the other saw the danger like a deadly map, was wise, careful, and useless. He had fancied that he would have to let himself vertically down the face of the whole building. When he dropped into the upper gallery he still felt as far from the terrestrial globe as if he had only dropped from the sun to the moon. He paused a little, panting in the gallery under the ball, and idly kicked his heels, moving a few yards along it. And as he did so a thunderbolt struck his soul. A man, a heavy, ordinary man, with a composed indifferent face, and a prosaic sort of uniform, with a row of buttons, blocked his way. Michael had no mind to wonder whether this solid astonished man, with the brown moustache and the nickel buttons, had also come on a flying ship. He merely let his mind float in an endless felicity about the man. He thought how nice it would be if he had to live up in that gallery with that one man for ever. He thought how he would luxuriate in the nameless shades of this man's soul and then hear with an endless excitement about the nameless shades of the souls of all his aunts and uncles. A moment before he had been dying alone. Now he was living in the same world with a man; an inexhaustible ecstasy. In the gallery below the ball Father Michael had found that man who is the noblest and most divine and most lovable of all men, better than all the saints, greater than all the heroes—man Friday.

In the confused colour and music of his new paradise, Michael heard only in a faint and distant fashion some remarks that this beautiful solid man seemed to be making to him; remarks about something or other being after hours and against orders. He also seemed to be asking how Michael "got up" there. This beautiful man evidently felt as Michael did that the earth was a star and was set in heaven.

At length Michael sated himself with the mere sensual music of the voice of the man in buttons. He began to listen to what he said, and even to make some attempt at answering a question which appeared to have been put several times and was now put with some excess of emphasis. Michael realized that the image of God in nickel buttons was asking him how he had come there. He said that he had come in Lucifer's ship. On his giving this answer the demeanour of the image of God underwent a remarkable change. From addressing Michael gruffly, as if he were a malefactor, he began suddenly to speak to him with a sort of eager and feverish amiability as if he were a child. He seemed particularly anxious to coax him away from the balustrade. He led him by the arm towards a door leading into the building itself, soothing him all the time. He gave what even Michael (slight as was his knowledge of the world) felt to be an improbable account of the sumptuous pleasures and varied advantages awaiting him downstairs. Michael followed him, however, if only out of politeness, down an apparently interminable spiral of staircase. At one point a door opened. Michael stepped through it, and the unaccountable man in buttons leapt after him and pinioned him where he stood. But he only wished to stand; to stand and stare. He had stepped as it were into another infinity, out under the dome of another heaven. But this was a dome of heaven made by man. The gold and green and crimson of its sunset were not in the shapeless clouds but in shapes of cherubim and seraphim, awful human shapes with a passionate plumage. Its stars were not above but far below, like fallen stars still in unbroken constellations; the dome itself was full of darkness. And far below, lower even than the lights, could be seen creeping or motionless, great black masses of men. The tongue of a terrible organ seemed to shake the very air in the whole void; and through it there came up to Michael the sound of a tongue more terrible; the dreadful everlasting voice of man, calling to his gods from the beginning to the end of the world. Michael felt almost as if he were a god, and all the voices were hurled at him.

"No, the pretty things aren't here," said the demi-god in buttons, caressingly. "The pretty things are downstairs. You come along with me. There's something that will surprise you downstairs; something you want very much to see."

Evidently the man in buttons did not feel like a god, so Michael made no attempt to explain his feelings to him, but followed him meekly enough down the trail of the serpentine staircase. He had no notion where or at what level he was. He was still full of the cold splendour of space, and of what a French writer has brilliantly named the "vertigo of the infinite," when another door opened, and with a shock indescribable he found himself on the familiar level, in a street full of faces, with the houses and even the lamp-posts above his head. He felt suddenly happy and suddenly indescribably small. He fancied he had been changed into a child again; his eyes sought the pavement seriously as children's do, as if it were a thing with which something satisfactory could be done. He felt the full warmth of that pleasure from which the proud shut themselves out; the pleasure which not only goes with humiliation, but which almost is humiliation. Men who have escaped death by a hair have it, and men whose love is returned by a woman unexpectedly, and men whose sins are forgiven them. Everything his eye fell on it feasted on, not aesthetically, but with a plain, jolly appetite as of a boy eating buns. He relished the squareness of the houses; he liked their clean angles as if he had just cut them with a knife. The lit squares of the shop windows excited him as the young are excited by the lit stage of some promising pantomime. He happened to see in one shop which projected with a bulging bravery on to the pavement some square tins of potted meat, and it seemed like a hint of a hundred hilarious high teas in a hundred streets of the world. He was, perhaps, the happiest of all the children of men. For in that unendurable instant when he hung, half slipping, to the ball of St. Paul's, the whole universe had been destroyed and re-created.

Suddenly through all the din of the dark streets came a crash of glass. With that mysterious suddenness of the Cockney mob, a rush was made in the right direction, a dingy office, next to the shop of the potted meat. The pane of glass was lying in splinters about the pavement. And the police already had their hands on a very tall young man, with dark, lank hair and dark, dazed eyes, with a grey plaid over his shoulder, who had just smashed the shop window with a single blow of his stick.

"I'd do it again," said the young man, with a furious white face. "Anybody would have done it. Did you see what it said? I swear I'd do it again." Then his eyes encountered the monkish habit of Michael, and he pulled off his grey tam-o'-shanter with the gesture of a Catholic.

"Father, did you see what they said?" he cried, trembling. "Did you see what they dared to say? I didn't understand it at first. I read it half through before I broke the window."

Michael felt he knew not how. The whole peace of the world was pent up painfully in his heart. The new and childlike world which he had seen so suddenly, men had not seen at all. Here they were still at their old bewildering, pardonable, useless quarrels, with so much to be said on both sides, and so little that need be said at all. A fierce inspiration fell on him suddenly; he would strike them where they stood with the love of God. They should not move till they saw their own sweet and startling existence. They should not go from that place till they went home embracing like brothers and shouting like men delivered. From the Cross from which he had fallen fell the shadow of its fantastic mercy; and the first three words he spoke in a voice like a silver trumpet, held men as still as stones. Perhaps if he had spoken there for an hour in his illumination he might have founded a religion on Ludgate Hill. But the heavy hand of his guide fell suddenly on his shoulder.

"This poor fellow is dotty," he said good-humouredly to the crowd. "I found him wandering in the Cathedral. Says he came in a flying ship. Is there a constable to spare to take care of him?"

There was a constable to spare. Two other constables attended to the tall young man in grey; a fourth concerned himself with the owner of the shop, who showed some tendency to be turbulent. They took the tall young man away to a magistrate, whither we shall follow him in an ensuing chapter. And they took the happiest man in the world away to an asylum.

II. THE RELIGION OF THE STIPENDIARY MAGISTRATE

The editorial office of *The Atheist* had for some years past become less and less prominently interesting as a feature of Ludgate Hill. The paper was unsuited to the atmosphere. It showed an interest in the Bible unknown in the district, and a knowledge of that volume to which nobody else on Ludgate Hill could make any conspicuous claim. It was in vain that the editor of *The Atheist* filled his front window with fierce and final demands as to what Noah in the Ark did with the neck of the giraffe. It was in vain that he asked violently, as for the last time, how the statement "God is Spirit" could be reconciled with the statement "The earth is His footstool." It was in vain that he cried with an accusing energy that the Bishop of London was paid L12,000 a year for pretending to believe that the whale swallowed Jonah. It was in vain that he hung in conspicuous places the most thrilling scientific calculations about the width of the throat of a whale. Was it nothing to them all they that passed by? Did his sudden and splendid and truly sincere indignation never stir any of the people pouring down Ludgate Hill? Never. The little man who edited *The Atheist* would rush from his shop on starlit evenings and shake his fist at St. Paul's in the passion of his holy war upon the holy place. He might have spared his emotion. The cross at the top of St. Paul's and *The Atheist* shop at the foot of it were alike remote from the world. The shop and the Cross were equally uplifted and alone in the empty heavens.

To the little man who edited *The Atheist*, a fiery little Scotchman, with fiery, red hair and beard, going by the name of Turnbull, all this decline in public importance seemed not so much sad or even mad, but merely bewildering and unaccountable. He had said the worst thing that could be said; and it seemed accepted and ignored like the ordinary second best of the politicians. Every day his blasphemies looked more glaring, and every day the dust lay thicker upon them. It made him feel as if he were moving in a world of idiots. He seemed among a race of men who smiled when told of their own death, or looked vacantly at the Day of Judgement. Year after year went by, and year after year the death of God in a shop in Ludgate became a less and less important occurrence. All the forward men of his age discouraged Turnbull. The socialists said he was cursing priests when he should be cursing capitalists. The artists said that the soul was most spiritual, not when freed from religion, but when freed from morality. Year after year went by, and at least a man came by who treated Mr. Turnbull's secularist shop with a real respect and seriousness. He was a young man in a grey plaid, and he smashed the window.

He was a young man, born in the Bay of Arisaig, opposite Rum and the Isle of Skye. His high, hawklike features and snaky black hair bore the mark of that unknown historic thing which is crudely called Celtic, but which is probably far older than the Celts, whoever they were. He was in name and stock a Highlander of the Macdonalds; but his family took, as was common in such cases, the name of a subordinate sept as a surname, and for all the purposes which could be answered in London, he called himself Evan MacIan. He had been brought up in some loneliness and seclusion as a strict Roman Catholic, in the midst of that little wedge of Roman Catholics which is driven into the Western Highlands. And he had found his way as far as Fleet Street, seeking some half-promised employment, without having properly realized that there were in the world any people who were not Roman Catholics. He had uncovered himself for a few moments before the statue of Queen Anne, in front of St. Paul's Cathedral, under the firm impression that it was a figure of the Virgin Mary. He was somewhat surprised at the lack of deference shown to the figure by the people bustling by. He did not understand that their one essential historical principle, the one law truly graven on their hearts, was the great and comforting statement that Queen Anne is dead. This faith was as fundamental as his faith, that Our Lady was alive. Any persons he had talked to since he had touched the fringe of our fashion or civilization had been by a coincidence, sympathetic or hypocritical. Or if they had spoken some established blasphemies, he had been unable to understand them merely owing to the preoccupied satisfaction of his mind.

On that fantastic fringe of the Gaelic land where he walked as a boy, the cliffs were as fantastic as the clouds. Heaven seemed to humble itself and come closer to the earth. The common paths of his little village began to climb quite suddenly and seemed resolved to go to heaven. The sky seemed to fall down towards the hills; the hills took hold upon the sky. In the sumptuous sunset of gold and purple and peacock green cloudlets and islets were the same. Evan lived like a man walking on a borderland, the borderland between this world and another. Like so many men and nations who grow up with nature and the common things, he understood the supernatural before he understood the natural. He had looked at dim angels standing knee-deep in the grass before he had looked at the grass. He knew that Our Lady's robes were blue before he knew the wild roses round her feet were red. The deeper his memory plunged into the dark house of childhood the nearer and nearer he came to the things that cannot be named. All through his life he thought of the daylight world as a sort of divine debris, the broken remainder of his first vision. The skies and mountains were the splendid off-scourings of another place. The stars were lost jewels of the Queen. Our Lady had gone and left the stars by accident.

His private tradition was equally wild and unworldly. His great-grandfather had been cut down at Culloden, certain in his last instant that God would restore the King. His grandfather, then a boy of ten, had taken the terrible claymore from the hand of the dead and hung it up in his house, burnishing it and sharpening it for sixty years, to be ready for the next rebellion. His father, the youngest son and the last left alive, had refused to attend on Queen Victoria in Scotland. And Evan himself had been of one piece with his progenitors; and was not dead with them, but alive in the twentieth century. He was not in the least the pathetic Jacobite of whom we read, left behind by a final advance of all things. He was, in his own fancy, a conspirator, fierce and up to date. In the long, dark afternoons of the Highland winter, he plotted and fumed in the dark. He drew plans of the capture of London on the desolate sand of Arisaig.

When he came up to capture London, it was not with an army of white cockades, but with a stick and a satchel. London overawed him a little, not because he thought it grand or even terrible, but because it bewildered him; it was not the Golden City or even hell; it was Limbo. He had one shock of sentiment, when he turned that wonderful corner of Fleet Street and saw St. Paul's sitting in the sky.

"Ah," he said, after a long pause, "that sort of thing was built under the Stuarts!" Then with a sour grin he asked himself what was the corresponding monument of the Brunswicks and the Protestant Constitution. After some warning, he selected a sky-sign of some pill.

Half an hour afterwards his emotions left him with an emptied mind on the same spot. And it was in a mood of mere idle investigation that he happened to come to a standstill opposite the office of *The Atheist*. He did not see the word "atheist", or if he did, it is quite possible that he did not know the meaning of the word. Even as it was, the document would not have shocked even the innocent Highlander, but for the troublesome and quite unforeseen fact that the innocent Highlander read it stolidly to the end; a thing unknown among the most enthusiastic subscribers to the paper, and calculated in any case to create a new situation.

With a smart journalistic instinct characteristic of all his school, the editor of *The Atheist* had put first in his paper and most prominently in his window an article called "The Mesopotamian Mythology and its Effects on Syriac Folk Lore." Mr. Evan MacIan began to read this quite idly, as he would have read a public statement beginning with a young girl dying in Brighton and ending with Bile Beans. He received the very considerable amount of information accumulated by the author with that tired clearness of the mind which children have on heavy summer afternoons—that tired clearness which leads them to go on asking questions long after they have lost interest in the subject and are as bored as their nurse. The streets were full of people and empty of adventures. He might as well know about the gods of Mesopotamia as not; so he flattened his long, lean face against the dim bleak pane of the window and read all there was to read about Mesopotamian gods. He read how the Mesopotamians had a god named Sho (sometimes pronounced Ji), and that he was described as being very powerful, a striking similarity to some expressions about Jahveh, who is also described as having power. Evan had never heard of Jahveh in his life, and imagining him to be some other Mesopotamian idol, read on with a dull curiosity. He learnt that the name Sho, under its third form of Psa, occurs in an early legend which describes how the deity, after the manner of Jupiter on so many occasions, seduced a Virgin and begat a hero. This hero, whose name is not essential to our existence, was, it was said, the chief hero and Saviour of the Mesopotamian ethical scheme. Then followed a paragraph giving other examples of such heroes and Saviours being born of some profligate intercourse between God and mortal. Then followed a paragraph—but Evan did not understand it. He read it again and then again. Then he did understand it. The glass fell in ringing fragments on to the pavement, and Evan sprang over the barrier into the shop, brandishing his stick.

"What is this?" cried little Mr. Turnbull, starting up with hair aflame. "How dare you break my window?"

"Because it was the quickest cut to you," cried Evan, stamping. "Stand up and fight, you crapulous coward. You dirty lunatic, stand up, will you? Have you any weapons here?"

"Are you mad?" asked Turnbull, glaring.

"Are you?" cried Evan. "Can you be anything else when you plaster your own house with that God-defying filth? Stand up and fight, I say."

A great light like dawn came into Mr. Turnbull's face. Behind his red hair and beard he turned deadly pale with pleasure. Here, after twenty lone years of useless toil, he had his reward. Someone was angry with the paper. He bounded to his feet like a boy; he saw a new youth opening before him. And as not unfrequently happens to middle-aged gentlemen when they see a new youth opening before them, he found himself in the presence of the police.

The policemen, after some ponderous questionings, collared both the two enthusiasts. They were more respectful, however, to the young man who had smashed the window, than to the miscreant who had had his window smashed. There was an air of refined mystery about Evan MacIan, which did not exist in the irate little shopkeeper, an air of refined mystery which appealed to the policemen, for policemen, like most other English types, are at once snobs and poets. MacIan might possibly be a gentleman, they felt; the editor manifestly was not. And the editor's fine rational republican appeals to his respect for law, and his ardour to be tried by his fellow citizens, seemed to the police quite as much gibberish as Evan's mysticism could have done. The police were not used to hearing principles, even the principles of their own existence.

The police magistrate, before whom they were hurried and tried, was a Mr. Cumberland Vane, a cheerful, middle-aged gentleman, honourably celebrated for the lightness of his sentences and the lightness of his conversation. He occasionally worked himself up into a sort of theoretic rage about certain particular offenders, such as the men who took pokers to their wives, talked in a loose, sentimental way about the desirability of flogging them, and was hopelessly bewildered by the fact that the wives seemed even more angry with him than with their husbands. He was a tall, spruce man, with a twist of black moustache and incomparable morning dress. He looked like a gentleman, and yet, somehow, like a stage gentleman.

He had often treated serious crimes against mere order or property with a humane flippancy. Hence, about the mere breaking of an editor's window, he was almost uproarious.

"Come, Mr. MacIan, come," he said, leaning back in his chair, "do you generally enter you friends' houses by walking through the glass?" (Laughter.)

"He is not my friend," said Evan, with the stolidity of a dull child.

"Not your friend, eh?" said the magistrate, sparkling. "Is he your brother-in-law?" (Loud and prolonged laughter.)

"He is my enemy," said Evan, simply; "he is the enemy of God."

Mr. Vane shifted sharply in his seat, dropping the eye-glass out of his eye in a momentary and not unmanly embarrassment.

"You mustn't talk like that here," he said, roughly, and in a kind of hurry, "that has nothing to do with us."

Evan opened his great, blue eyes; "God," he began.

"Be quiet," said the magistrate, angrily, "it is most undesirable that things of that sort should be spoken about—a—in public, and in an ordinary Court of Justice. Religion is—a—too personal a matter to be mentioned in such a place."

"Is it?" answered the Highlander, "then what did those policemen swear by just now?"

"That is no parallel," answered Vane, rather irritably; "of course there is a form of oath—to be taken reverently—reverently, and there's an end of it. But to talk in a public place about one's most sacred and private sentiments—well, I call it bad taste. (Slight applause.) I call it irreverent. I call it irreverent, and I'm not specially orthodox either."

"I see you are not," said Evan, "but I am."

"We are wondering from the point," said the police magistrate, pulling himself together.

"May I ask why you smashed this worthy citizen's window?"

Evan turned a little pale at the mere memory, but he answered with the same cold and deadly literalism that he showed throughout.

"Because he blasphemed Our Lady."

"I tell you once and for all," cried Mr. Cumberland Vane, rapping his knuckles angrily on the table, "I tell you, once and for all, my man, that I will not have you turning on any religious rant or cant here. Don't imagine that it will impress me. The most religious people are not those who talk about it. (Applause.) You answer the questions and do nothing else."

"I did nothing else," said Evan, with a slight smile.

"Eh," cried Vane, glaring through his eye-glass.

"You asked me why I broke his window," said MacIan, with a face of wood. "I answered, 'Because he blasphemed Our Lady.' I had no other reason. So I have no other answer." Vane continued to gaze at him with a sternness not habitual to him.

"You are not going the right way to work, Sir," he said, with severity. "You are not going the right way to work to—a—have your case treated with special consideration. If you had simply expressed regret for what you had done, I should have been strongly inclined to dismiss the matter as an outbreak of temper. Even now, if you say that you are sorry I shall only——"

"But I am not in the least sorry," said Evan, "I am very pleased."

"I really believe you are insane," said the stipendiary, indignantly, for he had really been doing his best as a good-natured man, to compose the dispute. "What conceivable right have you to break other people's windows because their opinions do not agree with yours? This man only gave expression to his sincere belief."

"So did I," said the Highlander.

"And who are you?" exploded Vane. "Are your views necessarily the right ones? Are you necessarily in possession of the truth?"

"Yes," said MacIan.

The magistrate broke into a contemptuous laugh.

"Oh, you want a nurse to look after you," he said. "You must pay L10."

Evan MacIan plunged his hands into his loose grey garment and drew out a queer looking leather purse. It contained exactly twelve sovereigns. He paid down the ten, coin by coin, in silence, and equally silently returned the remaining two to the receptacle. Then he said, "May I say a word, your worship?"

Cumberland Vane seemed half hypnotized with the silence and automatic movements of the stranger; he made a movement with his head which might have been either "yes" or "no". "I only wished to say, your worship," said MacIan, putting back the purse in his trouser pocket, "that smashing that shop window was, I confess, a useless and rather irregular business. It may be excused, however, as a mere preliminary to further proceedings, a sort of preface. Wherever and whenever I meet that man," and he pointed to the editor of The Atheist, "whether it be outside this door in ten minutes from now, or twenty years hence in some distant country, wherever and whenever I meet that man, I will fight him. Do not be afraid. I will not rush at him like a bully, or bear him down with any brute superiority. I will fight him like a gentleman; I will fight him as our fathers fought. He shall choose how, sword or pistol, horse or foot. But if he refuses, I will write his cowardice on every wall in the world. If he had said of my mother what he said of the Mother of God, there is not a club of clean men in Europe that would deny my right to call him out. If he had said it of my wife, you English would yourselves have pardoned me for beating him like a dog in the market place. Your worship, I have no mother; I have no wife. I have only that which the poor have equally with the rich; which the lonely have equally with the man of many friends. To me this whole strange world is homely, because in the heart of it there is a home; to me this cruel world is kindly, because higher than the heavens there is something more human than humanity. If a man must not fight for this, may he fight for anything? I would fight for my friend, but if I lost my friend, I should still be there. I would fight for my country, but if I lost my country, I should still exist. But if what that devil dreams were true, I should not be—I should burst like a bubble and be gone. I could not live in that imbecile universe. Shall I not fight for my own existence?"

The magistrate recovered his voice and his presence of mind. The first part of the speech, the bombastic and brutally practical challenge, stunned him with surprise; but the rest of Evan's remarks, branching off as they did into theoretic phrases, gave his vague and very English mind (full of memories of the hedging and compromise in English public speaking) an indistinct sensation of relief, as if the man, though mad, were not so dangerous as he had thought. He went into a sort of weary laughter.

"For Heaven's sake, man," he said, "don't talk so much. Let other people have a chance (laughter). I trust all that you said about asking Mr. Turnbull to fight, may be regarded as rubbish. In case of accidents, however, I must bind you over to keep the peace."

"To keep the peace," repeated Evan, "with whom?"

"With Mr. Turnbull," said Vane.

"Certainly not," answered MacIan. "What has he to do with peace?"

"Do you mean to say," began the magistrate, "that you refuse to..." The voice of Turnbull himself clove in for the first time.

"Might I suggest," he said, "That I, your worship, can settle to some extent this absurd matter myself. This rather wild gentleman promises that he will not attack me with any ordinary assault—and if he does, you may be sure the police shall hear of it. But he says he will not. He says he will challenge me to a duel; and I cannot say anything stronger about his mental state than to say that I think that it is highly probable that he will. (Laughter.) But it takes two to make a duel, your worship (renewed laughter). I do not in the least mind being described on every wall in the world as the coward who would not fight a man in Fleet Street, about whether the Virgin Mary had a parallel in Mesopotamian mythology. No, your worship. You need not trouble to bind him over to keep the peace. I bind myself over to keep the peace, and you may rest quite satisfied that there will be no duel with me in it."

Mr. Cumberland Vane rolled about, laughing in a sort of relief.

"You're like a breath of April, sir," he cried. "You're ozone after that fellow. You're perfectly right. Perhaps I have taken the thing too seriously. I should love to see him sending you challenges and to see you smiling. Well, well."

Evan went out of the Court of Justice free, but strangely shaken, like a sick man. Any punishment of suppression he would have felt as natural; but the sudden juncture between the laughter of his judge and the laughter of the man he had wronged, made him feel suddenly small, or at least, defeated. It was really true that the whole modern world regarded his world as a bubble. No cruelty could have shown it, but their kindness showed it with a ghastly clearness. As he was brooding, he suddenly became conscious of a small, stern figure, fronting him in silence. Its eyes were grey and awful, and its beard red. It was Turnbull.

"Well, sir," said the editor of *The Atheist*, "where is the fight to be? Name the field, sir."

Evan stood thunderstruck. He stammered out something, he knew not what; he only guessed it by the answer of the other.

"Do I want to fight? Do I want to fight?" cried the furious Free-thinker. "Why, you moonstruck scarecrow of superstition, do you think your dirty saints are the only people who can die? Haven't you hung atheists, and burned them, and boiled them, and did they ever deny their faith? Do you think we don't want to fight? Night and day I have prayed—I have longed—for an atheist revolution—I have longed to see your blood and ours on the streets. Let it be yours or mine?"

"But you said..." began MacIan.

"I know," said Turnbull scornfully. "And what did you say? You damned fool, you said things that might have got us locked up for a year, and shadowed by the coppers for half a decade. If you wanted to fight, why did you tell that ass you wanted to? I got you out, to fight if you want to. Now, fight if you dare."

"I swear to you, then," said MacIan, after a pause. "I swear to you that nothing shall come between us. I swear to you that nothing shall be in my heart or in my head till our swords clash together. I swear it by the God you have denied, by the Blessed Lady you have blasphemed; I swear it by the seven swords in her heart. I swear it by the Holy Island where my fathers are, by the honour of my mother, by the secret of my people, and by the chalice of the Blood of God."

The atheist drew up his head. "And I," he said, "give my word."

III. SOME OLD CURIOSITIES

The evening sky, a dome of solid gold, unflaked even by a single sunset cloud, steeped the meanest sights of London in a strange and mellow light. It made a little greasy street of St. Martin's Lane look as if it were paved with gold. It made the pawnbroker's half-way down it shine as if it were really that Mountain of Piety that the French poetic instinct has named it; it made the mean pseudo-French bookshop, next but one to it, a shop packed with dreary indecency, show for a moment a kind of Parisian colour. And the shop that stood between the pawnshop and the shop of dreary indecency, showed with quite a blaze of old world beauty, for it was, by accident, a shop not unbeautiful in itself. The front window had a glimmer of bronze and blue steel, lit, as by a few stars, by the sparks of what were alleged to be jewels; for it was in brief, a shop of brica-brac and old curiosities. A row of half-burnished seventeenth-century swords ran like an ornate railing along the front of the window; behind was a darker glimmer of old oak and old armour; and higher up hung the most extraordinary looking South Sea tools or utensils, whether designed for killing enemies or merely for cooking them, no mere white man could possibly conjecture. But the romance of the eye, which really on this rich evening, clung about the shop, had its main source in the accident of two doors standing open, the front door that opened on the street and a back door that opened on an odd green square of garden, that the sun turned to a square of gold. There is nothing more beautiful than thus to look as it were through the archway of a house; as if the open sky were an interior chamber, and the sun a secret lamp of the place.

I have suggested that the sunset light made everything lovely. To say that it made the keeper of the curiosity shop lovely would be a tribute to it perhaps too extreme. It would easily have made him beautiful if he had been merely squalid; if he had been a Jew of the Fagin type. But he was a Jew of another and much less admirable type; a Jew with a very well-sounding name. For though there are no hard tests for separating the tares and the wheat of any people, one rude but efficient guide is that the nice Jew is called Moses Solomon, and the nasty Jew is called Thornton Percy. The keeper of the curiosity shop was of the Thornton Percy branch of the chosen people; he belonged to those Lost Ten Tribes whose industrious object is to lose themselves. He was a man still young, but already corpulent, with sleek dark hair, heavy handsome clothes, and a full, fat, permanent smile, which looked at the first glance kindly, and at the second cowardly. The name over his shop was Henry Gordon, but two Scotchmen who were in his shop that evening could come upon no trace of a Scotch accent.

These two Scotchmen in this shop were careful purchasers, but free-handed payers. One of them who seemed to be the principal and the authority (whom, indeed, Mr. Henry Gordon fancied he had seen somewhere before), was a small, sturdy fellow, with fine grey eyes, a square red tie and a square red beard, that he carried aggressively forward as if he defied anyone to pull it. The other kept so much in the background in comparison that he looked almost ghostly in his grey cloak or plaid, a tall, sallow, silent young man.

The two Scotchmen were interested in seventeenth-century swords. They were fastidious about them. They had a whole armoury of these weapons brought out and rolled clattering about the counter, until they found two of precisely the same length. Presumably they desired the exact symmetry for some decorative trophy. Even then they felt the points, poised the swords for balance and bent them in a circle to see that they sprang straight again; which, for decorative purposes, seems carrying realism rather far.

"These will do," said the strange person with the red beard. "And perhaps I had better pay for them at once. And as you are the challenger, Mr. MacIan, perhaps you had better explain the situation."

The tall Scotchman in grey took a step forward and spoke in a voice quite clear and bold, and yet somehow lifeless, like a man going through an ancient formality.

"The fact is, Mr. Gordon, we have to place our honour in your hands. Words have passed between Mr. Turnbull and myself on a grave and invaluable matter, which can only be atoned for by fighting. Unfortunately, as the police are in some sense pursuing

G.K. CHESTERTON

us, we are hurried, and must fight now and without seconds. But if you will be so kind as to take us into your little garden and see far play, we shall feel how——"

The shopman recovered himself from a stunning surprise and burst out:

"Gentlemen, are you drunk? A duel! A duel in my garden. Go home, gentlemen, go home. Why, what did you quarrel about?"

"We quarrelled," said Evan, in the same dead voice, "about religion." The fat shopkeeper rolled about in his chair with enjoyment.

"Well, this is a funny game," he said. "So you want to commit murder on behalf of religion. Well, well my religion is a little respect for humanity, and——"

"Excuse me," cut in Turnbull, suddenly and fiercely, pointing towards the pawnbroker's next door. "Don't you own that shop?"

"Why—er—yes," said Gordon.

"And don't you own that shop?" repeated the secularist, pointing backward to the pornographic bookseller.

"What if I do?"

"Why, then," cried Turnbull, with grating contempt. "I will leave the religion of humanity confidently in your hands; but I am sorry I troubled you about such a thing as honour. Look here, my man. I do believe in humanity. I do believe in liberty. My father died for it under the swords of the Yeomanry. I am going to die for it, if need be, under that sword on your counter. But if there is one sight that makes me doubt it it is your foul fat face. It is hard to believe you were not meant to be ruled like a dog or killed like a cockroach. Don't try your slave's philosophy on me. We are going to fight, and we are going to fight in your garden, with your swords. Be still! Raise your voice above a whisper, and I run you through the body."

Turnbull put the bright point of the sword against the gay waistcoat of the dealer, who stood choking with rage and fear, and an astonishment so crushing as to be greater than either.

"MacIan," said Turnbull, falling almost into the familiar tone of a business partner, "MacIan, tie up this fellow and put a gag in his mouth. Be still, I say, or I kill you where you stand."

The man was too frightened to scream, but he struggled wildly, while Evan MacIan, whose long, lean hands were unusually powerful, tightened some old curtain cords round him, strapped a rope gag in his mouth and rolled him on his back on the floor.

"There's nothing very strong here," said Evan, looking about him. "I'm afraid he'll work through that gag in half an hour or so."

"Yes," said Turnbull, "but one of us will be killed by that time."

"Well, let's hope so," said the Highlander, glancing doubtfully at the squirming thing on the floor.

"And now," said Turnbull, twirling his fiery moustache and fingering his sword, "let us go into the garden. What an exquisite summer evening!"

MacIan said nothing, but lifting his sword from the counter went out into the sun.

The brilliant light ran along the blades, filling the channels of them with white fire; the combatants stuck their swords in the turf and took off their hats, coats, waistcoats, and boots. Evan said a short Latin prayer to himself, during which Turnbull made something of a parade of lighting a cigarette which he flung away the instant after,

222

when he saw MacIan apparently standing ready. Yet MacIan was not exactly ready. He stood staring like a man stricken with a trance.

"What are you staring at?" asked Turnbull. "Do you see the bobbies?"

"I see Jerusalem," said Evan, "all covered with the shields and standards of the Saracens."

"Jerusalem!" said Turnbull, laughing. "Well, we've taken the only inhabitant into captivity."

And he picked up his sword and made it whistle like a boy's wand.

"I beg your pardon," said MacIan, dryly. "Let us begin."

MacIan made a military salute with his weapon, which Turnbull copied or parodied with an impatient contempt; and in the stillness of the garden the swords came together with a clear sound like a bell. The instant the blades touched, each felt them tingle to their very points with a personal vitality, as if they were two naked nerves of steel. Evan had worn throughout an air of apathy, which might have been the stale apathy of one who wants nothing. But it was indeed the more dreadful apathy of one who wants something and will care for nothing else. And this was seen suddenly; for the instant Evan engaged he disengaged and lunged with an infernal violence. His opponent with a desperate promptitude parried and riposted; the parry only just succeeded, the riposte failed. Something big and unbearable seemed to have broken finally out of Evan in that first murderous lunge, leaving him lighter and cooler and quicker upon his feet. He fell to again, fiercely still, but now with a fierce caution. The next moment Turnbull lunged; MacIan seemed to catch the point and throw it away from him, and was thrusting back like a thunderbolt, when a sound paralysed him; another sound beside their ringing weapons. Turnbull, perhaps from an equal astonishment, perhaps from chivalry, stopped also and forebore to send his sword through his exposed enemy.

"What's that?" asked Evan, hoarsely.

A heavy scraping sound, as of a trunk being dragged along a littered floor, came from the dark shop behind them.

"The old Jew has broken one of his strings, and he's crawling about," said Turnbull. "Be quick! We must finish before he gets his gag out."

"Yes, yes, quick! On guard!" cried the Highlander. The blades crossed again with the same sound like song, and the men went to work again with the same white and watchful faces. Evan, in his impatience, went back a little to his wildness. He made windmills, as the French duellists say, and though he was probably a shade the better fencer of the two, he found the other's point pass his face twice so close as almost to graze his cheek. The second time he realized the actual possibility of defeat and pulled himself together under a shock of the sanity of anger. He narrowed, and, so to speak, tightened his operations: he fenced (as the swordsman's boast goes), in a wedding ring; he turned Turnbull's thrusts with a maddening and almost mechanical click, like that of a machine. Whenever Turnbull's sword sought to go over that other mere white streak it seemed to be caught in a complex network of steel. He turned one thrust, turned another, turned another. Then suddenly he went forward at the lunge with his whole living weight. Turnbull leaped back, but Evan lunged and lunged and lunged again like a devilish piston rod or battering ram. And high above all the sound of the struggle there broke into the silent evening a bellowing human voice, nasal, raucous, at the highest pitch of pain. "Help! Help! Police! Murder! Murder!" The gag was broken; and the tongue of terror was loose.

"Keep on!" gasped Turnbull. "One may be killed before they come."

The voice of the screaming shopkeeper was loud enough to drown not only the noise of the swords but all other noises around it, but even through its rending din there seemed to be some other stir or scurry. And Evan, in the very act of thrusting at Turnbull, saw something in his eyes that made him drop his sword. The atheist, with his grey eyes at their widest and wildest, was staring straight over his shoulder at the little archway of shop that opened on the street beyond. And he saw the archway blocked and blackened with strange figures.

"We must bolt, MacIan," he said abruptly. "And there isn't a damned second to lose either. Do as I do."

With a bound he was beside the little cluster of his clothes and boots that lay on the lawn; he snatched them up, without waiting to put any of them on; and tucking his sword under his other arm, went wildly at the wall at the bottom of the garden and swung himself over it. Three seconds after he had alighted in his socks on the other side, MacIan alighted beside him, also in his socks and also carrying clothes and sword in a desperate bundle.

They were in a by-street, very lean and lonely itself, but so close to a crowded thoroughfare that they could see the vague masses of vehicles going by, and could even see an individual hansom cab passing the corner at the instant. Turnbull put his fingers to his mouth like a gutter-snipe and whistled twice. Even as he did so he could hear the loud voices of the neighbours and the police coming down the garden.

The hansom swung sharply and came tearing down the little lane at his call. When the cabman saw his fares, however, two wild-haired men in their shirts and socks with naked swords under their arms, he not unnaturally brought his readiness to a rigid stop and stared suspiciously.

"You talk to him a minute," whispered Turnbull, and stepped back into the shadow of the wall.

"We want you," said MacIan to the cabman, with a superb Scotch drawl of indifference and assurance, "to drive us to St. Pancras Station—verra quick."

"Very sorry, sir," said the cabman, "but I'd like to know it was all right. Might I arst where you come from, sir?"

A second after he spoke MacIan heard a heavy voice on the other side of the wall, saying: "I suppose I'd better get over and look for them. Give me a back."

"Cabby," said MacIan, again assuming the most deliberate and lingering lowland Scotch intonation, "if ye're really verra anxious to ken whar a' come fra', I'll tell ye as a verra great secret. A' come from Scotland. And a'm gaein' to St. Pancras Station. Open the doors, cabby."

The cabman stared, but laughed. The heavy voice behind the wall said: "Now then, a better back this time, Mr. Price." And from the shadow of the wall Turnbull crept out. He had struggled wildly into his coat (leaving his waistcoat on the pavement), and he was with a fierce pale face climbing up the cab behind the cabman. MacIan had no glimmering notion of what he was up to, but an instinct of discipline, inherited from a hundred men of war, made him stick to his own part and trust the other man's.

"Open the doors, cabby," he repeated, with something of the obstinate solemnity of a drunkard, "open the doors. Did ye no hear me say St. Pancras Station?"

The top of a policeman's helmet appeared above the garden wall. The cabman did not see it, but he was still suspicious and began:

"Very sorry, sir, but..." and with that the catlike Turnbull tore him out of his seat and hurled him into the street below, where he lay suddenly stunned.

"Give me his hat," said Turnbull in a silver voice, that the other obeyed like a bugle. "And get inside with the swords."

And just as the red and raging face of a policeman appeared above the wall, Turnbull struck the horse with a terrible cut of the whip and the two went whirling away like a boomerang.

They had spun through seven streets and three or four squares before anything further happened. Then, in the neighbourhood of Maida Vale, the driver opened the trap and talked through it in a manner not wholly common in conversations through that aperture.

"Mr. MacIan," he said shortly and civilly.

"Mr. Turnbull," replied his motionless fare.

"Under circumstances such as those in which we were both recently placed there was no time for anything but very abrupt action. I trust therefore that you have no cause to complain of me if I have deferred until this moment a consultation with you on our present position or future action. Our present position, Mr. MacIan, I imagine that I am under no special necessity of describing. We have broken the law and we are fleeing from its officers. Our future action is a thing about which I myself entertain sufficiently strong views; but I have no right to assume or to anticipate yours, though I may have formed a decided conception of your character and a decided notion of what they will probably be. Still, by every principle of intellectual justice, I am bound to ask you now and seriously whether you wish to continue our interrupted relations."

MacIan leant his white and rather weary face back upon the cushions in order to speak up through the open door.

"Mr. Turnbull," he said, "I have nothing to add to what I have said before. It is strongly borne in upon me that you and I, the sole occupants of this runaway cab, are at this moment the two most important people in London, possibly in Europe. I have been looking at all the streets as we went past, I have been looking at all the shops as we went past, I have been looking at all the churches as we went past. At first, I felt a little dazed with the vastness of it all. I could not understand what it all meant. But now I know exactly what it all means. It means us. This whole civilization is only a dream. You and I are the realities."

"Religious symbolism," said Mr. Turnbull, through the trap, "does not, as you are probably aware, appeal ordinarily to thinkers of the school to which I belong. But in symbolism as you use it in this instance, I must, I think, concede a certain truth. We *must* fight this thing out somewhere; because, as you truly say, we have found each other's reality. We *must* kill each other—or convert each other. I used to think all Christians were hypocrites, and I felt quite mildly towards them really. But I know you are sincere—and my soul is mad against you. In the same way you used, I suppose, to think that all atheists thought atheism would leave them free for immorality—and yet in your heart you tolerated them entirely. Now you *know* that I am an honest man, and you are mad against me, as I am against you. Yes, that's it. You can't be angry with bad men. But a good man in the wrong—why one thirsts for his blood. Yes, you open for me a vista of thought."

"Don't run into anything," said Evan, immovably.

"There's something in that view of yours, too," said Turnbull, and shut down the trap.

They sped on through shining streets that shot by them like arrows. Mr. Turnbull had evidently a great deal of unused practical talent which was unrolling itself in this ridiculous adventure. They had got away with such stunning promptitude that the police chase had in all probability not even properly begun. But in case it had, the amateur cabman chose his dizzy course through London with a strange dexterity. He did not do what would have first occurred to any ordinary outsider desiring to destroy his tracks. He did not cut into by-ways or twist his way through mean streets. His amateur common sense told him that it was precisely the poor street, the side street, that would be likely to remember and report the passing of a hansom cab, like the passing of a royal procession. He kept chiefly to the great roads, so full of hansoms that a wilder pair than they might easily have passed in the press. In one of the quieter streets Evan put on his boots.

Towards the top of Albany Street the singular cabman again opened the trap.

"Mr. MacIan," he said, "I understand that we have now definitely settled that in the conventional language honour is not satisfied. Our action must at least go further than it has gone under recent interrupted conditions. That, I believe, is understood."

"Perfectly," replied the other with his bootlace in his teeth.

"Under those conditions," continued Turnbull, his voice coming through the hole with a slight note of trepidation very unusual with him, "I have a suggestion to make, if that can be called a suggestion, which has probably occurred to you as readily as to me. Until the actual event comes off we are practically in the position if not of comrades, at least of business partners. Until the event comes off, therefore I should suggest that quarrelling would be inconvenient and rather inartistic; while the ordinary exchange of politeness between man and man would be not only elegant but uncommonly practical."

"You are perfectly right," answered MacIan, with his melancholy voice, "in saying that all this has occurred to me. All duellists should behave like gentlemen to each other. But we, by the queerness of our position, are something much more than either duellists or gentlemen. We are, in the oddest and most exact sense of the term, brothers —in arms."

"Mr. MacIan," replied Turnbull, calmly, "no more need be said." And he closed the trap once more.

They had reached Finchley Road before he opened it again.

Then he said, "Mr. MacIan, may I offer you a cigar. It will be a touch of realism."

"Thank you," answered Evan. "You are very kind." And he began to smoke in the cab.

IV. A DISCUSSION AT DAWN

The duellists had from their own point of view escaped or conquered the chief powers of the modern world. They had satisfied the magistrate, they had tied the tradesman neck and heels, and they had left the police behind. As far as their own feelings went they had melted into a monstrous sea; they were but the fare and driver of one of the million hansoms that fill London streets. But they had forgotten something; they had forgotten journalism. They had forgotten that there exists in the modern world, perhaps for the first time in history, a class of people whose interest is not that things should happen well or happen badly, should happen successfully or happen unsuccessfully, should happen to the advantage of this party or the advantage of that part, but whose interest simply is that things should happen.

It is the one great weakness of journalism as a picture of our modern existence, that it must be a picture made up entirely of exceptions. We announce on flaring posters that a man has fallen off a scaffolding. We do not announce on flaring posters that a man has not fallen off a scaffolding. Yet this latter fact is fundamentally more exciting, as indicating that that moving tower of terror and mystery, a man, is still abroad upon the earth. That the man has not fallen off a scaffolding is really more sensational; and it is also some thousand times more common. But journalism cannot reasonably be expected thus to insist upon the permanent miracles. Busy editors cannot be expected to put on their posters, "Mr. Wilkinson Still Safe," or "Mr. Jones, of Worthing, Not Dead Yet." They cannot announce the happiness of mankind at all. They cannot describe all the forks that are not stolen, or all the marriages that are not judiciously dissolved. Hence the complete picture they give of life is of necessity fallacious; they can only represent what is unusual. However democratic they may be, they are only concerned with the minority.

The incident of the religious fanatic who broke a window on Ludgate Hill was alone enough to set them up in good copy for the night. But when the same man was brought before a magistrate and defied his enemy to mortal combat in the open court, then the columns would hardly hold the excruciating information, and the headlines were so large that there was hardly room for any of the text. The *Daily Telegraph* headed a column, "A Duel on Divinity," and there was a correspondence afterwards which lasted for months, about whether police magistrates ought to mention religion. The *Daily Mail* in its dull, sensible way, headed the events, "Wanted to fight for the Virgin." Mr. James Douglas, in *The Star*, presuming on his knowledge of philosophical and theological terms, described the Christian's outbreak under the title of "Dualist and Duellist." The *Daily News* inserted a colourless account of the matter, but was pursued and eaten up for some weeks, with letters from outlying ministers, headed "Murder and Mariolatry." But the journalistic temperature was steadily and consistently heated by all these influences; the journalists had tasted blood, prospectively, and were in the mood for more; everything in the matter prepared them for further outbursts of moral indignation. And when a gasping reporter rushed in in the last hours of the evening with the announcement that the two heroes of the Police Court had literally been found fighting in a London back garden, with a shopkeeper bound and gagged in the front of the house, the editors and sub-editors were stricken still as men are by great beatitudes.

The next morning, five or six of the great London dailies burst out simultaneously into great blossoms of eloquent leader-writing. Towards the end all the leaders tended to be the same, but they all began differently. The *Daily Telegraph*, for instance began, "There will be little difference among our readers or among all truly English and law-abiding men touching the, etc. etc." The *Daily Mail* said, "People must learn, in the modern world, to keep their theological differences to themselves. The fracas, etc. etc." The *Daily News* started, "Nothing could be more inimical to the cause of true religion than, etc. etc." The *Times* began with something about Celtic disturbances of the equilibrium of Empire, and the *Daily Express* distinguished itself splendidly by omitting altogether so controversial a matter and substituting a leader about goloshes.

And the morning after that, the editors and the newspapers were in such a state, that, as the phrase is, there was no holding them. Whatever secret and elvish thing it is that broods over editors and suddenly turns their brains, that thing had seized on the story of the broken glass and the duel in the garden. It became monstrous and omnipresent, as do in our time the unimportant doings of the sect of the Agapemonites, or as did at an earlier time the dreary dishonesties of the Rhodesian financiers. Questions were asked about it, and even answered, in the House of Commons. The Government was solemnly denounced in the papers for not having done something, nobody knew what, to prevent the window being broken. An enormous subscription was started to reimburse Mr. Gordon, the man who had been gagged in the shop. Mr. MacIan, one of the combatants, became for some mysterious reason, singly and hugely popular as a comic figure in the comic papers and on the stage of the music hall. He was always represented (in defiance of fact), with red whiskers, and a very red nose, and in full Highland costume. And a song, consisting of an unimaginable number of verses, in which his name was rhymed with flat iron, the British Lion, sly 'un, dandelion, Spion (With Kop in the next line), was sung to crowded houses every night. The papers developed a devouring thirst for the capture of the fugitives; and when they had not been caught for forty-eight hours, they suddenly turned the whole matter into a detective mystery. Letters under the heading, "Where are They," poured in to every paper, with every conceivable kind of explanation, running them to earth in the Monument, the Twopenny Tube, Epping Forest, Westminster Abbey, rolled up in carpets at Shoolbreds, locked up in safes in Chancery Lane. Yes, the papers were very interesting, and Mr. Turnbull unrolled a whole bundle of them for the amusement of Mr. MacIan as they sat on a high common to the north of London, in the coming of the white dawn.

The darkness in the east had been broken with a bar of grey; the bar of grey was split with a sword of silver and morning lifted itself laboriously over London. From the spot where Turnbull and MacIan were sitting on one of the barren steeps behind Hampstead, they could see the whole of London shaping itself vaguely and largely in the grey and growing light, until the white sun stood over it and it lay at their feet, the splendid monstrosity that it is. Its bewildering squares and parallelograms were compact and perfect as a Chinese puzzle; an enormous hieroglyphic which man must decipher or die. There fell upon both of them, but upon Turnbull more than the other, because he know more what the scene signified, that quite indescribable sense as of a sublime and passionate and heart-moving futility, which is never evoked by deserts or dead men or men neglected and barbarous, which can only be invoked by the sight of the enormous genius of man applied to anything other than the best. Turnbull, the old idealistic democrat, had so often reviled the democracy and reviled them justly for their supineness, their snobbishness, their evil reverence for idle things. He was right enough; for our democracy has only one great fault; it is not democratic. And after denouncing so justly average modern men for so many years as sophists and as slaves, he looked down from an empty slope in Hampstead and saw what gods they are. Their achievement seemed all the more heroic and divine, because it seemed doubtful whether it was worth doing at all. There seemed to be something greater than mere accuracy in making such a mistake as London. And what was to be the end of it all? what was to be the ultimate transformation of this common and incredible London man, this workman on a tram in Battersea, his clerk on an omnibus in Cheapside? Turnbull, as he stared drearily, murmured to himself the words of the old atheistic and revolutionary Swinburne who had intoxicated his youth:

> "And still we ask if God or man
> Can loosen thee Lazarus;
> Bid thee rise up republican,
> And save thyself and all of us.
> But no disciple's tongue can say
> If thou can'st take our sins away."

Turnbull shivered slightly as if behind the earthly morning he felt the evening of the world, the sunset of so many hopes. Those words were from "Songs before Sunrise". But Turnbull's songs at their best were songs after sunrise, and sunrise had been no such great thing after all. Turnbull shivered again in the sharp morning air. MacIan was also gazing with his face towards the city, but there was that about his blind and mystical stare that told one, so to speak, that his eyes were turned inwards. When Turnbull said something to him about London, they seemed to move as at a summons and come out like two householders coming out into their doorways.

"Yes," he said, with a sort of stupidity. "It's a very big place."

There was a somewhat unmeaning silence, and then MacIan said again:

"It's a very big place. When I first came into it I was frightened of it. Frightened exactly as one would be frightened at the sight of a man forty feet high. I am used to big things where I come from, big mountains that seem to fill God's infinity, and the big sea that goes to the end of the world. But then these things are all shapeless and confused things, not made in any familiar form. But to see the plain, square, human things as large as that, houses so large and streets so large, and the town itself so large, was like having screwed some devil's magnifying glass into one's eye. It was like seeing a porridge bowl as big as a house, or a mouse-trap made to catch elephants."

"Like the land of the Brobdingnagians," said Turnbull, smiling.

"Oh! Where is that?" said MacIan.

Turnbull said bitterly, "In a book," and the silence fell suddenly between them again.

They were sitting in a sort of litter on the hillside; all the things they had hurriedly collected, in various places, for their flight, were strewn indiscriminately round them. The two swords with which they had lately sought each other's lives were flung down on the grass at random, like two idle walking-sticks. Some provisions they had bought last night, at a low public house, in case of undefined contingencies, were tossed about like the materials of an ordinary picnic, here a basket of chocolate, and there a bottle of wine. And to add to the disorder finally, there were strewn on top of everything, the most disorderly of modern things, newspapers, and more newspapers, and yet again newspapers, the ministers of the modern anarchy. Turnbull picked up one of them drearily, and took out a pipe.

"There's a lot about us," he said. "Do you mind if I light up?"

"Why should I mind?" asked MacIan.

Turnbull eyed with a certain studious interest, the man who did not understand any of the verbal courtesies; he lit his pipe and blew great clouds out of it.

"Yes," he resumed. "The matter on which you and I are engaged is at this moment really the best copy in England. I am a journalist, and I know. For the first time, perhaps, for many generations, the English are really more angry about a wrong thing done in England than they are about a wrong thing done in France."

"It is not a wrong thing," said MacIan.

Turnbull laughed. "You seem unable to understand the ordinary use of the human language. If I did not suspect that you were a genius, I should certainly know you were a blockhead. I fancy we had better be getting along and collecting our baggage."

And he jumped up and began shoving the luggage into his pockets, or strapping it on to his back. As he thrust a tin of canned meat, anyhow, into his bursting side pocket, he said casually:

"I only meant that you and I are the most prominent people in the English papers."

"Well, what did you expect?" asked MacIan, opening his great grave blue eyes.

"The papers are full of us," said Turnbull, stooping to pick up one of the swords.

MacIan stooped and picked up the other.

"Yes," he said, in his simple way. "I have read what they have to say. But they don't seem to understand the point."

"The point of what?" asked Turnbull.

"The point of the sword," said MacIan, violently, and planted the steel point in the soil like a man planting a tree.

"That is a point," said Turnbull, grimly, "that we will discuss later. Come along."

Turnbull tied the last tin of biscuits desperately to himself with string; and then spoke, like a diver girt for plunging, short and sharp.

"Now, Mr. MacIan, you must listen to me. You must listen to me, not merely because I know the country, which you might learn by looking at a map, but because I know the people of the country, whom you could not know by living here thirty years. That infernal city down there is awake; and it is awake against us. All those endless rows of windows and windows are all eyes staring at us. All those forests of chimneys are fingers pointing at us, as we stand here on the hillside. This thing has caught on. For the next six mortal months they will think of nothing but us, as for six mortal months they thought of nothing but the Dreyfus case. Oh, I know it's funny. They let starving children, who don't want to die, drop by the score without looking round. But because two gentlemen, from private feelings of delicacy, do want to die, they will mobilize the army and navy to prevent them. For half a year or more, you and I, Mr. MacIan, will be an obstacle to every reform in the British Empire. We shall prevent the Chinese being sent out of the Transvaal and the blocks being stopped in the Strand. We shall be the conversational substitute when anyone recommends Home Rule, or complains of sky signs. Therefore, do not imagine, in your innocence, that we have only to melt away among those English hills as a Highland cateran might into your god-forsaken Highland mountains. We must be eternally on our guard; we must live the hunted life of two distinguished criminals. We must expect to be recognized as much as if we were Napoleon escaping from Elba. We must be prepared for our descriptions being sent to every tiny village, and for our faces being recognized by every ambitious policeman. We must often sleep under the stars as if we were in Africa. Last and most important we must not dream of effecting our—our final settlement, which will be a thing as famous as the Phoenix Park murders, unless we have made real and precise arrangements for our isolation—I will not say our safety. We must not, in short, fight until we have thrown them off our scent, if only for a moment. For, take my word for it, Mr. MacIan, if the British Public once catches us up, the British Public will prevent the duel, if it is only by locking us both up in asylums for the rest of our days."

MacIan was looking at the horizon with a rather misty look.

"I am not at all surprised," he said, "at the world being against us. It makes me feel I was right to——"

"Yes?" said Turnbull.

"To smash your window," said MacIan. "I have woken up the world."

"Very well, then," said Turnbull, stolidly. "Let us look at a few final facts. Beyond that hill there is comparatively clear country. Fortunately, I know the part well, and if you will follow me exactly, and, when necessary, on your stomach, we may be able to get ten miles out of London, literally without meeting anyone at all, which will be the best possible beginning, at any rate. We have provisions for at least two days and two nights, three days if we do it carefully. We may be able to get fifty or sixty miles away without even walking into an inn door. I have the biscuits and the tinned meat, and the milk. You have the chocolate, I think? And the brandy?"

"Yes," said MacIan, like a soldier taking orders.

"Very well, then, come on. March. We turn under that third bush and so down into the valley." And he set off ahead at a swinging walk.

Then he stopped suddenly; for he realized that the other was not following. Evan MacIan was leaning on his sword with a lowering face, like a man suddenly smitten still with doubt.

"What on earth is the matter?" asked Turnbull, staring in some anger.

Evan made no reply.

"What the deuce is the matter with you?" demanded the leader, again, his face slowly growing as red as his beard; then he said, suddenly, and in a more human voice, "Are you in pain, MacIan?"

"Yes," replied the Highlander, without lifting his face.

"Take some brandy," cried Turnbull, walking forward hurriedly towards him. "You've got it."

"It's not in the body," said MacIan, in his dull, strange way. "The pain has come into my mind. A very dreadful thing has just come into my thoughts."

"What the devil are you talking about?" asked Turnbull.

MacIan broke out with a queer and living voice.

"We must fight now, Turnbull. We must fight now. A frightful thing has come upon me, and I know it must be now and here. I must kill you here," he cried, with a sort of tearful rage impossible to describe. "Here, here, upon this blessed grass."

"Why, you idiot," began Turnbull.

"The hour has come—the black hour God meant for it. Quick, it will soon be gone. Quick!"

And he flung the scabbard from him furiously, and stood with the sunlight sparkling along his sword.

"You confounded fool," repeated Turnbull. "Put that thing up again, you ass; people will come out of that house at the first clash of the steel."

"One of us will be dead before they come," said the other, hoarsely, "for this is the hour God meant."

"Well, I never thought much of God," said the editor of *The Atheist*, losing all patience. "And I think less now. Never mind what God meant. Kindly enlighten my pagan darkness as to what the devil *you* mean."

"The hour will soon be gone. In a moment it will be gone," said the madman. "It is now, now, now that I must nail your blaspheming body to the earth—now, now that I must avenge Our Lady on her vile slanderer. Now or never. For the dreadful thought is in my mind."

"And what thought," asked Turnbull, with frantic composure, "occupies what you call your mind?"

"I must kill you now," said the fanatic, "because——"

"Well, because," said Turnbull, patiently.

"Because I have begun to like you."

Turnbull's face had a sudden spasm in the sunlight, a change so instantaneous that it left no trace behind it; and his features seemed still carved into a cold stare. But when he spoke again he seemed like a man who was placidly pretending to misunderstand something that he understood perfectly well.

"Your affection expresses itself in an abrupt form," he began, but MacIan broke the brittle and frivolous speech to pieces with a violent voice. "Do not trouble to talk like that," he said. "You know what I mean as well as I know it. Come on and fight, I say. Perhaps you are feeling just as I do."

Turnbull's face flinched again in the fierce sunlight, but his attitude kept its contemptuous ease.

"Your Celtic mind really goes too fast for me," he said; "let me be permitted in my heavy Lowland way to understand this new development. My dear Mr. MacIan, what do you really mean?"

MacIan still kept the shining sword-point towards the other's breast.

"You know what I mean. You mean the same yourself. We must fight now or else——"

"Or else?" repeated Turnbull, staring at him with an almost blinding gravity.

"Or else we may not want to fight at all," answered Evan, and the end of his speech was like a despairing cry.

Turnbull took out his own sword suddenly as if to engage; then planting it point downwards for a moment, he said, "Before we begin, may I ask you a question?"

MacIan bowed patiently, but with burning eyes.

"You said, just now," continued Turnbull, presently, "that if we did not fight now, we might not want to fight at all. How would you feel about the matter if we came not to want to fight at all?"

"I should feel," answered the other, "just as I should feel if you had drawn your sword, and I had run away from it. I should feel that because I had been weak, justice had not been done."

"Justice," answered Turnbull, with a thoughtful smile, "but we are talking about your feelings. And what do you mean by justice, apart from your feelings?"

MacIan made a gesture of weary recognition! "Oh, Nominalism," he said, with a sort of sigh, "we had all that out in the twelfth century."

"I wish we could have it out now," replied the other, firmly. "Do you really mean that if you came to think me right, you would be certainly wrong?"

"If I had a blow on the back of my head, I might come to think you a green elephant," answered MacIan, "but have I not the right to say now, that if I thought that I should think wrong?"

"Then you are quite certain that it would be wrong to like me?" asked Turnbull, with a slight smile.

"No," said Evan, thoughtfully, "I do not say that. It may not be the devil, it may be some part of God I am not meant to know. But I had a work to do, and it is making the work difficult."

"And I suppose," said the atheist, quite gently, "that you and I know all about which part of God we ought to know."

MacIan burst out like a man driven back and explaining everything.

"The Church is not a thing like the Athenaeum Club," he cried. "If the Athenaeum Club lost all its members, the Athenaeum Club would dissolve and cease to exist. But when we belong to the Church we belong to something which is outside all of us; which is outside everything you talk about, outside the Cardinals and the Pope. They belong to it, but it does not belong to them. If we all fell dead suddenly, the Church would still somehow exist in God. Confound it all, don't you see that I am more sure of its existence than I am of my own existence? And yet you ask me to trust my temperament, my own temperament, which can be turned upside down by two bottles of claret or an attack of the jaundice. You ask me to trust that when it softens towards you and not to trust the thing which I believe to be outside myself and more real than the blood in my body."

"Stop a moment," said Turnbull, in the same easy tone, "Even in the very act of saying that you believe this or that, you imply that there is a part of yourself that you trust even if there are many parts which you mistrust. If it is only you that like me, surely, also, it is only you that believe in the Catholic Church."

Evan remained in an unmoved and grave attitude. "There is a part of me which is divine," he answered, "a part that can be trusted, but there are also affections which are entirely animal and idle."

"And you are quite certain, I suppose," continued Turnbull, "that if even you esteem me the esteem would be wholly animal and idle?" For the first time MacIan started as if he had not expected the thing that was said to him. At last he said:

"Whatever in earth or heaven it is that has joined us two together, it seems to be something which makes it impossible to lie. No, I do not think that the movement in me towards you was...was that surface sort of thing. It may have been something deeper...something strange. I cannot understand the thing at all. But understand this and understand it thoroughly, if I loved you my love might be divine. No, it is not some trifle that we are fighting about. It is not some superstition or some symbol. When you wrote those words about Our Lady, you were in that act a wicked man doing a wicked thing. If I hate you it is because you have hated goodness. And if I like you...it is because you are good."

Turnbull's face wore an indecipherable expression.

"Well, shall we fight now?" he said.

"Yes," said MacIan, with a sudden contraction of his black brows, "yes, it must be now."

The bright swords crossed, and the first touch of them, travelling down blade and arm, told each combatant that the heart of the other was awakened. It was not in that way that the swords rang together when they had rushed on each other in the little garden behind the dealer's shop.

There was a pause, and then MacIan made a movement as if to thrust, and almost at the same moment Turnbull suddenly and calmly dropped his sword. Evan stared round in an unusual bewilderment, and then realized that a large man in pale clothes and a Panama hat was strolling serenely towards them.

V. THE PEACEMAKER

When the combatants, with crossed swords, became suddenly conscious of a third party, they each made the same movement. It was as quick as the snap of a pistol, and they altered it instantaneously and recovered their original pose, but they had both made it, they had both seen it, and they both knew what it was. It was not a movement of anger at being interrupted. Say or think what they would, it was a movement of relief. A force within them, and yet quite beyond them, seemed slowly and pitilessly washing away the adamant of their oath. As mistaken lovers might watch the inevitable sunset of first love, these men watched the sunset of their first hatred.

Their hearts were growing weaker and weaker against each other. When their weapons rang and riposted in the little London garden, they could have been very certain that if a third party had interrupted them something at least would have happened. They would have killed each other or they would have killed him. But now nothing could undo or deny that flash of fact, that for a second they had been glad to be interrupted. Some new and strange thing was rising higher and higher in their hearts like a high sea at night. It was something that seemed all the more merciless, because it might turn out an enormous mercy. Was there, perhaps, some such fatalism in friendship as all lovers talk about in love? Did God make men love each other against their will?

"I'm sure you'll excuse my speaking to you," said the stranger, in a voice at once eager and deprecating.

The voice was too polite for good manners. It was incongruous with the eccentric spectacle of the duellists which ought to have startled a sane and free man. It was also incongruous with the full and healthy, though rather loose physique of the man who spoke. At the first glance he looked a fine animal, with curling gold beard and hair, and blue eyes, unusually bright. It was only at the second glance that the mind felt a sudden and perhaps unmeaning irritation at the way in which the gold beard retreated backwards into the waistcoat, and the way in which the finely shaped nose went forward as if smelling its way. And it was only, perhaps, at the hundredth glance that the bright blue eyes, which normally before and after the instant seemed brilliant with intelligence, seemed as it were to be brilliant with idiocy. He was a heavy, healthy-looking man, who looked all the larger because of the loose, light coloured clothes that he wore, and that had in their extreme lightness and looseness, almost a touch of the tropics. But a closer examination of his attire would have shown that even in the tropics it would have been unique; but it was all woven according to some hygienic texture which no human being had ever heard of before, and which was absolutely necessary even for a day's health. He wore a huge broad-brimmed hat, equally hygienic, very much at the back of his head, and his voice coming out of so heavy and hearty a type of man was, as I have said, startlingly shrill and deferential.

"I'm sure you'll excuse my speaking to you," he said. "Now, I wonder if you are in some little difficulty which, after all, we could settle very comfortably together? Now, you don't mind my saying this, do you?"

The face of both combatants remained somewhat solid under this appeal. But the stranger, probably taking their silence for a gathering shame, continued with a kind of gaiety:

"So you are the young men I have read about in the papers. Well, of course, when one is young, one is rather romantic. Do you know what I always say to young people?"

A blank silence followed this gay inquiry. Then Turnbull said in a colourless voice:

"As I was forty-seven last birthday, I probably came into the world too soon for the experience."

"Very good, very good," said the friendly person. "Dry Scotch humour. Dry Scotch humour. Well now. I understand that you two people want to fight a duel. I suppose you aren't much up in the modern world. We've quite outgrown duelling, you know. In fact, Tolstoy tells us that we shall soon outgrow war, which he says is simply a duel between nations. A duel between nations. But there is no doubt about our having outgrown duelling."

Waiting for some effect upon his wooden auditors, the stranger stood beaming for a moment and then resumed:

"Now, they tell me in the newspapers that you are really wanting to fight about something connected with Roman Catholicism. Now, do you know what I always say to Roman Catholics?"

"No," said Turnbull, heavily. "Do *they*?" It seemed to be a characteristic of the hearty, hygienic gentleman that he always forgot the speech he had made the moment before. Without enlarging further on the fixed form of his appeal to the Church of Rome, he laughed cordially at Turnbull's answer; then his wandering blue eyes caught the sunlight on the swords, and he assumed a good-humoured gravity.

"But you know this is a serious matter," he said, eyeing Turnbull and MacIan, as if they had just been keeping the table in a roar with their frivolities. "I am sure that if I appealed to your higher natures...your higher natures. Every man has a higher nature and a lower nature. Now, let us put the matter very plainly, and without any romantic nonsense about honour or anything of that sort. Is not bloodshed a great sin?"

"No," said MacIan, speaking for the first time.

"Well, really, really!" said the peacemaker.

"Murder is a sin," said the immovable Highlander. "There is no sin of bloodshed."

"Well, we won't quarrel about a word," said the other, pleasantly.

"Why on earth not?" said MacIan, with a sudden asperity. "Why shouldn't we quarrel about a word? What is the good of words if they aren't important enough to quarrel over? Why do we choose one word more than another if there isn't any difference between them? If you called a woman a chimpanzee instead of an angel, wouldn't there be a quarrel about a word? If you're not going to argue about words, what are you going to argue about? Are you going to convey your meaning to me by moving your ears? The Church and the heresies always used to fight about words, because they are the only things worth fighting about. I say that murder is a sin, and bloodshed is not, and that there is as much difference between those words as there is between the word 'yes' and the word 'no'; or rather more difference, for 'yes' and 'no', at least, belong to the same category. Murder is a spiritual incident. Bloodshed is a physical incident. A surgeon commits bloodshed."

"Ah, you're a casuist!" said the large man, wagging his head. "Now, do you know what I always say to casuists...?"

MacIan made a violent gesture; and Turnbull broke into open laughter. The peacemaker did not seem to be in the least annoyed, but continued in unabated enjoyment.

"Well, well," he said, "let us get back to the point. Now Tolstoy has shown that force is no remedy; so you see the position in which I am placed. I am doing my best to stop what I'm sure you won't mind my calling this really useless violence, this really quite wrong violence of yours. But it's against my principles to call in the police against you, because the police are still on a lower moral plane, so to speak, because, in short, the police undoubtedly sometimes employ force. Tolstoy has shown that violence merely breeds violence in the person towards whom it is used, whereas Love, on the other hand, breeds Love. So you see how I am placed. I am reduced to use Love in order to stop you. I am obliged to use Love."

He gave to the word an indescribable sound of something hard and heavy, as if he were saying "boots". Turnbull suddenly gripped his sword and said, shortly, "I see how you are placed quite well, sir. You will not call the police. Mr. MacIan, shall we engage?" MacIan plucked his sword out of the grass.

"I must and will stop this shocking crime," cried the Tolstoian, crimson in the face. "It is against all modern ideas. It is against the principle of love. How you, sir, who pretend to be a Christian..."

MacIan turned upon him with a white face and bitter lip. "Sir," he said, "talk about the principle of love as much as you like. You seem to me colder than a lump of stone; but I am willing to believe that you may at some time have loved a cat, or a dog, or a child. When you were a baby, I suppose you loved your mother. Talk about love, then, till the world is sick of the word. But don't you talk about Christianity. Don't you dare to say one word, white or black, about it. Christianity is, as far as you are concerned, a horrible mystery. Keep clear of it, keep silent upon it, as you would upon an abomination. It is a thing that has made men slay and torture each other; and you will never know why. It is a thing that has made men do evil that good might come; and you will never understand the evil, let alone the good. Christianity is a thing that could only make you vomit, till you are other than you are. I would not justify it to you even if I could. Hate it, in God's name, as Turnbull does, who is a man. It is a monstrous thing, for which men die. And if you will stand here and talk about love for another ten minutes it is very probable that you will see a man die for it."

And he fell on guard. Turnbull was busy settling something loose in his elaborate hilt, and the pause was broken by the stranger.

"Suppose I call the police?" he said, with a heated face.

"And deny your most sacred dogma," said MacIan.

"Dogma!" cried the man, in a sort of dismay. "Oh, we have no *dogmas*, you know!"

There was another silence, and he said again, airily:

"You know, I think, there's something in what Shaw teaches about no moral principles being quite fixed. Have you ever read *The Quintessence of Ibsenism*? Of course he went very wrong over the war."

Turnbull, with a bent, flushed face, was tying up the loose piece of the pommel with string. With the string in his teeth, he said, "Oh, make up your damned mind and clear out!"

"It's a serious thing," said the philosopher, shaking his head. "I must be alone and consider which is the higher point of view. I rather feel that in a case so extreme as this..." and he went slowly away. As he disappeared among the trees, they heard him murmuring in a sing-song voice, "New occasions teach new duties," out of a poem by James Russell Lowell.

"Ah," said MacIan, drawing a deep breath. "Don't you believe in prayer now? I prayed for an angel."

"An hour ago," said the Highlander, in his heavy meditative voice, "I felt the devil weakening my heart and my oath against you, and I prayed that God would send an angel to my aid."

"Well?" inquired the other, finishing his mending and wrapping the rest of the string round his hand to get a firmer grip.

"Well?"

"Well, that man was an angel," said MacIan.

"I didn't know they were as bad as that," answered Turnbull.

"We know that devils sometimes quote Scripture and counterfeit good," replied the mystic. "Why should not angels sometimes come to show us the black abyss of evil on whose brink we stand. If that man had not tried to stop us...I might...I might have stopped."

"I know what you mean," said Turnbull, grimly.

"But then he came," broke out MacIan, "and my soul said to me: 'Give up fighting, and you will become like That. Give up vows and dogmas, and fixed things, and you may grow like That. You may learn, also, that fog of false philosophy. You may grow fond of that mire of crawling, cowardly morals, and you may come to think a blow bad, because it hurts, and not because it humiliates. You may come to think murder wrong, because it is violent, and not because it is unjust. Oh, you blasphemer of the good, an hour ago I almost loved you! But do not fear for me now. I have heard the word Love pronounced in *his* intonation; and I know exactly what it means. On guard!'"

The swords caught on each other with a dreadful clang and jar, full of the old energy and hate; and at once plunged and replunged. Once more each man's heart had become the magnet of a mad sword. Suddenly, furious as they were, they were frozen for a moment motionless.

"What noise is that?" asked the Highlander, hoarsely.

"I think I know," replied Turnbull.

"What?... What?" cried the other.

"The student of Shaw and Tolstoy has made up his remarkable mind," said Turnbull, quietly. "The police are coming up the hill."

VI. THE OTHER PHILOSOPHER

Between high hedges in Hertfordshire, hedges so high as to create a kind of grove, two men were running. They did not run in a scampering or feverish manner, but in the steady swing of the pendulum. Across the great plains and uplands to the right and left of the lane, a long tide of sunset light rolled like a sea of ruby, lighting up the long terraces of the hills and picking out the few windows of the scattered hamlets in startling blood-red sparks. But the lane was cut deep in the hill and remained in an abrupt shadow. The two men running in it had an impression not uncommonly experienced between those wild green English walls; a sense of being led between the walls of a maze.

Though their pace was steady it was vigorous; their faces were heated and their eyes fixed and bright. There was, indeed, something a little mad in the contrast between the evening's stillness over the empty country-side, and these two figures fleeing wildly from nothing. They had the look of two lunatics, possibly they were.

"Are you all right?" said Turnbull, with civility. "Can you keep this up?"

"Quite easily, thank you," replied MacIan. "I run very well."

"Is that a qualification in a family of warriors?" asked Turnbull.

"Undoubtedly. Rapid movement is essential," answered MacIan, who never saw a joke in his life.

Turnbull broke out into a short laugh, and silence fell between them, the panting silence of runners.

Then MacIan said: "We run better than any of those policemen. They are too fat. Why do you make your policemen so fat?"

"I didn't do much towards making them fat myself," replied Turnbull, genially, "but I flatter myself that I am now doing something towards making them thin. You'll see they will be as lean as rakes by the time they catch us. They will look like your friend, Cardinal Manning."

"But they won't catch us," said MacIan, in his literal way.

"No, we beat them in the great military art of running away," returned the other. "They won't catch us unless——"

MacIan turned his long equine face inquiringly. "Unless what?" he said, for Turnbull had gone silent suddenly, and seemed to be listening intently as he ran as a horse does with his ears turned back.

"Unless what?" repeated the Highlander.

"Unless they do—what they have done. Listen." MacIan slackened his trot, and turned his head to the trail they had left behind them. Across two or three billows of the up and down lane came along the ground the unmistakable throbbing of horses' hoofs.

238

"They have put the mounted police on us," said Turnbull, shortly. "Good Lord, one would think we were a Revolution."

"So we are," said MacIan calmly. "What shall we do? Shall we turn on them with our points?"

"It may come to that," answered Turnbull, "though if it does, I reckon that will be the last act. We must put it off if we can." And he stared and peered about him between the bushes. "If we could hide somewhere the beasts might go by us," he said. "The police have their faults, but thank God they're inefficient. Why, here's the very thing. Be quick and quiet. Follow me."

He suddenly swung himself up the high bank on one side of the lane. It was almost as high and smooth as a wall, and on the top of it the black hedge stood out over them as an angle, almost like a thatched roof of the lane. And the burning evening sky looked down at them through the tangle with red eyes as of an army of goblins.

Turnbull hoisted himself up and broke the hedge with his body. As his head and shoulders rose above it they turned to flame in the full glow as if lit up by an immense firelight. His red hair and beard looked almost scarlet, and his pale face as bright as a boy's. Something violent, something that was at once love and hatred, surged in the strange heart of the Gael below him. He had an unutterable sense of epic importance, as if he were somehow lifting all humanity into a prouder and more passionate region of the air. As he swung himself up also into the evening light he felt as if he were rising on enormous wings.

Legends of the morning of the world which he had heard in childhood or read in youth came back upon him in a cloudy splendour, purple tales of wrath and friendship, like Roland and Oliver, or Balin and Balan, reminding him of emotional entanglements. Men who had loved each other and then fought each other; men who had fought each other and then loved each other, together made a mixed but monstrous sense of momentousness. The crimson seas of the sunset seemed to him like a bursting out of some sacred blood, as if the heart of the world had broken.

Turnbull was wholly unaffected by any written or spoken poetry; his was a powerful and prosaic mind. But even upon him there came for the moment something out of the earth and the passionate ends of the sky. The only evidence was in his voice, which was still practical but a shade more quiet.

"Do you see that summer-house-looking thing over there?" he asked shortly. "That will do for us very well."

Keeping himself free from the tangle of the hedge he strolled across a triangle of obscure kitchen garden, and approached a dismal shed or lodge a yard or two beyond it. It was a weather-stained hut of grey wood, which with all its desolation retained a tag or two of trivial ornament, which suggested that the thing had once been a sort of summer-house, and the place probably a sort of garden.

"That is quite invisible from the road," said Turnbull, as he entered it, "and it will cover us up for the night."

MacIan looked at him gravely for a few moments. "Sir," he said, "I ought to say something to you. I ought to say——"

"Hush," said Turnbull, suddenly lifting his hand; "be still, man."

In the sudden silence, the drumming of the distant horses grew louder and louder with inconceivable rapidity, and the cavalcade of police rushed by below them in the lane, almost with the roar and rattle of an express train.

"I ought to tell you," continued MacIan, still staring stolidly at the other, "that you are a great chief, and it is good to go to war behind you."

Turnbull said nothing, but turned and looked out of the foolish lattice of the little windows, then he said, "We must have food and sleep first."

When the last echo of their eluded pursuers had died in the distant uplands, Turnbull began to unpack the provisions with the easy air of a man at a picnic. He had just laid out the last items, put a bottle of wine on the floor, and a tin of salmon on the window-ledge, when the bottomless silence of that forgotten place was broken. And it was broken by three heavy blows of a stick delivered upon the door.

Turnbull looked up in the act of opening a tin and stared silently at his companion. MacIan's long, lean mouth had shut hard.

"Who the devil can that be?" said Turnbull.

"God knows," said the other. "It might be God."

Again the sound of the wooden stick reverberated on the wooden door. It was a curious sound and on consideration did not resemble the ordinary effects of knocking on a door for admittance. It was rather as if the point of a stick were plunged again and again at the panels in an absurd attempt to make a hole in them.

A wild look sprang into MacIan's eyes and he got up half stupidly, with a kind of stagger, put his hand out and caught one of the swords. "Let us fight at once," he cried, "it is the end of the world."

"You're overdone, MacIan," said Turnbull, putting him on one side. "It's only someone playing the goat. Let me open the door."

But he also picked up a sword as he stepped to open it.

He paused one moment with his hand on the handle and then flung the door open. Almost as he did so the ferrule of an ordinary bamboo cane came at his eyes, so that he had actually to parry it with the naked weapon in his hands. As the two touched, the point of the stick was dropped very abruptly, and the man with the stick stepped hurriedly back.

Against the heraldic background of sprawling crimson and gold offered him by the expiring sunset, the figure of the man with the stick showed at first merely black and fantastic. He was a small man with two wisps of long hair that curled up on each side, and seen in silhouette, looked like horns. He had a bow tie so big that the two ends showed on each side of his neck like unnatural stunted wings. He had his long black cane still tilted in his hand like a fencing foil and half presented at the open door. His large straw hat had fallen behind him as he leapt backwards.

"With reference to your suggestion, MacIan," said Turnbull, placidly, "I think it looks more like the Devil."

"Who on earth are you?" cried the stranger in a high shrill voice, brandishing his cane defensively.

"Let me see," said Turnbull, looking round to MacIan with the same blandness. "Who are we?"

"Come out," screamed the little man with the stick.

"Certainly," said Turnbull, and went outside with the sword, MacIan following.

Seen more fully, with the evening light on his face, the strange man looked a little less like a goblin. He wore a square pale-grey jacket suit, on which the grey butterfly tie was the only indisputable touch of affectation. Against the great sunset his figure had looked merely small: seen in a more equal light it looked tolerably compact and shapely. His reddish-brown hair, combed into two great curls, looked like the long, slow curling hair of the women in some pre-Raphaelite pictures. But within this feminine frame of hair his face was unexpectedly impudent, like a monkey's.

"What are you doing here?" he said, in a sharp small voice.

"Well," said MacIan, in his grave childish way, "what are *you* doing here?"

"I," said the man, indignantly, "I'm in my own garden."

"Oh," said MacIan, simply, "I apologize."

Turnbull was coolly curling his red moustache, and the stranger stared from one to the other, temporarily stunned by their innocent assurance.

"But, may I ask," he said at last, "what the devil you are doing in my summer-house?"

"Certainly," said MacIan. "We were just going to fight."

"To fight!" repeated the man.

"We had better tell this gentleman the whole business," broke in Turnbull. Then turning to the stranger he said firmly, "I am sorry, sir, but we have something to do that must be done. And I may as well tell you at the beginning and to avoid waste of time or language, that we cannot admit any interference."

"We were just going to take some slight refreshment when you interrupted us..."

The little man had a dawning expression of understanding and stooped and picked up the unused bottle of wine, eyeing it curiously.

Turnbull continued:

"But that refreshment was preparatory to something which I fear you will find less comprehensible, but on which our minds are entirely fixed, sir. We are forced to fight a duel. We are forced by honour and an internal intellectual need. Do not, for your own sake, attempt to stop us. I know all the excellent and ethical things that you will want to say to us. I know all about the essential requirements of civil order: I have written leading articles about them all my life. I know all about the sacredness of human life; I have bored all my friends with it. Try and understand our position. This man and I are alone in the modern world in that we think that God is essentially important. I think He does not exist; that is where the importance comes in for me. But this man thinks that He does exist, and thinking that very properly thinks Him more important than anything else. Now we wish to make a great demonstration and assertion—something that will set the world on fire like the first Christian persecutions. If you like, we are attempting a mutual martyrdom. The papers have posted up every town against us. Scotland Yard has fortified every police station with our enemies; we are driven therefore to the edge of a lonely lane, and indirectly to taking liberties with your summer-house in order to arrange our..."

"Stop!" roared the little man in the butterfly necktie. "Put me out of my intellectual misery. Are you really the two tomfools I have read of in all the papers? Are you the two people who wanted to spit each other in the Police Court? Are you? Are you?"

"Yes," said MacIan, "it began in a Police Court."

The little man slung the bottle of wine twenty yards away like a stone.

"Come up to my place," he said. "I've got better stuff than that. I've got the best Beaune within fifty miles of here. Come up. You're the very men I wanted to see."

Even Turnbull, with his typical invulnerability, was a little taken aback by this boisterous and almost brutal hospitality.

"Why...sir..." he began.

"Come up! Come in!" howled the little man, dancing with delight. "I'll give you a dinner. I'll give you a bed! I'll give you a green smooth lawn and your choice of swords and pistols. Why, you fools, I adore fighting! It's the only good thing in God's world! I've walked about these damned fields and longed to see somebody cut up and killed and the blood running. Ha! Ha!"

And he made sudden lunges with his stick at the trunk of a neighbouring tree so that the ferrule made fierce prints and punctures in the bark.

"Excuse me," said MacIan suddenly with the wide-eyed curiosity of a child, "excuse me, but..."

"Well?" said the small fighter, brandishing his wooden weapon.

"Excuse me," repeated MacIan, "but was that what you were doing at the door?"

The little man stared an instant and then said: "Yes," and Turnbull broke into a guffaw.

"Come on!" cried the little man, tucking his stick under his arm and taking quite suddenly to his heels. "Come on! Confound me, I'll see both of you eat and then I'll see one of you die. Lord bless me, the gods must exist after all—they have sent me one of my day-dreams! Lord! A duel!"

He had gone flying along a winding path between the borders of the kitchen garden, and in the increasing twilight he was as hard to follow as a flying hare. But at length the path after many twists betrayed its purpose and led abruptly up two or three steps to the door of a tiny but very clean cottage. There was nothing about the outside to distinguish it from other cottages, except indeed its ominous cleanliness and one thing that was out of all the custom and tradition of all cottages under the sun. In the middle of the little garden among the stocks and marigolds there surged up in shapeless stone a South Sea Island idol. There was something gross and even evil in that eyeless and alien god among the most innocent of the English flowers.

"Come in!" cried the creature again. "Come in! it's better inside!"

Whether or no it was better inside it was at least a surprise. The moment the two duellists had pushed open the door of that inoffensive, whitewashed cottage they found that its interior was lined with fiery gold. It was like stepping into a chamber in the Arabian Nights. The door that closed behind them shut out England and all the energies of the West. The ornaments that shone and shimmered on every side of them were subtly mixed from many periods and lands, but were all oriental. Cruel Assyrian bas-reliefs ran along the sides of the passage; cruel Turkish swords and daggers glinted above and below them; the two were separated by ages and fallen civilizations. Yet they seemed to sympathize since they were both harmonious and both merciless. The house seemed to consist of chamber within chamber and created that impression as of a dream which belongs also to the Arabian Nights themselves. The innermost room of all was like the inside of a jewel. The little man who owned it all threw himself on a heap of scarlet and golden cushions and struck his hands together. A negro in a white robe and turban appeared suddenly and silently behind them.

"Selim," said the host, "these two gentlemen are staying with me tonight. Send up the very best wine and dinner at once. And Selim, one of these gentlemen will probably die tomorrow. Make arrangements, please."

The negro bowed and withdrew.

Evan MacIan came out the next morning into the little garden to a fresh silver day, his long face looking more austere than ever in that cold light, his eyelids a little heavy. He carried one of the swords. Turnbull was in the little house behind him, demolishing the end of an early breakfast and humming a tune to himself, which could be heard through the open window. A moment or two later he leapt to his feet and came out into the sunlight, still munching toast, his own sword stuck under his arm like a walking-stick.

Their eccentric host had vanished from sight, with a polite gesture, some twenty minutes before. They imagined him to be occupied on some concerns in the interior of the house, and they waited for his emergence, stamping the garden in silence—the garden of tall, fresh country flowers, in the midst of which the monstrous South Sea idol lifted itself as abruptly as the prow of a ship riding on a sea of red and white and gold.

It was with a start, therefore, that they came upon the man himself already in the garden. They were all the more startled because of the still posture in which they found him. He was on his knees in front of the stone idol, rigid and motionless, like a saint in a trance or ecstasy. Yet when Turnbull's tread broke a twig, he was on his feet in a flash.

"Excuse me," he said with an irradiation of smiles, but yet with a kind of bewilderment. "So sorry...family prayers...old fashioned...mother's knee. Let us go on to the lawn behind."

And he ducked rapidly round the statue to an open space of grass on the other side of it.

"This will do us best, Mr. MacIan," said he. Then he made a gesture towards the heavy stone figure on the pedestal which had now its blank and shapeless back turned towards them. "Don't you be afraid," he added, "he can still see us."

MacIan turned his blue, blinking eyes, which seemed still misty with sleep (or sleeplessness) towards the idol, but his brows drew together.

The little man with the long hair also had his eyes on the back view of the god. His eyes were at once liquid and burning, and he rubbed his hands slowly against each other.

"Do you know," he said, "I think he can see us better this way. I often think that this blank thing is his real face, watching, though it cannot be watched. He! he! Yes, I think he looks nice from behind. He looks more cruel from behind, don't you think?"

"What the devil is the thing?" asked Turnbull gruffly.

"It is the only Thing there is," answered the other. "It is Force."

"Oh!" said Turnbull shortly.

"Yes, my friends," said the little man, with an animated countenance, fluttering his fingers in the air, "it was no chance that led you to this garden; surely it was the caprice of some old god, some happy, pitiless god. Perhaps it was his will, for he loves blood; and on that stone in front of him men have been butchered by hundreds in the fierce, feasting islands of the South. In this cursed, craven place I have not been permitted to kill men on his altar. Only rabbits and cats, sometimes."

In the stillness MacIan made a sudden movement, unmeaning apparently, and then remained rigid.

"But today, today," continued the small man in a shrill voice. "Today his hour is come. Today his will is done on earth as it is in heaven. Men, men, men will bleed before him today." And he bit his forefinger in a kind of fever.

Still, the two duellists stood with their swords as heavily as statues, and the silence seemed to cool the eccentric and call him back to more rational speech.

"Perhaps I express myself a little too lyrically," he said with an amicable abruptness. "My philosophy has its higher ecstasies, but perhaps you are hardly worked up to them yet. Let us confine ourselves to the unquestioned. You have found your way, gentlemen, by a beautiful accident, to the house of the only man in England (probably) who will favour and encourage your most reasonable project. From Cornwall to Cape Wrath this county is one horrible, solid block of humanitarianism. You will find men who will defend this or that war in a distant continent. They will defend it on the contemptible ground of commerce or the more contemptible ground of social good. But do not fancy that you will find one other person who will comprehend a strong man taking the sword in his hand and wiping out his enemy. My name is Wimpey, Morrice Wimpey. I had a Fellowship at Magdalen. But I assure you I had to drop it, owing to my having said something in a public lecture infringing the popular prejudice against those great gentlemen, the assassins of the Italian Renaissance. They let me say it at dinner and so on, and seemed to like it. But in a public lecture...so inconsistent. Well, as I say, here is your only refuge and temple of honour. Here you can fall back on that naked and awful arbitration which is the only thing that balances the stars—a still, continuous violence. *Vae Victis!* Down, down, down with the defeated! Victory is the only ultimate fact. Carthage *was* destroyed, the Red Indians are being exterminated: that is the single certainty. In an hour from now that sun will still be shining and that grass growing, and one of you will be conquered; one of you will be the conqueror. When it has been done, nothing will alter it. Heroes, I give you the hospitality fit for heroes. And I salute the survivor. Fall on!"

The two men took their swords. Then MacIan said steadily: "Mr. Turnbull, lend me your sword a moment."

Turnbull, with a questioning glance, handed him the weapon. MacIan took the second sword in his left hand and, with a violent gesture, hurled it at the feet of little Mr. Wimpey.

"Fight!" he said in a loud, harsh voice. "Fight me now!"

Wimpey took a step backward, and bewildered words bubbled on his lips.

"Pick up that sword and fight me," repeated MacIan, with brows as black as thunder.

The little man turned to Turnbull with a gesture, demanding judgement or protection.

"Really, sir," he began, "this gentleman confuses..."

"You stinking little coward," roared Turnbull, suddenly releasing his wrath. "Fight, if you're so fond of fighting! Fight, if you're so fond of all that filthy philosophy! If winning is everything, go in and win! If the weak must go to the wall, go to the wall! Fight, you rat! Fight, or if you won't fight—run!"

And he ran at Wimpey, with blazing eyes.

Wimpey staggered back a few paces like a man struggling with his own limbs. Then he felt the furious Scotchman coming at him like an express train, doubling his size every second, with eyes as big as windows and a sword as bright as the sun. Something broke inside him, and he found himself running away, tumbling over his own feet in terror, and crying out as he ran.

"Chase him!" shouted Turnbull as MacIan snatched up the sword and joined in the scamper. "Chase him over a county! Chase him into the sea! Shoo! Shoo! Shoo!"

The little man plunged like a rabbit among the tall flowers, the two duellists after him. Turnbull kept at his tail with savage ecstasy, still shooing him like a cat. But MacIan, as he ran past the South Sea idol, paused an instant to spring upon its pedestal. For five seconds he strained against the inert mass. Then it stirred; and he sent it over with a great crash among the flowers, that engulfed it altogether. Then he went bounding after the runaway.

In the energy of his alarm the ex-Fellow of Magdalen managed to leap the paling of his garden. The two pursuers went over it after him like flying birds. He fled frantically down a long lane with his two terrors on his trail till he came to a gap in the hedge and went across a steep meadow like the wind. The two Scotchmen, as they ran, kept up a cheery bellowing and waved their swords. Up three slanting meadows, down four slanting meadows on the other side, across another road, across a heath of snapping bracken, through a wood, across another road, and to the brink of a big pool, they pursued the flying philosopher. But when he came to the pool his pace was so precipitate that he could not stop it, and with a kind of lurching stagger, he fell splash into the greasy water. Getting dripping to his feet, with the water up to his knees, the worshipper of force and victory waded disconsolately to the other side and drew himself on to the bank. And Turnbull sat down on the grass and went off into reverberations of laughter. A second afterwards the most extraordinary grimaces were seen to distort the stiff face of MacIan, and unholy sounds came from within. He had never practised laughing, and it hurt him very much.

VII. THE VILLAGE OF GRASSLEY-IN-THE-HOLE

At about half past one, under a strong blue sky, Turnbull got up out of the grass and fern in which he had been lying, and his still intermittent laughter ended in a kind of yawn.

"I'm hungry," he said shortly. "Are you?"

"I have not noticed," answered MacIan. "What are you going to do?"

"There's a village down the road, past the pool," answered Turnbull. "I can see it from here. I can see the whitewashed walls of some cottages and a kind of corner of the church. How jolly it all looks. It looks so—I don't know what the word is—so sensible. Don't fancy I'm under any illusions about Arcadian virtue and the innocent villagers. Men make beasts of themselves there with drink, but they don't deliberately make devils of themselves with mere talking. They kill wild animals in the wild woods, but they don't kill cats to the God of Victory. They don't——" He broke off and suddenly spat on the ground.

"Excuse me," he said; "it was ceremonial. One has to get the taste out of one's mouth."

"The taste of what?" asked MacIan.

"I don't know the exact name for it," replied Turnbull. "Perhaps it is the South Sea Islands, or it may be Magdalen College."

There was a long pause, and MacIan also lifted his large limbs off the ground—his eyes particularly dreamy.

"I know what you mean, Turnbull," he said, "but... I always thought you people agreed with all that."

"With all that about doing as one likes, and the individual, and Nature loving the strongest, and all the things which that cockroach talked about."

Turnbull's big blue-grey eyes stood open with a grave astonishment.

"Do you really mean to say, MacIan," he said, "that you fancied that we, the Free-thinkers, that Bradlaugh, or Holyoake, or Ingersoll, believe all that dirty, immoral mysticism about Nature? Damn Nature!"

"I supposed you did," said MacIan calmly. "It seems to me your most conclusive position."

"And you mean to tell me," rejoined the other, "that you broke my window, and challenged me to mortal combat, and tied a tradesman up with ropes, and chased an Oxford Fellow across five meadows—all under the impression that I am such an illiterate idiot as to believe in Nature!"

"I supposed you did," repeated MacIan with his usual mildness; "but I admit that I know little of the details of your belief—or disbelief."

Turnbull swung round quite suddenly, and set off towards the village.

"Come along," he cried. "Come down to the village. Come down to the nearest decent inhabitable pub. This is a case for beer."

"I do not quite follow you," said the Highlander.

"Yes, you do," answered Turnbull. "You follow me slap into the inn-parlour. I repeat, this is a case for beer. We must have the whole of this matter out thoroughly before we go a step farther. Do you know that an idea has just struck me of great simplicity and of some cogency. Do not by any means let us drop our intentions of settling our differences with two steel swords. But do you not think that with two pewter pots we might do what we really have never thought of doing yet—discover what our difference is?"

"It never occurred to me before," answered MacIan with tranquillity. "It is a good suggestion."

And they set out at an easy swing down the steep road to the village of Grassley-in-the-Hole.

Grassley-in-the-Hole was a rude parallelogram of buildings, with two thoroughfares which might have been called two high streets if it had been possible to call them streets. One of these ways was higher on the slope than the other, the whole parallelogram lying aslant, so to speak, on the side of the hill. The upper of these two roads was decorated with a big public house, a butcher's shop, a small public house, a sweetstuff shop, a very small public house, and an illegible signpost. The lower of the two roads boasted a horse-pond, a post office, a gentleman's garden with very high hedges, a microscopically small public house, and two cottages. Where all the people lived who supported all the public houses was in this, as in many other English villages, a silent and smiling mystery. The church lay a little above and beyond the village, with a square grey tower dominating it decisively.

But even the church was scarcely so central and solemn an institution as the large public house, the Valencourt Arms. It was named after some splendid family that had long gone bankrupt, and whose seat was occupied by a man who had invented a hygienic bootjack; but the unfathomable sentimentalism of the English people insisted in regarding the Inn, the seat and the sitter in it, as alike parts of a pure and marmoreal antiquity. And in the Valencourt Arms festivity itself had some solemnity and decorum; and beer was drunk with reverence, as it ought to be. Into the principal parlour of this place entered two strangers, who found themselves, as is always the case in such hostels, the object, not of fluttered curiosity or pert inquiry, but of steady, ceaseless, devouring ocular study. They had long coats down to their heels, and carried under each coat something that looked like a stick. One was tall and dark, the other short and red-haired. They ordered a pot of ale each.

"MacIan," said Turnbull, lifting his tankard, "the fool who wanted us to be friends made us want to go on fighting. It is only natural that the fool who wanted us to fight should make us friendly. MacIan, your health!"

Dusk was already dropping, the rustics in the tavern were already lurching and lumbering out of it by twos and threes, crying clamorous good nights to a solitary old toper that remained, before MacIan and Turnbull had reached the really important part of their discussion.

MacIan wore an expression of sad bewilderment not uncommon with him. "I am to understand, then," he said, "that you don't believe in nature."

"You may say so in a very special and emphatic sense," said Turnbull. "I do not believe in nature, just as I do not believe in Odin. She is a myth. It is not merely that I do not believe that nature can guide us. It is that I do not believe that nature exists."

"Exists?" said MacIan in his monotonous way, settling his pewter pot on the table.

"Yes, in a real sense nature does not exist. I mean that nobody can discover what the original nature of things would have been if things had not interfered with it. The first blade of grass began to tear up the earth and eat it; it was interfering with nature, if there is any nature. The first wild ox began to tear up the grass and eat it; he was interfering with nature, if there is any nature. In the same way," continued Turnbull, "the human when it asserts its dominance over nature is just as natural as the thing which it destroys."

"And in the same way," said MacIan almost dreamily, "the superhuman, the supernatural is just as natural as the nature which it destroys."

Turnbull took his head out of his pewter pot in some anger.

"The supernatural, of course," he said, "is quite another thing; the case of the supernatural is simple. The supernatural does not exist."

"Quite so," said MacIan in a rather dull voice; "you said the same about the natural. If the natural does not exist the supernatural obviously can't." And he yawned a little over his ale.

Turnbull turned for some reason a little red and remarked quickly, "That may be jolly clever, for all I know. But everyone does know that there is a division between the things that as a matter of fact do commonly happen and the things that don't. Things that break the evident laws of nature——"

"Which does not exist," put in MacIan sleepily. Turnbull struck the table with a sudden hand.

"Good Lord in heaven!" he cried——

"Who does not exist," murmured MacIan.

"Good Lord in heaven!" thundered Turnbull, without regarding the interruption. "Do you really mean to sit there and say that you, like anybody else, would not recognize the difference between a natural occurrence and a supernatural one—if there could be such a thing? If I flew up to the ceiling——"

"You would bump your head badly," cried MacIan, suddenly starting up. "One can't talk of this kind of thing under a ceiling at all. Come outside! Come outside and ascend into heaven!"

He burst the door open on a blue abyss of evening and they stepped out into it: it was suddenly and strangely cool.

"Turnbull," said MacIan, "you have said some things so true and some so false that I want to talk; and I will try to talk so that you understand. For at present you do not understand at all. We don't seem to mean the same things by the same words."

He stood silent for a second or two and then resumed.

"A minute or two ago I caught you out in a real contradiction. At that moment logically I was right. And at that moment I knew I was wrong. Yes, there is a real difference between the natural and the supernatural: if you flew up into that blue sky this instant, I should think that you were moved by God—or the devil. But if you want to know what I really think...I must explain."

He stopped again, abstractedly boring the point of his sword into the earth, and went on:

"I was born and bred and taught in a complete universe. The supernatural was not natural, but it was perfectly reasonable. Nay, the supernatural to me is more reasonable than the natural; for the supernatural is a direct message from God, who is reason. I was taught that some things are natural and some things divine. I mean that some things are mechanical and some things divine. But there is the great difficulty, Turnbull. The great difficulty is that, according to my teaching, you are divine."

"Me! Divine?" said Turnbull truculently. "What do you mean?"

"That is just the difficulty," continued MacIan thoughtfully. "I was told that there was a difference between the grass and a man's will; and the difference was that a man's will was special and divine. A man's free will, I heard, was supernatural."

"Rubbish!" said Turnbull.

"Oh," said MacIan patiently, "then if a man's free will isn't supernatural, why do your materialists deny that it exists?"

Turnbull was silent for a moment. Then he began to speak, but MacIan continued with the same steady voice and sad eyes:

"So what I feel is this: Here is the great divine creation I was taught to believe in. I can understand your disbelieving in it, but why disbelieve in a part of it? It was all one thing to me. God had authority because he was God. Man had authority because he was man. You cannot prove that God is better than a man; nor can you prove that a man is better than a horse. Why permit any ordinary thing? Why do you let a horse be saddled?"

"Some modern thinkers disapprove of it," said Turnbull a little doubtfully.

"I know," said MacIan grimly; "that man who talked about love, for instance."

Turnbull made a humorous grimace; then he said: "We seem to be talking in a kind of shorthand; but I won't pretend not to understand you. What you mean is this: that you learnt about all your saints and angels at the same time as you learnt about common morality, from the same people, in the same way. And you mean to say that if one may be disputed, so may the other. Well, let that pass for the moment. But let me ask you a question in turn. Did not this system of yours, which you swallowed whole, contain all sorts of things that were merely local, the respect for the chief of your clan, or such things; the village ghost, the family feud, or what not? Did you not take in those things, too, along with your theology?"

MacIan stared along the dim village road, down which the last straggler from the inn was trailing his way.

"What you say is not unreasonable," he said. "But it is not quite true. The distinction between the chief and us did exist; but it was never anything like the distinction between the human and the divine, or the human and the animal. It was more like the distinction between one animal and another. But——"

"Well?" said Turnbull.

MacIan was silent.

"Go on," repeated Turnbull; "what's the matter with you? What are you staring at?"

"I am staring," said MacIan at last, "at that which shall judge us both."

"Oh, yes," said Turnbull in a tired way, "I suppose you mean God."

"No, I don't," said MacIan, shaking his head. "I mean him."

And he pointed to the half-tipsy yokel who was ploughing down the road.

"What do you mean?" asked the atheist.

"I mean him," repeated MacIan with emphasis. "He goes out in the early dawn; he digs or he ploughs a field. Then he comes back and drinks ale, and then he sings a song. All your philosophies and political systems are young compared to him. All your hoary cathedrals, yes, even the Eternal Church on earth is new compared to him. The most mouldering gods in the British Museum are new facts beside him. It is he who in the end shall judge us all."

And MacIan rose to his feet with a vague excitement.

"What are you going to do?"

"I am going to ask him," cried MacIan, "which of us is right."

Turnbull broke into a kind of laugh. "Ask that intoxicated turnip-eater——" he began.

"Yes—which of us is right," cried MacIan violently. "Oh, you have long words and I have long words; and I talk of every man being the image of God; and you talk of every man being a citizen and enlightened enough to govern. But if every man typifies God, there is God. If every man is an enlightened citizen, there is your enlightened citizen. The first man one meets is always man. Let us catch him up."

And in gigantic strides the long, lean Highlander whirled away into the grey twilight, Turnbull following with a good-humoured oath.

The track of the rustic was easy to follow, even in the faltering dark; for he was enlivening his wavering walk with song. It was an interminable poem, beginning with some unspecified King William, who (it appeared) lived in London town and who after the second rise vanished rather abruptly from the train of thought. The rest was almost entirely about beer and was thick with local topography of a quite unrecognizable kind. The singer's step was neither very rapid, nor, indeed, exceptionally secure; so the song grew louder and louder and the two soon overtook him.

He was a man elderly or rather of any age, with lean grey hair and a lean red face, but with that remarkable rustic physiognomy in which it seems that all the features stand out independently from the face; the rugged red nose going out like a limb; the bleared blue eyes standing out like signals.

He gave them greeting with the elaborate urbanity of the slightly intoxicated. MacIan, who was vibrating with one of his silent, violent decisions, opened the question without delay. He explained the philosophic position in words as short and simple as possible. But the singular old man with the lank red face seemed to think uncommonly little of the short words. He fixed with a fierce affection upon one or two of the long ones.

"Atheists!" he repeated with luxurious scorn. "Atheists! I know their sort, master. Atheists! Don't talk to me about 'un. Atheists!"

The grounds of his disdain seemed a little dark and confused; but they were evidently sufficient. MacIan resumed in some encouragement:

"You think as I do, I hope; you think that a man should be connected with the Church; with the common Christian——"

The old man extended a quivering stick in the direction of a distant hill.

"There's the church," he said thickly. "Grassley old church that is. Pulled down it was, in the old squire's time, and——"

"I mean," explained MacIan elaborately, "that you think that there should be someone typifying religion, a priest——"

"Priests!" said the old man with sudden passion. "Priests! I know 'un. What they want in England? That's what I say. What they want in England?"

"They want you," said MacIan.

"Quite so," said Turnbull, "and me; but they won't get us. MacIan, your attempt on the primitive innocence does not seem very successful. Let me try. What you want, my friend, is your rights. You don't want any priests or churches. A vote, a right to speak is what you——"

"Who says I a'n't got a right to speak?" said the old man, facing round in an irrational frenzy. "I got a right to speak. I'm a man, I am. I don't want no votin' nor priests. I say a man's a man; that's what I say. If a man a'n't a man, what is he? That's what I say, if a man a'n't a man, what is he? When I sees a man, I sez 'e's a man."

"Quite so," said Turnbull, "a citizen."

"I say he's a man," said the rustic furiously, stopping and striking his stick on the ground. "Not a city or owt else. He's a man."

"You're perfectly right," said the sudden voice of MacIan, falling like a sword. "And you have kept close to something the whole world of today tries to forget."

"Good night."

And the old man went on wildly singing into the night.

"A jolly old creature," said Turnbull; "he didn't seem able to get much beyond that fact that a man is a man."

"Has anybody got beyond it?" asked MacIan.

Turnbull looked at him curiously. "Are you turning an agnostic?" he asked.

"Oh, you do not understand!" cried out MacIan. "We Catholics are all agnostics. We

Catholics have only in that sense got as far as realizing that man is a man. But your Ibsens and your Zolas and your Shaws and your Tolstoys have not even got so far."

VIII. AN INTERLUDE OF ARGUMENT

Morning broke in bitter silver along the grey and level plain; and almost as it did so Turnbull and MacIan came out of a low, scrubby wood on to the empty and desolate flats. They had walked all night.

They had walked all night and talked all night also, and if the subject had been capable of being exhausted they would have exhausted it. Their long and changing argument had taken them through districts and landscapes equally changing. They had discussed Haeckel upon hills so high and steep that in spite of the coldness of the night it seemed as if the stars might burn them. They had explained and re-explained the Massacre of St. Bartholomew in little white lanes walled in with standing corn as with walls of gold. They had talked about Mr. Kensit in dim and twinkling pine woods, amid the bewildering monotony of the pines. And it was with the end of a long speech from MacIan, passionately defending the practical achievements and the solid prosperity of the Catholic tradition, that they came out upon the open land.

MacIan had learnt much and thought more since he came out of the cloudy hills of Arisaig. He had met many typical modern figures under circumstances which were sharply symbolic; and, moreover, he had absorbed the main modern atmosphere from the mere presence and chance phrases of Turnbull, as such atmospheres can always be absorbed from the presence and the phrases of any man of great mental vitality. He had at last begun thoroughly to understand what are the grounds upon which the mass of the modern world solidly disapprove of her creed; and he threw himself into replying to them with a hot intellectual enjoyment.

"I begin to understand one or two of your dogmas, Mr. Turnbull," he had said emphatically as they ploughed heavily up a wooded hill. "And every one that I understand I deny. Take any one of them you like. You hold that your heretics and sceptics have helped the world forward and handed on a lamp of progress. I deny it. Nothing is plainer from real history than that each of your heretics invented a complete cosmos of his own which the next heretic smashed entirely to pieces. Who knows now exactly what Nestorius taught? Who cares? There are only two things that we know for certain about it. The first is that Nestorius, as a heretic, taught something quite opposite to the teaching of Arius, the heretic who came before him, and something quite useless to James Turnbull, the heretic who comes after. I defy you to go back to the Free-thinkers of the past and find any habitation for yourself at all. I defy you to read Godwin or Shelley or the deists of the eighteenth century of the nature-worshipping humanists of the Renaissance, without discovering that you differ from them twice as much as you differ from the Pope. You are a nineteenth-century sceptic, and you are always telling me that I ignore the cruelty of nature. If you had been an eighteenth-century sceptic you would have told me that I ignore the kindness and benevolence of nature. You are an atheist, and you praise the deists of the eighteenth century. Read them instead of praising them, and you will find that their whole universe stands or falls with the deity. You are a materialist, and you think Bruno a scientific hero. See what he said and you will think him an insane mystic. No, the great Free-thinker, with his genuine ability and honesty, does not in practice destroy Christianity. What he does destroy is the Free-thinker who went before. Free-thought may be suggestive, it may be inspiriting, it may have as much as you please of the merits that come from vivacity and variety. But there is one thing Free-thought can never be by any possibility—Free-thought can never be progressive. It can never be progressive because it will accept nothing from the past; it begins every time again from the beginning; and it goes every time in a different direction. All the rational philosophers have gone along different roads, so it is impossible to say which has gone farthest. Who can discuss whether Emerson was a better optimist than Schopenhauer was pessimist? It is like asking if this corn is as yellow as that hill is steep. No; there are only two things that really progress; and they both accept accumulations of authority. They may be progressing uphill and down; they may be growing steadily better or steadily worse; but they have steadily increased in certain definable matters; they have steadily advanced in a certain definable direction; they are the only two things, it seems, that ever *can* progress. The first is strictly physical science. The second is the Catholic Church."

"Physical science and the Catholic Church!" said Turnbull sarcastically; "and no doubt the first owes a great deal to the second."

"If you pressed that point I might reply that it was very probable," answered MacIan calmly. "I often fancy that your historical generalizations rest frequently on random instances; I should not be surprised if your vague notions of the Church as the persecutor of science was a generalization from Galileo. I should not be at all surprised if, when you counted the scientific investigations and discoveries since the fall of Rome, you found that a great mass of them had been made by monks. But the matter is irrelevant to my meaning. I say that if you want an example of anything which has progressed in the moral world by the same method as science in the material world, by continually adding to without unsettling what was there before, then I say that there *is* only one example of it. And that is Us."

"With this enormous difference," said Turnbull, "that however elaborate be the calculations of physical science, their net result can be tested. Granted that it took millions of books I never read and millions of men I never heard of to discover the electric light. Still I can see the electric light. But I cannot see the supreme virtue which is the result of all your theologies and sacraments."

"Catholic virtue is often invisible because it is the normal," answered MacIan. "Christianity is always out of fashion because it is always sane; and all fashions are mild insanities. When Italy is mad on art the Church seems too Puritanical; when England is mad on Puritanism the Church seems too artistic. When you quarrel with us now you class us with kingship and despotism; but when you quarrelled with us first it was because we would not accept the divine despotism of Henry VIII. The Church always seems to be behind the times, when it is really beyond the times; it is waiting till the last fad shall have seen its last summer. It keeps the key of a permanent virtue."

"Oh, I have heard all that!" said Turnbull with genial contempt. "I have heard that Christianity keeps the key of virtue, and that if you read Tom Paine you will cut your throat at Monte Carlo. It is such rubbish that I am not even angry at it. You say that Christianity is the prop of morals; but what more do you do? When a doctor attends you and could poison you with a pinch of salt, do you ask whether he is a Christian? You ask whether he is a gentleman, whether he is an M.D.—anything but that. When a soldier enlists to die for his country or disgrace it, do you ask whether he is a Christian? You are more likely to ask whether he is Oxford or Cambridge at the boat race. If you think your creed essential to morals why do you not make it a test for these things?"

"We once did make it a test for these things," said MacIan smiling, "and then you told us that we were imposing by force a faith unsupported by argument. It seems rather hard that having first been told that our creed must be false because we did use tests, we should now be told that it must be false because we don't. But I notice that most anti-Christian arguments are in the same inconsistent style."

"That is all very well as a debating-club answer," replied Turnbull good-humouredly, "but the question still remains: Why don't you confine yourself more to Christians if Christians are the only really good men?"

"Who talked of such folly?" asked MacIan disdainfully. "Do you suppose that the Catholic Church ever held that Christians were the only good men? Why, the Catholics of the Catholic Middle Ages talked about the virtues of all the virtuous Pagans until humanity was sick of the subject. No, if you really want to know what we mean when we say that Christianity has a special power of virtue, I will tell you. The Church is the only thing on earth that can perpetuate a type of virtue and make it something more than a fashion. The thing is so plain and historical that I hardly think you will ever deny it. You cannot deny that it is perfectly possible that tomorrow morning, in Ireland or in Italy, there might appear a man not only as good but good in exactly the same way as St. Francis of Assisi. Very well, now take the other types of human virtue; many of them splendid. The English gentleman of Elizabeth was chivalrous and idealistic. But can you stand still here in this meadow and be an English gentleman of Elizabeth? The austere republican of the eighteenth century, with his stern patriotism and his simple life, was a fine fellow. But have you ever seen him? have you ever seen an austere republican? Only a hundred years have passed and that volcano of revolutionary truth and valour is as cold as the mountains of the moon. And so it is and so it will be with the ethics which are buzzing down Fleet Street at this instant as I speak. What phrase would inspire the London clerk or workman just now? Perhaps that he is a son of the British Empire on which the sun never sets; perhaps that he is a prop of his Trades Union, or a class-conscious proletarian something or other; perhaps merely that he is a gentleman when he obviously is not. Those names and notions are all honourable; but how long will they last? Empires break; industrial conditions change; the suburbs will not last for ever. What will remain? I will tell you. The Catholic Saint will remain."

"And suppose I don't like him?" said Turnbull.

"On my theory the question is rather whether he will like you: or more probably whether he will ever have heard of you. But I grant the reasonableness of your query. You have a right, if you speak as the ordinary man, to ask if you will like the saint. But as the ordinary man you do like him. You revel in him. If you dislike him it is not because you are a nice ordinary man, but because you are (if you will excuse me) a sophisticated prig of a Fleet Street editor. That is just the funny part of it. The human race has always admired the Catholic virtues, however little it can practise them; and oddly enough it has admired most those of them that the modern world most sharply disputes. You complain of Catholicism for setting up an ideal of virginity; it did nothing of the kind. The whole human race set up an ideal of virginity; the Greeks in Athene, the Romans in the Vestal fire, set up an ideal of virginity. What then is your real quarrel with Catholicism? Your quarrel can only be, your quarrel really only is, that Catholicism has *achieved* an ideal of virginity; that it is no longer a mere piece of floating poetry. But if you, and a few feverish men, in top hats, running about in a street in London, choose to differ as to the ideal itself, not only from the Church, but from the Parthenon whose name means virginity, from the Roman Empire which went outwards from the virgin flame, from the whole legend and tradition of Europe, from the lion who will not touch virgins, from the unicorn who respects them, and who make up together the bearers of your own national shield, from the most living and lawless of your own poets, from Massinger, who wrote the *Virgin Martyr*, from Shakespeare, who wrote *Measure for Measure*—if you in Fleet Street differ from all this human experience, does it never strike you that it may be Fleet Street that is wrong?"

"No," answered Turnbull; "I trust that I am sufficiently fair-minded to canvass and consider the idea; but having considered it, I think Fleet Street is right, yes—even if the Parthenon is wrong. I think that as the world goes on new psychological atmospheres are generated, and in these atmospheres it is possible to find delicacies and combinations which in other times would have to be represented by some ruder symbol. Every man feels the need of some element of purity in sex; perhaps they can only typify purity as the absence of sex. You will laugh if I suggest that we may have made in Fleet Street an atmosphere in which a man can be so passionate as Sir Lancelot and as pure as Sir Galahad. But, after all, we have in the modern world erected many such atmospheres. We have, for instance, a new and imaginative appreciation of children."

"Quite so," replied MacIan with a singular smile. "It has been very well put by one of the brightest of your young authors, who said: 'Unless you become as little children ye shall in no wise enter the kingdom of heaven.' But you are quite right; there is a modern worship of children. And what, I ask you, is this modern worship of children? What, in the name of all the angels and devils, is it except a worship of virginity? Why should anyone worship a thing merely because it is small or immature? No; you have tried to escape from this thing, and the very thing you point to as the goal of your escape is only the thing again. Am I wrong in saying that these things seem to be eternal?"

And it was with these words that they came in sight of the great plains. They went a little way in silence, and then James Turnbull said suddenly, "But I *cannot* believe in the thing." MacIan answered nothing to the speech; perhaps it is unanswerable. And indeed they scarcely spoke another word to each other all that day.

IX. THE STRANGE LADY

Moonrise with a great and growing moon opened over all those flats, making them seem flatter and larger than they were, turning them to a lake of blue light. The two companions trudged across the moonlit plain for half an hour in full silence. Then MacIan stopped suddenly and planted his sword-point in the ground like one who plants his tent-pole for the night. Leaving it standing there, he clutched his black-haired skull with his great claws of hands, as was his custom when forcing the pace of his brain. Then his hands dropped again and he spoke.

"I'm sure you're thinking the same as I am," he said; "how long are we to be on this damned seesaw?"

The other did not answer, but his silence seemed somehow solid as assent; and MacIan went on conversationally. Neither noticed that both had instinctively stood still before the sign of the fixed and standing sword.

"It is hard to guess what God means in this business. But he means something—or the other thing, or both. Whenever we have tried to fight each other something has stopped us. Whenever we have tried to be reconciled to each other, something has stopped us again. By the run of our luck we have never had time to be either friends or enemies. Something always jumped out of the bushes."

Turnbull nodded gravely and glanced round at the huge and hedgeless meadow which fell away towards the horizon into a glimmering high road.

"Nothing will jump out of bushes here anyhow," he said.

"That is what I meant," said MacIan, and stared steadily at the heavy hilt of his standing sword, which in the slight wind swayed on its tempered steel like some huge thistle on its stalk.

"That is what I meant; we are quite alone here. I have not heard a horse-hoof or a footstep or the hoot of a train for miles. So I think we might stop here and ask for a miracle."

"Oh! might we?" said the atheistic editor with a sort of gusto of disgust.

"I beg your pardon," said MacIan, meekly. "I forgot your prejudices." He eyed the wind-swung sword-hilt in sad meditation and resumed: "What I mean is, we might find out in this quiet place whether there really is any fate or any commandment against our enterprise. I will engage on my side, like Elijah, to accept a test from heaven. Turnbull, let us draw swords here in this moonlight and this monstrous solitude. And if here in this moonlight and solitude there happens anything to interrupt us—if it be lightning striking our sword-blades or a rabbit running under our legs—I will take it as a sign from God and we will shake hands for ever."

Turnbull's mouth twitched in angry humour under his red moustache. He said: "I will wait for signs from God until I have any signs of His existence; but God—or Fate—forbid that a man of scientific culture should refuse any kind of experiment."

"Very well, then," said MacIan, shortly. "We are more quiet here than anywhere else; let us engage." And he plucked his sword-point out of the turf.

Turnbull regarded him for a second and a half with a baffling visage almost black against the moonrise; then his hand made a sharp movement to his hip and his sword shone in the moon.

As old chess-players open every game with established gambits, they opened with a thrust and parry, orthodox and even frankly ineffectual. But in MacIan's soul more formless storms were gathering, and he made a lunge or two so savage as first to surprise and then to enrage his opponent. Turnbull ground his teeth, kept his temper, and waiting for the third lunge, and the worst, had almost spitted the lunger when a shrill, small cry came from behind him, a cry such as is not made by any of the beasts that perish.

Turnbull must have been more superstitious than he knew, for he stopped in the act of going forward. MacIan was brazenly superstitious, and he dropped his sword. After all, he had challenged the universe to send an interruption; and this was an interruption, whatever else it was. An instant afterwards the sharp, weak cry was repeated. This time it was certain that it was human and that it was female.

MacIan stood rolling those great blue Gaelic eyes that contrasted with his dark hair. "It is the voice of God," he said again and again.

"God hasn't got much of a voice," said Turnbull, who snatched at every chance of cheap profanity. "As a matter of fact, MacIan, it isn't the voice of God, but it's something a jolly sight more important—it is the voice of man—or rather of woman. So I think we'd better scoot in its direction."

MacIan snatched up his fallen weapon without a word, and the two raced away towards that part of the distant road from which the cry was now constantly renewed.

They had to run over a curve of country that looked smooth but was very rough; a neglected field which they soon found to be full of the tallest grasses and the deepest rabbit-holes. Moreover, that great curve of the countryside which looked so slow and gentle when you glanced over it, proved to be highly precipitous when you scampered over it; and Turnbull was twice nearly flung on his face. MacIan, though much heavier, avoided such an overthrow only by having the quick and incalculable feet of the mountaineer; but both of them may be said to have leapt off a low cliff when they leapt into the road.

The moonlight lay on the white road with a more naked and electric glare than on the grey-green upland, and though the scene which it revealed was complicated, it was not difficult to get its first features at a glance.

A small but very neat black-and-yellow motor-car was standing stolidly, slightly to the left of the road. A somewhat larger light-green motor-car was tipped half-way into a ditch on the same side, and four flushed and staggering men in evening dress were tipped out of it. Three of them were standing about the road, giving their opinions to the moon with vague but echoing violence. The fourth, however, had already advanced on the chauffeur of the black-and-yellow car, and was threatening him with a stick. The chauffeur had risen to defend himself. By his side sat a young lady.

She was sitting bolt upright, a slender and rigid figure gripping the sides of her seat, and her first few cries had ceased. She was clad in close-fitting dark costume, a mass of warm brown hair went out in two wings or waves on each side of her forehead; and even at that distance it could be seen that her profile was of the aquiline and eager sort, like a young falcon hardly free of the nest.

Turnbull had concealed in him somewhere a fund of common sense and knowledge of the world of which he himself and his best friends were hardly aware. He was one of those who take in much of the shows of things absent-mindedly, and in an irrelevant reverie. As he stood at the door of his editorial shop on Ludgate Hill and meditated on the non-existence of God, he silently absorbed a good deal of varied knowledge about the existence of men. He had come to know types by instinct and dilemmas with a glance; he saw the crux of the situation in the road, and what he saw made him redouble his pace.

He knew that the men were rich; he knew that they were drunk; and he knew, what was worst of all, that they were fundamentally frightened. And he knew this also, that no common ruffian (such as attacks ladies in novels) is ever so savage and ruthless as a coarse kind of gentleman when he is really alarmed. The reason is not recondite; it is simply because the police-court is not such a menacing novelty to the poor ruffian as it is to the rich. When they came within hail and heard the voices, they confirmed all Turnbull's anticipations. The man in the middle of the road was shouting in a hoarse and groggy voice that the chauffeur had smashed their car on purpose; that they must get to the Cri that evening, and that he would jolly well have to take them there. The chauffeur had mildly objected that he was driving a lady. "Oh! we'll take care of the lady," said the red-faced young man, and went off into gurgling and almost senile laughter.

By the time the two champions came up, things had grown more serious. The intoxication of the man talking to the chauffeur had taken one of its perverse and catlike jumps into mere screaming spite and rage. He lifted his stick and struck at the chauffeur, who caught hold of it, and the drunkard fell backwards, dragging him out of his seat on the car. Another of the rowdies rushed forward booing in idiot excitement, fell over the chauffeur, and, either by accident or design, kicked him as he lay. The drunkard got to his feet again; but the chauffeur did not.

The man who had kicked kept a kind of half-witted conscience or cowardice, for he stood staring at the senseless body and murmuring words of inconsequent self-justification, making gestures with his hands as if he were arguing with somebody. But the other three, with a mere whoop and howl of victory, were boarding the car on three sides at once. It was exactly at this moment that Turnbull fell among them like one fallen from the sky. He tore one of the climbers backward by the collar, and with a hearty push sent him staggering over into the ditch upon his nose. One of the remaining two, who was too far gone to notice anything, continued to clamber ineffectually over the high back of the car, kicking and pouring forth a rivulet of soliloquy. But the other dropped at the interruption, turned upon Turnbull and began a battering bout of fisticuffs. At the same moment the man crawled out of the ditch in a masquerade of mud and rushed at his old enemy from behind. The whole had not taken a second; and an instant after MacIan was in the midst of them.

Turnbull had tossed away his sheathed sword, greatly preferring his hands, except in the avowed etiquette of the duel; for he had learnt to use his hands in the old street-battles of Bradlaugh. But to MacIan the sword even sheathed was a more natural weapon, and he laid about him on all sides with it as with a stick. The man who had the walking-stick found his blows parried with promptitude; and a second after, to his great astonishment, found his own stick fly up in the air as by a conjuring trick, with a turn of the swordsman's wrist. Another of the revellers picked the stick out of the ditch and ran in upon MacIan, calling to his companion to assist him.

"I haven't got a stick," grumbled the disarmed man, and looked vaguely about the ditch.

"Perhaps," said MacIan, politely, "you would like this one." With the word the drunkard found his hand that had grasped the stick suddenly twisted and empty; and the stick lay at the feet of his companion on the other side of the road. MacIan felt a faint stir behind him; the girl had risen to her feet and was leaning forward to stare at the fighters. Turnbull was still engaged in countering and pommelling with the third young man. The fourth young man was still engaged with himself, kicking his legs in helpless rotation on the back of the car and talking with melodious rationality.

At length Turnbull's opponent began to back before the battery of his heavy hands, still fighting, for he was the soberest and boldest of the four. If these are annals of military glory, it is due to him to say that he need not have abandoned the conflict; only that as he backed to the edge of the ditch his foot caught in a loop of grass and he went over in a flat and comfortable position from which it took him a considerable time to rise. By the time he had risen, Turnbull had come to the rescue of MacIan, who was at bay but belabouring his two enemies handsomely. The sight of the liberated reserve was to them like that of Blucher at Waterloo; the two set off at a sullen trot down the road, leaving even the walking-stick lying behind them in the moonlight. MacIan plucked the struggling and aspiring idiot off the back of the car like a stray cat, and left him swaying unsteadily in the moon. Then he approached the front part of the car in a somewhat embarrassed manner and pulled off his cap.

For some solid seconds the lady and he merely looked at each other, and MacIan had an irrational feeling of being in a picture hung on a wall. That is, he was motionless, even lifeless, and yet staringly significant, like a picture. The white moonlight on the road, when he was not looking at it, gave him a vision of the road being white with snow. The motor-car, when he was not looking at it, gave him a rude impression of a captured coach in the old days of highwaymen. And he whose whole soul was with the swords and stately manners of the eighteenth century, he who was a Jacobite risen from the dead, had an overwhelming sense of being once more in the picture, when he had so long been out of the picture.

In that short and strong silence he absorbed the lady from head to foot. He had never really looked at a human being before in his life. He saw her face and hair first, then that she had long suede gloves; then that there was a fur cap at the back of her brown hair. He might, perhaps, be excused for this hungry attention. He had prayed that some sign might come from heaven; and after an almost savage scrutiny he came to the conclusion that his one did. The lady's instantaneous arrest of speech might need more explaining; but she may well have been stunned with the squalid attack and the abrupt rescue. Yet it was she who remembered herself first and suddenly called out with self-accusing horror:

"Oh, that poor, poor man!"

They both swung round abruptly and saw that Turnbull, with his recovered sword under his arm-pit, was already lifting the fallen chauffeur into the car. He was only stunned and was slowly awakening, feebly waving his left arm.

The lady in long gloves and the fur cap leapt out and ran rapidly towards them, only to be reassured by Turnbull, who (unlike many of his school) really knew a little science when he invoked it to redeem the world. "He's all right," said he; "he's quite safe. But I'm afraid he won't be able to drive the car for half an hour or so."

"I can drive the car," said the young woman in the fur cap with stony practicability.

"Oh, in that case," began MacIan, uneasily; and that paralysing shyness which is a part of romance induced him to make a backward movement as if leaving her to herself. But Turnbull was more rational than he, being more indifferent.

"I don't think you ought to drive home alone, ma'am," he said, gruffly. "There seem to be a lot of rowdy parties along this road, and the man will be no use for an hour. If you will tell us where you are going, we will see you safely there and say good night."

The young lady exhibited all the abrupt disturbance of a person who is not commonly disturbed. She said almost sharply and yet with evident sincerity: "Of course

I am awfully grateful to you for all you've done—and there's plenty of room if you'll come in."

Turnbull, with the complete innocence of an absolutely sound motive, immediately jumped into the car; but the girl cast an eye at MacIan, who stood in the road for an instant as if rooted like a tree. Then he also tumbled his long legs into the tonneau, having that sense of degradedly diving into heaven which so many have known in so many human houses when they consented to stop to tea or were allowed to stop to supper. The slowly reviving chauffeur was set in the back seat; Turnbull and MacIan had fallen into the middle one; the lady with a steely coolness had taken the driver's seat and all the handles of that headlong machine. A moment afterwards the engine started, with a throb and leap unfamiliar to Turnbull, who had only once been in a motor during a general election, and utterly unknown to MacIan, who in his present mood thought it was the end of the world. Almost at the same instant that the car plucked itself out of the mud and whipped away up the road, the man who had been flung into the ditch rose waveringly to his feet. When he saw the car escaping he ran after it and shouted something which, owing to the increasing distance, could not be heard. It is awful to reflect that, if his remark was valuable, it is quite lost to the world.

The car shot on up and down the shining moonlit lanes, and there was no sound in it except the occasional click or catch of its machinery; for through some cause or other no soul inside it could think of a word to say. The lady symbolized her feelings, whatever they were, by urging the machine faster and faster until scattered woodlands went by them in one black blotch and heavy hills and valleys seemed to ripple under the wheels like mere waves. A little while afterwards this mood seemed to slacken and she fell into a more ordinary pace; but still she did not speak. Turnbull, who kept a more common and sensible view of the case than anyone else, made some remark about the moonlight; but something indescribable made him also relapse into silence.

All this time MacIan had been in a sort of monstrous delirium, like some fabulous hero snatched up into the moon. The difference between this experience and common experiences was analogous to that between waking life and a dream. Yet he did not feel in the least as if he were dreaming; rather the other way; as waking was more actual than dreaming, so this seemed by another degree more actual than waking itself. But it was another life altogether, like a cosmos with a new dimension.

He felt he had been hurled into some new incarnation: into the midst of new relations, wrongs and rights, with towering responsibilities and almost tragic joys which he had as yet had no time to examine. Heaven had not merely sent him a message; Heaven itself had opened around him and given him an hour of its own ancient and star-shattering energy. He had never felt so much alive before; and yet he was like a man in a trance. And if you had asked him on what his throbbing happiness hung, he could only have told you that it hung on four or five visible facts, as a curtain hangs on four of five fixed nails. The fact that the lady had a little fur at her throat; the fact that the curve of her cheek was a low and lean curve and that the moonlight caught the height of her cheek-bone; the fact that her hands were small but heavily gloved as they gripped the steering-wheel; the fact that a white witch light was on the road; the fact that the brisk breeze of their passage stirred and fluttered a little not only the brown hair of her head but the black fur on her cap. All these facts were to him certain and incredible, like sacraments.

When they had driven half a mile farther, a big shadow was flung across the path, followed by its bulky owner, who eyed the car critically but let it pass. The silver moonlight picked out a piece or two of pewter ornament on his blue uniform; and as they went by they knew it was a sergeant of police. Three hundred yards farther on another policeman stepped out into the road as if to stop them, then seemed to doubt his own authority and stepped back again. The girl was a daughter of the rich; and this police suspicion (under which all the poor live day and night) stung her for the first time into speech.

"What can they mean?" she cried out in a kind of temper; "this car's going like a snail."

There was a short silence, and then Turnbull said: "It is certainly very odd, you are driving quietly enough."

"You are driving nobly," said MacIan, and his words (which had no meaning whatever) sounded hoarse and ungainly even in his own ears.

They passed the next mile and a half swiftly and smoothly; yet among the many things which they passed in the course of it was a clump of eager policemen standing at a cross-road. As they passed, one of the policemen shouted something to the others; but nothing else happened. Eight hundred yards farther on, Turnbull stood up suddenly in the swaying car.

"My God, MacIan!" he called out, showing his first emotion of that night. "I don't believe it's the pace; it couldn't be the pace. I believe it's us."

MacIan sat motionless for a few moments and then turned up at his companion a face that was as white as the moon above it.

"You may be right," he said at last; "if you are, I must tell her."

"I will tell the lady if you like," said Turnbull, with his unconquered good temper.

"You!" said MacIan, with a sort of sincere and instinctive astonishment. "Why should you—no, I must tell her, of course——"

And he leant forward and spoke to the lady in the fur cap.

"I am afraid, madam, that we may have got you into some trouble," he said, and even as he said it it sounded wrong, like everything he said to this particular person in the long gloves. "The fact is," he resumed, desperately, "the fact is, we are being chased by the police." Then the last flattening hammer fell upon poor Evan's embarrassment; for the fluffy brown head with the furry black cap did not turn by a section of the compass.

"We are chased by the police," repeated MacIan, vigorously; then he added, as if beginning an explanation, "You see, I am a Catholic."

The wind whipped back a curl of the brown hair so as to necessitate a new theory of aesthetics touching the line of the cheek-bone; but the head did not turn.

"You see," began MacIan, again blunderingly, "this gentleman wrote in his newspaper that Our Lady was a common woman, a bad woman, and so we agreed to fight; and we were fighting quite a little time ago—but that was before we saw you."

The young lady driving her car had half turned her face to listen; and it was not a reverent or a patient face that she showed him. Her Norman nose was tilted a trifle too high upon the slim stalk of her neck and body.

When MacIan saw that arrogant and uplifted profile pencilled plainly against the moonshine, he accepted an ultimate defeat. He had expected the angels to despise him if he were wrong, but not to despise him so much as this.

"You see," said the stumbling spokesman, "I was angry with him when he insulted the Mother of God, and I asked him to fight a duel with me; but the police are all trying to stop it."

Nothing seemed to waver or flicker in the fair young falcon profile; and it only opened its lips to say, after a silence: "I thought people in our time were supposed to respect each other's religion."

Under the shadow of that arrogant face MacIan could only fall back on the obvious answer: "But what about a man's irreligion?" The face only answered: "Well, you ought to be more broadminded."

If anyone else in the world had said the words, MacIan would have snorted with his equine neigh of scorn. But in this case he seemed knocked down by a superior simplicity, as if his eccentric attitude were rebuked by the innocence of a child. He could not dissociate anything that this woman said or did or wore from an idea of spiritual rarity and virtue. Like most others under the same elemental passion, his soul was at present soaked in ethics. He could have applied moral terms to the material objects of her environment. If someone had spoken of "her generous ribbon" or "her chivalrous gloves" or "her merciful shoe-buckle," it would not have seemed to him nonsense.

He was silent, and the girl went on in a lower key as if she were momentarily softened and a little saddened also. "It won't do, you know," she said; "you can't find out the truth in that way. There are such heaps of churches and people thinking different things nowadays, and they all think they are right. My uncle was a Swedenborgian."

MacIan sat with bowed head, listening hungrily to her voice but hardly to her words, and seeing his great world drama grow smaller and smaller before his eyes till it was no bigger than a child's toy theatre.

"The time's gone by for all that," she went on; "you can't find out the real thing like that—if there is really anything to find——" and she sighed rather drearily; for, like many of the women of our wealthy class, she was old and broken in thought, though young and clean enough in her emotions.

"Our object," said Turnbull, shortly, "is to make an effective demonstration"; and after that word, MacIan looked at his vision again and found it smaller than ever.

"It would be in the newspapers, of course," said the girl. "People read the newspapers, but they don't believe them, or anything else, I think." And she sighed again.

She drove in silence a third of a mile before she added, as if completing the sentence: "Anyhow, the whole thing's quite absurd."

"I don't think," began Turnbull, "that you quite realize——Hullo! hullo—hullo—what's this?"

The amateur chauffeur had been forced to bring the car to a staggering stoppage, for a file of fat, blue policemen made a wall across the way. A sergeant came to the side and touched his peaked cap to the lady.

"Beg your pardon, miss," he said with some embarrassment, for he knew her for a daughter of a dominant house, "but we have reason to believe that the gentlemen in your car are——" and he hesitated for a polite phrase.

"I am Evan MacIan," said that gentleman, and stood up in a sort of gloomy pomp, not wholly without a touch of the sulks of a schoolboy.

"Yes, we will get out, sergeant," said Turnbull, more easily; "my name is James Turnbull. We must not incommode the lady."

"What are you taking them up for?" asked the young woman, looking straight in front of her along the road.

"It's under the new act," said the sergeant, almost apologetically. "Incurable disturbers of the peace."

"What will happen to them?" she asked, with the same frigid clearness.

"Westgate Adult Reformatory," he replied, briefly.

"Until when?"

"Until they are cured," said the official.

"Very well, sergeant," said the young lady, with a sort of tired common sense. "I am sure I don't want to protect criminals or go against the law; but I must tell you that these gentlemen have done me a considerable service; you won't mind drawing your men a little farther off while I say good night to them. Men like that always misunderstand."

The sergeant was profoundly disquieted from the beginning at the mere idea of arresting anyone in the company of a great lady; to refuse one of her minor requests was quite beyond his courage. The police fell back to a few yards behind the car. Turnbull took up the two swords that were their only luggage; the swords that, after so many half duels, they were now to surrender at last. MacIan, the blood thundering in his brain at the thought of that instant of farewell, bent over, fumbled at the handle and flung open the door to get out.

But he did not get out. He did not get out, because it is dangerous to jump out of a car when it is going at full speed. And the car was going at full speed, because the young lady, without turning her head or so much as saying a syllable, had driven down a handle that made the machine plunge forward like a buffalo and then fly over the landscape like a greyhound. The police made one rush to follow, and then dropped so grotesque and hopeless a chase. Away in the vanishing distance they could see the sergeant furiously making notes.

The open door, still left loose on its hinges, swung and banged quite crazily as they went whizzing up one road and down another. Nor did MacIan sit down; he stood up stunned and yet staring, as he would have stood up at the trumpet of the Last Day. A black dot in the distance sprang up a tall black forest, swallowed them and spat them out again at the other end. A railway bridge grew larger and larger till it leapt upon their backs bellowing, and was in its turn left behind. Avenues of poplars on both sides of the road chased each other like the figures in a zoetrope. Now and then with a shock and rattle they went through sleeping moonlit villages, which must have stirred an instant in their sleep as at the passing of a fugitive earthquake. Sometimes in an outlying house a light in one erratic, unexpected window would give them a nameless hint of the hundred human secrets which they left behind them with their dust. Sometimes even a slouching rustic would be afoot on the road and would look after them, as after a flying phantom. But still MacIan stood up staring at earth and heaven; and still the door he had flung open flapped loose like a flag. Turnbull, after a few minutes of dumb amazement, had yielded to the healthiest element in his nature and gone off into uncontrollable fits of laughter. The girl had not stirred an inch.

After another half mile that seemed a mere flash, Turnbull leant over and locked the door. Evan staggered at last into his seat and hid his throbbing head in his hands; and still the car flew on and its driver sat inflexible and silent. The moon had already gone down, and the whole darkness was faintly troubled with twilight and the first movement of beasts and fowls. It was that mysterious moment when light is coming as if it were something unknown whose nature one could not guess—a mere alteration in everything. They looked at the sky and it seemed as dark as ever; then they saw the black shape of a tower or tree against it and knew that it was already grey. Save that they were driving southward and had certainly passed the longitude of London, they knew nothing of their direction; but Turnbull, who had spent a year on the Hampshire coast in his youth, began to recognize the unmistakable but quite indescribable villages of the English south. Then a white witch fire began to burn between the black stems of the fir-trees; and, like so many things in nature, though not in books on evolution, the daybreak, when it did come, came much quicker than one would think. The gloomy heavens were ripped up and rolled away like a scroll, revealing splendours, as the car went roaring up the curve of a great hill; and above them and black against the broadening light, there stood one of those crouching and fantastic trees that are first signals of the sea.

X. THE SWORDS REJOINED

As they came over the hill and down on the other side of it, it is not too much to say that the whole universe of God opened over them and under them, like a thing unfolding to five times its size. Almost under their feet opened the enormous sea, at the bottom of a steep valley which fell down into a bay; and the sea under their feet blazed at them almost as lustrous and almost as empty as the sky. The sunrise opened above them like some cosmic explosion, shining and shattering and yet silent; as if the world were blown to pieces without a sound. Round the rays of the victorious sun swept a sort of rainbow of confused and conquered colours—brown and blue and green and flaming rose-colour; as though gold were driving before it all the colours of the world. The lines of the landscape down which they sped, were the simple, strict, yet swerving, lines of a rushing river; so that it was almost as if they were being sucked down in a huge still whirlpool. Turnbull had some such feeling, for he spoke for the first time for many hours.

"If we go down at this rate we shall be over the sea cliff," he said.

"How glorious!" said MacIan.

When, however, they had come into the wide hollow at the bottom of that landslide, the car took a calm and graceful curve along the side of the sea, melted into the fringe of a few trees, and quietly, yet astonishingly, stopped. A belated light was burning in the broad morning in the window of a sort of lodge- or gate-keepers' cottage; and the girl stood up in the car and turned her splendid face to the sun.

Evan seemed startled by the stillness, like one who had been born amid sound and speed. He wavered on his long legs as he stood up; he pulled himself together, and the only consequence was that he trembled from head to foot. Turnbull had already opened the door on his side and jumped out.

The moment he had done so the strange young woman had one more mad movement, and deliberately drove the car a few yards farther. Then she got out with an almost cruel coolness and began pulling off her long gloves and almost whistling.

"You can leave me here," she said, quite casually, as if they had met five minutes before. "That is the lodge of my father's place. Please come in, if you like—but I understood that you had some business."

Evan looked at that lifted face and found it merely lovely; he was far too much of a fool to see that it was working with a final fatigue and that its austerity was agony. He was even fool enough to ask it a question. "Why did you save us?" he said, quite humbly.

The girl tore off one of her gloves, as if she were tearing off her hand. "Oh, I don't know," she said, bitterly. "Now I come to think of it, I can't imagine."

Evan's thoughts, that had been piled up to the morning star, abruptly let him down with a crash into the very cellars of the emotional universe. He remained in a stunned silence for a long time; and that, if he had only known, was the wisest thing that he could possibly do at the moment.

Indeed, the silence and the sunrise had their healing effect, for when the extraordinary lady spoke again, her tone was more friendly and apologetic. "I'm not really ungrateful," she said; "it was very good of you to save me from those men."

"But why?" repeated the obstinate and dazed MacIan, "why did you save us from the other men? I mean the policemen?"

The girl's great brown eyes were lit up with a flash that was at once final desperation and the loosening of some private and passionate reserve.

"Oh, God knows!" she cried. "God knows that if there is a God He has turned His big back on everything. God knows I have had no pleasure in my life, though I am pretty and young and father has plenty of money. And then people come and tell me that I ought to do things and I do them and it's all drivel. They want you to do work among the poor; which means reading Ruskin and feeling self-righteous in the best room in a poor tenement. Or to help some cause or other, which always means bundling people out of crooked houses, in which they've always lived, into straight houses, in which they often die. And all the time you have inside only the horrid irony of your own empty head and empty heart. I am to give to the unfortunate, when my whole misfortune is that I have nothing to give. I am to teach, when I believe nothing at all that I was taught. I am to save the children from death, and I am not even certain that I should not be better dead. I suppose if I actually saw a child drowning I should save it. But that would be from the same motive from which I have saved you, or destroyed you, whichever it is that I have done."

"What was the motive?" asked Evan, in a low voice.

"My motive is too big for my mind," answered the girl.

Then, after a pause, as she stared with a rising colour at the glittering sea, she said: "It can't be described, and yet I am trying to describe it. It seems to me not only that I am unhappy, but that there is no way of being happy. Father is not happy, though he is a Member of Parliament——" She paused a moment and added with a ghost of a smile: "Nor Aunt Mabel, though a man from India has told her the secret of all creeds. But I may be wrong; there may be a way out. And for one stark, insane second, I felt that, after all, you had got the way out and that was why the world hated you. You see, if there were a way out, it would be sure to be something that looked very queer."

Evan put his hand to his forehead and began stumblingly: "Yes, I suppose we do seem——"

"Oh, yes, you look queer enough," she said, with ringing sincerity. "You'll be all the better for a wash and brush up."

"You forget our business, madam," said Evan, in a shaking voice; "we have no concern but to kill each other."

"Well, I shouldn't be killed looking like that if I were you," she replied, with inhuman honesty.

Evan stood and rolled his eyes in masculine bewilderment. Then came the final change in this Proteus, and she put out both her hands for an instant and said in a low tone on which he lived for days and nights:

"Don't you understand that I did not dare to stop you? What you are doing is so mad that it may be quite true. Somehow one can never really manage to be an atheist."

Turnbull stood staring at the sea; but his shoulders showed that he heard, and after one minute he turned his head. But the girl had only brushed Evan's hand with hers and had fled up the dark alley by the lodge gate.

Evan stood rooted upon the road, literally like some heavy statue hewn there in the age of the Druids. It seemed impossible that he should ever move. Turnbull grew restless with this rigidity, and at last, after calling his companion twice or thrice, went up and clapped him impatiently on one of his big shoulders. Evan winced and leapt away from him with a repulsion which was not the hate of an unclean thing nor the dread of a dangerous one, but was a spasm of awe and separation from something from which he was now sundered as by the sword of God. He did not hate the atheist; it is possible that he loved him. But Turnbull was now something more dreadful than an enemy: he was a thing sealed and devoted—a thing now hopelessly doomed to be either a corpse or an executioner.

"What is the matter with you?" asked Turnbull, with his hearty hand still in the air; and yet he knew more about it than his innocent action would allow.

"James," said Evan, speaking like one under strong bodily pain, "I asked for God's answer and I have got it—got it in my vitals. He knows how weak I am, and that I might forget the peril of the faith, forget the face of Our Lady—yes, even with your blow upon her cheek. But the honour of this earth has just this about it, that it can make a man's heart like iron. I am from the Lords of the Isles and I dare not be a mere deserter. Therefore, God has tied me by the chain of my worldly place and word, and there is nothing but fighting now."

"I think I understand you," said Turnbull, "but you say everything tail foremost."

"She wants us to do it," said Evan, in a voice crushed with passion. "She has hurt herself so that we might do it. She has left her good name and her good sleep and all her habits and dignity flung away on the other side of England in the hope that she may hear of us and that we have broken some hole into heaven."

"I thought I knew what you mean," said Turnbull, biting his beard; "it does seem as if we ought to do something after all she has done this night."

"I never liked you so much before," said MacIan, in bitter sorrow.

As he spoke, three solemn footmen came out of the lodge gate and assembled to assist the chauffeur to his room. The mere sight of them made the two wanderers flee as from a too frightful incongruity, and before they knew where they were, they were well upon the grassy ledge of England that overlooks the Channel. Evan said suddenly: "Will they let me see her in heaven once in a thousand ages?" and addressed the remark to the editor of *The Atheist*, as on which he would be likely or qualified to answer. But no answer came; a silence sank between the two.

Turnbull strode sturdily to the edge of the cliff and looked out, his companion following, somewhat more shaken by his recent agitation.

"If that's the view you take," said Turnbull, "and I don't say you are wrong, I think I know where we shall be best off for the business. As it happens, I know this part of the south coast pretty well. And unless I am mistaken there's a way down the cliff just here which will land us on a stretch of firm sand where no one is likely to follow us."

The Highlander made a gesture of assent and came also almost to the edge of the precipice. The sunrise, which was broadening over sea and shore, was one of those rare and splendid ones in which there seems to be no mist or doubt, and nothing but a universal clarification more and more complete. All the colours were transparent. It seemed like a triumphant prophecy of some perfect world where everything being innocent will be intelligible; a world where even our bodies, so to speak, may be as of burning glass. Such a world is faintly though fiercely figured in the coloured windows of Christian architecture. The sea that lay before them was like a pavement of emerald, bright and almost brittle; the sky against which its strict horizon hung was almost absolutely white, except that close to the sky line, like scarlet braids on the hem of a garment, lay strings of flaky cloud of so gleaming and gorgeous a red that they seemed cut out of some strange blood-red celestial metal, of which the mere gold of this earth is but a drab yellow imitation.

"The hand of Heaven is still pointing," muttered the man of superstition to himself. "And now it is a blood-red hand."

The cool voice of his companion cut in upon his monologue, calling to him from a little farther along the cliff, to tell him that he had found the ladder of descent. It began as a steep and somewhat greasy path, which then tumbled down twenty or thirty feet in the form of a fall of rough stone steps. After that, there was a rather awkward drop on to a ledge of stone and then the journey was undertaken easily and even elegantly by the remains of an ornamental staircase, such as might have belonged to some long-disused watering-place. All the time that the two travellers sank from stage to stage of this downward journey, there closed over their heads living bridges and caverns of the most varied foliage, all of which grew greener, redder, or more golden, in the growing sunlight of the morning. Life, too, of the more moving sort rose at the sun on every side of them. Birds whirred and fluttered in the undergrowth, as if imprisoned in green cages. Other birds were shaken up in great clouds from the tree-tops, as if they were blossoms detached and scattered up to heaven. Animals which Turnbull was too much of a Londoner and MacIan too much of a Northerner to know, slipped by among the tangle or ran pattering up the tree-trunks. Both the men, according to their several creeds, felt the full thunder of the psalm of life as they had never heard it before; MacIan felt God the Father, benignant in all His energies, and Turnbull that ultimate anonymous energy, that *Natura Naturans,* which is the whole theme of Lucretius. It was down this clamorous ladder of life that they went down to die.

They broke out upon a brown semicircle of sand, so free from human imprint as to justify Turnbull's profession. They strode out upon it, stuck their swords in the sand, and had a pause too important for speech. Turnbull eyed the coast curiously for a moment, like one awakening memories of childhood; then he said abruptly, like a man remembering somebody's name: "But, of course, we shall be better off still round the corner of Cragness Point; nobody ever comes there at all." And picking up his sword again, he began striding towards a big bluff of the rocks which stood out upon their left. MacIan followed him round the corner and found himself in what was certainly an even finer fencing court, of flat, firm sand, enclosed on three sides by white walls of rock, and on the fourth by the green wall of the advancing sea.

"We are quite safe here," said Turnbull, and, to the other's surprise, flung himself down, sitting on the brown beach.

"You see, I was brought up near here," he explained. "I was sent from Scotland to stop with my aunt. It is highly probable that I may die here. Do you mind if I light a pipe?"

"Of course, do whatever you like," said MacIan, with a choking voice, and he went and walked alone by himself along the wet, glistening sands.

Ten minutes afterwards he came back again, white with his own whirlwind of emotions; Turnbull was quite cheerful and was knocking out the end of his pipe.

"You see, we have to do it," said MacIan. "She tied us to it."

"Of course, my dear fellow," said the other, and leapt up as lightly as a monkey.

They took their places gravely in the very centre of the great square of sand, as if they had thousands of spectators. Before saluting, MacIan, who, being a mystic, was one inch nearer to Nature, cast his eye round the huge framework of their heroic folly. The three walls of rock all leant a little outward, though at various angles; but this impression was exaggerated in the direction of the incredible by the heavy load of living trees and thickets which each wall wore on its top like a huge shock of hair. On all that luxurious crest of life the risen and victorious sun was beating, burnishing it all like gold, and every bird that rose with that sunrise caught a light like a star upon it like the dove of the Holy Spirit. Imaginative life had never so much crowded upon MacIan. He felt that he could write whole books about the feelings of a single bird. He felt that for two centuries he would not tire of being a rabbit. He was in the Palace of Life, of which the very tapestries and curtains were alive. Then he recovered himself, and remembered his affairs. Both men saluted, and iron rang upon iron. It was exactly at the same moment that he realized that his enemy's left ankle was encircled with a ring of salt water that had crept up to his feet.

"What is the matter?" said Turnbull, stopping an instant, for he had grown used to every movement of his extraordinary fellow-traveller's face.

MacIan glanced again at that silver anklet of sea-water and then looked beyond at the next promontory round which a deep sea was boiling and leaping. Then he turned and looked back and saw heavy foam being shaken up to heaven about the base of Cragness Point.

"The sea has cut us off," he said, curtly.

"I have noticed it," said Turnbull with equal sobriety. "What view do you take of the development?"

Evan threw away his weapon, and, as his custom was, imprisoned his big head in his hands. Then he let them fall and said: "Yes, I know what it means; and I think it is the fairest thing. It is the finger of God—red as blood—still pointing. But now it points to two graves."

There was a space filled with the sound of the sea, and then MacIan spoke again in a voice pathetically reasonable: "You see, we both saved her—and she told us both to fight—and it would not be just that either should fail and fall alone, while the other——"

"You mean," said Turnbull, in a voice surprisingly soft and gentle, "that there is something fine about fighting in a place where even the conqueror must die?"

"Oh, you have got it right, you have got it right!" cried out Evan, in an extraordinary childish ecstasy. "Oh, I'm sure that you really believe in God!"

Turnbull answered not a word, but only took up his fallen sword.

For the third time Evan MacIan looked at those three sides of English cliff hung with their noisy load of life. He had been at a loss to understand the almost ironical magnificence of all those teeming creatures and tropical colours and smells that smoked happily to heaven. But now he knew that he was in the closed court of death and that all the gates were sealed.

He drank in the last green and the last red and the last gold, those unique and indescribable things of God, as a man drains good wine at the bottom of his glass. Then he turned and saluted his enemy once more, and the two stood up and fought till the foam flowed over their knees.

Then MacIan stepped backward suddenly with a splash and held up his hand. "Turnbull!" he cried; "I can't help it—fair fighting is more even than promises. And this is not fair fighting."

"What the deuce do you mean?" asked the other, staring.

"I've only just thought of it," cried Evan, brokenly. "We're very well matched—it may go on a good time—the tide is coming up fast—and I'm a foot and a half taller. You'll be washed away like seaweed before it's above my breeches. I'll not fight foul for all the girls and angels in the universe."

"Will you oblige me," said Turnbull, with staring grey eyes and a voice of distinct and violent politeness; "will you oblige me by jolly well minding your own business? Just you stand up and fight, and we'll see who will be washed away like seaweed. You wanted to finish this fight and you shall finish it, or I'll denounce you as a coward to the whole of that assembled company."

Evan looked very doubtful and offered a somewhat wavering weapon; but he was quickly brought back to his senses by his opponent's sword-point, which shot past him, shaving his shoulder by a hair. By this time the waves were well up Turnbull's thigh, and what was worse, they were beginning to roll and break heavily around them.

MacIan parried this first lunge perfectly, the next less perfectly; the third in all human probability he would not have parried at all; the Christian champion would have been pinned like a butterfly, and the atheistic champion left to drown like a rat, with such consolation as his view of the cosmos afforded him. But just as Turnbull launched his heaviest stroke, the sea, in which he stood up to his hips, launched a yet heavier one. A wave breaking beyond the others smote him heavily like a hammer of water. One leg gave way, he was swung round and sucked into the retreating sea, still gripping his sword.

MacIan put his sword between his teeth and plunged after his disappearing enemy. He had the sense of having the whole universe on top of him as crest after crest struck him down. It seemed to him quite a cosmic collapse, as if all the seven heavens were falling on him one after the other. But he got hold of the atheist's left leg and he did not let it go.

After some ten minutes of foam and frenzy, in which all the senses at once seemed blasted by the sea, Evan found himself laboriously swimming on a low, green swell, with the sword still in his teeth and the editor of *The Atheist* still under his arm. What he was going to do he had not even the most glimmering idea; so he merely kept his grip and swam somehow with one hand.

He ducked instinctively as there bulked above him a big, black wave, much higher than any that he had seen. Then he saw that it was hardly the shape of any possible wave. Then he saw that it was a fisherman's boat, and, leaping upward, caught hold of the bow. The boat pitched forward with its stern in the air for just as much time as was needed to see that there was nobody in it. After a moment or two of desperate clambering, however, there were two people in it, Mr. Evan MacIan, panting and sweating, and Mr. James Turnbull, uncommonly close to being drowned. After ten minutes' aimless tossing in the empty fishing-boat he recovered, however, stirred, stretched himself, and looked round on the rolling waters. Then, while taking no notice of the streams of salt water that were pouring from his hair, beard, coat, boots, and trousers, he carefully wiped the wet off his sword-blade to preserve it from the possibilities of rust.

MacIan found two oars in the bottom of the deserted boat and began somewhat drearily to row.

A rainy twilight was clearing to cold silver over the moaning sea, when the battered boat that had rolled and drifted almost aimlessly all night, came within sight of land, though of land which looked almost as lost and savage as the waves. All night there had been but little lifting in the leaden sea, only now and then the boat had been heaved up, as on a huge shoulder which slipped from under it; such occasional sea-quakes came probably from the swell of some steamer that had passed it in the dark; otherwise the waves were harmless though restless. But it was piercingly cold, and there was, from time to time, a splutter of rain like the splutter of the spray, which seemed almost to freeze as it fell. MacIan, more at home than his companion in this quite barbarous and elemental sort of adventure, had rowed toilsomely with the heavy oars whenever he saw anything that looked like land; but for the most part had trusted with grim transcendentalism to wind and tide. Among the implements of their first outfit the brandy alone had remained to him, and he gave it to his freezing companion in quantities which greatly alarmed that temperate Londoner; but MacIan came from the cold seas and mists where a man can drink a tumbler of raw whisky in a boat without it making him wink.

When the Highlander began to pull really hard upon the oars, Turnbull craned his dripping red head out of the boat to see the goal of his exertions. It was a sufficiently uninviting one; nothing so far as could be seen but a steep and shelving bank of shingle, made of loose little pebbles such as children like, but slanting up higher than a house. On the top of the mound, against the sky line, stood up the brown skeleton of some broken fence or breakwater. With the grey and watery dawn crawling up behind it, the fence really seemed to say to our philosophic adventurers that they had come at last to the other end of nowhere.

Bent by necessity to his labour, MacIan managed the heavy boat with real power and skill, and when at length he ran it up on a smoother part of the slope it caught and held so that they could clamber out, not sinking farther than their knees into the water and the shingle. A foot or two farther up their feet found the beach firmer, and a few moments afterwards they were leaning on the ragged breakwater and looking back at the sea they had escaped.

They had a dreary walk across wastes of grey shingle in the grey dawn before they began to come within hail of human fields or roads; nor had they any notion of what fields or roads they would be. Their boots were beginning to break up and the confusion of stones tried them severely, so that they were glad to lean on their swords, as if they were the staves of pilgrims. MacIan thought vaguely of a weird ballad of his own country which describes the soul in Purgatory as walking on a plain full of sharp stones, and only saved by its own charities upon earth.

> If ever thou gavest hosen and shoon
> Every night and all,
> Sit thee down and put them on,
> And Christ receive thy soul.

Turnbull had no such lyrical meditations, but he was in an even worse temper.

At length they came to a pale ribbon of road, edged by a shelf of rough and almost colourless turf; and a few feet up the slope there stood grey and weather-stained, one of those big wayside crucifixes which are seldom seen except in Catholic countries.

MacIan put his hand to his head and found that his bonnet was not there. Turnbull gave one glance at the crucifix—a glance at once sympathetic and bitter, in which was concentrated the whole of Swinburne's poem on the same occasion.

> O hidden face of man, whereover
> The years have woven a viewless veil,
> If thou wert verily man's lover
> What did thy love or blood avail?
> Thy blood the priests mix poison of,
> And in gold shekels coin thy love.

Then, leaving MacIan in his attitude of prayer, Turnbull began to look right and left very sharply, like one looking for something. Suddenly, with a little cry, he saw it and ran forward. A few yards from them along the road a lean and starved sort of hedge came pitifully to an end. Caught upon its prickly angle, however, there was a very small and very dirty scrap of paper that might have hung there for months, since it escaped from someone tearing up a letter or making a spill out of a newspaper. Turnbull snatched at it and found it was the corner of a printed page, very coarsely printed, like a cheap novelette, and just large enough to contain the words: "*et c'est elle qui*——"

"Hurrah!" cried Turnbull, waving his fragment; "we are safe at last. We are free at last. We are somewhere better than England or Eden or Paradise. MacIan, we are in the Land of the Duel!"

"Where do you say?" said the other, looking at him heavily and with knitted brows, like one almost dazed with the grey doubts of desolate twilight and drifting sea.

"We are in France!" cried Turnbull, with a voice like a trumpet, "in the land where things really happen—*Tout arrive en France*. We arrive in France. Look at this little message," and he held out the scrap of paper. "There's an omen for you superstitious hill folk. *C'est elle qui—Mais oui, mais oui, c'est elle qui sauvera encore le monde*."

"France!" repeated MacIan, and his eyes awoke again in his head like large lamps lighted.

"Yes, France!" said Turnbull, and all the rhetorical part of him came to the top, his face growing as red as his hair. "France, that has always been in rebellion for liberty and reason. France, that has always assailed superstition with the club of Rabelais or the rapier of Voltaire. France, at whose first council table sits the sublime figure of Julian the Apostate. France, where a man said only the other day those splendid unanswerable words"—with a superb gesture—"'we have extinguished in heaven those lights that men shall never light again.'"

"No," said MacIan, in a voice that shook with a controlled passion. "But France, which was taught by St. Bernard and led to war by Joan of Arc. France that made the crusades. France that saved the Church and scattered the heresies by the mouths of Bossuet and Massillon. France, which shows today the conquering march of Catholicism, as brain after brain surrenders to it, Brunetière, Coppée, Hauptmann, Barrès, Bourget, Lemaître."

"France!" asserted Turnbull with a sort of rollicking self-exaggeration, very unusual with him, "France, which is one torrent of splendid scepticism from Abelard to Anatole France."

"France," said MacIan, "which is one cataract of clear faith from St. Louis to Our Lady of Lourdes."

"France at least," cried Turnbull, throwing up his sword in schoolboy triumph, "in which these things are thought about and fought about. France, where reason and religion clash in one continual tournament. France, above all, where men understand the pride and passion which have plucked our blades from their scabbards. Here, at least, we shall not be chased and spied on by sickly parsons and greasy policemen, because we wish to put our lives on the game. Courage, my friend, we have come to the country of honour."

MacIan did not even notice the incongruous phrase "my friend", but nodding again and again, drew his sword and flung the scabbard far behind him in the road.

"Yes," he cried, in a voice of thunder, "we will fight here and *He* shall look on at it."

Turnbull glanced at the crucifix with a sort of scowling good-humour and then said: "He may look and see His cross defeated."

"The cross cannot be defeated," said MacIan, "for it is Defeat."

A second afterwards the two bright, blood-thirsty weapons made the sign of the cross in horrible parody upon each other.

They had not touched each other twice, however, when upon the hill, above the crucifix, there appeared another horrible parody of its shape; the figure of a man who appeared for an instant waving his outspread arms. He had vanished in an instant; but MacIan, whose fighting face was set that way, had seen the shape momentarily but quite photographically. And while it was like a comic repetition of the cross, it was also, in that place and hour, something more incredible. It had been only instantaneously on the retina of his eye; but unless his eye and mind were going mad together, the figure was that of an ordinary London policeman.

He tried to concentrate his senses on the sword-play; but one half of his brain was wrestling with the puzzle; the apocalyptic and almost seraphic apparition of a stout constable out of Clapham on top of a dreary and deserted hill in France. He did not, however, have to puzzle long. Before the duellists had exchanged half a dozen passes, the big, blue policeman appeared once more on the top of the hill, a palpable monstrosity in the eye of heaven. He was waving only one arm now and seemed to be shouting directions. At the same moment a mass of blue blocked the corner of the road behind the small, smart figure of Turnbull, and a small company of policemen in the English uniform came up at a kind of half-military double.

Turnbull saw the stare of consternation in his enemy's face and swung round to share its cause. When he saw it, cool as he was, he staggered back.

"What the devil are you doing here?" he called out in a high, shrill voice of authority, like one who finds a tramp in his own larder.

"Well, sir," said the sergeant in command, with that sort of heavy civility shown only to the evidently guilty, "seems to me we might ask what are you doing here?"

"We are having an affair of honour," said Turnbull, as if it were the most rational thing in the world. "If the French police like to interfere, let them interfere. But why the blue blazes should you interfere, you great blue blundering sausages?"

"I'm afraid, sir," said the sergeant with restraint, "I'm afraid I don't quite follow you."

"I mean, why don't the French police take this up if it's got to be taken up? I always heard that they were spry enough in their own way."

"Well, sir," said the sergeant reflectively, "you see, sir, the French police don't take this up—well, because you see, sir, this ain't France. This is His Majesty's dominions, same as 'Ampstead 'eath."

"Not France?" repeated Turnbull, with a sort of dull incredulity.

"No, sir," said the sergeant; "though most of the people talk French. This is the island called St. Loup, sir, an island in the Channel. We've been sent down specially from London, as you were such specially distinguished criminals, if you'll allow me to say so. Which reminds me to warn you that anything you say may be used against you at your trial."

"Quite so," said Turnbull, and lurched suddenly against the sergeant, so as to tip him over the edge of the road with a crash into the shingle below. Then leaving MacIan and the policemen equally and instantaneously nailed to the road, he ran a little way along it, leapt off on to a part of the beach, which he had found in his journey to be firmer, and went across it with a clatter of pebbles. His sudden calculation was successful; the police, unacquainted with the various levels of the loose beach, tried to overtake him by the shorter cut and found themselves, being heavy men, almost up to their knees in shoals of slippery shingle. Two who had been slower with their bodies were quicker with their minds, and seeing Turnbull's trick, ran along the edge of the road after him. Then MacIan finally awoke, and leaving half his sleeve in the grip of the only man who tried to hold him, took the two policemen in the small of their backs with the impetus of a cannon-ball and, sending them also flat among the stones, went tearing after his twin defier of the law.

As they were both good runners, the start they had gained was decisive. They dropped over a high breakwater farther on upon the beach, turned sharply, and scrambled up a line of ribbed rocks, crowned with a thicket, crawled through it, scratching their hands and faces, and dropped into another road; and there found that they could slacken their speed into a steady trot. In all this desperate dart and scramble, they still kept hold of their drawn swords, which now, indeed, in the vigorous phrase of Bunyan, seemed almost to grow out of their hands.

They had run another half mile or so when it became apparent that they were entering a sort of scattered village. One or two whitewashed cottages and even a shop had appeared along the side of the road. Then, for the first time, Turnbull twisted round his red bear to get a glimpse of his companion, who was a foot or two behind, and remarked abruptly: "Mr. MacIan, we've been going the wrong way to work all along. We're traced everywhere, because everybody knows about us. It's as if one went about with Kruger's beard on Mafeking Night."

"What do you mean?" said MacIan, innocently.

"I mean," said Turnbull, with steady conviction, "that what we want is a little diplomacy, and I am going to buy some in a shop."

XI. A SCANDAL IN THE VILLAGE

In the little hamlet of Haroc, in the Isle of St. Loup, there lived a man who—though living under the English flag—was absolutely untypical of the French tradition. He was quite unnoticeable, but that was exactly where he was quite himself. He was not even extraordinarily French; but then it is against the French tradition to be extraordinarily French. Ordinary Englishmen would only have thought him a little old-fashioned; imperialistic Englishmen would really have mistaken him for the old John Bull of the caricatures. He was stout; he was quite undistinguished; and he had side-whiskers, worn just a little longer than John Bull's. He was by name Pierre Durand; he was by trade a wine merchant; he was by politics a conservative republican; he had been brought up a Catholic, had always thought and acted as an agnostic, and was very mildly returning to the Church in his later years. He had a genius (if one can even use so wild a word in connexion with so tame a person) a genius for saying the conventional thing on every conceivable subject; or rather what we in England would call the conventional thing. For it was not convention with him, but solid and manly conviction. Convention implies cant or affectation, and he had not the faintest smell of either. He was simply an ordinary citizen with ordinary views; and if you had told him so he would have taken it as an ordinary compliment. If you had asked him about women, he would have said that one must preserve their domesticity and decorum; he would have used the stalest words, but he would have in reserve the strongest arguments. If you had asked him about government, he would have said that all citizens were free and equal, but he would have meant what he said. If you had asked him about education, he would have said that the young must be trained up in habits of industry and of respect for their parents. Still he would have set them the example of industry, and he would have been one of the parents whom they could respect. A state of mind so hopelessly central is depressing to the English instinct. But then in England a man announcing these platitudes is generally a fool and a frightened fool, announcing them out of mere social servility. But Durand was anything but a fool; he had read all the eighteenth century, and could have defended his platitudes round every angle of eighteenth-century argument. And certainly he was anything but a coward: swollen and sedentary as he was, he could have hit any man back who touched him with the instant violence of an automatic machine; and dying in a uniform would have seemed to him only the sort of thing that sometimes happens. I am afraid it is impossible to explain this monster amid the exaggerative sects and the eccentric clubs of my country. He was merely a man.

He lived in a little villa which was furnished well with comfortable chairs and tables and highly uncomfortable classical pictures and medallions. The art in his home contained nothing between the two extremes of hard, meagre designs of Greek heads and Roman togas, and on the other side a few very vulgar Catholic images in the crudest colours; these were mostly in his daughter's room. He had recently lost his wife, whom he had loved heartily and rather heavily in complete silence, and upon whose grave he was constantly in the habit of placing hideous little wreaths, made out of a sort of black-and-white beads. To his only daughter he was equally devoted, though he restricted her a good deal under a sort of theoretic alarm about her innocence; an alarm which was peculiarly unnecessary, first, because she was an exceptionally reticent and religious girl, and secondly, because there was hardly anybody else in the place.

Madeleine Durand was physically a sleepy young woman, and might easily have been supposed to be morally a lazy one. It is, however, certain that the work of her house was done somehow, and it is even more rapidly ascertainable that nobody else did it. The logician is, therefore, driven back upon the assumption that she did it; and that lends a sort of mysterious interest to her personality at the beginning. She had very broad, low, and level brows, which seemed even lower because her warm yellow hair clustered down to her eyebrows; and she had a face just plump enough not to look as powerful as it was. Anything that was heavy in all this was abruptly lightened by two large, light china-blue eyes, lightened all of a sudden as if it had been lifted into the air by two big blue butterflies. The rest of her was less than middle-sized, and was of a casual and comfortable sort; and she had this difference from such girls as the girl in the motor-car, that one did not incline to take in her figure at all, but only her broad and leonine and innocent head.

Both the father and the daughter were of the sort that would normally have avoided all observation; that is, all observation in that extraordinary modern world which calls out everything except strength. Both of them had strength below the surface; they were like quiet peasants owning enormous and unquarried mines. The father with his square face and grey side whiskers, the daughter with her square face and golden fringe of hair, were both stronger than they know; stronger than anyone knew. The father believed in civilization, in the storied tower we have erected to affront nature; that is, the father believed in Man. The daughter believed in God; and was even stronger. They neither of them believed in themselves; for that is a decadent weakness.

The daughter was called a devotee. She left upon ordinary people the impression—the somewhat irritating impression—produced by such a person; it can only be described as the sense of strong water being perpetually poured into some abyss. She did her housework easily; she achieved her social relations sweetly; she was never neglectful and never unkind. This accounted for all that was soft in her, but not for all that was hard. She trod firmly as if going somewhere; she flung her face back as if defying something; she hardly spoke a cross word, yet there was often battle in her eyes. The modern man asked doubtfully where all this silent energy went to. He would have stared still more doubtfully if he had been told that it all went into her prayers.

The conventions of the Isle of St. Loup were necessarily a compromise or confusion between those of France and England; and it was vaguely possible for a respectable young lady to have half-attached lovers, in a way that would be impossible to the *bourgeoisie* of France. One man in particular had made himself an unmistakable figure in the track of this girl as she went to church. He was a short, prosperous-looking man, whose long, bushy black beard and clumsy black umbrella made him seem both shorter and older than he really was; but whose big, bold eyes, and step that spurned the ground, gave him an instant character of youth.

His name was Camille Bert, and he was a commercial traveller who had only been in the island an idle week before he began to hover in the tracks of Madeleine Durand. Since everyone knows everyone in so small a place, Madeleine certainly knew him to speak to; but it is not very evident that she ever spoke. He haunted her, however; especially at church, which was, indeed, one of the few certain places for finding her. In her home she had a habit of being invisible, sometimes through insatiable domesticity, sometimes through an equally insatiable solitude. M. Bert did not give the impression of a pious man, though he did give, especially with his eyes, the impression of an honest one. But he went to Mass with a simple exactitude that could not be mistaken for a pose, or even for a vulgar fascination. It was perhaps this religious regularity which eventually drew Madeleine into recognition of him. At least it is certain that she twice spoke to him with her square and open smile in the porch of the church; and there was human nature enough in the hamlet to turn even that into gossip.

But the real interest arose suddenly as a squall arises with the extraordinary affair that occurred about five days after. There was about a third of a mile beyond the village of Haroc a large but lonely hotel upon the London or Paris model, but commonly almost entirely empty. Among the accidental group of guests who had come to it at this season was a man whose nationality no one could fix and who bore the non-committal name of Count Gregory. He treated everybody with complete civility and almost in complete silence. On the few occasions when he spoke, he spoke either French, English, or once (to the priest) Latin; and the general opinion was that he spoke them all wrong. He was a large, lean man, with the stoop of an aged eagle, and even the eagle's nose to complete it; he had old-fashioned military whiskers and moustache dyed with a garish and highly incredible yellow. He had the dress of a showy gentleman and the manners of a decayed gentleman; he seemed (as with a sort of simplicity) to be trying to be a dandy when he was too old even to know that he was old. Ye he was decidedly a handsome figure with his curled yellow hair and lean fastidious face; and he wore a peculiar frock-coat of bright turquoise blue, with an unknown order pinned to it, and he carried a huge and heavy cane. Despite his silence and his dandified dress and whiskers, the island might never have heard of him but for the extraordinary event of which I have spoken, which fell about in the following way:

In such casual atmospheres only the enthusiastic go to Benediction; and as the warm blue twilight closed over the little candle-lit church and village, the line of worshippers who went home from the former to the latter thinned out until it broke. On one such evening at least no one was in church except the quiet, unconquerable Madeleine, four old women, one fisherman, and, of course, the irrepressible M. Camille Bert. The others seemed to melt away afterwards into the peacock colours of the dim green grass and the dark blue sky. Even Durand was invisible instead of being merely reverentially remote; and Madeleine set forth through the patch of black forest alone. She was not in the least afraid of loneliness, because she was not afraid of devils. I think they were afraid of her.

In a clearing of the wood, however, which was lit up with a last patch of the perishing sunlight, there advanced upon her suddenly one who was more startling than a devil. The incomprehensible Count Gregory, with his yellow hair like flame and his face like the white ashes of the flame, was advancing bareheaded towards her, flinging out his arms and his long fingers with a frantic gesture.

"We are alone here," he cried, "and you would be at my mercy, only that I am at yours."

Then his frantic hands fell by his sides and he looked up under his brows with an expression that went well with his hard breathing. Madeleine Durand had come to a halt at first in childish wonder, and now, with more than masculine self-control, "I fancy I know your face, sir," she said, as if to gain time.

"I know I shall not forget yours," said the other, and extended once more his ungainly arms in an unnatural gesture. Then of a sudden there came out of him a spout of wild and yet pompous phrases. "It is as well that you should know the worst and the best. I am a man who knows no limit; I am the most callous of criminals, the most unrepentant of sinners. There is no man in my dominions so vile as I. But my dominions stretch from the olives of Italy to the fir-woods of Denmark, and there is no nook of all of them in which I have not done a sin. But when I bear you away I shall be doing my first sacrilege, and also my first act of virtue." He seized her suddenly by the elbow; and she did not scream but only pulled and tugged. Yet though she had not screamed, someone astray in the woods seemed to have heard the struggle. A short but nimble figure came along the woodland path like a humming bullet and had caught Count Gregory a crack across the face before his own could be recognized. When it was recognized it was that of Camille, with the black elderly beard and the young ardent eyes.

Up to the moment when Camille had hit the Count, Madeleine had entertained no doubt that the Count was merely a madman. Now she was startled with a new sanity; for the tall man in the yellow whiskers and yellow moustache first returned the blow of Bert, as if it were a sort of duty, and then stepped back with a slight bow and an easy smile.

"This need go no further here, M. Bert," he said. "I need not remind you how far it should go elsewhere."

"Certainly, you need remind me of nothing," answered Camille, stolidly. "I am glad that you are just not too much of a scoundrel for a gentleman to fight."

"We are detaining the lady," said Count Gregory, with politeness; and, making a gesture suggesting that he would have taken off his hat if he had had one, he strode away up the avenue of trees and eventually disappeared. He was so complete an aristocrat that he could offer his back to them all the way up that avenue; and his back never once looked uncomfortable.

"You must allow me to see you home," said Bert to the girl, in a gruff and almost stifled voice; "I think we have only a little way to go."

"Only a little way," she said, and smiled once more that night, in spite of fatigue and fear and the world and the flesh and the devil. The glowing and transparent blue of twilight had long been covered by the opaque and slatelike blue of night, when he handed her into the lamp-lit interior of her home. He went out himself into the darkness, walking sturdily, but tearing at his black beard.

All the French or semi-French gentry of the district considered this a case in which a duel was natural and inevitable, and neither party had any difficulty in finding seconds, strangers as they were in the place. Two small landowners, who were careful, practising Catholics, willingly undertook to represent that strict church-goer Camille Burt; while the profligate but apparently powerful Count Gregory found friends in an energetic local doctor who was ready for social promotion and an accidental Californian tourist who was ready for anything. As no particular purpose could be served by delay, it was arranged that the affair should fall out three days afterwards. And when this was settled the whole community, as it were, turned over again in bed and thought no more about the matter. At least there was only one member of it who seemed to be restless, and that was she who was commonly most restful. On the next night Madeleine Durand went to church as usual; and as usual the stricken Camille was there also. What was not so usual was that when they were a bow-shot from the church Madeleine turned round and walked back to him. "Sir," she began, "it is not wrong of me to speak to you," and the very words gave him a jar of unexpected truth; for in all the novels he had ever read she would have begun: "It is wrong of me to speak to you." She went on with wide and serious eyes like an animal's: "It is not wrong of me to speak to you, because your soul, or anybody's soul, matters so much more than what the world says about anybody. I want to talk to you about what you are going to do."

Bert saw in front of him the inevitable heroine of the novels trying to prevent bloodshed; and his pale firm face became implacable.

"I would do anything but that for you," he said; "but no man can be called less than a man."

She looked at him for a moment with a face openly puzzled, and then broke into an odd and beautiful half-smile.

"Oh, I don't mean that," she said; "I don't talk about what I don't understand. No one has ever hit me; and if they had I should not feel as a man may. I am sure it is not the best thing to fight. It would be better to forgive—if one could really forgive. But when people dine with my father and say that fighting a duel is mere murder—of course I can see that is not just. It's all so different—having a reason—and letting the other man know—and using the same guns and things—and doing it in front of your friends. I'm awfully stupid, but I know that men like you aren't murderers. But it wasn't that that I meant."

"What did you mean?" asked the other, looking broodingly at the earth.

"Don't you know," she said, "there is only one more celebration? I thought that as you always go to church—I thought you would communicate this morning."

Bert stepped backward with a sort of action she had never seen in him before. It seemed to alter his whole body.

"You may be right or wrong to risk dying," said the girl, simply; "the poor women in our village risk it whenever they have a baby. You men are the other half of the world. I know nothing about when you ought to die. But surely if you are daring to try and find God beyond the grave and appeal to Him—you ought to let Him find you when He comes and stands there every morning in our little church."

And placid as she was, she made a little gesture of argument, of which the pathos wrung the heart.

M. Camille Bert was by no means placid. Before that incomplete gesture and frankly pleading face he retreated as if from the jaws of a dragon. His dark black hair and beard looked utterly unnatural against the startling pallor of his face. When at last he said something it was: "O God! I can't stand this!" He did not say it in French. Nor did he, strictly speaking, say it in English. The truth (interesting only to anthropologists) is that he said it in Scotch.

"There will be another mass in a matter of eight hours," said Madeleine, with a sort of business eagerness and energy, "and you can do it then before the fighting. You must forgive me, but I was so frightened that you would not do it at all."

Bert seemed to crush his teeth together until they broke, and managed to say between them: "And why should you suppose that I shouldn't do as you say—I mean not to do it at all?"

"You always go to Mass," answered the girl, opening her wide blue eyes, "and the Mass is very long and tiresome unless one loves God."

Then it was that Bert exploded with a brutality which might have come from Count Gregory, his criminal opponent. He advanced upon Madeleine with flaming eyes, and almost took her by the two shoulders. "I do not love God," he cried, speaking French with the broadest Scotch accent; "I do not want to find Him; I do not think He is there to be found. I must burst up the show; I must and will say everything. You are the happiest and honestest thing I ever saw in this godless universe. And I am the dirtiest and most dishonest."

Madeleine looked at him doubtfully for an instant, and then said with a sudden simplicity and cheerfulness: "Oh, but if you are really sorry it is all right. If you are horribly sorry it is all the better. You have only to go and tell the priest so and he will give you God out of his own hands."

"I hate your priest and I deny your God!" cried the man, "and I tell you God is a lie and a fable and a mask. And for the first time in my life I do not feel superior to God."

"What can it all mean?" said Madeleine, in massive wonder.

"Because I am a fable also and a mask," said the man. He had been plucking fiercely at his black beard and hair all the time; now he suddenly plucked them off and flung them like moulted feathers in the mire. This extraordinary spoliation left in the sunlight the same face, but a much younger head—a head with close chestnut curls and a short chestnut beard.

"Now you know the truth," he answered, with hard eyes. "I am a cad who has played a crooked trick on a quiet village and a decent woman for a private reason of his own. I might have played it successfully on any other woman; I have hit the one woman on whom it cannot be played. It's just like my damned luck. The plain truth is," and here when he came to the plain truth he boggled and blundered as Evan had done in telling it to the girl in the motor-car.

"The plain truth is," he said at last, "that I am James Turnbull the atheist. The police are after me; not for atheism but for being ready to fight for it."

"I saw something about you in a newspaper," said the girl, with a simplicity which even surprise could never throw off its balance.

"Evan MacIan said there was a God," went on the other, stubbornly, "and I say there isn't. And I have come to fight for the fact that there is no God; it is for that that I have seen this cursed island and your blessed face."

"You want me really to believe," said Madeleine, with parted lips, "that you think——"

"I want you to hate me!" cried Turnbull, in agony. "I want you to be sick when you think of my name. I am sure there is no God."

"But there is," said Madeleine, quite quietly, and rather with the air of one telling children about an elephant. "Why, I touched His body only this morning."

"You touched a bit of bread," said Turnbull, biting his knuckles. "Oh, I will say anything that can madden you!"

"You think it is only a bit of bread," said the girl, and her lips tightened ever so little.

"I know it is only a bit of bread," said Turnbull, with violence.

She flung back her open face and smiled. "Then why did you refuse to eat it?" she said.

James Turnbull made a little step backward, and for the first time in his life there seemed to break out and blaze in his head thoughts that were not his own.

"Why, how silly of them," cried out Madeleine, with quite a schoolgirl gaiety, "why, how silly of them to call *you* a blasphemer! Why, you have wrecked your whole business because you would not commit blasphemy."

The man stood, a somewhat comic figure in his tragic bewilderment, with the honest red head of James Turnbull sticking out of the rich and fictitious garments of Camille Bert. But the startled pain of his face was strong enough to obliterate the oddity.

"You come down here," continued the lady, with that female emphasis which is so pulverizing in conversation and so feeble at a public meeting, "you and your MacIan come down here and put on false beards or noses in order to fight. You pretend to be a Catholic commercial traveller from France. Poor Mr. MacIan has to pretend to be a dissolute nobleman from nowhere. Your scheme succeeds; you pick a quite convincing quarrel; you arrange a quite respectable duel; the duel you have planned so long will come off tomorrow with absolute certainty and safety. And then you throw off your wig and throw up your scheme and throw over your colleague, because I ask you to go into a building and eat a bit of bread. And *then* you dare to tell me that you are sure there is nothing watching us. Then you say you know there is nothing on the very altar you run away from. You know——"

"I only know," said Turnbull, "that I must run away from you. This has got beyond any talking." And he plunged along into the village, leaving his black wig and beard lying behind him on the road.

As the market-place opened before him he saw Count Gregory, that distinguished foreigner, standing and smoking in elegant meditation at the corner of the local café. He immediately made his way rapidly towards him, considering that a consultation was urgent. But he had hardly crossed half of that stony quadrangle when a window burst open above him and a head was thrust out, shouting. The man was in his woollen undershirt, but Turnbull knew the energetic, apologetic head of the sergeant of police. He pointed furiously at Turnbull and shouted his name. A policeman ran excitedly from under an archway and tried to collar him. Two men selling vegetables dropped their baskets and joined in the chase. Turnbull dodged the constable, upset one of the men into his own basket, and bounding towards the distinguished foreign Count, called to him clamorously: "Come on, MacIan, the hunt is up again."

The prompt reply of Count Gregory was to pull off his large yellow whiskers and scatter them on the breeze with an air of considerable relief. Then he joined the flight of Turnbull, and even as he did so, with one wrench of his powerful hands rent and split the strange, thick stick that he carried. Inside it was a naked old-fashioned rapier. The two got a good start up the road before the whole town was awakened behind them; and half-way up it a similar transformation was seen to take place in Mr. Turnbull's singular umbrella.

The two had a long race for the harbour; but the English police were heavy and the French inhabitants were indifferent. In any case, they got used to the notion of the road being clear; and just as they had come to the cliffs MacIan banged into another gentleman with unmistakable surprise. How he knew he was another gentleman merely by banging into him, must remain a mystery. MacIan was a very poor and very sober Scotch gentleman. The other was a very drunk and very wealthy English gentleman. But there was something in the staggered and openly embarrassed apologies that made them understand each other as readily and as quickly and as much as two men talking French in the middle of China. The nearest expression of the type is that it either hits or apologizes; and in this case both apologized.

"You seem to be in a hurry," said the unknown Englishman, falling back a step or two in order to laugh with an unnatural heartiness. "What's it all about, eh?" Then before MacIan could get past his sprawling and staggering figure he ran forward again and said with a sort of shouting and ear-shattering whisper: "I say, my name is Wilkinson. *You* know—Wilkinson's Entire was my grandfather. Can't drink beer myself. Liver." And he shook his head with extraordinary sagacity.

"We really are in a hurry, as you say," said MacIan, summoning a sufficiently pleasant smile, "so if you will let us pass——"

"I'll tell you what, you fellows," said the sprawling gentleman, confidentially, while Evan's agonized ears heard behind him the first paces of the pursuit, "if you really are, as you say, in a hurry, I know what it is to be in a hurry—Lord, what a hurry I was in when we all came out of Cartwright's rooms—if you really are in a hurry"—and he seemed to steady his voice into a sort of solemnity—"if you are in a hurry, there's nothing like a good yacht for a man in a hurry."

"No doubt you're right," said MacIan, and dashed past him in despair. The head of the pursuing host was just showing over the top of the hill behind him. Turnbull had already ducked under the intoxicated gentleman's elbow and fled far in front.

"No, but look here," said Mr. Wilkinson, enthusiastically running after MacIan and catching him by the sleeve of his coat. "If you want to hurry you should take a yacht, and if"—he said, with a burst of rationality, like one leaping to a further point in logic —"if you want a yacht—you can have mine."

Evan pulled up abruptly and looked back at him. "We are really in the devil of a hurry," he said, "and if you really have a yacht, the truth is that we would give our ears for it."

"You'll find it in harbour," said Wilkinson, struggling with his speech. "Left side of harbour—called *Gibson Girl*—can't think why, old fellow, I never lent it you before."

With these words the benevolent Mr. Wilkinson fell flat on his face in the road, but continued to laugh softly, and turned towards his flying companion a face of peculiar peace and benignity. Evan's mind went through a crisis of instantaneous casuistry, in which it may be that he decided wrongly; but about how he decided his biographer can profess no doubt. Two minutes afterwards he had overtaken Turnbull and told the tale; ten minutes afterwards he and Turnbull had somehow tumbled into the yacht called the *Gibson Girl* and had somehow pushed off from the Isle of St. Loup.

XII. THE DESERT ISLAND

Those who happen to hold the view (and Mr. Evan MacIan, now alive and comfortable, is among the number) that something supernatural, some eccentric kindness from god or fairy had guided our adventurers through all their absurd perils, might have found his strongest argument perhaps in their management or mismanagement of Mr. Wilkinson's yacht. Neither of them had the smallest qualification for managing such a vessel; but MacIan had a practical knowledge of the sea in much smaller and quite different boats, while Turnbull had an abstract knowledge of science and some of its applications to navigation, which was worse. The presence of the god or fairy can only be deduced from the fact that they never definitely ran into anything, either a boat, a rock, a quicksand, or a man-of-war. Apart from this negative description, their voyage would be difficult to describe. It took at least a fortnight, and MacIan, who was certainly the shrewder sailor of the two, realized that they were sailing west into the Atlantic and were probably by this time past the Scilly Isles. How much farther they stood out into the western sea it was impossible to conjecture. But they felt certain, at least, that they were far enough into that awful gulf between us and America to make it unlikely that they would soon see land again. It was therefore with legitimate excitement that one rainy morning after daybreak they saw that distinct shape of a solitary island standing up against the encircling strip of silver which ran round the skyline and separated the grey and green of the billows from the grey and mauve of the morning clouds.

"What can it be?" cried MacIan, in a dry-throated excitement. "I didn't know there were any Atlantic islands so far beyond the Scillies—Good Lord, it can't be Madeira, yet?"

"I thought you were fond of legends and lies and fables," said Turnbull, grimly. "Perhaps it's Atlantis."

"Of course, it might be," answered the other, quite innocently and gravely; "but I never thought the story about Atlantis was very solidly established."

"Whatever it is, we are running on to it," said Turnbull, equably, "and we shall be shipwrecked twice, at any rate."

The naked-looking nose of land projecting from the unknown island was, indeed, growing larger and larger, like the trunk of some terrible and advancing elephant. There seemed to be nothing in particular, at least on this side of the island, except shoals of shellfish lying so thick as almost to make it look like one of those toy grottos that the children make. In one place, however, the coast offered a soft, smooth bay of sand, and even the rudimentary ingenuity of the two amateur mariners managed to run up the little ship with her prow well on shore and her bowsprit pointing upward, as in a sort of idiotic triumph.

They tumbled on shore and began to unload the vessel, setting the stores out in rows upon the sand with something of the solemnity of boys playing at pirates. There were Mr. Wilkinson's cigar-boxes and Mr. Wilkinson's dozen of champagne and Mr. Wilkinson's tinned salmon and Mr. Wilkinson's tinned tongue and Mr. Wilkinson's tinned sardines, and every sort of preserved thing that could be seen at the Army and Navy stores. Then MacIan stopped with a jar of pickles in his hand and said abruptly:

"I don't know why we're doing all this; I suppose we ought really to fall to and get it over."

Then he added more thoughtfully: "Of course this island seems rather bare and the survivor——"

"The question is," said Turnbull, with cheerful speculation, "whether the survivor will be in a proper frame of mind for potted prawns."

MacIan looked down at the rows of tins and bottles, and the cloud of doubt still lowered upon his face.

"You will permit me two liberties, my dear sir," said Turnbull at last: "The first is to break open this box and light one of Mr. Wilkinson's excellent cigars, which will, I am sure, assist my meditations; the second is to offer a penny for your thoughts; or rather to convulse the already complex finances of this island by betting a penny that I know them."

"What on earth are you talking about?" asked MacIan, listlessly, in the manner of an inattentive child.

"I know what you are really thinking, MacIan," repeated Turnbull, laughing. "I know what I am thinking, anyhow. And I rather fancy it's the same."

"What are you thinking?" asked Evan.

"I am thinking and you are thinking," said Turnbull, "that it is damned silly to waste all that champagne."

Something like the spectre of a smile appeared on the unsmiling visage of the Gael; and he made at least no movement of dissent.

"We could drink all the wine and smoke all the cigars easily in a week," said Turnbull; "and that would be to die feasting like heroes."

"Yes, and there is something else," said MacIan, with slight hesitation. "You see, we are on an almost unknown rock, lost in the Atlantic. The police will never catch us; but then neither may the public ever hear of us; and that was one of the things we wanted."

Then, after a pause, he said, drawing in the sand with his sword-point: "She may never hear of it at all."

"Well?" inquired the other, puffing at his cigar.

"Well," said MacIan, "we might occupy a day or two in drawing up a thorough and complete statement of what we did and why we did it, and all about both our points of view. Then we could leave one copy on the island whatever happens to us and put another in an empty bottle and send it out to sea, as they do in the books."

"A good idea," said Turnbull, "and now let us finish unpacking."

As MacIan, a tall, almost ghostly figure, paced along the edge of sand that ran round the islet, the purple but cloudy poetry which was his native element was piled up at its thickest upon his soul. The unique island and the endless sea emphasized the thing solely as an epic. There were no ladies or policemen here to give him a hint either of its farce or its tragedy.

"Perhaps when the morning stars were made," he said to himself, "God built this island up from the bottom of the world to be a tower and a theatre for the fight between yea and nay."

Then he wandered up to the highest level of the rock, where there was a roof or plateau of level stone. Half an hour afterwards, Turnbull found him clearing away the loose sand from this table-land and making it smooth and even.

"We will fight up here, Turnbull," said MacIan, "when the time comes. And till the time comes this place shall be sacred."

"I thought of having lunch up here," said Turnbull, who had a bottle of champagne in his hand.

"No, no—not up here," said MacIan, and came down from the height quite hastily. Before he descended, however, he fixed the two swords upright, one at each end of the platform, as if they were human sentinels to guard it under the stars.

Then they came down and lunched plentifully in a nest of loose rocks. In the same place that night they supped more plentifully still. The smoke of Mr. Wilkinson's cigars went up ceaseless and strong smelling, like a pagan sacrifice; the golden glories of Mr. Wilkinson's champagne rose to their heads and poured out of them in fancies and philosophies. And occasionally they would look up at the starlight and the rock and see the space guarded by the two cross-hilted swords, which looked like two black crosses at either end of a grave.

In this primitive and Homeric truce the week passed by; it consisted almost entirely of eating, drinking, smoking, talking, and occasionally singing. They wrote their records and cast loose their bottle. They never ascended to the ominous plateau; they had never stood there save for that single embarrassed minute when they had had no time to take stock of the seascape or the shape of the land. They did not even explore the island; for MacIan was partly concerned in prayer and Turnbull entirely concerned with tobacco; and both these forms of inspiration can be enjoyed by the secluded and even the sedentary. It was on a golden afternoon, the sun sinking over the sea, rayed like the very head of Apollo, when Turnbull tossed off the last half-pint from the emptied Wilkinsonian bottle, hurled the bottle into the sea with objectless energy, and went up to where his sword stood waiting for him on the hill. MacIan was already standing heavily by his with bent head and eyes reading the ground. He had not even troubled to throw a glance round the island or the horizon. But Turnbull being of a more active and birdlike type of mind did throw a glance round the scene. The consequence of which was that he nearly fell off the rock.

On three sides of this shelly and sandy islet the sea stretched blue and infinite without a speck of land or sail; the same as Turnbull had first seen it, except that the tide being out it showed a few yards more of slanting sand under the roots of the rocks. But on the fourth side the island exhibited a more extraordinary feature. In fact, it exhibited the extraordinary feature of not being an island at all. A long, curving neck of sand, as smooth and wet as the neck of the sea serpent, ran out into the sea and joined their rock to a line of low, billowing, and glistening sand-hills, which the sinking sea had just bared to the sun. Whether they were firm sand or quicksand it was difficult to guess; but there was at least no doubt that they lay on the edge of some larger land; for colourless hills appeared faintly behind them and no sea could be seen beyond.

"Sakes alive!" cried Turnbull, with rolling eyes; "this ain't an island in the Atlantic. We've butted the bally continent of America."

MacIan turned his head, and his face, already pale, grew a shade paler. He was by this time walking in a world of omens and hieroglyphics, and he could not read anything but what was baffling or menacing in this brown gigantic arm of the earth stretched out into the sea to seize him.

"MacIan," said Turnbull, in his temperate way, "whatever our eternal interrupted tete-a-tetes have taught us or not taught us, at least we need not fear the charge of fear. If it is essential to your emotions, I will cheerfully finish the fight here and now; but I must confess that if you kill me here I shall die with my curiosity highly excited and unsatisfied upon a minor point of geography."

"I do not want to stop now," said the other, in his elephantine simplicity, "but we must stop for a moment, because it is a sign—perhaps it is a miracle. We must see what is at the end of the road of sand; it may be a bridge built across the gulf by God."

"So long as you gratify my query," said Turnbull, laughing and letting back his blade into the sheath, "I do not care for what reason you choose to stop."

They clambered down the rocky peninsula and trudged along the sandy isthmus with the plodding resolution of men who seemed almost to have made up their minds to be wanderers on the face of the earth. Despite Turnbull's air of scientific eagerness, he was really the less impatient of the two; and the Highlander went on well ahead of him with passionate strides. By the time they had walked for about half an hour in the ups and downs of those dreary sands, the distance between the two had lengthened and MacIan was only a tall figure silhouetted for an instant upon the crest of some sand-dune and then disappearing behind it. This rather increased the Robinson Crusoe feeling in Mr. Turnbull, and he looked about almost disconsolately for some sign of life. What sort of life he expected it to be if it appeared, he did not very clearly know. He has since confessed that he thinks that in his subconsciousness he expected an alligator.

The first sign of life that he did see, however, was something more extraordinary than the largest alligator. It was nothing less than the notorious Mr. Evan MacIan coming bounding back across the sand-heaps breathless, without his cap and keeping the sword in his hand only by a habit now quite hardened.

"Take care, Turnbull," he cried out from a good distance as he ran, "I've seen a native."

THE BALL AND THE CROSS

"A native?" repeated his companion, whose scenery had of late been chiefly of shellfish, "what the deuce! Do you mean an oyster?"

"No," said MacIan, stopping and breathing hard, "I mean a savage. A black man."

"Why, where did you see him?" asked the staring editor.

"Over there—behind that hill," said the gasping MacIan. "He put up his black head and grinned at me."

Turnbull thrust his hands through his red hair like one who gives up the world as a bad riddle. "Lord love a duck," said he, "can it be Jamaica?"

Then glancing at his companion with a small frown, as of one slightly suspicious, he said: "I say, don't think me rude—but you're a visionary kind of fellow—and then we drank a great deal. Do you mind waiting here while I go and see for myself?"

"Shout if you get into trouble," said the Celt, with composure; "you will find it as I say."

Turnbull ran off ahead with a rapidity now far greater than his rival's, and soon vanished over the disputed sand-hill. Then five minutes passed, and then seven minutes; and MacIan bit his lip and swung his sword, and the other did not reappear. Finally, with a Gaelic oath, Evan started forward to the rescue, and almost at the same moment the small figure of the missing man appeared on the ridge against the sky.

Even at that distance, however, there was something odd about his attitude; so odd that MacIan continued to make his way in that direction. It looked as if he were wounded; or, still more, as if he were ill. He wavered as he came down the slope and seemed flinging himself into peculiar postures. But it was only when he came within three feet of MacIan's face, that that observer of mankind fully realized that Mr. James Turnbull was roaring with laughter.

"You are quit right," sobbed that wholly demoralized journalist. "He's black, oh, there's no doubt the black's all right—as far as it goes." And he went off again into convulsions of his humorous ailment.

"What ever is the matter with you?" asked MacIan, with stern impatience. "Did you see the negro——"

"I saw the negro," gasped Turnbull. "I saw the splendid barbarian Chief. I saw the Emperor of Ethiopia—oh, I saw him all right. The negro's hands and face are a lovely colour—and the negro——" And he was overtaken once more.

"Well, well, well," said Evan, stamping each monosyllable on the sand, "what about the negro?"

"Well, the truth is," said Turnbull, suddenly and startlingly, becoming quite grave and precise, "the truth is, the negro is a Margate negro, and we are now on the edge of the Isle of Thanet, a few miles from Margate."

Then he had a momentary return of his hysteria and said: "I say, old boy, I should like to see a chart of our fortnight's cruise in Wilkinson's yacht."

MacIan had no smile in answer, but his eager lips opened as if parched for the truth. "You mean to say," he began——

"Yes, I mean to say," said Turnbull, "and I mean to say something funnier still. I have learnt everything I wanted to know from the partially black musician over there, who has taken a run in his war-paint to meet a friend in a quiet pub along the coast— the noble savage has told me all about it. The bottle containing our declaration, doctrines, and dying sentiments was washed up on Margate beach yesterday in the presence of one alderman, two bathing-machine men, three policemen, seven doctors, and a hundred and thirteen London clerks on a holiday, to all of whom, whether directly or indirectly, our composition gave enormous literary pleasure. Buck up, old man, this story of ours is a switchback. I have begun to understand the pulse and the time of it; now we are up in a cathedral and then we are down in a theatre, where they only play farces. Come, I am quite reconciled—let us enjoy the farce."

But MacIan said nothing, and an instant afterwards Turnbull himself called out in an entirely changed voice: "Oh, this is damnable! This is not to be borne!"

MacIan followed his eye along the sand-hills. He saw what looked like the momentary and waving figure of the negro minstrel, and then he saw a heavy running policeman take the turn of the sand-hill with the smooth solemnity of a railway train.

XIII. THE GARDEN OF PEACE

Up to this instant Evan MacIan had really understood nothing; but when he saw the policeman he saw everything. He saw his enemies, all the powers and princes of the earth. He suddenly altered from a staring statue to a leaping man of the mountains.

"We must break away from him here," he cried, briefly, and went like a whirlwind over the sand ridge in a straight line and at a particular angle. When the policeman had finished his admirable railway curve, he found a wall of failing sand between him and the pursued. By the time he had scaled it thrice, slid down twice, and crested it in the third effort, the two flying figures were far in front. They found the sand harder farther on; it began to be crusted with scraps of turf and in a few moments they were flying easily over an open common of rank sea-grass. They had no easy business, however; for the bottle which they had so innocently sent into the chief gate of Thanet had called to life the police of half a county on their trail. From every side across the grey-green common figures could be seen running and closing in; and it was only when MacIan with his big body broke down the tangled barrier of a little wood, as men break down a door with the shoulder; it was only when they vanished crashing into the underworld of the black wood, that their hunters were even instantaneously thrown off the scent.

At the risk of struggling a little longer like flies in that black web of twigs and trunks, Evan (who had an instinct of the hunter or the hunted) took an incalculable course through the forest, which let them out at last by a forest opening—quite forgotten by the leaders of the chase. They ran a mile or two farther along the edge of the wood until they reached another and somewhat similar opening. Then MacIan stood utterly still and listened, as animals listen, for every sound in the universe. Then he said: "We are quit of them." And Turnbull said: "Where shall we go now?"

MacIan looked at the silver sunset that was closing in, barred by plumy lines of purple cloud; he looked at the high tree-tops that caught the last light and at the birds going heavily homeward, just as if all these things were bits of written advice that he could read.

Then he said: "The best place we can go to is to bed. If we can get some sleep in this wood, now everyone has cleared out of it, it will be worth a handicap of two hundred yards tomorrow."

Turnbull, who was exceptionally lively and laughing in his demeanour, kicked his legs about like a schoolboy and said he did not want to go to sleep. He walked incessantly and talked very brilliantly. And when at last he lay down on the hard earth, sleep struck him senseless like a hammer.

Indeed, he needed the strongest sleep he could get; for the earth was still full of darkness and a kind of morning fog when his fellow-fugitive shook him awake.

"No more sleep, I'm afraid," said Evan, in a heavy, almost submissive, voice of apology. "They've gone on past us right enough for a good thirty miles; but now they've found out their mistake, and they're coming back."

"Are you sure?" said Turnbull, sitting up and rubbing his red eyebrows with his hand.

The next moment, however, he had jumped up alive and leaping like a man struck with a shock of cold water, and he was plunging after MacIan along the woodland path. The shape of their old friend the constable had appeared against the pearl and pink of the sunrise. Somehow, it always looked a very funny shape when seen against the sunrise.

❦

A wash of weary daylight was breaking over the country-side, and the fields and roads were full of white mist—the kind of white mist that clings in corners like cotton wool. The empty road, along which the chase had taken its turn, was overshadowed on one side by a very high discoloured wall, stained, and streaked green, as with seaweed— evidently the high-shouldered sentinel of some great gentleman's estate. A yard or two from the wall ran parallel to it a linked and tangled line of lime-trees, forming a kind of cloister along the side of the road. It was under this branching colonnade that the two fugitives fled, almost concealed from their pursuers by the twilight, the mist and the leaping zoetrope of shadows. Their feet, though beating the ground furiously, made but a faint noise; for they had kicked away their boots in the wood; their long, antiquated weapons made no jingle or clatter, for they had strapped them across their backs like guitars. They had all the advantages that invisibility and silence can add to speed.

A hundred and fifty yards behind them down the centre of the empty road the first of their pursuers came pounding and panting—a fat but powerful policeman who had distanced all the rest. He came on at a splendid pace for so portly a figure; but, like all heavy bodies in motion, he gave the impression that it would be easier for him to increase his pace than to slacken it suddenly. Nothing short of a brick wall could have abruptly brought him up. Turnbull turned his head slightly and found breath to say something to MacIan. MacIan nodded.

Pursuer and pursued were fixed in their distance as they fled, for some quarter of a mile, when they came to a place where two or three of the trees grew twistedly together, making a special obscurity. Past this place the pursuing policeman went thundering without thought or hesitation. But he was pursuing his shadow or the wind; for Turnbull had put one foot in a crack of the tree and gone up it as quickly and softly as a cat. Somewhat more laboriously but in equal silence the long legs of the Highlander had followed; and crouching in crucial silence in the cloud of leaves, they saw the whole posse of their pursuers go by and die into the dust and mists of the distance.

The white vapour lay, as it often does, in lean and palpable layers; and even the head of the tree was above it in the half-daylight, like a green ship swinging on a sea of foam.

287

But higher yet behind them, and readier to catch the first coming of the sun, ran the rampart of the top of the wall, which in their excitement of escape looked at once indispensable and unattainable, like the wall of heaven. Here, however, it was MacIan's turn to have the advantage; for, though less light-limbed and feline, he was longer and stronger in the arms. In two seconds he had tugged up his chin over the wall like a horizontal bar; the next he sat astride of it, like a horse of stone. With his assistance Turnbull vaulted to the same perch, and the two began cautiously to shift along the wall in the direction by which they had come, doubling on their tracks to throw off the last pursuit. MacIan could not rid himself of the fancy of bestriding a steed; the long, grey coping of the wall shot out in front of him, like the long, grey neck of some nightmare Rosinante. He had the quaint thought that he and Turnbull were two knights on one steed on the old shield of the Templars.

The nightmare of the stone horse was increased by the white fog, which seemed thicker inside the wall than outside. They could make nothing of the enclosure upon which they were partial trespassers, except that the green and crooked branches of a big apple-tree came crawling at them out of the mist, like the tentacles of some green cuttlefish. Anything would serve, however, that was likely to confuse their trail, so they both decided without need of words to use this tree also as a ladder—a ladder of descent. When they dropped from the lowest branch to the ground their stockinged feet felt hard gravel beneath them.

They had alighted in the middle of a very broad garden path, and the clearing mist permitted them to see the edge of a well-clipped lawn. Though the white vapour was still a veil, it was like the gauzy veil of a transformation scene in a pantomime; for through it there glowed shapeless masses of colour, masses which might be clouds of sunrise or mosaics of gold and crimson, or ladies robed in ruby and emerald draperies. As it thinned yet farther they saw that it was only flowers; but flowers in such insolent mass and magnificence as can seldom be seen out of the tropics. Purple and crimson rhododendrons rose arrogantly, like rampant heraldic animals against their burning background of laburnum gold. The roses were red hot; the clematis was, so to speak, blue hot. And yet the mere whiteness of the syringa seemed the most violent colour of all. As the golden sunlight gradually conquered the mists, it had really something of the sensational sweetness of the slow opening of the gates of Eden. MacIan, whose mind was always haunted with such seraphic or titanic parallels, made some such remark to his companion. But Turnbull only cursed and said that it was the back garden of some damnable rich man.

When the last haze had faded from the ordered paths, the open lawns, and the flaming flower-beds, the two realized, not without an abrupt re-examination of their position, that they were not alone in the garden.

Down the centre of the central garden path, preceded by a blue cloud from a cigarette, was walking a gentleman who evidently understood all the relish of a garden in the very early morning. He was a slim yet satisfied figure, clad in a suit of pale-grey tweed, so subdued that the pattern was imperceptible—a costume that was casual but not by any means careless. His face, which was reflective and somewhat over-refined, was the face of a quite elderly man, though his stringy hair and moustache were still quite yellow. A double eye-glass, with a broad, black ribbon, drooped from his aquiline nose, and he smiled, as he communed with himself, with a self-content which was rare and almost irritating. The straw panama on his head was many shades shabbier than his clothes, as if he had caught it up by accident.

It needed the full shock of the huge shadow of MacIan, falling across his sunlit path, to rouse him from his smiling reverie. When this had fallen on him he lifted his head a little and blinked at the intruders with short-sighted benevolence, but with far less surprise than might have been expected. He was a gentleman; that is, he had social presence of mind, whether for kindness or for insolence.

"Can I do anything for you?" he said, at last.

MacIan bowed. "You can extend to us your pardon," he said, for he also came of a whole race of gentlemen—of gentlemen without shirts to their backs. "I am afraid we are trespassing. We have just come over the wall."

"Over the wall?" repeated the smiling old gentleman, still without letting his surprise come uppermost.

"I suppose I am not wrong, sir," continued MacIan, "in supposing that these grounds inside the wall belong to you?"

The man in the panama looked at the ground and smoked thoughtfully for a few moments, after which he said, with a sort of matured conviction:

"Yes, certainly; the grounds inside the wall really belong to me, and the grounds outside the wall, too."

"A large proprietor, I imagine," said Turnbull, with a truculent eye.

"Yes," answered the old gentleman, looking at him with a steady smile. "A large proprietor."

Turnbull's eye grew even more offensive, and he began biting his red beard; but MacIan seemed to recognize a type with which he could deal and continued quite easily:

"I am sure that a man like you will not need to be told that one sees and does a good many things that do not get into the newspapers. Things which, on the whole, had better not get into the newspapers."

The smile of the large proprietor broadened for a moment under his loose, light moustache, and the other continued with increased confidence:

"One sometimes wants to have it out with another man. The police won't allow it in the streets—and then there's the County Council—and in the fields even nothing's allowed but posters of pills. But in a gentleman's garden, now——"

The strange gentleman smiled again and said, easily enough: "Do you want to fight? What do you want to fight about?"

MacIan had understood his man pretty well up to that point; an instinct common to all men with the aristocratic tradition of Europe had guided him. He knew that the kind of man who in his own back garden wears good clothes and spoils them with a bad hat is not the kind of man who has an abstract horror of illegal actions of violence or the evasion of the police. But a man may understand ragging and yet be very far from understanding religious ragging. This seeming host of theirs might comprehend a quarrel of husband and lover or a difficulty at cards or even escape from a pursuing tailor; but it still remained doubtful whether he would feel the earth fail under him in that earthquake instant when the Virgin is compared to a goddess of Mesopotamia. Even MacIan, therefore (whose tact was far from being his strong point), felt the necessity for some compromise in the mode of approach. At last he said, and even then with hesitation:

"We are fighting about God; there can be nothing so important as that."

The tilted eye-glasses of the old gentleman fell abruptly from his nose, and he thrust his aristocratic chin so far forward that his lean neck seemed to shoot out longer like a telescope.

"About God?" he queried, in a key completely new.

"Look here!" cried Turnbull, taking his turn roughly, "I'll tell you what it's all about. I think that there's no God. I take it that it's nobody's business but mine—or God's, if there is one. This young gentleman from the Highlands happens to think that it's his business. In consequence, he first takes a walking-stick and smashes my shop; then he takes the same walking-stick and tries to smash me. To this I naturally object. I suggest that if it comes to that we should both have sticks. He improves on the suggestion and proposes that we should both have steel-pointed sticks. The police (with characteristic unreasonableness) will not accept either of our proposals; the result is that we run about dodging the police and have jumped over our garden wall into your magnificent garden to throw ourselves on your magnificent hospitality."

The face of the old gentleman had grown redder and redder during this address, but it was still smiling; and when he broke out it was with a kind of guffaw.

"So you really want to fight with drawn swords in my garden," he asked, "about whether there is really a God?"

"Why not?" said MacIan, with his simple monstrosity of speech; "all man's worship began when the Garden of Eden was founded."

"Yes, by——!" said Turnbull, with an oath, "and ended when the Zoological Gardens were founded."

"In this garden! In my presence!" cried the stranger, stamping up and down the gravel and choking with laughter, "whether there is a God!" And he went stamping up and down the garden, making it echo with his unintelligible laughter. Then he came back to them more composed and wiping his eyes.

"Why, how small the world is!" he cried at last. "I can settle the whole matter. Why, I am God!"

And he suddenly began to kick and wave his well-clad legs about the lawn.

"You are what?" repeated Turnbull, in a tone which is beyond description.

"Why, God, of course!" answered the other, thoroughly amused. "How funny it is to think that you have tumbled over a garden wall and fallen exactly on the right person! You might have gone floundering about in all sorts of churches and chapels and colleges and schools of philosophy looking for some evidence of the existence of God. Why, there is no evidence, except seeing him. And now you've seen him. You've seen him dance!"

And the obliging old gentleman instantly stood on one leg without relaxing at all the grave and cultured benignity of his expression.

"I understood that this garden——" began the bewildered MacIan.

"Quite so! Quite so!" said the man on one leg, nodding gravely. "I said this garden belonged to me and the land outside it. So they do. So does the country beyond that and the sea beyond that and all the rest of the earth. So does the moon. So do the sun and stars." And he added, with a smile of apology: "You see, I'm God."

Turnbull and MacIan looked at him for one moment with a sort of notion that perhaps he was not too old to be merely playing the fool. But after staring steadily for an instant Turnbull saw the hard and horrible earnestness in the man's eyes behind all his empty animation. Then Turnbull looked very gravely at the strict gravel walls and the gay flower-beds and the long rectangular red-brick building, which the mist had left evident beyond them. Then he looked at MacIan.

Almost at the same moment another man came walking quickly round the regal clump of rhododendrons. He had the look of a prosperous banker, wore a good tall silk hat, was almost stout enough to burst the buttons of a fine frock-coat; but he was talking to himself, and one of his elbows had a singular outward jerk as he went by.

XIV. A MUSEUM OF SOULS

The man with the good hat and the jumping elbow went by very quickly; yet the man with the bad hat, who thought he was God, overtook him. He ran after him and jumped over a bed of geraniums to catch him.

"I beg your Majesty's pardon," he said, with mock humility, "but here is a quarrel which you ought really to judge."

Then as he led the heavy, silk-hatted man back towards the group, he caught MacIan's ear in order to whisper: "This poor gentleman is mad; he thinks he is Edward VII." At this the self-appointed Creator slightly winked. "Of course you won't trust him much; come to me for everything. But in my position one has to meet so many people. One has to be broadminded."

The big banker in the black frock-coat and hat was standing quite grave and dignified on the lawn, save for his slight twitch of one limb, and he did not seem by any means unworthy of the part which the other promptly forced upon him.

"My dear fellow," said the man in the straw hat, "these two gentlemen are going to fight a duel of the utmost importance. Your own royal position and my much humbler one surely indicate us as the proper seconds. Seconds—yes, seconds——" and here the speaker was once more shaken with his old malady of laughter.

"Yes, you and I are both seconds—and these two gentlemen can obviously fight in front of us. You, he-he, are the king. I am God; really, they could hardly have better supporters. They have come to the right place."

Then Turnbull, who had been staring with a frown at the fresh turf, burst out with a rather bitter laugh and cried, throwing his red head in the air:

"Yes, by God, MacIan, I think we have come to the right place!" And MacIan answered, with an adamantine stupidity:

"Any place is the right place where they will let us do it."

There was a long stillness, and their eyes involuntarily took in the landscape, as they had taken in all the landscapes of their everlasting combat; the bright, square garden behind the shop; the whole lift and leaning of the side of Hampstead Heath; the little garden of the decadent choked with flowers; the square of sand beside the sea at sunrise. They both felt at the same moment all the breadth and blossoming beauty of that paradise, the coloured trees, the natural and restful nooks and also the great wall of stone—more awful than the wall of China—from which no flesh could flee.

Turnbull was moodily balancing his sword in his hand as the other spoke; then he started, for a mouth whispered quite close to his ear. With a softness incredible in any cat, the huge, heavy man in the black hat and frock-coat had crept across the lawn from his own side and was saying in his ear: "Don't trust that second of yours. He's mad and not so mad, either; for he frightfully cunning and sharp. Don't believe the story he tells you about why I hate him. I know the story he'll tell; I overheard it when the housekeeper was talking to the postman. It's too long to talk about now, and I expect we're watched, but——"

Something in Turnbull made him want suddenly to be sick on the grass; the mere healthy and heathen horror of the unclean; the mere inhumane hatred of the inhuman state of madness. He seemed to hear all round him the hateful whispers of that place, innumerable as leaves whispering in the wind, and each of them telling eagerly some evil that had not happened or some terrific secret which was not true. All the rationalist and plain man revolted within him against bowing down for a moment in that forest of deception and egotistical darkness. He wanted to blow up that palace of delusions with dynamite; and in some wild way, which I will not defend, he tried to do it.

He looked across at MacIan and said: "Oh, I can't stand this!"

"Can't stand what?" asked his opponent, eyeing him doubtfully.

"Shall we say the atmosphere?" replied Turnbull; "one can't use uncivil expressions even to a—deity. The fact is, I don't like having God for my second."

"Sir!" said that being in a state of great offence, "in my position I am not used to having my favours refused. Do you know who I am?"

The editor of *The Atheist* turned upon him like one who has lost all patience, and exploded: "Yes, you are God, aren't you?" he said, abruptly, "why do we have two sets of teeth?"

"Teeth?" spluttered the genteel lunatic; "teeth?"

"Yes," cried Turnbull, advancing on him swiftly and with animated gestures, "why does teething hurt? Why do growing pains hurt? Why are measles catching? Why does a rose have thorns? Why do rhinoceroses have horns? Why is the horn on the top of the nose? Why haven't I a horn on the top of my nose, eh?" And he struck the bridge of his nose smartly with his forefinger to indicate the place of the omission and then wagged the finger menacingly at the Creator.

"I've often wanted to meet you," he resumed, sternly, after a pause, "to hold you accountable for all the idiocy and cruelty of this muddled and meaningless world of yours. You make a hundred seeds and only one bears fruit. You make a million worlds and only one seems inhabited. What do you mean by it, eh? What do you mean by it?"

The unhappy lunatic had fallen back before this quite novel form of attack, and lifted his burnt-out cigarette almost like one warding off a blow. Turnbull went on like a torrent.

"A man died yesterday in Ealing. You murdered him. A girl had the toothache in Croydon. You gave it her. Fifty sailors were drowned off Selsey Bill. You scuttled their ship. What have you got to say for yourself, eh?"

The representative of omnipotence looked as if he had left most of these things to his subordinates; he passed a hand over his wrinkling brow and said in a voice much saner than any he had yet used:

"Well, if you dislike my assistance, of course—perhaps the other gentleman——"

"The other gentleman," cried Turnbull, scornfully, "is a submissive and loyal and obedient gentleman. He likes the people who wear crowns, whether of diamonds or of stars. He believes in the divine right of kings, and it is appropriate enough that he should have the king for his second. But it is not appropriate to me that I should have God for my second. God is not good enough. I dislike and I deny the divine right of kings. But I dislike more and I deny more the divine right of divinity."

Then after a pause in which he swallowed his passion, he said to MacIan: "You have got the right second, anyhow."

The Highlander did not answer, but stood as if thunderstruck with one long and heavy thought. Then at last he turned abruptly to his second in the silk hat and said: "Who are you?"

The man in the silk hat blinked and bridled in affected surprise, like one who was in truth accustomed to be doubted.

"I am King Edward VII," he said, with shaky arrogance. "Do you doubt my word?"

"I do not doubt it in the least," answered MacIan.

"Then, why," said the large man in the silk hat, trembling from head to foot, "why do you wear your hat before the king?"

"Why should I take it off," retorted MacIan, with equal heat, "before a usurper?"

Turnbull swung round on his heel. "Well, really," he said, "I thought at least you were a loyal subject."

"I am the only loyal subject," answered the Gael. "For nearly thirty years I have walked these islands and have not found another."

"You are always hard to follow," remarked Turnbull, genially, "and sometimes so much so as to be hardly worth following."

"I alone am loyal," insisted MacIan; "for I alone am in rebellion. I am ready at any instant to restore the Stuarts. I am ready at any instant to defy the Hanoverian brood— and I defy it now even when face to face with the actual ruler of the enormous British Empire!"

And folding his arms and throwing back his lean, hawklike face, he haughtily confronted the man with the formal frock-coat and the eccentric elbow.

"What right had you stunted German squires," he cried, "to interfere in a quarrel between Scotch and English and Irish gentlemen? Who made you, whose fathers could not splutter English while they walked in Whitehall, who made you the judge between the republic of Sidney and the monarchy of Montrose? What had your sires to do with England that they should have the foul offering of the blood of Derwentwater and the heart of Jimmy Dawson? Where are the corpses of Culloden? Where is the blood of Lochiel?" MacIan advanced upon his opponent with a bony and pointed finger, as if indicating the exact pocket in which the blood of that Cameron was probably kept; and Edward VII fell back a few paces in considerable confusion.

"What good have you ever done to us?" he continued in harsher and harsher accents, forcing the other back towards the flower-beds. "What good have you ever done, you race of German sausages? Yards of barbarian etiquette, to throttle the freedom of aristocracy! Gas of northern metaphysics to blow up Broad Church bishops like balloons. Bad pictures and bad manners and pantheism and the Albert Memorial. Go back to Hanover, you humbug? Go to——"

Before the end of this tirade the arrogance of the monarch had entirely given way; he had fairly turned tail and was trundling away down the path. MacIan strode after him still preaching and flourishing his large, lean hands. The other two remained in the centre of the lawn—Turnbull in convulsions of laughter, the lunatic in convulsions of disgust. Almost at the same moment a third figure came stepping swiftly across the lawn.

The advancing figure walked with a stoop, and yet somehow flung his forked and narrow beard forward. That carefully cut and pointed yellow beard was, indeed, the most emphatic thing about him. When he clasped his hands behind him, under the tails of his coat, he would wag his beard at a man like a big forefinger. It performed almost all his gestures; it was more important than the glittering eye-glasses through which he looked or the beautiful bleating voice in which he spoke. His face and neck were of a lusty red, but lean and stringy; he always wore his expensive gold-rim eye-glasses slightly askew upon his aquiline nose; and he always showed two gleaming foreteeth under his moustache, in a smile so perpetual as to earn the reputation of a sneer. But for the crooked glasses his dress was always exquisite; and but for the smile he was perfectly and perennially depressed.

"Don't you think," said the new-comer, with a sort of supercilious entreaty, "that we had better all come into breakfast? It is such a mistake to wait for breakfast. It spoils one's temper so much."

"Quite so," replied Turnbull, seriously.

"There seems almost to have been a little quarrelling here," said the man with the goatish beard.

"It is rather a long story," said Turnbull, smiling. "Originally, it might be called a phase in the quarrel between science and religion."

The new-comer started slightly, and Turnbull replied to the question on his face.

"Oh, yes," he said, "I am science!"

"I congratulate you heartily," answered the other, "I am Doctor Quayle."

Turnbull's eyes did not move, but he realized that the man in the panama hat had lost all his ease of a landed proprietor and had withdrawn to a distance of thirty yards, where he stood glaring with all the contraction of fear and hatred that can stiffen a cat.

⚜

MacIan was sitting somewhat disconsolately on a stump of tree, his large black head half buried in his large brown hands, when Turnbull strode up to him chewing a cigarette. He did not look up, but his comrade and enemy addressed him like one who must free himself of his feelings.

"Well, I hope, at any rate," he said, "that you like your precious religion now. I hope you like the society of this poor devil whom your damned tracts and hymns and priests have driven out of his wits. Five men in this place, they tell me, five men in this place who might have been fathers of families, and every one of them thinks he is God the Father. Oh! you may talk about the ugliness of science, but there is no one here who thinks he is Protoplasm."

"They naturally prefer a bright part," said MacIan, wearily. "Protoplasm is not worth going mad about."

"At least," said Turnbull, savagely, "it was your Jesus Christ who started all this bosh about being God."

294

For one instant MacIan opened the eyes of battle; then his tightened lips took a crooked smile and he said, quite calmly:

"No, the idea is older; it was Satan who first said that he was God."

"Then, what," asked Turnbull, very slowly, as he softly picked a flower, "what is the difference between Christ and Satan?"

"It is quite simple," replied the Highlander. "Christ descended into hell; Satan fell into it."

"Does it make much odds?" asked the free-thinker.

"It makes all the odds," said the other. "One of them wanted to go up and went down; the other wanted to go down and went up. A god can be humble, a devil can only be humbled."

"Why are you always wanting to humble a man?" asked Turnbull, knitting his brows. "It affects me as ungenerous."

"Why were you wanting to humble a god when you found him in this garden?" asked MacIan.

"That was an extreme case of impudence," said Turnbull.

"Granting the man his almighty pretensions, I think he was very modest," said MacIan. "It is we who are arrogant, who know we are only men. The ordinary man in the street is more of a monster than that poor fellow; for the man in the street treats himself as God Almighty when he knows he isn't. He expects the universe to turn round him, though he knows he isn't the centre."

"Well," said Turnbull, sitting down on the grass, "this is a digression, anyhow. What I want to point out is, that your faith does end in asylums and my science doesn't."

"Doesn't it, by George!" cried MacIan, scornfully. "There are a few men here who are mad on God and a few who are mad on the Bible. But I bet there are many more who are simply mad on madness."

"Do you really believe it?" asked the other.

"Scores of them, I should say," answered MacIan. "Fellows who have read medical books or fellows whose fathers and uncles had something hereditary in their heads—the whole air they breathe is mad."

"All the same," said Turnbull, shrewdly, "I bet you haven't found a madman of that sort."

"I bet I have!" cried Evan, with unusual animation. "I've been walking about the garden talking to a poor chap all the morning. He's simply been broken down and driven raving by your damned science. Talk about believing one is God—why, it's quite an old, comfortable, fireside fancy compared with the sort of things this fellow believes. He believes that there is a God, but that he is better than God. He says God will be afraid to face him. He says one is always progressing beyond the best. He put his arm in mine and whispered in my ear, as if it were the apocalypse: 'Never trust a God that you can't improve on.'"

"What can he have meant?" said the atheist, with all his logic awake. "Obviously one should not trust any God that one can improve on."

"It is the way he talks," said MacIan, almost indifferently; "but he says rummier things than that. He says that a man's doctor ought to decide what woman he marries; and he says that children ought not to be brought up by their parents, because a physical partiality will then distort the judgement of the educator."

"Oh, dear!" said Turnbull, laughing, "you have certainly come across a pretty bad case, and incidentally proved your own. I suppose some men do lose their wits through science as through love and other good things."

"And he says," went on MacIan, monotonously, "that he cannot see why anyone should suppose that a triangle is a three-sided figure. He says that on some higher plane——"

Turnbull leapt to his feet as by an electric shock. "I never could have believed," he cried, "that you had humour enough to tell a lie. You've gone a bit too far, old man, with your little joke. Even in a lunatic asylum there can't be anybody who, having thought about the matter, thinks that a triangle has not got three sides. If he exists he must be a new era in human psychology. But he doesn't exist."

"I will go and fetch him," said MacIan, calmly; "I left the poor fellow wandering about by the nasturtium bed."

MacIan vanished, and in a few moments returned, trailing with him his own discovery among lunatics, who was a slender man with a fixed smile and an unfixed and rolling head. He had a goatlike beard just long enough to be shaken in a strong wind. Turnbull sprang to his feet and was like one who is speechless through choking a sudden shout of laughter.

"Why, you great donkey," he shouted, in an ear-shattering whisper, "that's not one of the patients at all. That's one of the doctors."

Evan looked back at the leering head with the long-pointed beard and repeated the word inquiringly: "One of the doctors?"

"Oh, you know what I mean," said Turnbull, impatiently. "The medical authorities of the place."

Evan was still staring back curiously at the beaming and bearded creature behind him.

"The mad doctors," said Turnbull, shortly.

"Quite so," said MacIan.

After a rather restless silence Turnbull plucked MacIan by the elbow and pulled him aside.

"For goodness sake," he said, "don't offend this fellow; he may be as mad as ten hatters, if you like, but he has us between his finger and thumb. This is the very time he appointed to talk with us about our—well, our exeat."

"But what can it matter?" asked the wondering MacIan. "He can't keep us in the asylum. We're not mad."

"Jackass!" said Turnbull, heartily, "of course we're not mad. Of course, if we are medically examined and the thing is thrashed out, they will find we are not mad. But don't you see that if the thing is thrashed out it will mean letters to this reference and telegrams to that; and at the first word of who we are, we shall be taken out of a madhouse, where we may smoke, to a jail, where we mayn't. No, if we manage this very quietly, he may merely let us out at the front door as stray revellers. If there's half an hour of inquiry, we are cooked."

MacIan looked at the grass frowningly for a few seconds, and then said in a new, small and childish voice: "I am awfully stupid, Mr. Turnbull; you must be patient with me."

Turnbull caught Evan's elbow again with quite another gesture. "Come," he cried, with the harsh voice of one who hides emotion, "come and let us be tactful in chorus."

The doctor with the pointed beard was already slanting it forward at a more than usually acute angle, with the smile that expressed expectancy.

"I hope I do not hurry you, gentlemen," he said, with the faintest suggestion of a sneer at their hurried consultation, "but I believe you wanted to see me at half past eleven."

"I am most awfully sorry, Doctor," said Turnbull, with ready amiability; "I never meant to keep you waiting; but the silly accident that has landed us in your garden may have some rather serious consequences to our friends elsewhere, and my friend here was just drawing my attention to some of them."

"Quite so! Quite so!" said the doctor, hurriedly. "If you really want to put anything before me, I can give you a few moments in my consulting-room."

He led them rapidly into a small but imposing apartment, which seemed to be built and furnished entirely in red-varnished wood. There was one desk occupied with carefully docketed papers; and there were several chairs of the red-varnished wood—though of different shape. All along the wall ran something that might have been a bookcase, only that it was not filled with books, but with flat, oblong slabs or cases of the same polished dark-red consistency. What those flat wooden cases were they could form no conception.

The doctor sat down with a polite impatience on his professional perch; MacIan remained standing, but Turnbull threw himself almost with luxury into a hard wooden arm-chair.

"This is a most absurd business, Doctor," he said, "and I am ashamed to take up the time of busy professional men with such pranks from outside. The plain fact is, that he and I and a pack of silly men and girls have organized a game across this part of the country—a sort of combination of hare and hounds and hide and seek—I dare say you've heard of it. We are the hares, and, seeing your high wall look so inviting, we tumbled over it, and naturally were a little startled with what we found on the other side."

"Quite so!" said the doctor, mildly. "I can understand that you were startled."

Turnbull had expected him to ask what place was the headquarters of the new exhilarating game, and who were the male and female enthusiasts who had brought it to such perfection; in fact, Turnbull was busy making up these personal and topographical particulars. As the doctor did not ask the question, he grew slightly uneasy, and risked the question: "I hope you will accept my assurance that the thing was an accident and that no intrusion was meant."

"Oh, yes, sir," replied the doctor, smiling, "I accept everything that you say."

"In that case," said Turnbull, rising genially, "we must not further interrupt your important duties. I suppose there will be someone to let us out?"

"No," said the doctor, still smiling steadily and pleasantly, "there will be no one to let you out."

"Can we let ourselves out, then?" asked Turnbull, in some surprise.

"Why, of course not," said the beaming scientist; "think how dangerous that would be in a place like this."

"Then, how the devil are we to get out?" cried Turnbull, losing his manners for the first time.

"It is a question of time, of receptivity, and treatment," said the doctor, arching his eyebrows indifferently. "I do not regard either of your cases as incurable."

And with that the man of the world was struck dumb, and, as in all intolerable moments, the word was with the unworldly.

MacIan took one stride to the table, leant across it, and said: "We can't stop here, we're not mad people!"

"We don't use the crude phrase," said the doctor, smiling at his patent-leather boots.

"But you *can't* think us mad," thundered MacIan. "You never saw us before. You know nothing about us. You haven't even examined us."

The doctor threw back his head and beard. "Oh, yes," he said, "very thoroughly."

"But you can't shut a man up on your mere impressions without documents or certificates or anything?"

The doctor got languidly to his feet. "Quite so," he said. "You certainly ought to see the documents."

He went across to the curious mock book-shelves and took down one of the flat mahogany cases. This he opened with a curious key at his watch-chain, and laying back a flap revealed a quire of foolscap covered with close but quite clear writing. The first three words were in such large copy-book hand that they caught the eye even at a distance. They were: "MacIan, Evan Stuart."

Evan bent his angry eagle face over it; yet something blurred it and he could never swear he saw it distinctly. He saw something that began: "Prenatal influences predisposing to mania. Grandfather believed in return of the Stuarts. Mother carried bone of St. Eulalia with which she touched children in sickness. Marked religious mania at early age——"

Evan fell back and fought for his speech. "Oh!" he burst out at last. "Oh! if all this world I have walked in had been as sane as my mother was."

Then he compressed his temples with his hands, as if to crush them. And then lifted suddenly a face that looked fresh and young, as if he had dipped and washed it in some holy well.

"Very well," he cried; "I will take the sour with the sweet. I will pay the penalty of having enjoyed God in this monstrous modern earth that cannot enjoy man or beast. I will die happy in your madhouse, only because I know what I know. Let it be granted, then—MacIan is a mystic; MacIan is a maniac. But this honest shopkeeper and editor whom I have dragged on my inhuman escapades, you cannot keep him. He will go free, thank God, he is not down in any damned document. His ancestor, I am certain, did not die at Culloden. His mother, I swear, had no relics. Let my friend out of your front door, and as for me——"

The doctor had already gone across to the laden shelves, and after a few minutes' short-sighted peering, had pulled down another parallelogram of dark-red wood.

This also he unlocked on the table, and with the same unerring egotistic eye on of the company saw the words, written in large letters: "Turnbull, James."

Hitherto Turnbull himself had somewhat scornfully surrendered his part in the whole business; but he was too honest and unaffected not to start at his own name. After the name, the inscription appeared to run: "Unique case of Eleutheromania.

Parentage, as so often in such cases, prosaic and healthy. Eleutheromaniac signs occurred early, however, leading him to attach himself to the individualist Bradlaugh. Recent outbreak of pure anarchy——"

Turnbull slammed the case to, almost smashing it, and said with a burst of savage laughter: "Oh! come along, MacIan; I don't care so much, even about getting out of the madhouse, if only we get out of this room. You were right enough, MacIan, when you spoke about—about mad doctors."

Somehow they found themselves outside in the cool, green garden, and then, after a stunned silence, Turnbull said: "There is one thing that was puzzling me all the time, and I understand it now."

"What do you mean?" asked Evan.

"No man by will or wit," answered Turnbull, "can get out of this garden; and yet we got into it merely by jumping over a garden wall. The whole thing explains itself easily enough. That undefended wall was an open trap. It was a trap laid for two celebrated lunatics. They saw us get in right enough. And they will see that we do not get out."

Evan gazed at the garden wall, gravely for more than a minute, and then he nodded without a word.

XV. THE DREAM OF MACIAN

The system of espionage in the asylum was so effective and complete that in practice the patients could often enjoy a sense of almost complete solitude. They could stray up so near to the wall in an apparently unwatched garden as to find it easy to jump over it. They would only have found the error of their calculations if they had tried to jump.

Under this insulting liberty, in this artificial loneliness, Evan MacIan was in the habit of creeping out into the garden after dark—especially upon moonlight nights. The moon, indeed, was for him always a positive magnet in a manner somewhat hard to explain to those of a robuster attitude. Evidently, Apollo is to the full as poetical as Diana; but it is not a question of poetry in the matured and intellectual sense of the word. It is a question of a certain solid and childish fancy. The sun is in the strict and literal sense invisible; that is to say, that by our bodily eyes it cannot properly be seen. But the moon is a much simpler thing; a naked and nursery sort of thing. It hangs in the sky quite solid and quite silver and quite useless; it is one huge celestial snowball. It was at least some such infantile facts and fancies which led Evan again and again during his dehumanized imprisonment to go out as if to shoot the moon.

He was out in the garden on one such luminous and ghostly night, when the steady moonshine toned down all the colours of the garden until almost the strongest tints to be seen were the strong soft blue of the sky and the large lemon moon. He was walking with his face turned up to it in that rather half-witted fashion which might have excused the error of his keepers; and as he gazed he became aware of something little and lustrous flying close to the lustrous orb, like a bright chip knocked off the moon. At first he thought it was a mere sparkle or refraction in his own eyesight; he blinked and cleared his eyes. Then he thought it was a falling star; only it did not fall. It jerked awkwardly up and down in a way unknown among meteors and strangely reminiscent of the works of man. The next moment the thing drove right across the moon, and from being silver upon blue, suddenly became black upon silver; then although it passed the field of light in a flash its outline was unmistakable though eccentric. It was a flying ship.

The vessel took one long and sweeping curve across the sky and came nearer and nearer to MacIan, like a steam-engine coming round a bend. It was of pure white steel, and in the moon it gleamed like the armour of Sir Galahad. The simile of such virginity is not inappropriate; for, as it grew larger and larger and lower and lower, Evan saw that the only figure in it was robed in white from head to foot and crowned with snow-white hair, on which the moonshine lay like a benediction. The figure stood so still that he could easily have supposed it to be a statue. Indeed, he thought it was until it spoke.

"Evan," said the voice, and it spoke with the simple authority of some forgotten father revisiting his children, "you have remained here long enough, and your sword is wanted elsewhere."

"Wanted for what?" asked the young man, accepting the monstrous event with a queer and clumsy naturalness; "what is my sword wanted for?"

"For all that you hold dear," said the man standing in the moonlight; "for the thrones of authority and for all ancient loyalty to law."

Evan looked up at the lunar orb again as if in irrational appeal—a moon calf bleating to his mother the moon. But the face of Luna seemed as witless as his own; there is no help in nature against the supernatural; and he looked again at the tall marble figure that might have been made out of solid moonlight.

Then he said in a loud voice: "Who are you?" and the next moment was seized by a sort of choking terror lest his question should be answered. But the unknown preserved an impenetrable silence for a long space and then only answered: "I must not say who I am until the end of the world; but I may say what I am. I am the law."

And he lifted his head so that the moon smote full upon his beautiful and ancient face.

The face was the face of a Greek god grown old, but not grown either weak or ugly; there was nothing to break its regularity except a rather long chin with a cleft in it, and this rather added distinction than lessened beauty. His strong, well-opened eyes were very brilliant but quite colourless like steel.

MacIan was one of those to whom a reverence and self-submission in ritual come quite easy, and are ordinary things. It was not artificial in him to bend slightly to this solemn apparition or to lower his voice when he said: "Do you bring me some message?"

"I do bring you a message," answered the man of moon and marble. "The king has returned."

Evan did not ask for or require any explanation. "I suppose you can take me to the war," he said, and the silent silver figure only bowed its head again. MacIan clambered into the silver boat, and it rose upward to the stars.

To say that it rose to the stars is no mere metaphor, for the sky had cleared to that occasional and astonishing transparency in which one can see plainly both stars and moon.

As the white-robed figure went upward in his white chariot, he said quite quietly to Evan: "There is an answer to all the folly talked about equality. Some stars are big and some small; some stand still and some circle around them as they stand. They can be orderly, but they cannot be equal."

"They are all very beautiful," said Evan, as if in doubt.

"They are all beautiful," answered the other, "because each is in his place and owns his superior. And now England will be beautiful after the same fashion. The earth will be as beautiful as the heavens, because our kings have come back to us."

"The Stuart——" began Evan, earnestly.

"Yes," answered the old man, "that which has returned is Stuart and yet older than Stuart. It is Capet and Plantagenet and Pendragon. It is all that good old time of which proverbs tell, that golden reign of Saturn against which gods and men were rebels. It is all that was ever lost by insolence and overwhelmed in rebellion. It is your own forefather, MacIan with the broken sword, bleeding without hope at Culloden. It is Charles refusing to answer the questions of the rebel court. It is Mary of the magic face confronting the gloomy and grasping peers and the boorish moralities of Knox. It is Richard, the last Plantagenet, giving his crown to Bolingbroke as to a common brigand. It is Arthur, overwhelmed in Lyonesse by heathen armies and dying in the mist, doubtful if ever he shall return."

"But now——" said Evan, in a low voice.

"But now!" said the old man; "he has returned."

"Is the war still raging?" asked MacIan.

"It rages like the pit itself beyond the sea whither I am taking you," answered the other. "But in England the king enjoys his own again. The people are once more taught and ruled as is best; they are happy knights, happy squires, happy servants, happy serfs, if you will; but free at last of that load of vexation and lonely vanity which was called being a citizen."

"Is England, indeed, so secure?" asked Evan.

"Look out and see," said the guide. "I fancy you have seen this place before."

They were driving through the air towards one region of the sky where the hollow of night seemed darkest and which was quite without stars. But against this black background there sprang up, picked out in glittering silver, a dome and a cross. It seemed that it was really newly covered with silver, which in the strong moonlight was like white flame. But, however, covered or painted, Evan had no difficult in knowing the place again. He saw the great thoroughfare that sloped upward to the base of its huge pedestal of steps. And he wondered whether the little shop was still by the side of it and whether its window had been mended.

As the flying ship swept round the dome he observed other alterations. The dome had been redecorated so as to give it a more solemn and somewhat more ecclesiastical note; the ball was draped or destroyed, and round the gallery, under the cross, ran what looked like a ring of silver statues, like the little leaden images that stood round the hat of Louis XI. Round the second gallery, at the base of the dome, ran a second rank of such images, and Evan thought there was another round the steps below. When they came closer he saw that they were figures in complete armour of steel or silver, each with a naked sword, point upward; and then he saw one of the swords move. These were not statues but an armed order of chivalry thrown in three circles round the cross. MacIan drew in his breath, as children do at anything they think utterly beautiful. For he could imagine nothing that so echoed his own visions of pontifical or chivalric art as this white dome sitting like a vast silver tiara over London, ringed with a triple crown of swords.

As they went sailing down Ludgate Hill, Evan saw that the state of the streets fully answered his companion's claim about the reintroduction of order. All the old blackcoated bustle with its cockney vivacity and vulgarity had disappeared. Groups of labourers, quietly but picturesquely clad, were passing up and down in sufficiently large numbers; but it required but a few mounted men to keep the streets in order. The mounted men were not common policemen, but knights with spurs and plume whose smooth and splendid armour glittered like diamond rather than steel. Only in one place —at the corner of Bouverie Street—did there appear to be a moment's confusion, and that was due to hurry rather than resistance. But one old grumbling man did not get out of the way quick enough, and the man on horseback struck him, not severely, across the shoulders with the flat of his sword.

"The soldier had no business to do that," said MacIan, sharply. "The old man was moving as quickly as he could."

"We attach great importance to discipline in the streets," said the man in white, with a slight smile.

"Discipline is not so important as justice," said MacIan.

The other did not answer.

Then after a swift silence that took them out across St. James's Park, he said: "The people must be taught to obey; they must learn their own ignorance. And I am not sure," he continued, turning his back on Evan and looking out of the prow of the ship into the darkness, "I am not sure that I agree with your little maxim about justice. Discipline for the whole society is surely more important than justice to an individual."

Evan, who was also leaning over the edge, swung round with startling suddenness and stared at the other's back.

"Discipline for society——" he repeated, very staccato, "more important—justice to individual?"

Then after a long silence he called out: "Who and what are you?"

"I am an angel," said the white-robed figure, without turning round.

"You are not a Catholic," said MacIan.

The other seemed to take no notice, but reverted to the main topic.

"In our armies up in heaven we learn to put a wholesome fear into subordinates."

MacIan sat craning his neck forward with an extraordinary and unaccountable eagerness.

"Go on!" he cried, twisting and untwisting his long, bony fingers, "go on!"

"Besides," continued he, in the prow, "you must allow for a certain high spirit and haughtiness in the superior type."

"Go on!" said Evan, with burning eyes.

"Just as the sight of sin offends God," said the unknown, "so does the sight of ugliness offend Apollo. The beautiful and princely must, of necessity, be impatient with the squalid and——"

"Why, you great fool!" cried MacIan, rising to the top of his tremendous stature, "did you think I would have doubted only for that rap with a sword? I know that noble orders have bad knights, that good knights have bad tempers, that the Church has rough priests and coarse cardinals; I have known it ever since I was born. You fool! you had only to say, 'Yes, it is rather a shame,' and I should have forgotten the affair. But I saw on your mouth the twitch of your infernal sophistry; I knew that something was wrong with you and your cathedrals. Something is wrong; everything is wrong. You are not an angel. That is not a church. It is not the rightful king who has come home."

"That is unfortunate," said the other, in a quiet but hard voice, "because you are going to see his Majesty."

"No," said MacIan, "I am going to jump over the side."

"Do you desire death?"

"No," said Evan, quite composedly, "I desire a miracle."

"From whom do you ask it? To whom do you appeal?" said his companion, sternly. "You have betrayed the king, renounced his cross on the cathedral, and insulted an archangel."

"I appeal to God," said Evan, and sprang up and stood upon the edge of the swaying ship.

The being in the prow turned slowly round; he looked at Evan with eyes which were like two suns, and put his hand to his mouth just too late to hide an awful smile.

"And how do you know," he said, "how do you know that I am not God?"

MacIan screamed. "Ah!" he cried. "Now I know who you really are. You are not God. You are not one of God's angels. But you were once."

The being's hand dropped from his mouth and Evan dropped out of the car.

XVI. THE DREAM OF TURNBULL

Turnbull was walking rather rampantly up and down the garden on a gusty evening chewing his cigar and in that mood when every man suppresses an instinct to spit. He was not, as a rule, a man much acquainted with moods; and the storms and sunbursts of MacIan's soul passed before him as an impressive but unmeaning panorama, like the anarchy of Highland scenery. Turnbull was one of those men in whom a continuous appetite and industry of the intellect leave the emotions very simple and steady. His heart was in the right place; but he was quite content to leave it there. It was his head that was his hobby. His mornings and evenings were marked not by impulses or thirsty desires, not by hope or by heart-break; they were filled with the fallacies he had detected, the problems he had made plain, the adverse theories he had wrestled with and thrown, the grand generalizations he had justified. But even the cheerful inner life of a logician may be upset by a lunatic asylum, to say nothing of whiffs of memory from a lady in Jersey, and the little red-bearded man on this windy evening was in a dangerous frame of mind.

Plain and positive as he was, the influence of earth and sky may have been greater on him than he imagined; and the weather that walked the world at that moment was as red and angry as Turnbull. Long strips and swirls of tattered and tawny cloud were dragged downward to the west exactly as torn red raiment would be dragged. And so strong and pitiless was the wind that it whipped away fragments of red-flowering bushes or of copper beech, and drove them also across the garden, a drift of red leaves, like the leaves of autumn, as in parody of the red and driven rags of cloud.

There was a sense in earth and heaven as of everything breaking up, and all the revolutionist in Turnbull rejoiced that it was breaking up. The trees were breaking up under the wind, even in the tall strength of their bloom: the clouds were breaking up and losing even their large heraldic shapes. Shards and shreds of copper cloud split off continually and floated by themselves, and for some reason the truculent eye of Turnbull was attracted to one of these careering cloudlets, which seemed to him to career in an exaggerated manner. Also it kept its shape, which is unusual with clouds shaken off; also its shape was of an odd sort.

Turnbull continued to stare at it, and in a little time occurred that crucial instant when a thing, however incredible, is accepted as a fact. The copper cloud was tumbling down towards the earth, like some gigantic leaf from the copper beeches. And as it came nearer it was evident, first, that it was not a cloud, and, second, that it was not itself of the colour of copper; only, being burnished like a mirror, it had reflected the red-brown colours of the burning clouds. As the thing whirled like a windswept leaf down towards the wall of the garden it was clear that it was some sort of air-ship made of metal, and slapping the air with big broad fins of steel. When it came about a hundred feet above the garden, a shaggy, lean figure leapt up in it, almost black against the bronze and scarlet of the west, and, flinging out a kind of hook or anchor, caught on to the green apple-tree just under the wall; and from that fixed holding ground the ship swung in the red tempest like a captive balloon.

While our friend stood frozen for an instant by his astonishment, the queer figure in the airy car tipped the vehicle almost upside down by leaping over the side of it, seemed to slide or drop down the rope like a monkey, and alighted (with impossible precision and placidity) seated on the edge of the wall, over which he kicked and dangled his legs as he grinned at Turnbull. The wind roared in the trees yet more ruinous and desolate, the red tails of the sunset were dragged downward like red dragons sucked down to death, and still on the top of the asylum wall sat the sinister figure with the grimace, swinging his feet in tune with the tempest; while above him, at the end of its tossing or tightened cord, the enormous iron air-ship floated as light and as little noticed as a baby's balloon upon its string.

Turnbull's first movement after sixty motionless seconds was to turn round and look at the large, luxuriant parallelogram of the garden and the long, low rectangular building beyond. There was not a soul or a stir of life within sight. And he had a quite meaningless sensation, as if there never really had been any one else there except he since the foundation of the world.

Stiffening in himself the masculine but mirthless courage of the atheist, he drew a little nearer to the wall and, catching the man at a slightly different angle of the evening light, could see his face and figure quite plain. Two facts about him stood out in the picked colours of some piratical schoolboy's story. The first was that his lean brown body was bare to the belt of his loose white trousers; the other that through hygiene, affectation, or whatever other cause, he had a scarlet handkerchief tied tightly but somewhat aslant across his brow. After these two facts had become emphatic, others appeared sufficiently important. One was that under the scarlet rag the hair was plentiful, but white as with the last snows of mortality. Another was that under the mop of white and senile hair the face was strong, handsome, and smiling, with a well-cut profile and a long cloven chin. The length of this lower part of the face and the strange cleft in it (which gave the man, in quite another sense from the common one, a double chin) faintly spoilt the claim of the face to absolute regularity, but it greatly assisted it in wearing the expression of half-smiling and half-sneering arrogance with which it was staring at all the stones, all the flowers, but especially at the solitary man.

"What do you want?" shouted Turnbull.

"I want you, Jimmy," said the eccentric man on the wall, and with the very word he had let himself down with a leap on to the centre of the lawn, where he bounded once literally like an India-rubber ball and then stood grinning with his legs astride. The only three facts that Turnbull could now add to his inventory were that the man had an ugly-looking knife swinging at his trousers belt, that his brown feet were as bare as his bronzed trunk and arms, and that his eyes had a singular bleak brilliancy which was of no particular colour.

"Excuse my not being in evening dress," said the newcomer with an urbane smile. "We scientific men, you know—I have to work my own engines—electrical engineer— very hot work."

"Look here," said Turnbull, sturdily clenching his fists in his trousers pockets, "I am bound to expect lunatics inside these four walls; but I do bar their coming from outside, bang out of the sunset clouds."

"And yet you came from the outside, too, Jim," said the stranger in a voice almost affectionate.

"What do you want?" asked Turnbull, with an explosion of temper as sudden as a pistol shot.

"I have already told you," said the man, lowering his voice and speaking with evident sincerity; "I want you."

"What do you want with me?"

"I want exactly what you want," said the new-comer with a new gravity. "I want the Revolution."

Turnbull looked at the fire-swept sky and the wind-stricken woodlands, and kept on repeating the word voicelessly to himself—the word that did indeed so thoroughly express his mood of rage as it had been among those red clouds and rocking tree-tops. "Revolution!" he said to himself. "The Revolution—yes, that is what I want right enough—anything, so long as it is a Revolution."

To some cause he could never explain he found himself completing the sentence on the top of the wall, having automatically followed the stranger so far. But when the stranger silently indicated the rope that led to the machine, he found himself pausing and saying: "I can't leave MacIan behind in this den."

"We are going to destroy the Pope and all the kings," said the new-comer. "Would it be wiser to take him with us?"

Somehow the muttering Turnbull found himself in the flying ship also, and it swung up into the sunset.

"All the great rebels have been very little rebels," said the man with the red scarf. "They have been like fourth-form boys who sometimes venture to hit a fifth-form boy. That was all the worth of their French Revolution and regicide. The boys never really dared to defy the schoolmaster."

"Whom do you mean by the schoolmaster?" asked Turnbull.

"You know whom I mean," answered the strange man, as he lay back on cushions and looked up into the angry sky.

They seemed rising into stronger and stronger sunlight, as if it were sunrise rather than sunset. But when they looked down at the earth they saw it growing darker and darker. The lunatic asylum in its large rectangular grounds spread below them in a foreshortened and infantile plan, and looked for the first time the grotesque thing that it was. But the clear colours of the plan were growing darker every moment. The masses of rose or rhododendron deepened from crimson to violet. The maze of gravel pathways faded from gold to brown. By the time they had risen a few hundred feet higher nothing could be seen of that darkening landscape except the lines of lighted windows, each one of which, at least, was the light of one lost intelligence. But on them as they swept upward better and braver winds seemed to blow, and on them the ruby light of evening seemed struck, and splashed like red spurts from the grapes of Dionysus. Below them the fallen lights were literally the fallen stars of servitude. And above them all the red and raging clouds were like the leaping flags of liberty.

The man with the cloven chin seemed to have a singular power of understanding thoughts; for, as Turnbull felt the whole universe tilt and turn over his head, the stranger said exactly the right thing.

"Doesn't it seem as if everything were being upset?" said he; "and if once everything is upset, He will be upset on top of it."

Then, as Turnbull made no answer, his host continued:

"That is the really fine thing about space. It is topsy-turvy. You have only to climb far enough towards the morning star to feel that you are coming down to it. You have only to dive deep enough into the abyss to feel that you are rising. That is the only glory of this universe—it is a giddy universe."

Then, as Turnbull was still silent, he added:

"The heavens are full of revolution—of the real sort of revolution. All the high things are sinking low and all the big things looking small. All the people who think they are aspiring find they are falling head foremost. And all the people who think they are condescending find they are climbing up a precipice. That is the intoxication of space. That is the only joy of eternity—doubt. There is only one pleasure the angels can possibly have in flying, and that is, that they do not know whether they are on their head or their heels."

Then, finding his companion still mute, he fell himself into a smiling and motionless meditation, at the end of which he said suddenly:

"So MacIan converted you?"

Turnbull sprang up as if spurning the steel car from under his feet. "Converted me!" he cried. "What the devil do you mean? I have known him for a month, and I have not retracted a single——"

"This Catholicism is a curious thing," said the man of the cloven chin in uninterrupted reflectiveness, leaning his elegant elbows over the edge of the vessel; "it soaks and weakens men without their knowing it, just as I fear it has soaked and weakened you."

Turnbull stood in an attitude which might well have meant pitching the other man out of the flying ship.

"I am an atheist," he said, in a stifled voice. "I have always been an atheist. I am still an atheist." Then, addressing the other's indolent and indifferent back, he cried: "In God's name what do you mean?"

And the other answered without turning round:

"I mean nothing in God's name."

Turnbull spat over the edge of the car and fell back furiously into his seat.

The other continued still unruffled, and staring over the edge idly as an angler stares down at a stream.

"The truth is that we never thought that you could have been caught," he said; "we counted on you as the one red-hot revolutionary left in the world. But, of course, these men like MacIan are awfully clever, especially when they pretend to be stupid."

Turnbull leapt up again in a living fury and cried: "What have I got to do with MacIan? I believe all I ever believed, and disbelieve all I ever disbelieved. What does all this mean, and what do you want with me here?"

Then for the first time the other lifted himself from the edge of the car and faced him.

"I have brought you here," he answered, "to take part in the last war of the world."

"The last war!" repeated Turnbull, even in his dazed state a little touchy about such a dogma; "how do you know it will be the last?"

The man laid himself back in his reposeful attitude, and said:

"It is the last war, because if it does not cure the world for ever, it will destroy it."

"What do you mean?"

"I only mean what you mean," answered the unknown in a temperate voice. "What was it that you always meant on those million and one nights when you walked outside your Ludgate Hill shop and shook your hand in the air?"

"Still I do not see," said Turnbull, stubbornly.

"You will soon," said the other, and abruptly bent downward one iron handle of his huge machine. The engine stopped, stooped, and dived almost as deliberately as a man bathing; in their downward rush they swept within fifty yards of a big bulk of stone that Turnbull knew only too well. The last red anger of the sunset was ended; the dome of heaven was dark; the lanes of flaring light in the streets below hardly lit up the base of the building. But he saw that it was St. Paul's Cathedral, and he saw that on the top of it the ball was still standing erect, but the cross was stricken and had fallen sideways. Then only he cared to look down into the streets, and saw that they were inflamed with uproar and tossing passions.

"We arrive at a happy moment," said the man steering the ship. "The insurgents are bombarding the city, and a cannon-ball has just hit the cross. Many of the insurgents are simple people, and they naturally regard it as a happy omen."

"Quite so," said Turnbull, in a rather colourless voice.

"Yes," replied the other. "I thought you would be glad to see your prayer answered. Of course I apologize for the word prayer."

"Don't mention it," said Turnbull.

The flying ship had come down upon a sort of curve, and was now rising again. The higher and higher it rose the broader and broader became the scenes of flame and desolation underneath.

Ludgate Hill indeed had been an uncaptured and comparatively quiet height, altered only by the startling coincidence of the cross fallen awry. All the other thoroughfares on all sides of that hill were full of the pulsation and the pain of battle, full of shaking torches and shouting faces. When at length they had risen high enough to have a bird's-eye view of the whole campaign, Turnbull was already intoxicated. He had smelt gunpowder, which was the incense of his own revolutionary religion.

"Have the people really risen?" he asked, breathlessly. "What are they fighting about?"

"The programme is rather elaborate," said his entertainer with some indifference. "I think Dr. Hertz drew it up."

Turnbull wrinkled his forehead. "Are all the poor people with the Revolution?" he asked.

The other shrugged his shoulders. "All the instructed and class-conscious part of them without exception," he replied. "There were certainly a few districts; in fact, we are passing over them just now——"

Turnbull looked down and saw that the polished car was literally lit up from underneath by the far-flung fires from below. Underneath whole squares and solid districts were in flames, like prairies or forests on fire.

"Dr. Hertz has convinced everybody," said Turnbull's cicerone in a smooth voice, "that nothing can really be done with the real slums. His celebrated maxim has been quite adopted. I mean the three celebrated sentences: 'No man should be unemployed. Employ the employables. Destroy the unemployables.'"

There was a silence, and then Turnbull said in a rather strained voice: "And do I understand that this good work is going on under here?"

"Going on splendidly," replied his companion in the heartiest voice. "You see, these people were much too tired and weak even to join the social war. They were a definite hindrance to it."

"And so you are simply burning them out?"

"It *does* seem absurdly simple," said the man, with a beaming smile, "when one thinks of all the worry and talk about helping a hopeless slave population, when the future obviously was only crying to be rid of them. There are happy babes unborn ready to burst the doors when these drivellers are swept away."

"Will you permit me to say," said Turnbull, after reflection, "that I don't like all this?"

"And will you permit me to say," said the other, with a snap, "that I don't like Mr. Evan MacIan?"

Somewhat to the speaker's surprise this did not inflame the sensitive sceptic; he had the air of thinking thoroughly, and then he said: "No, I don't think it's my friend MacIan that taught me that. I think I should always have said that I don't like this. These people have rights."

"Rights!" repeated the unknown in a tone quite indescribable. Then he added with a more open sneer: "Perhaps they also have souls."

"They have lives!" said Turnbull, sternly; "that is quite enough for me. I understood you to say that you thought life sacred."

"Yes, indeed!" cried his mentor with a sort of idealistic animation. "Yes, indeed! Life is sacred—but lives are not sacred. We are improving Life by removing lives. Can you, as a free-thinker, find any fault in that?"

"Yes," said Turnbull with brevity.

"Yet you applaud tyrannicide," said the stranger with rationalistic gaiety. "How inconsistent! It really comes to this: You approve of taking away life from those to whom it is a triumph and a pleasure. But you will not take away life from those to whom it is a burden and a toil."

Turnbull rose to his feet in the car with considerable deliberation, but his face seemed oddly pale. The other went on with enthusiasm.

"Life, yes, Life is indeed sacred!" he cried; "but new lives for old! Good lives for bad! On that very place where now there sprawls one drunken wastrel of a pavement artist more or less wishing he were dead—on that very spot there shall in the future be living pictures; there shall be golden girls and boys leaping in the sun."

Turnbull, still standing up, opened his lips. "Will you put me down, please?" he said, quite calmly, like on stopping an omnibus.

"Put you down—what do you mean?" cried his leader. "I am taking you to the front of the revolutionary war, where you will be one of the first of the revolutionary leaders."

"Thank you," replied Turnbull with the same painful constraint. "I have heard about your revolutionary war, and I think on the whole that I would rather be anywhere else."

"Do you want to be taken to a monastery," snarled the other, "with MacIan and his winking Madonnas."

"I want to be taken to a madhouse," said Turnbull distinctly, giving the direction with a sort of precision. "I want to go back to exactly the same lunatic asylum from which I came."

"Why?" asked the unknown.

"Because I want a little sane and wholesome society," answered Turnbull.

There was a long and peculiar silence, and then the man driving the flying machine said quite coolly: "I won't take you back."

And then Turnbull said equally coolly: "Then I'll jump out of the car."

The unknown rose to his full height, and the expression in his eyes seemed to be made of ironies behind ironies, as two mirrors infinitely reflect each other. At last he said, very gravely: "Do you think I am the devil?"

"Yes," said Turnbull, violently. "For I think the devil is a dream, and so are you. I don't believe in you or your flying ship or your last fight of the world. It is all a nightmare. I say as a fact of dogma and faith that it is all a nightmare. And I will be a martyr for my faith as much as St. Catherine, for I will jump out of this ship and risk waking up safe in bed."

After swaying twice with the swaying vessel he dived over the side as one dives into the sea. For some incredible moments stars and space and planets seemed to shoot up past him as the sparks fly upward; and yet in that sickening descent he was full of some unnatural happiness. He could connect it with no idea except one that half escaped him —what Evan had said of the difference between Christ and Satan; that it was by Christ's own choice that He descended into hell.

When he again realized anything, he was lying on his elbow on the lawn of the lunatic asylum, and the last red of the sunset had not yet disappeared.

XVII. THE IDIOT

Evan MacIan was standing a few yards off looking at him in absolute silence.

He had not the moral courage to ask MacIan if there had been anything astounding in the manner of his coming there, nor did MacIan seem to have any question to ask, or perhaps any need to ask it. The two men came slowly towards each other, and found the same expression on each other's faces. Then, for the first time in all their acquaintance, they shook hands.

Almost as if this were a kind of unconscious signal, it brought Dr. Quayle bounding out of a door and running across the lawn.

"Oh, there you are!" he exclaimed with a relieved giggle. "Will you come inside, please? I want to speak to you both."

They followed him into his shiny wooden office where their damning record was kept. Dr. Quayle sat down on a swivel chair and swung round to face them. His carved smile had suddenly disappeared.

"I will be plain with you gentlemen," he said, abruptly; "you know quite well we do our best for everybody here. Your cases have been under special consideration, and the Master himself has decided that you ought to be treated specially and—er—under somewhat simpler conditions."

"You mean treated worse, I suppose," said Turnbull, gruffly.

The doctor did not reply, and MacIan said: "I expected this." His eyes had begun to glow.

The doctor answered, looking at his desk and playing with a key: "Well, in certain cases that give anxiety—it is often better——"

"Give anxiety," said Turnbull, fiercely. "Confound your impudence! What do you mean? You imprison two perfectly sane men in a madhouse because you have made up a long word. They take it in good temper, walk and talk in your garden like monks who have found a vocation, are civil even to you, you damned druggists' hack! Behave not only more sanely than any of your patients, but more sanely than half the sane men outside, and you have the soul-stifling cheek to say that they give anxiety."

"The head of the asylum has settled it all," said Dr. Quayle, still looking down.

MacIan took one of his immense strides forward and stood over the doctor with flaming eyes.

"If the head has settled it let the head announce it," he said. "I won't take it from you. I believe you to be a low, gibbering degenerate. Let us see the head of the asylum."

"See the head of the asylum," repeated Dr. Quayle. "Certainly not."

The tall Highlander, bending over him, put one hand on his shoulder with fatherly interest.

"You don't seem to appreciate the peculiar advantages of my position as a lunatic," he said. "I could kill you with my left hand before such a rat as you could so much as squeak. And I wouldn't be hanged for it."

"I certainly agree with Mr. MacIan," said Turnbull with sobriety and perfect respectfulness, "that you had better let us see the head of the institution."

Dr. Quayle got to his feet in a mixture of sudden hysteria and clumsy presence of mind.

"Oh, certainly," he said with a weak laugh. "You can see the head of the asylum if you particularly want to." He almost ran out of the room, and the two followed swiftly on his flying coat tails. He knocked at an ordinary varnished door in the corridor. When a voice said, "Come in," MacIan's breath went hissing back through his teeth into his chest. Turnbull was more impetuous, and opened the door.

It was a neat and well-appointed room entirely lined with a medical library. At the other end of it was a ponderous and polished desk with an incandescent lamp on it, the light of which was just sufficient to show a slender, well-bred figure in an ordinary medical black frock-coat, whose head, quite silvered with age, was bent over neat piles of notes. This gentleman looked up for an instant as they entered, and the lamplight fell on his glittering spectacles and long, clean-shaven face—a face which would have been simply like an aristocrat's but that a certain lion poise of the head and long cleft in the chin made it look more like a very handsome actor's. It was only for a flash that his face was thus lifted. Then he bent his silver head over his notes once more, and said, without looking up again:

"I told you, Dr. Quayle, that these men were to go to cells B and C."

Turnbull and MacIan looked at each other, and said more than they could ever say with tongues or swords. Among other things they said that to that particular Head of the institution it was a waste of time to appeal, and they followed Dr. Quayle out of the room.

The instant they stepped out into the corridor four sturdy figures stepped from four sides, pinioned them, and ran them along the galleries. They might very likely have thrown their captors right and left had they been inclined to resist, but for some nameless reason they were more inclined to laugh. A mixture of mad irony with childish curiosity made them feel quite inclined to see what next twist would be taken by their imbecile luck. They were dragged down countless cold avenues lined with glazed tiles, different only in being of different lengths and set at different angles. They were so many and so monotonous that to escape back by them would have been far harder than fleeing from the Hampton Court maze. Only the fact that windows grew fewer, coming at longer intervals, and the fact that when the windows did come they seemed shadowed and let in less light, showed that they were winding into the core or belly of some enormous building. After a little time the glazed corridors began to be lit by electricity.

At last, when they had walked nearly a mile in those white and polished tunnels, they came with quite a shock to the futile finality of a cul-de-sac. All that white and weary journey ended suddenly in an oblong space and a blank white wall. But in the white wall there were two iron doors painted white on which were written, respectively, in neat black capitals B and C.

"You go in here, sir," said the leader of the officials, quite respectfully, "and you in here."

But before the doors had clanged upon their dazed victims, MacIan had been able to say to Turnbull with a strange drawl of significance: "I wonder who A is."

Turnbull made an automatic struggle before he allowed himself to be thrown into the cell. Hence it happened that he was the last to enter, and was still full of the exhilaration of the adventures for at least five minutes after the echo of the clanging door had died away.

Then, when silence had sunk deep and nothing happened for two and a half hours, it suddenly occurred to him that this was the end of his life. He was hidden and sealed up in this little crack of stone until the flesh should fall off his bones. He was dead, and the world had won.

His cell was of an oblong shape, but very long in comparison with its width. It was just wide enough to permit the arms to be fully extended with the dumb-bells, which were hung up on the left wall, very dusty. It was, however, long enough for a man to walk one thirty-fifth part of a mile if he traversed it entirely. On the same principle a row of fixed holes, quite close together, let in to the cells by pipes what was alleged to be the freshest air. For these great scientific organizers insisted that a man should be healthy even if he was miserable. They provided a walk long enough to give him exercise and holes large enough to give him oxygen. There their interest in human nature suddenly ceased. It seemed never to have occurred to them that the benefit of exercise belongs partly to the benefit of liberty. They had not entertained the suggestion that the open air is only one of the advantages of the open sky. They administered air in secret, but in sufficient doses, as if it were a medicine. They suggested walking, as if no man had ever felt inclined to walk. Above all, the asylum authorities insisted on their own extraordinary cleanliness. Every morning, while Turnbull was still half asleep on his iron bedstead which was lifted half-way up the wall and clamped to it with iron, four sluices or metal mouths opened above him at the four corners of the chamber and washed it white of any defilement. Turnbull's solitary soul surged up against this sickening daily solemnity.

"I am buried alive!" he cried, bitterly; "they have hidden me under mountains. I shall be here till I rot. Why the blazes should it matter to them whether I am dirty or clean."

Every morning and evening an iron hatchway opened in his oblong cell, and a brown hairy hand or two thrust in a plate of perfectly cooked lentils and a big bowl of cocoa. He was not underfed any more than he was underexercised or asphyxiated. He had ample walking space, ample air, ample and even filling food. The only objection was that he had nothing to walk towards, nothing to feast about, and no reason whatever for drawing the breath of life.

Even the shape of his cell especially irritated him. It was a long, narrow parallelogram, which had a flat wall at one end and ought to have had a flat wall at the other; but that end was broken by a wedge or angle of space, like the prow of a ship. After three days of silence and cocoa, this angle at the end began to infuriate Turnbull. It maddened him to think that two lines came together and pointed at nothing. After the fifth day he was reckless, and poked his head into the corner. After twenty-five days he almost broke his head against it. Then he became quite cool and stupid again, and began to examine it like a sort of Robinson Crusoe.

Almost unconsciously it was his instinct to examine outlets, and he found himself paying particular attention to the row of holes which let in the air into his last house of life. He soon discovered that these air-holes were all the ends and mouths of long leaden tubes which doubtless carried air from some remote watering-place near Margate. One evening while he was engaged in the fifth investigation he noticed something like twilight in one of these dumb mouths, as compared with the darkness of the others. Thrusting his finger in as far as it would go, he found a hole and flapping edge in the tube. This he rent open and instantly saw a light behind; it was at least certain that he had struck some other cell.

It is a characteristic of all things now called "efficient", which means mechanical and calculated, that if they go wrong at all they go entirely wrong. There is no power of retrieving a defeat, as in simpler and more living organisms. A strong gun can conquer a strong elephant, but a wounded elephant can easily conquer a broken gun. Thus the Prussian monarchy in the eighteenth century, or now, can make a strong army merely by making the men afraid. But it does it with the permanent possibility that the men may some day be more afraid of their enemies than of their officers. Thus the drainage in our cities so long as it is quite solid means a general safety, but if there is one leak it means concentrated poison—an explosion of deathly germs like dynamite, a spirit of stink. Thus, indeed, all that excellent machinery which is the swiftest thing on earth in saving human labour is also the slowest thing on earth in resisting human interference. It may be easier to get chocolate for nothing out of a shopkeeper than out of an automatic machine. But if you did manage to steal the chocolate, the automatic machine would be much less likely to run after you.

Turnbull was not long in discovering this truth in connexion with the cold and colossal machinery of this great asylum. He had been shaken by many spiritual states since the instant when he was pitched head foremost into that private cell which was to be his private room till death. He had felt a high fit of pride and poetry, which had ebbed away and left him deadly cold. He had known a period of mere scientific curiosity, in the course of which he examined all the tiles of his cell, with the gratifying conclusion that they were all the same shape and size; but was greatly puzzled about the angle in the wall at the end, and also about an iron peg or spike that stood out from the wall, the object of which he does not know to this day. Then he had a period of mere madness not to be written of by decent men, but only by those few dirty novelists hallooed on by the infernal huntsman to hunt down and humiliate human nature. This also passed, but left behind it a feverish distaste for many of the mere objects around him. Long after he had returned to sanity and such hopeless cheerfulness as a man might have on a desert island, he disliked the regular squares of the pattern of wall and floor and the triangle that terminated his corridor. Above all, he had a hatred, deep as the hell he did not believe in, for the objectless iron peg in the wall.

But in all his moods, sane or insane, intolerant or stoical, he never really doubted this: that the machine held him as light and as hopelessly as he had from his birth been held by the hopeless cosmos of his own creed. He knew well the ruthless and inexhaustible resources of our scientific civilization. He no more expected rescue from a medical certificate than rescue from the solar system. In many of his Robinson Crusoe moods he thought kindly of MacIan as of some quarrelsome school-fellow who had long been dead. He thought of leaving in the cell when he died a rigid record of his opinions, and when he began to write them down on scraps of envelope in his pocket, he was startled to discover how much they had changed. Then he remembered the Beauchamp Tower, and tried to write his blazing scepticism on the wall, and discovered that it was all shiny tiles on which nothing could be either drawn or carved. Then for an instant there hung and broke above him like a high wave the whole horror of scientific imprisonment, which manages to deny a man not only liberty, but every accidental comfort of bondage. In the old filthy dungeons men could carve their prayers or protests in the rock. Here the white and slippery walls escaped even from bearing witness. The old prisoners could make a pet of a mouse or a beetle strayed out of a hole. Here the unpierceable walls were washed every morning by an automatic sluice. There was no natural corruption and no merciful decay by which a living thing could enter in. Then James Turnbull looked up and saw the high invincible hatefulness of the society in which he lived, and saw the hatefulness of something else also, which he told himself again and again was not the cosmos in which he believed. But all the time he had never once doubted that the five sides of his cell were for him the wall of the world henceforward, and it gave him a shock of surprise even to discover the faint light through the aperture in the ventilation tube. But he had forgotten how close efficiency has to pack everything together and how easily, therefore, a pipe here or there may leak.

Turnbull thrust his first finger down the aperture, and at last managed to make a slight further fissure in the piping. The light that came up from beyond was very faint, and apparently indirect; it seemed to fall from some hole or window higher up. As he was screwing his eye to peer at this grey and greasy twilight he was astonished to see another human finger very long and lean come down from above towards the broken pipe and hook it up to something higher. The lighted aperture was abruptly blackened and blocked, presumably by a face and mouth, for something human spoke down the tube, though the words were not clear.

"Who is that?" asked Turnbull, trembling with excitement, yet wary and quite resolved not to spoil any chance.

After a few indistinct sounds the voice came down with a strong Argyllshire accent: "I say, Turnbull, we couldn't fight through this tube, could we?"

Sentiments beyond speech surged up in Turnbull and silenced him for a space just long enough to be painful. Then he said with his old gaiety: "I vote we talk a little first; I don't want to murder the first man I have met for ten million years."

"I know what you mean," answered the other. "It has been awful. For a mortal month I have been alone with God."

Turnbull started, and it was on the tip of his tongue to answer: "Alone with God! Then you do not know what loneliness is."

But he answered, after all, in his old defiant style: "Alone with God, were you? And I suppose you found his Majesty's society rather monotonous?"

"Oh, no," said MacIan, and his voice shuddered; "it was a great deal too exciting."

After a very long silence the voice of MacIan said: "What do you really hate most in your place?"

"You'd think I was really mad if I told you," answered Turnbull, bitterly.

"Then I expect it's the same as mine," said the other voice.

"I am sure it's not the same as anybody's," said Turnbull, "for it has no rhyme or reason. Perhaps my brain really has gone, but I detest that iron spike in the left wall more than the damned desolation or the damned cocoa. Have you got one in your cell?"

"Not now," replied MacIan with serenity. "I've pulled it out."

His fellow-prisoner could only repeat the words.

"I pulled it out the other day when I was off my head," continued the tranquil Highland voice. "It looked so unnecessary."

"You must be ghastly strong," said Turnbull.

"One is, when one is mad," was the careless reply, "and it had worn a little loose in the socket. Even now I've got it out I can't discover what it was for. But I've found out something a long sight funnier."

"What do you mean?" asked Turnbull.

"I have found out where A is," said the other.

Three weeks afterwards MacIan had managed to open up communications which made his meaning plain. By that time the two captives had fully discovered and demonstrated that weakness in the very nature of modern machinery to which we have already referred. The very fact that they were isolated from all companions meant that they were free from all spies, and as there were no gaolers to be bribed, so there were none to be baffled. Machinery brought them their cocoa and cleaned their cells; that machinery was as helpless as it was pitiless. A little patient violence, conducted day after day amid constant mutual suggestion, opened an irregular hole in the wall, large enough to let in a small man, in the exact place where there had been before the tiny ventilation holes. Turnbull tumbled somehow into MacIan's apartment, and his first glance found out that the iron spike was indeed plucked from its socket, and left, moreover, another ragged hole into some hollow place behind. But for this MacIan's cell was the duplicate of Turnbull's—a long oblong ending in a wedge and lined with cold and lustrous tiles. The small hole from which the peg had been displaced was in that short oblique wall at the end nearest to Turnbull's. That individual looked at it with a puzzled face.

"What is in there?" he asked.

MacIan answered briefly: "Another cell."

"But where can the door of it be?" said his companion, even more puzzled; "the doors of our cells are at the other end."

"It has no door," said Evan.

In the pause of perplexity that followed, an eerie and sinister feeling crept over Turnbull's stubborn soul in spite of himself. The notion of the doorless room chilled him with that sense of half-witted curiosity which one has when something horrible is half understood.

"James Turnbull," said MacIan, in a low and shaken voice, "these people hate us more than Nero hated Christians, and fear us more than any man feared Nero. They have filled England with frenzy and galloping in order to capture us and wipe us out— in order to kill us. And they have killed us, for you and I have only made a hole in our coffins. But though this hatred that they felt for us is bigger than they felt for Bonaparte, and more plain and practical than they would feel for Jack the Ripper, yet it is not we whom the people of this place hate most."

A cold and quivering impatience continued to crawl up Turnbull's spine; he had never felt so near to superstition and supernaturalism, and it was not a pretty sort of superstition either.

"There is another man more fearful and hateful," went on MacIan, in his low monotone voice, "and they have buried him even deeper. God knows how they did it, for he was let in by neither door nor window, nor lowered through any opening above. I expect these iron handles that we both hate have been part of some damned machinery for walling him up. He is there. I have looked through the hole at him; but I cannot stand looking at him long, because his face is turned away from me and he does not move."

Al Turnbull's unnatural and uncompleted feelings found their outlet in rushing to the aperture and looking into the unknown room.

It was a third oblong cell exactly like the other two except that it was doorless, and except that on one of the walls was painted a large black A like the B and C outside their own doors. The letter in this case was not painted outside, because this prison had no outside.

On the same kind of tiled floor, of which the monotonous squares had maddened

Turnbull's eye and brain, was sitting a figure which was startlingly short even for a child, only that the enormous head was ringed with hair of a frosty grey. The figure was draped, both insecurely and insufficiently, in what looked like the remains of a brown flannel dressing-gown; an emptied cup of cocoa stood on the floor beside it, and the creature had his big grey head cocked at a particular angle of inquiry or attention which amid all that gathering gloom and mystery struck one as comic if not cocksure.

After six still seconds Turnbull could stand it no longer, but called out to the dwarfish thing—in what words heaven knows. The thing got up with the promptitude of an animal, and turning round offered the spectacle of two owlish eyes and a huge grey-and-white beard not unlike the plumage of an owl. This extraordinary beard covered him literally to his feet (not that that was very far), and perhaps it was as well that it did, for portions of his remaining clothing seemed to fall off whenever he moved. One talks trivially of a face like parchment, but this old man's face was so wrinkled that it was like a parchment loaded with hieroglyphics. The lines of his face were so deep and complex that one could see five or ten different faces besides the real one, as one can see them in an elaborate wall-paper. And yet while his face seemed like a scripture older than the gods, his eyes were quite bright, blue, and startled like those of a baby. They looked as if they had only an instant before been fitted into his head.

Everything depended so obviously upon whether this buried monster spoke that Turnbull did not know or care whether he himself had spoken. He said something or nothing. And then he waited for this dwarfish voice that had been hidden under the mountains of the world. At last it did speak, and spoke in English, with a foreign accent that was neither Latin nor Teutonic. He suddenly stretched out a long and very dirty forefinger, and cried in a voice of clear recognition, like a child's: "That's a hole."

He digested the discovery for some seconds, sucking his finger, and then he cried, with a crow of laughter: "And that's a head come through it."

The hilarious energy in this idiot attitude gave Turnbull another sick turn. He had grown to tolerate those dreary and mumbling madmen who trailed themselves about the beautiful asylum gardens. But there was something new and subversive of the universe in the combination of so much cheerful decision with a body without a brain.

"Why did they put you in such a place?" he asked at last with embarrassment.

"Good place. Yes," said the old man, nodding a great many times and beaming like a flattered landlord. "Good shape. Long and narrow, with a point. Like this," and he made lovingly with his hands a map of the room in the air.

"But that's not the best," he added, confidentially. "Squares very good; I have a nice long holiday, and can count them. But that's not the best."

"What is the best?" asked Turnbull in great distress.

"Spike is the best," said the old man, opening his blue eyes blazing; "it sticks out."

The words Turnbull spoke broke out of him in pure pity. "Can't we do anything for you?" he said.

"I am very happy," said the other, alphabetically. "You are a good man. Can I help you?"

"No, I don't think you can, sir," said Turnbull with rough pathos; "I am glad you are contented at least."

The weird old person opened his broad blue eyes and fixed Turnbull with a stare extraordinarily severe. "You are quite sure," he said, "I cannot help you?"

"Quite sure, thank you," said Turnbull with broken brevity. "Good day."

Then he turned to MacIan who was standing close behind him, and whose face, now familiar in all its moods, told him easily that Evan had heard the whole of the strange dialogue.

"Curse those cruel beasts!" cried Turnbull. "They've turned him to an imbecile just by burying him alive. His brain's like a pin-point now."

"You are sure he is a lunatic?" said Evan, slowly.

"Not a lunatic," said Turnbull, "an idiot. He just points to things and says that they stick out."

"He had a notion that he could help us," said MacIan moodily, and began to pace towards the other end of his cell.

"Yes, it was a bit pathetic," assented Turnbull; "such a Thing offering help, and besides—— Hallo! Hallo! What's the matter?"

"God Almighty guide us all!" said MacIan.

He was standing heavy and still at the other end of the room and staring quietly at the door which for thirty days had sealed them up from the sun. Turnbull, following the other's eye, stared at the door likewise, and then he also uttered an exclamation. The iron door was standing about an inch and a half open.

"He said——" began Evan, in a trembling voice—"he offered——"

"Come along, you fool!" shouted Turnbull with a sudden and furious energy. "I see it all now, and it's the best stroke of luck in the world. You pulled out that iron handle that had screwed up his cell, and it somehow altered the machinery and opened all the doors."

Seizing MacIan by the elbow he bundled him bodily out into the open corridor and ran him on till they saw daylight through a half-darkened window.

"All the same," said Evan, like one answering in an ordinary conversation, "he did ask you whether he could help you."

All this wilderness of windowless passages was so built into the heart of that fortress of fear that it seemed more than an hour before the fugitives had any good glimpse of the outer world. They did not even know what hour of the day it was; and when, turning a corner, they saw the bare tunnel of the corridor end abruptly in a shining square of garden, the grass burning in that strong evening sunshine which makes it burnished gold rather than green, the abrupt opening on to the earth seemed like a hole knocked in the wall of heaven. Only once or twice in life is it permitted to a man thus to see the very universe from outside, and feel existence itself as an adorable adventure not yet begun. As they found this shining escape out of that hellish labyrinth they both had simultaneously the sensation of being babes unborn, of being asked by God if they would like to live upon the earth. They were looking in at one of the seven gates of Eden.

Turnbull was the first to leap into the garden, with an earth-spurning leap like that of one who could really spread his wings and fly. MacIan, who came an instant after, was less full of mere animal gusto and fuller of a more fearful and quivering pleasure in the clear and innocent flower colours and the high and holy trees. With one bound they were in that cool and cleared landscape, and they found just outside the door the black-clad gentleman with the cloven chin smilingly regarding them; and his chin seemed to grow longer and longer as he smiled.

XVIII. A RIDDLE OF FACES

Just behind him stood two other doctors: one, the familiar Dr. Quayle, of the blinking eyes and bleating voice; the other, a more commonplace but much more forcible figure, a stout young doctor with short, well-brushed hair and a round but resolute face. At the sight of the escape these two subordinates uttered a cry and sprang forward, but their superior remained motionless and smiling, and somehow the lack of his support seemed to arrest and freeze them in the very gesture of pursuit.

"Let them be," he cried in a voice that cut like a blade of ice; and not only of ice, but of some awful primordial ice that had never been water.

"I want no devoted champions," said the cutting voice; "even the folly of one's friends bores one at last. You don't suppose I should have let these lunatics out of their cells without good reason. I have the best and fullest reason. They can be let out of their cell today, because today the whole world has become their cell. I will have no more medieval mummery of chains and doors. Let them wander about the earth as they wandered about this garden, and I shall still be their easy master. Let them take the wings of the morning and abide in the uttermost parts of the sea—I am there. Whither shall they go from my presence and whither shall they flee from my spirit? Courage, Dr. Quayle, and do not be downhearted; the real days of tyranny are only beginning on this earth."

And with that the Master laughed and swung away from them, almost as if his laugh was a bad thing for people to see.

"Might I speak to you a moment?" said Turnbull, stepping forward with a respectful resolution. But the shoulders of the Master only seemed to take on a new and unexpected angle of mockery as he strode away.

Turnbull swung round with great abruptness to the other two doctors, and said, harshly: "What in snakes does he mean—and who are you?"

"My name is Hutton," said the short, stout man, "and I am—well, one of those whose business it is to uphold this establishment."

"My name is Turnbull," said the other; "I am one of those whose business it is to tear it to the ground."

The small doctor smiled, and Turnbull's anger seemed suddenly to steady him.

"But I don't want to talk about that," he said, calmly; "I only want to know what the Master of this asylum really means."

Dr. Hutton's smile broke into a laugh which, short as it was, had the suspicion of a shake in it. "I suppose you think that quite a simple question," he said.

"I think it a plain question," said Turnbull, "and one that deserves a plain answer. Why did the Master lock us up in a couple of cupboards like jars of pickles for a mortal month, and why does he now let us walk free in the garden again?"

"I understand," said Hutton, with arched eyebrows, "that your complaint is that you are now free to walk in the garden."

"My complaint is," said Turnbull, stubbornly, "that if I am fit to walk freely now, I have been as fit for the last month. No one has examined me, no one has come near me. Your chief says that I am only free because he has made other arrangements. What are those arrangements?"

The young man with the round face looked down for a little while and smoked reflectively. The other and elder doctor had gone pacing nervously by himself upon the lawn. At length the round face was lifted again, and showed two round blue eyes with a certain frankness in them.

"Well, I don't see that it can do any harm to tell you know," he said. "You were shut up just then because it was just during that month that the Master was bringing off his big scheme. He was getting his bill through Parliament, and organizing the new medical police. But of course you haven't heard of all that; in fact, you weren't meant to."

"Heard of all what?" asked the impatient inquirer.

"There's a new law now, and the asylum powers are greatly extended. Even if you did escape now, any policeman would take you up in the next town if you couldn't show a certificate of sanity from us."

"Well," continued Dr. Hutton, "the Master described before both Houses of Parliament the real scientific objection to all existing legislation about lunacy. As he very truly said, the mistake was in supposing insanity to be merely an exception or an extreme. Insanity, like forgetfulness, is simply a quality which enters more or less into all human beings; and for practical purposes it is more necessary to know whose mind is really trustworthy than whose has some accidental taint. We have therefore reversed the existing method, and people now have to prove that they are sane. In the first village you entered, the village constable would notice that you were not wearing on the left lapel of your coat the small pewter S which is now necessary to any one who walks about beyond asylum bounds or outside asylum hours."

"You mean to say," said Turnbull, "that this was what the Master of the asylum urged before the House of Commons?"

Dr. Hutton nodded with gravity.

"And you mean to say," cried Turnbull, with a vibrant snort, "that that proposal was passed in an assembly that calls itself democratic?"

The doctor showed his whole row of teeth in a smile. "Oh, the assembly calls itself Socialist now," he said, "But we explained to them that this was a question for men of science."

Turnbull gave one stamp upon the gravel, then pulled himself together, and resumed: "But why should your infernal head medicine-man lock us up in separate cells while he was turning England into a madhouse? I'm not the Prime Minister; we're not the House of Lords."

"He wasn't afraid of the Prime Minister," replied Dr. Hutton; "he isn't afraid of the House of Lords. But——"

"Well?" inquired Turnbull, stamping again.

"He is afraid of you," said Hutton, simply. "Why, didn't you know?"

MacIan, who had not spoken yet, made one stride forward and stood with shaking limbs and shining eyes.

"He was afraid!" began Evan, thickly. "You mean to say that we——"

"I mean to say the plain truth now that the danger is over," said Hutton, calmly; "most certainly you two were the only people he ever was afraid of." Then he added in a low but not inaudible voice: "Except one—whom he feared worse, and has buried deeper."

"Come away," cried MacIan, "this has to be thought about."

Turnbull followed him in silence as he strode away, but just before he vanished, turned and spoke again to the doctors.

"But what has got hold of people?" he asked, abruptly. "Why should all England have gone dotty on the mere subject of dottiness?"

Dr. Hutton smiled his open smile once more and bowed slightly. "As to that also," he replied, "I don't want to make you vain."

Turnbull swung round without a word, and he and his companion were lost in the lustrous leafage of the garden. They noticed nothing special about the scene, except that the garden seemed more exquisite than ever in the deepening sunset, and that there seemed to be many more people, whether patients or attendants, walking about in it.

From behind the two black-coated doctors as they stood on the lawn another figure somewhat similarly dressed strode hurriedly past them, having also grizzled hair and an open flapping frock-coat. Both his decisive step and dapper black array marked him out as another medical man, or at least a man in authority, and as he passed Turnbull the latter was aroused by a strong impression of having seen the man somewhere before. It was no one that he knew well, yet he was certain that it was someone at whom he had at sometime or other looked steadily. It was neither the face of a friend nor of an enemy; it aroused neither irritation nor tenderness, yet it was a face which had for some reason been of great importance in his life. Turning and returning, and making detours about the garden, he managed to study the man's face again and again—a moustached, somewhat military face with a monocle, the sort of face that is aristocratic without being distinguished. Turnbull could not remember any particular doctors in his decidedly healthy existence. Was the man a long-lost uncle, or was he only somebody who had sat opposite him regularly in a railway train? At that moment the man knocked down his own eye-glass with a gesture of annoyance; Turnbull remembered the gesture, and the truth sprang up solid in front of him. The man with the moustaches was Cumberland Vane, the London police magistrate before whom he and MacIan had once stood on their trial. The magistrate must have been transferred to some other official duties—to something connected with the inspection of asylums.

Turnbull's heart gave a leap of excitement which was half hope. As a magistrate Mr. Cumberland Vane had been somewhat careless and shallow, but certainly kindly, and not inaccessible to common sense so long as it was put to him in strictly conventional language. He was at least an authority of a more human and refreshing sort than the crank with the wagging beard or the fiend with the forked chin.

He went straight up to the magistrate, and said: "Good evening, Mr. Vane; I doubt if you remember me."

Cumberland Vane screwed the eye-glass into his scowling face for an instant, and then said curtly but not uncivilly: "Yes, I remember you, sir; assault or battery, wasn't it? —a fellow broke your window. A tall fellow—McSomething—case made rather a noise afterwards."

"MacIan is the name, sir," said Turnbull, respectfully; "I have him here with me."

"Eh!" said Vane very sharply. "Confound him! Has he got anything to do with this game?"

"Mr. Vane," said Turnbull, pacifically, "I will not pretend that either he or I acted quite decorously on that occasion. You were very lenient with us, and did not treat us as criminals when you very well might. So I am sure you will give us your testimony that, even if we were criminals, we are not lunatics in any legal or medical sense whatever. I am sure you will use your influence for us."

"My influence!" repeated the magistrate, with a slight start. "I don't quite understand you."

"I don't know in what capacity you are here," continued Turnbull, gravely, "but a legal authority of your distinction must certainly be here in an important one. Whether you are visiting and inspecting the place, or attached to it as some kind of permanent legal adviser, your opinion must still——"

Cumberland Vane exploded with a detonation of oaths; his face was transfigured with fury and contempt, and yet in some odd way he did not seem specially angry with Turnbull.

"But Lord bless us and save us!" he gasped, at length; "I'm not here as an official at all. I'm here as a patient. The cursed pack of rat-catching chemists all say that I've lost my wits."

"You!" cried Turnbull with terrible emphasis. "You! Lost your wits!"

In the rush of his real astonishment at this towering unreality Turnbull almost added: "Why, you haven't got any to lose." But he fortunately remembered the remains of his desperate diplomacy.

"This can't go on," he said, positively. "Men like MacIan and I may suffer unjustly all our lives, but a man like you must have influence."

"There is only one man who has any influence in England now," said Vane, and his high voice fell to a sudden and convincing quietude.

"Whom do you mean?" asked Turnbull.

"I mean that cursed fellow with the long split chin," said the other.

"Is it really true," asked Turnbull, "that he has been allowed to buy up and control such a lot? What put the country into such a state?"

Mr. Cumberland Vane laughed outright. "What put the country into such a state?" he asked. "Why, you did. When you were fool enough to agree to fight MacIan, after all, everybody was ready to believe that the Bank of England might paint itself pink with white spots."

"I don't understand," answered Turnbull. "Why should you be surprised at my fighting? I hope I have always fought."

"Well," said Cumberland Vane, airily, "you didn't believe in religion, you see—so we thought you were safe at any rate. You went further in your language than most of us wanted to go; no good in just hurting one's mother's feelings, I think. But of course we all knew you were right, and, really, we relied on you."

"Did you?" said the editor of *The Atheist* with a bursting heart. "I am sorry you did not tell me so at the time."

He walked away very rapidly and flung himself on a garden seat, and for some six minutes his own wrongs hid from him the huge and hilarious fact that Cumberland Vane had been locked up as a lunatic.

The garden of the madhouse was so perfectly planned, and answered so exquisitely to every hour of daylight, that one could almost fancy that the sunlight was caught there tangled in its tinted trees, as the wise men of Gotham tried to chain the spring to a bush. Or it seemed as if this ironic paradise still kept its unique dawn or its special sunset while the rest of the earthly globe rolled through its ordinary hours. There was one evening, or late afternoon, in particular, which Evan MacIan will remember in the last moments of death. It was what artists call a daffodil sky, but it is coarsened even by reference to a daffodil. It was of that innocent lonely yellow which has never heard of orange, though it might turn quite unconsciously into green. Against it the tops, one might say the turrets, of the clipt and ordered trees were outlined in that shade of veiled violet which tints the tops of lavender. A white early moon was hardly traceable upon that delicate yellow. MacIan, I say, will remember this tender and transparent evening, partly because of its virgin gold and silver, and partly because he passed beneath it through the most horrible instant of his life.

Turnbull was sitting on his seat on the lawn, and the golden evening impressed even his positive nature, as indeed it might have impressed the oxen in a field. He was shocked out of his idle mood of awe by seeing MacIan break from behind the bushes and run across the lawn with an action he had never seen in the man before, with all his experience of the eccentric humours of this Celt. MacIan fell on the bench, shaking it so that it rattled, and gripped it with his knees like one in dreadful pain of body. That particular run and tumble is typical only of a man who has been hit by some sudden and incurable evil, who is bitten by a viper or condemned to be hanged. Turnbull looked up in the white face of his friend and enemy, and almost turned cold at what he saw there. He had seen the blue but gloomy eyes of the western Highlander troubled by as many tempests as his own west Highland seas, but there had always been a fixed star of faith behind the storms. Now the star had gone out, and there was only misery.

Yet MacIan had the strength to answer the question where Turnbull, taken by surprise, had not the strength to ask it.

"They are right, they are right!" he cried. "O my God! they are right, Turnbull. I ought to be here!"

He went on with shapeless fluency as if he no longer had the heart to choose or check his speech. "I suppose I ought to have guessed long ago—all my big dreams and schemes—and everyone being against us—but I was stuck up, you know."

"Do tell me about it, really," cried the atheist, and, faced with the furnace of the other's pain, he did not notice that he spoke with the affection of a father.

"I am mad, Turnbull," said Evan, with a dead clearness of speech, and leant back against the garden seat.

"Nonsense," said the other, clutching at the obvious cue of benevolent brutality, "this is one of your silly moods."

MacIan shook his head. "I know enough about myself," he said, "to allow for any mood, though it opened heaven or hell. But to see things—to see them walking solid in the sun—things that can't be there—real mystics never do that, Turnbull."

"What things?" asked the other, incredulously.

MacIan lowered his voice. "I saw *her*," he said, "three minutes ago—walking here in this hell yard."

Between trying to look scornful and really looking startled, Turnbull's face was confused enough to emit no speech, and Evan went on in monotonous sincerity:

"I saw her walk behind those blessed trees against that holy sky of gold as plain as I can see her whenever I shut my eyes. I did shut them, and opened them again, and she was still there—that is, of course, she wasn't—— She still had a little fur round her neck, but her dress was a shade brighter than when I really saw her."

"My dear fellow," cried Turnbull, rallying a hearty laugh, "the fancies have really got hold of you. You mistook some other poor girl here for her."

"Mistook some other——" said MacIan, and words failed him altogether.

They sat for some moments in the mellow silence of the evening garden, a silence that was stifling for the sceptic, but utterly empty and final for the man of faith. At last he broke out again with the words: "Well, anyhow, if I'm mad, I'm glad I'm mad on that."

Turnbull murmured some clumsy deprecation, and sat stolidly smoking to collect his thoughts; the next instant he had all his nerves engaged in the mere effort to sit still.

Across the clear space of cold silver and a pale lemon sky which was left by the gap in the ilex-trees there passed a slim, dark figure, a profile and the poise of a dark head like a bird's, which really pinned him to his seat with the point of coincidence. With an effort he got to his feet, and said with a voice of affected insouciance: "By George! MacIan, she is uncommonly like——"

"What!" cried MacIan, with a leap of eagerness that was heart-breaking, "do you see her, too?" And the blaze came back into the centre of his eyes.

Turnbull's tawny eyebrows were pulled together with a peculiar frown of curiosity, and all at once he walked quickly across the lawn. MacIan sat rigid, but peered after him with open and parched lips. He saw the sight which either proved him sane or proved the whole universe half-witted; he saw the man of flesh approach that beautiful phantom, saw their gestures of recognition, and saw them against the sunset joining hands.

He could stand it no longer, but ran across to the path, turned the corner and saw standing quite palpable in the evening sunlight, talking with a casual grace to Turnbull, the face and figure which had filled his midnights with frightfully vivid or desperately half-forgotten features. She advanced quite pleasantly and coolly, and put out her hand. The moment that he touched it he knew that he was sane even if the solar system was crazy.

She was entirely elegant and unembarrassed. That is the awful thing about women —they refuse to be emotional at emotional moments, upon some such ludicrous pretext as there being someone else there. But MacIan was in a condition of criticism much less than the average masculine one, being in fact merely overturned by the rushing riddle of the events.

Evan does not know to this day what particular question he asked, but he vividly remembers that she answered, and every line or fluctuation of her face as she said it.

"Oh, don't you know?" she said, smiling, and suddenly lifting her level brown eyebrows. "Haven't you heard the news? I'm a lunatic."

Then she added after a short pause, and with a sort of pride: "I've got a certificate."

Her manner, by the matchless social stoicism of her sex, was entirely suited to a drawing-room, but Evan's reply fell somewhat far short of such a standard, as he only said: "What the devil in hell does all this nonsense mean?"

"Really," said the young lady, and laughed.

"I beg your pardon," said the unhappy young man, rather wildly, "but what I mean is, why are you here in an asylum?"

The young woman broke again into one of the maddening and mysterious laughs of femininity. Then she composed her features, and replied with equal dignity: "Well, if it comes to that, why are you?"

The fact that Turnbull had strolled away and was investigating rhododendrons may have been due to Evan's successful prayers to the other world, or possibly to his own pretty successful experience of this one. But though they two were as isolated as a new Adam and Eve in a pretty ornamental Eden, the lady did not relax by an inch the rigour of her badinage.

"I am locked up in the madhouse," said Evan, with a sort of stiff pride, "because I tried to keep my promise to you."

"Quite so," answered the inexplicable lady, nodding with a perfectly blazing smile, "and I am locked up because it was to me you promised."

"It is outrageous!" cried Evan; "it is impossible!"

"Oh, you can see my certificate if you like," she replied with some hauteur.

MacIan stared at her and then at his boots, and then at the sky and then at her again. He was quite sure now that he himself was not mad, and the fact rather added to his perplexity.

Then he drew nearer to her, and said in a dry and dreadful voice: "Oh, don't condescend to play the fool with such a fool as me. Are you really locked up here as a patient—because you helped us to escape?"

"Yes," she said, still smiling, but her steady voice had a shake in it.

Evan flung his big elbow across his forehead and burst into tears.

The pure lemon of the sky faded into purer white as the great sunset silently collapsed. The birds settled back into the trees; the moon began to glow with its own light. Mr. James Turnbull continued his botanical researches into the structure of the rhododendron. But the lady did not move an inch until Evan had flung up his face again; and when he did he saw by the last gleam of sunlight that it was not only his face that was wet.

Mr. James Turnbull had all his life professed a profound interest in physical science, and the phenomena of a good garden were really a pleasure to him; but after three-quarters of an hour or so even the apostle of science began to find rhododendrus a bore, and was somewhat relieved when an unexpected development of events obliged him to transfer his researches to the equally interesting subject of hollyhocks, which grew some fifty feet farther along the path. The ostensible cause of his removal was the unexpected reappearance of his two other acquaintances walking and talking laboriously along the way, with the black head bent close to the brown one. Even hollyhocks detained Turnbull but a short time. Having rapidly absorbed all the important principles affecting the growth of those vegetables, he jumped over a flower-bed and walked back into the building. The other two came up along the slow course of the path talking and talking. No one but God knows what they said (for they certainly have forgotten), and if I remembered it I would not repeat it. When they parted at the head of the walk she put out her hand again in the same well-bred way, although it trembled; he seemed to restrain a gesture as he let it fall.

"If it is really always to be like this," he said, thickly, "it would not matter if we were here for ever."

"You tried to kill yourself four times for me," she said, unsteadily, "and I have been chained up as a madwoman for you. I really think that after that——"

"Yes, I know," said Evan in a low voice, looking down. "After that we belong to each other. We are sort of sold to each other—until the stars fall." Then he looked up suddenly, and said: "By the way, what is your name?"

"My name is Beatrice Drake," she replied with complete gravity. "You can see it on my certificate of lunacy."

XIX. THE LAST PARLEY

Turnbull walked away, wildly trying to explain to himself the presence of two personal acquaintances so different as Vane and the girl. As he skirted a low hedge of laurel, an enormously tall young man leapt over it, stood in front of him, and almost fell on his neck as if seeking to embrace him.

"Don't you know me?" almost sobbed the young man, who was in the highest spirits. "Ain't I written on your heart, old boy? I say, what did you do with my yacht?"

"Take your arms off my neck," said Turnbull, irritably. "Are you mad?"

The young man sat down on the gravel path and went into ecstasies of laughter. "No, that's just the fun of it—I'm not mad," he replied. "They've shut me up in this place, and I'm not mad." And he went off again into mirth as innocent as wedding-bells.

Turnbull, whose powers of surprise were exhausted, rolled his round grey eyes and said, "Mr. Wilkinson, I think," because he could not think of anything else to say.

The tall man sitting on the gravel bowed with urbanity, and said: "Quite at your service. Not to be confused with the Wilkinsons of Cumberland; and as I say, old boy, what have you done with my yacht? You see, they've locked me up here—in this garden —and a yacht would be a sort of occupation for an unmarried man."

"I am really horribly sorry," began Turnbull, in the last stage of bated bewilderment and exasperation, "but really——"

"Oh, I can see you can't have it on you at the moment," said Mr. Wilkinson with much intellectual magnanimity.

"Well, the fact is——" began Turnbull again, and then the phrase was frozen on his mouth, for round the corner came the goatlike face and gleaming eye-glasses of Dr. Quayle.

"Ah, my dear Mr. Wilkinson," said the doctor, as if delighted at a coincidence; "and Mr. Turnbull, too. Why, I want to speak to Mr. Turnbull."

Mr. Turnbull made some movement rather of surrender than assent, and the doctor caught it up exquisitely, showing even more of his two front teeth. "I am sure Mr. Wilkinson will excuse us a moment." And with flying frock-coat he led Turnbull rapidly round the corner of a path.

"My dear sir," he said, in a quite affectionate manner, "I do not mind telling you— you are such a very hopeful case—you understand so well the scientific point of view; and I don't like to see you bothered by the really hopeless cases. They are monotonous and maddening. The man you have just been talking to, poor fellow, is one of the strongest cases of pure *idee fixe* that we have. It's very sad, and I'm afraid utterly incurable. He keeps on telling everybody"—and the doctor lowered his voice confidentially—"he tells everybody that two people have taken is yacht. His account of how he lost it is quite incoherent."

Turnbull stamped his foot on the gravel path, and called out: "Oh, I can't stand this. Really——"

"I know, I know," said the psychologist, mournfully; "it is a most melancholy case, and also fortunately a very rare one. It is so rare, in fact, that in one classification of these maladies it is entered under a heading by itself—Perdinavititis, mental inflammation creating the impression that one has lost a ship. Really," he added, with a kind of half-embarrassed guilt, "it's rather a feather in my cap. I discovered the only existing case of perdinavititis."

"But this won't do, doctor," said Turnbull, almost tearing his hair, "this really won't do. The man really did lose a ship. Indeed, not to put too fine a point on it, I took his ship."

Dr. Quayle swung round for an instant so that his silk-lined overcoat rustled, and stared singularly at Turnbull. Then he said with hurried amiability: "Why, of course you did. Quite so, quite so," and with courteous gestures went striding up the garden path. Under the first laburnum-tree he stopped, however, and pulling out his pencil and notebook wrote down feverishly: "Singular development in the Elenthero-maniac, Turnbull. Sudden manifestation of Rapinavititis—the delusion that one has stolen a ship. First case ever recorded."

Turnbull stood for an instant staggered into stillness. Then he ran raging round the garden to find MacIan, just as a husband, even a bad husband, will run raging to find his wife if he is full of a furious query. He found MacIan stalking moodily about the half-lit garden, after his extraordinary meeting with Beatrice. No one who saw his slouching stride and sunken head could have known that his soul was in the seventh heaven of ecstasy. He did not think; he did not even very definitely desire. He merely wallowed in memories, chiefly in material memories; words said with a certain cadence or trivial turns of the neck or wrist. Into the middle of his stationary and senseless enjoyment were thrust abruptly the projecting elbow and the projecting red beard of Turnbull. MacIan stepped back a little, and the soul in his eyes came very slowly to its windows. When James Turnbull had the glittering sword-point planted upon his breast he was in far less danger. For three pulsating seconds after the interruption MacIan was in a mood to have murdered his father.

And yet his whole emotional anger fell from him when he saw Turnbull's face, in which the eyes seemed to be bursting from the head like bullets. All the fire and fragrance even of young and honourable love faded for a moment before that stiff agony of interrogation.

"Are you hurt, Turnbull?" he asked, anxiously.

"I am dying," answered the other quite calmly. "I am in the quite literal sense of the words dying to know something. I want to know what all this can possibly mean."

MacIan did not answer, and he continued with asperity: "You are still thinking about that girl, but I tell you the whole thing is incredible. She's not the only person here. I've met the fellow Wilkinson, whose yacht we lost. I've met the very magistrate you were hauled up to when you broke my window. What can it mean—meeting all these old people again? One never meets such old friends again except in a dream."

Then after a silence he cried with a rending sincerity: "Are you really there, Evan? Have you ever been really there? Am I simply dreaming?"

MacIan had been listening with a living silence to every word, and now his face flamed with one of his rare revelations of life.

"No, you good atheist," he cried; "no, you clean, courteous, reverent, pious old blasphemer. No, you are not dreaming—you are waking up."

"What do you mean?"

"There are two states where one meets so many old friends," said MacIan; "one is a dream, the other is the end of the world."

"And you say——"

"I say this is not a dream," said Evan in a ringing voice.

"You really mean to suggest——" began Turnbull.

"Be silent! or I shall say it all wrong," said MacIan, breathing hard. "It's hard to explain, anyhow. An apocalypse is the opposite of a dream. A dream is falser than the outer life. But the end of the world is more actual than the world it ends. I don't say this is really the end of the world, but it's something like that—it's the end of something. All the people are crowding into one corner. Everything is coming to a point."

"What is the point?" asked Turnbull.

"I can't see it," said Evan; "it is too large and plain."

Then after a silence he said: "I can't see it—and yet I will try to describe it. Turnbull, three days ago I saw quite suddenly that our duel was not right after all."

"Three days ago!" repeated Turnbull. "When and why did this illumination occur?"

"I knew I was not quite right," answered Evan, "the moment I saw the round eyes of that old man in the cell."

"Old man in the cell!" repeated his wondering companion. "Do you mean the poor old idiot who likes spikes to stick out?"

"Yes," said MacIan, after a slight pause, "I mean the poor old idiot who likes spikes to stick out. When I saw his eyes and heard his old croaking accent, I knew that it would not really have been right to kill you. It would have been a venial sin."

"I am much obliged," said Turnbull, gruffly.

"You must give me time," said MacIan, quite patiently, "for I am trying to tell the whole truth. I am trying to tell more of it than I know."

"So you see I confess"—he went on with laborious distinctness—"I confess that all the people who called our duel mad were right in a way. I would confess it to old Cumberland Vane and his eye-glass. I would confess it even to that old ass in brown flannel who talked to us about Love. Yes, they are right in a way. I am a little mad."

He stopped and wiped his brow as if he were literally doing heavy labour. Then he went on:

"I am a little mad; but, after all, it is only a little madness. When hundreds of high-minded men had fought duels about a jostle with the elbow or the ace of spades, the whole world need not have gone wild over my one little wildness. Plenty of other people have killed themselves between then and now. But all England has gone into captivity in order to take us captive. All England has turned into a lunatic asylum in order to prove us lunatics. Compared with the general public, I might positively be called sane."

He stopped again, and went on with the same air of travailing with the truth:

"When I saw that, I saw everything; I saw the Church and the world. The Church in its earthly action has really touched morbid things—tortures and bleeding visions and blasts of extermination. The Church has had her madnesses, and I am one of them. I am the massacre of St. Bartholomew. I am the Inquisition of Spain. I do not say that we have never gone mad, but I say that we are fit to act as keepers to our enemies. Massacre is wicked even with a provocation, as in the Bartholomew. But your modern Nietzsche will tell you that massacre would be glorious without a provocation. Torture should be violently stopped, though the Church is doing it. But your modern Tolstoy will tell you that it ought not to be violently stopped whoever is doing it. In the long run, which is most mad—the Church or the world? Which is madder, the Spanish priest who permitted tyranny, or the Prussian sophist who admired it? Which is madder, the Russian priest who discourages righteous rebellion, or the Russian novelist who forbids it? That is the final and blasting test. The world left to itself grows wilder than any creed. A few days ago you and I were the maddest people in England. Now, by God! I believe we are the sanest. That is the only real question—whether the Church is really madder than the world. Let the rationalists run their own race, and let us see where *they* end. If the world has some healthy balance other than God, let the world find it. Does the world find it? Cut the world loose," he cried with a savage gesture. "Does the world stand on its own end? Does it stand, or does it stagger?"

Turnbull remained silent, and MacIan said to him, looking once more at the earth: "It staggers, Turnbull. It cannot stand by itself; you know it cannot. It has been the sorrow of your life. Turnbull, this garden is not a dream, but an apocalyptic fulfilment. This garden is the world gone mad."

Turnbull did not move his head, and he had been listening all the time; yet, somehow, the other knew that for the first time he was listening seriously.

"The world has gone mad," said MacIan, "and it has gone mad about Us. The world takes the trouble to make a big mistake about every little mistake made by the Church. That is why they have turned ten counties to a madhouse; that is why crowds of kindly people are poured into this filthy melting-pot. Now is the judgement of this world. The Prince of this World is judged, and he is judged exactly because he is judging. There is at last one simple solution to the quarrel between the ball and the cross——"

Turnbull for the first time started.

"The ball and——" he repeated.

"What is the matter with you?" asked MacIan.

"I had a dream," said Turnbull, thickly and obscurely, "in which I saw the cross struck crooked and the ball secure——"

"I had a dream," said MacIan, "in which I saw the cross erect and the ball invisible. They were both dreams from hell. There must be some round earth to plant the cross upon. But here is the awful difference—that the round world will not consent even to continue round. The astronomers are always telling us that it is shaped like an orange, or like an egg, or like a German sausage. They beat the old world about like a bladder and thump it into a thousand shapeless shapes. Turnbull, we cannot trust the ball to be always a ball; we cannot trust reason to be reasonable. In the end the great terrestrial globe will go quite lop-sided, and only the cross will stand upright."

There was a long silence, and then Turnbull said, hesitatingly: "Has it occurred to you that since—since those two dreams, or whatever they were——"

"Well?" murmured MacIan.

"Since then," went on Turnbull, in the same low voice, "since then we have never even looked for our swords."

"You are right," answered Evan almost inaudibly. "We have found something which we both hate more than we ever hated each other, and I think I know its name."

Turnbull seemed to frown and flinch for a moment. "It does not much matter what you call it," he said, "so long as you keep out of its way."

The bushes broke and snapped abruptly behind them, and a very tall figure towered above Turnbull with an arrogant stoop and a projecting chin, a chin of which the shape showed queerly even in its shadow upon the path.

"You see that is not so easy," said MacIan between his teeth.

They looked up into the eyes of the Master, but looked only for a moment. The eyes were full of a frozen and icy wrath, a kind of utterly heartless hatred. His voice was for the first time devoid of irony. There was no more sarcasm in it than there is in an iron club.

"You will be inside the building in three minutes," he said, with pulverizing precision, "or you will be fired on by the artillery at all the windows. There is too much talking in this garden; we intend to close it. You will be accommodated indoors."

"Ah!" said MacIan, with a long and satisfied sigh, "then I was right."

And he turned his back and walked obediently towards the building. Turnbull seemed to canvass for a few minutes the notion of knocking the Master down, and then fell under the same almost fairy fatalism as his companion. In some strange way it did seem that the more smoothly they yielded, the more swiftly would events sweep on to some great collision.

XX. DIES IRAE

As they advanced towards the asylum they looked up at its rows on rows of windows, and understood the Master's material threat. By means of that complex but concealed machinery which ran like a network of nerves over the whole fabric, there had been shot out under every window-ledge rows and rows of polished-steel cylinders, the cold miracles of modern gunnery. They commanded the whole garden and the whole country-side, and could have blown to pieces an army corps.

This silent declaration of war had evidently had its complete effect. As MacIan and Turnbull walked steadily but slowly towards the entrance hall of the institution, they could see that most, or at least many, of the patients had already gathered there as well as the staff of doctors and the whole regiment of keepers and assistants. But when they entered the lamp-lit hall, and the high iron door was clashed to and locked behind them, yet a new amazement leapt into their eyes, and the stalwart Turnbull almost fell. For he saw a sight which was indeed, as MacIan had said—either the Day of Judgement or a dream.

Within a few feet of him at one corner of the square of standing people stood the girl he had known in Jersey, Madeleine Durand. She looked straight at him with a steady smile which lit up the scene of darkness and unreason like the light of some honest fireside. Her square face and throat were thrown back, as her habit was, and there was something almost sleepy in the geniality of her eyes. He saw her first, and for a few seconds saw her only; then the outer edge of his eyesight took in all the other staring faces, and he saw all the faces he had ever seen for weeks and months past. There was the Tolstoyan in Jaeger flannel, with the yellow beard that went backward and the foolish nose and eyes that went forward, with the curiosity of a crank. He was talking eagerly to Mr. Gordon, the corpulent Jew shopkeeper whom they had once gagged in his own shop. There was the tipsy old Hertfordshire rustic; he was talking energetically to himself. There was not only Mr. Vane the magistrate, but the clerk of Mr. Vane, the magistrate. There was not only Miss Drake of the motor-car, but also Miss Drake's chauffeur. Nothing wild or unfamiliar could have produced upon Turnbull such a nightmare impression as that ring of familiar faces. Yet he had one intellectual shock which was greater than all the others. He stepped impulsively forward towards Madeleine, and then wavered with a kind of wild humility. As he did so he caught sight of another square face behind Madeleine's, a face with long grey whiskers and an austere stare. It was old Durand, the girls' father; and when Turnbull saw him he saw the last and worst marvel of that monstrous night. He remembered Durand; he remembered his monotonous, everlasting lucidity, his stupefyingly sensible views of everything, his colossal contentment with truisms merely because they were true. "Confound it all!" cried Turnbull to himself, "if *he* is in the asylum, there can't be anyone outside." He drew nearer to Madeleine, but still doubtfully and all the more so because she still smiled at him. MacIan had already gone across to Beatrice with an air of fright.

Then all these bewildered but partly amicable recognitions were cloven by a cruel voice which always made all human blood turn bitter. The Master was standing in the middle of the room surveying the scene like a great artist looking at a completed picture. Handsome as he looked, they had never seen so clearly what was really hateful in his face; and even then they could only express it by saying that the arched brows and the long emphatic chin gave it always a look of being lit from below, like the face of some infernal actor.

"This is indeed a cosy party," he said, with glittering eyes.

The Master evidently meant to say more, but before he could say anything M. Durand had stepped right up to him and was speaking.

He was speaking exactly as a French bourgeois speaks to the manager of a restaurant. That is, he spoke with rattling and breathless rapidity, but with no incoherence, and therefore with no emotion. It was a steady, monotonous vivacity, which came not seemingly from passion, but merely from the reason having been sent off at a gallop. He was saying something like this:

"You refuse me my half-bottle of Medoc, the drink the most wholesome and the most customary. You refuse me the company and obedience of my daughter, which Nature herself indicates. You refuse me the beef and mutton, without pretence that it is a fast of the Church. You now forbid me the promenade, a thing necessary to a person of my age. It is useless to tell me that you do all this by law. Law rests upon the social contract. If the citizen finds himself despoiled of such pleasures and powers as he would have had even in the savage state, the social contract is annulled."

"It's no good chattering away, Monsieur," said Hutton, for the Master was silent. "The place is covered with machine-guns. We've got to obey our orders, and so have you."

"The machinery is of the most perfect," assented Durand, somewhat irrelevantly;

"worked by petroleum, I believe. I only ask you to admit that if such things fall below the comfort of barbarism, the social contract is annulled. It is a pretty little point of theory."

"Oh! I dare say," said Hutton.

Durand bowed quite civilly and withdrew.

"A cosy party," resumed the Master, scornfully, "and yet I believe some of you are in doubt about how we all came together. I will explain it, ladies and gentlemen; I will explain everything. To whom shall I specially address myself? To Mr. James Turnbull. He has a scientific mind."

Turnbull seemed to choke with sudden protest. The Master seemed only to cough out of pure politeness and proceeded: "Mr. Turnbull will agree with me," he said, "when I say that we long felt in scientific circles that great harm was done by such a legend as that of the Crucifixion."

Turnbull growled something which was presumably assent.

The Master went on smoothly: "It was in vain for us to urge that the incident was irrelevant; that there were many such fanatics, many such executions. We were forced to take the thing thoroughly in hand, to investigate it in the spirit of scientific history, and with the assistance of Mr. Turnbull and others we were happy in being able to announce that this alleged Crucifixion never occurred at all."

MacIan lifted his head and looked at the Master steadily, but Turnbull did not look up.

"This, we found, was the only way with all superstitions," continued the speaker; "it was necessary to deny them historically, and we have done it with great success in the case of miracles and such things. Now within our own time there arose an unfortunate fuss which threatened (as Mr. Turnbull would say) to galvanize the corpse of Christianity into a fictitious life—the alleged case of a Highland eccentric who wanted to fight for the Virgin."

MacIan, quite white, made a step forward, but the speaker did not alter his easy attitude or his flow of words. "Again we urged that this duel was not to be admired, that it was a mere brawl, but the people were ignorant and romantic. There were signs of treating this alleged Highlander and his alleged opponent as heroes. We tried all other means of arresting this reactionary hero worship. Working men who betted on the duel were imprisoned for gambling. Working men who drank the health of a duellist were imprisoned for drunkenness. But the popular excitement about the alleged duel continued, and we had to fall back on our old historical method. We investigated, on scientific principles, the story of MacIan's challenge, and we are happy to be able to inform you that the whole story of the attempted duel is a fable. There never was any challenge. There never was any man named MacIan. It is a melodramatic myth, like Calvary."

Not a soul moved save Turnbull, who lifted his head; yet there was the sense of a silent explosion.

"The whole story of the MacIan challenge," went on the Master, beaming at them all with a sinister benignity, "has been found to originate in the obsessions of a few pathological types, who are now all fortunately in our care. There is, for instance, a person here of the name of Gordon, formerly the keeper of a curiosity shop. He is a victim of the disease called Vinculomania—the impression that one has been bound or tied up. We have also a case of Fugacity (Mr. Whimpey), who imagines that he was chased by two men."

The indignant faces of the Jew shopkeeper and the Magdalen Don started out of the crowd in their indignation, but the speaker continued:

"One poor woman we have with us," he said, in a compassionate voice, "believes she was in a motor-car with two such men; this is the well-known illusion of speed on which I need not dwell. Another wretched woman has the simple egotistic mania that she has caused the duel. Madeleine Durand actually professes to have been the subject of the fight between MacIan and his enemy, a fight which, if it occurred at all, certainly began long before. But it never occurred at all. We have taken in hand every person who professed to have seen such a thing, and proved them all to be unbalanced. That is why they are here."

The Master looked round the room, just showing his perfect teeth with the perfection of artistic cruelty, exalted for a moment in the enormous simplicity of his success, and then walked across the hall and vanished through an inner door. His two lieutenants, Quayle and Hutton, were left standing at the head of the great army of servants and keepers.

"I hope we shall have no more trouble," said Dr. Quayle pleasantly enough, and addressing Turnbull, who was leaning heavily upon the back of a chair.

Still looking down, Turnbull lifted the chair an inch or two from the ground. Then he suddenly swung it above his head and sent it at the inquiring doctor with an awful crash which sent one of its wooden legs loose along the floor and crammed the doctor gasping into a corner. MacIan gave a great shout, snatched up the loose chair-leg, and, rushing on the other doctor, felled him with a blow. Twenty attendants rushed to capture the rebels; MacIan flung back three of them and Turnbull went over on top of one, when from behind them all came a shriek as of something quite fresh and frightful.

Two of the three passages leading out of the hall were choked with blue smoke. Another instant and the hall was full of the fog of it, and red sparks began to swarm like scarlet bees.

"The place is on fire!" cried Quayle with a scream of indecent terror. "Oh, who can have done it? How can it have happened?"

A light had come into Turnbull's eyes. "How did the French Revolution happen?" he asked.

"Oh, how should I know!" wailed the other.

"Then I will tell you," said Turnbull; "it happened because some people fancied that a French grocer was as respectable as he looked."

Even as he spoke, as if by confirmation, old Mr. Durand re-entered the smoky room quite placidly, wiping the petroleum from his hands with a handkerchief. He had set fire to the building in accordance with the strict principles of the social contract.

But MacIan had taken a stride forward and stood there shaken and terrible. "Now," he cried, panting, "now is the judgement of the world. The doctors will leave this place; the keepers will leave this place. They will leave us in charge of the machinery and the machine-guns at the windows. But we, the lunatics, will wait to be burned alive if only we may see them go."

"How do you know we shall go?" asked Hutton, fiercely.

"You believe nothing," said MacIan, simply, "and you are insupportably afraid of death."

"So this is suicide," sneered the doctor; "a somewhat doubtful sign of sanity."

"Not at all—this is vengeance," answered Turnbull, quite calmly; "a thing which is completely healthy."

"You think the doctors will go," said Hutton, savagely.

"The keepers have gone already," said Turnbull.

Even as they spoke the main doors were burst open in mere brutal panic, and all the officers and subordinates of the asylum rushed away across the garden pursued by the smoke. But among the ticketed maniacs not a man or woman moved.

"We hate dying," said Turnbull, with composure, "but we hate you even more. This is a successful revolution."

In the roof above their heads a panel shot back, showing a strip of star-lit sky and a huge thing made of white metal, with the shape and fins of a fish, swinging as if at anchor. At the same moment a steel ladder slid down from the opening and struck the floor, and the cleft chin of the mysterious Master was thrust into the opening. "Quayle, Hutton," he said, "you will escape with me." And they went up the ladder like automata of lead.

Long after they had clambered into the car, the creature with the cloven face continued to leer down upon the smoke-stung crowd below. Then at last he said in a silken voice and with a smile of final satisfaction:

"By the way, I fear I am very absent minded. There is one man specially whom, somehow, I always forget. I always leave him lying about. Once I mislaid him on the Cross of St. Paul's. So silly of me; and now I've forgotten him in one of those little cells where your fire is burning. Very unfortunate—especially for him." And nodding genially, he climbed into his flying ship.

MacIan stood motionless for two minutes, and then rushed down one of the suffocating corridors till he found the flames. Turnbull looked once at Madeleine, and followed.

⁂

MacIan, with singed hair, smoking garments, and smarting hands and face, had already broken far enough through the first barriers of burning timber to come within cry of the cells he had once known. It was impossible, however, to see the spot where the old man lay dead or alive; not now through darkness, but through scorching and aching light. The site of the old half-wit's cell was now the heart of a standing forest of fire—the flames as thick and yellow as a cornfield. Their incessant shrieking and crackling was like a mob shouting against an orator. Yet through all that deafening density MacIan thought he heard a small and separate sound. When he heard it he rushed forward as if to plunge into that furnace, but Turnbull arrested him by an elbow.

"Let me go!" cried Evan, in agony; "it's the poor old beggar's voice—he's still alive, and shouting for help."

"Listen!" said Turnbull, and lifted one finger from his clenched hand.

"Or else he is shrieking with pain," protested MacIan. "I will not endure it."

"Listen!" repeated Turnbull, grimly. "Did you ever hear anyone shout for help or shriek with pain in that voice?"

The small shrill sounds which came through the crash of the conflagration were indeed of an odd sort, and MacIan turned a face of puzzled inquiry to his companion.

"He is singing," said Turnbull, simply.

A remaining rampart fell, crushing the fire, and through the diminished din of it the voice of the little old lunatic came clearer. In the heart of that white-hot hell he was singing like a bird. What he was singing it was not very easy to follow, but it seemed to be something about playing in the golden hay.

"Good Lord!" cried Turnbull, bitterly, "there seem to be some advantages in really being an idiot." Then advancing to the fringe of the fire he called out on chance to the invisible singer: "Can you come out? Are you cut off?"

"God help us all!" said MacIan, with a shudder; "he's laughing now."

At whatever stage of being burned alive the invisible now found himself, he was now shaking out peals of silvery and hilarious laughter. As he listened, MacIan's two eyes began to glow, as if a strange thought had come into his head.

"Fool, come out and save yourself!" shouted Turnbull.

"No, by Heaven! that is not the way," cried Evan, suddenly. "Father," he shouted, "come out and save us all!"

The fire, though it had dropped in one or two places, was, upon the whole, higher and more unconquerable than ever. Separate tall flames shot up and spread out above them like the fiery cloisters of some infernal cathedral, or like a grove of red tropical trees in the garden of the devil. Higher yet in the purple hollow of the night the topmost flames leapt again and again fruitlessly at the stars, like golden dragons chained but struggling. The towers and domes of the oppressive smoke seemed high and far enough to drown distant planets in a London fog. But if we exhausted all frantic similes for that frantic scene, the main impression about the fire would still be its ranked upstanding rigidity and a sort of roaring stillness. It was literally a wall of fire.

"Father," cried MacIan, once more, "come out of it and save us all!" Turnbull was staring at him as he cried.

The tall and steady forest of fire must have been already a portent visible to the whole circle of land and sea. The red flush of it lit up the long sides of white ships far out in the German Ocean, and picked out like piercing rubies the windows in the villages on the distant heights. If any villagers or sailors were looking towards it they must have seen a strange sight as MacIan cried out for the third time.

That forest of fire wavered, and was cloven in the centre; and then the whole of one half of it leaned one way as a cornfield leans all one way under the load of the wind. Indeed, it looked as if a great wind had sprung up and driven the great fire aslant. Its smoke was no longer sent up to choke the stars, but was trailed and dragged across county after county like one dreadful banner of defeat.

But it was not the wind; or, if it was the wind, it was two winds blowing in opposite directions. For while one half of the huge fire sloped one way towards the inland heights, the other half, at exactly the same angle, sloped out eastward towards the sea. So that earth and ocean could behold, where there had been a mere fiery mass, a thing divided like a V—a cloven tongue of flame. But if it were a prodigy for those distant, it was something beyond speech for those quite near. As the echoes of Evan's last appeal rang and died in the universal uproar, the fiery vault over his head opened down the middle, and, reeling back in two great golden billows, hung on each side as huge and harmless as two sloping hills lie on each side of a valley. Down the centre of this trough, or chasm, a little path ran, cleared of all but ashes, and down this little path was walking a little old man singing as if he were alone in a wood in spring.

When James Turnbull saw this he suddenly put out a hand and seemed to support himself on the strong shoulder of Madeleine Durand. Then after a moment's hesitation he put his other hand on the shoulder of MacIan. His blue eyes looked extraordinarily brilliant and beautiful. In many sceptical papers and magazines afterwards he was sadly or sternly rebuked for having abandoned the certainties of materialism. All his life up to that moment he had been most honestly certain that materialism was a fact. But he was unlike the writers in the magazines precisely in this—that he preferred a fact even to materialism.

As the little singing figure came nearer and nearer, Evan fell on his knees, and after an instant Beatrice followed; then Madeleine fell on her knees, and after a longer instant Turnbull followed. Then the little old man went past them singing down that corridor of flames. They had not looked at his face.

When he had passed they looked up. While the first light of the fire had shot east and west, painting the sides of ships with fire-light or striking red sparks out of windowed houses, it had not hitherto struck upward, for there was above it the ponderous and rococo cavern of its own monstrous coloured smoke. But now the fire was turned to left and right like a woman's hair parted in the middle, and now the shafts of its light could shoot up into empty heavens and strike anything, either bird or cloud. But it struck something that was neither cloud nor bird. Far, far away up in those huge hollows of space something was flying swiftly and shining brightly, something that shone too bright and flew too fast to be any of the fowls of the air, though the red light lit it from underneath like the breast of a bird. Everyone knew it was a flying ship, and everyone knew whose.

As they stared upward the little speck of light seemed slightly tilted, and two black dots dropped from the edge of it. All the eager, upturned faces watched the two dots as they grew bigger and bigger in their downward rush. Then someone screamed, and no one looked up any more. For the two bodies, larger every second flying, spread out and sprawling in the fire-light, were the dead bodies of the two doctors whom Professor Lucifer had carried with him—the weak and sneering Quayle, the cold and clumsy Hutton. They went with a crash into the thick of the fire.

"They are gone!" screamed Beatrice, hiding her head. "O God! They are lost!"

Evan put his arm about her, and remembered his own vision.

"No, they are not lost," he said. "They are saved. He has taken away no souls with him, after all."

He looked vaguely about at the fire that was already fading, and there among the ashes lay two shining things that had survived the fire, his sword and Turnbull's, fallen haphazard in the pattern of a cross.

MANALIVE

I

THE ENIGMAS OF INNOCENT SMITH

1. HOW THE GREAT WIND CAME TO BEACON HOUSE

A wind sprang high in the west, like a wave of unreasonable happiness, and tore eastward across England, trailing with it the frosty scent of forests and the cold intoxication of the sea. In a million holes and corners it refreshed a man like a flagon, and astonished him like a blow. In the inmost chambers of intricate and embowered houses it woke like a domestic explosion, littering the floor with some professor's papers till they seemed as precious as fugitive, or blowing out the candle by which a boy read "Treasure Island" and wrapping him in roaring dark. But everywhere it bore drama into undramatic lives, and carried the trump of crisis across the world. Many a harassed mother in a mean backyard had looked at five dwarfish shirts on the clothes-line as at some small, sick tragedy; it was as if she had hanged her five children. The wind came, and they were full and kicking as if five fat imps had sprung into them; and far down in her oppressed subconscious she half-remembered those coarse comedies of her fathers when the elves still dwelt in the homes of men. Many an unnoticed girl in a dank walled garden had tossed herself into the hammock with the same intolerant gesture with which she might have tossed herself into the Thames; and that wind rent the waving wall of woods and lifted the hammock like a balloon, and showed her shapes of quaint clouds far beyond, and pictures of bright villages far below, as if she rode heaven in a fairy boat. Many a dusty clerk or cleric, plodding a telescopic road of poplars, thought for the hundredth time that they were like the plumes of a hearse; when this invisible energy caught and swung and clashed them round his head like a wreath or salutation of seraphic wings. There was in it something more inspired and authoritative even than the old wind of the proverb; for this was the good wind that blows nobody harm.

The flying blast struck London just where it scales the northern heights, terrace above terrace, as precipitous as Edinburgh. It was round about this place that some

339

poet, probably drunk, looked up astonished at all those streets gone skywards, and (thinking vaguely of glaciers and roped mountaineers) gave it the name of Swiss Cottage, which it has never been able to shake off. At some stage of those heights a terrace of tall gray houses, mostly empty and almost as desolate as the Grampians, curved round at the western end, so that the last building, a boarding establishment called "Beacon House," offered abruptly to the sunset its high, narrow and towering termination, like the prow of some deserted ship.

The ship, however, was not wholly deserted. The proprietor of the boarding-house, a Mrs. Duke, was one of those helpless persons against whom fate wars in vain; she smiled vaguely both before and after all her calamities; she was too soft to be hurt. But by the aid (or rather under the orders) of a strenuous niece she always kept the remains of a clientele, mostly of young but listless folks. And there were actually five inmates standing disconsolately about the garden when the great gale broke at the base of the terminal tower behind them, as the sea bursts against the base of an outstanding cliff.

All day that hill of houses over London had been domed and sealed up with cold cloud. Yet three men and two girls had at last found even the gray and chilly garden more tolerable than the black and cheerless interior. When the wind came it split the sky and shouldered the cloudland left and right, unbarring great clear furnaces of evening gold. The burst of light released and the burst of air blowing seemed to come almost simultaneously; and the wind especially caught everything in a throttling violence. The bright short grass lay all one way like brushed hair. Every shrub in the garden tugged at its roots like a dog at the collar, and strained every leaping leaf after the hunting and exterminating element. Now and again a twig would snap and fly like a bolt from an arbalist. The three men stood stiffly and aslant against the wind, as if leaning against a wall. The two ladies disappeared into the house; rather, to speak truly, they were blown into the house. Their two frocks, blue and white, looked like two big broken flowers, driving and drifting upon the gale. Nor is such a poetic fancy inappropriate, for there was something oddly romantic about this inrush of air and light after a long, leaden and unlifting day. Grass and garden trees seemed glittering with something at once good and unnatural, like a fire from fairyland. It seemed like a strange sunrise at the wrong end of the day.

The girl in white dived in quickly enough, for she wore a white hat of the proportions of a parachute, which might have wafted her away into the coloured clouds of evening. She was their one splash of splendour, and irradiated wealth in that impecunious place (staying there temporarily with a friend), an heiress in a small way, by name Rosamund Hunt, brown-eyed, round-faced, but resolute and rather boisterous. On top of her wealth she was good-humoured and rather good-looking; but she had not married, perhaps because there was always a crowd of men around her. She was not fast (though some might have called her vulgar), but she gave irresolute youths an impression of being at once popular and inaccessible. A man felt as if he had fallen in love with Cleopatra, or as if he were asking for a great actress at the stage door. Indeed, some theatrical spangles seemed to cling about Miss Hunt; she played the guitar and the mandoline; she always wanted charades; and with that great rending of the sky by sun and storm, she felt a girlish melodrama swell again within her. To the crashing orchestration of the air the clouds rose like the curtain of some long-expected pantomime.

Nor, oddly, was the girl in blue entirely unimpressed by this apocalypse in a private garden; though she was one of most prosaic and practical creatures alive. She was, indeed, no other than the strenuous niece whose strength alone upheld that mansion of decay. But as the gale swung and swelled the blue and white skirts till they took on the monstrous contours of Victorian crinolines, a sunken memory stirred in her that was almost romance—a memory of a dusty volume of *Punch* in an aunt's house in infancy: pictures of crinoline hoops and croquet hoops and some pretty story, of which perhaps they were a part. This half-perceptible fragrance in her thoughts faded almost instantly, and Diana Duke entered the house even more promptly than her companion. Tall, slim, aquiline, and dark, she seemed made for such swiftness. In body she was of the breed of those birds and beasts that are at once long and alert, like greyhounds or herons or even like an innocent snake. The whole house revolved on her as on a rod of steel. It would be wrong to say that she commanded; for her own efficiency was so impatient that she obeyed herself before any one else obeyed her. Before electricians could mend a bell or locksmiths open a door, before dentists could pluck a tooth or butlers draw a tight cork, it was done already with the silent violence of her slim hands. She was light; but there was nothing leaping about her lightness. She spurned the ground, and she meant to spurn it. People talk of the pathos and failure of plain women; but it is a more terrible thing that a beautiful woman may succeed in everything but womanhood.

"It's enough to blow your head off," said the young woman in white, going to the looking-glass.

The young woman in blue made no reply, but put away her gardening gloves, and then went to the sideboard and began to spread out an afternoon cloth for tea.

"Enough to blow your head off, I say," said Miss Rosamund Hunt, with the unruffled cheeriness of one whose songs and speeches had always been safe for an encore.

"Only your hat, I think," said Diana Duke, "but I dare say that is sometimes more important."

Rosamund's face showed for an instant the offence of a spoilt child, and then the humour of a very healthy person. She broke into a laugh and said, "Well, it would have to be a big wind to blow your head off."

There was another silence; and the sunset breaking more and more from the sundering clouds, filled the room with soft fire and painted the dull walls with ruby and gold.

"Somebody once told me," said Rosamund Hunt, "that it's easier to keep one's head when one has lost one's heart."

"Oh, don't talk such rubbish," said Diana with savage sharpness.

Outside, the garden was clad in a golden splendour; but the wind was still stiffly blowing, and the three men who stood their ground might also have considered the problem of hats and heads. And, indeed, their position, touching hats, was somewhat typical of them. The tallest of the three abode the blast in a high silk hat, which the wind seemed to charge as vainly as that other sullen tower, the house behind him. The second man tried to hold on a stiff straw hat at all angles, and ultimately held it in his hand. The third had no hat, and, by his attitude, seemed never to have had one in his life. Perhaps this wind was a kind of fairy wand to test men and women, for there was much of the three men in this difference.

The man in the solid silk hat was the embodiment of silkiness and solidity. He was a big, bland, bored and (as some said) boring man, with flat fair hair and handsome heavy features; a prosperous young doctor by the name of Warner. But if his blondness and blandness seemed at first a little fatuous, it is certain that he was no fool. If Rosamund Hunt was the only person there with much money, he was the only person who had as yet found any kind of fame. His treatise on "The Probable Existence of Pain in the Lowest Organisms" had been universally hailed by the scientific world as at once solid and daring. In short, he undoubtedly had brains; and perhaps it was not his fault if they were the kind of brains that most men desire to analyze with a poker.

The young man who put his hat off and on was a scientific amateur in a small way, and worshipped the great Warner with a solemn freshness. It was, in fact, at his invitation that the distinguished doctor was present; for Warner lived in no such ramshackle lodging-house, but in a professional palace in Harley Street. This young man was really the youngest and best-looking of the three. But he was one of those persons, both male and female, who seem doomed to be good-looking and insignificant. Brown-haired, high-coloured, and shy, he seemed to lose the delicacy of his features in a sort of blur of brown and red as he stood blushing and blinking against the wind. He was one of those obvious unnoticeable people: every one knew that he was Arthur Inglewood, unmarried, moral, decidedly intelligent, living on a little money of his own, and hiding himself in the two hobbies of photography and cycling. Everybody knew him and forgot him; even as he stood there in the glare of golden sunset there was something about him indistinct, like one of his own red-brown amateur photographs.

The third man had no hat; he was lean, in light, vaguely sporting clothes, and the large pipe in his mouth made him look all the leaner. He had a long ironical face, blue-black hair, the blue eyes of an Irishman, and the blue chin of an actor. An Irishman he was, an actor he was not, except in the old days of Miss Hunt's charades, being, as a matter of fact, an obscure and flippant journalist named Michael Moon. He had once been hazily supposed to be reading for the Bar; but (as Warner would say with his rather elephantine wit) it was mostly at another kind of bar that his friends found him. Moon, however, did not drink, nor even frequently get drunk; he simply was a gentleman who liked low company. This was partly because company is quieter than society: and if he enjoyed talking to a barmaid (as apparently he did), it was chiefly because the barmaid did the talking. Moreover he would often bring other talent to assist her. He shared that strange trick of all men of his type, intellectual and without ambition—the trick of going about with his mental inferiors. There was a small resilient Jew named Moses Gould in the same boarding-house, a man whose negro vitality and vulgarity amused Michael so much that he went round with him from bar to bar, like the owner of a performing monkey.

The colossal clearance which the wind had made of that cloudy sky grew clearer and clearer; chamber within chamber seemed to open in heaven. One felt one might at last find something lighter than light. In the fullness of this silent effulgence all things collected their colours again: the gray trunks turned silver, and the drab gravel gold. One bird fluttered like a loosened leaf from one tree to another, and his brown feathers were brushed with fire.

"Inglewood," said Michael Moon, with his blue eye on the bird, "have you any friends?"

Dr. Warner mistook the person addressed, and turning a broad beaming face, said,—
"Oh yes, I go out a great deal."

Michael Moon gave a tragic grin, and waited for his real informant, who spoke a moment after in a voice curiously cool, fresh and young, as coming out of that brown and even dusty interior.

"Really," answered Inglewood, "I'm afraid I've lost touch with my old friends. The greatest friend I ever had was at school, a fellow named Smith. It's odd you should mention it, because I was thinking of him to-day, though I haven't seen him for seven or eight years. He was on the science side with me at school— a clever fellow though queer; and he went up to Oxford when I went to Germany. The fact is, it's rather a sad story. I often asked him to come and see me, and when I heard nothing I made inquiries, you know. I was shocked to learn that poor Smith had gone off his head. The accounts were a bit cloudy, of course, some saying that he had recovered again; but they always say that. About a year ago I got a telegram from him myself. The telegram, I'm sorry to say, put the matter beyond a doubt."

"Quite so," assented Dr. Warner stolidly; "insanity is generally incurable."

"So is sanity," said the Irishman, and studied him with a dreary eye.

"Symptoms?" asked the doctor. "What was this telegram?"

"It's a shame to joke about such things," said Inglewood, in his honest, embarrassed way; "the telegram was Smith's illness, not Smith. The actual words were, 'Man found alive with two legs.'"

"Alive with two legs," repeated Michael, frowning. "Perhaps a version of alive and kicking? I don't know much about people out of their senses; but I suppose they ought to be kicking."

"And people in their senses?" asked Warner, smiling.

"Oh, they ought to be kicked," said Michael with sudden heartiness.

"The message is clearly insane," continued the impenetrable Warner. "The best test is a reference to the undeveloped normal type. Even a baby does not expect to find a man with three legs."

"Three legs," said Michael Moon, "would be very convenient in this wind."

A fresh eruption of the atmosphere had indeed almost thrown them off their balance and broken the blackened trees in the garden. Beyond, all sorts of accidental objects could be seen scouring the wind-scoured sky—straws, sticks, rags, papers, and, in the distance, a disappearing hat. Its disappearance, however, was not final; after an interval of minutes they saw it again, much larger and closer, like a white panama, towering up into the heavens like a balloon, staggering to and fro for an instant like a stricken kite, and then settling in the centre of their own lawn as falteringly as a fallen leaf.

"Somebody's lost a good hat," said Dr. Warner shortly.

Almost as he spoke, another object came over the garden wall, flying after the fluttering panama. It was a big green umbrella. After that came hurtling a huge yellow Gladstone bag, and after that came a figure like a flying wheel of legs, as in the shield of the Isle of Man.

But though for a flash it seemed to have five or six legs, it alighted upon two, like the man in the queer telegram. It took the form of a large light-haired man in gay green holiday clothes. He had bright blonde hair that the wind brushed back like a German's, a flushed eager face like a cherub's, and a prominent pointing nose, a little like a dog's.

His head, however, was by no means cherubic in the sense of being without a body. On the contrary, on his vast shoulders and shape generally gigantesque, his head looked oddly and unnaturally small. This gave rise to a scientific theory (which his conduct fully supported) that he was an idiot.

Inglewood had a politeness instinctive and yet awkward. His life was full of arrested half gestures of assistance. And even this prodigy of a big man in green, leaping the wall like a bright green grasshopper, did not paralyze that small altruism of his habits in such a matter as a lost hat. He was stepping forward to recover the green gentleman's head-gear, when he was struck rigid with a roar like a bull's.

"Unsportsmanlike!" bellowed the big man. "Give it fair play, give it fair play!" And he came after his own hat quickly but cautiously, with burning eyes. The hat had seemed at first to droop and dawdle as in ostentatious langour on the sunny lawn; but the wind again freshening and rising, it went dancing down the garden with the devilry of a ~pas de quatre~. The eccentric went bounding after it with kangaroo leaps and bursts of breathless speech, of which it was not always easy to pick up the thread: "Fair play, fair play . . . sport of kings . . . chase their crowns . . . quite humane . . . tramontana . . . cardinals chase red hats . . . old English hunting . . . started a hat in Bramber Combe . . . hat at bay . . . mangled hounds . . . Got him!"

As the wind rose out of a roar into a shriek, he leapt into the sky on his strong, fantastic legs, snatched at the vanishing hat, missed it, and pitched sprawling face foremost on the grass. The hat rose over him like a bird in triumph. But its triumph was premature; for the lunatic, flung forward on his hands, threw up his boots behind, waved his two legs in the air like symbolic ensigns (so that they actually thought again of the telegram), and actually caught the hat with his feet. A prolonged and piercing yell of wind split the welkin from end to end. The eyes of all the men were blinded by the invisible blast, as by a strange, clear cataract of transparency rushing between them and all objects about them. But as the large man fell back in a sitting posture and solemnly crowned himself with the hat, Michael found, to his incredulous surprise, that he had been holding his breath, like a man watching a duel.

While that tall wind was at the top of its sky-scraping energy, another short cry was heard, beginning very querulous, but ending very quick, swallowed in abrupt silence. The shiny black cylinder of Dr. Warner's official hat sailed off his head in the long, smooth parabola of an airship, and in almost cresting a garden tree was caught in the topmost branches. Another hat was gone. Those in that garden felt themselves caught in an unaccustomed eddy of things happening; no one seemed to know what would blow away next. Before they could speculate, the cheering and hallooing hat-hunter was already halfway up the tree, swinging himself from fork to fork with his strong, bent, grasshopper legs, and still giving forth his gasping, mysterious comments.

"Tree of life . . . Ygdrasil . . . climb for centuries perhaps . . . owls nesting in the hat . . . remotest generations of owls . . . still usurpers . . . gone to heaven . . . man in the moon wears it . . . brigand . . . not yours . . . belongs to depressed medical man . . . in garden . . . give it up . . . give it up!"

The tree swung and swept and thrashed to and fro in the thundering wind like a thistle, and flamed in the full sunshine like a bonfire. The green, fantastic human figure, vivid against its autumn red and gold, was already among its highest and craziest branches, which by bare luck did not break with the weight of his big body. He was up there among the last tossing leaves and the first twinkling stars of evening, still talking to himself cheerfully, reasoningly, half apologetically, in little gasps. He might well be out of breath, for his whole preposterous raid had gone with one rush; he had bounded the wall once like a football, swept down the garden like a slide, and shot up the tree like a rocket. The other three men seemed buried under incident piled on incident— a wild world where one thing began before another thing left off. All three had the first thought. The tree had been there for the five years they had known the boarding-house. Each one of them was active and strong. No one of them had even thought of climbing it. Beyond that, Inglewood felt first the mere fact of colour. The bright brisk leaves, the bleak blue sky, the wild green arms and legs, reminded him irrationally of something glowing in his infancy, something akin to a gaudy man on a golden tree; perhaps it was only painted monkey on a stick. Oddly enough, Michael Moon, though more of a humourist, was touched on a tenderer nerve, half remembered the old, young theatricals with Rosamund, and was amused to find himself almost quoting Shakespeare—

> "For valour. Is not love a Hercules,
> Still climbing trees in the Hesperides?"

Even the immovable man of science had a bright, bewildered sensation that the Time Machine had given a great jerk, and gone forward with rather rattling rapidity.

He was not, however, wholly prepared for what happened next. The man in green, riding the frail topmost bough like a witch on a very risky broomstick, reached up and rent the black hat from its airy nest of twigs. It had been broken across a heavy bough in the first burst of its passage, a tangle of branches in torn and scored and scratched it in every direction, a clap of wind and foliage had flattened it like a concertina; nor can it be said that the obliging gentleman with the sharp nose showed any adequate tenderness for its structure when he finally unhooked it from its place. When he had found it, however, his proceedings were by some counted singular. He waved it with a loud whoop of triumph, and then immediately appeared to fall backwards off the tree, to which, however, he remained attached by his long strong legs, like a monkey swung by his tail. Hanging thus head downwards above the unhelmed Warner, he gravely proceeded to drop the battered silk cylinder upon his brows. "Every man a king," explained the inverted philosopher, "every hat (consequently) a crown. But this is a crown out of heaven."

And he again attempted the coronation of Warner, who, however, moved away with great abruptness from the hovering diadem; not seeming, strangely enough, to wish for his former decoration in its present state.

"Wrong, wrong!" cried the obliging person hilariously. "Always wear uniform, even if it's shabby uniform! Ritualists may always be untidy. Go to a dance with soot on your shirt-front; but go with a shirt-front. Huntsman wears old coat, but old pink coat. Wear a topper, even if it's got no top. It's the symbol that counts, old cock. Take your hat, because it is your hat after all; its nap rubbed all off by the bark, dears, and its brim not the least bit curled; but for old sakes' sake it is still, dears, the nobbiest tile in the world."

Speaking thus, with a wild comfortableness, he settled or smashed the shapeless silk hat over the face of the disturbed physician, and fell on his feet among the other men, still talking, beaming and breathless.

"Why don't they make more games out of wind?" he asked in some excitement. "Kites are all right, but why should it only be kites? Why, I thought of three other games for a windy day while I was climbing that tree. Here's one of them: you take a lot of pepper—"

"I think," interposed Moon, with a sardonic mildness, "that your games are already sufficiently interesting. Are you, may I ask, a professional acrobat on a tour, or a travelling advertisement of Sunny Jim? How and why do you display all this energy for clearing walls and climbing trees in our melancholy, but at least rational, suburbs?"

The stranger, so far as so loud a person was capable of it, appeared to grow confidential.

"Well, it's a trick of my own," he confessed candidly. "I do it by having two legs."

Arthur Inglewood, who had sunk into the background of this scene of folly, started and stared at the newcomer with his short-sighted eyes screwed up and his high colour slightly heightened.

"Why, I believe you're Smith," he cried with his fresh, almost boyish voice; and then after an instant's stare, "and yet I'm not sure."

"I have a card, I think," said the unknown, with baffling solemnity—"a card with my real name, my titles, offices, and true purpose on this earth."

He drew out slowly from an upper waistcoat pocket a scarlet card-case, and as slowly produced a very large card. Even in the instant of its production, they fancied it was of a queer shape, unlike the cards of ordinary gentlemen. But it was there only for an instant; for as it passed from his fingers to Arthur's, one or another slipped his hold. The strident, tearing gale in that garden carried away the stranger's card to join the wild waste paper of the universe; and that great western wind shook the whole house and passed.

2. THE LUGGAGE OF AN OPTIMIST

We all remember the fairy tales of science in our infancy, which played with the supposition that large animals could jump in the proportion of small ones. If an elephant were as strong as a grasshopper, he could (I suppose) spring clean out of the Zoological Gardens and alight trumpeting upon Primrose Hill. If a whale could leap from the sea like a trout, perhaps men might look up and see one soaring above Yarmouth like the winged island of Laputa. Such natural energy, though sublime, might certainly be inconvenient, and much of this inconvenience attended the gaiety and good intentions of the man in green. He was too large for everything, because he was lively as well as large. By a fortunate physical provision, most very substantial creatures are also reposeful; and middle-class boarding-houses in the lesser parts of London are not built for a man as big as a bull and excitable as a kitten.

When Inglewood followed the stranger into the boarding-house, he found him talking earnestly (and in his own opinion privately) to the helpless Mrs. Duke. That fat, faint lady could only goggle up like a dying fish at the enormous new gentleman, who politely offered himself as a lodger, with vast gestures of the wide white hat in one hand, and the yellow Gladstone bag in the other. Fortunately, Mrs. Duke's more efficient niece and partner was there to complete the contract; for, indeed, all the people of the house had somehow collected in the room. This fact, in truth, was typical of the whole episode. The visitor created an atmosphere of comic crisis; and from the time he came into the house to the time he left it, he somehow got the company to gather and even follow (though in derision) as children gather and follow a Punch and Judy. An hour ago, and for four years previously, these people had avoided each other, even when they had really liked each other. They had slid in and out of dismal and deserted rooms in search of particular newspapers or private needlework. Even now they all came casually, as with varying interests; but they all came. There was the embarrassed Inglewood, still a sort of red shadow; there was the unembarrassed Warner, a pallid but solid substance. There was Michael Moon offering like a riddle the contrast of the horsy crudeness of his clothes and the sombre sagacity of his visage. He was now joined by his yet more comic crony, Moses Gould. Swaggering on short legs with a prosperous purple tie, he was the gayest of godless little dogs; but like a dog also in this, that however he danced and wagged with delight, the two dark eyes on each side of his protuberant nose glistened gloomily like black buttons. There was Miss Rosamund Hunt, still with the fine white hat framing her square, good-looking face, and still with her native air of being dressed for some party that never came off. She also, like Mr. Moon, had a new companion, new so far as this narrative goes, but in reality an old friend and a protegee. This was a slight young woman in dark gray, and in no way notable but for a load of dull red hair, of which the shape somehow gave her pale face that triangular, almost peaked, appearance which was given by the lowering headdress and deep rich ruff of the Elizabethan beauties. Her surname seemed to be Gray, and Miss Hunt called her Mary, in that indescribable tone applied to a dependent who has practically become a friend. She wore a small silver cross on her very business-like gray clothes, and was the only member of the party who went to church. Last, but the reverse of least, there was Diana Duke, studying the newcomer with eyes of steel, and listening carefully to every idiotic word he said. As for Mrs. Duke, she smiled up at him, but never dreamed of listening to him. She had never really listened to any one in her life; which, some said, was why she had survived.

Nevertheless, Mrs. Duke was pleased with her new guest's concentration of courtesy upon herself; for no one ever spoke seriously to her any more than she listened seriously to any one. And she almost beamed as the stranger, with yet wider and almost whirling gestures of explanation with his huge hat and bag, apologized for having entered by the wall instead of the front door. He was understood to put it down to an unfortunate family tradition of neatness and care of his clothes.

"My mother was rather strict about it, to tell the truth," he said, lowering his voice, to Mrs. Duke. "She never liked me to lose my cap at school. And when a man's been taught to be tidy and neat it sticks to him."

Mrs. Duke weakly gasped that she was sure he must have had a good mother; but her niece seemed inclined to probe the matter further.

"You've got a funny idea of neatness," she said, "if it's jumping garden walls and clambering up garden trees. A man can't very well climb a tree tidily."

"He can clear a wall neatly," said Michael Moon; "I saw him do it."

Smith seemed to be regarding the girl with genuine astonishment. "My dear young lady," he said, "I was tidying the tree. You don't want last year's hats there, do you, any more than last year's leaves? The wind takes off the leaves, but it couldn't manage the hat; that wind, I suppose, has tidied whole forests to-day. Rum idea this is, that tidiness is a timid, quiet sort of thing; why, tidiness is a toil for giants. You can't tidy anything without untidying yourself; just look at my trousers. Don't you know that? Haven't you ever had a spring cleaning?"

"Oh yes, sir," said Mrs. Duke, almost eagerly. "You will find everything of that sort quite nice." For the first time she had heard two words that she could understand.

Miss Diana Duke seemed to be studying the stranger with a sort of spasm of calculation; then her black eyes snapped with decision, and she said that he could have a particular bedroom on the top floor if he liked: and the silent and sensitive Inglewood, who had been on the rack through these cross-purposes, eagerly offered to show him up to the room. Smith went up the stairs four at a time, and when he bumped his head against the ultimate ceiling, Inglewood had an odd sensation that the tall house was much shorter than it used to be.

Arthur Inglewood followed his old friend—or his new friend, for he did not very clearly know which he was. The face looked very like his old schoolfellow's at one second and very unlike at another. And when Inglewood broke through his native politeness so far as to say suddenly, "Is your name Smith?" he received only the unenlightening reply, "Quite right; quite right. Very good. Excellent!" Which appeared to Inglewood, on reflection, rather the speech of a new-born babe accepting a name than of a grown-up man admitting one.

Despite these doubts about identity, the hapless Inglewood watched the other unpack, and stood about his bedroom in all the impotent attitudes of the male friend. Mr. Smith unpacked with the same kind of whirling accuracy with which he climbed a tree—throwing things out of his bag as if they were rubbish, yet managing to distribute quite a regular pattern all round him on the floor.

As he did so he continued to talk in the same somewhat gasping manner (he had come upstairs four steps at a time, but even without this his style of speech was breathless and fragmentary), and his remarks were still a string of more or less significant but often separate pictures.

"Like the day of judgement," he said, throwing a bottle so that it somehow settled, rocking on its right end. "People say vast universe . . . infinity and astronomy; not sure . . . I think things are too close together . . . packed up; for travelling . . . stars too close, really . . . why, the sun's a star, too close to be seen properly; the earth's a star, too close to be seen at all . . . too many pebbles on the beach; ought all to be put in rings; too many blades of grass to study . . . feathers on a bird make the brain reel; wait till the big bag is unpacked . . . may all be put in our right places then."

Here he stopped, literally for breath—throwing a shirt to the other end of the room, and then a bottle of ink so that it fell quite neatly beyond it. Inglewood looked round on this strange, half-symmetrical disorder with an increasing doubt.

In fact, the more one explored Mr. Smith's holiday luggage, the less one could make anything of it. One peculiarity of it was that almost everything seemed to be there for the wrong reason; what is secondary with every one else was primary with him. He would wrap up a pot or pan in brown paper; and the unthinking assistant would discover that the pot was valueless or even unnecessary, and that it was the brown paper that was truly precious. He produced two or three boxes of cigars, and explained with plain and perplexing sincerity that he was no smoker, but that cigar-box wood was by far the best for fretwork. He also exhibited about six small bottles of wine, white and red, and Inglewood, happening to note a Volnay which he knew to be excellent, supposed at first that the stranger was an epicure in vintages. He was therefore surprised to find that the next bottle was a vile sham claret from the colonies, which even colonials (to do them justice) do not drink. It was only then that he observed that all six bottles had those bright metallic seals of various tints, and seemed to have been chosen solely because they have the three primary and three secondary colours: red, blue, and yellow; green, violet and orange. There grew upon Inglewood an almost creepy sense of the real childishness of this creature. For Smith was really, so far as human psychology can be, innocent. He had the sensualities of innocence: he loved the stickiness of gum, and he cut white wood greedily as if he were cutting a cake. To this man wine was not a doubtful thing to be defended or denounced; it was a quaintly coloured syrup, such as a child sees in a shop window. He talked dominantly and rushed the social situation; but he was not asserting himself, like a superman in a modern play. He was simply forgetting himself, like a little boy at a party. He had somehow made the giant stride from babyhood to manhood, and missed that crisis in youth when most of us grow old.

As he shunted his big bag, Arthur observed the initials I. S. printed on one side of it, and remembered that Smith had been called Innocent Smith at school, though whether as a formal Christian name or a moral description he could not remember. He was just about to venture another question, when there was a knock at the door, and the short figure of Mr. Gould offered itself, with the melancholy Moon, standing like his tall crooked shadow, behind him. They had drifted up the stairs after the other two men with the wandering gregariousness of the male.

"Hope there's no intrusion," said the beaming Moses with a glow of good nature, but not the airiest tinge of apology.

"The truth is," said Michael Moon with comparative courtesy, "we thought we might see if they had made you comfortable. Miss Duke is rather—"

"I know," cried the stranger, looking up radiantly from his bag; "magnificent, isn't she? Go close to her—hear military music going by, like Joan of Arc."

Inglewood stared and stared at the speaker like one who has just heard a wild fairy tale, which nevertheless contains one small and forgotten fact. For he remembered how he had himself thought of Jeanne d'Arc years ago, when, hardly more than a schoolboy, he had first come to the boarding-house. Long since the pulverizing rationalism of his friend Dr. Warner had crushed such youthful ignorances and disproportionate dreams. Under the Warnerian scepticism and science of hopeless human types, Inglewood had long come to regard himself as a timid, insufficient, and "weak" type, who would never marry; to regard Diana Duke as a materialistic maidservant; and to regard his first fancy for her as the small, dull farce of a collegian kissing his landlady's daughter. And yet the phrase about military music moved him queerly, as if he had heard those distant drums.

"She has to keep things pretty tight, as is only natural," said Moon, glancing round the rather dwarfish room, with its wedge of slanted ceiling, like the conical hood of a dwarf.

"Rather a small box for you, sir," said the waggish Mr. Gould.

"Splendid room, though," answered Mr. Smith enthusiastically, with his head inside his Gladstone bag. "I love these pointed sorts of rooms, like Gothic. By the way," he cried out, pointing in quite a startling way, "where does that door lead to?"

"To certain death, I should say," answered Michael Moon, staring up at a dust-stained and disused trapdoor in the sloping roof of the attic. "I don't think there's a loft there; and I don't know what else it could lead to." Long before he had finished his sentence the man with the strong green legs had leapt at the door in the ceiling, swung himself somehow on to the ledge beneath it, wrenched it open after a struggle, and clambered through it. For a moment they saw the two symbolic legs standing like a truncated statue; then they vanished. Through the hole thus burst in the roof appeared the empty and lucid sky of evening, with one great many-coloured cloud sailing across it like a whole county upside down.

"Hullo, you fellows!" came the far cry of Innocent Smith, apparently from some remote pinnacle. "Come up here; and bring some of my things to eat and drink. It's just the spot for a picnic."

With a sudden impulse Michael snatched two of the small bottles of wine, one in each solid fist; and Arthur Inglewood, as if mesmerized, groped for a biscuit tin and a big jar of ginger. The enormous hand of Innocent Smith appearing through the aperture, like a giant's in a fairy tale, received these tributes and bore them off to the eyrie; then they both hoisted themselves out of the window. They were both athletic, and even gymnastic; Inglewood through his concern for hygiene, and Moon through his concern for sport, which was not quite so idle and inactive as that of the average sportsman. Also they both had a light-headed burst of celestial sensation when the door was burst in the roof, as if a door had been burst in the sky, and they could climb out on to the very roof of the universe. They were both men who had long been unconsciously imprisoned in the commonplace, though one took it comically, and the other seriously. They were both men, nevertheless, in whom sentiment had never died. But Mr. Moses Gould had an equal contempt for their suicidal athletics and their subconscious transcendentalism, and he stood and laughed at the thing with the shameless rationality of another race.

When the singular Smith, astride of a chimney-pot, learnt that Gould was not following, his infantile officiousness and good nature forced him to dive back into the attic to comfort or persuade; and Inglewood and Moon were left alone on the long gray-green ridge of the slate roof, with their feet against gutters and their backs against chimney-pots, looking agnostically at each other. Their first feeling was that they had come out into eternity, and that eternity was very like topsy-turvydom. One definition occurred to both of them—that he had come out into the light of that lucid and radiant ignorance in which all beliefs had begun. The sky above them was full of mythology. Heaven seemed deep enough to hold all the gods. The round of the ether turned from green to yellow gradually like a great unripe fruit. All around the sunken sun it was like a lemon; round all the east it was a sort of golden green, more suggestive of a greengage; but the whole had still the emptiness of daylight and none of the secrecy of dusk. Tumbled here and there across this gold and pale green were shards and shattered masses of inky purple cloud, which seemed falling towards the earth in every kind of colossal perspective. One of them really had the character of some many-mitred, many-bearded, many-winged Assyrian image, huge head downwards, hurled out of heaven—a sort of false Jehovah, who was perhaps Satan.

All the other clouds had preposterous pinnacled shapes, as if the god's palaces had been flung after him.

And yet, while the empty heaven was full of silent catastrophe, the height of human buildings above which they sat held here and there a tiny trivial noise that was the exact antithesis; and they heard some six streets below a newsboy calling, and a bell bidding to chapel. They could also hear talk out of the garden below; and realized that the irrepressible Smith must have followed Gould downstairs, for his eager and pleading accents could be heard, followed by the half-humourous protests of Miss Duke and the full and very youthful laughter of Rosamund Hunt. The air had that cold kindness that comes after a storm. Michael Moon drank it in with as serious a relish as he had drunk the little bottle of cheap claret, which he had emptied almost at a draught. Inglewood went on eating ginger very slowly and with a solemnity unfathomable as the sky above him. There was still enough stir in the freshness of the atmosphere to make them almost fancy they could smell the garden soil and the last roses of autumn. Suddenly there came from the darkening room a silvery ping and pong which told them that Rosamund had brought out the long-neglected mandoline. After the first few notes there was more of the distant bell-like laughter.

"Inglewood," said Michael Moon, "have you ever heard that I am a blackguard?"

"I haven't heard it, and I don't believe it," answered Inglewood, after an odd pause. "But I have heard you were—what they call rather wild."

"If you have heard that I am wild, you can contradict the rumour," said Moon, with an extraordinary calm; "I am tame. I am quite tame; I am about the tamest beast that crawls. I drink too much of the same kind of whisky at the same time every night. I even drink about the same amount too much. I go to the same number of public-houses. I meet the same damned women with mauve faces. I hear the same number of dirty stories— generally the same dirty stories. You may assure my friends, Inglewood, that you see before you a person whom civilization has thoroughly tamed."

Arthur Inglewood was staring with feelings that made him nearly fall off the roof, for indeed the Irishman's face, always sinister, was now almost demoniacal.

"Christ confound it!" cried out Moon, suddenly clutching the empty claret bottle, "this is about the thinnest and filthiest wine I ever uncorked, and it's the only drink I have really enjoyed for nine years. I was never wild until just ten minutes ago." And he sent the bottle whizzing, a wheel of glass, far away beyond the garden into the road, where, in the profound evening silence, they could even hear it break and part upon the stones.

"Moon," said Arthur Inglewood, rather huskily, "you mustn't be so bitter about it. Everyone has to take the world as he finds it; of course one often finds it a bit dull—"

"That fellow doesn't," said Michael decisively; "I mean that fellow Smith. I have a fancy there's some method in his madness. It looks as if he could turn into a sort of wonderland any minute by taking one step out of the plain road. Who would have thought of that trapdoor? Who would have thought that this cursed colonial claret could taste quite nice among the chimney-pots? Perhaps that is the real key of fairyland. Perhaps Nosey Gould's beastly little Empire Cigarettes ought only to be smoked on stilts, or something of that sort. Perhaps Mrs. Duke's cold leg of mutton would seem quite appetizing at the top of a tree. Perhaps even my damned, dirty, monotonous drizzle of Old Bill Whisky—"

"Don't be so rough on yourself," said Inglewood, in serious distress. "The dullness isn't your fault or the whisky's. Fellows who don't— fellows like me I mean—have just the same feeling that it's all rather flat and a failure. But the world's made like that; it's all survival. Some people are made to get on, like Warner; and some people are made to stick quiet, like me. You can't help your temperament. I know you're much cleverer than I am; but you can't help having all the loose ways of a poor literary chap, and I can't help having all the doubts and helplessness of a small scientific chap, any more than a fish can help floating or a fern can help curling up. Humanity, as Warner said so well in that lecture, really consists of quite different tribes of animals all disguised as men."

In the dim garden below the buzz of talk was suddenly broken by Miss Hunt's musical instrument banging with the abruptness of artillery into a vulgar but spirited tune.

Rosamund's voice came up rich and strong in the words of some fatuous, fashionable coon song:-

"Darkies sing a song on the old plantation, Sing it as we sang it in days long since gone by."

Inglewood's brown eyes softened and saddened still more as he continued his monologue of resignation to such a rollicking and romantic tune. But the blue eyes of Michael Moon brightened and hardened with a light that Inglewood did not understand. Many centuries, and many villages and valleys, would have been happier if Inglewood or Inglewood's countrymen had ever understood that light, or guessed at the first blink that it was the battle star of Ireland.

"Nothing can ever alter it; it's in the wheels of the universe," went on Inglewood, in a low voice: "some men are weak and some strong, and the only thing we can do is to know that we are weak. I have been in love lots of times, but I could not do anything, for I remembered my own fickleness. I have formed opinions, but I haven't the cheek to push them, because I've so often changed them. That's the upshot, old fellow. We can't trust ourselves— and we can't help it."

Michael had risen to his feet, and stood poised in a perilous position at the end of the roof, like some dark statue hung above its gable. Behind him, huge clouds of an almost impossible purple turned slowly topsy-turvy in the silent anarchy of heaven. Their gyration made the dark figure seem yet dizzier.

"Let us . . . " he said, and was suddenly silent.

"Let us what?" asked Arthur Inglewood, rising equally quick though somewhat more cautiously, for his friend seemed to find some difficulty in speech.

"Let us go and do some of these things we can't do," said Michael.

At the same moment there burst out of the trapdoor below them the cockatoo hair and flushed face of Innocent Smith, calling to them that they must come down as the "concert" was in full swing, and Mr. Moses Gould was about to recite "Young Lochinvar."

As they dropped into Innocent's attic they nearly tumbled over its entertaining impedimenta again. Inglewood, staring at the littered floor, thought instinctively of the littered floor of a nursery. He was therefore the more moved, and even shocked, when his eye fell on a large well-polished American revolver.

"Hullo!" he cried, stepping back from the steely glitter as men step back from a serpent; "are you afraid of burglars? or when and why do you deal death out of that machine gun?"

"Oh, that!" said Smith, throwing it a single glance; "I deal life out of that," and he went bounding down the stairs.

3. THE BANNER OF BEACON

All next day at Beacon House there was a crazy sense that it was everybody's birthday. It is the fashion to talk of institutions as cold and cramping things. The truth is that when people are in exceptionally high spirits, really wild with freedom and invention, they always must, and they always do, create institutions. When men are weary they fall into anarchy; but while they are gay and vigorous they invariably make rules. This, which is true of all the churches and republics of history, is also true of the most trivial parlour game or the most unsophisticated meadow romp. We are never free until some institution frees us; and liberty cannot exist till it is declared by authority. Even the wild authority of the harlequin Smith was still authority, because it produced everywhere a crop of crazy regulations and conditions. He filled every one with his own half-lunatic life; but it was not expressed in destruction, but rather in a dizzy and toppling construction. Each person with a hobby found it turning into an institution. Rosamund's songs seemed to coalesce into a kind of opera; Michael's jests and paragraphs into a magazine. His pipe and her mandoline seemed between them to make a sort of smoking concert. The bashful and bewildered Arthur Inglewood almost struggled against his own growing importance. He felt as if, in spite of him, his photographs were turning into a picture gallery, and his bicycle into a gymkhana. But no one had any time to criticize these impromptu estates and offices, for they followed each other in wild succession like the topics of a rambling talker.

Existence with such a man was an obstacle race made out of pleasant obstacles. Out of any homely and trivial object he could drag reels of exaggeration, like a conjurer. Nothing could be more shy and impersonal than poor Arthur's photography. Yet the preposterous Smith was seen assisting him eagerly through sunny morning hours, and an indefensible sequence described as "Moral Photography" began to unroll about the boarding-house. It was only a version of the old photographer's joke which produces the same figure twice on one plate, making a man play chess with himself, dine with himself, and so on. But these plates were more hysterical and ambitious—as, "Miss Hunt forgets Herself," showing that lady answering her own too rapturous recognition with a most appalling stare of ignorance; or "Mr. Moon questions Himself," in which Mr. Moon appeared as one driven to madness under his own legal cross-examination, which was conducted with a long forefinger and an air of ferocious waggery. One highly successful trilogy—representing Inglewood recognizing Inglewood, Inglewood prostrating himself before Inglewood, and Inglewood severely beating Inglewood with an umbrella— Innocent Smith wanted to have enlarged and put up in the hall, like a sort of fresco, with the inscription,—

"Self-reverence, self-knowledge, self-control— These three alone will make a man a prig."

— TENNYSON

Nothing, again, could be more prosaic and impenetrable than the domestic energies of Miss Diana Duke. But Innocent had somehow blundered on the discovery that her thrifty dressmaking went with a considerable feminine care for dress—the one feminine thing that had never failed her solitary self-respect. In consequence Smith pestered her with a theory (which he really seemed to take seriously) that ladies might combine economy with magnificence if they would draw light chalk patterns on a plain dress and then dust them off again. He set up "Smith's Lightning Dressmaking Company," with two screens, a cardboard placard, and box of bright soft crayons; and Miss Diana actually threw him an abandoned black overall or working dress on which to exercise the talents of a modiste. He promptly produced for her a garment aflame with red and gold sunflowers; she held it up an instant to her shoulders, and looked like an empress. And Arthur Inglewood, some hours afterwards cleaning his bicycle (with his usual air of being inextricably hidden in it), glanced up; and his hot face grew hotter, for Diana stood laughing for one flash in the doorway, and her dark robe was rich with the green and purple of great decorative peacocks, like a secret garden in the "Arabian Nights." A pang too swift to be named pain or pleasure went through his heart like an old-world rapier. He remembered how pretty he thought her years ago, when he was ready to fall in love with anybody; but it was like remembering a worship of some Babylonian princess in some previous existence. At his next glimpse of her (and he caught himself awaiting it) the purple and green chalk was dusted off, and she went by quickly in her working clothes.

As for Mrs. Duke, none who knew that matron could conceive her as actively resisting this invasion that had turned her house upside down. But among the most exact observers it was seriously believed that she liked it. For she was one of those women who at bottom regard all men as equally mad, wild animals of some utterly separate species. And it is doubtful if she really saw anything more eccentric or inexplicable in Smith's chimney-pot picnics or crimson sunflowers than she had in the chemicals of Inglewood or the sardonic speeches of Moon. Courtesy, on the other hand, is a thing that anybody can understand, and Smith's manners were as courteous as they were unconventional. She said he was "a real gentleman," by which she simply meant a kind-hearted man, which is a very different thing. She would sit at the head of the table with fat, folded hands and a fat, folded smile for hours and hours, while every one else was talking at once. At least, the only other exception was Rosamund's companion, Mary Gray, whose silence was of a much more eager sort. Though she never spoke she always looked as if she might speak any minute. Perhaps this is the very definition of a companion. Innocent Smith seemed to throw himself, as into other adventures, into the adventure of making her talk. He never succeeded, yet he was never snubbed; if he achieved anything, it was only to draw attention to this quiet figure, and to turn her, by ever so little, from a modesty to a mystery. But if she was a riddle, every one recognized that she was a fresh and unspoilt riddle, like the riddle of the sky and the woods in spring. Indeed, though she was rather older than the other two girls, she had an early morning ardour, a fresh earnestness of youth, which Rosamund seemed to have lost in the mere spending of money, and Diana in the mere guarding of it. Smith looked at her again and again. Her eyes and mouth were set in her face the wrong way—which was really the right way. She had the knack of saying everything with her face: her silence was a sort of steady applause.

But among the hilarious experiments of that holiday (which seemed more like a week's holiday than a day's) one experiment towers supreme, not because it was any sillier or more successful than the others, but because out of this particular folly flowed all of the odd events that were to follow. All the other practical jokes exploded of themselves, and left vacancy; all the other fictions returned upon themselves, and were finished like a song. But the string of solid and startling events— which were to include a hansom cab, a detective, a pistol, and a marriage licence—were all made primarily possible by the joke about the High Court of Beacon.

It had originated, not with Innocent Smith, but with Michael Moon. He was in a strange glow and pressure of spirits, and talked incessantly; yet he had never been more sarcastic, and even inhuman. He used his old useless knowledge as a barrister to talk entertainingly of a tribunal that was a parody on the pompous anomalies of English law. The High Court of Beacon, he declared, was a splendid example of our free and sensible constitution. It had been founded by King John in defiance of the Magna Carta, and now held absolute power over windmills, wine and spirit licences, ladies traveling in Turkey, revision of sentences for dog-stealing and parricide, as well as anything whatever that happened in the town of Market Bosworth. The whole hundred and nine seneschals of the High Court of Beacon met once in every four centuries; but in the intervals (as Mr. Moon explained) the whole powers of the institution were vested in Mrs. Duke. Tossed about among the rest of the company, however, the High Court did not retain its historical and legal seriousness, but was used somewhat unscrupulously in a riot of domestic detail. If somebody spilt the Worcester Sauce on the tablecloth, he was quite sure it was a rite without which the sittings and findings of the Court would be invalid; or if somebody wanted a window to remain shut, he would suddenly remember that none but the third son of the lord of the manor of Penge had the right to open it. They even went to the length of making arrests and conducting criminal inquiries. The proposed trial of Moses Gould for patriotism was rather above the heads of the company, especially of the criminal; but the trial of Inglewood on a charge of photographic libel, and his triumphant acquittal upon a plea of insanity, were admitted to be in the best tradition of the Court.

But when Smith was in wild spirits he grew more and more serious, not more and more flippant like Michael Moon. This proposal of a private court of justice, which Moon had thrown off with the detachment of a political humourist, Smith really caught hold of with the eagerness of an abstract philosopher. It was by far the best thing they could do, he declared, to claim sovereign powers even for the individual household.

"You believe in Home Rule for Ireland; I believe in Home Rule for homes," he cried eagerly to Michael. "It would be better if every father COULD kill his son, as with the old Romans; it would be better, because nobody would be killed. Let's issue a Declaration of Independence from Beacon House. We could grow enough greens in that garden to support us, and when the tax-collector comes let's tell him we're self-supporting, and play on him with the hose . . . . Well, perhaps, as you say, we couldn't very well have a hose, as that comes from the main; but we could sink a well in this chalk, and a lot could be done with water-jugs . . . . Let this really be Beacon House. Let's light a bonfire of independence on the roof, and see house after house answering it across the valley of the Thames! Let us begin the League of the Free Families! Away with Local Government! A fig for Local Patriotism! Let every house be a sovereign state as this is, and judge its own children by its own law, as we do by the Court of Beacon. Let us cut the painter, and begin to be happy together, as if we were on a desert island."

"I know that desert island," said Michael Moon; "it only exists in the `Swiss Family Robinson.' A man feels a strange desire for some sort of vegetable milk, and crash comes down some unexpected cocoa-nut from some undiscovered monkey. A literary man feels inclined to pen a sonnet, and at once an officious porcupine rushes out of a thicket and shoots out one of his quills."

"Don't you say a word against the `Swiss Family Robinson,'" cried Innocent with great warmth. "It mayn't be exact science, but it's dead accurate philosophy. When you're really shipwrecked, you do really find what you want. When you're really on a desert island, you never find it a desert. If we were really besieged in this garden, we'd find a hundred English birds and English berries that we never knew were here. If we were snowed up in this room, we'd be the better for reading scores of books in that bookcase that we don't even know are there; we'd have talks with each other, good, terrible talks, that we shall go to the grave without guessing; we'd find materials for everything— christening, marriage, or funeral; yes, even for a coronation— if we didn't decide to be a republic."

"A coronation on `Swiss Family' lines, I suppose," said Michael, laughing. "Oh, I know you would find everything in that atmosphere. If we wanted such a simple thing, for instance, as a Coronation Canopy, we should walk down beyond the geraniums and find the Canopy Tree in full bloom. If we wanted such a trifle as a crown of gold, why, we should be digging up dandelions, and we should find a gold mine under the lawn. And when we wanted oil for the ceremony, why I suppose a great storm would wash everything on shore, and we should find there was a Whale on the premises."

"And so there IS a whale on the premises for all you know," asseverated Smith, striking the table with passion. "I bet you've never examined the premises! I bet you've never been round at the back as I was this morning— for I found the very thing you say could only grow on a tree. There's an old sort of square tent up against the dustbin; it's got three holes in the canvas, and a pole's broken, so it's not much good as a tent, but as a Canopy—" And his voice quite failed him to express its shining adequacy; then he went on with controversial eagerness: "You see I take every challenge as you make it. I believe every blessed thing you say couldn't be here has been here all the time. You say you want a whale washed up for oil. Why, there's oil in that cruet-stand at your elbow; and I don't believe anybody has touched it or thought of it for years. And as for your gold crown, we're none of us wealthy here, but we could collect enough ten-shilling bits from our own pockets to string round a man's head for half an hour; or one of Miss Hunt's gold bangles is nearly big enough to—"

The good-humoured Rosamund was almost choking with laughter. "All is not gold that glitters," she said, "and besides—"

"What a mistake that is!" cried Innocent Smith, leaping up in great excitement. "All is gold that glitters— especially now we are a Sovereign State. What's the good of a Sovereign State if you can't define a sovereign? We can make anything a precious metal, as men could in the morning of the world. They didn't choose gold because it was rare; your scientists can tell you twenty sorts of slime much rarer. They chose gold because it was bright—because it was a hard thing to find, but pretty when you've found it. You can't fight with golden swords or eat golden biscuits; you can only look at it—and you can look at it out here."

With one of his incalculable motions he sprang back and burst open the doors into the garden. At the same time also, with one of his gestures that never seemed at the instant so unconventional as they were, he stretched out his hand to Mary Gray, and led her out on to the lawn as if for a dance.

The French windows, thus flung open, let in an evening even lovelier than that of the day before. The west was swimming with sanguine colours, and a sort of sleepy flame lay along the lawn. The twisted shadows of the one or two garden trees showed upon this sheen, not gray or black, as in common daylight, but like arabesques written in vivid violet ink on some page of Eastern gold. The sunset was one of those festive and yet mysterious conflagrations in which common things by their colours remind us of costly or curious things. The slates upon the sloping roof burned like the plumes of a vast peacock, in every mysterious blend of blue and green. The red-brown bricks of the wall glowed with all the October tints of strong ruby and tawny wines. The sun seemed to set each object alight with a different coloured flame, like a man lighting fireworks; and even Innocent's hair, which was of a rather colourless fairness, seemed to have a flame of pagan gold on it as he strode across the lawn towards the one tall ridge of rockery.

"What would be the good of gold," he was saying, "if it did not glitter? Why should we care for a black sovereign any more than for a black sun at noon? A black button would do just as well. Don't you see that everything in this garden looks like a jewel? And will you kindly tell me what the deuce is the good of a jewel except that it looks like a jewel? Leave off buying and selling, and start looking! Open your eyes, and you'll wake up in the New Jerusalem.

"All is gold that glitters— Tree and tower of brass; Rolls the golden evening air Down the golden grass. Kick the cry to Jericho, How yellow mud is sold; All is gold that glitters, For the glitter is the gold."

"And who wrote that?" asked Rosamund, amused.

"No one will ever write it," answered Smith, and cleared the rockery with a flying leap.

"Really," said Rosamund to Michael Moon, "he ought to be sent to an asylum. Don't you think so?"

"I beg your pardon," inquired Michael, rather sombrely; his long, swarthy head was dark against the sunset, and, either by accident or mood, he had the look of something isolated and even hostile amid the social extravagance of the garden.

"I only said Mr. Smith ought to go to an asylum," repeated the lady.

The lean face seemed to grow longer and longer, for Moon was unmistakably sneering. "No," he said; "I don't think it's at all necessary."

"What do you mean?" asked Rosamund quickly. "Why not?"

"Because he is in one now," answered Michael Moon, in a quiet but ugly voice. "Why, didn't you know?"

"What?" cried the girl, and there was a break in her voice; for the Irishman's face and voice were really almost creepy. With his dark figure and dark sayings in all that sunshine he looked like the devil in paradise.

"I'm sorry," he continued, with a sort of harsh humility. "Of course we don't talk about it much . . . but I thought we all really knew."

"Knew what?"

"Well," answered Moon, "that Beacon House is a certain rather singular sort of house—a house with the tiles loose, shall we say? Innocent Smith is only the doctor that visits us; hadn't you come when he called before? As most of our maladies are melancholic, of course he has to be extra cheery. Sanity, of course, seems a very bumptious eccentric thing to us. Jumping over a wall, climbing a tree—that's his bedside manner."

"You daren't say such a thing!" cried Rosamund in a rage. "You daren't suggest that I—"

"Not more than I am," said Michael soothingly; "not more than the rest of us. Haven't you ever noticed that Miss Duke never sits still—a notorious sign? Haven't you ever observed that Inglewood is always washing his hands— a known mark of mental disease? I, of course, am a dipsomaniac."

"I don't believe you," broke out his companion, not without agitation. "I've heard you had some bad habits—"

"All habits are bad habits," said Michael, with deadly calm. "Madness does not come by breaking out, but by giving in; by settling down in some dirty, little, self-repeating circle of ideas; by being tamed. YOU went mad about money, because you're an heiress."

"It's a lie," cried Rosamund furiously. "I never was mean about money."

"You were worse," said Michael, in a low voice and yet violently. "You thought that other people were. You thought every man who came near you must be a fortune-hunter; you would not let yourself go and be sane; and now you're mad and I'm mad, and serve us right."

"You brute!" said Rosamund, quite white. "And is this true?"

With the intellectual cruelty of which the Celt is capable when his abysses are in revolt, Michael was silent for some seconds, and then stepped back with an ironical bow. "Not literally true, of course," he said; "only really true. An allegory, shall we say? a social satire."

"And I hate and despise your satires," cried Rosamund Hunt, letting loose her whole forcible female personality like a cyclone, and speaking every word to wound. "I despise it as I despise your rank tobacco, and your nasty, loungy ways, and your snarling, and your Radicalism, and your old clothes, and your potty little newspaper, and your rotten failure at everything. I don't care whether you call it snobbishness or not, I like life and success, and jolly things to look at, and action. You won't frighten me with Diogenes; I prefer Alexander."

"Victrix causa deae—" said Michael gloomily; and this angered her more, as, not knowing what it meant, she imagined it to be witty.

"Oh, I dare say you know Greek," she said, with cheerful inaccuracy; "you haven't done much with that either." And she crossed the garden, pursuing the vanished Innocent and Mary.

In doing so she passed Inglewood, who was returning to the house slowly, and with a thought-clouded brow. He was one of those men who are quite clever, but quite the reverse of quick. As he came back out of the sunset garden into the twilight parlour,

Diana Duke slipped swiftly to her feet and began putting away the tea things. But it was not before Inglewood had seen an instantaneous picture so unique that he might well have snapshotted it with his everlasting camera. For Diana had been sitting in front of her unfinished work with her chin on her hand, looking straight out of the window in pure thoughtless thought.

"You are busy," said Arthur, oddly embarrassed with what he had seen, and wishing to ignore it.

"There's no time for dreaming in this world," answered the young lady with her back to him.

"I have been thinking lately," said Inglewood in a low voice, "that there's no time for waking up."

She did not reply, and he walked to the window and looked out on the garden.

"I don't smoke or drink, you know," he said irrelevantly, "because I think they're drugs. And yet I fancy all hobbies, like my camera and bicycle, are drugs too. Getting under a black hood, getting into a dark room—getting into a hole anyhow. Drugging myself with speed, and sunshine, and fatigue, and fresh air. Pedalling the machine so fast that I turn into a machine myself. That's the matter with all of us. We're too busy to wake up."

"Well," said the girl solidly, "what is there to wake up to?"

"There must be!" cried Inglewood, turning round in a singular excitement—"there must be something to wake up to! All we do is preparations—your cleanliness, and my healthiness, and Warner's scientific appliances. We're always preparing for something—something that never comes off. I ventilate the house, and you sweep the house; but what is going to HAPPEN in the house?"

She was looking at him quietly, but with very bright eyes, and seemed to be searching for some form of words which she could not find.

Before she could speak the door burst open, and the boisterous Rosamund Hunt, in her flamboyant white hat, boa, and parasol, stood framed in the doorway. She was in a breathing heat, and on her open face was an expression of the most infantile astonishment.

"Well, here's a fine game!" she said, panting. "What am I to do now, I wonder? I've wired for Dr. Warner; that's all I can think of doing."

"What is the matter?" asked Diana, rather sharply, but moving forward like one used to be called upon for assistance.

"It's Mary," said the heiress, "my companion Mary Gray: that cracked friend of yours called Smith has proposed to her in the garden, after ten hours' acquaintance, and he wants to go off with her now for a special licence."

Arthur Inglewood walked to the open French windows and looked out on the garden, still golden with evening light. Nothing moved there but a bird or two hopping and twittering; but beyond the hedge and railings, in the road outside the garden gate, a hansom cab was waiting, with the yellow Gladstone bag on top of it.

4. THE GARDEN OF THE GOD

Diana Duke seemed inexplicably irritated at the abrupt entrance and utterance of the other girl.

"Well," she said shortly, "I suppose Miss Gray can decline him if she doesn't want to marry him."

"But she DOES want to marry him!" cried Rosamund in exasperation. "She's a wild, wicked fool, and I won't be parted from her."

"Perhaps," said Diana icily, "but I really don't see what we can do."

"But the man's balmy, Diana," reasoned her friend angrily. "I can't let my nice governess marry a man that's balmy! You or somebody MUST stop it!—Mr. Inglewood, you're a man; go and tell them they simply can't."

"Unfortunately, it seems to me they simply can," said Inglewood, with a depressed air. "I have far less right of intervention than Miss Duke, besides having, of course, far less moral force than she."

"You haven't either of you got much," cried Rosamund, the last stays of her formidable temper giving way; "I think I'll go somewhere else for a little sense and pluck. I think I know some one who will help me more than you do, at any rate . . . he's a cantankerous beast, but he's a man, and has a mind, and knows it . . . " And she flung out into the garden, with cheeks aflame, and the parasol whirling like a Catherine wheel.

She found Michael Moon standing under the garden tree, looking over the hedge; hunched like a bird of prey, with his large pipe hanging down his long blue chin. The very hardness of his expression pleased her, after the nonsense of the new engagement and the shilly-shallying of her other friends.

"I am sorry I was cross, Mr. Moon," she said frankly. "I hated you for being a cynic; but I've been well punished, for I want a cynic just now. I've had my fill of sentiment— I'm fed up with it. The world's gone mad, Mr. Moon—all except the cynics, I think. That maniac Smith wants to marry my old friend Mary, and she— and she—doesn't seem to mind."

Seeing his attentive face still undisturbedly smoking, she added smartly, "I'm not joking; that's Mr. Smith's cab outside. He swears he'll take her off now to his aunt's, and go for a special licence. Do give me some practical advice, Mr. Moon."

Mr. Moon took his pipe out of his mouth, held it in his hand for an instant reflectively, and then tossed it to the other side of the garden. "My practical advice to you is this," he said: "Let him go for his special licence, and ask him to get another one for you and me."

"Is that one of your jokes?" asked the young lady. "Do say what you really mean."

"I mean that Innocent Smith is a man of business," said Moon with ponderous precision—"a plain, practical man: a man of affairs; a man of facts and the daylight. He has let down twenty ton of good building bricks suddenly on my head, and I am glad to say they have woken me up. We went to sleep a little while ago on this very lawn, in this very sunlight. We have had a little nap for five years or so, but now we're going to be married, Rosamund, and I can't see why that cab . . . "

"Really," said Rosamund stoutly, "I don't know what you mean."

"What a lie!" cried Michael, advancing on her with brightening eyes. "I'm all for lies in an ordinary way; but don't you see that to-night they won't do? We've wandered into a world of facts, old girl. That grass growing, and that sun going down, and that cab at the door, are facts. You used to torment and excuse yourself by saying I was after your money, and didn't really love you. But if I stood here now and told you I didn't love you—you wouldn't believe me: for truth is in this garden to-night."

"Really, Mr. Moon . . . " said Rosamund, rather more faintly.

He kept two big blue magnetic eyes fixed on her face. "Is my name Moon?" he asked. "Is your name Hunt? On my honour, they sound to me as quaint and as distant as Red Indian names. It's as if your name was `Swim' and my name was `Sunrise.' But our real names are Husband and Wife, as they were when we fell asleep."

"It is no good," said Rosamund, with real tears in her eyes; "one can never go back."

"I can go where I damn please," said Michael, "and I can carry you on my shoulder."

"But really, Michael, really, you must stop and think!" cried the girl earnestly. "You could carry me off my feet, I dare say, soul and body, but it may be bitter bad business for all that. These things done in that romantic rush, like Mr. Smith's, they— they do attract women, I don't deny it. As you say, we're all telling the truth to-night. They've attracted poor Mary, for one. They attract me, Michael. But the cold fact remains: imprudent marriages do lead to long unhappiness and disappointment— you've got used to your drinks and things—I shan't be pretty much longer—"

"Imprudent marriages!" roared Michael. "And pray where in earth or heaven are there any prudent marriages? Might as well talk about prudent suicides. You and I have dawdled round each other long enough, and are we any safer than Smith and Mary Gray, who met last night? You never know a husband till you marry him. Unhappy! of course you'll be unhappy. Who the devil are you that you shouldn't be unhappy, like the mother that bore you? Disappointed! of course we'll be disappointed. I, for one, don't expect till I die to be so good a man as I am at this minute— a tower with all the trumpets shouting."

"You see all this," said Rosamund, with a grand sincerity in her solid face, "and do you really want to marry me?"

"My darling, what else is there to do?" reasoned the Irishman. "What other occupation is there for an active man on this earth, except to marry you? What's the alternative to marriage, barring sleep? It's not liberty, Rosamund. Unless you marry God, as our nuns do in Ireland, you must marry Man—that is Me. The only third thing is to marry yourself— yourself, yourself, yourself—the only companion that is never satisfied— and never satisfactory."

"Michael," said Miss Hunt, in a very soft voice, "if you won't talk so much, I'll marry you."

"It's no time for talking," cried Michael Moon; "singing is the only thing. Can't you find that mandoline of yours, Rosamund?"

"Go and fetch it for me," said Rosamund, with crisp and sharp authority.

The lounging Mr. Moon stood for one split second astonished; then he shot away across the lawn, as if shod with the feathered shoes out of the Greek fairy tale. He cleared three yards and fifteen daisies at a leap, out of mere bodily levity; but when he came within a yard or two of the open parlour windows, his flying feet fell in their old manner like lead; he twisted round and came back slowly, whistling. The events of that enchanted evening were not at an end.

Inside the dark sitting-room of which Moon had caught a glimpse a curious thing had happened, almost an instant after the intemperate exit of Rosamund. It was something which, occurring in that obscure parlour, seemed to Arthur Inglewood like heaven and earth turning head over heels, the sea being the ceiling and the stars the floor. No words can express how it astonished him, as it astonishes all simple men when it happens. Yet the stiffest female stoicism seems separated from it only by a sheet of paper or a sheet of steel. It indicates no surrender, far less any sympathy. The most rigid and ruthless woman can begin to cry, just as the most effeminate man can grow a beard. It is a separate sexual power, and proves nothing one way or the other about force of character. But to young men ignorant of women, like Arthur Inglewood, to see Diana Duke crying was like seeing a motor-car shedding tears of petrol.

He could never have given (even if his really manly modesty had permitted it) any vaguest vision of what he did when he saw that portent. He acted as men do when a theatre catches fire—very differently from how they would have conceived themselves as acting, whether for better or worse. He had a faint memory of certain half-stifled explanations, that the heiress was the one really paying guest, and she would go, and the bailiffs (in consequence) would come; but after that he knew nothing of his own conduct except by the protests it evoked.

"Leave me alone, Mr. Inglewood—leave me alone; that's not the way to help."

"But I can help you," said Arthur, with grinding certainty; "I can, I can, I can . . . "

"Why, you said," cried the girl, "that you were much weaker than me."

"So I am weaker than you," said Arthur, in a voice that went vibrating through everything, "but not just now."

"Let go my hands!" cried Diana. "I won't be bullied."

In one element he was much stronger than she—the matter of humour. This leapt up in him suddenly, and he laughed, saying: "Well, you are mean. You know quite well you'll bully me all the rest of my life. You might allow a man the one minute of his life when he's allowed to bully."

It was as extraordinary for him to laugh as for her to cry, and for the first time since her childhood Diana was entirely off her guard.

"Do you mean you want to marry me?" she said.

"Why, there's a cab at the door!" cried Inglewood, springing up with an unconscious energy and bursting open the glass doors that led into the garden.

As he led her out by the hand they realized somehow for the first time that the house and garden were on a steep height over London. And yet, though they felt the place to be uplifted, they felt it also to be secret: it was like some round walled garden on the top of one of the turrets of heaven.

Inglewood looked around dreamily, his brown eyes devouring all sorts of details with a senseless delight. He noticed for the first time that the railings of the gate beyond the garden bushes were moulded like little spearheads and painted blue. He noticed that one of the blue spears was loosened in its place, and hung sideways; and this almost made him laugh. He thought it somehow exquisitely harmless and funny that the railing should be crooked; he thought he should like to know how it happened, who did it, and how the man was getting on.

When they were gone a few feet across that fiery grass they realized that they were not alone. Rosamund Hunt and the eccentric Mr. Moon, both of whom they had last seen in the blackest temper of detachment, were standing together on the lawn. They were standing in quite an ordinary manner, and yet they looked somehow like people in a book.

"Oh," said Diana, "what lovely air!"

"I know," called out Rosamund, with a pleasure so positive that it rang out like a complaint. "It's just like that horrid, beastly fizzy stuff they gave me that made me feel happy."

"Oh, it isn't like anything but itself!" answered Diana, breathing deeply. "Why, it's all cold, and yet it feels like fire."

"Balmy is the word we use in Fleet Street," said Mr. Moon. "Balmy—especially on the crumpet." And he fanned himself quite unnecessarily with his straw hat. They were all full of little leaps and pulsations of objectless and airy energy. Diana stirred and stretched her long arms rigidly, as if crucified, in a sort of excruciating restfulness; Michael stood still for long intervals, with gathered muscles, then spun round like a teetotum, and stood still again; Rosamund did not trip, for women never trip, except when they fall on their noses, but she struck the ground with her foot as she moved, as if to some inaudible dance tune; and Inglewood, leaning quite quietly against a tree, had unconsciously clutched a branch and shaken it with a creative violence. Those giant gestures of Man, that made the high statues and the strokes of war, tossed and tormented all their limbs. Silently as they strolled and stood they were bursting like batteries with an animal magnetism.

"And now," cried Moon quite suddenly, stretching out a hand on each side, "let's dance round that bush!"

"Why, what bush do you mean?" asked Rosamund, looking round with a sort of radiant rudeness.

"The bush that isn't there," said Michael—"the Mulberry Bush."

They had taken each other's hands, half laughing and quite ritually; and before they could disconnect again Michael spun them all round, like a demon spinning the world for a top. Diana felt, as the circle of the horizon flew instantaneously around her, a far aerial sense of the ring of heights beyond London and corners where she had climbed as a child; she seemed almost to hear the rooks cawing about the old pines on Highgate, or to see the glowworms gathering and kindling in the woods of Box Hill.

The circle broke—as all such perfect circles of levity must break— and sent its author, Michael, flying, as by centrifugal force, far away against the blue rails of the gate. When reeling there he suddenly raised shout after shout of a new and quite dramatic character.

"Why, it's Warner!" he shouted, waving his arms. "It's jolly old Warner— with a new silk hat and the old silk moustache!"

"Is that Dr. Warner?" cried Rosamund, bounding forward in a burst of memory, amusement, and distress. "Oh, I'm so sorry! Oh, do tell him it's all right!"

"Let's take hands and tell him," said Michael Moon. For indeed, while they were talking, another hansom cab had dashed up behind the one already waiting, and Dr. Herbert Warner, leaving a companion in the cab, had carefully deposited himself on the pavement.

Now, when you are an eminent physician and are wired for by an heiress to come to a case of dangerous mania, and when, as you come in through the garden to the house, the heiress and her landlady and two of the gentlemen boarders join hands and dance round you in a ring, calling out, "It's all right! it's all right!" you are apt to be flustered and even displeased. Dr. Warner was a placid but hardly a placable person. The two things are by no means the same; and even when Moon explained to him that he, Warner, with his high hat and tall, solid figure, was just such a classic figure as OUGHT to be danced round by a ring of laughing maidens on some old golden Greek seashore — even then he seemed to miss the point of the general rejoicing.

"Inglewood!" cried Dr. Warner, fixing his former disciple with a stare, "are you mad?"

Arthur flushed to the roots of his brown hair, but he answered, easily and quietly enough, "Not now. The truth is, Warner, I've just made a rather important medical discovery—quite in your line."

"What do you mean?" asked the great doctor stiffly—"what discovery?"

"I've discovered that health really is catching, like disease," answered Arthur.

"Yes; sanity has broken out, and is spreading," said Michael, performing a ~pas seul~ with a thoughtful expression. "Twenty thousand more cases taken to the hospitals; nurses employed night and day."

Dr. Warner studied Michael's grave face and lightly moving legs with an unfathomed wonder. "And is THIS, may I ask," he said, "the sanity that is spreading?"

"You must forgive me, Dr. Warner," cried Rosamund Hunt heartily. "I know I've treated you badly; but indeed it was all a mistake. I was in a frightfully bad temper when I sent for you, but now it all seems like a dream—and Mr. Smith is the sweetest, most sensible, most delightful old thing that ever existed, and he may marry any one he likes—except me."

"I should suggest Mrs. Duke," said Michael.

The gravity of Dr. Warner's face increased. He took a slip of pink paper from his waistcoat pocket, with his pale blue eyes quietly fixed on Rosamund's face all the time. He spoke with a not inexcusable frigidity.

"Really, Miss Hunt," he said, "you are not yet very reassuring. You sent me this wire only half an hour ago: `Come at once, if possible, with another doctor. Man—Innocent Smith—gone mad on premises, and doing dreadful things. Do you know anything of him?' I went round at once to a distinguished colleague of mine, a doctor who is also a private detective and an authority on criminal lunacy; he has come round with me, and is waiting in the cab. Now you calmly tell me that this criminal madman is a highly sweet and sane old thing, with accompaniments that set me speculating on your own definition of sanity. I hardly comprehend the change."

"Oh, how can one explain a change in sun and moon and everybody's soul?" cried Rosamund, in despair. "Must I confess we had got so morbid as to think him mad merely because he wanted to get married; and that we didn't even know it was only because we wanted to get married ourselves? We'll humiliate ourselves, if you like, doctor; we're happy enough."

"Where is Mr. Smith?" asked Warner of Inglewood very sharply.

Arthur started; he had forgotten all about the central figure of their farce, who had not been visible for an hour or more.

"I—I think he's on the other side of the house, by the dustbin," he said.

"He may be on the road to Russia," said Warner, "but he must be found." And he strode away and disappeared round a corner of the house by the sunflowers.

"I hope," said Rosamund, "he won't really interfere with Mr. Smith."

"Interfere with the daisies!" said Michael with a snort. "A man can't be locked up for falling in love—at least I hope not."

"No; I think even a doctor couldn't make a disease out of him. He'd throw off the doctor like the disease, don't you know? I believe it's a case of a sort of holy well. I believe Innocent Smith is simply innocent, and that is why he is so extraordinary."

It was Rosamund who spoke, restlessly tracing circles in the grass with the point of her white shoe.

"I think," said Inglewood, "that Smith is not extraordinary at all. He's comic just because he's so startlingly commonplace. Don't you know what it is to be all one family circle, with aunts and uncles, when a schoolboy comes home for the holidays? That bag there on the cab is only a schoolboy's hamper. This tree here in the garden is only the sort of tree that any schoolboy would have climbed. Yes, that's the thing that has haunted us all about him, the thing we could never fit a word to. Whether he is my old schoolfellow or no, at least he is all my old schoolfellows. He is the endless bun-eating, ball-throwing animal that we have all been."

"That is only you absurd boys," said Diana. "I don't believe any girl was ever so silly, and I'm sure no girl was ever so happy, except—" and she stopped.

"I will tell you the truth about Innocent Smith," said Michael Moon in a low voice. "Dr. Warner has gone to look for him in vain. He is not there. Haven't you noticed that we never saw him since we found ourselves? He was an astral baby born on all four of us; he was only our own youth returned. Long before poor old Warner had clambered out of his cab, the thing we called Smith had dissolved into dew and light on this lawn. Once or twice more, by the mercy of God, we may feel the thing, but the man we shall never see. In a spring garden before breakfast we shall smell the smell called Smith. In the snapping of brisk twigs in tiny fires we shall hear a noise named Smith. Everything insatiable and innocent in the grasses that gobble up the earth like babies at a bun feast, in the white mornings that split the sky as a boy splits up white firwood, we may feel for one instant the presence of an impetuous purity; but his innocence was too close to the unconsciousness of inanimate things not to melt back at a mere touch into the mild hedges and heavens; he—"

He was interrupted from behind the house by a bang like that of a bomb. Almost at the same instant the stranger in the cab sprang out of it, leaving it rocking upon the stones of the road. He clutched the blue railings of the garden, and peered eagerly over them in the direction of the noise. He was a small, loose, yet alert man, very thin, with a face that seemed made out of fish bones, and a silk hat quite as rigid and resplendent as Warner's, but thrust back recklessly on the hinder part of his head.

"Murder!" he shrieked, in a high and feminine but very penetrating voice. "Stop that murderer there!"

Even as he shrieked a second shot shook the lower windows of the house, and with the noise of it Dr. Herbert Warner came flying round the corner like a leaping rabbit. Yet before he had reached the group a third discharge had deafened them, and they saw with their own eyes two spots of white sky drilled through the second of the unhappy Herbert's high hats. The next moment the fugitive physician fell over a flowerpot, and came down on all fours, staring like a cow. The hat with the two shot-holes in it rolled upon the gravel path before him, and Innocent Smith came round the corner like a railway train. He was looking twice his proper size—a giant clad in green, the big revolver still smoking in his hand, his face sanguine and in shadow, his eyes blazing like all stars, and his yellow hair standing out all ways like Struwelpeter's.

Though this startling scene hung but an instant in stillness, Inglewood had time to feel once more what he had felt when he saw the other lovers standing on the lawn— the sensation of a certain cut and coloured clearness that belongs rather to the things of art than to the things of experience. The broken flowerpot with its red-hot geraniums, the green bulk of Smith and the black bulk of Warner, the blue-spiked railings behind, clutched by the stranger's yellow vulture claws and peered over by his long vulture neck, the silk hat on the gravel, and the little cloudlet of smoke floating across the garden as innocently as the puff of a cigarette— all these seemed unnaturally distinct and definite. They existed, like symbols, in an ecstasy of separation. Indeed, every object grew more and more particular and precious because the whole picture was breaking up. Things look so bright just before they burst.

Long before his fancies had begun, let alone ceased, Arthur had stepped across and taken one of Smith's arms. Simultaneously the little stranger had run up the steps and taken the other. Smith went into peals of laughter, and surrendered his pistol with perfect willingness. Moon raised the doctor to his feet, and then went and leaned sullenly on the garden gate. The girls were quiet and vigilant, as good women mostly are in instants of catastrophe, but their faces showed that, somehow or other, a light had been dashed out of the sky. The doctor himself, when he had risen, collected his hat and wits, and dusting himself down with an air of great disgust, turned to them in brief apology. He was very white with his recent panic, but he spoke with perfect self-control.

"You will excuse us, ladies," he said; "my friend and Mr. Inglewood are both scientists in their several ways. I think we had better all take Mr. Smith indoors, and communicate with you later."

And under the guard of the three natural philosophers the disarmed Smith was led tactfully into the house, still roaring with laughter.

From time to time during the next twenty minutes his distant boom of mirth could again be heard through the half-open window; but there came no echo of the quiet voices of the physicians. The girls walked about the garden together, rubbing up each other's spirits as best they might; Michael Moon still hung heavily against the gate. Somewhere about the expiration of that time Dr. Warner came out of the house with a face less pale but even more stern, and the little man with the fish-bone face advanced gravely in his rear. And if the face of Warner in the sunlight was that of a hanging judge, the face of the little man behind was more like a death's head.

"Miss Hunt," said Dr. Herbert Warner, "I only wish to offer you my warm thanks and admiration. By your prompt courage and wisdom in sending for us by wire this evening, you have enabled us to capture and put out of mischief one of the most cruel and terrible of the enemies of humanity— a criminal whose plausibility and pitilessness have never been before combined in flesh."

Rosamund looked across at him with a white, blank face and blinking eyes. "What do you mean?" she asked. "You can't mean Mr. Smith?"

"He has gone by many other names," said the doctor gravely, "and not one he did not leave to be cursed behind him. That man, Miss Hunt, has left a track of blood and tears across the world. Whether he is mad as well as wicked, we are trying, in the interests of science, to discover. In any case, we shall have to take him to a magistrate first, even if only on the road to a lunatic asylum. But the lunatic asylum in which he is confined will have to be sealed with wall within wall, and ringed with guns like a fortress, or he will break out again to bring forth carnage and darkness on the earth."

Rosamund looked at the two doctors, her face growing paler and paler. Then her eyes strayed to Michael, who was leaning on the gate; but he continued to lean on it without moving, with his face turned away towards the darkening road.

5. THE ALLEGORICAL PRACTICAL JOKER

The criminal specialist who had come with Dr. Warner was a somewhat more urbane and even dapper figure than he had appeared when clutching the railings and craning his neck into the garden. He even looked comparatively young when he took his hat off, having fair hair parted in the middle and carefully curled on each side, and lively movements, especially of the hands. He had a dandified monocle slung round his neck by a broad black ribbon, and a big bow tie, as if a big American moth had alighted on him. His dress and gestures were bright enough for a boy's; it was only when you looked at the fish-bone face that you beheld something acrid and old. His manners were excellent, though hardly English, and he had two half-conscious tricks by which people who only met him once remembered him. One was a trick of closing his eyes when he wished to be particularly polite; the other was one of lifting his joined thumb and forefinger in the air as if holding a pinch of snuff, when he was hesitating or hovering over a word. But those who were longer in his company tended to forget these oddities in the stream of his quaint and solemn conversation and really singular views.

"Miss Hunt," said Dr. Warner, "this is Dr. Cyrus Pym."

Dr. Cyrus Pym shut his eyes during the introduction, rather as if he were "playing fair" in some child's game, and gave a prompt little bow, which somehow suddenly revealed him as a citizen of the United States.

"Dr. Cyrus Pym," continued Warner (Dr. Pym shut his eyes again), "is perhaps the first criminological expert of America. We are very fortunate to be able to consult with him in this extraordinary case—"

"I can't make head or tail of anything," said Rosamund. "How can poor Mr. Smith be so dreadful as he is by your account?"

"Or by your telegram," said Herbert Warner, smiling.

"Oh, you don't understand," cried the girl impatiently. "Why, he's done us all more good than going to church."

"I think I can explain to the young lady," said Dr. Cyrus Pym. "This criminal or maniac Smith is a very genius of evil, and has a method of his own, a method of the most daring ingenuity. He is popular wherever he goes, for he invades every house as an uproarious child. People are getting suspicious of all the respectable disguises for a scoundrel; so he always uses the disguise of—what shall I say—the Bohemian, the blameless Bohemian. He always carries people off their feet. People are used to the mask of conventional good conduct. He goes in for eccentric good-nature. You expect a Don Juan to dress up as a solemn and solid Spanish merchant; but you're not prepared when he dresses up as Don Quixote. You expect a humbug to behave like Sir Charles Grandison; because (with all respect, Miss Hunt, for the deep, tear-moving tenderness of Samuel Richardson) Sir Charles Grandison so often behaved like a humbug. But no real red-blooded citizen is quite ready for a humbug that models himself not on Sir Charles Grandison but on Sir Roger de Coverly. Setting up to be a good man a little cracked is a new criminal incognito, Miss Hunt. It's been a great notion, and uncommonly successful; but its success just makes it mighty cruel. I can forgive Dick Turpin if he impersonates Dr. Busby; I can't forgive him when he impersonates Dr. Johnson. The saint with a tile loose is a bit too sacred, I guess, to be parodied."

"But how do you know," cried Rosamund desperately, "that Mr. Smith is a known criminal?"

"I collated all the documents," said the American, "when my friend Warner knocked me up on receipt of your cable. It is my professional affair to know these facts, Miss Hunt; and there's no more doubt about them than about the Bradshaw down at the depot. This man has hitherto escaped the law, through his admirable affectations of infancy or insanity. But I myself, as a specialist, have privately authenticated notes of some eighteen or twenty crimes attempted or achieved in this manner. He comes to houses as he has to this, and gets a grand popularity. He makes things go. They do go; when he's gone the things are gone. Gone, Miss Hunt, gone, a man's life or a man's spoons, or more often a woman. I assure you I have all the memoranda."

"I have seen them," said Warner solidly, "I can assure you that all this is correct."

"The most unmanly aspect, according to my feelings," went on the American doctor, "is this perpetual deception of innocent women by a wild simulation of innocence. From almost every house where this great imaginative devil has been, he has taken some poor girl away with him; some say he's got a hypnotic eye with his other queer features, and that they go like automata. What's become of all those poor girls nobody knows. Murdered, I dare say; for we've lots of instances, besides this one, of his turning his hand to murder, though none ever brought him under the law. Anyhow, our most modern methods of research can't find any trace of the wretched women. It's when I think of them that I am really moved, Miss Hunt. And I've really nothing else to say just now except what Dr. Warner has said."

"Quite so," said Warner, with a smile that seemed moulded in marble—"that we all have to thank you very much for that telegram."

The little Yankee scientist had been speaking with such evident sincerity that one forgot the tricks of his voice and manner— the falling eyelids, the rising intonation, and the poised finger and thumb—which were at other times a little comic. It was not so much that he was cleverer than Warner; perhaps he was not so clever, though he was more celebrated. But he had what Warner never had, a fresh and unaffected seriousness — the great American virtue of simplicity. Rosamund knitted her brows and looked gloomily toward the darkening house that contained the dark prodigy.

Broad daylight still endured; but it had already changed from gold to silver, and was changing from silver to gray. The long plumy shadows of the one or two trees in the garden faded more and more upon a dead background of dusk. In the sharpest and deepest shadow, which was the entrance to the house by the big French windows, Rosamund could watch a hurried consultation between Inglewood (who was still left in charge of the mysterious captive) and Diana, who had moved to his assistance from without. After a few minutes and gestures they went inside, shutting the glass doors upon the garden; and the garden seemed to grow grayer still.

The American gentleman named Pym seemed to be turning and on the move in the same direction; but before he started he spoke to Rosamund with a flash of that guileless tact which redeemed much of his childish vanity, and with something of that spontaneous poetry which made it difficult, pedantic as he was, to call him a pedant.

"I'm vurry sorry, Miss Hunt," he said; "but Dr. Warner and I, as two quali-FIED practitioners, had better take Mr. Smith away in that cab, and the less said about it the better. Don't you agitate yourself, Miss Hunt. You've just got to think that we're taking away a monstrosity, something that oughtn't to be at all—something like one of those gods in your Britannic Museum, all wings, and beards, and legs, and eyes, and no shape. That's what Smith is, and you shall soon be quit of him."

He had already taken a step towards the house, and Warner was about to follow him, when the glass doors were opened again and Diana Duke came out with more than her usual quickness across the lawn. Her face was aquiver with worry and excitement, and her dark earnest eyes fixed only on the other girl.

"Rosamund," she cried in despair, "what shall I do with her?"

"With her?" cried Miss Hunt, with a violent jump. "O lord, he isn't a woman too, is he?"

"No, no, no," said Dr. Pym soothingly, as if in common fairness. "A woman? no, really, he is not so bad as that."

"I mean your friend Mary Gray," retorted Diana with equal tartness. "What on earth am I to do with her?"

"How can we tell her about Smith, you mean," answered Rosamund, her face at once clouded and softening. "Yes, it will be pretty painful."

"But I HAVE told her," exploded Diana, with more than her congenital exasperation. "I have told her, and she doesn't seem to mind. She still says she's going away with Smith in that cab."

"But it's impossible!" ejaculated Rosamund. "Why, Mary is really religious. She—"

She stopped in time to realize that Mary Gray was comparatively close to her on the lawn. Her quiet companion had come down very quietly into the garden, but dressed very decisively for travel. She had a neat but very ancient blue tam-o'-shanter on her head, and was pulling some rather threadbare gray gloves on to her hands. Yet the two tints fitted excellently with her heavy copper-coloured hair; the more excellently for the touch of shabbiness: for a woman's clothes never suit her so well as when they seem to suit her by accident.

But in this case the woman had a quality yet more unique and attractive. In such gray hours, when the sun is sunk and the skies are already sad, it will often happen that one reflection at some occasional angle will cause to linger the last of the light. A scrap of window, a scrap of water, a scrap of looking-glass, will be full of the fire that is lost to all the rest of the earth. The quaint, almost triangular face of Mary Gray was like some triangular piece of mirror that could still repeat the splendour of hours before. Mary, though she was always graceful, could never before have properly been called beautiful; and yet her happiness amid all that misery was so beautiful as to make a man catch his breath.

"O Diana," cried Rosamund in a lower voice and altering her phrase; "but how did you tell her?"

"It is quite easy to tell her," answered Diana sombrely; "it makes no impression at all."

"I'm afraid I've kept everything waiting," said Mary Gray apologetically, "and now we must really say good-bye. Innocent is taking me to his aunt's over at Hampstead, and I'm afraid she goes to bed early."

Her words were quite casual and practical, but there was a sort of sleepy light in her eyes that was more baffling than darkness; she was like one speaking absently with her eye on some very distant object.

"Mary, Mary," cried Rosamund, almost breaking down, "I'm so sorry about it, but the thing can't be at all. We—we have found out all about Mr. Smith."

"All?" repeated Mary, with a low and curious intonation; "why, that must be awfully exciting."

There was no noise for an instant and no motion except that the silent Michael Moon, leaning on the gate, lifted his head, as it might be to listen. Then Rosamund remaining speechless, Dr. Pym came to her rescue in a definite way.

"To begin with," he said, "this man Smith is constantly attempting murder. The Warden of Brakespeare College—"

"I know," said Mary, with a vague but radiant smile. "Innocent told me."

"I can't say what he told you," replied Pym quickly, "but I'm very much afraid it wasn't true. The plain truth is that the man's stained with every known human crime. I assure you I have all the documents. I have evidence of his committing burglary, signed by a most eminent English curate. I have—"

"Oh, but there were two curates," cried Mary, with a certain gentle eagerness; "that was what made it so much funnier."

The darkened glass doors of the house opened once more, and Inglewood appeared for an instant, making a sort of signal. The American doctor bowed, the English doctor did not, but they both set out stolidly towards the house. No one else moved, not even Michael hanging on the gate; but the back of his head and shoulders had still an indescribable indication that he was listening to every word.

"But don't you understand, Mary," cried Rosamund in despair; "don't you know that awful things have happened even before our very eyes. I should have thought you would have heard the revolver shots upstairs."

"Yes, I heard the shots," said Mary almost brightly; "but I was busy packing just then. And Innocent had told me he was going to shoot at Dr. Warner; so it wasn't worth while to come down."

"Oh, I don't understand what you mean," cried Rosamund Hunt, stamping, "but you must and shall understand what I mean. I don't care how cruelly I put it, if only I can save you. I mean that your Innocent Smith is the most awfully wicked man in the world. He has sent bullets at lots of other men and gone off in cabs with lots of other women. And he seems to have killed the women too, for nobody can find them."

"He is really rather naughty sometimes," said Mary Gray, laughing softly as she buttoned her old gray gloves.

"Oh, this is really mesmerism, or something," said Rosamund, and burst into tears.

At the same moment the two black-clad doctors appeared out of the house with their great green-clad captive between them. He made no resistance, but was still laughing in a groggy and half-witted style. Arthur Inglewood followed in the rear, a dark and red study in the last shades of distress and shame. In this black, funereal, and painfully realistic style the exit from Beacon House was made by a man whose entrance a day before had been effected by the happy leaping of a wall and the hilarious climbing of a tree. No one moved of the groups in the garden except Mary Gray, who stepped forward quite naturally, calling out, "Are you ready, Innocent? Our cab's been waiting such a long time."

"Ladies and gentlemen," said Dr. Warner firmly, "I must insist on asking this lady to stand aside. We shall have trouble enough as it is, with the three of us in a cab."

"But it IS our cab," persisted Mary. "Why, there's Innocent's yellow bag on the top of it."

"Stand aside," repeated Warner roughly. "And you, Mr. Moon, please be so obliging as to move a moment. Come, come! the sooner this ugly business is over the better—and how can we open the gate if you will keep leaning on it?"

Michael Moon looked at his long lean forefinger, and seemed to consider and reconsider this argument. "Yes," he said at last; "but how can I lean on this gate if you keep on opening it?"

"Oh, get out of the way!" cried Warner, almost good-humouredly. "You can lean on the gate any time."

"No," said Moon reflectively. "Seldom the time and the place and the blue gate altogether; and it all depends whether you come of an old country family. My ancestors leaned on gates before any one had discovered how to open them."

"Michael!" cried Arthur Inglewood in a kind of agony, "are you going to get out of the way?"

"Why, no; I think not," said Michael, after some meditation, and swung himself slowly round, so that he confronted the company, while still, in a lounging attitude, occupying the path.

"Hullo!" he called out suddenly; "what are you doing to Mr. Smith?"

"Taking him away," answered Warner shortly, "to be examined."

"Matriculation?" asked Moon brightly.

"By a magistrate," said the other curtly.

"And what other magistrate," cried Michael, raising his voice, "dares to try what befell on this free soil, save only the ancient and independent Dukes of Beacon? What other court dares to try one of our company, save only the High Court of Beacon? Have you forgotten that only this afternoon we flew the flag of independence and severed ourselves from all the nations of the earth?"

"Michael," cried Rosamund, wringing her hands, "how can you stand there talking nonsense? Why, you saw the dreadful thing yourself. You were there when he went mad. It was you that helped the doctor up when he fell over the flower-pot."

"And the High Court of Beacon," replied Moon with hauteur, "has special powers in all cases concerning lunatics, flower-pots, and doctors who fall down in gardens. It's in our very first charter from Edward I: `Si medicus quisquam in horto prostratus—'"

"Out of the way!" cried Warner with sudden fury, "or we will force you out of it."

"What!" cried Michael Moon, with a cry of hilarious fierceness. "Shall I die in defence of this sacred pale? Will you paint these blue railings red with my gore?" and he laid hold of one of the blue spikes behind him. As Inglewood had noticed earlier in the evening, the railing was loose and crooked at this place, and the painted iron staff and spearhead came away in Michael's hand as he shook it.

"See!" he cried, brandishing this broken javelin in the air, "the very lances round Beacon Tower leap from their places to defend it. Ah, in such a place and hour it is a fine thing to die alone!" And in a voice like a drum he rolled the noble lines of Ronsard—

"Ou pour l'honneur de Dieu, ou pour le droit de mon prince, Navre, poitrine ouverte, au bord de mon province."

"Sakes alive!" said the American gentleman, almost in an awed tone. Then he added, "Are there two maniacs here?"

"No; there are five," thundered Moon. "Smith and I are the only sane people left."

"Michael!" cried Rosamund; "Michael, what does it mean?"

"It means bosh!" roared Michael, and slung his painted spear hurtling to the other end of the garden. "It means that doctors are bosh, and criminology is bosh, and Americans are bosh— much more bosh than our Court of Beacon. It means, you fatheads, that Innocent Smith is no more mad or bad than the bird on that tree."

"But, my dear Moon," began Inglewood in his modest manner, "these gentlemen—"

"On the word of two doctors," exploded Moon again, without listening to anybody else, "shut up in a private hell on the word of two doctors! And such doctors! Oh, my hat! Look at 'em!—do just look at 'em! Would you read a book, or buy a dog, or go to a hotel on the advice of twenty such? My people came from Ireland, and were Catholics. What would you say if I called a man wicked on the word of two priests?"

"But it isn't only their word, Michael," reasoned Rosamund; "they've got evidence too."

"Have you looked at it?" asked Moon.

"No," said Rosamund, with a sort of faint surprise; "these gentlemen are in charge of it."

"And of everything else, it seems to me," said Michael. "Why, you haven't even had the decency to consult Mrs. Duke."

"Oh, that's no use," said Diana in an undertone to Rosamund; "Auntie can't say 'Bo!' to a goose."

"I am glad to hear it," answered Michael, "for with such a flock of geese to say it to, the horrid expletive might be constantly on her lips. For my part, I simply refuse to let things be done in this light and airy style. I appeal to Mrs. Duke—it's her house."

"Mrs. Duke?" repeated Inglewood doubtfully.

"Yes, Mrs. Duke," said Michael firmly, "commonly called the Iron Duke."

"If you ask Auntie," said Diana quietly, "she'll only be for doing nothing at all. Her only idea is to hush things up or to let things slide. That just suits her."

"Yes," replied Michael Moon; "and, as it happens, it just suits all of us. You are impatient with your elders, Miss Duke; but when you are as old yourself you will know what Napoleon knew— that half one's letters answer themselves if you can only refrain from the fleshly appetite of answering them."

He was still lounging in the same absurd attitude, with his elbow on the grate, but his voice had altered abruptly for the third time; just as it had changed from the mock heroic to the humanly indignant, it now changed to the airy incisiveness of a lawyer giving good legal advice.

"It isn't only your aunt who wants to keep this quiet if she can," he said; "we all want to keep it quiet if we can. Look at the large facts—the big bones of the case. I believe those scientific gentlemen have made a highly scientific mistake. I believe Smith is as blameless as a buttercup. I admit buttercups don't often let off loaded pistols in private houses; I admit there is something demanding explanation. But I am morally certain there's some blunder, or some joke, or some allegory, or some accident behind all this. Well, suppose I'm wrong. We've disarmed him; we're five men to hold him; he may as well go to a lock-up later on as now. But suppose there's even a chance of my being right. Is it anybody's interest here to wash this linen in public?

"Come, I'll take each of you in order. Once take Smith outside that gate, and you take him into the front page of the evening papers. I know; I've written the front page myself. Miss Duke, do you or your aunt want a sort of notice stuck up over your boarding-house—`Doctors shot here.'? No, no—doctors are rubbish, as I said; but you don't want the rubbish shot here. Arthur, suppose I am right, or suppose I am wrong. Smith has appeared as an old schoolfellow of yours. Mark my words, if he's proved guilty, the Organs of Public Opinion will say you introduced him. If he's proved innocent, they will say you helped to collar him. Rosamund, my dear, suppose I am right or wrong. If he's proved guilty, they'll say you engaged your companion to him. If he's proved innocent, they'll print that telegram. I know the Organs, damn them."

He stopped an instant; for this rapid rationalism left him more breathless than had either his theatrical or his real denunciation. But he was plainly in earnest, as well as positive and lucid; as was proved by his proceeding quickly the moment he had found his breath.

"It is just the same," he cried, "with our medical friends. You will say that Dr. Warner has a grievance. I agree. But does he want specially to be snapshotted by all the journalists ~prostratus in horto~? It was no fault of his, but the scene was not very dignified even for him. He must have justice; but does he want to ask for justice, not only on his knees, but on his hands and knees? Does he want to enter the court of justice on all fours? Doctors are not allowed to advertise; and I'm sure no doctor wants to advertise himself as looking like that. And even for our American guest the interest is the same. Let us suppose that he has conclusive documents. Let us assume that he has revelations really worth reading. Well, in a legal inquiry (or a medical inquiry, for that matter) ten to one he won't be allowed to read them. He'll be tripped up every two or three minutes with some tangle of old rules. A man can't tell the truth in public nowadays. But he can still tell it in private; he can tell it inside that house."

"It is quite true," said Dr. Cyrus Pym, who had listened throughout the speech with a seriousness which only an American could have retained through such a scene. "It is true that I have been per-ceptibly less hampered in private inquiries."

"Dr. Pym!" cried Warner in a sort of sudden anger. "Dr. Pym! you aren't really going to admit—"

"Smith may be mad," went on the melancholy Moon in a monologue that seemed as heavy as a hatchet, "but there was something after all in what he said about Home Rule for every home. Yes, there is something, when all's said and done, in the High Court of Beacon. It is really true that human beings might often get some sort of domestic justice where just now they can only get legal injustice—oh, I am a lawyer too, and I know that as well. It is true that there's too much official and indirect power. Often and often the thing a whole nation can't settle is just the thing a family could settle. Scores of young criminals have been fined and sent to jail when they ought to have been thrashed and sent to bed. Scores of men, I am sure, have had a lifetime at Hanwell when they only wanted a week at Brighton. There IS something in Smith's notion of domestic self-government; and I propose that we put it into practice. You have the prisoner; you have the documents. Come, we are a company of free, white, Christian people, such as might be besieged in a town or cast up on a desert island. Let us do this thing ourselves. Let us go into that house there and sit down and find out with our own eyes and ears whether this thing is true or not; whether this Smith is a man or a monster. If we can't do a little thing like that, what right have we to put crosses on ballot papers?"

Inglewood and Pym exchanged a glance; and Warner, who was no fool, saw in that glance that Moon was gaining ground. The motives that led Arthur to think of surrender were indeed very different from those which affected Dr. Cyrus Pym. All Arthur's instincts were on the side of privacy and polite settlement; he was very English and would often endure wrongs rather than right them by scenes and serious rhetoric. To play at once the buffoon and the knight-errant, like his Irish friend, would have been absolute torture to him; but even the semi-official part he had played that afternoon was very painful. He was not likely to be reluctant if any one could convince him that his duty was to let sleeping dogs lie.

On the other hand, Cyrus Pym belonged to a country in which things are possible that seem crazy to the English. Regulations and authorities exactly like one of Innocent's pranks or one of Michael's satires really exist, propped by placid policemen and imposed on bustling business men. Pym knew whole States which are vast and yet secret and fanciful; each is as big as a nation yet as private as a lost village, and as unexpected as an apple-pie bed. States where no man may have a cigarette, States where any man may have ten wives, very strict prohibition States, very lax divorce States—all these large local vagaries had prepared Cyrus Pym's mind for small local vagaries in a smaller country. Infinitely more remote from England than any Russian or Italian, utterly incapable of even conceiving what English conventions are, he could not see the social impossibility of the Court of Beacon. It is firmly believed by those who shared the experiment, that to the very end Pym believed in that phantasmal court and supposed it to be some Britannic institution.

Towards the synod thus somewhat at a standstill there approached through the growing haze and gloaming a short dark figure with a walk apparently founded on the imperfect repression of a negro breakdown. Something at once in the familiarity and the incongruity of this being moved Michael to even heartier outbursts of a healthy and humane flippancy.

"Why, here's little Nosey Gould," he exclaimed. "Isn't the mere sight of him enough to banish all your morbid reflections?"

"Really," replied Dr. Warner, "I really fail to see how Mr. Gould affects the question; and I once more demand—"

"Hello! what's the funeral, gents?" inquired the newcomer with the air of an uproarious umpire. "Doctor demandin' something? Always the way at a boarding-house, you know. Always lots of demand. No supply."

As delicately and impartially as he could, Michael restated his position, and indicated generally that Smith had been guilty of certain dangerous and dubious acts, and that there had even arisen an allegation that he was insane.

"Well, of course he is," said Moses Gould equably; "it don't need old 'Olmes to see that. The 'awk-like face of 'Olmes," he added with abstract relish, "showed a shide of disappointment, the sleuth-like Gould 'avin' got there before 'im."

"If he is mad," began Inglewood.

"Well," said Moses, "when a cove gets out on the tile the first night there's generally a tile loose."

"You never objected before," said Diana Duke rather stiffly, "and you're generally pretty free with your complaints."

"I don't compline of him," said Moses magnanimously, "the poor chap's 'armless enough; you might tie 'im up in the garden here and 'e'd make noises at the burglars."

"Moses," said Moon with solemn fervour, "you are the incarnation of Common Sense. You think Mr. Innocent is mad. Let me introduce you to the incarnation of Scientific Theory. He also thinks Mr. Innocent is mad.—Doctor, this is my friend Mr. Gould.—Moses, this is the celebrated Dr. Pym." The celebrated Dr. Cyrus Pym closed his eyes and bowed. He also murmured his national war-cry in a low voice, which sounded like "Pleased to meet you."

"Now you two people," said Michael cheerfully, "who both think our poor friend mad, shall jolly well go into that house over there and prove him mad. What could be more powerful than the combination of Scientific Theory with Common Sense? United you stand; divided you fall. I will not be so uncivil as to suggest that Dr. Pym has no common sense; I confine myself to recording the chronological accident that he has not shown us any so far. I take the freedom of an old friend in staking my shirt that Moses has no scientific theory. Yet against this strong coalition I am ready to appear, armed with nothing but an intuition—which is American for a guess."

"Distinguished by Mr. Gould's assistance," said Pym, opening his eyes suddenly. "I gather that though he and I are identical in primary di-agnosis there is yet between us something that cannot be called a disagreement, something which we may perhaps call a—" He put the points of thumb and forefinger together, spreading the other fingers exquisitely in the air, and seemed to be waiting for somebody else to tell him what to say.

"Catchin' flies?" inquired the affable Moses.

"A divergence," said Dr. Pym, with a refined sigh of relief; "a divergence. Granted that the man in question is deranged, he would not necessarily be all that science requires in a homicidal maniac—"

"Has it occurred to you," observed Moon, who was leaning on the gate again, and did not turn round, "that if he were a homicidal maniac he might have killed us all here while we were talking."

Something exploded silently underneath all their minds, like sealed dynamite in some forgotten cellars. They all remembered for the first time for some hour or two that the monster of whom they were talking was standing quietly among them. They had left him in the garden like a garden statue; there might have been a dolphin coiling round his legs, or a fountain pouring out of his mouth, for all the notice they had taken of Innocent Smith. He stood with his crest of blonde, blown hair thrust somewhat forward, his fresh-coloured, rather short-sighted face looking patiently downwards at nothing in particular, his huge shoulders humped, and his hands in his trousers pockets. So far as they could guess he had not moved at all. His green coat might have been cut out of the green turf on which he stood. In his shadow Pym had expounded and Rosamund expostulated, Michael had ranted and Moses had ragged. He had remained like a thing graven; the god of the garden. A sparrow had perched on one of his heavy shoulders; and then, after correcting its costume of feathers, had flown away.

"Why," cried Michael, with a shout of laughter, "the Court of Beacon has opened— and shut up again too. You all know now I am right. Your buried common sense has told you what my buried common sense has told me. Smith might have fired off a hundred cannons instead of a pistol, and you would still know he was harmless as I know he is harmless. Back we all go to the house and clear a room for discussion. For the High Court of Beacon, which has already arrived at its decision, is just about to begin its inquiry."

"Just a goin' to begin!" cried little Mr. Moses in an extraordinary sort of disinterested excitement, like that of an animal during music or a thunderstorm. "Follow on to the 'Igh Court of Eggs and Bacon; 'ave a kipper from the old firm! 'Is Lordship complimented Mr. Gould on the 'igh professional delicacy 'e had shown, and which was worthy of the best traditions of the Saloon Bar— and three of Scotch hot, miss! Oh, chase me, girls!"

The girls betraying no temptation to chase him, he went away in a sort of waddling dance of pure excitement; and had made a circuit of the garden before he reappeared, breathless but still beaming. Moon had known his man when he realized that no people presented to Moses Gould could be quite serious, even if they were quite furious. The glass doors stood open on the side nearest to Mr. Moses Gould; and as the feet of that festive idiot were evidently turned in the same direction, everybody else went that way with the unanimity of some uproarious procession. Only Diana Duke retained enough rigidity to say the thing that had been boiling at her fierce feminine lips for the last few hours. Under the shadow of tragedy she had kept it back as unsympathetic. "In that case," she said sharply, "these cabs can be sent away."

"Well, Innocent must have his bag, you know," said Mary with a smile. "I dare say the cabman would get it down for us."

"I'll get the bag," said Smith, speaking for the first time in hours; his voice sounded remote and rude, like the voice of a statue.

Those who had so long danced and disputed round his immobility were left breathless by his precipitance. With a run and spring he was out of the garden into the street; with a spring and one quivering kick he was actually on the roof of the cab. The cabman happened to be standing by the horse's head, having just removed its emptied nose-bag. Smith seemed for an instant to be rolling about on the cab's back in the embraces of his Gladstone bag. The next instant, however, he had rolled, as if by a royal luck, into the high seat behind, and with a shriek of piercing and appalling suddenness had sent the horse flying and scampering down the street.

His evanescence was so violent and swift, that this time it was all the other people who were turned into garden statues. Mr. Moses Gould, however, being ill-adapted both physically and morally for the purposes of permanent sculpture, came to life some time before the rest, and, turning to Moon, remarked, like a man starting chattily with a stranger on an omnibus, "Tile loose, eh? Cab loose anyhow." There followed a fatal silence; and then Dr. Warner said, with a sneer like a club of stone,—

"This is what comes of the Court of Beacon, Mr. Moon. You have let loose a maniac on the whole metropolis."

Beacon House stood, as has been said, at the end of a long crescent of continuous houses. The little garden that shut it in ran out into a sharp point like a green cape pushed out into the sea of two streets. Smith and his cab shot up one side of the triangle, and certainly most of those standing inside of it never expected to see him again. At the apex, however, he turned the horse sharply round and drove with equal violence up the other side of the garden, visible to all those in the group. With a common impulse the little crowd ran across the lawn as if to stop him, but they soon had reason to duck and recoil. Even as he vanished up street for the second time, he let the big yellow bag fly from his hand, so that it fell in the centre of the garden, scattering the company like a bomb, and nearly damaging Dr. Warner's hat for the third time. Long before they had collected themselves, the cab had shot away with a shriek that went into a whisper.

"Well," said Michael Moon, with a queer note in his voice; "you may as well all go inside anyhow. We've got two relics of Mr. Smith at least; his fiancee and his trunk."

"Why do you want us to go inside?" asked Arthur Inglewood, in whose red brow and rough brown hair botheration seemed to have reached its limit.

"I want the rest to go in," said Michael in a clear voice, "because I want the whole of this garden in which to talk to you."

There was an atmosphere of irrational doubt; it was really getting colder, and a night wind had begun to wave the one or two trees in the twilight. Dr. Warner, however, spoke in a voice devoid of indecision.

"I refuse to listen to any such proposal," he said; "you have lost this ruffian, and I must find him."

"I don't ask you to listen to any proposal," answered Moon quietly; "I only ask you to listen."

He made a silencing movement with his hand, and immediately the whistling noise that had been lost in the dark streets on one side of the house could be heard from quite a new quarter on the other side. Through the night-maze of streets the noise increased with incredible rapidity, and the next moment the flying hoofs and flashing wheels had swept up to the blue-railed gate at which they had originally stood. Mr. Smith got down from his perch with an air of absent-mindedness, and coming back into the garden stood in the same elephantine attitude as before.

"Get inside! get inside!" cried Moon hilariously, with the air of one shooing a company of cats. "Come, come, be quick about it! Didn't I tell you I wanted to talk to Inglewood?"

How they were all really driven into the house again it would have been difficult afterwards to say. They had reached the point of being exhausted with incongruities, as people at a farce are ill with laughing, and the brisk growth of the storm among the trees seemed like a final gesture of things in general. Inglewood lingered behind them, saying with a certain amicable exasperation, "I say, do you really want to speak to me?"

"I do," said Michael, "very much."

Night had come as it generally does, quicker than the twilight had seemed to promise. While the human eye still felt the sky as light gray, a very large and lustrous moon appearing abruptly above a bulk of roofs and trees, proved by contrast that the sky was already a very dark gray indeed. A drift of barren leaves across the lawn, a drift of riven clouds across the sky, seemed to be lifted on the same strong and yet laborious wind.

"Arthur," said Michael, "I began with an intuition; but now I am sure. You and I are going to defend this friend of yours before the blessed Court of Beacon, and to clear him too—clear him of both crime and lunacy. Just listen to me while I preach to you for a bit." They walked up and down the darkening garden together as Michael Moon went on.

"Can you," asked Michael, "shut your eyes and see some of those queer old hieroglyphics they stuck up on white walls in the old hot countries. How stiff they were in shape and yet how gaudy in colour. Think of some alphabet of arbitrary figures picked out in black and red, or white and green, with some old Semitic crowd of Nosey Gould's ancestors staring at it, and try to think why the people put it up at all."

Inglewood's first instinct was to think that his perplexing friend had really gone off his head at last; there seemed so reckless a flight of irrelevancy from the tropic-pictured walls he was asked to imagine to the gray, wind-swept, and somewhat chilly suburban garden in which he was actually kicking his heels. How he could be more happy in one by imagining the other he could not conceive. Both (in themselves) were unpleasant.

"Why does everybody repeat riddles," went on Moon abruptly, "even if they've forgotten the answers? Riddles are easy to remember because they are hard to guess. So were those stiff old symbols in black, red, or green easy to remember because they had been hard to guess. Their colours were plain. Their shapes were plain. Everything was plain except the meaning."

Inglewood was about to open his mouth in an amiable protest, but Moon went on, plunging quicker and quicker up and down the garden and smoking faster and faster. "Dances, too," he said; "dances were not frivolous. Dances were harder to understand than inscriptions and texts. The old dances were stiff, ceremonial, highly coloured but silent. Have you noticed anything odd about Smith?"

"Well, really," cried Inglewood, left behind in a collapse of humour, "have I noticed anything else?"

"Have you noticed this about him," asked Moon, with unshaken persistency, "that he has done so much and said so little? When first he came he talked, but in a gasping, irregular sort of way, as if he wasn't used to it. All he really did was actions—painting red flowers on black gowns or throwing yellow bags on to the grass. I tell you that big green figure is figurative— like any green figure capering on some white Eastern wall."

"My dear Michael," cried Inglewood, in a rising irritation which increased with the rising wind, "you are getting absurdly fanciful."

"I think of what has just happened," said Michael steadily. "The man has not spoken for hours; and yet he has been speaking all the time. He fired three shots from a six-shooter and then gave it up to us, when he might have shot us dead in our boots. How could he express his trust in us better than that? He wanted to be tried by us. How could he have shown it better than by standing quite still and letting us discuss it? He wanted to show that he stood there willingly, and could escape if he liked. How could he have shown it better than by escaping in the cab and coming back again? Innocent

Smith is not a madman—he is a ritualist. He wants to express himself, not with his tongue, but with his arms and legs— with my body I thee worship, as it says in the marriage service. I begin to understand the old plays and pageants. I see why the mutes at a funeral were mute. I see why the mummers were mum. They MEANT something; and Smith means something too. All other jokes have to be noisy—like little Nosey Gould's jokes, for instance. The only silent jokes are the practical jokes. Poor Smith, properly considered, is an allegorical practical joker. What he has really done in this house has been as frantic as a war-dance, but as silent as a picture."

"I suppose you mean," said the other dubiously, "that we have got to find out what all these crimes meant, as if they were so many coloured picture-puzzles. But even supposing that they do mean something—why, Lord bless my soul!—"

Taking the turn of the garden quite naturally, he had lifted his eyes to the moon, by this time risen big and luminous, and had seen a huge, half-human figure sitting on the garden wall. It was outlined so sharply against the moon that for the first flash it was hard to be certain even that it was human: the hunched shoulders and outstanding hair had rather the air of a colossal cat. It resembled a cat also in the fact that when first startled it sprang up and ran with easy activity along the top of the wall. As it ran, however, its heavy shoulders and small stooping head rather suggested a baboon. The instant it came within reach of a tree it made an ape-like leap and was lost in the branches. The gale, which by this time was shaking every shrub in the garden, made the identification yet more difficult, since it melted the moving limbs of the fugitive in the multitudinous moving limbs of the tree.

"Who is there?" shouted Arthur. "Who are you? Are you Innocent?"

"Not quite," answered an obscure voice among the leaves. "I cheated you once about a penknife."

The wind in the garden had gathered strength, and was throwing the tree backwards and forwards with the man in the thick of it, just as it had on the gay and golden afternoon when he had first arrived.

"But are you Smith?" asked Inglewood as in an agony.

"Very nearly," said the voice out of the tossing tree.

"But you must have some real names," shrieked Inglewood in despair. "You must call yourself something."

"Call myself something," thundered the obscure voice, shaking the tree so that all its ten thousand leaves seemed to be talking at once. "I call myself Roland Oliver Isaiah Charlemagne Arthur Hildebrand Homer Danton Michaelangelo Shakespeare Brakespeare—"

"But, manalive!" began Inglewood in exasperation.

"That's right! that's right!" came with a roar out of the rocking tree; "that's my real name." And he broke a branch, and one or two autumn leaves fluttered away across the moon.

THE EXPLANATIONS OF INNOCENT SMITH

1. THE EYE OF DEATH; OR, THE MURDER CHARGE

The dining-room of the Dukes had been set out for the Court of Beacon with a certain impromptu pomposity that seemed somehow to increase its cosiness. The big room was, as it were, cut up into small rooms, with walls only waist high—the sort of separation that children make when they are playing at shops. This had been done by Moses Gould and Michael Moon (the two most active members of this remarkable inquiry) with the ordinary furniture of the place. At one end of the long mahogany table was set the one enormous garden chair, which was surmounted by the old torn tent or umbrella which Smith himself had suggested as a coronation canopy. Inside this erection could be perceived the dumpy form of Mrs. Duke, with cushions and a form of countenance that already threatened slumber. At the other end sat the accused Smith, in a kind of dock; for he was carefully fenced in with a quadrilateral of light bedroom chairs, any of which he could have tossed out the window with his big toe. He had been provided with pens and paper, out of the latter of which he made paper boats, paper darts, and paper dolls contentedly throughout the whole proceedings. He never spoke or even looked up, but seemed as unconscious as a child on the floor of an empty nursery.

On a row of chairs raised high on the top of a long settee sat the three young ladies with their backs up against the window, and Mary Gray in the middle; it was something between a jury box and the stall of the Queen of Beauty at a tournament. Down the centre of the long table Moon had built a low barrier out of eight bound volumes of "Good Words" to express the moral wall that divided the conflicting parties. On the right side sat the two advocates of the prosecution, Dr. Pym and Mr. Gould; behind a barricade of books and documents, chiefly (in the case of Dr. Pym) solid volumes of criminology. On the other side, Moon and Inglewood, for the defence, were also fortified with books and papers; but as these included several old yellow volumes by

380

Ouida and Wilkie Collins, the hand of Mr. Moon seemed to have been somewhat careless and comprehensive. As for the victim and prosecutor, Dr. Warner, Moon wanted at first to have him kept entirely behind a high screen in the corner, urging the indelicacy of his appearance in court, but privately assuring him of an unofficial permission to peep over the top now and then. Dr. Warner, however, failed to rise to the chivalry of such a course, and after some little disturbance and discussion he was accommodated with a seat on the right side of the table in a line with his legal advisers.

It was before this solidly-established tribunal that Dr. Cyrus Pym, after passing a hand through the honey-coloured hair over each ear, rose to open the case. His statement was clear and even restrained, and such flights of imagery as occurred in it only attracted attention by a certain indescribable abruptness, not uncommon in the flowers of American speech.

He planted the points of his ten frail fingers on the mahogany, closed his eyes, and opened his mouth. "The time has gone by," he said, "when murder could be regarded as a moral and individual act, important perhaps to the murderer, perhaps to the murdered. Science has profoundly . . . " here he paused, poising his compressed finger and thumb in the air as if he were holding an elusive idea very tight by its tail, then he screwed up his eyes and said "modified," and let it go—"has profoundly Modified our view of death. In superstitious ages it was regarded as the termination of life, catastrophic, and even tragic, and was often surrounded by solemnity. Brighter days, however, have dawned, and we now see death as universal and inevitable, as part of that great soul-stirring and heart-upholding average which we call for convenience the order of nature. In the same way we have come to consider murder SOCIALLY. Rising above the mere private feelings of a man while being forcibly deprived of life, we are privileged to behold murder as a mighty whole, to see the rich rotation of the cosmos, bringing, as it brings the golden harvests and the golden-bearded harvesters, the return for ever of the slayers and the slain."

He looked down, somewhat affected with his own eloquence, coughed slightly, putting up four of his pointed fingers with the excellent manners of Boston, and continued: "There is but one result of this happier and humaner outlook which concerns the wretched man before us. It is that thoroughly elucidated by a Milwaukee doctor, our great secret-guessing Sonnenschein, in his great work, `The Destructive Type.' We do not denounce Smith as a murderer, but rather as a murderous man. The type is such that its very life— I might say its very health—is in killing. Some hold that it is not properly an aberration, but a newer and even a higher creature. My dear old friend Dr. Bulger, who kept ferrets—" (here Moon suddenly ejaculated a loud "hurrah!" but so instantaneously resumed his tragic expression that Mrs. Duke looked everywhere else for the sound); Dr. Pym continued somewhat sternly—"who, in the interests of knowledge, kept ferrets, felt that the creature's ferocity is not utilitarian, but absolutely an end in itself. However this may be with ferrets, it is certainly so with the prisoner. In his other iniquities you may find the cunning of the maniac; but his acts of blood have almost the simplicity of sanity. But it is the awful sanity of the sun and the elements—a cruel, an evil sanity. As soon stay the iris-leapt cataracts of our virgin West as stay the natural force that sends him forth to slay. No environment, however scientific, could have softened him. Place that man in the silver-silent purity of the palest cloister, and there will be some deed of violence done with the crozier or the alb.

Rear him in a happy nursery, amid our brave-browed Anglo-Saxon infancy, and he will find some way to strangle with the skipping-rope or brain with the brick. Circumstances may be favourable, training may be admirable, hopes may be high, but the huge elemental hunger of Innocent Smith for blood will in its appointed season burst like a well-timed bomb."

Arthur Inglewood glanced curiously for an instant at the huge creature at the foot of the table, who was fitting a paper figure with a cocked hat, and then looked back at Dr. Pym, who was concluding in a quieter tone.

"It only remains for us," he said, "to bring forward actual evidence of his previous attempts. By an agreement already made with the Court and the leaders of the defence, we are permitted to put in evidence authentic letters from witnesses to these scenes, which the defence is free to examine. Out of several cases of such outrages we have decided to select one— the clearest and most scandalous. I will therefore, without further delay, call on my junior, Mr. Gould, to read two letters—one from the Sub-Warden and the other from the porter of Brakespeare College, in Cambridge University."

Gould jumped up with a jerk like a jack-in-the-box, an academic-looking paper in his hand and a fever of importance on his face. He began in a loud, high, cockney voice that was as abrupt as a cock-crow:—

"Sir,—Hi am the Sub-Warden of Brikespeare College, Cambridge—"

"Lord have mercy on us," muttered Moon, making a backward movement as men do when a gun goes off.

"Hi am the Sub-Warden of Brikespeare College, Cambridge," proclaimed the uncompromising Moses, "and I can endorse the description you gave of the un'appy Smith. It was not alone my unfortunate duty to rebuke many of the lesser violences of his undergraduate period, but I was actually a witness to the last iniquity which terminated that period. Hi happened to passing under the house of my friend the Warden of Brikespeare, which is semi-detached from the College and connected with it by two or three very ancient arches or props, like bridges, across a small strip of water connected with the river. To my grive astonishment I be'eld my eminent friend suspended in mid-air and clinging to one of these pieces of masonry, his appearance and attitude indicatin' that he suffered from the grivest apprehensions. After a short time I heard two very loud shots, and distinctly perceived the unfortunate undergraduate Smith leaning far out of the Warden's window and aiming at the Warden repeatedly with a revolver. Upon seeing me, Smith burst into a loud laugh (in which impertinence was mingled with insanity), and appeared to desist. I sent the college porter for a ladder, and he succeeded in detaching the Warden from his painful position. Smith was sent down. The photograph I enclose is from the group of the University Rifle Club prizemen, and represents him as he was when at the College.— Hi am, your obedient servant, Amos Boulter.

"The other letter," continued Gould in a glow of triumph, "is from the porter, and won't take long to read.

"Dear Sir,—It is quite true that I am the porter of Brikespeare College, and that I 'elped the Warden down when the young man was shooting at him, as Mr. Boulter has said in his letter. The young man who was shooting at him was Mr. Smith, the same that is in the photograph Mr. Boulter sends.— Yours respectfully, Samuel Barker."

Gould handed the two letters across to Moon, who examined them. But for the vocal divergences in the matter of h's and a's, the Sub-Warden's letter was exactly as Gould had rendered it; and both that and the porter's letter were plainly genuine. Moon handed them to Inglewood, who handed them back in silence to Moses Gould.

"So far as this first charge of continual attempted murder is concerned," said Dr. Pym, standing up for the last time, "that is my case."

Michael Moon rose for the defence with an air of depression which gave little hope at the outset to the sympathizers with the prisoner. He did not, he said, propose to follow the doctor into the abstract questions. "I do not know enough to be an agnostic," he said, rather wearily, "and I can only master the known and admitted elements in such controversies. As for science and religion, the known and admitted facts are plain enough. All that the parsons say is unproved. All that the doctors say is disproved. That's the only difference between science and religion there's ever been, or will be. Yet these new discoveries touch me, somehow," he said, looking down sorrowfully at his boots. "They remind me of a dear old great-aunt of mine who used to enjoy them in her youth. It brings tears to my eyes. I can see the old bucket by the garden fence and the line of shimmering poplars behind—"

"Hi! here, stop the 'bus a bit," cried Mr. Moses Gould, rising in a sort of perspiration. "We want to give the defence a fair run—like gents, you know; but any gent would draw the line at shimmering poplars."

"Well, hang it all," said Moon, in an injured manner, "if Dr. Pym may have an old friend with ferrets, why mayn't I have an old aunt with poplars?"

"I am sure," said Mrs. Duke, bridling, with something almost like a shaky authority, "Mr. Moon may have what aunts he likes."

"Why, as to liking her," began Moon, "I—but perhaps, as you say, she is scarcely the core of the question. I repeat that I do not mean to follow the abstract speculations. For, indeed, my answer to Dr. Pym is simple and severely concrete. Dr. Pym has only treated one side of the psychology of murder. If it is true that there is a kind of man who has a natural tendency to murder, is it not equally true"—here he lowered his voice and spoke with a crushing quietude and earnestness—"is it not equally true that there is a kind of man who has a natural tendency to get murdered? Is it not at least a hypothesis holding the field that Dr. Warner is such a man? I do not speak without the book, any more than my learned friend. The whole matter is expounded in Dr. Moonenschein's monumental work, 'The Destructible Doctor,' with diagrams, showing the various ways in which such a person as Dr. Warner may be resolved into his elements. In the light of these facts—"

"Hi, stop the 'bus! stop the 'bus!" cried Moses, jumping up and down and gesticulating in great excitement. "My principal's got something to say! My principal wants to do a bit of talkin'."

Dr. Pym was indeed on his feet, looking pallid and rather vicious. "I have strictly CON-fined myself," he said nasally, "to books to which immediate reference can be made. I have Sonnenschein's 'Destructive Type' here on the table, if the defence wish to see it. Where is this wonderful work on Destructability Mr. Moon is talking about? Does it exist? Can he produce it?"

"Produce it!" cried the Irishman with a rich scorn. "I'll produce it in a week if you'll pay for the ink and paper."

"Would it have much authority?" asked Pym, sitting down.

"Oh, authority!" said Moon lightly; "that depends on a fellow's religion."

Dr. Pym jumped up again. "Our authority is based on masses of accurate detail," he said. "It deals with a region in which things can be handled and tested. My opponent will at least admit that death is a fact of experience."

"Not of mine," said Moon mournfully, shaking his head. "I've never experienced such a thing in all my life."

"Well, really," said Dr. Pym, and sat down sharply amid a crackle of papers.

"So we see," resumed Moon, in the same melancholy voice, "that a man like Dr. Warner is, in the mysterious workings of evolution, doomed to such attacks. My client's onslaught, even if it occurred, was not unique. I have in my hand letters from more than one acquaintance of Dr. Warner whom that remarkable man has affected in the same way. Following the example of my learned friends I will read only two of them. The first is from an honest and laborious matron living off the Harrow Road.

"Mr. Moon, Sir,—Yes, I did throw a sorsepan at him. Wot then? It was all I had to throw, all the soft things being porned, and if your Docter Warner doesn't like having sorsepans thrown at him, don't let him wear his hat in a respectable woman's parler, and tell him to leave orf smiling or tell us the joke.—Yours respectfully, Hannah Miles.

"The other letter is from a physician of some note in Dublin, with whom Dr. Warner was once engaged in consultation. He writes as follows:—

"Dear Sir,—The incident to which you refer is one which I regret, and which, moreover, I have never been able to explain. My own branch of medicine is not mental; and I should be glad to have the view of a mental specialist on my singular momentary and indeed almost automatic action. To say that I 'pulled Dr. Warner's nose,' is, however, inaccurate in a respect that strikes me as important. That I punched his nose I must cheerfully admit (I need not say with what regret); but pulling seems to me to imply a precision of objective with which I cannot reproach myself. In comparison with this, the act of punching was an outward, instantaneous, and even natural gesture.—Believe me, yours faithfully, Burton Lestrange.

"I have numberless other letters," continued Moon, "all bearing witness to this widespread feeling about my eminent friend; and I therefore think that Dr. Pym should have admitted this side of the question in his survey. We are in the presence, as Dr. Pym so truly says, of a natural force. As soon stay the cataract of the London water-works as stay the great tendency of Dr. Warner to be assassinated by somebody. Place that man in a Quakers' meeting, among the most peaceful of Christians, and he will immediately be beaten to death with sticks of chocolate. Place him among the angels of the New Jerusalem, and he will be stoned to death with precious stones. Circumstances may be beautiful and wonderful, the average may be heart-upholding, the harvester may be golden-bearded, the doctor may be secret-guessing, the cataract may be iris-leapt, the Anglo-Saxon infant may be brave-browed, but against and above all these prodigies the grand simple tendency of Dr. Warner to get murdered will still pursue its way until it happily and triumphantly succeeds at last."

He pronounced this peroration with an appearance of strong emotion. But even stronger emotions were manifesting themselves on the other side of the table. Dr. Warner had leaned his large body quite across the little figure of Moses Gould and was talking in excited whispers to Dr. Pym. That expert nodded a great many times and finally started to his feet with a sincere expression of sternness.

"Ladies and gentlemen," he cried indignantly, "as my colleague has said, we should be delighted to give any latitude to the defence—if there were a defence. But Mr. Moon seems to think he is there to make jokes— very good jokes I dare say, but not at all adapted to assist his client. He picks holes in science. He picks holes in my client's social popularity. He picks holes in my literary style, which doesn't seem to suit his high-toned European taste. But how does this picking of holes affect the issue? This Smith has picked two holes in my client's hat, and with an inch better aim would have picked two holes in his head. All the jokes in the world won't unpick those holes or be any use for the defence."

Inglewood looked down in some embarrassment, as if shaken by the evident fairness of this, but Moon still gazed at his opponent in a dreamy way. "The defence?" he said vaguely—"oh, I haven't begun that yet."

"You certainly have not," said Pym warmly, amid a murmur of applause from his side, which the other side found it impossible to answer. "Perhaps, if you have any defence, which has been doubtful from the very beginning—"

"While you're standing up," said Moon, in the same almost sleepy style, "perhaps I might ask you a question."

"A question? Certainly," said Pym stiffly. "It was distinctly arranged between us that as we could not cross-examine the witnesses, we might vicariously cross-examine each other. We are in a position to invite all such inquiry."

"I think you said," observed Moon absently, "that none of the prisoner's shots really hit the doctor."

"For the cause of science," cried the complacent Pym, "fortunately not."

"Yet they were fired from a few feet away?"

"Yes; about four feet."

"And no shots hit the Warden, though they were fired quite close to him too?" asked Moon.

"That is so," said the witness gravely.

"I think," said Moon, suppressing a slight yawn, "that your Sub-Warden mentioned that Smith was one of the University's record men for shooting."

"Why, as to that—" began Pym, after an instant of stillness.

"A second question," continued Moon, comparatively curtly. "You said there were other cases of the accused trying to kill people. Why have you not got evidence of them?"

The American planted the points of his fingers on the table again. "In those cases," he said precisely, "there was no evidence from outsiders, as in the Cambridge case, but only the evidence of the actual victims."

"Why didn't you get their evidence?"

"In the case of the actual victims," said Pym, "there was some difficulty and reluctance, and—"

"Do you mean," asked Moon, "that none of the actual victims would appear against the prisoner?"

"That would be exaggerative," began the other.

"A third question," said Moon, so sharply that every one jumped. "You've got the evidence of the Sub-Warden who heard some shots; where's the evidence of the Warden himself who was shot at? The Warden of Brakespeare lives, a prosperous gentleman."

"We did ask for a statement from him," said Pym a little nervously; "but it was so eccentrically expressed that we suppressed it out of deference to an old gentleman whose past services to science have been great."

Moon leaned forward. "You mean, I suppose," he said, "that his statement was favourable to the prisoner."

"It might be understood so," replied the American doctor; "but, really, it was difficult to understand at all. In fact, we sent it back to him."

"You have no longer, then, any statement signed by the Warden of Brakespeare."

"No."

"I only ask," said Michael quietly, "because we have. To conclude my case I will ask my junior, Mr. Inglewood, to read a statement of the true story—a statement attested as true by the signature of the Warden himself."

Arthur Inglewood rose with several papers in his hand, and though he looked somewhat refined and self-effacing, as he always did, the spectators were surprised to feel that his presence was, upon the whole, more efficient and sufficing than his leader's. He was, in truth, one of those modest men who cannot speak until they are told to speak; and then can speak well. Moon was entirely the opposite. His own impudences amused him in private, but they slightly embarrassed him in public; he felt a fool while he was speaking, whereas Inglewood felt a fool only because he could not speak. The moment he had anything to say he could speak; and the moment he could speak, speaking seemed quite natural. Nothing in this universe seemed quite natural to Michael Moon.

"As my colleague has just explained," said Inglewood, "there are two enigmas or inconsistencies on which we base the defence. The first is a plain physical fact. By the admission of everybody, by the very evidence adduced by the prosecution, it is clear that the accused was celebrated as a specially good shot. Yet on both the occasions complained of he shot from a distance of four or five feet, and shot at him four or five times, and never hit him once. That is the first startling circumstance on which we base our argument. The second, as my colleague has urged, is the curious fact that we cannot find a single victim of these alleged outrages to speak for himself. Subordinates speak for him. Porters climb up ladders to him. But he himself is silent. Ladies and gentlemen, I propose to explain on the spot both the riddle of the shots and the riddle of the silence. I will first of all read the covering letter in which the true account of the Cambridge incident is contained, and then that document itself. When you have heard both, there will be no doubt about your decision. The covering letter runs as follows:—

"Dear Sir,—The following is a very exact and even vivid account of the incident as it really happened at Brakespeare College. We, the undersigned, do not see any particular reason why we should refer it to any isolated authorship. The truth is, it has been a composite production; and we have even had some difference of opinion about the adjectives. But every word of it is true.—We are, yours faithfully,

"Wilfred Emerson Eames, "Warden of Brakespeare College, Cambridge.

"Innocent Smith.

"The enclosed statement," continued Inglewood, "runs as follows:—

"A celebrated English university backs so abruptly on the river, that it has, so to speak, to be propped up and patched with all sorts of bridges and semi-detached buildings. The river splits itself into several small streams and canals, so that in one or two corners the place has almost the look of Venice. It was so especially in the case with which we are concerned, in which a few flying buttresses or airy ribs of stone sprang across a strip of water to connect Brakespeare College with the house of the Warden of Brakespeare.

"The country around these colleges is flat; but it does not seem flat when one is thus in the midst of the colleges. For in these flat fens there are always wandering lakes and lingering rivers of water. And these always change what might have been a scheme of horizontal lines into a scheme of vertical lines. Wherever there is water the height of high buildings is doubled, and a British brick house becomes a Babylonian tower. In that shining unshaken surface the houses hang head downwards exactly to their highest or lowest chimney. The coral-coloured cloud seen in that abyss is as far below the world as its original appears above it. Every scrap of water is not only a window but a skylight. Earth splits under men's feet into precipitous aerial perspectives, into which a bird could as easily wing its way as—"

Dr. Cyrus Pym rose in protest. The documents he had put in evidence had been confined to cold affirmation of fact. The defence, in a general way, had an indubitable right to put their case in their own way, but all this landscape gardening seemed to him (Dr. Cyrus Pym) to be not up to the business. "Will the leader of the defence tell me," he asked, "how it can possibly affect this case, that a cloud was cor'l-coloured, or that a bird could have winged itself anywhere?"

"Oh, I don't know," said Michael, lifting himself lazily; "you see, you don't know yet what our defence is. Till you know that, don't you see, anything may be relevant. Why, suppose," he said suddenly, as if an idea had struck him, "suppose we wanted to prove the old Warden colour-blind. Suppose he was shot by a black man with white hair, when he thought he was being shot by a white man with yellow hair! To ascertain if that cloud was really and truly coral-coloured might be of the most massive importance."

He paused with a seriousness which was hardly generally shared, and continued with the same fluency: "Or suppose we wanted to maintain that the Warden committed suicide—that he just got Smith to hold the pistol as Brutus's slave held the sword. Why, it would make all the difference whether the Warden could see himself plain in still water. Still water has made hundreds of suicides: one sees oneself so very—well, so very plain."

"Do you, perhaps," inquired Pym with austere irony, "maintain that your client was a bird of some sort—say, a flamingo?"

"In the matter of his being a flamingo," said Moon with sudden severity, "my client reserves his defence."

No one quite knowing what to make of this, Mr. Moon resumed his seat and Inglewood resumed the reading of his document:—

"There is something pleasing to a mystic in such a land of mirrors. For a mystic is one who holds that two worlds are better than one. In the highest sense, indeed, all thought is reflection.

"This is the real truth, in the saying that second thoughts are best. Animals have no second thoughts; man alone is able to see his own thought double, as a drunkard sees a lamp-post; man alone is able to see his own thought upside down as one sees a house in a puddle. This duplication of mentality, as in a mirror, is (we repeat) the inmost thing of human philosophy. There is a mystical, even a monstrous truth, in the statement that two heads are better than one. But they ought both to grow on the same body."

"I know it's a little transcendental at first," interposed Inglewood, beaming round with a broad apology, "but you see this document was written in collaboration by a don and a—"

"Drunkard, eh?" suggested Moses Gould, beginning to enjoy himself.

"I rather think," proceeded Inglewood with an unruffled and critical air, "that this part was written by the don. I merely warn the Court that the statement, though indubitably accurate, bears here and there the trace of coming from two authors."

"In that case," said Dr. Pym, leaning back and sniffing, "I cannot agree with them that two heads are better than one."

"The undersigned persons think it needless to touch on a kindred problem so often discussed at committees for University Reform: the question of whether dons see double because they are drunk, or get drunk because they see double. It is enough for them (the undersigned persons) if they are able to pursue their own peculiar and profitable theme—which is puddles. What (the undersigned persons ask themselves) is a puddle? A puddle repeats infinity, and is full of light; nevertheless, if analyzed objectively, a puddle is a piece of dirty water spread very thin on mud. The two great historic universities of England have all this large and level and reflective brilliance. Nevertheless, or, rather, on the other hand, they are puddles—puddles, puddles, puddles, puddles. The undersigned persons ask you to excuse an emphasis inseparable from strong conviction."

Inglewood ignored a somewhat wild expression on the faces of some present, and continued with eminent cheerfulness:—

"Such were the thoughts that failed to cross the mind of the undergraduate Smith as he picked his way among the stripes of canal and the glittering rainy gutters into which the water broke up round the back of Brakespeare College. Had these thoughts crossed his mind he would have been much happier than he was. Unfortunately he did not know that his puzzles were puddles. He did not know that the academic mind reflects infinity and is full of light by the simple process of being shallow and standing still. In his case, therefore, there was something solemn, and even evil about the infinity implied. It was half-way through a starry night of bewildering brilliancy; stars were both above and below. To young Smith's sullen fancy the skies below seemed even hollower than the skies above; he had a horrible idea that if he counted the stars he would find one too many in the pool.

"In crossing the little paths and bridges he felt like one stepping on the black and slender ribs of some cosmic Eiffel Tower. For to him, and nearly all the educated youth of that epoch, the stars were cruel things. Though they glowed in the great dome every night, they were an enormous and ugly secret; they uncovered the nakedness of nature; they were a glimpse of the iron wheels and pulleys behind the scenes. For the young men of that sad time thought that the god always comes from the machine. They did not know that in reality the machine only comes from the god. In short, they were all pessimists, and starlight was atrocious to them— atrocious because it was true. All their universe was black with white spots.

"Smith looked up with relief from the glittering pools below to the glittering skies and the great black bulk of the college. The only light other than stars glowed through one peacock-green curtain in the upper part of the building, marking where Dr. Emerson Eames always worked till morning and received his friends and favourite pupils at any hour of the night. Indeed, it was to his rooms that the melancholy Smith was bound. Smith had been at Dr. Eames's lecture for the first half of the morning, and at pistol practice and fencing in a saloon for the second half. He had been sculling madly for the first half of the afternoon and thinking idly (and still more madly) for the second half. He had gone to a supper where he was uproarious, and on to a debating club where he was perfectly insufferable, and the melancholy Smith was melancholy still. Then, as he was going home to his diggings he remembered the eccentricity of his friend and master, the Warden of Brakespeare, and resolved desperately to turn in to that gentleman's private house.

"Emerson Eames was an eccentric in many ways, but his throne in philosophy and metaphysics was of international eminence; the university could hardly have afforded to lose him, and, moreover, a don has only to continue any of his bad habits long enough to make them a part of the British Constitution. The bad habits of Emerson Eames were to sit up all night and to be a student of Schopenhauer. Personally, he was a lean, lounging sort of man, with a blond pointed beard, not so very much older than his pupil Smith in the matter of mere years, but older by centuries in the two essential respects of having a European reputation and a bald head.

"`I came, against the rules, at this unearthly hour,' said Smith, who was nothing to the eye except a very big man trying to make himself small, `because I am coming to the conclusion that existence is really too rotten. I know all the arguments of the thinkers that think otherwise—bishops, and agnostics, and those sort of people. And knowing you were the greatest living authority on the pessimist thinkers—'

"`All thinkers,' said Eames, `are pessimist thinkers.'

"After a patch of pause, not the first—for this depressing conversation had gone on for some hours with alternations of cynicism and silence— the Warden continued with his air of weary brilliancy: `It's all a question of wrong calculation. The moth flies into the candle because he doesn't happen to know that the game is not worth the candle. The wasp gets into the jam in hearty and hopeful efforts to get the jam into him. IN the same way the vulgar people want to enjoy life just as they want to enjoy gin—because they are too stupid to see that they are paying too big a price for it. That they never find happiness—that they don't even know how to look for it—is proved by the paralyzing clumsiness and ugliness of everything they do. Their discordant colours are cries of pain. Look at the brick villas beyond the college on this side of the river. There's one with spotted blinds; look at it! just go and look at it!'

"`Of course,' he went on dreamily, `one or two men see the sober fact a long way off —they go mad. Do you notice that maniacs mostly try either to destroy other things, or (if they are thoughtful) to destroy themselves? The madman is the man behind the scenes, like the man that wanders about the coulisse of a theater. He has only opened the wrong door and come into the right place. He sees things at the right angle. But the common world—'

"`Oh, hang the common world!' said the sullen Smith, letting his fist fall on the table in an idle despair.

"`Let's give it a bad name first,' said the Professor calmly, `and then hang it. A

389

puppy with hydrophobia would probably struggle for life while we killed it; but if we were kind we should kill it. So an omniscient god would put us out of our pain. He would strike us dead.'

"'Why doesn't he strike us dead?' asked the undergraduate abstractedly, plunging his hands into his pockets.

"'He is dead himself,' said the philosopher; `that is where he is really enviable.'

"'To any one who thinks,' proceeded Eames, `the pleasures of life, trivial and soon tasteless, are bribes to bring us into a torture chamber. We all see that for any thinking man mere extinction is the . . . What are you doing? . . . Are you mad? . . . Put that thing down.'

"Dr. Eames had turned his tired but still talkative head over his shoulder, and had found himself looking into a small round black hole, rimmed by a six-sided circlet of steel, with a sort of spike standing up on the top. It fixed him like an iron eye. Through those eternal instants during which the reason is stunned he did not even know what it was. Then he saw behind it the chambered barrel and cocked hammer of a revolver, and behind that the flushed and rather heavy face of Smith, apparently quite unchanged, or even more mild than before.

"'I'll help you out of your hole, old man,' said Smith, with rough tenderness. `I'll put the puppy out of his pain.'

"Emerson Eames retreated towards the window. `Do you mean to kill me?' he cried.

"'It's not a thing I'd do for every one,' said Smith with emotion; `but you and I seem to have got so intimate to-night, somehow. I know all your troubles now, and the only cure, old chap.'

"'Put that thing down,' shouted the Warden.

"'It'll soon be over, you know,' said Smith with the air of a sympathetic dentist. And as the Warden made a run for the window and balcony, his benefactor followed him with a firm step and a compassionate expression.

"Both men were perhaps surprised to see that the gray and white of early daybreak had already come. One of them, however, had emotions calculated to swallow up surprise. Brakespeare College was one of the few that retained real traces of Gothic ornament, and just beneath Dr. Eames's balcony there ran out what had perhaps been a flying buttress, still shapelessly shaped into gray beasts and devils, but blinded with mosses and washed out with rains. With an ungainly and most courageous leap, Eames sprang out on this antique bridge, as the only possible mode of escape from the maniac. He sat astride of it, still in his academic gown, dangling his long thin legs, and considering further chances of flight. The whitening daylight opened under as well as over him that impression of vertical infinity already remarked about the little lakes round Brakespeare. Looking down and seeing the spires and chimneys pendent in the pools, they felt alone in space. They felt as if they were looking over the edge from the North Pole and seeing the South Pole below.

"'Hang the world, we said,' observed Smith, `and the world is hanged. "He has hanged the world upon nothing," says the Bible. Do you like being hanged upon nothing? I'm going to be hanged upon something myself. I'm going to swing for you . . . Dear, tender old phrase,' he murmured; `never true till this moment. I am going to swing for you. For you, dear friend. For your sake. At your express desire.'

"'Help!' cried the Warden of Brakespeare College; `help!'

"'The puppy struggles,' said the undergraduate, with an eye of pity, 'the poor puppy struggles. How fortunate it is that I am wiser and kinder than he,' and he sighted his weapon so as exactly to cover the upper part of Eames's bald head.

"'Smith,' said the philosopher with a sudden change to a sort of ghastly lucidity, 'I shall go mad.'

"'And so look at things from the right angle,' observed Smith, sighing gently. 'Ah, but madness is only a palliative at best, a drug. The only cure is an operation—an operation that is always successful: death.'

"As he spoke the sun rose. It seemed to put colour into everything, with the rapidity of a lightning artist. A fleet of little clouds sailing across the sky changed from pigeon-gray to pink. All over the little academic town the tops of different buildings took on different tints: here the sun would pick out the green enameled on a pinnacle, there the scarlet tiles of a villa; here the copper ornament on some artistic shop, and there the sea-blue slates of some old and steep church roof. All these coloured crests seemed to have something oddly individual and significant about them, like crests of famous knights pointed out in a pageant or a battlefield: they each arrested the eye, especially the rolling eye of Emerson Eames as he looked round on the morning and accepted it as his last. Through a narrow chink between a black timber tavern and a big gray college he could see a clock with gilt hands which the sunshine set on fire. He stared at it as though hypnotized; and suddenly the clock began to strike, as if in personal reply. As if at a signal, clock after clock took up the cry: all the churches awoke like chickens at cockcrow. The birds were already noisy in the trees behind the college. The sun rose, gathering glory that seemed too full for the deep skies to hold, and the shallow waters beneath them seemed golden and brimming and deep enough for the thirst of the gods. Just round the corner of the College, and visible from his crazy perch, were the brightest specks on that bright landscape, the villa with the spotted blinds which he had made his text that night. He wondered for the first time what people lived in them.

"Suddenly he called out with mere querulous authority, as he might have called to a student to shut a door.

"'Let me come off this place,' he cried; 'I can't bear it.'

"'I rather doubt if it will bear you,' said Smith critically; 'but before you break your neck, or I blow out your brains, or let you back into this room (on which complex points I am undecided) I want the metaphysical point cleared up. Do I understand that you want to get back to life?'

"'I'd give anything to get back,' replied the unhappy professor.

"'Give anything!' cried Smith; 'then, blast your impudence, give us a song!'

"'What song do you mean?' demanded the exasperated Eames; 'what song?'

"'A hymn, I think, would be most appropriate,' answered the other gravely. 'I'll let you off if you'll repeat after me the words—

"'I thank the goodness and the grace That on my birth have smiled. And perched me on this curious place, A happy English child.'

"Dr. Emerson Eames having briefly complied, his persecutor abruptly told him to hold his hands up in the air. Vaguely connecting this proceeding with the usual conduct of brigands and bushrangers, Mr. Eames held them up, very stiffly, but without marked surprise. A bird alighting on his stone seat took no more notice of him than of a comic statue.

"'You are now engaged in public worship,' remarked Smith severely, `and before I have done with you, you shall thank God for the very ducks on the pond.'

"The celebrated pessimist half articulately expressed his perfect readiness to thank God for the ducks on the pond.

"'Not forgetting the drakes,' said Smith sternly. (Eames weakly conceded the drakes.) `Not forgetting anything, please. You shall thank heaven for churches and chapels and villas and vulgar people and puddles and pots and pans and sticks and rags and bones and spotted blinds.'

"'All right, all right,' repeated the victim in despair; `sticks and rags and bones and blinds.'

"'Spotted blinds, I think we said,' remarked Smith with a rogueish ruthlessness, and wagging the pistol-barrel at him like a long metallic finger.

"'Spotted blinds,' said Emerson Eames faintly.

"'You can't say fairer than that,' admitted the younger man, `and now I'll just tell you this to wind up with. If you really were what you profess to be, I don't see that it would matter to snail or seraph if you broke your impious stiff neck and dashed out all your drivelling devil-worshipping brains. But in strict biographical fact you are a very nice fellow, addicted to talking putrid nonsense, and I love you like a brother. I shall therefore fire off all my cartridges round your head so as not to hit you (I am a good shot, you may be glad to hear), and then we will go in and have some breakfast.'

"He then let off two barrels in the air, which the Professor endured with singular firmness, and then said, `But don't fire them all off.'

"'Why not' asked the other buoyantly.

"'Keep them,' asked his companion, `for the next man you meet who talks as we were talking.'

"It was at this moment that Smith, looking down, perceived apoplectic terror upon the face of the Sub-Warden, and heard the refined shriek with which he summoned the porter and the ladder.

"It took Dr. Eames some little time to disentangle himself from the ladder, and some little time longer to disentangle himself from the Sub-Warden. But as soon as he could do so unobtrusively, he rejoined his companion in the late extraordinary scene. He was astonished to find the gigantic Smith heavily shaken, and sitting with his shaggy head on his hands. When addressed, he lifted a very pale face.

"'Why, what is the matter?' asked Eames, whose own nerves had by this time twittered themselves quiet, like the morning birds.

"'I must ask your indulgence,' said Smith, rather brokenly. `I must ask you to realize that I have just had an escape from death.'

"'YOU have had an escape from death?' repeated the Professor in not unpardonable irritation. `Well, of all the cheek—'

"'Oh, don't you understand, don't you understand?' cried the pale young man impatiently. `I had to do it, Eames; I had to prove you wrong or die. When a man's young, he nearly always has some one whom he thinks the top-water mark of the mind of man— some one who knows all about it, if anybody knows.

"'Well, you were that to me; you spoke with authority, and not as the scribes. Nobody could comfort me if YOU said there was no comfort. If you really thought there was nothing anywhere, it was because you had been there to see. Don't you see that I HAD to prove you didn't really mean it?— or else drown myself in the canal.'

"`Well,' said Eames hesitatingly, `I think perhaps you confuse—'

"`Oh, don't tell me that!' cried Smith with the sudden clairvoyance of mental pain; `don't tell me I confuse enjoyment of existence with the Will to Live! That's German, and German is High Dutch, and High Dutch is Double Dutch. The thing I saw shining in your eyes when you dangled on that bridge was enjoyment of life and not "the Will to Live." What you knew when you sat on that damned gargoyle was that the world, when all is said and done, is a wonderful and beautiful place; I know it, because I knew it at the same minute. I saw the gray clouds turn pink, and the little gilt clock in the crack between the houses. It was THOSE things you hated leaving, not Life, whatever that is. Eames, we've been to the brink of death together; won't you admit I'm right?'

"`Yes,' said Eames very slowly, `I think you are right. You shall have a First!'

"`Right!' cried Smith, springing up reanimated. `I've passed with honours, and now let me go and see about being sent down.'

"`You needn't be sent down,' said Eames with the quiet confidence of twelve years of intrigue. `Everything with us comes from the man on top to the people just round him: I am the man on top, and I shall tell the people round me the truth.'

"The massive Mr. Smith rose and went firmly to the window, but he spoke with equal firmness. `I must be sent down,' he said, `and the people must not be told the truth.'

"`And why not' asked the other.

"`Because I mean to follow your advice,' answered the massive youth, `I mean to keep the remaining shots for people in the shameful state you and I were in last night— I wish we could even plead drunkenness. I mean to keep those bullets for pessimists— pills for pale people. And in this way I want to walk the world like a wonderful surprise — to float as idly as the thistledown, and come as silently as the sunrise; not to be expected any more than the thunderbolt, not to be recalled any more than the dying breeze. I don't want people to anticipate me as a well-known practical joke. I want both my gifts to come virgin and violent, the death and the life after death. I am going to hold a pistol to the head of the Modern Man. But I shall not use it to kill him—only to bring him to life. I begin to see a new meaning in being the skeleton at the feast.'

"`You can scarcely be called a skeleton,' said Dr. Eames, smiling.

"`That comes of being so much at the feast,' answered the massive youth. `No skeleton can keep his figure if he is always dining out. But that is not quite what I meant: what I mean is that I caught a kind of glimpse of the meaning of death and all that—the skull and cross-bones, the ~memento mori~. It isn't only meant to remind us of a future life, but to remind us of a present life too. With our weak spirits we should grow old in eternity if we were not kept young by death. Providence has to cut immortality into lengths for us, as nurses cut the bread and butter into fingers.'

"Then he added suddenly in a voice of unnatural actuality, `But I know something now, Eames. I knew it when I saw the clouds turn pink.'

"`What do you mean?' asked Eames. `What did you know?'

"`I knew for the first time that murder is really wrong.'

"He gripped Dr. Eames's hand and groped his way somewhat unsteadily to the door. Before he had vanished through it he had added, `It's very dangerous, though, when a man thinks for a split second that he understands death.'

"Dr. Eames remained in repose and rumination some hours after his late assailant had left. Then he rose, took his hat and umbrella, and went for a brisk if rotatory walk. Several times, however, he stood outside the villa with the spotted blinds, studying them intently with his head slightly on one side. Some took him for a lunatic and some for an intending purchaser. He is not yet sure that the two characters would be widely different.

"The above narrative has been constructed on a principle which is, in the opinion of the undersigned persons, new in the art of letters. Each of the two actors is described as he appeared to the other. But the undersigned persons absolutely guarantee the exactitude of the story; and if their version of the thing be questioned, they, the undersigned persons, would deucedly well like to know who does know about it if they don't.

"The undersigned persons will now adjourn to `The Spotted Dog' for beer. Farewell.

"(Signed) James Emerson Eames, "Warden of Brakespeare College, Cambridge.

"Innocent Smith."

2. THE TWO CURATES; OR, THE BURGLARY CHARGE

Arthur Inglewood handed the document he had just read to the leaders of the prosecution, who examined it with their heads together. Both the Jew and the American were of sensitive and excitable stocks, and they revealed by the jumpings and bumpings of the black head and the yellow that nothing could be done in the way of denial of the document. The letter from the Warden was as authentic as the letter from the Sub-Warden, however regrettably different in dignity and social tone.

"Very few words," said Inglewood, "are required to conclude our case in this matter. Surely it is now plain that our client carried his pistol about with the eccentric but innocent purpose of giving a wholesome scare to those whom he regarded as blasphemers. In each case the scare was so wholesome that the victim himself has dated from it as from a new birth. Smith, so far from being a madman, is rather a mad doctor — he walks the world curing frenzies and not distributing them. That is the answer to the two unanswerable questions which I put to the prosecutors. That is why they dared not produce a line by any one who had actually confronted the pistol. All who had actually confronted the pistol confessed that they had profited by it. That was why Smith, though a good shot, never hit anybody. He never hit anybody because he was a good shot. His mind was as clear of murder as his hands are of blood. This, I say, is the only possible explanation of these facts and of all the other facts. No one can possibly explain the Warden's conduct except by believing the Warden's story. Even Dr. Pym, who is a very factory of ingenious theories, could find no other theory to cover the case."

"There are promising per-spectives in hypnotism and dual personality," said Dr. Cyrus Pym dreamily; "the science of criminology is in its infancy, and—"

"Infancy!" cried Moon, jerking his red pencil in the air with a gesture of enlightenment; "why, that explains it!"

"I repeat," proceeded Inglewood, "that neither Dr. Pym nor any one else can account on any other theory but ours for the Warden's signature, for the shots missed and the witnesses missing."

The little Yankee had slipped to his feet with some return of a cock-fighting coolness. "The defence," he said, "omits a coldly colossal fact. They say we produce none of the actual victims. Wal, here is one victim—England's celebrated and stricken Warner. I reckon he is pretty well produced. And they suggest that all the outrages were followed by reconciliation. Wal, there's no flies on England's Warner; and he isn't reconciled much."

"My learned friend," said Moon, getting elaborately to his feet, "must remember that the science of shooting Dr. Warner is in its infancy. Dr. Warner would strike the idlest eye as one specially difficult to startle into any recognition of the glory of God. We admit that our client, in this one instance, failed, and that the operation was not successful. But I am empowered to offer, on behalf of my client, a proposal for operating on Dr. Warner again, at his earliest convenience, and without further fees."

"'Ang it all, Michael," cried Gould, quite serious for the first time in his life, "you might give us a bit of bally sense for a chinge."

"What was Dr. Warner talking about just before the first shot?" asked Moon sharply.

"The creature," said Dr. Warner superciliously, "asked me, with characteristic rationality, whether it was my birthday."

"And you answered, with characteristic swank," cried Moon, shooting out a long lean finger, as rigid and arresting as the pistol of Smith, "that you didn't keep your birthday."

"Something like that," assented the doctor.

"Then," continued Moon, "he asked you why not, and you said it was because you didn't see that birth was anything to rejoice over. Agreed? Now is there any one who doubts that our tale is true?"

There was a cold crash of stillness in the room; and Moon said, "Pax populi vox Dei; it is the silence of the people that is the voice of God. Or in Dr. Pym's more civilized language, it is up to him to open the next charge. On this we claim an acquittal."

It was about an hour later. Dr. Cyrus Pym had remained for an unprecedented time with his eyes closed and his thumb and finger in the air. It almost seemed as if he had been "struck so," as the nurses say; and in the deathly silence Michael Moon felt forced to relieve the strain with some remark. For the last half-hour or so the eminent criminologist had been explaining that science took the same view of offences against property as it did of offences against life. "Most murder," he had said, "is a variation of homicidal mania, and in the same way most theft is a version of kleptomania. I cannot entertain any doubt that my learned friends opposite adequately con-ceive how this must involve a scheme of punishment more tol'rant and humane than the cruel methods of ancient codes. They will doubtless exhibit consciousness of a chasm so eminently yawning, so thought-arresting, so—" It was here that he paused and indulged in the delicate gesture to which allusion has been made; and Michael could bear it no longer.

"Yes, yes," he said impatiently, "we admit the chasm. The old cruel codes accuse a man of theft and send him to prison for ten years. The tolerant and humane ticket accuses him of nothing and sends him to prison for ever. We pass the chasm."

It was characteristic of the eminent Pym, in one of his trances of verbal fastidiousness, that he went on, unconscious not only of his opponent's interruption, but even of his own pause.

"So stock-improving," continued Dr. Cyrus Pym, "so fraught with real high hopes of the future. Science therefore regards thieves, in the abstract, just as it regards murderers. It regards them not as sinners to be punished for an arbitrary period, but as patients to be detained and cared for," (his first two digits closed again as he hesitated)—"in short, for the required period. But there is something special in the case we investigate here. Kleptomania commonly con-joins itself—"

"I beg pardon," said Michael; "I did not ask just now because, to tell the truth, I really thought Dr. Pym, though seemingly vertical, was enjoying well-earned slumber, with a pinch in his fingers of scentless and delicate dust. But now that things are moving a little more, there is something I should really like to know. I have hung on Dr. Pym's lips, of course, with an interest that it were weak to call rapture, but I have so far been unable to form any conjecture about what the accused, in the present instance, is supposed to have been and gone and done."

"If Mr. Moon will have patience," said Pym with dignity, "he will find that this was the very point to which my exposition was di-rected. Kleptomania, I say, exhibits itself as a kind of physical attraction to certain defined materials; and it has been held (by no less a man than Harris) that this is the ultimate explanation of the strict specialism and vurry narrow professional outlook of most criminals. One will have an irresistible physical impulsion towards pearl sleeve-links, while he passes over the most elegant and celebrated diamond sleeve-links, placed about in the most conspicuous locations. Another will impede his flight with no less than forty-seven buttoned boots, while elastic-sided boots leave him cold, and even sarcastic. The specialism of the criminal, I repeat, is a mark rather of insanity than of any brightness of business habits; but there is one kind of depredator to whom this principle is at first sight hard to apply. I allude to our fellow-citizen the housebreaker.

"It has been maintained by some of our boldest young truth-seekers, that the eye of a burglar beyond the back-garden wall could hardly be caught and hypnotized by a fork that is insulated in a locked box under the butler's bed. They have thrown down the gauntlet to American science on this point. They declare that diamond links are not left about in conspicuous locations in the haunts of the lower classes, as they were in the great test experiment of Calypso College. We hope this experiment here will be an answer to that young ringing challenge, and will bring the burglar once more into line and union with his fellow criminals."

Moon, whose face had gone through every phase of black bewilderment for five minutes past, suddenly lifted his hand and struck the table in explosive enlightenment.

"Oh, I see!" he cried; "you mean that Smith is a burglar."

"I thought I made it quite ad'quately lucid," said Mr. Pym, folding up his eyelids. It was typical of this topsy-turvy private trial that all the eloquent extras, all the rhetoric or digression on either side, was exasperating and unintelligible to the other. Moon could not make head or tail of the solemnity of a new civilization. Pym could not make head or tail of the gaiety of an old one.

"All the cases in which Smith has figured as an expropriator," continued the American doctor, "are cases of burglary. Pursuing the same course as in the previous case, we select the indubitable instance from the rest, and we take the most correct cast-iron evidence. I will now call on my colleague, Mr. Gould, to read a letter we have received from the earnest, unspotted Canon of Durham, Canon Hawkins."

Mr. Moses Gould leapt up with his usual alacrity to read the letter from the earnest and unspotted Hawkins. Moses Gould could imitate a farmyard well, Sir Henry Irving not so well, Marie Lloyd to a point of excellence, and the new motor horns in a manner that put him upon the platform of great artists. But his imitation of a Canon of Durham was not convincing; indeed, the sense of the letter was so much obscured by the extraordinary leaps and gasps of his pronunciation that it is perhaps better to print it here as Moon read it when, a little later, it was handed across the table.

"Dear Sir,—I can scarcely feel surprise that the incident you mention, private as it was, should have filtered through our omnivorous journals to the mere populace; for the position I have since attained makes me, I conceive, a public character, and this was certainly the most extraordinary incident in a not uneventful and perhaps not an unimportant career. I am by no means without experience in scenes of civil tumult. I have faced many a political crisis in the old Primrose League days at Herne Bay, and, before I broke with the wilder set, have spent many a night at the Christian Social Union. But this other experience was quite inconceivable. I can only describe it as the letting loose of a place which it is not for me, as a clergyman, to mention.

"It occurred in the days when I was, for a short period, a curate at Hoxton; and the other curate, then my colleague, induced me to attend a meeting which he described, I must say profanely described, as calculated to promote the kingdom of God. I found, on the contrary, that it consisted entirely of men in corduroys and greasy clothes whose manners were coarse and their opinions extreme.

"Of my colleague in question I wish to speak with the fullest respect and friendliness, and I will therefore say little. No one can be more convinced than I of the evil of politics in the pulpit; and I never offer my congregation any advice about voting except in cases in which I feel strongly that they are likely to make an erroneous selection. But, while I do not mean to touch at all upon political or social problems, I must say that for a clergyman to countenance, even in jest, such discredited nostrums of dissipated demagogues as Socialism or Radicalism partakes of the character of the betrayal of a sacred trust. Far be it from me to say a word against the Reverend Raymond Percy, the colleague in question. He was brilliant, I suppose, and to some apparently fascinating; but a clergyman who talks like a Socialist, wears his hair like a pianist, and behaves like an intoxicated person, will never rise in his profession, or even obtain the admiration of the good and wise. Nor is it for me to utter my personal judgements of the appearance of the people in the hall. Yet a glance round the room, revealing ranks of debased and envious faces—"

"Adopting," said Moon explosively, for he was getting restive—"adopting the reverend gentleman's favourite figure of logic, may I say that while tortures would not tear from me a whisper about his intellect, he is a blasted old jackass."

"Really!" said Dr. Pym; "I protest."

"You must keep quiet, Michael," said Inglewood; "they have a right to read their story."

"Chair! Chair! Chair!" cried Gould, rolling about exuberantly in his own; and Pym glanced for a moment towards the canopy which covered all the authority of the Court of Beacon.

"Oh, don't wake the old lady," said Moon, lowering his voice in a moody good-humour. "I apologize. I won't interrupt again."

Before the little eddy of interruption was ended the reading of the clergyman's letter was already continuing.

"The proceedings opened with a speech from my colleague, of which I will say nothing. It was deplorable. Many of the audience were Irish, and showed the weakness of that impetuous people. When gathered together into gangs and conspiracies they seem to lose altogether that lovable good-nature and readiness to accept anything one tells them which distinguishes them as individuals."

With a slight start, Michael rose to his feet, bowed solemnly, and sat down again.

"These persons, if not silent, were at least applausive during the speech of Mr. Percy. He descended to their level with witticisms about rent and a reserve of labour. Confiscation, expropriation, arbitration, and such words with which I cannot soil my lips, recurred constantly. Some hours afterward the storm broke. I had been addressing the meeting for some time, pointing out the lack of thrift in the working classes, their insufficient attendance at evening service, their neglect of the Harvest Festival, and of many other things that might materially help them to improve their lot. It was, I think, about this time that an extraordinary interruption occurred. An enormous, powerful man, partly concealed with white plaster, arose in the middle of the hall, and offered (in a loud, roaring voice, like a bull's) some observations which seemed to be in a foreign language. Mr. Raymond Percy, my colleague, descended to his level by entering into a duel of repartee, in which he appeared to be the victor. The meeting began to behave more respectfully for a little; yet before I had said twelve sentences more the rush was made for the platform. The enormous plasterer, in particular, plunged towards us, shaking the earth like an elephant; and I really do not know what would have happened if a man equally large, but not quite so ill-dressed, had not jumped up also and held him away. This other big man shouted a sort of speech to the mob as he was shoving them back. I don't know what he said, but, what with shouting and shoving and such horseplay, he got us out at a back door, while the wretched people went roaring down another passage.

"Then follows the truly extraordinary part of my story. When he had got us outside, in a mean backyard of blistered grass leading into a lane with a very lonely-looking lamp-post, this giant addressed me as follows: 'You're well out of that, sir; now you'd better come along with me. I want you to help me in an act of social justice, such as we've all been talking about. Come along!' And turning his big back abruptly, he led us down the lean old lane with the one lean old lamp-post, we scarcely knowing what to do but to follow him. He had certainly helped us in a most difficult situation, and, as a gentleman, I could not treat such a benefactor with suspicion without grave grounds. Such also was the view of my Socialistic colleague, who (with all his dreadful talk of arbitration) is a gentleman also. In fact, he comes of the Staffordshire Percys, a branch of the old house and has the black hair and pale, clear-cut face of the whole family. I cannot but refer it to vanity that he should heighten his personal advantages with black velvet or a red cross of considerable ostentation, and certainly—but I digress.

"A fog was coming up the street, and that last lost lamp-post faded behind us in a way that certainly depressed the mind. The large man in front of us looked larger and larger in the haze. He did not turn round, but he said with his huge back to us, `All that talking's no good; we want a little practical Socialism.'

"`I quite agree,' said Percy; `but I always like to understand things in theory before I put them into practice.'

"`Oh, you just leave that to me,' said the practical Socialist, or whatever he was, with the most terrifying vagueness. `I have a way with me. I'm a Permeator.'

"I could not imagine what he meant, but my companion laughed, so I was sufficiently reassured to continue the unaccountable journey for the present. It led us through most singular ways; out of the lane, where we were already rather cramped, into a paved passage, at the end of which we passed through a wooden gate left open. We then found ourselves, in the increasing darkness and vapour, crossing what appeared to be a beaten path across a kitchen garden. I called out to the enormous person going on in front, but he answered obscurely that it was a short cut.

"I was just repeating my very natural doubt to my clerical companion when I was brought up against a short ladder, apparently leading to a higher level of road. My thoughtless colleague ran up it so quickly that I could not do otherwise than follow as best I could. The path on which I then planted my feet was quite unprecedentedly narrow. I had never had to walk along a thoroughfare so exiguous. Along one side of it grew what, in the dark and density of air, I first took to be some short, strong thicket of shrubs. Then I saw that they were not short shrubs; they were the tops of tall trees. I, an English gentleman and clergyman of the Church of England—I was walking along the top of a garden wall like a tom cat.

"I am glad to say that I stopped within my first five steps, and let loose my just reprobation, balancing myself as best I could all the time.

"`It's a right-of-way,' declared my indefensible informant. `It's closed to traffic once in a hundred years.'

"`Mr. Percy, Mr. Percy!' I called out; `you are not going on with this blackguard?'

"`Why, I think so,' answered my unhappy colleague flippantly. `I think you and I are bigger blackguards than he is, whatever he is.'

"`I am a burglar,' explained the big creature quite calmly. `I am a member of the Fabian Society. I take back the wealth stolen by the capitalist, not by sweeping civil war and revolution, but by reform fitted to the special occasion—here a little and there a little. Do you see that fifth house along the terrace with the flat roof? I'm permeating that one to-night.'

"`Whether this is a crime or a joke,' I cried, `I desire to be quit of it.'

"`The ladder is just behind you,' answered the creature with horrible courtesy; `and, before you go, do let me give you my card.'

"If I had had the presence of mind to show any proper spirit I should have flung it away, though any adequate gesture of the kind would have gravely affected my equilibrium upon the wall. As it was, in the wildness of the moment, I put it in my waistcoat pocket, and, picking my way back by wall and ladder, landed in the respectable streets once more. Not before, however, I had seen with my own eyes the two awful and lamentable facts— that the burglar was climbing up a slanting roof towards the chimneys, and that Raymond Percy (a priest of God and, what was worse, a gentleman) was crawling up after him. I have never seen either of them since that day.

"In consequence of this soul-searching experience I severed my connection with the wild set. I am far from saying that every member of the Christian Social Union must necessarily be a burglar. I have no right to bring any such charge. But it gave me a hint of what such courses may lead to in many cases; and I saw them no more.

"I have only to add that the photograph you enclose, taken by a Mr. Inglewood, is undoubtedly that of the burglar in question. When I got home that night I looked at his card, and he was inscribed there under the name of Innocent Smith.—Yours faithfully, "John Clement Hawkins."

Moon merely went through the form of glancing at the paper. He knew that the prosecutors could not have invented so heavy a document; that Moses Gould (for one) could no more write like a canon than he could read like one. After handing it back he rose to open the defence on the burglary charge.

"We wish," said Michael, "to give all reasonable facilities to the prosecution; especially as it will save the time of the whole court. The latter object I shall once again pursue by passing over all those points of theory which are so dear to Dr. Pym. I know how they are made. Perjury is a variety of aphasia, leading a man to say one thing instead of another. Forgery is a kind of writer's cramp, forcing a man to write his uncle's name instead of his own. Piracy on the high seas is probably a form of sea-sickness. But it is unnecessary for us to inquire into the causes of a fact which we deny. Innocent Smith never did commit burglary at all.

"I should like to claim the power permitted by our previous arrangement, and ask the prosecution two or three questions."

Dr. Cyrus Pym closed his eyes to indicate a courteous assent.

"In the first place," continued Moon, "have you the date of Canon Hawkins's last glimpse of Smith and Percy climbing up the walls and roofs?"

"Ho, yus!" called out Gould smartly. "November thirteen, eighteen ninety-one."

"Have you," continued Moon, "identified the houses in Hoxton up which they climbed?"

"Must have been Ladysmith Terrace out of the highroad," answered Gould with the same clockwork readiness.

"Well," said Michael, cocking an eyebrow at him, "was there any burglary in that terrace that night? Surely you could find that out."

"There may well have been," said the doctor primly, after a pause, "an unsuccessful one that led to no legalities."

"Another question," proceeded Michael. "Canon Hawkins, in his blood-and-thunder boyish way, left off at the exciting moment. Why don't you produce the evidence of the other clergyman, who actually followed the burglar and presumably was present at the crime?"

Dr. Pym rose and planted the points of his fingers on the table, as he did when he was specially confident of the clearness of his reply.

"We have entirely failed," he said, "to track the other clergyman, who seems to have melted into the ether after Canon Hawkins had seen him as-cending the gutters and the leads. I am fully aware that this may strike many as sing'lar; yet, upon reflection, I think it will appear pretty natural to a bright thinker. This Mr. Raymond Percy is admittedly, by the canon's evidence, a minister of eccentric ways. His con-nection with England's proudest and fairest does not seemingly prevent a taste for the society of the real low-down. On the other hand, the prisoner Smith is, by general agreement, a man of irr'sistible fascination. I entertain no doubt that Smith led the Revered Percy into the crime and forced him to hide his head in the real crim'nal class. That would fully account for his non-appearance, and the failure of all attempts to trace him."

"It is impossible, then, to trace him?" asked Moon.

"Impossible," repeated the specialist, shutting his eyes.

"You are sure it's impossible?"

"Oh dry up, Michael," cried Gould, irritably. "We'd 'ave found 'im if we could, for you bet 'e saw the burglary. Don't YOU start looking for 'im. Look for your own 'ead in the dustbin. You'll find that—after a bit," and his voice died away in grumbling.

"Arthur," directed Michael Moon, sitting down, "kindly read Mr. Raymond Percy's letter to the court."

"Wishing, as Mr. Moon has said, to shorten the proceedings as much as possible," began Inglewood, "I will not read the first part of the letter sent to us. It is only fair to the prosecution to admit the account given by the second clergyman fully ratifies, as far as facts are concerned, that given by the first clergyman. We concede, then, the canon's story so far as it goes. This must necessarily be valuable to the prosecutor and also convenient to the court. I begin Mr. Percy's letter, then, at the point when all three men were standing on the garden wall:—

"As I watched Hawkins wavering on the wall, I made up my own mind not to waver. A cloud of wrath was on my brain, like the cloud of copper fog on the houses and gardens round. My decision was violent and simple; yet the thoughts that led up to it were so complicated and contradictory that I could not retrace them now. I knew Hawkins was a kind, innocent gentleman; and I would have given ten pounds for the pleasure of kicking him down the road. That God should allow good people to be as bestially stupid as that— rose against me like a towering blasphemy.

"At Oxford, I fear, I had the artistic temperament rather badly; and artists love to be limited. I liked the church as a pretty pattern; discipline was mere decoration. I delighted in mere divisions of time; I liked eating fish on Friday. But then I like fish; and the fast was made for men who like meat. Then I came to Hoxton and found men who had fasted for five hundred years; men who had to gnaw fish because they could not get meat—and fish-bones when they could not get fish. As too many British officers treat the army as a review, so I had treated the Church Militant as if it were the Church Pageant. Hoxton cures that. Then I realized that for eighteen hundred years the Church Militant had not been a pageant, but a riot—and a suppressed riot. There, still living patiently in Hoxton, were the people to whom the tremendous promises had been made. In the face of that I had to become a revolutionary if I was to continue to be religious. In Hoxton one cannot be a conservative without being also an atheist— and a pessimist. Nobody but the devil could want to conserve Hoxton.

"On the top of all this comes Hawkins. If he had cursed all the Hoxton men, excommunicated them, and told them they were going to hell, I should have rather admired him. If he had ordered them all to be burned in the market-place, I should still have had that patience that all good Christians have with the wrongs inflicted on other people. But there is no priestcraft about Hawkins—nor any other kind of craft. He is as perfectly incapable of being a priest as he is of being a carpenter or a cabman or a gardener or a plasterer. He is a perfect gentleman; that is his complaint. He does not impose his creed, but simply his class. He never said a word of religion in the whole of his damnable address. He simply said all the things his brother, the major, would have said. A voice from heaven assures me that he has a brother, and that this brother is a major.

"When this helpless aristocrat had praised cleanliness in the body and convention in the soul to people who could hardly keep body and soul together, the stampede against our platform began. I took part in his undeserved rescue, I followed his obscure deliverer, until (as I have said) we stood together on the wall above the dim gardens, already clouding with fog. Then I looked at the curate and at the burglar, and decided, in a spasm of inspiration, that the burglar was the better man of the two. The burglar seemed quite as kind and human as the curate was— and he was also brave and self-reliant, which the curate was not. I knew there was no virtue in the upper class, for I belong to it myself; I knew there was not so very much in the lower class, for I had lived with it a long time. Many old texts about the despised and persecuted came back to my mind, and I thought that the saints might well be hidden in the criminal class. About the time Hawkins let himself down the ladder I was crawling up a low, sloping, blue-slate roof after the large man, who went leaping in front of me like a gorilla.

"This upward scramble was short, and we soon found ourselves tramping along a broad road of flat roofs, broader than many big thoroughfares, with chimney-pots here and there that seemed in the haze as bulky as small forts. The asphyxiation of the fog seemed to increase the somewhat swollen and morbid anger under which my brain and body laboured. The sky and all those things that are commonly clear seemed overpowered by sinister spirits. Tall spectres with turbans of vapour seemed to stand higher than the sun or moon, eclipsing both. I thought dimly of illustrations to the `Arabian Nights' on brown paper with rich but sombre tints, showing genii gathering round the Seal of Solomon. By the way, what was the Seal of Solomon? Nothing to do with sealing-wax really, I suppose; but my muddled fancy felt the thick clouds as being of that heavy and clinging substance, of strong opaque colour, poured out of boiling pots and stamped into monstrous emblems.

"The first effect of the tall turbaned vapours was that discoloured look of pea-soup or coffee brown of which Londoners commonly speak. But the scene grew subtler with familiarity. We stood above the average of the housetops and saw something of that thing called smoke, which in great cities creates the strange thing called fog. Beneath us rose a forest of chimney-pots. And there stood in every chimney-pot, as if it were a flower-pot, a brief shrub or a tall tree of coloured vapour. The colours of the smoke were various; for some chimneys were from firesides and some from factories, and some again from mere rubbish heaps. And yet, though the tints were all varied, they all seemed unnatural, like fumes from a witch's pot. It was as if the shameful and ugly shapes growing shapeless in the cauldron sent up each its separate spurt of steam, coloured according to the fish or flesh consumed. Here, aglow from underneath, were dark red clouds, such as might drift from dark jars of sacrificial blood; there the vapour was dark indigo gray, like the long hair of witches steeped in the hell-broth. In another place the smoke was of an awful opaque ivory yellow, such as might be the disembodiment of one of their old, leprous waxen images. But right across it ran a line of bright, sinister, sulphurous green, as clear and crooked as Arabic—"

Mr. Moses Gould once more attempted the arrest of the 'bus. He was understood to suggest that the reader should shorten the proceedings by leaving out all the adjectives.

Mrs. Duke, who had woken up, observed that she was sure it was all very nice, and the decision was duly noted down by Moses with a blue, and by Michael with a red pencil. Inglewood then resumed the reading of the document.

"Then I read the writing of the smoke. Smoke was like the modern city that makes it; it is not always dull or ugly, but it is always wicked and vain.

"Modern England was like a cloud of smoke; it could carry all colours, but it could leave nothing but a stain. It was our weakness and not our strength that put a rich refuse in the sky. These were the rivers of our vanity pouring into the void. We had taken the sacred circle of the whirlwind, and looked down on it, and seen it as a whirlpool. And then we had used it as a sink. It was a good symbol of the mutiny in my own mind. Only our worst things were going to heaven. Only our criminals could still ascend like angels.

"As my brain was blinded with such emotions, my guide stopped by one of the big chimney-pots that stood at the regular intervals like lamp-posts along that uplifted and aerial highway. He put his heavy hand upon it, and for the moment I thought he was merely leaning on it, tired with his steep scramble along the terrace. So far as I could guess from the abysses, full of fog on either side, and the veiled lights of red brown and old gold glowing through them now and again, we were on the top of one of those long, consecutive, and genteel rows of houses which are still to be found lifting their heads above poorer districts, the remains of some rage of optimism in earlier speculative builders. Probably enough, they were entirely untenanted, or tenanted only by such small clans of the poor as gather also in the old emptied palaces of Italy. Indeed, some little time later, when the fog had lifted a little, I discovered that we were walking round a semi-circle of crescent which fell away below us into one flat square or wide street below another, like a giant stairway, in a manner not unknown in the eccentric building of London, and looking like the last ledges of the land. But a cloud sealed the giant stairway as yet.

"My speculations about the sullen skyscape, however, were interrupted by something as unexpected as the moon falling from the sky. Instead of my burglar lifting his hand from the chimney he leaned on, he leaned on it a little more heavily, and the whole chimney-pot turned over like the opening top of an inkstand. I remembered the short ladder leaning against the low wall and felt sure he had arranged his criminal approach long before.

"The collapse of the big chimney-pot ought to have been the culmination of my chaotic feelings; but, to tell the truth, it produced a sudden sense of comedy and even of comfort. I could not recall what connected this abrupt bit of housebreaking with some quaint but still kindly fancies. Then I remembered the delightful and uproarious scenes of roofs and chimneys in the harlequinades of my childhood, and was darkly and quite irrationally comforted by a sense of unsubstantiality in the scene, as if the houses were of lath and paint and pasteboard, and were only meant to be tumbled in and out of by policemen and pantaloons. The law-breaking of my companion seemed not only seriously excusable, but even comically excusable. Who were all these pompous preposterous people with their footmen and their foot-scrapers, their chimney-pots and their chimney-pot hats, that they should prevent a poor clown from getting sausages if he wanted them? One would suppose that property was a serious thing. I had reached, as it were, a higher level of that mountainous and vapourous visions, the heaven of a higher levity.

"My guide had jumped down into the dark cavity revealed by the displaced chimney-pot. He must have landed at a level considerably lower, for, tall as he was, nothing but his weirdly tousled head remained visible. Something again far off, and yet familiar, pleased me about this way of invading the houses of men. I thought of little chimney-sweeps, and 'The Water Babies;' but I decided that it was not that. Then I remembered what it was that made me connect such topsy-turvy trespass with ideas quite opposite to the idea of crime. Christmas Eve, of course, and Santa Claus coming down the chimney.

"Almost at the same instant the hairy head disappeared into the black hole; but I heard a voice calling to me from below. A second or two afterwards, the hairy head reappeared; it was dark against the more fiery part of the fog, and nothing could be spelt of its expression, but its voice called on me to follow with that enthusiastic impatience proper only among old friends. I jumped into the gulf, and as blindly as Curtius, for I was still thinking of Santa Claus and the traditional virtue of such vertical entrance.

"In every well-appointed gentleman's house, I reflected, there was the front door for the gentlemen, and the side door for the tradesmen; but there was also the top door for the gods. The chimney is, so to speak, the underground passage between earth and heaven. By this starry tunnel Santa Claus manages—like the skylark— to be true to the kindred points of heaven and home. Nay, owing to certain conventions, and a widely distributed lack of courage for climbing, this door was, perhaps, little used. But Santa Claus's door was really the front door: it was the door fronting the universe.

"I thought this as I groped my way across the black garret, or loft below the roof, and scrambled down the squat ladder that let us down into a yet larger loft below. Yet it was not till I was half-way down the ladder that I suddenly stood still, and thought for an instant of retracing all my steps, as my companion had retraced them from the beginning of the garden wall. The name of Santa Claus had suddenly brought me back to my senses. I remembered why Santa Clause came, and why he was welcome.

"I was brought up in the propertied classes, and with all their horror of offences against property. I had heard all the regular denunciations of robbery, both right and wrong; I had read the Ten Commandments in church a thousand times. And then and there, at the age of thirty-four, half-way down a ladder in a dark room in the bodily act of burglar, I saw suddenly for the first time that theft, after all, is really wrong.

"It was too late to turn back, however, and I followed the strangely soft footsteps of my huge companion across the lower and larger loft, till he knelt down on a part of the bare flooring and, after a few fumbling efforts, lifted a sort of trapdoor. This released a light from below, and we found ourselves looking down into a lamp-lit sitting room, of the sort that in large houses often leads out of a bedroom, and is an adjunct to it. Light thus breaking from beneath our feet like a soundless explosion, showed that the trapdoor just lifted was clogged with dust and rust, and had doubtless been long disused until the advent of my enterprising friend. But I did not look at this long, for the sight of the shining room underneath us had an almost unnatural attractiveness. To enter a modern interior at so strange an angle, by so forgotten a door, was an epoch in one's psychology. It was like having found a fourth dimension.

"My companion dropped from the aperture into the room so suddenly and soundlessly, that I could do nothing but follow him; though, for lack of practice in crime, I was by no means soundless. Before the echo of my boots had died away, the big burglar had gone quickly to the door, half opened it, and stood looking down the staircase and listening. Then, leaving the door still half open, he came back into the middle of the room, and ran his roving blue eye round its furniture and ornament. The room was comfortably lined with books in that rich and human way that makes the walls seem alive; it was a deep and full, but slovenly, bookcase, of the sort that is constantly ransacked for the purposes of reading in bed. One of those stunted German stoves that look like red goblins stood in a corner, and a sideboard of walnut wood with closed doors in its lower part. There were three windows, high but narrow. After another glance round, my housebreaker plucked the walnut doors open and rummaged inside. He found nothing there, apparently, except an extremely handsome cut-glass decanter, containing what looked like port. Somehow the sight of the thief returning with this ridiculous little luxury in his hand woke within me once more all the revelation and revulsion I had felt above.

"'Don't do it!' I cried quite incoherently, `Santa Claus—'

"'Ah,' said the burglar, as he put the decanter on the table and stood looking at me, `you've thought about that, too.'

"'I can't express a millionth part of what I've thought of,' I cried, `but it's something like this . . . oh, can't you see it? Why are children not afraid of Santa Claus, though he comes like a thief in the night? He is permitted secrecy, trespass, almost treachery— because there are more toys where he has been. What should we feel if there were less? Down what chimney from hell would come the goblin that should take away the children's balls and dolls while they slept? Could a Greek tragedy be more gray and cruel than that daybreak and awakening? Dog-stealer, horse-stealer, man-stealer—can you think of anything so base as a toy-stealer?'

"The burglar, as if absently, took a large revolver from his pocket and laid it on the table beside the decanter, but still kept his blue reflective eyes fixed on my face.

"'Man!' I said, `all stealing is toy-stealing. That's why it's really wrong. The goods of the unhappy children of men should be really respected because of their worthlessness. I know Naboth's vineyard is as painted as Noah's Ark. I know Nathan's ewe-lamb is really a woolly baa-lamb on a wooden stand. That is why I could not take them away. I did not mind so much, as long as I thought of men's things as their valuables; but I dare not put a hand upon their vanities.'

"After a moment I added abruptly, `Only saints and sages ought to be robbed. They may be stripped and pillaged; but not the poor little worldly people of the things that are their poor little pride.'

"He set out two wineglasses from the cupboard, filled them both, and lifted one of them with a salutation towards his lips.

"'Don't do it!' I cried. `It might be the last bottle of some rotten vintage or other. The master of this house may be quite proud of it. Don't you see there's something sacred in the silliness of such things?'

"'It's not the last bottle,' answered my criminal calmly; `there's plenty more in the cellar.'

"'You know the house, then?' I said.

"'Too well,' he answered, with a sadness so strange as to have something eerie about it. 'I am always trying to forget what I know— and to find what I don't know.' He drained his glass. 'Besides,' he added, 'it will do him good.'

"'What will do him good?'

"'The wine I'm drinking,' said the strange person.

"'Does he drink too much, then?' I inquired.

"'No,' he answered, 'not unless I do.'

"'Do you mean,' I demanded, 'that the owner of this house approves of all you do?'

"'God forbid,' he answered; 'but he has to do the same.'

"The dead face of the fog looking in at all three windows unreasonable increased a sense of riddle, and even terror, about this tall, narrow house we had entered out of the sky. I had once more the notion about the gigantic genii— I fancied that enormous Egyptian faces, of the dead reds and yellows of Egypt, were staring in at each window of our little lamp-lit room as at a lighted stage of marionettes. My companion went on playing with the pistol in front of him, and talking with the same rather creepy confidentialness.

"'I am always trying to find him—to catch him unawares. I come in through skylights and trapdoors to find him; but whenever I find him—he is doing what I am doing.'

"I sprang to my feet with a thrill of fear. 'There is some one coming,' I cried, and my cry had something of a shriek in it. Not from the stairs below, but along the passage from the inner bedchamber (which seemed somehow to make it more alarming), footsteps were coming nearer. I am quite unable to say what mystery, or monster, or double, I expected to see when the door was pushed open from within. I am only quite certain that I did not expect to see what I did see.

"Framed in the open doorway stood, with an air of great serenity, a rather tall young woman, definitely though indefinably artistic— her dress the colour of spring and her hair of autumn leaves, with a face which, though still comparatively young, conveyed experience as well as intelligence. All she said was, 'I didn't hear you come in.'

"'I came in another way,' said the Permeator, somewhat vaguely. 'I'd left my latchkey at home.'

"I got to my feet in a mixture of politeness and mania. 'I'm really very sorry,' I cried. 'I know my position is irregular. Would you be so obliging as to tell me whose house this is?'

"'Mine,' said the burglar, 'May I present you to my wife?'

"I doubtfully, and somewhat slowly, resumed my seat; and I did not get out of it till nearly morning. Mrs. Smith (such was the prosaic name of this far from prosaic household) lingered a little, talking slightly and pleasantly. She left on my mind the impression of a certain odd mixture of shyness and sharpness; as if she knew the world well, but was still a little harmlessly afraid of it. Perhaps the possession of so jumpy and incalculable a husband had left her a little nervous. Anyhow, when she had retired to the inner chamber once more, that extraordinary man poured forth his apologia and autobiography over the dwindling wine.

"He had been sent to Cambridge with a view to a mathematical and scientific, rather than a classical or literary, career. A starless nihilism was then the philosophy of the schools; and it bred in him a war between the members and the spirit, but one in which the members were right. While his brain accepted the black creed, his very body rebelled against it. As he put it, his right hand taught him terrible things. As the authorities of Cambridge University put it, unfortunately, it had taken the form of his right hand flourishing a loaded firearm in the very face of a distinguished don, and driving him to climb out of the window and cling to a waterspout. He had done it solely because the poor don had professed in theory a preference for non-existence. For this very unacademic type of argument he had been sent down. Vomiting as he was with revulsion, from the pessimism that had quailed under his pistol, he made himself a kind of fanatic of the joy of life. He cut across all the associations of serious-minded men. He was gay, but by no means careless. His practical jokes were more in earnest than verbal ones. Though not an optimist in the absurd sense of maintaining that life is all beer and skittles, he did really seem to maintain that beer and skittles are the most serious part of it. `What is more immortal,' he would cry, `than love and war? Type of all desire and joy—beer. Type of all battle and conquest—skittles.'

"There was something in him of what the old world called the solemnity of revels— when they spoke of `solemnizing' a mere masquerade or wedding banquet. Nevertheless he was not a mere pagan any more than he was a mere practical joker. His eccentricities sprang from a static fact of faith, in itself mystical, and even childlike and Christian.

"`I don't deny,' he said, `that there should be priests to remind men that they will one day die. I only say that at certain strange epochs it is necessary to have another kind of priests, called poets, actually to remind men that they are not dead yet. The intellectuals among whom I moved were not even alive enough to fear death. They hadn't enough blood in them to be cowards. Until a pistol barrel was poked under their very noses they never even knew they had been born. For ages looking up an eternal perspective it might be true that life is a learning to die. But for these little white rats it was just as true that death was their only chance of learning to live.'

"His creed of wonder was Christian by this absolute test; that he felt it continually slipping from himself as much as from others. He had the same pistol for himself, as Brutus said of the dagger. He continually ran preposterous risks of high precipice or headlong speed to keep alive the mere conviction that he was alive. He treasured up trivial and yet insane details that had once reminded him of the awful subconscious reality. When the don had hung on the stone gutter, the sight of his long dangling legs, vibrating in the void like wings, somehow awoke the naked satire of the old definition of man as a two-legged animal without feathers. The wretched professor had been brought into peril by his head, which he had so elaborately cultivated, and only saved by his legs, which he had treated with coldness and neglect. Smith could think of no other way of announcing or recording this, except to send a telegram to an old friend (by this time a total stranger) to say that he had just seen a man with two legs; and that the man was alive.

"The uprush of his released optimism burst into stars like a rocket when he suddenly fell in love. He happened to be shooting a high and very headlong weir in a canoe, by way of proving to himself that he was alive; and he soon found himself involved in some doubt about the continuance of the fact. What was worse, he found he had equally jeopardized a harmless lady alone in a rowing-boat, and one who had provoked death by no professions of philosophic negation. He apologized in wild gasps through all his wild wet labours to bring her to the shore, and when he had done so at last, he seems to have proposed to her on the bank. Anyhow, with the same impetuosity with which he had nearly murdered her, he completely married her; and she was the lady in green to whom I had recently said `good-night.'

"They had settled down in these high narrow houses near Highbury. Perhaps, indeed, that is hardly the word. One could strictly say that Smith was married, that he was very happily married, that he not only did not care for any woman but his wife, but did not seem to care for any place but his home; but perhaps one could hardly say that he had settled down. `I am a very domestic fellow,' he explained with gravity, `and have often come in through a broken window rather than be late for tea.'

"He lashed his soul with laughter to prevent it falling asleep. He lost his wife a series of excellent servants by knocking at the door as a total stranger, and asking if Mr. Smith lived there and what kind of a man he was. The London general servant is not used to the master indulging in such transcendental ironies. And it was found impossible to explain to her that he did it in order to feel the same interest in his own affairs that he always felt in other people's.

"`I know there's a fellow called Smith,' he said in his rather weird way, `living in one of the tall houses in this terrace. I know he is really happy, and yet I can never catch him at it.'

"Sometimes he would, of a sudden, treat his wife with a kind of paralyzed politeness, like a young stranger struck with love at first sight. Sometimes he would extend this poetic fear to the very furniture; would seem to apologize to the chair he sat on, and climb the staircase as cautiously as a cragsman, to renew in himself the sense of their skeleton of reality. Every stair is a ladder and every stool a leg, he said. And at other times he would play the stranger exactly in the opposite sense, and would enter by another way, so as to feel like a thief and a robber. He would break and violate his own home, as he had done with me that night. It was near morning before I could tear myself from this queer confidence of the Man Who Would Not Die, and as I shook hands with him on the doorstep the last load of fog was lifting, and rifts of daylight revealed the stairway of irregular street levels that looked like the end of the world.

"It will be enough for many to say that I had passed a night with a maniac. What other term, it will be said, could be applied to such a being? A man who reminds himself that he is married by pretending not to be married! A man who tries to covet his own goods instead of his neighbor's! On this I have but one word to say, and I feel it of my honour to say it, though no one understands. I believe the maniac was one of those who do not merely come, but are sent; sent like a great gale upon ships by Him who made His angels winds and His messengers a flaming fire. This, at least, I know for certain. Whether such men have laughed or wept, we have laughed at their laughter as much as at their weeping. Whether they cursed or blessed the world, they have never fitted it. It is true that men have shrunk from the sting of a great satirist as if from the sting of an adder. But it is equally true that men flee from the embrace of a great optimist as from the embrace of a bear. Nothing brings down more curses than a real benediction. For the goodness of good things, like the badness of bad things, is a prodigy past speech; it is to be pictured rather than spoken. We shall have gone deeper than the deeps of heaven and grown older than the oldest angels before we feel, even in its first faint vibrations, the everlasting violence of that double passion with which God hates and loves the world.—I am, yours faithfully, "Raymond Percy."

"Oh, 'oly, 'oly, 'oly!" said Mr. Moses Gould.

The instant he had spoken all the rest knew they had been in an almost religious state of submission and assent. Something had bound them together; something in the sacred tradition of the last two words of the letter; something also in the touching and boyish embarrassment with which Inglewood had read them— for he had all the thin-skinned reverence of the agnostic. Moses Gould was as good a fellow in his way as ever lived; far kinder to his family than more refined men of pleasure, simple and steadfast in his admiration, a thoroughly wholesome animal and a thoroughly genuine character. But wherever there is conflict, crises come in which any soul, personal or racial, unconsciously turns on the world the most hateful of its hundred faces. English reverence, Irish mysticism, American idealism, looked up and saw on the face of Moses a certain smile. It was that smile of the Cynic Triumphant, which has been the tocsin for many a cruel riot in Russian villages or mediaeval towns.

"Oh, 'oly, 'oly, 'oly!" said Moses Gould.

Finding that this was not well received, he explained further, exuberance deepening on his dark exuberant features.

"Always fun to see a bloke swallow a wasp when 'e's corfin' up a fly," he said pleasantly. "Don't you see you've bunged up old Smith anyhow. If this parson's tale's O.K.—why, Smith is 'ot. 'E's pretty 'ot. We find him elopin' with Miss Gray (best respects!) in a cab. Well, what abart this Mrs. Smith the curate talks of, with her blarsted shyness—transmigogrified into a blighted sharpness? Miss Gray ain't been very sharp, but I reckon she'll be pretty shy."

"Don't be a brute," growled Michael Moon.

None could lift their eyes to look at Mary; but Inglewood sent a glance along the table at Innocent Smith. He was still bowed above his paper toys, and a wrinkle was on his forehead that might have been worry or shame. He carefully plucked out one corner of a complicated paper and tucked it in elsewhere; then the wrinkle vanished and he looked relieved.

3. THE ROUND ROAD; OR, THE DESERTION CHARGE

Pym rose with sincere embarrassment; for he was an American, and his respect for ladies was real, and not at all scientific.

"Ignoring," he said, "the delicate and considerable knightly protests that have been called forth by my colleague's native sense of oration, and apologizing to all for whom our wild search for truth seems unsuitable to the grand ruins of a feudal land, I still think my colleague's question by no means devoid of rel'vancy. The last charge against the accused was one of burglary; the next charge on the paper is of bigamy and desertion. It does without question appear that the defence, in aspiring to rebut this last charge, have really admitted the next. Either Innocent Smith is still under a charge of attempted burglary, or else that is exploded; but he is pretty well fixed for attempted bigamy. It all depends on what view we take of the alleged letter from Curate Percy. Under these conditions I feel justified in claiming my right to questions. May I ask how the defence got hold of the letter from Curate Percy? Did it come direct from the prisoner?"

"We have had nothing direct from the prisoner," said Moon quietly. "The few documents which the defence guarantees came to us from another quarter."

"From what quarter?" asked Dr. Pym.

"If you insist," answered Moon, "we had them from Miss Gray."

"Dr. Cyrus Pym quite forgot to close his eyes, and, instead, opened them very wide.

"Do you really mean to say," he said, "that Miss Gray was in possession of this document testifying to a previous Mrs. Smith?"

"Quite so," said Inglewood, and sat down.

The doctor said something about infatuation in a low and painful voice, and then with visible difficulty continued his opening remarks.

"Unfortunately the tragic truth revealed by Curate Percy's narrative is only too crushingly confirmed by other and shocking documents in our own possession. Of these the principal and most certain is the testimony of Innocent Smith's gardener, who was present at the most dramatic and eye-opening of his many acts of marital infidelity. Mr. Gould, the gardener, please."

Mr. Gould, with his tireless cheerfulness, arose to present the gardener. That functionary explained that he had served Mr. and Mrs. Innocent Smith when they had a little house on the edge of Croydon. From the gardener's tale, with its many small allusions, Inglewood grew certain he had seen the place. It was one of those corners of town or country that one does not forget, for it looked like a frontier. The garden hung very high above the lane, and its end was steep and sharp, like a fortress. Beyond was a roll of real country, with a white path sprawling across it, and the roots, boles, and branches of great gray trees writhing and twisting against the sky. But as if to assert that the lane itself was suburban, were sharply relieved against that gray and tossing upland a lamp-post painted a peculiar yellow-green and a red pillar-box that stood exactly at the corner. Inglewood was sure of the place; he had passed it twenty times in his constitutionals on the bicycle; he had always dimly felt it was a place where something might occur. But it gave him quite a shiver to feel that the face of his frightful friend or enemy Smith might at any time have appeared over the garden bushes above. The gardener's account, unlike the curate's, was quite free from decorative adjectives, however many he may have uttered privately when writing it. He simply said that on a particular morning Mr. Smith came out and began to play about with a rake, as he often did. Sometimes he would tickle the nose of his eldest child (he had two children); sometimes he would hook the rake on to the branch of a tree, and hoist himself up with horrible gymnastic jerks, like those of a giant frog in its final agony. Never, apparently, did he think of putting the rake to any of its proper uses, and the gardener, in consequence, treated his actions with coldness and brevity. But the gardener was certain that on one particular morning in October he (the gardener) had come round the corner of the house carrying the hose, had seen Mr. Smith standing on the lawn in a striped red and white jacket (which might have been his smoking-jacket, but was quite as like a part of his pyjamas), and had heard him then and there call out to his wife, who was looking out of the bedroom window on to the garden, these decisive and very loud expressions—

"I won't stay here any longer. I've got another wife and much better children a long way from here. My other wife's got redder hair than yours, and my other garden's got a much finer situation; and I'm going off to them."

With these words, apparently, he sent the rake flying far up into the sky, higher than many could have shot an arrow, and caught it again. Then he cleared the hedge at a leap and alighted on his feet down in the lane below, and set off up the road without even a hat. Much of the picture was doubtless supplied by Inglewood's accidental memory of the place. He could see with his mind's eye that big bare-headed figure with the ragged rake swaggering up the crooked woodland road, and leaving lamp-post and pillar-box behind. But the gardener, on his own account, was quite prepared to swear to the public confession of bigamy, to the temporary disappearance of the rake in the sky, and the final disappearance of the man up the road. Moreover, being a local man, he could swear that, beyond some local rumours that Smith had embarked on the south-eastern coast, nothing was known of him again.

This impression was somewhat curiously clinched by Michael Moon in the few but clear phrases in which he opened the defence upon the third charge. So far from denying that Smith had fled from Croydon and disappeared on the Continent, he seemed prepared to prove all this on his own account. "I hope you are not so insular," he said, "that you will not respect the word of a French innkeeper as much as that of an English gardener. By Mr. Inglewood's favour we will hear the French innkeeper."

Before the company had decided the delicate point Inglewood was already reading the account in question. It was in French. It seemed to them to run something like this:
—

"Sir,—Yes; I am Durobin of Durobin's Cafe on the sea-front at Gras, rather north of Dunquerque. I am willing to write all I know of the stranger out of the sea.

"I have no sympathy with eccentrics or poets. A man of sense looks for beauty in things deliberately intended to be beautiful, such as a trim flower-bed or an ivory statuette. One does not permit beauty to pervade one's whole life, just as one does not pave all the roads with ivory or cover all the fields with geraniums. My faith, but we should miss the onions!

"But whether I read things backwards through my memory, or whether there are indeed atmospheres of psychology which the eye of science cannot as yet pierce, it is the humiliating fact that on that particular evening I felt like a poet—like any little rascal of a poet who drinks absinthe in the mad Montmartre.

"Positively the sea itself looked like absinthe, green and bitter and poisonous. I had never known it look so unfamiliar before. In the sky was that early and stormy darkness that is so depressing to the mind, and the wind blew shrilly round the little lonely coloured kiosk where they sell the newspapers, and along the sand-hills by the shore. There I saw a fishing-boat with a brown sail standing in silently from the sea. It was already quite close, and out of it clambered a man of monstrous stature, who came wading to shore with the water not up to his knees, though it would have reached the hips of many men. He leaned on a long rake or pole, which looked like a trident, and made him look like a Triton. Wet as he was, and with strips of seaweed clinging to him, he walked across to my cafe, and, sitting down at a table outside, asked for cherry brandy, a liqueur which I keep, but is seldom demanded. Then the monster, with great politeness, invited me to partake of a vermouth before my dinner, and we fell into conversation. He had apparently crossed from Kent by a small boat got at a private bargain because of some odd fancy he had for passing promptly in an easterly direction, and not waiting for any of the official boats. He was, he somewhat vaguely explained, looking for a house. When I naturally asked him where the house was, he answered that he did not know; it was on an island; it was somewhere to the east; or, as he expressed it with a hazy and yet impatient gesture, `over there.'

"I asked him how, if he did not know the place, he would know it when he saw it. Here he suddenly ceased to be hazy, and became alarmingly minute. He gave a description of the house detailed enough for an auctioneer. I have forgotten nearly all the details except the last two, which were that the lamp-post was painted green, and that there was a red pillar-box at the corner.

"`A red pillar-box!' I cried in astonishment. `Why, the place must be in England!'

"`I had forgotten,' he said, nodding heavily. `That is the island's name.'

"`But, ~nom du nom~,' I cried testily, `you've just come from England, my boy.'

"`They SAID it was England,' said my imbecile, conspiratorially. `They said it was Kent. But Kentish men are such liars one can't believe anything they say.'

"`Monsieur,' I said, `you must pardon me. I am elderly, and the ~fumisteries~ of the young men are beyond me. I go by common sense, or, at the largest, by that extension of applied common sense called science.'

"`Science!' cried the stranger. `There is only one good thing science ever discovered —a good thing, good tidings of great joy— that the world is round.'

"I told him with civility that his words conveyed no impression to my intelligence. `I mean,' he said, `that going right round the world is the shortest way to where you are already.'

"`Is it not even shorter,' I asked, `to stop where you are?'

"`No, no, no!' he cried emphatically. `That way is long and very weary. At the end of the world, at the back of the dawn, I shall find the wife I really married and the house that is really mine. And that house will have a greener lamp-post and a redder pillar-box. Do you,' he asked with a sudden intensity, `do you never want to rush out of your house in order to find it?'

"`No, I think not,' I replied; `reason tells a man from the first to adapt his desires to the probable supply of life. I remain here, content to fulfil the life of man. All my interests are here, and most of my friends, and—'

"`And yet,' he cried, starting to his almost terrific height, `you made the French Revolution!'

"`Pardon me,' I said, `I am not quite so elderly. A relative perhaps.'

"`I mean your sort did!' exclaimed this personage. `Yes, your damned smug, settled, sensible sort made the French Revolution. Oh! I know some say it was no good, and you're just back where you were before. Why, blast it all, that's just where we all want to be—back where we were before! That is revolution—going right round! Every revolution, like a repentance, is a return.'

"He was so excited that I waited till he had taken his seat again, and then said something indifferent and soothing; but he struck the tiny table with his colossal fist and went on.

"`I am going to have a revolution, not a French Revolution, but an English Revolution. God has given to each tribe its own type of mutiny. The Frenchmen march against the citadel of the city together; the Englishman marches to the outskirts of the city, and alone. But I am going to turn the world upside down, too. I'm going to turn myself upside down. I'm going to walk upside down in the cursed upsidedownland of the Antipodes, where trees and men hang head downward in the sky. But my revolution, like yours, like the earth's, will end up in the holy, happy place— the celestial, incredible place—the place where we were before.'

"With these remarks, which can scarcely be reconciled with reason, he leapt from the seat and strode away into the twilight, swinging his pole and leaving behind him an excessive payment, which also pointed to some loss of mental balance. This is all I know of the episode of the man landed from the fishing-boat, and I hope it may serve the interests of justice.— Accept, Sir, the assurances of the very high consideration, with which I have the honour to be your obedient servant, "Jules Durobin."

"The next document in our dossier," continued Inglewood, "comes from the town of Crazok, in the central plains of Russia, and runs as follows:—

"Sir,—My name is Paul Nickolaiovitch: I am the stationmaster at the station near Crazok. The great trains go by across the plains taking people to China, but very few people get down at the platform where I have to watch. This makes my life rather lonely, and I am thrown back much upon the books I have. But I cannot discuss these very much with my neighbours, for enlightened ideas have not spread in this part of Russia so much as in other parts. Many of the peasants round here have never heard of Bernard Shaw.

"I am a Liberal, and do my best to spread Liberal ideas; but since the failure of the revolution this has been even more difficult. The revolutionists committed many acts contrary to the pure principles of humanitarianism, with which indeed, owing to the scarcity of books, they were ill acquainted. I did not approve of these cruel acts, though provoked by the tyranny of the government; but now there is a tendency to reproach all Intelligents with the memory of them. This is very unfortunate for Intelligents.

"It was when the railway strike was almost over, and a few trains came through at long intervals, that I stood one day watching a train that had come in. Only one person got out of the train, far away up at the other end of it, for it was a very long train. It was evening, with a cold, greenish sky. A little snow had fallen, but not enough to whiten the plain, which stretched away a sort of sad purple in all directions, save where the flat tops of some distant tablelands caught the evening light like lakes. As the solitary man came stamping along on the thin snow by the train he grew larger and larger; I thought I had never seen so large a man. But he looked even taller than he was, I think, because his shoulders were very big and his head comparatively little. From the big shoulders hung a tattered old jacket, striped dull red and dirty white, very thin for the winter, and one hand rested on a huge pole such as peasants rake in weeds with to burn them.

"Before he had traversed the full length of the train he was entangled in one of those knots of rowdies that were the embers of the extinct revolution, though they mostly disgraced themselves upon the government side. I was just moving to his assistance, when he whirled up his rake and laid out right and left with such energy that he came through them without scathe and strode right up to me, leaving them staggered and really astonished.

"Yet when he reached me, after so abrupt an assertion of his aim, he could only say rather dubiously in French that he wanted a house.

"'There are not many houses to be had round here,' I answered in the same

413

language, `the district has been very disturbed. A revolution, as you know, has recently been suppressed. Any further building—'

"`Oh! I don't mean that,' he cried; `I mean a real house—a live house. It really is a live house, for it runs away from me.'

"`I am ashamed to say that something in his phrase or gesture moved me profoundly. We Russians are brought up in an atmosphere of folk-lore, and its unfortunate effects can still be seen in the bright colours of the children's dolls and of the ikons. For an instant the idea of a house running away from a man gave me pleasure, for the enlightenment of man moves slowly.

"`Have you no other house of your own?' I asked.

"`I have left it,' he said very sadly. `It was not the house that grew dull, but I that grew dull in it. My wife was better than all women, and yet I could not feel it.'

"`And so,' I said with sympathy, `you walked straight out of the front door, like a masculine Nora.'

"`Nora?' he inquired politely, apparently supposing it to be a Russian word.

"`I mean Nora in "The Doll's House,"' I replied.

"At this he looked very much astonished, and I knew he was an Englishman; for Englishmen always think that Russians study nothing but `ukases.'

"`"The Doll's House"?' he cried vehemently; `why, that is just where Ibsen was so wrong! Why, the whole aim of a house is to be a doll's house. Don't you remember, when you were a child, how those little windows WERE windows, while the big windows weren't. A child has a doll's house, and shrieks when a front door opens inwards. A banker has a real house, yet how numerous are the bankers who fail to emit the faintest shriek when their real front doors open inwards.'

"Something from the folk-lore of my infancy still kept me foolishly silent; and before I could speak, the Englishman had leaned over and was saying in a sort of loud whisper, `I have found out how to make a big thing small. I have found out how to turn a house into a doll's house. Get a long way off it: God lets us turn all things into toys by his great gift of distance. Once let me see my old brick house standing up quite little against the horizon, and I shall want to go back to it again. I shall see the funny little toy lamp-post painted green against the gate, and all the dear little people like dolls looking out of the window. For the windows really open in my doll's house.'

"`But why?' I asked, `should you wish to return to that particular doll's house? Having taken, like Nora, the bold step against convention, having made yourself in the conventional sense disreputable, having dared to be free, why should you not take advantage of your freedom? As the greatest modern writers have pointed out, what you called your marriage was only your mood. You have a right to leave it all behind, like the clippings of your hair or the parings of your nails. Having once escaped, you have the world before you. Though the words may seem strange to you, you are free in Russia.'

"He sat with his dreamy eyes on the dark circles of the plains, where the only moving thing was the long and labouring trail of smoke out of the railway engine, violet in tint, volcanic in outline, the one hot and heavy cloud of that cold clear evening of pale green.

"`Yes,' he said with a huge sigh, `I am free in Russia. You are right. I could really walk into that town over there and have love all over again, and perhaps marry some beautiful woman and begin again, and nobody could ever find me. Yes, you have certainly convinced me of something.'

"His tone was so queer and mystical that I felt impelled to ask him what he meant, and of what exactly I had convinced him.

"'You have convinced me,' he said with the same dreamy eye, 'why it is really wicked and dangerous for a man to run away from his wife.'

"'And why is it dangerous?' I inquired.

"'Why, because nobody can find him,' answered this odd person, 'and we all want to be found.'

"'The most original modern thinkers,' I remarked, 'Ibsen, Gorki, Nietzsche, Shaw, would all rather say that what we want most is to be lost: to find ourselves in untrodden paths, and to do unprecedented things: to break with the past and belong to the future.'

"He rose to his whole height somewhat sleepily, and looked round on what was, I confess, a somewhat desolate scene—the dark purple plains, the neglected railroad, the few ragged knots of malcontents. 'I shall not find the house here,' he said. 'It is still eastward— further and further eastward.'

"Then he turned upon me with something like fury, and struck the foot of his pole upon the frozen earth.

"'And if I do go back to my country,' he cried, 'I may be locked up in a madhouse before I reach my own house. I have been a bit unconventional in my time! Why, Nietzsche stood in a row of ramrods in the silly old Prussian army, and Shaw takes temperance beverages in the suburbs; but the things I do are unprecedented things. This round road I am treading is an untrodden path. I do believe in breaking out; I am a revolutionist. But don't you see that all these real leaps and destructions and escapes are only attempts to get back to Eden— to something we have had, to something we at least have heard of? Don't you see one only breaks the fence or shoots the moon in order to get HOME?'

"'No,' I answered after due reflection, 'I don't think I should accept that.'

"'Ah,' he said with a sort of a sigh, 'then you have explained a second thing to me.'

"'What do you mean?' I asked; 'what thing?'

"'Why your revolution has failed,' he said; and walking across quite suddenly to the train he got into it just as it was steaming away at last. And as I saw the long snaky tail of it disappear along the darkening flats.

"I saw no more of him. But though his views were adverse to the best advanced thought, he struck me as an interesting person: I should like to find out if he has produced any literary works.—Yours, etc., "Paul Nickolaiovitch."

There was something in this odd set of glimpses into foreign lives which kept the absurd tribunal quieter than it had hitherto been, and it was again without interruption that Inglewood opened another paper upon his pile. "The Court will be indulgent," he said, "if the next note lacks the special ceremonies of our letter-writing. It is ceremonious enough in its own way:—

"The Celestial Principles are permanent: Greeting.—I am Wong-Hi, and I tend the temple of all the ancestors of my family in the forest of Fu. The man that broke through the sky and came to me said that it must be very dull, but I showed him the wrongness of his thought. I am indeed in one place, for my uncle took me to this temple when I was a boy, and in this I shall doubtless die. But if a man remain in one place he shall see that the place changes. The pagoda of my temple stands up silently out of all the trees, like a yellow pagoda above many green pagodas. But the skies are sometimes blue like porcelain, and sometimes green like jade, and sometimes red like garnet. But the night is always ebony and always returns, said the Emperor Ho.

"The sky-breaker came at evening very suddenly, for I had hardly seen any stirring in the tops of the green trees over which I look as over a sea, when I go to the top of the temple at morning. And yet when he came, it was as if an elephant had strayed from the armies of the great kings of India. For palms snapped, and bamboos broke, and there came forth in the sunshine before the temple one taller than the sons of men.

"Strips of red and white hung about him like ribbons of a carnival, and he carried a pole with a row of teeth on it like the teeth of a dragon. His face was white and discomposed, after the fashion of the foreigners, so that they look like dead men filled with devils; and he spoke our speech brokenly.

"He said to me, `This is only a temple; I am trying to find a house.' And then he told me with indelicate haste that the lamp outside his house was green, and that there was a red post at the corner of it.

"`I have not seen your house nor any houses,' I answered. `I dwell in this temple and serve the gods.'

"`Do you believe in the gods?' he asked with hunger in his eyes, like the hunger of dogs. And this seemed to me a strange question to ask, for what should a man do except what men have done?

"`My Lord,' I said, `it must be good for men to hold up their hands even if the skies are empty. For if there are gods, they will be pleased, and if there are none, then there are none to be displeased. Sometimes the skies are gold and sometimes porphyry and sometimes ebony, but the trees and the temple stand still under it all. So the great Confucius taught us that if we do always the same things with our hands and our feet as do the wise beasts and birds, with our heads we may think many things: yes, my Lord, and doubt many things. So long as men offer rice at the right season, and kindle lanterns at the right hour, it matters little whether there be gods or no. For these things are not to appease gods, but to appease men.'

"He came yet closer to me, so that he seemed enormous; yet his look was very gentle.

"`Break your temple,' he said, `and your gods will be freed.'

"And I, smiling at his simplicity, answered: `And so, if there be no gods, I shall have nothing but a broken temple.'

"And at this, that giant from whom the light of reason was withheld threw out his mighty arms and asked me to forgive him. And when I asked him for what he should be forgiven he answered: `For being right.'

"`Your idols and emperors are so old and wise and satisfying,' he cried, `it is a shame that they should be wrong. We are so vulgar and violent, we have done you so many iniquities— it is a shame we should be right after all.'

"And I, still enduring his harmlessness, asked him why he thought that he and his people were right.

"And he answered: `We are right because we are bound where men should be bound, and free where men should be free. We are right because we doubt and destroy laws and customs— but we do not doubt our own right to destroy them. For you live by customs, but we live by creeds. Behold me! In my country I am called Smip. My country is abandoned, my name is defiled, because I pursue around the world what really belongs to me. You are steadfast as the trees because you do not believe. I am as fickle as the tempest because I do believe. I do believe in my own house, which I shall find again. And at the last remaineth the green lantern and the red post.'

"I said to him: `At the last remaineth only wisdom.'

"But even as I said the word he uttered a horrible shout, and rushing forward disappeared among the trees. I have not seen this man again nor any other man. The virtues of the wise are of fine brass. "Wong-Hi."

"The next letter I have to read," proceeded Arthur Inglewood, "will probably make clear the nature of our client's curious but innocent experiment. It is dated from a mountain village in California, and runs as follows:—

"Sir,—A person answering to the rather extraordinary description required certainly went, some time ago, over the high pass of the Sierras on which I live and of which I am probably the sole stationary inhabitant. I keep a rudimentary tavern, rather ruder than a hut, on the very top of this specially steep and threatening pass. My name is Louis Hara, and the very name may puzzle you about my nationality. Well, it puzzles me a great deal. When one has been for fifteen years without society it is hard to have patriotism; and where there is not even a hamlet it is difficult to invent a nation. My father was an Irishman of the fiercest and most free-shooting of the old Californian kind. My mother was a Spaniard, proud of descent from the old Spanish families round San Francisco, yet accused for all that of some admixture of Red Indian blood. I was well educated and fond of music and books. But, like many other hybrids, I was too good or too bad for the world; and after attempting many things I was glad enough to get a sufficient though a lonely living in this little cabaret in the mountains. In my solitude I fell into many of the ways of a savage. Like an Eskimo, I was shapeless in winter; like a Red Indian, I wore in hot summers nothing but a pair of leather trousers, with a great straw hat as big as a parasol to defend me from the sun. I had a bowie knife at my belt and a long gun under my arm; and I dare say I produced a pretty wild impression on the few peaceable travellers that could climb up to my place. But I promise you I never looked as mad as that man did. Compared with him I was Fifth Avenue.

"I dare say that living under the very top of the Sierras has an odd effect on the mind; one tends to think of those lonely rocks not as peaks coming to a point, but rather as pillars holding up heaven itself. Straight cliffs sail up and away beyond the hope of the eagles; cliffs so tall that they seem to attract the stars and collect them as sea-crags collect a mere glitter of phosphorous. These terraces and towers of rock do not, like smaller crests, seem to be the end of the world. Rather they seem to be its awful beginning: its huge foundations. We could almost fancy the mountain branching out above us like a tree of stone, and carrying all those cosmic lights like a candelabrum. For just as the peaks failed us, soaring impossibly far, so the stars crowded us (as it seemed), coming impossibly near. The spheres burst about us more like thunderbolts hurled at the earth than planets circling placidly about it.

"All this may have driven me mad; I am not sure. I know there is one angle of the road down the pass where the rock leans out a little, and on windy nights I seem to hear it clashing overhead with other rocks— yes, city against city and citadel against citadel, far up into the night. It was on such an evening that the strange man struggled up the pass. Broadly speaking, only strange men did struggle up the pass. But I had never seen one like this one before.

"He carried (I cannot conceive why) a long, dilapidated garden rake, all bearded and bedraggled with grasses, so that it looked like the ensign of some old barbarian tribe. His hair, which was as long and rank as the grass, hung down below his huge shoulders; and such clothes as clung about him were rags and tongues of red and yellow, so that he had the air of being dressed like an Indian in feathers or autumn leaves. The rake or pitchfork, or whatever it was, he used sometimes as an alpenstock, sometimes (I was told) as a weapon. I do not know why he should have used it as a weapon, for he had, and afterwards showed me, an excellent six-shooter in his pocket. `But THAT,' he said, `I use only for peaceful purposes.' I have no notion what he meant.

"He sat down on the rough bench outside my inn and drank some wine from the vineyards below, sighing with ecstasy over it like one who had travelled long among alien, cruel things and found at last something that he knew. Then he sat staring rather foolishly at the rude lantern of lead and coloured glass that hangs over my door. It is old, but of no value; my grandmother gave it to me long ago: she was devout, and it happens that the glass is painted with a crude picture of Bethlehem and the Wise Men and the Star. He seemed so mesmerized with the transparent glow of Our Lady's blue gown and the big gold star behind, that he led me also to look at the thing, which I had not done for fourteen years.

"Then he slowly withdrew his eyes from this and looked out eastward where the road fell away below us. The sunset sky was a vault of rich velvet, fading away into mauve and silver round the edges of the dark mountain amphitheatre; and between us and the ravine below rose up out of the deeps and went up into the heights the straight solitary rock we call Green Finger. Of a queer volcanic colour, and wrinkled all over with what looks undecipherable writing, it hung there like a Babylonian pillar or needle.

"The man silently stretched out his rake in that direction, and before he spoke I knew what he meant. Beyond the great green rock in the purple sky hung a single star.

"`A star in the east,' he said in a strange hoarse voice like one of our ancient eagles'. `The wise men followed the star and found the house. But if I followed the star, should I find the house?'

"`It depends perhaps,' I said, smiling, `on whether you are a wise man.' I refrained from adding that he certainly didn't look it.

"`You may judge for yourself,' he answered. `I am a man who left his own house because he could no longer bear to be away from it.'

"`It certainly sounds paradoxical,' I said.

"`I heard my wife and children talking and saw them moving about the room,' he continued, `and all the time I knew they were walking and talking in another house thousands of miles away, under the light of different skies, and beyond the series of the seas. I loved them with a devouring love, because they seemed not only distant but unattainable. Never did human creatures seem so dear and so desirable: but I seemed like a cold ghost; therefore I cast off their dust from my feet for a testimony. Nay, I did more. I spurned the world under my feet so that it swung full circle like a treadmill.'

"'Do you really mean,' I cried, 'that you have come right round the world? Your speech is English, yet you are coming from the west.'

"'My pilgrimage is not yet accomplished,' he replied sadly. 'I have become a pilgrim to cure myself of being an exile.'

"Something in the word 'pilgrim' awoke down in the roots of my ruinous experience memories of what my fathers had felt about the world, and of something from whence I came. I looked again at the little pictured lantern at which I had not looked for fourteen years.

"'My grandmother,' I said in a low tone, 'would have said that we were all in exile, and that no earthly house could cure the holy home-sickness that forbids us rest.'

"He was silent a long while, and watched a single eagle drift out beyond the Green Finger into the darkening void.

"Then he said, 'I think your grandmother was right,' and stood up leaning on his grassy pole. 'I think that must be the reason,' he said—'the secret of this life of man, so ecstatic and so unappeased. But I think there is more to be said. I think God has given us the love of special places, of a hearth and of a native land, for a good reason.'

"'I dare say,' I said. 'What reason?'

"'Because otherwise,' he said, pointing his pole out at the sky and the abyss, 'we might worship that.'

"'What do you mean?' I demanded.

"'Eternity,' he said in his harsh voice, 'the largest of the idols— the mightiest of the rivals of God.'

"'You mean pantheism and infinity and all that,' I suggested.

"'I mean,' he said with increasing vehemence, 'that if there be a house for me in heaven it will either have a green lamp-post and a hedge, or something quite as positive and personal as a green lamp-post and a hedge. I mean that God bade me love one spot and serve it, and do all things however wild in praise of it, so that this one spot might be a witness against all the infinities and the sophistries, that Paradise is somewhere and not anywhere, is something and not anything. And I would not be so very much surprised if the house in heaven had a real green lamp-post after all.'

"With which he shouldered his pole and went striding down the perilous paths below, and left me alone with the eagles. But since he went a fever of homelessness will often shake me. I am troubled by rainy meadows and mud cabins that I have never seen; and I wonder whether America will endure.— Yours faithfully, Louis Hara."

After a short silence Inglewood said: "And, finally, we desire to put in as evidence the following document:—

"This is to say that I am Ruth Davis, and have been housemaid to Mrs. I. Smith at 'The Laurels' in Croydon for the last six months. When I came the lady was alone, with two children; she was not a widow, but her husband was away. She was left with plenty of money and did not seem disturbed about him, though she often hoped he would be back soon. She said he was rather eccentric and a little change did him good. One evening last week I was bringing the tea-things out on to the lawn when I nearly dropped them. The end of a long rake was suddenly stuck over the hedge, and planted like a jumping-pole; and over the hedge, just like a monkey on a stick, came a huge, horrible man, all hairy and ragged like Robinson Crusoe. I screamed out, but my mistress didn't even get out of her chair, but smiled and said he wanted shaving. Then he sat down quite calmly at the garden table and took a cup of tea, and then I realized that this must be Mr. Smith himself. He has stopped here ever since and does not really give much trouble, though I sometimes fancy he is a little weak in his head. "Ruth Davis.

"P.S.—I forgot to say that he looked round at the garden and said, very loud and strong: `Oh, what a lovely place you've got;' just as if he'd never seen it before."

The room had been growing dark and drowsy; the afternoon sun sent one heavy shaft of powdered gold across it, which fell with an intangible solemnity upon the empty seat of Mary Gray, for the younger women had left the court before the more recent of the investigations. Mrs. Duke was still asleep, and Innocent Smith, looking like a large hunchback in the twilight, was bending closer and closer to his paper toys. But the five men really engaged in the controversy, and concerned not to convince the tribunal but to convince each other, still sat round the table like the Committee of Public Safety.

Suddenly Moses Gould banged one big scientific book on top of another, cocked his little legs up against the table, tipped his chair backwards so far as to be in direct danger of falling over, emitted a startling and prolonged whistle like a steam engine, and asserted that it was all his eye.

When asked by Moon what was all his eye, he banged down behind the books again and answered with considerable excitement, throwing his papers about. "All those fairy-tales you've been reading out," he said. "Oh! don't talk to me! I ain't littery and that, but I know fairy-tales when I hear 'em. I got a bit stumped in some of the philosophical bits and felt inclined to go out for a B. and S. But we're living in West 'Ampstead and not in 'Ell; and the long and the short of it is that some things 'appen and some things don't 'appen. Those are the things that don't 'appen."

"I thought," said Moon gravely, "that we quite clearly explained—"

"Oh yes, old chap, you quite clearly explained," assented Mr. Gould with extraordinary volubility. "You'd explain an elephant off the doorstep, you would. I ain't a clever chap like you; but I ain't a born natural, Michael Moon, and when there's an elephant on my doorstep I don't listen to no explanations. `It's got a trunk,' I says.—`My trunk,' you says: `I'm fond of travellin', and a change does me good.'— `But the blasted thing's got tusks,' I says.—`Don't look a gift 'orse in the mouth,' you says, `but thank the goodness and the graice that on your birth 'as smiled.'—`But it's nearly as big as the 'ouse,' I says.—`That's the bloomin' perspective,' you says, `and the sacred magic of distance.'—`Why, the elephant's trumpetin' like the Day of Judgement,' I says.—`That's your own conscience a-talking to you, Moses Gould,' you says in a grive and tender voice. Well, I 'ave got a conscience as much as you. I don't believe most of the things they tell you in church on Sundays; and I don't believe these 'ere things any more because you goes on about 'em as if you was in church. I believe an elephant's a great big ugly dingerous beast— and I believe Smith's another."

"Do you mean to say," asked Inglewood, "that you still doubt the evidence of exculpation we have brought forward?"

"Yes, I do still doubt it," said Gould warmly. "It's all a bit too far-fetched, and some of it a bit too far off. 'Ow can we test all those tales? 'Ow can we drop in and buy the `Pink 'Un' at the railway station at Kosky Wosky or whatever it was? 'Ow can we go and do a gargle at the saloon-bar on top of the Sierra Mountains? But anybody can go and see Bunting's boarding-house at Worthing."

Moon regarded him with an expression of real or assumed surprise.

"Any one," continued Gould, "can call on Mr. Trip."

"It is a comforting thought," replied Michael with restraint; "but why should any one call on Mr. Trip?"

"For just exactly the sime reason," cried the excited Moses, hammering on the table with both hands, "for just exactly the sime reason that he should communicate with Messrs. 'Anbury and Bootle of Paternoster Row and with Miss Gridley's 'igh class Academy at 'Endon, and with old Lady Bullingdon who lives at Penge."

"Again, to go at once to the moral roots of life," said Michael, "why is it among the duties of man to communicate with old Lady Bullingdon who lives at Penge?"

"It ain't one of the duties of man," said Gould, "nor one of his pleasures, either, I can tell you. She takes the crumpet, does Lady Bullingdon at Penge. But it's one of the duties of a prosecutor pursuin' the innocent, blameless butterfly career of your friend Smith, and it's the sime with all the others I mentioned."

"But why do you bring in these people here?" asked Inglewood.

"Why! Because we've got proof enough to sink a steamboat," roared Moses; "because I've got the papers in my very 'and; because your precious Innocent is a blackguard and 'ome smasher, and these are the 'omes he's smashed. I don't set up for a 'oly man; but I wouldn't 'ave all those poor girls on my conscience for something. And I think a chap that's capable of deserting and perhaps killing 'em all is about capable of cracking a crib or shootin' an old schoolmaster—so I don't care much about the other yarns one way or another."

"I think," said Dr. Cyrus Pym with a refined cough, "that we are approaching this matter rather irregularly. This is really the fourth charge on the charge sheet, and perhaps I had better put it before you in an ordered and scientific manner."

Nothing but a faint groan from Michael broke the silence of the darkening room.

4. THE WILD WEDDINGS; OR, THE POLYGAMY CHARGE

"A modern man," said Dr. Cyrus Pym, "must, if he be thoughtful, approach the problem of marriage with some caution. Marriage is a stage—doubtless a suitable stage —in the long advance of mankind towards a goal which we cannot as yet conceive; which we are not, perhaps, as yet fitted even to desire. What, gentlemen, is the ethical position of marriage? Have we outlived it?"

"Outlived it?" broke out Moon; "why, nobody's ever survived it! Look at all the people married since Adam and Eve—and all as dead as mutton."

"This is no doubt an inter-pellation joc'lar in its character," said Dr. Pym frigidly. "I cannot tell what may be Mr. Moon's matured and ethical view of marriage—"

"I can tell," said Michael savagely, out of the gloom. "Marriage is a duel to the death, which no man of honour should decline."

"Michael," said Arthur Inglewood in a low voice, "you MUST keep quiet."

"Mr. Moon," said Pym with exquisite good temper, "probably regards the institution in a more antiquated manner. Probably he would make it stringent and uniform. He would treat divorce in some great soul of steel—the divorce of a Julius Caesar or of a

G.K. CHESTERTON

Salt Ring Robinson— exactly as he would treat some no-account tramp or labourer who scoots from his wife. Science has views broader and more humane. Just as murder for the scientist is a thirst for absolute destruction, just as theft for the scientist is a hunger for monotonous acquisition, so polygamy for the scientist is an extreme development of the instinct for variety. A man thus afflicted is incapable of constancy. Doubtless there is a physical cause for this flitting from flower to flower— as there is, doubtless, for the intermittent groaning which appears to afflict Mr. Moon at the present moment. Our own world-scorning Winterbottom has even dared to say, `For a certain rare and fine physical type polygamy is but the realization of the variety of females, as comradeship is the realization of the variety of males.' In any case, the type that tends to variety is recognized by all authoritative inquirers. Such a type, if the widower of a negress, does in many ascertained cases espouse ~en seconde noces~ an albino; such a type, when freed from the gigantic embraces of a female Patagonian, will often evolve from its own imaginative instinct the consoling figure of an Eskimo. To such a type there can be no doubt that the prisoner belongs. If blind doom and unbearable temptation constitute any slight excuse for a man, there is no doubt that he has these excuses.

"Earlier in the inquiry the defence showed real chivalric ideality in admitting half of our story without further dispute. We should like to acknowledge and imitate so eminently large-hearted a style by conceding also that the story told by Curate Percy about the canoe, the weir, and the young wife seems to be substantially true. Apparently Smith did marry a young woman he had nearly run down in a boat; it only remains to be considered whether it would not have been kinder of him to have murdered her instead of marrying her. In confirmation of this fact I can now con-cede to the defence an unquestionable record of such a marriage."

So saying, he handed across to Michael a cutting from the "Maidenhead Gazette" which distinctly recorded the marriage of the daughter of a "coach," a tutor well known in the place, to Mr. Innocent Smith, late of Brakespeare College, Cambridge.

When Dr. Pym resumed it was realized that his face had grown at once both tragic and triumphant.

"I pause upon this pre-liminary fact," he said seriously, "because this fact alone would give us the victory, were we aspiring after victory and not after truth. As far as the personal and domestic problem holds us, that problem is solved. Dr. Warner and I entered this house at an instant of highly emotional diff'culty. England's Warner has entered many houses to save human kind from sickness; this time he entered to save an innocent lady from a walking pestilence. Smith was just about to carry away a young girl from this house; his cab and bag were at the very door. He had told her she was going to await the marriage license at the house of his aunt. That aunt," continued Cyrus Pym, his face darkening grandly—"that visionary aunt had been the dancing will-o'-the-wisp who had led many a high-souled maiden to her doom. Into how many virginal ears has he whispered that holy word? When he said `aunt' there glowed about her all the merriment and high morality of the Anglo-Saxon home. Kettles began to hum, pussy cats to purr, in that very wild cab that was being driven to destruction."

Inglewood looked up, to find, to his astonishment (as many another denizen of the eastern hemisphere has found), that the American was not only perfectly serious, but was really eloquent and affecting— when the difference of the hemispheres was adjusted.

"It is therefore atrociously evident that the man Smith has at least represented himself to one innocent female of this house as an eligible bachelor, being, in fact, a married man. I agree with my colleague, Mr. Gould, that no other crime could approximate to this. As to whether what our ancestors called purity has any ultimate ethical value indeed, science hesitates with a high, proud hesitation. But what hesitation can there be about the baseness of a citizen who ventures, by brutal experiments upon living females, to anticipate the verdict of science on such a point?

"The woman mentioned by Curate Percy as living with Smith in Highbury may or may not be the same as the lady he married in Maidenhead. If one short sweet spell of constancy and heart repose interrupted the plunging torrent of his profligate life, we will not deprive him of that long past possibility. After that conjectural date, alas, he seems to have plunged deeper and deeper into the shaking quagmires of infidelity and shame."

Dr. Pym closed his eyes, but the unfortunate fact that there was no more light left this familiar signal without its full and proper moral effect. After a pause, which almost partook of the character of prayer, he continued.

"The first instance of the accused's repeated and irregular nuptials," he exclaimed, "comes from Lady Bullingdon, who expresses herself with the high haughtiness which must be excused in those who look out upon all mankind from the turrets of a Norman and ancestral keep. The communication she has sent to us runs as follows:—

"Lady Bullingdon recalls the painful incident to which reference is made, and has no desire to deal with it in detail. The girl Polly Green was a perfectly adequate dressmaker, and lived in the village for about two years. Her unattached condition was bad for her as well as for the general morality of the village. Lady Bullingdon, therefore, allowed it to be understood that she favoured the marriage of the young woman. The villagers, naturally wishing to oblige Lady Bullingdon, came forward in several cases; and all would have been well had it not been for the deplorable eccentricity or depravity of the girl Green herself. Lady Bullingdon supposes that where there is a village there must be a village idiot, and in her village, it seems, there was one of these wretched creatures. Lady Bullingdon only saw him once, and she is quite aware that it is really difficult to distinguish between actual idiots and the ordinary heavy type of the rural lower classes. She noticed, however, the startling smallness of his head in comparison to the rest of his body; and, indeed, the fact of his having appeared upon election day wearing the rosette of both the two opposing parties appears to Lady Bullingdon to put the matter quite beyond doubt. Lady Bullingdon was astounded to learn that this afflicted being had put himself forward as one of the suitors of the girl in question. Lady Bullingdon's nephew interviewed the wretch upon the point, telling him that he was a `donkey' to dream of such a thing, and actually received, along with an imbecile grin, the answer that donkeys generally go after carrots. But Lady Bullingdon was yet further amazed to find the unhappy girl inclined to accept this monstrous proposal, though she was actually asked in marriage by Garth, the undertaker, a man in a far superior position to her own. Lady Bullingdon could not, of course, countenance such an arrangement for a moment, and the two unhappy persons escaped for a clandestine marriage. Lady Bullingdon cannot exactly recall the man's name, but thinks it was Smith. He was always called in the village the Innocent. Later, Lady Bullingdon believes he murdered Green in a mental outbreak."

"The next communication," proceeded Pym, "is more conspicuous for brevity, but I am of the opinion that it will adequately convey the upshot. It is dated from the offices of Messrs. Hanbury and Bootle, publishers, and is as follows:—

"Sir,—Yrs. rcd. and conts. noted. Rumour re typewriter possibly refers to a Miss Blake or similar name, left here nine years ago to marry an organ-grinder. Case was undoubtedly curious, and attracted police attention. Girl worked excellently till about Oct. 1907, when apparently went mad. Record was written at the time, part of which I enclose.— Yrs., etc., W. Trip.

"The fuller statement runs as follows:—

"On October 12 a letter was sent from this office to Messrs. Bernard and Juke, bookbinders. Opened by Mr. Juke, it was found to contain the following: `Sir, our Mr. Trip will call at 3, as we wish to know whether it is really decided 00000073*bb* !!!!! *xy*.' To this Mr. Juke, a person of a playful mind, returned the answer: `Sir, I am in a position to give it as my most decided opinion that it is not really decided that 00000073*bb* !!!!! *xy*. Yrs., etc., `J. Juke.'

"On receiving this extraordinary reply, our Mr. Trip asked for the original letter sent from him, and found that the typewriter had indeed substituted these demented hieroglyphics for the sentences really dictated to her. Our Mr. Trip interviewed the girl, fearing that she was in an unbalanced state, and was not much reassured when she merely remarked that she always went like that when she heard the barrel organ. Becoming yet more hysterical and extravagant, she made a series of most improbable statements—as, that she was engaged to the barrel-organ man, that he was in the habit of serenading her on that instrument, that she was in the habit of playing back to him upon the typewriter (in the style of King Richard and Blondel), and that the organ man's musical ear was so exquisite and his adoration of herself so ardent that he could detect the note of the different letters on the machine, and was enraptured by them as by a melody. To all these statements of course our Mr. Trip and the rest of us only paid that sort of assent that is paid to persons who must as quickly as possible be put in the charge of their relations. But on our conducting the lady downstairs, her story received the most startling and even exasperating confirmation; for the organ-grinder, an enormous man with a small head and manifestly a fellow-lunatic, had pushed his barrel organ in at the office doors like a battering-ram, and was boisterously demanding his alleged fiancee. When I myself came on the scene he was flinging his great, ape-like arms about and reciting a poem to her. But we were used to lunatics coming and reciting poems in our office, and we were not quite prepared for what followed. The actual verse he uttered began, I think,

`O vivid, inviolate head, Ringed —'

but he never got any further. Mr. Trip made a sharp movement towards him, and the next moment the giant picked up the poor lady typewriter like a doll, sat her on top of the organ, ran it with a crash out of the office doors, and raced away down the street like a flying wheelbarrow. I put the police upon the matter; but no trace of the amazing pair could be found. I was sorry myself; for the lady was not only pleasant but unusually cultivated for her position. As I am leaving the service of Messrs. Hanbury and Bootle, I put these things in a record and leave it with them. (Signed) Aubrey Clarke, Publishers' Reader.

"And the last document," said Dr. Pym complacently, "is from one of those high-souled women who have in this age introduced your English girlhood to hockey, the higher mathematics, and every form of ideality.

"Dear Sir (she writes),—I have no objection to telling you the facts about the absurd incident you mention; though I would ask you to communicate them with some caution, for such things, however entertaining in the abstract, are not always auxiliary to the success of a girls' school. The truth is this: I wanted some one to deliver a lecture on a philological or historical question—a lecture which, while containing solid educational matter, should be a little more popular and entertaining than usual, as it was the last lecture of the term. I remembered that a Mr. Smith of Cambridge had written somewhere or other an amusing essay about his own somewhat ubiquitous name— an essay which showed considerable knowledge of genealogy and topography. I wrote to him, asking if he would come and give us a bright address upon English surnames; and he did. It was very bright, almost too bright. To put the matter otherwise, by the time that he was halfway through it became apparent to the other mistresses and myself that the man was totally and entirely off his head. He began rationally enough by dealing with the two departments of place names and trade names, and he said (quite rightly, I dare say) that the loss of all significance in names was an instance of the deadening of civilization. But then he went on calmly to maintain that every man who had a place name ought to go to live in that place, and that every man who had a trade name ought instantly to adopt that trade; that people named after colours should always dress in those colours, and that people named after trees or plants (such as Beech or Rose) ought to surround and decorate themselves with these vegetables. In a slight discussion that arose afterwards among the elder girls the difficulties of the proposal were clearly, and even eagerly, pointed out. It was urged, for instance, by Miss Younghusband that it was substantially impossible for her to play the part assigned to her; Miss Mann was in a similar dilemma, from which no modern views on the sexes could apparently extricate her; and some young ladies, whose surnames happened to be Low, Coward, and Craven, were quite enthusiastic against the idea. But all this happened afterwards. What happened at the crucial moment was that the lecturer produced several horseshoes and a large iron hammer from his bag, announced his immediate intention of setting up a smithy in the neighbourhood, and called on every one to rise in the same cause as for a heroic revolution. The other mistresses and I attempted to stop the wretched man, but I must confess that by an accident this very intercession produced the worst explosion of his insanity. He was waving the hammer, and wildly demanding the names of everybody; and it so happened that Miss Brown, one of the younger teachers, was wearing a brown dress—a reddish-brown dress that went quietly enough with the warmer colour of her hair, as well she knew. She was a nice girl, and nice girls do know about those things. But when our maniac discovered that we really had a Miss Brown who WAS brown, his ~idee fixe~ blew up like a powder magazine, and there, in the presence of all the mistresses and girls, he publicly proposed to the lady in the red-brown dress. You can imagine the effect of such a scene at a girls' school. At least, if you fail to imagine it, I certainly fail to describe it.

"Of course, the anarchy died down in a week or two, and I can think of it now as a joke. There was only one curious detail, which I will tell you, as you say your inquiry is vital; but I should desire you to consider it a little more confidential than the rest. Miss

Brown, who was an excellent girl in every way, did quite suddenly and surreptitiously leave us only a day or two afterwards. I should never have thought that her head would be the one to be really turned by so absurd an excitement.—Believe me, yours faithfully, Ada Gridley.

"I think," said Pym, with a really convincing simplicity and seriousness, "that these letters speak for themselves."

Mr. Moon rose for the last time in a darkness that gave no hint of whether his native gravity was mixed with his native irony.

"Throughout this inquiry," he said, "but especially in this its closing phase, the prosecution has perpetually relied upon one argument; I mean the fact that no one knows what has become of all the unhappy women apparently seduced by Smith. There is no sort of proof that they were murdered, but that implication is perpetually made when the question is asked as to how they died. Now I am not interested in how they died, or when they died, or whether they died. But I am interested in another analogous question—that of how they were born, and when they were born, and whether they were born. Do not misunderstand me. I do not dispute the existence of these women, or the veracity of those who have witnessed to them. I merely remark on the notable fact that only one of these victims, the Maidenhead girl, is described as having any home or parents. All the rest are boarders or birds of passage—a guest, a solitary dressmaker, a bachelor-girl doing typewriting. Lady Bullingdon, looking from her turrets, which she bought from the Whartons with the old soap-boiler's money when she jumped at marrying an unsuccessful gentleman from Ulster—Lady Bullingdon, looking out from those turrets, did really see an object which she describes as Green. Mr. Trip, of Hanbury and Bootle, really did have a typewriter betrothed to Smith. Miss Gridley, though idealistic, is absolutely honest. She did house, feed, and teach a young woman whom Smith succeeded in decoying away. We admit that all these women really lived. But we still ask whether they were ever born?"

"Oh, crikey!" said Moses Gould, stifled with amusement.

"There could hardly," interposed Pym with a quiet smile, "be a better instance of the neglect of true scientific process. The scientist, when once convinced of the fact of vitality and consciousness, would infer from these the previous process of generation."

"If these gals," said Gould impatiently—"if these gals were all alive (all alive O!) I'd chance a fiver they were all born."

"You'd lose your fiver," said Michael, speaking gravely out of the gloom. "All those admirable ladies were alive. They were more alive for having come into contact with Smith. They were all quite definitely alive, but only one of them was ever born."

"Are you asking us to believe—" began Dr. Pym.

"I am asking you a second question," said Moon sternly. "Can the court now sitting throw any light on a truly singular circumstance? Dr. Pym, in his interesting lecture on what are called, I believe, the relations of the sexes, said that Smith was the slave of a lust for variety which would lead a man first to a negress and then to an albino, first to a Patagonian giantess and then to a tiny Eskimo. But is there any evidence of such variety here? Is there any trace of a gigantic Patagonian in the story? Was the typewriter an Eskimo? So picturesque a circumstance would not surely have escaped remark. Was Lady Bullingdon's dressmaker a negress? A voice in my bosom answers, `No!' Lady

Bullingdon, I am sure, would think a negress so conspicuous as to be almost Socialistic, and would feel something a little rakish even about an albino.

"But was there in Smith's taste any such variety as the learned doctor describes? So far as our slight materials go, the very opposite seems to be the case. We have only one actual description of any of the prisoner's wives— the short but highly poetic account by the aesthetic curate. 'Her dress was the colour of spring, and her hair of autumn leaves.' Autumn leaves, of course, are of various colours, some of which would be rather startling in hair (green, for instance); but I think such an expression would be most naturally used of the shades from red-brown to red, especially as ladies with their coppery-coloured hair do frequently wear light artistic greens. Now when we come to the next wife, we find the eccentric lover, when told he is a donkey, answering that donkeys always go after carrots; a remark which Lady Bullingdon evidently regarded as pointless and part of the natural table-talk of a village idiot, but which has an obvious meaning if we suppose that Polly's hair was red. Passing to the next wife, the one he took from the girls' school, we find Miss Gridley noticing that the schoolgirl in question wore 'a reddish-brown dress, that went quietly enough with the warmer colour of her hair.' In other words, the colour of the girl's hair was something redder than red-brown. Lastly, the romantic organ-grinder declaimed in the office some poetry that only got as far as the words,—

'O vivid, inviolate head, Ringed —'

But I think that a wide study of the worst modern poets will enable us to guess that 'ringed with a glory of red,' or 'ringed with its passionate red,' was the line that rhymed to 'head.' In this case once more, therefore, there is good reason to suppose that Smith fell in love with a girl with some sort of auburn or darkish-red hair—rather," he said, looking down at the table, "rather like Miss Gray's hair."

Cyrus Pym was leaning forward with lowered eyelids, ready with one of his more pedantic interpellations; but Moses Gould suddenly struck his forefinger on his nose, with an expression of extreme astonishment and intelligence in his brilliant eyes.

"Mr. Moon's contention at present," interposed Pym, "is not, even if veracious, inconsistent with the lunatico-criminal view of I. Smith, which we have nailed to the mast. Science has long anticipated such a complication. An incurable attraction to a particular type of physical woman is one of the commonest of criminal per-versities, and when not considered narrowly, but in the light of induction and evolution—"

"At this late stage," said Michael Moon very quietly, "I may perhaps relieve myself of a simple emotion that has been pressing me throughout the proceedings, by saying that induction and evolution may go and boil themselves. The Missing Link and all that is well enough for kids, but I'm talking about things we know here. All we know of the Missing Link is that he is missing—and he won't be missed either. I know all about his human head and his horrid tail; they belong to a very old game called 'Heads I win, tails you lose.' If you do find a fellow's bones, it proves he lived a long while ago; if you don't find his bones, it proves how long ago he lived. That is the game you've been playing with this Smith affair. Because Smith's head is small for his shoulders you call him microcephalous; if it had been large, you'd have called it water-on-the-brain. As long as poor old Smith's seraglio seemed pretty various, variety was the sign of madness: now, because it's turning out to be a bit monochrome—now monotony is the sign of madness. I suffer from all the disadvantages of being a grown-up person, and

I'm jolly well going to get some of the advantages too; and with all politeness I propose not to be bullied with long words instead of short reasons, or consider your business a triumphant progress merely because you're always finding out that you were wrong. Having relieved myself of these feelings, I have merely to add that I regard Dr. Pym as an ornament to the world far more beautiful than the Parthenon, or the monument on Bunker's Hill, and that I propose to resume and conclude my remarks on the many marriages of Mr. Innocent Smith.

"Besides this red hair, there is another unifying thread that runs through these scattered incidents. There is something very peculiar and suggestive about the names of these women. Mr. Trip, you will remember, said he thought the typewriter's name was Blake, but could not remember exactly. I suggest that it might have been Black, and in that case we have a curious series: Miss Green in Lady Bullingdon's village; Miss Brown at the Hendon School; Miss Black at the publishers. A chord of colours, as it were, which ends up with Miss Gray at Beacon House, West Hampstead."

Amid a dead silence Moon continued his exposition. "What is the meaning of this queer coincidence about colours? Personally I cannot doubt for a moment that these names are purely arbitrary names, assumed as part of some general scheme or joke. I think it very probable that they were taken from a series of costumes— that Polly Green only meant Polly (or Mary) when in green, and that Mary Gray only means Mary (or Polly) when in gray. This would explain—"

Cyrus Pym was standing up rigid and almost pallid. "Do you actually mean to suggest—" he cried.

"Yes," said Michael; "I do mean to suggest that. Innocent Smith has had many wooings, and many weddings for all I know; but he has had only one wife. She was sitting on that chair an hour ago, and is now talking to Miss Duke in the garden.

"Yes, Innocent Smith has behaved here, as he has on hundreds of other occasions, upon a plain and perfectly blameless principle. It is odd and extravagant in the modern world, but not more than any other principle plainly applied in the modern world would be. His principle can be quite simply stated: he refuses to die while he is still alive. He seeks to remind himself, by every electric shock to the intellect, that he is still a man alive, walking on two legs about the world. For this reason he fires bullets at his best friends; for this reason he arranges ladders and collapsible chimneys to steal his own property; for this reason he goes plodding around a whole planet to get back to his own home; and for this reason he has been in the habit of taking the woman whom he loved with a permanent loyalty, and leaving her about (so to speak) at schools, boarding-houses, and places of business, so that he might recover her again and again with a raid and a romantic elopement. He seriously sought by a perpetual recapture of his bride to keep alive the sense of her perpetual value, and the perils that should be run for her sake.

"So far his motives are clear enough; but perhaps his convictions are not quite so clear. I think Innocent Smith has an idea at the bottom of all this. I am by no means sure that I believe it myself, but I am quite sure that it is worth a man's uttering and defending.

"The idea that Smith is attacking is this. Living in an entangled civilization, we have come to think certain things wrong which are not wrong at all. We have come to think outbreak and exuberance, banging and barging, rotting and wrecking, wrong. In themselves they are not merely pardonable; they are unimpeachable. There is nothing wicked about firing a pistol off even at a friend, so long as you do not mean to hit him and know you won't. It is no more wrong than throwing a pebble at the sea—less, for you do occasionally hit the sea. There is nothing wrong in bashing down a chimney-pot and breaking through a roof, so long as you are not injuring the life or property of other men. It is no more wrong to choose to enter a house from the top than to choose to open a packing-case from the bottom. There is nothing wicked about walking round the world and coming back to your own house; it is no more wicked than walking round the garden and coming back to your own house. And there is nothing wicked about picking up your wife here, there, and everywhere, if, forsaking all others, you keep only to her so long as you both shall live. It is as innocent as playing a game of hide-and-seek in the garden. You associate such acts with blackguardism by a mere snobbish association, as you think there is something vaguely vile about going (or being seen going) into a pawnbroker's or a public-house. You think there is something squalid and commonplace about such a connection. You are mistaken.

"This man's spiritual power has been precisely this, that he has distinguished between custom and creed. He has broken the conventions, but he has kept the commandments. It is as if a man were found gambling wildly in a gambling hell, and you found that he only played for trouser buttons. It is as if you found a man making a clandestine appointment with a lady at a Covent Garden ball, and then you found it was his grandmother. Everything is ugly and discreditable, except the facts; everything is wrong about him, except that he has done no wrong.

"It will then be asked, `Why does Innocent Smith continue far into his middle age a farcical existence, that exposes him to so many false charges?' To this I merely answer that he does it because he really is happy, because he really is hilarious, because he really is a man and alive. He is so young that climbing garden trees and playing silly practical jokes are still to him what they once were to us all. And if you ask me yet again why he alone among men should be fed with such inexhaustible follies, I have a very simple answer to that, though it is one that will not be approved.

"There is but one answer, and I am sorry if you don't like it. If Innocent is happy, it is because he IS innocent. If he can defy the conventions, it is just because he can keep the commandments. It is just because he does not want to kill but to excite to life that a pistol is still as exciting to him as it is to a schoolboy. It is just because he does not want to steal, because he does not covet his neighbour's goods, that he has captured the trick (oh, how we all long for it!), the trick of coveting his own goods. It is just because he does not want to commit adultery that he achieves the romance of sex; it is just because he loves one wife that he has a hundred honeymoons. If he had really murdered a man, if he had really deserted a woman, he would not be able to feel that a pistol or a love-letter was like a song— at least, not a comic song."

"Do not imagine, please, that any such attitude is easy to me or appeals in any particular way to my sympathies. I am an Irishman, and a certain sorrow is in my bones, bred either of the persecutions of my creed, or of my creed itself. Speaking singly, I feel as if man was tied to tragedy, and there was no way out of the trap of old age and doubt. But if there is a way out, then, by Christ and St. Patrick, this is the way out. If one could keep as happy as a child or a dog, it would be by being as innocent as a child, or as sinless as a dog. Barely and brutally to be good—that may be the road, and he may have found it. Well, well, well, I see a look of skepticism on the face of my old friend Moses. Mr. Gould does not believe that being perfectly good in all respects would make a man merry."

"No," said Gould, with an unusual and convincing gravity; "I do not believe that being perfectly good in all respects would make a man merry."

"Well," said Michael quietly, "will you tell me one thing? Which of us has ever tried it?"

A silence ensued, rather like the silence of some long geological epoch which awaits the emergence of some unexpected type; for there rose at last in the stillness a massive figure that the other men had almost completely forgotten.

"Well, gentlemen," said Dr. Warner cheerfully, "I've been pretty well entertained with all this pointless and incompetent tomfoolery for a couple of days; but it seems to be wearing rather thin, and I'm engaged for a city dinner. Among the hundred flowers of futility on both sides I was unable to detect any sort of reason why a lunatic should be allowed to shoot me in the back garden."

He had settled his silk hat on his head and gone out sailing placidly to the garden gate, while the almost wailing voice of Pym still followed him: "But really the bullet missed you by several feet." And another voice added: "The bullet missed him by several years."

There was a long and mainly unmeaning silence, and then Moon said suddenly, "We have been sitting with a ghost. Dr. Herbert Warner died years ago."

5. HOW THE GREAT WIND WENT FROM BEACON HOUSE

Mary was walking between Diana and Rosamund slowly up and down the garden; they were silent, and the sun had set. Such spaces of daylight as remained open in the west were of a warm-tinted white, which can be compared to nothing but a cream cheese; and the lines of plumy cloud that ran across them had a soft but vivid violet bloom, like a violet smoke. All the rest of the scene swept and faded away into a dove-like gray, and seemed to melt and mount into Mary's dark-gray figure until she seemed clothed with the garden and the skies. There was something in these last quiet colours that gave her a setting and a supremacy; and the twilight, which concealed Diana's statelier figure and Rosamund's braver array, exhibited and emphasized her, leaving her the lady of the garden, and alone.

When they spoke at last it was evident that a conversation long fallen silent was being revived.

"But where is your husband taking you?" asked Diana in her practical voice.

"To an aunt," said Mary; "that's just the joke. There really is an aunt, and we left the children with her when I arranged to be turned out of the other boarding-house down the road. We never take more than a week of this kind of holiday, but sometimes we take two of them together."

"Does the aunt mind much?" asked Rosamund innocently. "Of course, I dare say it's very narrow-minded and—what's that other word?— you know, what Goliath was— but I've known many aunts who would think it—well, silly."

"Silly?" cried Mary with great heartiness. "Oh, my Sunday hat! I should think it was silly! But what do you expect? He really is a good man, and it might have been snakes or something."

"Snakes?" inquired Rosamund, with a slightly puzzled interest.

"Uncle Harry kept snakes, and said they loved him," replied Mary with perfect simplicity. "Auntie let him have them in his pockets, but not in the bedroom."

"And you—" began Diana, knitting her dark brows a little.

"Oh, I do as auntie did," said Mary; "as long as we're not away from the children more than a fortnight together I play the game. He calls me 'Manalive;' and you must write it all one word, or he's quite flustered."

"But if men want things like that," began Diana.

"Oh, what's the good of talking about men?" cried Mary impatiently; "why, one might as well be a lady novelist or some horrid thing. There aren't any men. There are no such people. There's a man; and whoever he is he's quite different."

"So there is no safety," said Diana in a low voice.

"Oh, I don't know," answered Mary, lightly enough; "there's only two things generally true of them. At certain curious times they're just fit to take care of us, and they're never fit to take care of themselves."

"There is a gale getting up," said Rosamund suddenly. "Look at those trees over there, a long way off, and the clouds going quicker."

"I know what you're thinking about," said Mary; "and don't you be silly fools. Don't you listen to the lady novelists. You go down the king's highway; for God's truth, it is God's. Yes, my dear Michael will often be extremely untidy. Arthur Inglewood will be worse—he'll be untidy. But what else are all the trees and clouds for, you silly kittens?"

"The clouds and trees are all waving about," said Rosamund. "There is a storm coming, and it makes me feel quite excited, somehow. Michael is really rather like a storm: he frightens me and makes me happy."

"Don't you be frightened," said Mary. "All over, these men have one advantage; they are the sort that go out."

A sudden thrust of wind through the trees drifted the dying leaves along the path, and they could hear the far-off trees roaring faintly.

"I mean," said Mary, "they are the kind that look outwards and get interested in the world. It doesn't matter a bit whether it's arguing, or bicycling, or breaking down the ends of the earth as poor old Innocent does. Stick to the man who looks out of the window and tries to understand the world. Keep clear of the man who looks in at the window and tries to understand you. When poor old Adam had gone out gardening (Arthur will go out gardening), the other sort came along and wormed himself in, nasty old snake."

"You agree with your aunt," said Rosamund, smiling: "no snakes in the bedroom."

"I didn't agree with my aunt very much," replied Mary simply, "but I think she was right to let Uncle Harry collect dragons and griffins, so long as it got him out of the house."

Almost at the same moment lights sprang up inside the darkened house, turning the two glass doors into the garden into gates of beaten gold. The golden gates were burst open, and the enormous Smith, who had sat like a clumsy statue for so many hours, came flying and turning cart-wheels down the lawn and shouting, "Acquitted!

acquitted!" Echoing the cry, Michael scampered across the lawn to Rosamund and wildly swung her into a few steps of what was supposed to be a waltz. But the company knew Innocent and Michael by this time, and their extravagances were gaily taken for granted; it was far more extraordinary that Arthur Inglewood walked straight up to Diana and kissed her as if it had been his sister's birthday. Even Dr. Pym, though he refrained from dancing, looked on with real benevolence; for indeed the whole of the absurd revelation had disturbed him less than the others; he half supposed that such irresponsible tribunals and insane discussions were part of the mediaeval mummeries of the Old Land.

While the tempest tore the sky as with trumpets, window after window was lighted up in the house within; and before the company, broken with laughter and the buffeting of the wind, had groped their way to the house again, they saw that the great apish figure of Innocent Smith had clambered out of his own attic window, and roaring again and again, "Beacon House!" whirled round his head a huge log or trunk from the wood fire below, of which the river of crimson flame and purple smoke drove out on the deafening air.

He was evident enough to have been seen from three counties; but when the wind died down, and the party, at the top of their evening's merriment, looked again for Mary and for him, they were not to be found.

THE MAN WHO KNEW
TOO MUCH

THE FACE IN THE TARGET

Harold March, the rising reviewer and social critic, was walking vigorously across a great tableland of moors and commons, the horizon of which was fringed with the far-off woods of the famous estate of Torwood Park. He was a good-looking young man in tweeds, with very pale curly hair and pale clear eyes. Walking in wind and sun in the very landscape of liberty, he was still young enough to remember his politics and not merely try to forget them. For his errand at Torwood Park was a political one; it was the place of appointment named by no less a person than the Chancellor of the Exchequer, Sir Howard Horne, then introducing his so-called Socialist budget, and prepared to expound it in an interview with so promising a penman. Harold March was the sort of man who knows everything about politics, and nothing about politicians. He also knew a great deal about art, letters, philosophy, and general culture; about almost everything, indeed, except the world he was living in.

Abruptly, in the middle of those sunny and windy flats, he came upon a sort of cleft almost narrow enough to be called a crack in the land. It was just large enough to be the water-course for a small stream which vanished at intervals under green tunnels of undergrowth, as if in a dwarfish forest. Indeed, he had an odd feeling as if he were a giant looking over the valley of the pygmies. When he dropped into the hollow, however, the impression was lost; the rocky banks, though hardly above the height of a cottage, hung over and had the profile of a precipice. As he began to wander down the course of the stream, in idle but romantic curiosity, and saw the water shining in short strips between the great gray boulders and bushes as soft as great green mosses, he fell into quite an opposite vein of fantasy. It was rather as if the earth had opened and swallowed him into a sort of underworld of dreams. And when he became conscious of a human figure dark against the silver stream, sitting on a large boulder and looking rather like a large bird, it was perhaps with some of the premonitions proper to a man who meets the strangest friendship of his life.

The man was apparently fishing; or at least was fixed in a fisherman's attitude with more than a fisherman's immobility. March was able to examine the man almost as if he had been a statue for some minutes before the statue spoke. He was a tall, fair man, cadaverous, and a little lackadaisical, with heavy eyelids and a highbridged nose. When his face was shaded with his wide white hat, his light mustache and lithe figure gave him a look of youth. But the Panama lay on the moss beside him; and the spectator could see that his brow was prematurely bald; and this, combined with a certain hollowness about the eyes, had an air of headwork and even headache. But the most curious thing about him, realized after a short scrutiny, was that, though he looked like a fisherman, he was not fishing.

He was holding, instead of a rod, something that might have been a landing-net which some fishermen use, but which was much more like the ordinary toy net which children carry, and which they generally use indifferently for shrimps or butterflies. He was dipping this into the water at intervals, gravely regarding its harvest of weed or mud, and emptying it out again.

"No, I haven't caught anything," he remarked, calmly, as if answering an unspoken query. "When I do I have to throw it back again; especially the big fish. But some of the little beasts interest me when I get 'em."

"A scientific interest, I suppose?" observed March.

"Of a rather amateurish sort, I fear," answered the strange fisherman. "I have a sort of hobby about what they call 'phenomena of phosphorescence.' But it would be rather awkward to go about in society carrying stinking fish."

"I suppose it would," said March, with a smile.

"Rather odd to enter a drawing-room carrying a large luminous cod," continued the stranger, in his listless way. "How quaint it would be if one could carry it about like a lantern, or have little sprats for candles. Some of the seabeasts would really be very pretty like lampshades; the blue sea-snail that glitters all over like starlight; and some of the red starfish really shine like red stars. But, naturally, I'm not looking for them here."

March thought of asking him what he was looking for; but, feeling unequal to a technical discussion at least as deep as the deep-sea fishes, he returned to more ordinary topics.

"Delightful sort of hole this is," he said. "This little dell and river here. It's like those places Stevenson talks about, where something ought to happen."

"I know," answered the other. "I think it's because the place itself, so to speak, seems to happen and not merely to exist. Perhaps that's what old Picasso and some of the Cubists are trying to express by angles and jagged lines. Look at that wall like low cliffs that juts forward just at right angles to the slope of turf sweeping up to it. That's like a silent collision. It's like a breaker and the back-wash of a wave."

March looked at the low-browed crag overhanging the green slope and nodded. He was interested in a man who turned so easily from the technicalities of science to those of art; and asked him if he admired the new angular artists.

"As I feel it, the Cubists are not Cubist enough," replied the stranger. "I mean they're not thick enough. By making things mathematical they make them thin. Take the living lines out of that landscape, simplify it to a right angle, and you flatten it out to a mere diagram on paper. Diagrams have their own beauty; but it is of just the other sort. They stand for the unalterable things; the calm, eternal, mathematical sort of truths; what somebody calls the 'white radiance of'—"

He stopped, and before the next word came something had happened almost too quickly and completely to be realized. From behind the overhanging rock came a noise and rush like that of a railway train; and a great motor car appeared. It topped the crest of cliff, black against the sun, like a battle-chariot rushing to destruction in some wild epic. March automatically put out his hand in one futile gesture, as if to catch a falling tea-cup in a drawing-room.

For the fraction of a flash it seemed to leave the ledge of rock like a flying ship; then the very sky seemed to turn over like a wheel, and it lay a ruin amid the tall grasses below, a line of gray smoke going up slowly from it into the silent air. A little lower the figure of a man with gray hair lay tumbled down the steep green slope, his limbs lying all at random, and his face turned away.

The eccentric fisherman dropped his net and walked swiftly toward the spot, his new acquaintance following him. As they drew near there seemed a sort of monstrous irony in the fact that the dead machine was still throbbing and thundering as busily as a factory, while the man lay so still.

He was unquestionably dead. The blood flowed in the grass from a hopelessly fatal fracture at the back of the skull; but the face, which was turned to the sun, was uninjured and strangely arresting in itself. It was one of those cases of a strange face so unmistakable as to feel familiar. We feel, somehow, that we ought to recognize it, even though we do not. It was of the broad, square sort with great jaws, almost like that of a highly intellectual ape; the wide mouth shut so tight as to be traced by a mere line; the nose short with the sort of nostrils that seem to gape with an appetite for the air. The oddest thing about the face was that one of the eyebrows was cocked up at a much sharper angle than the other. March thought he had never seen a face so naturally alive as that dead one. And its ugly energy seemed all the stranger for its halo of hoary hair. Some papers lay half fallen out of the pocket, and from among them March extracted a card-case. He read the name on the card aloud.

"Sir Humphrey Turnbull. I'm sure I've heard that name somewhere."

His companion only gave a sort of a little sigh and was silent for a moment, as if ruminating, then he merely said, "The poor fellow is quite gone," and added some scientific terms in which his auditor once more found himself out of his depth.

"As things are," continued the same curiously well-informed person, "it will be more legal for us to leave the body as it is until the police are informed. In fact, I think it will be well if nobody except the police is informed. Don't be surprised if I seem to be keeping it dark from some of our neighbors round here." Then, as if prompted to regularize his rather abrupt confidence, he said: "I've come down to see my cousin at Torwood; my name is Horne Fisher. Might be a pun on my pottering about here, mightn't it?"

"Is Sir Howard Horne your cousin?" asked March. "I'm going to Torwood Park to see him myself; only about his public work, of course, and the wonderful stand he is making for his principles. I think this Budget is the greatest thing in English history. If it fails, it will be the most heroic failure in English history. Are you an admirer of your great kinsman, Mr. Fisher?"

"Rather," said Mr. Fisher. "He's the best shot I know."

Then, as if sincerely repentant of his nonchalance, he added, with a sort of enthusiasm:

"No, but really, he's a *beautiful* shot."

As if fired by his own words, he took a sort of leap at the ledges of the rock above him, and scaled them with a sudden agility in startling contrast to his general lassitude. He had stood for some seconds on the headland above, with his aquiline profile under the Panama hat relieved against the sky and peering over the countryside before his companion had collected himself sufficiently to scramble up after him.

The level above was a stretch of common turf on which the tracks of the fated car were plowed plainly enough; but the brink of it was broken as with rocky teeth; broken boulders of all shapes and sizes lay near the edge; it was almost incredible that any one could have deliberately driven into such a death trap, especially in broad daylight.

"I can't make head or tail of it," said March. "Was he blind? Or blind drunk?"

"Neither, by the look of him," replied the other.

"Then it was suicide."

"It doesn't seem a cozy way of doing it," remarked the man called Fisher. "Besides, I don't fancy poor old Puggy would commit suicide, somehow."

"Poor old who?" inquired the wondering journalist. "Did you know this unfortunate man?"

"Nobody knew him exactly," replied Fisher, with some vagueness. "But one *knew* him, of course. He'd been a terror in his time, in Parliament and the courts, and so on; especially in that row about the aliens who were deported as undesirables, when he wanted one of 'em hanged for murder. He was so sick about it that he retired from the bench. Since then he mostly motored about by himself; but he was coming to Torwood, too, for the week-end; and I don't see why he should deliberately break his neck almost at the very door. I believe Hoggs—I mean my cousin Howard—was coming down specially to meet him."

"Torwood Park doesn't belong to your cousin?" inquired March.

"No; it used to belong to the Winthrops, you know," replied the other. "Now a new man's got it; a man from Montreal named Jenkins. Hoggs comes for the shooting; I told you he was a lovely shot."

This repeated eulogy on the great social statesman affected Harold March as if somebody had defined Napoleon as a distinguished player of nap. But he had another half-formed impression struggling in this flood of unfamiliar things, and he brought it to the surface before it could vanish.

"Jenkins," he repeated. "Surely you don't mean Jefferson Jenkins, the social reformer? I mean the man who's fighting for the new cottage-estate scheme. It would be as interesting to meet him as any Cabinet Minister in the world, if you'll excuse my saying so."

"Yes; Hoggs told him it would have to be cottages," said Fisher. "He said the breed of cattle had improved too often, and people were beginning to laugh. And, of course, you must hang a peerage on to something; though the poor chap hasn't got it yet. Hullo, here's somebody else."

They had started walking in the tracks of the car, leaving it behind them in the hollow, still humming horribly like a huge insect that had killed a man. The tracks took them to the corner of the road, one arm of which went on in the same line toward the distant gates of the park. It was clear that the car had been driven down the long straight road, and then, instead of turning with the road to the left, had gone straight on over the turf to its doom. But it was not this discovery that had riveted Fisher's eye, but something even more solid. At the angle of the white road a dark and solitary figure was standing almost as still as a finger post. It was that of a big man in rough shooting-clothes, bareheaded, and with tousled curly hair that gave him a rather wild look. On a nearer approach this first more fantastic impression faded; in a full light the figure took on more conventional colors, as of an ordinary gentleman who happened to have come out without a hat and without very studiously brushing his hair. But the massive stature remained, and something deep and even cavernous about the setting of the eyes redeemed his animal good looks from the commonplace. But March had no time to study the man more closely, for, much to his astonishment, his guide merely observed, "Hullo, Jack!" and walked past him as if he had indeed been a signpost, and without attempting to inform him of the catastrophe beyond the rocks. It was relatively a small thing, but it was only the first in a string of singular antics on which his new and eccentric friend was leading him.

The man they had passed looked after them in rather a suspicious fashion, but Fisher continued serenely on his way along the straight road that ran past the gates of the great estate.

"That's John Burke, the traveler," he condescended to explain. "I expect you've heard of him; shoots big game and all that. Sorry I couldn't stop to introduce you, but I dare say you'll meet him later on."

"I know his book, of course," said March, with renewed interest. "That is certainly a fine piece of description, about their being only conscious of the closeness of the elephant when the colossal head blocked out the moon."

"Yes, young Halkett writes jolly well, I think. What? Didn't you know Halkett wrote Burke's book for him? Burke can't use anything except a gun; and you can't write with that. Oh, he's genuine enough in his way, you know, as brave as a lion, or a good deal braver by all accounts."

"You seem to know all about him," observed March, with a rather bewildered laugh, "and about a good many other people."

Fisher's bald brow became abruptly corrugated, and a curious expression came into his eyes.

"I know too much," he said. "That's what's the matter with me. That's what's the matter with all of us, and the whole show; we know too much. Too much about one another; too much about ourselves. That's why I'm really interested, just now, about one thing that I don't know."

"And that is?" inquired the other.

"Why that poor fellow is dead."

They had walked along the straight road for nearly a mile, conversing at intervals in this fashion; and March had a singular sense of the whole world being turned inside out. Mr. Horne Fisher did not especially abuse his friends and relatives in fashionable society; of some of them he spoke with affection. But they seemed to be an entirely new set of men and women, who happened to have the same nerves as the men and women mentioned most often in the newspapers. Yet no fury of revolt could have seemed to him more utterly revolutionary than this cold familiarity. It was like daylight on the other side of stage scenery.

They reached the great lodge gates of the park, and, to March's surprise, passed them and continued along the interminable white, straight road. But he was himself too early for his appointment with Sir Howard, and was not disinclined to see the end of his new friend's experiment, whatever it might be. They had long left the moorland behind them, and half the white road was gray in the great shadow of the Torwood pine forests, themselves like gray bars shuttered against the sunshine and within, amid that clear noon, manufacturing their own midnight. Soon, however, rifts began to appear in them like gleams of colored windows; the trees thinned and fell away as the road went forward, showing the wild, irregular copses in which, as Fisher said, the house-party had been blazing away all day. And about two hundred yards farther on they came to the first turn of the road.

At the corner stood a sort of decayed inn with the dingy sign of The Grapes. The signboard was dark and indecipherable by now, and hung black against the sky and the gray moorland beyond, about as inviting as a gallows. March remarked that it looked like a tavern for vinegar instead of wine.

"A good phrase," said Fisher, "and so it would be if you were silly enough to drink wine in it. But the beer is very good, and so is the brandy."

March followed him to the bar parlor with some wonder, and his dim sense of repugnance was not dismissed by the first sight of the innkeeper, who was widely different from the genial innkeepers of romance, a bony man, very silent behind a black mustache, but with black, restless eyes. Taciturn as he was, the investigator succeeded at last in extracting a scrap of information from him, by dint of ordering beer and talking to him persistently and minutely on the subject of motor cars. He evidently regarded the innkeeper as in some singular way an authority on motor cars; as being deep in the secrets of the mechanism, management, and mismanagement of motor cars; holding the man all the time with a glittering eye like the Ancient Mariner. Out of all this rather mysterious conversation there did emerge at last a sort of admission that one particular motor car, of a given description, had stopped before the inn about an hour before, and that an elderly man had alighted, requiring some mechanical assistance. Asked if the visitor required any other assistance, the innkeeper said shortly that the old gentleman had filled his flask and taken a packet of sandwiches. And with these words the somewhat inhospitable host had walked hastily out of the bar, and they heard him banging doors in the dark interior.

Fisher's weary eye wandered round the dusty and dreary inn parlor and rested dreamily on a glass case containing a stuffed bird, with a gun hung on hooks above it, which seemed to be its only ornament.

"Puggy was a humorist," he observed, "at least in his own rather grim style. But it seems rather too grim a joke for a man to buy a packet of sandwiches when he is just going to commit suicide."

"If you come to that," answered March, "it isn't very usual for a man to buy a packet of sandwiches when he's just outside the door of a grand house he's going to stop at."

"No . . . no," repeated Fisher, almost mechanically; and then suddenly cocked his eye at his interlocutor with a much livelier expression.

"By Jove! that's an idea. You're perfectly right. And that suggests a very queer idea, doesn't it?"

There was a silence, and then March started with irrational nervousness as the door of the inn was flung open and another man walked rapidly to the counter. He had struck it with a coin and called out for brandy before he saw the other two guests, who were sitting at a bare wooden table under the window. When he turned about with a rather wild stare, March had yet another unexpected emotion, for his guide hailed the man as Hoggs and introduced him as Sir Howard Horne.

He looked rather older than his boyish portraits in the illustrated papers, as is the way of politicians; his flat, fair hair was touched with gray, but his face was almost comically round, with a Roman nose which, when combined with his quick, bright eyes, raised a vague reminiscence of a parrot. He had a cap rather at the back of his head and a gun under his arm. Harold March had imagined many things about his meeting with the great political reformer, but he had never pictured him with a gun under his arm, drinking brandy in a public house.

"So you're stopping at Jink's, too," said Fisher. "Everybody seems to be at Jink's."

"Yes," replied the Chancellor of the Exchequer. "Jolly good shooting. At least all of it that isn't Jink's shooting. I never knew a chap with such good shooting that was such a bad shot. Mind you, he's a jolly good fellow and all that; I don't say a word against him. But he never learned to hold a gun when he was packing pork or whatever he did. They say he shot the cockade off his own servant's hat; just like him to have cockades, of course. He shot the weathercock off his own ridiculous gilded summerhouse. It's the only cock he'll ever kill, I should think. Are you coming up there now?"

Fisher said, rather vaguely, that he was following soon, when he had fixed something up; and the Chancellor of the Exchequer left the inn. March fancied he had been a little upset or impatient when he called for the brandy; but he had talked himself back into a satisfactory state, if the talk had not been quite what his literary visitor had expected. Fisher, a few minutes afterward, slowly led the way out of the tavern and stood in the middle of the road, looking down in the direction from which they had traveled. Then he walked back about two hundred yards in that direction and stood still again.

"I should think this is about the place," he said.

"What place?" asked his companion.

"The place where the poor fellow was killed," said Fisher, sadly.

"What do you mean?" demanded March.

"He was smashed up on the rocks a mile and a half from here."

"No, he wasn't," replied Fisher. "He didn't fall on the rocks at all. Didn't you notice that he only fell on the slope of soft grass underneath? But I saw that he had a bullet in him already."

Then after a pause he added:

"He was alive at the inn, but he was dead long before he came to the rocks. So he was shot as he drove his car down this strip of straight road, and I should think somewhere about here. After that, of course, the car went straight on with nobody to stop or turn it. It's really a very cunning dodge in its way; for the body would be found far away, and most people would say, as you do, that it was an accident to a motorist. The murderer must have been a clever brute."

"But wouldn't the shot be heard at the inn or somewhere?" asked March.

"It would be heard. But it would not be noticed. That," continued the investigator, "is where he was clever again. Shooting was going on all over the place all day; very likely he timed his shot so as to drown it in a number of others. Certainly he was a first-class criminal. And he was something else as well."

"What do you mean?" asked his companion, with a creepy premonition of something coming, he knew not why.

"He was a first-class shot," said Fisher. He had turned his back abruptly and was walking down a narrow, grassy lane, little more than a cart track, which lay opposite the inn and marked the end of the great estate and the beginning of the open moors. March plodded after him with the same idle perseverance, and found him staring through a gap in giant weeds and thorns at the flat face of a painted paling. From behind the paling rose the great gray columns of a row of poplars, which filled the heavens above them with dark-green shadow and shook faintly in a wind which had sunk slowly into a breeze. The afternoon was already deepening into evening, and the titanic shadows of the poplars lengthened over a third of the landscape.

"Are you a first-class criminal?" asked Fisher, in a friendly tone. "I'm afraid I'm not. But I think I can manage to be a sort of fourth-rate burglar."

And before his companion could reply he had managed to swing himself up and over the fence; March followed without much bodily effort, but with considerable mental disturbance. The poplars grew so close against the fence that they had some difficulty in slipping past them, and beyond the poplars they could see only a high hedge of laurel, green and lustrous in the level sun. Something in this limitation by a series of living walls made him feel as if he were really entering a shattered house instead of an open field. It was as if he came in by a disused door or window and found the way blocked by furniture. When they had circumvented the laurel hedge, they came out on a sort of terrace of turf, which fell by one green step to an oblong lawn like a bowling green. Beyond this was the only building in sight, a low conservatory, which seemed far away from anywhere, like a glass cottage standing in its own fields in fairyland. Fisher knew that lonely look of the outlying parts of a great house well enough. He realized that it is more of a satire on aristocracy than if it were choked with weeds and littered with ruins. For it is not neglected and yet it is deserted; at any rate, it is disused. It is regularly swept and garnished for a master who never comes.

Looking over the lawn, however, he saw one object which he had not apparently expected. It was a sort of tripod supporting a large disk like the round top of a table tipped sideways, and it was not until they had dropped on to the lawn and walked across to look at it that March realized that it was a target. It was worn and weatherstained; the gay colors of its concentric rings were faded; possibly it had been set up in those far-off Victorian days when there was a fashion of archery. March had one of his vague visions of ladies in cloudy crinolines and gentlemen in outlandish hats and whiskers revisiting that lost garden like ghosts.

Fisher, who was peering more closely at the target, startled him by an exclamation.

"Hullo!" he said. "Somebody has been peppering this thing with shot, after all, and quite lately, too. Why, I believe old Jink's been trying to improve his bad shooting here."

"Yes, and it looks as if it still wanted improving," answered March, laughing. "Not one of these shots is anywhere near the bull's-eye; they seem just scattered about in the wildest way."

"In the wildest way," repeated Fisher, still peering intently at the target. He seemed merely to assent, but March fancied his eye was shining under its sleepy lid and that he straightened his stooping figure with a strange effort.

"Excuse me a moment," he said, feeling in his pockets. "I think I've got some of my chemicals; and after that we'll go up to the house." And he stooped again over the target, putting something with his finger over each of the shot-holes, so far as March could see merely a dull-gray smear. Then they went through the gathering twilight up the long green avenues to the great house.

Here again, however, the eccentric investigator did not enter by the front door. He walked round the house until he found a window open, and, leaping into it, introduced his friend to what appeared to be the gun-room. Rows of the regular instruments for bringing down birds stood against the walls; but across a table in the window lay one or two weapons of a heavier and more formidable pattern.

"Hullo! these are Burke's big-game rifles," said Fisher. "I never knew he kept them here." He lifted one of them, examined it briefly, and put it down again, frowning heavily. Almost as he did so a strange young man came hurriedly into the room. He was dark and sturdy, with a bumpy forehead and a bulldog jaw, and he spoke with a curt apology.

"I left Major Burke's guns here," he said, "and he wants them packed up. He's going away to-night."

And he carried off the two rifles without casting a glance at the stranger; through the open window they could see his short, dark figure walking away across the glimmering garden. Fisher got out of the window again and stood looking after him.

"That's Halkett, whom I told you about," he said. "I knew he was a sort of secretary and had to do with Burke's papers; but I never knew he had anything to do with his guns. But he's just the sort of silent, sensible little devil who might be very good at anything; the sort of man you know for years before you find he's a chess champion."

He had begun to walk in the direction of the disappearing secretary, and they soon came within sight of the rest of the house-party talking and laughing on the lawn. They could see the tall figure and loose mane of the lion-hunter dominating the little group.

"By the way," observed Fisher, "when we were talking about Burke and Halkett, I said that a man couldn't very well write with a gun. Well, I'm not so sure now. Did you ever hear of an artist so clever that he could draw with a gun? There's a wonderful chap loose about here."

Sir Howard hailed Fisher and his friend the journalist with almost boisterous amiability. The latter was presented to Major Burke and Mr. Halkett and also (by way of a parenthesis) to his host, Mr. Jenkins, a commonplace little man in loud tweeds, whom everybody else seemed to treat with a sort of affection, as if he were a baby.

The irrepressible Chancellor of the Exchequer was still talking about the birds he had brought down, the birds that Burke and Halkett had brought down, and the birds that Jenkins, their host, had failed to bring down. It seemed to be a sort of sociable monomania.

"You and your big game," he ejaculated, aggressively, to Burke. "Why, anybody could shoot big game. You want to be a shot to shoot small game."

"Quite so," interposed Horne Fisher. "Now if only a hippopotamus could fly up in the air out of that bush, or you preserved flying elephants on the estate, why, then—"

"Why even Jink might hit that sort of bird," cried Sir Howard, hilariously slapping his host on the back. "Even he might hit a haystack or a hippopotamus."

"Look here, you fellows," said Fisher. "I want you to come along with me for a minute and shoot at something else. Not a hippopotamus. Another kind of queer animal I've found on the estate. It's an animal with three legs and one eye, and it's all the colors of the rainbow."

"What the deuce are you talking about?" asked Burke.

"You come along and see," replied Fisher, cheerfully.

Such people seldom reject anything nonsensical, for they are always seeking for something new. They gravely rearmed themselves from the gun-room and trooped along at the tail of their guide, Sir Howard only pausing, in a sort of ecstasy, to point out the celebrated gilt summerhouse on which the gilt weathercock still stood crooked. It was dusk turning to dark by the time they reached the remote green by the poplars and accepted the new and aimless game of shooting at the old mark.

The last light seemed to fade from the lawn, and the poplars against the sunset were like great plumes upon a purple hearse, when the futile procession finally curved round, and came out in front of the target. Sir Howard again slapped his host on the shoulder, shoving him playfully forward to take the first shot. The shoulder and arm he touched seemed unnaturally stiff and angular. Mr. Jenkins was holding his gun in an attitude more awkward than any that his satiric friends had seen or expected.

At the same instant a horrible scream seemed to come from nowhere. It was so unnatural and so unsuited to the scene that it might have been made by some inhuman thing flying on wings above them or eavesdropping in the dark woods beyond. But Fisher knew that it had started and stopped on the pale lips of Jefferson Jenkins, of Montreal, and no one at that moment catching sight of Jefferson Jenkins's face would have complained that it was commonplace. The next moment a torrent of guttural but good-humored oaths came from Major Burke as he and the two other men saw what was in front of them. The target stood up in the dim grass like a dark goblin grinning at them, and it was literally grinning. It had two eyes like stars, and in similar livid points of light were picked out the two upturned and open nostrils and the two ends of the wide and tight mouth. A few white dots above each eye indicated the hoary eyebrows; and one of them ran upward almost erect. It was a brilliant caricature done in bright dotted lines and March knew of whom. It shone in the shadowy grass, smeared with sea fire as if one of the submarine monsters had crawled into the twilight garden; but it had the head of a dead man.

"It's only luminous paint," said Burke. "Old Fisher's been having a joke with that phosphorescent stuff of his."

"Seems to be meant for old Puggy"' observed Sir Howard. "Hits him off very well."

With that they all laughed, except Jenkins. When they had all done, he made a noise like the first effort of an animal to laugh, and Horne Fisher suddenly strode across to him and said:

"Mr. Jenkins, I must speak to you at once in private."

It was by the little watercourse in the moors, on the slope under the hanging rock, that March met his new friend Fisher, by appointment, shortly after the ugly and almost grotesque scene that had broken up the group in the garden.

"It was a monkey-trick of mine," observed Fisher, gloomily, "putting phosphorus on the target; but the only chance to make him jump was to give him the horrors suddenly. And when he saw the face he'd shot at shining on the target he practiced on, all lit up with an infernal light, he did jump. Quite enough for my own intellectual satisfaction."

"I'm afraid I don't quite understand even now," said March, "exactly what he did or why he did it."

"You ought to," replied Fisher, with his rather dreary smile, "for you gave me the first suggestion yourself. Oh yes, you did; and it was a very shrewd one. You said a man wouldn't take sandwiches with him to dine at a great house. It was quite true; and the inference was that, though he was going there, he didn't mean to dine there. Or, at any rate, that he might not be dining there. It occurred to me at once that he probably expected the visit to be unpleasant, or the reception doubtful, or something that would prevent his accepting hospitality. Then it struck me that Turnbull was a terror to certain shady characters in the past, and that he had come down to identify and denounce one of them. The chances at the start pointed to the host—that is, Jenkins. I'm morally certain now that Jenkins was the undesirable alien Turnbull wanted to convict in another shooting-affair, but you see the shooting gentleman had another shot in his locker."

"But you said he would have to be a very good shot," protested March.

"Jenkins is a very good shot," said Fisher. "A very good shot who can pretend to be a very bad shot. Shall I tell you the second hint I hit on, after yours, to make me think it was Jenkins? It was my cousin's account of his bad shooting. He'd shot a cockade off a hat and a weathercock off a building. Now, in fact, a man must shoot very well indeed to shoot so badly as that. He must shoot very neatly to hit the cockade and not the head, or even the hat. If the shots had really gone at random, the chances are a thousand to one that they would not have hit such prominent and picturesque objects. They were chosen because they were prominent and picturesque objects. They make a story to go the round of society. He keeps the crooked weathercock in the summerhouse to perpetuate the story of a legend. And then he lay in wait with his evil eye and wicked gun, safely ambushed behind the legend of his own incompetence.

"But there is more than that. There is the summerhouse itself. I mean there is the whole thing. There's all that Jenkins gets chaffed about, the gilding and the gaudy colors and all the vulgarity that's supposed to stamp him as an upstart. Now, as a matter of fact, upstarts generally don't do this. God knows there's enough of 'em in society; and one knows 'em well enough. And this is the very last thing they do. They're generally only too keen to know the right thing and do it; and they instantly put themselves body and soul into the hands of art decorators and art experts, who do the whole thing for them. There's hardly another millionaire alive who has the moral courage to have a gilt monogram on a chair like that one in the gun-room. For that matter, there's the name as well as the monogram. Names like Tompkins and Jenkins and Jinks are funny without being vulgar; I mean they are vulgar without being common. If you prefer it, they are commonplace without being common. They are just the names to be chosen to *look* ordinary, but they're really rather extraordinary. Do you know many people called Tompkins? It's a good deal rarer than Talbot. It's pretty much the same with the comic clothes of the parvenu. Jenkins dresses like a character in Punch. But that's because he is a character in Punch. I mean he's a fictitious character. He's a fabulous animal. He doesn't exist.

"Have you ever considered what it must be like to be a man who doesn't exist? I mean to be a man with a fictitious character that he has to keep up at the expense not merely of personal talents: To be a new kind of hypocrite hiding a talent in a new kind of napkin. This man has chosen his hypocrisy very ingeniously; it was really a new one. A subtle villain has dressed up as a dashing gentleman and a worthy business man and a philanthropist and a saint; but the loud checks of a comical little cad were really rather a new disguise. But the disguise must be very irksome to a man who can really do things. This is a dexterous little cosmopolitan guttersnipe who can do scores of things, not only shoot, but draw and paint, and probably play the fiddle. Now a man like that may find the hiding of his talents useful; but he could never help wanting to use them where they were useless. If he can draw, he will draw absent-mindedly on blotting paper. I suspect this rascal has often drawn poor old Puggy's face on blotting paper. Probably he began doing it in blots as he afterward did it in dots, or rather shots. It was the same sort of thing; he found a disused target in a deserted yard and couldn't resist indulging in a little secret shooting, like secret drinking. You thought the shots all scattered and irregular, and so they were; but not accidental. No two distances were alike; but the different points were exactly where he wanted to put them. There's nothing needs such mathematical precision as a wild caricature. I've dabbled a little in drawing myself, and I assure you that to put one dot where you want it is a marvel with a pen close to a piece of paper. It was a miracle to do it across a garden with a gun. But a man who can work those miracles will always itch to work them, if it's only in the dark."

After a pause March observed, thoughtfully, "But he couldn't have brought him down like a bird with one of those little guns."

"No; that was why I went into the gun-room," replied Fisher. "He did it with one of Burke's rifles, and Burke thought he knew the sound of it. That's why he rushed out without a hat, looking so wild. He saw nothing but a car passing quickly, which he followed for a little way, and then concluded he'd made a mistake."

There was another silence, during which Fisher sat on a great stone as motionless as on their first meeting, and watched the gray and silver river eddying past under the bushes. Then March said, abruptly, "Of course he knows the truth now."

"Nobody knows the truth but you and I," answered Fisher, with a certain softening in his voice. "And I don't think you and I will ever quarrel."

"What do you mean?" asked March, in an altered accent. "What have you done about it?"

Horne Fisher continued to gaze steadily at the eddying stream. At last he said, "The police have proved it was a motor accident."

"But you know it was not."

"I told you that I know too much," replied Fisher, with his eye on the river. "I know that, and I know a great many other things. I know the atmosphere and the way the whole thing works. I know this fellow has succeeded in making himself something incurably commonplace and comic. I know you can't get up a persecution of old Toole or Little Tich. If I were to tell Hoggs or Halkett that old Jink was an assassin, they would almost die of laughter before my eyes. Oh, I don't say their laughter's quite innocent, though it's genuine in its way. They want old Jink, and they couldn't do without him. I don't say I'm quite innocent. I like Hoggs; I don't want him to be down and out; and he'd be done for if Jink can't pay for his coronet. They were devilish near the line at the last election. But the only real objection to it is that it's impossible. Nobody would believe it; it's not in the picture. The crooked weathercock would always turn it into a joke."

"Don't you think this is infamous?" asked March, quietly.

"I think a good many things," replied the other. "If you people ever happen to blow the whole tangle of society to hell with dynamite, I don't know that the human race will be much the worse. But don't be too hard on me merely because I know what society is. That's why I moon away my time over things like stinking fish."

There was a pause as he settled himself down again by the stream; and then he added:

"I told you before I had to throw back the big fish."

THE VANISHING PRINCE

This tale begins among a tangle of tales round a name that is at once recent and legendary. The name is that of Michael O'Neill, popularly called Prince Michael, partly because he claimed descent from ancient Fenian princes, and partly because he was credited with a plan to make himself prince president of Ireland, as the last Napoleon did of France. He was undoubtedly a gentleman of honorable pedigree and of many accomplishments, but two of his accomplishments emerged from all the rest. He had a talent for appearing when he was not wanted and a talent for disappearing when he was wanted, especially when he was wanted by the police. It may be added that his disappearances were more dangerous than his appearances. In the latter he seldom went beyond the sensational—pasting up seditious placards, tearing down official placards, making flamboyant speeches, or unfurling forbidden flags. But in order to effect the former he would sometimes fight for his freedom with startling energy, from which men were sometimes lucky to escape with a broken head instead of a broken neck. His most famous feats of escape, however, were due to dexterity and not to violence. On a cloudless summer morning he had come down a country road white with dust, and, pausing outside a farmhouse, had told the farmer's daughter, with elegant indifference, that the local police were in pursuit of him. The girl's name was Bridget Royce, a somber and even sullen type of beauty, and she looked at him darkly, as if in doubt, and said, "Do you want me to hide you?" Upon which he only laughed, leaped lightly over the stone wall, and strode toward the farm, merely throwing over his shoulder the remark, "Thank you, I have generally been quite capable of hiding myself." In which proceeding he acted with a tragic ignorance of the nature of women; and there fell on his path in that sunshine a shadow of doom.

While he disappeared through the farmhouse the girl remained for a few moments looking up the road, and two perspiring policemen came plowing up to the door where she stood. Though still angry, she was still silent, and a quarter of an hour later the officers had searched the house and were already inspecting the kitchen garden and cornfield behind it. In the ugly reaction of her mood she might have been tempted even to point out the fugitive, but for a small difficulty that she had no more notion than the policemen had of where he could possibly have gone. The kitchen garden was inclosed by a very low wall, and the cornfield beyond lay aslant like a square patch on a great green hill on which he could still have been seen even as a dot in the distance. Everything stood solid in its familiar place; the apple tree was too small to support or hide a climber; the only shed stood open and obviously empty; there was no sound save the droning of summer flies and the occasional flutter of a bird unfamiliar enough to be surprised by the scarecrow in the field; there was scarcely a shadow save a few blue lines that fell from the thin tree; every detail was picked out by the brilliant day light as if in a microscope. The girl described the scene later, with all the passionate realism of her race, and, whether or no the policemen had a similar eye for the picturesque, they had at least an eye for the facts of the case, and were compelled to give up the chase and retire from the scene. Bridget Royce remained as if in a trance, staring at the sunlit garden in which a man had just vanished like a fairy. She was still in a sinister mood, and the miracle took in her mind a character of unfriendliness and fear, as if the fairy were decidedly a bad fairy. The sun upon the glittering garden depressed her more than the darkness, but she continued to stare at it. Then the world itself went half-witted and she screamed. The scarecrow moved in the sun light. It had stood with its back to her in a battered old black hat and a tattered garment, and with all its tatters flying, it strode away across the hill.

She did not analyze the audacious trick by which the man had turned to his advantage the subtle effects of the expected and the obvious; she was still under the cloud of more individual complexities, and she noticed most of all that the vanishing scarecrow did not even turn to look at the farm. And the fates that were running so adverse to his fantastic career of freedom ruled that his next adventure, though it had the same success in another quarter, should increase the danger in this quarter. Among the many similar adventures related of him in this manner it is also said that some days afterward another girl, named Mary Cregan, found him concealed on the farm where she worked; and if the story is true, she must also have had the shock of an uncanny experience, for when she was busy at some lonely task in the yard she heard a voice speaking out of the well, and found that the eccentric had managed to drop himself into the bucket which was some little way below, the well only partly full of water. In this case, however, he had to appeal to the woman to wind up the rope. And men say it was when this news was told to the other woman that her soul walked over the border line of treason.

Such, at least, were the stories told of him in the countryside, and there were many more—as that he had stood insolently in a splendid green dressing gown on the steps of a great hotel, and then led the police a chase through a long suite of grand apartments, and finally through his own bedroom on to a balcony that overhung the river. The moment the pursuers stepped on to the balcony it broke under them, and they dropped pell-mell into the eddying waters, while Michael, who had thrown off his gown and dived, was able to swim away. It was said that he had carefully cut away the props so that they would not support anything so heavy as a policeman. But here again he was immediately fortunate, yet ultimately unfortunate, for it is said that one of the men was drowned, leaving a family feud which made a little rift in his popularity. These stories can now be told in some detail, not because they are the most marvelous of his many adventures, but because these alone were not covered with silence by the loyalty of the peasantry. These alone found their way into official reports, and it is these which three of the chief officials of the country were reading and discussing when the more remarkable part of this story begins.

Night was far advanced and the lights shone in the cottage that served for a temporary police station near the coast. On one side of it were the last houses of the straggling village, and on the other nothing but a waste moorland stretching away toward the sea, the line of which was broken by no landmark except a solitary tower of the prehistoric pattern still found in Ireland, standing up as slender as a column, but pointed like a pyramid. At a wooden table in front of the window, which normally looked out on this landscape, sat two men in plain clothes, but with something of a military bearing, for indeed they were the two chiefs of the detective service of that district. The senior of the two, both in age and rank, was a sturdy man with a short white beard, and frosty eyebrows fixed in a frown which suggested rather worry than severity.

His name was Morton, and he was a Liverpool man long pickled in the Irish quarrels, and doing his duty among them in a sour fashion not altogether unsympathetic. He had spoken a few sentences to his companion, Nolan, a tall, dark man with a cadaverous equine Irish face, when he seemed to remember something and touched a bell which rang in another room. The subordinate he had summoned immediately appeared with a sheaf of papers in his hand.

"Sit down, Wilson," he said. "Those are the depositions, I suppose."

"Yes," replied the third officer. "I think I've got all there is to be got out of them, so I sent the people away."

"Did Mary Cregan give evidence?" asked Morton, with a frown that looked a little heavier than usual.

"No, but her master did," answered the man called Wilson, who had flat, red hair and a plain, pale face, not without sharpness. "I think he's hanging round the girl himself and is out against a rival. There's always some reason of that sort when we are told the truth about anything. And you bet the other girl told right enough."

"Well, let's hope they'll be some sort of use," remarked Nolan, in a somewhat hopeless manner, gazing out into the darkness.

"Anything is to the good," said Morton, "that lets us know anything about him."

"Do we know anything about him?" asked the melancholy Irishman.

"We know one thing about him," said Wilson, "and it's the one thing that nobody ever knew before. We know where he is."

"Are you sure?" inquired Morton, looking at him sharply.

"Quite sure," replied his assistant. "At this very minute he is in that tower over there by the shore. If you go near enough you'll see the candle burning in the window."

As he spoke the noise of a horn sounded on the road outside, and a moment after they heard the throbbing of a motor car brought to a standstill before the door. Morton instantly sprang to his feet.

"Thank the Lord that's the car from Dublin," he said. "I can't do anything without special authority, not if he were sitting on the top of the tower and putting out his tongue at us. But the chief can do what he thinks best."

He hurried out to the entrance and was soon exchanging greetings with a big handsome man in a fur coat, who brought into the dingy little station the indescribable glow of the great cities and the luxuries of the great world.

For this was Sir Walter Carey, an official of such eminence in Dublin Castle that nothing short of the case of Prince Michael would have brought him on such a journey in the middle of the night. But the case of Prince Michael, as it happened, was complicated by legalism as well as lawlessness. On the last occasion he had escaped by a forensic quibble and not, as usual, by a private escapade; and it was a question whether at the moment he was amenable to the law or not. It might be necessary to stretch a point, but a man like Sir Walter could probably stretch it as far as he liked.

Whether he intended to do so was a question to be considered. Despite the almost aggressive touch of luxury in the fur coat, it soon became apparent that Sir Walter's large leonine head was for use as well as ornament, and he considered the matter soberly and sanely enough. Five chairs were set round the plain deal table, for who should Sir Walter bring with him but his young relative and secretary, Horne Fisher. Sir Walter listened with grave attention, and his secretary with polite boredom, to the string of episodes by which the police had traced the flying rebel from the steps of the hotel to the solitary tower beside the sea. There at least he was cornered between the moors and the breakers; and the scout sent by Wilson reported him as writing under a solitary candle, perhaps composing another of his tremendous proclamations. Indeed, it would have been typical of him to choose it as the place in which finally to turn to bay. He had some remote claim on it, as on a family castle; and those who knew him thought him capable of imitating the primitive Irish chieftains who fell fighting against the sea.

"I saw some queer-looking people leaving as I came in," said Sir Walter Carey. "I suppose they were your witnesses. But why do they turn up here at this time of night?"

Morton smiled grimly. "They come here by night because they would be dead men if they came here by day. They are criminals committing a crime that is more horrible here than theft or murder."

"What crime do you mean?" asked the other, with some curiosity.

"They are helping the law," said Morton.

There was a silence, and Sir Walter considered the papers before him with an abstracted eye. At last he spoke.

"Quite so; but look here, if the local feeling is as lively as that there are a good many points to consider. I believe the new Act will enable me to collar him now if I think it best. But is it best? A serious rising would do us no good in Parliament, and the government has enemies in England as well as Ireland. It won't do if I have done what looks a little like sharp practice, and then only raised a revolution."

"It's all the other way," said the man called Wilson, rather quickly. "There won't be half so much of a revolution if you arrest him as there will if you leave him loose for three days longer. But, anyhow, there can't be anything nowadays that the proper police can't manage."

"Mr. Wilson is a Londoner," said the Irish detective, with a smile.

"Yes, I'm a cockney, all right," replied Wilson, "and I think I'm all the better for that. Especially at this job, oddly enough."

Sir Walter seemed slightly amused at the pertinacity of the third officer, and perhaps even more amused at the slight accent with which he spoke, which rendered rather needless his boast about his origin.

"Do you mean to say," he asked, "that you know more about the business here because you have come from London?"

"Sounds funny, I know, but I do believe it," answered Wilson. "I believe these affairs want fresh methods. But most of all I believe they want a fresh eye."

The superior officers laughed, and the redhaired man went on with a slight touch of temper:

"Well, look at the facts. See how the fellow got away every time, and you'll understand what I mean. Why was he able to stand in the place of the scarecrow, hidden by nothing but an old hat? Because it was a village policeman who knew the scarecrow was there, was expecting it, and therefore took no notice of it. Now I never expect a scarecrow. I've never seen one in the street, and I stare at one when I see it in the field. It's a new thing to me and worth noticing. And it was just the same when he hid in the well. You are ready to find a well in a place like that; you look for a well, and so you don't see it. I don't look for it, and therefore I do look at it."

"It is certainly an idea," said Sir Walter, smiling, "but what about the balcony? Balconies are occasionally seen in London."

"But not rivers right under them, as if it was in Venice," replied Wilson.

"It is certainly a new idea," repeated Sir Walter, with something like respect. He had all the love of the luxurious classes for new ideas. But he also had a critical faculty, and was inclined to think, after due reflection, that it was a true idea as well.

Growing dawn had already turned the window panes from black to gray when Sir Walter got abruptly to his feet. The others rose also, taking this for a signal that the arrest was to be undertaken. But their leader stood for a moment in deep thought, as if conscious that he had come to a parting of the ways.

Suddenly the silence was pierced by a long, wailing cry from the dark moors outside. The silence that followed it seemed more startling than the shriek itself, and it lasted until Nolan said, heavily:

"'Tis the banshee. Somebody is marked for the grave."

His long, large-featured face was as pale as a moon, and it was easy to remember that he was the only Irishman in the room.

"Well, I know that banshee," said Wilson, cheerfully, "ignorant as you think I am of these things. I talked to that banshee myself an hour ago, and I sent that banshee up to the tower and told her to sing out like that if she could get a glimpse of our friend writing his proclamation."

"Do you mean that girl Bridget Royce?" asked Morton, drawing his frosty brows together. "Has she turned king's evidence to that extent?"

"Yes," answered Wilson. "I know very little of these local things, you tell me, but I reckon an angry woman is much the same in all countries."

Nolan, however, seemed still moody and unlike himself. "It's an ugly noise and an ugly business altogether," he said. "If it's really the end of Prince Michael it may well be the end of other things as well. When the spirit is on him he would escape by a ladder of dead men, and wade through that sea if it were made of blood."

"Is that the real reason of your pious alarms?" asked Wilson, with a slight sneer.

The Irishman's pale face blackened with a new passion.

"I have faced as many murderers in County Clare as you ever fought with in Clapham Junction, Mr. Cockney," he said.

"Hush, please," said Morton, sharply. "Wilson, you have no kind of right to imply doubt of your superior's conduct. I hope you will prove yourself as courageous and trustworthy as he has always been."

The pale face of the red-haired man seemed a shade paler, but he was silent and composed, and Sir Walter went up to Nolan with marked courtesy, saying, "Shall we go outside now, and get this business done?"

Dawn had lifted, leaving a wide chasm of white between a great gray cloud and the great gray moorland, beyond which the tower was outlined against the daybreak and the sea.

Something in its plain and primitive shape vaguely suggested the dawn in the first days of the earth, in some prehistoric time when even the colors were hardly created, when there was only blank daylight between cloud and clay. These dead hues were relieved only by one spot of gold—the spark of the candle alight in the window of the lonely tower, and burning on into the broadening daylight. As the group of detectives, followed by a cordon of policemen, spread out into a crescent to cut off all escape, the light in the tower flashed as if it were moved for a moment, and then went out. They knew the man inside had realized the daylight and blown out his candle.

"There are other windows, aren't there?" asked Morton, "and a door, of course, somewhere round the corner? Only a round tower has no corners."

"Another example of my small suggestion," observed Wilson, quietly. "That queer tower was the first thing I saw when I came to these parts; and I can tell you a little more about it—or, at any rate, the outside of it. There are four windows altogether, one a little way from this one, but just out of sight. Those are both on the ground floor, and so is the third on the other side, making a sort of triangle. But the fourth is just above the third, and I suppose it looks on an upper floor."

"It's only a sort of loft, reached by a ladder, said Nolan. "I've played in the place when I was a child. It's no more than an empty shell." And his sad face grew sadder, thinking perhaps of the tragedy of his country and the part that he played in it.

"The man must have got a table and chair, at any rate," said Wilson, "but no doubt he could have got those from some cottage. If I might make a suggestion, sir, I think we ought to approach all the five entrances at once, so to speak. One of us should go to the door and one to each window; Macbride here has a ladder for the upper window."

Mr. Horne Fisher languidly turned to his distinguished relative and spoke for the first time.

"I am rather a convert to the cockney school of psychology," he said in an almost inaudible voice.

The others seemed to feel the same influence in different ways, for the group began to break up in the manner indicated. Morton moved toward the window immediately in front of them, where the hidden outlaw had just snuffed the candle; Nolan, a little farther westward to the next window; while Wilson, followed by Macbride with the ladder, went round to the two windows at the back. Sir Walter Carey himself, followed by his secretary, began to walk round toward the only door, to demand admittance in a more regular fashion.

"He will be armed, of course," remarked Sir Walter, casually.

"By all accounts," replied Horne Fisher, "he can do more with a candlestick than most men with a pistol. But he is pretty sure to have the pistol, too."

Even as he spoke the question was answered with a tongue of thunder. Morton had just placed himself in front of the nearest window, his broad shoulders blocking the aperture. For an instant it was lit from within as with red fire, followed by a thundering throng of echoes. The square shoulders seemed to alter in shape, and the sturdy figure collapsed among the tall, rank grasses at the foot of the tower. A puff of smoke floated from the window like a little cloud. The two men behind rushed to the spot and raised him, but he was dead.

Sir Walter straightened himself and called out something that was lost in another noise of firing; it was possible that the police were already avenging their comrade from the other side. Fisher had already raced round to the next window, and a new cry of astonishment from him brought his patron to the same spot. Nolan, the Irish policeman, had also fallen, sprawling all his great length in the grass, and it was red with his blood. He was still alive when they reached him, but there was death on his face, and he was only able to make a final gesture telling them that all was over; and, with a broken word and a heroic effort, motioning them on to where his other comrades were besieging the back of the tower. Stunned by these rapid and repeated shocks, the two men could only vaguely obey the gesture, and, finding their way to the other windows at the back, they discovered a scene equally startling, if less final and tragic. The other two officers were not dead or mortally wounded, but Macbride lay with a broken leg and his ladder on top of him, evidently thrown down from the top window of the tower; while Wilson lay on his face, quite still as if stunned, with his red head among the gray and silver of the sea holly. In him, however, the impotence was but momentary, for he began to move and rise as the others came round the tower.

"My God! it's like an explosion!" cried Sir Walter; and indeed it was the only word for this unearthly energy, by which one man had been able to deal death or destruction on three sides of the same small triangle at the same instant.

Wilson had already scrambled to his feet and with splendid energy flew again at the window, revolver in hand. He fired twice into the opening and then disappeared in his own smoke; but the thud of his feet and the shock of a falling chair told them that the intrepid Londoner had managed at last to leap into the room. Then followed a curious silence; and Sir Walter, walking to the window through the thinning smoke, looked into the hollow shell of the ancient tower. Except for Wilson, staring around him, there was nobody there.

The inside of the tower was a single empty room, with nothing but a plain wooden chair and a table on which were pens, ink and paper, and the candlestick. Halfway up the high wall there was a rude timber platform under the upper window, a small loft which was more like a large shelf. It was reached only by a ladder, and it seemed to be as bare as the bare walls. Wilson completed his survey of the place and then went and stared at the things on the table. Then he silently pointed with his lean forefinger at the open page of the large notebook. The writer had suddenly stopped writing, even in the middle of a word.

"I said it was like an explosion," said Sir Walter Carey at last. "And really the man himself seems to have suddenly exploded. But he has blown himself up somehow without touching the tower. He's burst more like a bubble than a bomb."

"He has touched more valuable things than the tower," said Wilson, gloomily.

There was a long silence, and then Sir Walter said, seriously: "Well, Mr. Wilson, I am not a detective, and these unhappy happenings have left you in charge of that branch of the business. We all lament the cause of this, but I should like to say that I myself have the strongest confidence in your capacity for carrying on the work. What do you think we should do next?"

Wilson seemed to rouse himself from his depression and acknowledged the speaker's words with a warmer civility than he had hitherto shown to anybody. He called in a few of the police to assist in routing out the interior, leaving the rest to spread themselves in a search party outside.

"I think," he said, "the first thing is to make quite sure about the inside of this place, as it was hardly physically possible for him to have got outside. I suppose poor Nolan would have brought in his banshee and said it was supernaturally possible. But I've got no use for disembodied spirits when I'm dealing with facts. And the facts before me are an empty tower with a ladder, a chair, and a table."

"The spiritualists," said Sir Walter, with a smile, "would say that spirits could find a great deal of use for a table."

"I dare say they could if the spirits were on the table—in a bottle," replied Wilson, with a curl of his pale lip. "The people round here, when they're all sodden up with Irish whisky, may believe in such things. I think they want a little education in this country."

Horne Fisher's heavy eyelids fluttered in a faint attempt to rise, as if he were tempted to a lazy protest against the contemptuous tone of the investigator.

"The Irish believe far too much in spirits to believe in spiritualism," he murmured. "They know too much about 'em. If you want a simple and childlike faith in any spirit that comes along you can get it in your favorite London."

"I don't want to get it anywhere," said Wilson, shortly. "I say I'm dealing with much simpler things than your simple faith, with a table and a chair and a ladder. Now what I want to say about them at the start is this. They are all three made roughly enough of plain wood. But the table and the chair are fairly new and comparatively clean. The ladder is covered with dust and there is a cobweb under the top rung of it. That means that he borrowed the first two quite recently from some cottage, as we supposed, but the ladder has been a long time in this rotten old dustbin. Probably it was part of the original furniture, an heirloom in this magnificent palace of the Irish kings."

Again Fisher looked at him under his eyelids, but seemed too sleepy to speak, and Wilson went on with his argument.

"Now it's quite clear that something very odd has just happened in this place. The chances are ten to one, it seems to me, that it had something specially to do with this place. Probably he came here because he could do it only here; it doesn't seem very inviting otherwise. But the man knew it of old; they say it belonged to his family, so that altogether, I think, everything points to something in the construction of the tower itself."

"Your reasoning seems to me excellent," said Sir Walter, who was listening attentively. "But what could it be?"

"You see now what I mean about the ladder," went on the detective; "it's the only old piece of furniture here and the first thing that caught that cockney eye of mine. But there is something else. That loft up there is a sort of lumber room without any lumber. So far as I can see, it's as empty as everything else; and, as things are, I don't see the use of the ladder leading to it. It seems to me, as I can't find anything unusual down here, that it might pay us to look up there."

He got briskly off the table on which he was sitting (for the only chair was allotted to Sir Walter) and ran rapidly up the ladder to the platform above. He was soon followed by the others, Mr. Fisher going last, however, with an appearance of considerable nonchalance.

At this stage, however, they were destined to disappointment; Wilson nosed in every corner like a terrier and examined the roof almost in the posture of a fly, but half an hour afterward they had to confess that they were still without a clew. Sir Walter's private secretary seemed more and more threatened with inappropriate slumber, and, having been the last to climb up the ladder, seemed now to lack the energy even to climb down again.

"Come along, Fisher," called out Sir Walter from below, when the others had regained the floor. "We must consider whether we'll pull the whole place to pieces to see what it's made of."

"I'm coming in a minute," said the voice from the ledge above their heads, a voice somewhat suggestive of an articulate yawn.

"What are you waiting for?" asked Sir Walter, impatiently. "Can you see anything there?"

"Well, yes, in a way," replied the voice, vaguely. "In fact, I see it quite plain now."

"What is it?" asked Wilson, sharply, from the table on which he sat kicking his heels restlessly.

"Well, it's a man," said Horne Fisher.

Wilson bounded off the table as if he had been kicked off it. "What do you mean?" he cried. "How can you possibly see a man?"

"I can see him through the window," replied the secretary, mildly. "I see him coming across the moor. He's making a bee line across the open country toward this tower. He evidently means to pay us a visit. And, considering who it seems to be, perhaps it would be more polite if we were all at the door to receive him." And in a leisurely manner the secretary came down the ladder.

"Who it seems to be!" repeated Sir Walter in astonishment.

"Well, I think it's the man you call Prince Michael," observed Mr. Fisher, airily. "In fact, I'm sure it is. I've seen the police portraits of him."

There was a dead silence, and Sir Walter's usually steady brain seemed to go round like a windmill.

"But, hang it all!" he said at last, "even supposing his own explosion could have thrown him half a mile away, without passing through any of the windows, and left him alive enough for a country walk—even then, why the devil should he walk in this direction? The murderer does not generally revisit the scene of his crime so rapidly as all that."

"He doesn't know yet that it is the scene of his crime," answered Horne Fisher.

"What on earth do you mean? You credit him with rather singular absence of mind."

"Well, the truth is, it isn't the scene of his crime," said Fisher, and went and looked out of the window.

There was another silence, and then Sir Walter said, quietly: "What sort of notion have you really got in your head, Fisher? Have you developed a new theory about how this fellow escaped out of the ring round him?"

"He never escaped at all," answered the man at the window, without turning round. "He never escaped out of the ring because he was never inside the ring. He was not in this tower at all, at least not when we were surrounding it."

He turned and leaned back against the window, but, in spite of his usual listless manner, they almost fancied that the face in shadow was a little pale.

"I began to guess something of the sort when we were some way from the tower," he said. "Did you notice that sort of flash or flicker the candle gave before it was extinguished? I was almost certain it was only the last leap the flame gives when a candle burns itself out. And then I came into this room and I saw that."

He pointed at the table and Sir Walter caught his breath with a sort of curse at his own blindness. For the candle in the candlestick had obviously burned itself away to nothing and left him, mentally, at least, very completely in the dark.

"Then there is a sort of mathematical question," went on Fisher, leaning back in his limp way and looking up at the bare walls, as if tracing imaginary diagrams there. "It's not so easy for a man in the third angle to face the other two at the same moment, especially if they are at the base of an isosceles. I am sorry if it sounds like a lecture on geometry, but—"

"I'm afraid we have no time for it," said Wilson, coldly. "If this man is really coming back, I must give my orders at once."

"I think I'll go on with it, though," observed Fisher, staring at the roof with insolent serenity.

"I must ask you, Mr. Fisher, to let me conduct my inquiry on my own lines," said Wilson, firmly. "I am the officer in charge now."

"Yes," remarked Horne Fisher, softly, but with an accent that somehow chilled the hearer. "Yes. But why?"

Sir Walter was staring, for he had never seen his rather lackadaisical young friend look like that before. Fisher was looking at Wilson with lifted lids, and the eyes under them seemed to have shed or shifted a film, as do the eyes of an eagle.

"Why are you the officer in charge now?" he asked. "Why can you conduct the inquiry on your own lines now? How did it come about, I wonder, that the elder officers are not here to interfere with anything you do?"

Nobody spoke, and nobody can say how soon anyone would have collected his wits to speak when a noise came from without. It was the heavy and hollow sound of a blow upon the door of the tower, and to their shaken spirits it sounded strangely like the hammer of doom.

The wooden door of the tower moved on its rusty hinges under the hand that struck it and Prince Michael came into the room. Nobody had the smallest doubt about his identity. His light clothes, though frayed with his adventures, were of fine and almost foppish cut, and he wore a pointed beard, or imperial, perhaps as a further reminiscence of Louis Napoleon; but he was a much taller and more graceful man that his prototype. Before anyone could speak he had silenced everyone for an instant with a slight but splendid gesture of hospitality.

"Gentlemen," he said, "this is a poor place now, but you are heartily welcome."

Wilson was the first to recover, and he took a stride toward the newcomer.

"Michael O'Neill, I arrest you in the king's name for the murder of Francis Morton and James Nolan. It is my duty to warn you—"

"No, no, Mr. Wilson," cried Fisher, suddenly. "You shall not commit a third murder."

Sir Walter Carey rose from his chair, which fell over with a crash behind him. "What does all this mean?" he called out in an authoritative manner.

"It means," said Fisher, "that this man, Hooker Wilson, as soon as he had put his head in at that window, killed his two comrades who had put their heads in at the other windows, by firing across the empty room. That is what it means. And if you want to know, count how many times he is supposed to have fired and then count the charges left in his revolver."

Wilson, who was still sitting on the table, abruptly put a hand out for the weapon that lay beside him. But the next movement was the most unexpected of all, for the prince standing in the doorway passed suddenly from the dignity of a statue to the swiftness of an acrobat and rent the revolver out of the detective's hand.

"You dog!" he cried. "So you are the type of English truth, as I am of Irish tragedy— you who come to kill me, wading through the blood of your brethren. If they had fallen in a feud on the hillside, it would be called murder, and yet your sin might be forgiven you. But I, who am innocent, I was to be slain with ceremony. There would be long speeches and patient judges listening to my vain plea of innocence, noting down my despair and disregarding it. Yes, that is what I call assassination. But killing may be no murder; there is one shot left in this little gun, and I know where it should go."

Wilson turned quickly on the table, and even as he turned he twisted in agony, for Michael shot him through the body where he sat, so that he tumbled off the table like lumber.

The police rushed to lift him; Sir Walter stood speechless; and then, with a strange and weary gesture, Horne Fisher spoke.

"You are indeed a type of the Irish tragedy," he said. "You were entirely in the right, and you have put yourself in the wrong."

The prince's face was like marble for a space then there dawned in his eyes a light not unlike that of despair. He laughed suddenly and flung the smoking pistol on the ground.

"I am indeed in the wrong," he said. "I have committed a crime that may justly bring a curse on me and my children."

Horne Fisher did not seem entirely satisfied with this very sudden repentance; he kept his eyes on the man and only said, in a low voice, "What crime do you mean?"

"I have helped English justice," replied Prince Michael. "I have avenged your king's officers; I have done the work of his hangman. For that truly I deserve to be hanged."

And he turned to the police with a gesture that did not so much surrender to them, but rather command them to arrest him.

This was the story that Horne Fisher told to Harold March, the journalist, many years after, in a little, but luxurious, restaurant near Piccadilly. He had invited March to dinner some time after the affair he called "The Face in the Target," and the conversation had naturally turned on that mystery and afterward on earlier memories of Fisher's life and the way in which he was led to study such problems as those of Prince Michael. Horne Fisher was fifteen years older; his thin hair had faded to frontal baldness, and his long, thin hands dropped less with affectation and more with fatigue. And he told the story of the Irish adventure of his youth, because it recorded the first occasion on which he had ever come in contact with crime, or discovered how darkly and how terribly crime can be entangled with law.

"Hooker Wilson was the first criminal I ever knew, and he was a policeman," explained Fisher, twirling his wine glass. "And all my life has been a mixed-up business of the sort. He was a man of very real talent, and perhaps genius, and well worth studying, both as a detective and a criminal. His white face and red hair were typical of him, for he was one of those who are cold and yet on fire for fame; and he could control anger, but not ambition. He swallowed the snubs of his superiors in that first quarrel, though he boiled with resentment; but when he suddenly saw the two heads dark against the dawn and framed in the two windows, he could not miss the chance, not only of revenge, but of the removal of the two obstacles to his promotion. He was a dead shot and counted on silencing both, though proof against him would have been hard in any case. But, as a matter of fact, he had a narrow escape, in the case of Nolan, who lived just long enough to say, 'Wilson' and point. We thought he was summoning help for his comrade, but he was really denouncing his murderer. After that it was easy to throw down the ladder above him (for a man up a ladder cannot see clearly what is below and behind) and to throw himself on the ground as another victim of the catastrophe.

"But there was mixed up with his murderous ambition a real belief, not only in his own talents, but in his own theories. He did believe in what he called a fresh eye, and he did want scope for fresh methods. There was something in his view, but it failed where such things commonly fail, because the fresh eye cannot see the unseen. It is true about the ladder and the scarecrow, but not about the life and the soul; and he made a bad mistake about what a man like Michael would do when he heard a woman scream. All Michael's very vanity and vainglory made him rush out at once; he would have walked into Dublin Castle for a lady's glove. Call it his pose or what you will, but he would have done it. What happened when he met her is another story, and one we may never know, but from tales I've heard since, they must have been reconciled. Wilson was wrong there; but there was something, for all that, in his notion that the newcomer sees most, and that the man on the spot may know too much to know anything. He was right about some things. He was right about me."

"About you?" asked Harold March in some wonder.

"I am the man who knows too much to know anything, or, at any rate, to do anything," said Horne Fisher. "I don't mean especially about Ireland. I mean about England. I mean about the whole way we are governed, and perhaps the only way we can be governed. You asked me just now what became of the survivors of that tragedy. Well, Wilson recovered and we managed to persuade him to retire. But we had to pension that damnable murderer more magnificently than any hero who ever fought for England. I managed to save Michael from the worst, but we had to send that perfectly innocent man to penal servitude for a crime we know he never committed, and it was only afterward that we could connive in a sneakish way at his escape. And Sir Walter Carey is Prime Minister of this country, which he would probably never have been if the truth had been told of such a horrible scandal in his department. It might have done for us altogether in Ireland; it would certainly have done for him. And he is my father's old friend, and has always smothered me with kindness. I am too tangled up with the whole thing, you see, and I was certainly never born to set it right. You look distressed, not to say shocked, and I'm not at all offended at it. Let us change the subject by all means, if you like. What do you think of this Burgundy? It's rather a discovery of mine, like the restaurant itself."

And he proceeded to talk learnedly and luxuriantly on all the wines of the world; on which subject, also, some moralists would consider that he knew too much.

❧ 3 ❧

THE SOUL OF THE SCHOOLBOY

A large map of London would be needed to display the wild and zigzag course of one day's journey undertaken by an uncle and his nephew; or, to speak more truly, of a nephew and his uncle. For the nephew, a schoolboy on a holiday, was in theory the god in the car, or in the cab, tram, tube, and so on, while his uncle was at most a priest dancing before him and offering sacrifices. To put it more soberly, the schoolboy had something of the stolid air of a young duke doing the grand tour, while his elderly relative was reduced to the position of a courier, who nevertheless had to pay for everything like a patron. The schoolboy was officially known as Summers Minor, and in a more social manner as Stinks, the only public tribute to his career as an amateur photographer and electrician. The uncle was the Rev. Thomas Twyford, a lean and lively old gentleman with a red, eager face and white hair. He was in the ordinary way a country clergyman, but he was one of those who achieve the paradox of being famous in an obscure way, because they are famous in an obscure world. In a small circle of ecclesiastical archaeologists, who were the only people who could even understand one another's discoveries, he occupied a recognized and respectable place. And a critic might have found even in that day's journey at least as much of the uncle's hobby as of the nephew's holiday.

His original purpose had been wholly paternal and festive. But, like many other intelligent people, he was not above the weakness of playing with a toy to amuse himself, on the theory that it would amuse a child. His toys were crowns and miters and croziers and swords of state; and he had lingered over them, telling himself that the boy ought to see all the sights of London. And at the end of the day, after a tremendous tea, he rather gave the game away by winding up with a visit in which hardly any human boy could be conceived as taking an interest—an underground chamber supposed to have been a chapel, recently excavated on the north bank of the Thames, and containing literally nothing whatever but one old silver coin. But the coin, to those who knew, was more solitary and splendid than the Koh-i-noor. It was Roman, and was said to bear the head of St. Paul; and round it raged the most vital controversies about the ancient British Church. It could hardly be denied, however, that the controversies left Summers Minor comparatively cold.

Indeed, the things that interested Summers Minor, and the things that did not interest him, had mystified and amused his uncle for several hours. He exhibited the English schoolboy's startling ignorance and startling knowledge—knowledge of some special classification in which he can generally correct and confound his elders. He considered himself entitled, at Hampton Court on a holiday, to forget the very names of Cardinal Wolsey or William of Orange; but he could hardly be dragged from some details about the arrangement of the electric bells in the neighboring hotel. He was solidly dazed by Westminster Abbey, which is not so unnatural since that church became the lumber room of the larger and less successful statuary of the eighteenth century. But he had a magic and minute knowledge of the Westminster omnibuses, and indeed of the whole omnibus system of London, the colors and numbers of which he knew as a herald knows heraldry. He would cry out against a momentary confusion between a light-green Paddington and a dark-green Bayswater vehicle, as his uncle would at the identification of a Greek ikon and a Roman image.

"Do you collect omnibuses like stamps?" asked his uncle. "They must need a rather large album. Or do you keep them in your locker?"

"I keep them in my head," replied the nephew, with legitimate firmness.

"It does you credit, I admit," replied the clergyman. "I suppose it were vain to ask for what purpose you have learned that out of a thousand things. There hardly seems to be a career in it, unless you could be permanently on the pavement to prevent old ladies getting into the wrong bus. Well, we must get out of this one, for this is our place. I want to show you what they call St. Paul's Penny."

"Is it like St. Paul's Cathedral?" asked the youth with resignation, as they alighted.

At the entrance their eyes were arrested by a singular figure evidently hovering there with a similar anxiety to enter. It was that of a dark, thin man in a long black robe rather like a cassock; but the black cap on his head was of too strange a shape to be a biretta. It suggested, rather, some archaic headdress of Persia or Babylon. He had a curious black beard appearing only at the corners of his chin, and his large eyes were oddly set in his face like the flat decorative eyes painted in old Egyptian profiles. Before they had gathered more than a general impression of him, he had dived into the doorway that was their own destination.

Nothing could be seen above ground of the sunken sanctuary except a strong wooden hut, of the sort recently run up for many military and official purposes, the wooden floor of which was indeed a mere platform over the excavated cavity below. A soldier stood as a sentry outside, and a superior soldier, an Anglo-Indian officer of distinction, sat writing at the desk inside. Indeed, the sightseers soon found that this particular sight was surrounded with the most extraordinary precautions. I have compared the silver coin to the Koh-i-noor, and in one sense it was even conventionally comparable, since by a historical accident it was at one time almost counted among the Crown jewels, or at least the Crown relics, until one of the royal princes publicly restored it to the shrine to which it was supposed to belong. Other causes combined to concentrate official vigilance upon it; there had been a scare about spies carrying explosives in small objects, and one of those experimental orders which pass like waves over bureaucracy had decreed first that all visitors should change their clothes for a sort of official sackcloth, and then (when this method caused some murmurs) that they should at least turn out their pockets. Colonel Morris, the officer in charge, was a short, active man with a grim and leathery face, but a lively and humorous eye—a contradiction borne out by his conduct, for he at once derided the safeguards and yet insisted on them.

"I don't care a button myself for Paul's Penny, or such things," he admitted in answer to some antiquarian openings from the clergyman who was slightly acquainted with him, "but I wear the King's coat, you know, and it's a serious thing when the King's uncle leaves a thing here with his own hands under my charge. But as for saints and relics and things, I fear I'm a bit of a Voltairian; what you would call a skeptic."

"I'm not sure it's even skeptical to believe in the royal family and not in the 'Holy' Family," replied Mr. Twyford. "But, of course, I can easily empty my pockets, to show I don't carry a bomb."

The little heap of the parson's possessions which he left on the table consisted chiefly of papers, over and above a pipe and a tobacco pouch and some Roman and Saxon coins. The rest were catalogues of old books, and pamphlets, like one entitled "The Use of Sarum," one glance at which was sufficient both for the colonel and the schoolboy. They could not see the use of Sarum at all. The contents of the boy's pockets naturally made a larger heap, and included marbles, a ball of string, an electric torch, a magnet, a small catapult, and, of course, a large pocketknife, almost to be described as a small tool box, a complex apparatus on which he seemed disposed to linger, pointing out that it included a pair of nippers, a tool for punching holes in wood, and, above all, an instrument for taking stones out of a horse's hoof. The comparative absence of any horse he appeared to regard as irrelevant, as if it were a mere appendage easily supplied. But when the turn came of the gentleman in the black gown, he did not turn out his pockets, but merely spread out his hands.

"I have no possessions," he said.

"I'm afraid I must ask you to empty your pockets and make sure," observed the colonel, gruffly.

"I have no pockets," said the stranger.

Mr. Twyford was looking at the long black gown with a learned eye.

"Are you a monk?" he asked, in a puzzled fashion.

"I am a magus," replied the stranger. "You have heard of the magi, perhaps? I am a magician."

"Oh, I say!" exclaimed Summers Minor, with prominent eyes.

"But I was once a monk," went on the other. "I am what you would call an escaped monk. Yes, I have escaped into eternity. But the monks held one truth at least, that the highest life should be without possessions. I have no pocket money and no pockets, and all the stars are my trinkets."

"They are out of reach, anyhow," observed Colonel Morris, in a tone which suggested that it was well for them. "I've known a good many magicians myself in India—mango plant and all. But the Indian ones are all frauds, I'll swear. In fact, I had a good deal of fun showing them up. More fun than I have over this dreary job, anyhow. But here comes Mr. Symon, who will show you over the old cellar downstairs."

Mr. Symon, the official guardian and guide, was a young man, prematurely gray, with a grave mouth which contrasted curiously with a very small, dark mustache with waxed points, that seemed somehow, separate from it, as if a black fly had settled on his face. He spoke with the accent of Oxford and the permanent official, but in as dead a fashion as the most indifferent hired guide. They descended a dark stone staircase, at the floor of which Symon pressed a button and a door opened on a dark room, or, rather, a room which had an instant before been dark. For almost as the heavy iron door swung open an almost blinding blaze of electric lights filled the whole interior. The fitful enthusiasm of Stinks at once caught fire, and he eagerly asked if the lights and the door worked together.

"Yes, it's all one system," replied Symon. "It was all fitted up for the day His Royal Highness deposited the thing here. You see, it's locked up behind a glass case exactly as he left it."

A glance showed that the arrangements for guarding the treasure were indeed as strong as they were simple. A single pane of glass cut off one corner of the room, in an iron framework let into the rock walls and the wooden roof above; there was now no possibility of reopening the case without elaborate labor, except by breaking the glass, which would probably arouse the night watchman who was always within a few feet of it, even if he had fallen asleep. A close examination would have showed many more ingenious safeguards; but the eye of the Rev. Thomas Twyford, at least, was already riveted on what interested him much more—the dull silver disk which shone in the white light against a plain background of black velvet.

"St. Paul's Penny, said to commemorate the visit of St. Paul to Britain, was probably preserved in this chapel until the eighth century," Symon was saying in his clear but colorless voice. "In the ninth century it is supposed to have been carried away by the barbarians, and it reappears, after the conversion of the northern Goths, in the possession of the royal family of Gothland. His Royal Highness, the Duke of Gothland, retained it always in his own private custody, and when he decided to exhibit it to the public, placed it here with his own hand. It was immediately sealed up in such a manner—"

Unluckily at this point Summers Minor, whose attention had somewhat strayed from the religious wars of the ninth century, caught sight of a short length of wire appearing in a broken patch in the wall. He precipitated himself at it, calling out, "I say, does that connect?"

It was evident that it did connect, for no sooner had the boy given it a twitch than the whole room went black, as if they had all been struck blind, and an instant afterward they heard the dull crash of the closing door.

"Well, you've done it now," said Symon, in his tranquil fashion. Then after a pause he added, "I suppose they'll miss us sooner or later, and no doubt they can get it open; but it may take some little time."

There was a silence, and then the unconquerable Stinks observed:

"Rotten that I had to leave my electric torch."

"I think," said his uncle, with restraint, "that we are sufficiently convinced of your interest in electricity."

Then after a pause he remarked, more amiably: "I suppose if I regretted any of my own impedimenta, it would be the pipe. Though, as a matter of fact, it's not much fun smoking in the dark. Everything seems different in the dark."

"Everything is different in the dark," said a third voice, that of the man who called himself a magician. It was a very musical voice, and rather in contrast with his sinister and swarthy visage, which was now invisible. "Perhaps you don't know how terrible a truth that is. All you see are pictures made by the sun, faces and furniture and flowers and trees. The things themselves may be quite strange to you. Something else may be standing now where you saw a table or a chair. The face of your friend may be quite different in the dark."

A short, indescribable noise broke the stillness. Twyford started for a second, and then said, sharply:

"Really, I don't think it's a suitable occasion for trying to frighten a child."

"Who's a child?" cried the indignant Summers, with a voice that had a crow, but also something of a crack in it. "And who's a funk, either? Not me."

"I will be silent, then," said the other voice out of the darkness. "But silence also makes and unmakes."

The required silence remained unbroken for a long time until at last the clergyman said to Symon in a low voice:

"I suppose it's all right about air?"

"Oh, yes," replied the other aloud; "there's a fireplace and a chimney in the office just by the door."

A bound and the noise of a falling chair told them that the irrepressible rising generation had once more thrown itself across the room. They heard the ejaculation: "A chimney! Why, I'll be—" and the rest was lost in muffled, but exultant, cries.

The uncle called repeatedly and vainly, groped his way at last to the opening, and, peering up it, caught a glimpse of a disk of daylight, which seemed to suggest that the fugitive had vanished in safety. Making his way back to the group by the glass case, he fell over the fallen chair and took a moment to collect himself again. He had opened his mouth to speak to Symon, when he stopped, and suddenly found himself blinking in the full shock of the white light, and looking over the other man's shoulder, he saw that the door was standing open.

"So they've got at us at last," he observed to Symon.

The man in the black robe was leaning against the wall some yards away, with a smile carved on his face.

"Here comes Colonel Morris," went on Twyford, still speaking to Symon. "One of us will have to tell him how the light went out. Will you?"

But Symon still said nothing. He was standing as still as a statue, and looking steadily at the black velvet behind the glass screen. He was looking at the black velvet because there was nothing else to look at. St. Paul's Penny was gone.

Colonel Morris entered the room with two new visitors; presumably two new sightseers delayed by the accident. The foremost was a tall, fair, rather languid-looking man with a bald brow and a high-bridged nose; his companion was a younger man with light, curly hair and frank, and even innocent, eyes. Symon scarcely seemed to hear the newcomers; it seemed almost as if he had not realized that the return of the light revealed his brooding attitude. Then he started in a guilty fashion, and when he saw the elder of the two strangers, his pale face seemed to turn a shade paler.

"Why it's Horne Fisher!" and then after a pause he said in a low voice, "I'm in the devil of a hole, Fisher."

"There does seem a bit of a mystery to be cleared up," observed the gentleman so addressed.

"It will never be cleared up," said the pale Symon. "If anybody could clear it up, you could. But nobody could."

"I rather think I could," said another voice from outside the group, and they turned in surprise to realize that the man in the black robe had spoken again.

"You!" said the colonel, sharply. "And how do you propose to play the detective?"

"I do not propose to play the detective," answered the other, in a clear voice like a bell. "I propose to play the magician. One of the magicians you show up in India, Colonel."

No one spoke for a moment, and then Horne Fisher surprised everybody by saying, "Well, let's go upstairs, and this gentleman can have a try."

He stopped Symon, who had an automatic finger on the button, saying: "No, leave all the lights on. It's a sort of safeguard."

"The thing can't be taken away now," said Symon, bitterly.

"It can be put back," replied Fisher.

Twyford had already run upstairs for news of his vanishing nephew, and he received news of him in a way that at once puzzled and reassured him. On the floor above lay one of those large paper darts which boys throw at each other when the schoolmaster is out of the room. It had evidently been thrown in at the window, and on being unfolded displayed a scrawl of bad handwriting which ran: "Dear Uncle; I am all right. Meet you at the hotel later on," and then the signature.

Insensibly comforted by this, the clergyman found his thoughts reverting voluntarily to his favorite relic, which came a good second in his sympathies to his favorite nephew, and before he knew where he was he found himself encircled by the group discussing its loss, and more or less carried away on the current of their excitement. But an undercurrent of query continued to run in his mind, as to what had really happened to the boy, and what was the boy's exact definition of being all right.

Meanwhile Horne Fisher had considerably puzzled everybody with his new tone and attitude. He had talked to the colonel about the military and mechanical arrangements, and displayed a remarkable knowledge both of the details of discipline and the technicalities of electricity. He had talked to the clergyman, and shown an equally surprising knowledge of the religious and historical interests involved in the relic. He had talked to the man who called himself a magician, and not only surprised but scandalized the company by an equally sympathetic familiarity with the most fantastic forms of Oriental occultism and psychic experiment. And in this last and least respectable line of inquiry he was evidently prepared to go farthest; he openly encouraged the magician, and was plainly prepared to follow the wildest ways of investigation in which that magus might lead him.

"How would you begin now?" he inquired, with an anxious politeness that reduced the colonel to a congestion of rage.

"It is all a question of a force; of establishing communications for a force," replied that adept, affably, ignoring some military mutterings about the police force. "It is what you in the West used to call animal magnetism, but it is much more than that. I had better not say how much more. As to setting about it, the usual method is to throw some susceptible person into a trance, which serves as a sort of bridge or cord of communication, by which the force beyond can give him, as it were, an electric shock, and awaken his higher senses. It opens the sleeping eye of the mind."

"I'm suspectible," said Fisher, either with simplicity or with a baffling irony. "Why not open my mind's eye for me? My friend Harold March here will tell you I sometimes see things, even in the dark."

"Nobody sees anything except in the dark," said the magician.

Heavy clouds of sunset were closing round the wooden hut, enormous clouds, of which only the corners could be seen in the little window, like purple horns and tails, almost as if some huge monsters were prowling round the place. But the purple was already deepening to dark gray; it would soon be night.

"Do not light the lamp," said the magus with quiet authority, arresting a movement in that direction. "I told you before that things happen only in the dark."

How such a topsy-turvy scene ever came to be tolerated in the colonel's office, of all places, was afterward a puzzle in the memory of many, including the colonel. They recalled it like a sort of nightmare, like something they could not control. Perhaps there was really a magnetism about the mesmerist; perhaps there was even more magnetism about the man mesmerized. Anyhow, the man was being mesmerized, for Horne Fisher had collapsed into a chair with his long limbs loose and sprawling and his eyes staring at vacancy; and the other man was mesmerizing him, making sweeping movements with his darkly draped arms as if with black wings. The colonel had passed the point of explosion, and he dimly realized that eccentric aristocrats are allowed their fling. He comforted himself with the knowledge that he had already sent for the police, who would break up any such masquerade, and with lighting a cigar, the red end of which, in the gathering darkness, glowed with protest.

"Yes, I see pockets," the man in the trance was saying. "I see many pockets, but they are all empty. No; I see one pocket that is not empty."

There was a faint stir in the stillness, and the magician said, "Can you see what is in the pocket?"

"Yes," answered the other; "there are two bright things. I think they are two bits of steel. One of the pieces of steel is bent or crooked."

"Have they been used in the removal of the relic from downstairs?"

"Yes."

There was another pause and the inquirer added, "Do you see anything of the relic itself?"

"I see something shining on the floor, like the shadow or the ghost of it. It is over there in the corner beyond the desk."

There was a movement of men turning and then a sudden stillness, as of their stiffening, for over in the corner on the wooden floor there was really a round spot of pale light. It was the only spot of light in the room. The cigar had gone out.

"It points the way," came the voice of the oracle. "The spirits are pointing the way to penitence, and urging the thief to restitution. I can see nothing more." His voice trailed off into a silence that lasted solidly for many minutes, like the long silence below when the theft had been committed. Then it was broken by the ring of metal on the floor, and the sound of something spinning and falling like a tossed halfpenny.

"Light the lamp!" cried Fisher in a loud and even jovial voice, leaping to his feet with far less languor than usual. "I must be going now, but I should like to see it before I go. Why, I came on purpose to see it."

The lamp was lit, and he did see it, for St. Paul's Penny was lying on the floor at his feet.

"Oh, as for that," explained Fisher, when he was entertaining March and Twyford at lunch about a month later, "I merely wanted to play with the magician at his own game."

"I thought you meant to catch him in his own trap," said Twyford. "I can't make head or tail of anything yet, but to my mind he was always the suspect. I don't think he was necessarily a thief in the vulgar sense. The police always seem to think that silver is stolen for the sake of silver, but a thing like that might well be stolen out of some religious mania. A runaway monk turned mystic might well want it for some mystical purpose."

"No," replied Fisher, "the runaway monk is not a thief. At any rate he is not the thief. And he's not altogether a liar, either. He said one true thing at least that night."

"And what was that?" inquired March.

"He said it was all magnetism. As a matter of fact, it was done by means of a magnet." Then, seeing they still looked puzzled, he added, "It was that toy magnet belonging to your nephew, Mr. Twyford."

"But I don't understand," objected March. "If it was done with the schoolboy's magnet, I suppose it was done by the schoolboy."

"Well," replied Fisher, reflectively, "it rather depends which schoolboy."

"What on earth do you mean?"

"The soul of a schoolboy is a curious thing," Fisher continued, in a meditative manner. "It can survive a great many things besides climbing out of a chimney. A man can grow gray in great campaigns, and still have the soul of a schoolboy. A man can return with a great reputation from India and be put in charge of a great public treasure, and still have the soul of a schoolboy, waiting to be awakened by an accident. And it is ten times more so when to the schoolboy you add the skeptic, who is generally a sort of stunted schoolboy. You said just now that things might be done by religious mania. Have you ever heard of irreligious mania? I assure you it exists very violently, especially in men who like showing up magicians in India. But here the skeptic had the temptation of showing up a much more tremendous sham nearer home."

A light came into Harold March's eyes as he suddenly saw, as if afar off, the wider implication of the suggestion. But Twyford was still wrestling with one problem at a time.

"Do you really mean," he said, "that Colonel Morris took the relic?"

"He was the only person who could use the magnet," replied Fisher. "In fact, your obliging nephew left him a number of things he could use. He had a ball of string, and an instrument for making a hole in the wooden floor—I made a little play with that hole in the floor in my trance, by the way; with the lights left on below, it shone like a new shilling." Twyford suddenly bounded on his chair. "But in that case," he cried, in a new and altered voice, "why then of course— You said a piece of steel—?"

"I said there were two pieces of steel," said Fisher. "The bent piece of steel was the boy's magnet. The other was the relic in the glass case."

"But that is silver," answered the archaeologist, in a voice now almost unrecognizable.

"Oh," replied Fisher, soothingly, "I dare say it was painted with silver a little."

There was a heavy silence, and at last Harold March said, "But where is the real relic?"

"Where it has been for five years," replied Horne Fisher, "in the possession of a mad millionaire named Vandam, in Nebraska. There was a playful little photograph about him in a society paper the other day, mentioning his delusion, and saying he was always being taken in about relics."

Harold March frowned at the tablecloth; then, after an interval, he said: "I think I understand your notion of how the thing was actually done; according to that, Morris just made a hole and fished it up with a magnet at the end of a string. Such a monkey trick looks like mere madness, but I suppose he was mad, partly with the boredom of watching over what he felt was a fraud, though he couldn't prove it. Then came a chance to prove it, to himself at least, and he had what he called 'fun' with it. Yes, I think I see a lot of details now. But it's just the whole thing that knocks me. How did it all come to be like that?"

Fisher was looking at him with level lids and an immovable manner.

"Every precaution was taken," he said. "The Duke carried the relic on his own person, and locked it up in the case with his own hands."

March was silent; but Twyford stammered. "I don't understand you. You give me the creeps. Why don't you speak plainer?"

"If I spoke plainer you would understand me less," said Horne Fisher.

"All the same I should try," said March, still without lifting his head.

"Oh, very well," replied Fisher, with a sigh; "the plain truth is, of course, that it's a bad business. Everybody knows it's a bad business who knows anything about it. But it's always happening, and in one way one can hardly blame them. They get stuck on to a foreign princess that's as stiff as a Dutch doll, and they have their fling. In this case it was a pretty big fling."

The face of the Rev. Thomas Twyford certainly suggested that he was a little out of his depth in the seas of truth, but as the other went on speaking vaguely the old gentleman's features sharpened and set.

"If it were some decent morganatic affair I wouldn't say; but he must have been a fool to throw away thousands on a woman like that. At the end it was sheer blackmail; but it's something that the old ass didn't get it out of the taxpayers. He could only get it out of the Yank, and there you are."

The Rev. Thomas Twyford had risen to his feet.

"Well, I'm glad my nephew had nothing to do with it," he said. "And if that's what the world is like, I hope he will never have anything to do with it."

"I hope not," answered Horne Fisher. "No one knows so well as I do that one can have far too much to do with it."

For Summers Minor had indeed nothing to do with it; and it is part of his higher significance that he has really nothing to do with the story, or with any such stories. The boy went like a bullet through the tangle of this tale of crooked politics and crazy mockery and came out on the other side, pursuing his own unspoiled purposes. From the top of the chimney he climbed he had caught sight of a new omnibus, whose color and name he had never known, as a naturalist might see a new bird or a botanist a new flower. And he had been sufficiently enraptured in rushing after it, and riding away upon that fairy ship.

4

THE BOTTOMLESS WELL

In an oasis, or green island, in the red and yellow seas of sand that stretch beyond Europe toward the sunrise, there can be found a rather fantastic contrast, which is none the less typical of such a place, since international treaties have made it an outpost of the British occupation. The site is famous among archaeologists for something that is hardly a monument, but merely a hole in the ground. But it is a round shaft, like that of a well, and probably a part of some great irrigation works of remote and disputed date, perhaps more ancient than anything in that ancient land. There is a green fringe of palm and prickly pear round the black mouth of the well; but nothing of the upper masonry remains except two bulky and battered stones standing like the pillars of a gateway of nowhere, in which some of the more transcendental archaeologists, in certain moods at moonrise or sunset, think they can trace the faint lines of figures or features of more than Babylonian monstrosity; while the more rationalistic archaeologists, in the more rational hours of daylight, see nothing but two shapeless rocks. It may have been noticed, however, that all Englishmen are not archaeologists. Many of those assembled in such a place for official and military purposes have hobbies other than archaeology. And it is a solemn fact that the English in this Eastern exile have contrived to make a small golf links out of the green scrub and sand; with a comfortable clubhouse at one end of it and this primeval monument at the other. They did not actually use this archaic abyss as a bunker, because it was by tradition unfathomable, and even for practical purposes unfathomed. Any sporting projectile sent into it might be counted most literally as a lost ball. But they often sauntered round it in their interludes of talking and smoking cigarettes, and one of them had just come down from the clubhouse to find another gazing somewhat moodily into the well.

Both the Englishmen wore light clothes and white pith helmets and puggrees, but there, for the most part, their resemblance ended. And they both almost simultaneously said the same word, but they said it on two totally different notes of the voice.

"Have you heard the news?" asked the man from the club. "Splendid."

471

"Splendid," replied the man by the well. But the first man pronounced the word as a young man might say it about a woman, and the second as an old man might say it about the weather, not without sincerity, but certainly without fervor.

And in this the tone of the two men was sufficiently typical of them. The first, who was a certain Captain Boyle, was of a bold and boyish type, dark, and with a sort of native heat in his face that did not belong to the atmosphere of the East, but rather to the ardors and ambitions of the West. The other was an older man and certainly an older resident, a civilian official—Horne Fisher; and his drooping eyelids and drooping light mustache expressed all the paradox of the Englishman in the East. He was much too hot to be anything but cool.

Neither of them thought it necessary to mention what it was that was splendid. That would indeed have been superfluous conversation about something that everybody knew. The striking victory over a menacing combination of Turks and Arabs in the north, won by troops under the command of Lord Hastings, the veteran of so many striking victories, was already spread by the newspapers all over the Empire, let alone to this small garrison so near to the battlefield.

"Now, no other nation in the world could have done a thing like that," cried Captain Boyle, emphatically.

Horne Fisher was still looking silently into the well; a moment later he answered: "We certainly have the art of unmaking mistakes. That's where the poor old Prussians went wrong. They could only make mistakes and stick to them. There is really a certain talent in unmaking a mistake."

"What do you mean," asked Boyle, "what mistakes?"

"Well, everybody knows it looked like biting off more than he could chew," replied Horne Fisher. It was a peculiarity of Mr. Fisher that he always said that everybody knew things which about one person in two million was ever allowed to hear of. "And it was certainly jolly lucky that Travers turned up so well in the nick of time. Odd how often the right thing's been done for us by the second in command, even when a great man was first in command. Like Colborne at Waterloo."

"It ought to add a whole province to the Empire," observed the other.

"Well, I suppose the Zimmernes would have insisted on it as far as the canal," observed Fisher, thoughtfully, "though everybody knows adding provinces doesn't always pay much nowadays."

Captain Boyle frowned in a slightly puzzled fashion. Being cloudily conscious of never having heard of the Zimmernes in his life, he could only remark, stolidly:

"Well, one can't be a Little Englander."

Horne Fisher smiled, and he had a pleasant smile.

"Every man out here is a Little Englander," he said. "He wishes he were back in Little England."

"I don't know what you're talking about, I'm afraid," said the younger man, rather suspiciously. "One would think you didn't really admire Hastings or—or —anything."

"I admire him no end," replied Fisher. "He's by far the best man for this post; he understands the Moslems and can do anything with them. That's why I'm all against pushing Travers against him, merely because of this last affair."

"I really don't understand what you're driving at," said the other, frankly.

"Perhaps it isn't worth understanding," answered Fisher, lightly, "and, anyhow, we needn't talk politics. Do you know the Arab legend about that well?"

"I'm afraid I don't know much about Arab legends," said Boyle, rather stiffly.

"That's rather a mistake," replied Fisher, "especially from your point of view. Lord Hastings himself is an Arab legend. That is perhaps the very greatest thing he really is. If his reputation went it would weaken us all over Asia and Africa. Well, the story about that hole in the ground, that goes down nobody knows where, has always fascinated me, rather. It's Mohammedan in form now, but I shouldn't wonder if the tale is a long way older than Mohammed. It's all about somebody they call the Sultan Aladdin, not our friend of the lamp, of course, but rather like him in having to do with genii or giants or something of that sort. They say he commanded the giants to build him a sort of pagoda, rising higher and higher above all the stars. The Utmost for the Highest, as the people said when they built the Tower of Babel. But the builders of the Tower of Babel were quite modest and domestic people, like mice, compared with old Aladdin. They only wanted a tower that would reach heaven— a mere trifle. He wanted a tower that would pass heaven and rise above it, and go on rising for ever and ever. And Allah cast him down to earth with a thunderbolt, which sank into the earth, boring a hole deeper and deeper, till it made a well that was without a bottom as the tower was to have been without a top. And down that inverted tower of darkness the soul of the proud Sultan is falling forever and ever."

"What a queer chap you are," said Boyle. "You talk as if a fellow could believe those fables."

"Perhaps I believe the moral and not the fable," answered Fisher. "But here comes Lady Hastings. You know her, I think."

The clubhouse on the golf links was used, of course, for many other purposes besides that of golf. It was the only social center of the garrison beside the strictly military headquarters; it had a billiard room and a bar, and even an excellent reference library for those officers who were so perverse as to take their profession seriously. Among these was the great general himself, whose head of silver and face of bronze, like that of a brazen eagle, were often to be found bent over the charts and folios of the library. The great Lord Hastings believed in science and study, as in other severe ideals of life, and had given much paternal advice on the point to young Boyle, whose appearances in that place of research were rather more intermittent. It was from one of these snatches of study that the young man had just come out through the glass doors of the library on to the golf links. But, above all, the club was so appointed as to serve the social conveniences of ladies at least as much as gentlemen, and Lady Hastings was able to play the queen in such a society almost as much as in her own ballroom. She was eminently calculated and, as some said, eminently inclined to play such a part. She was much younger than her husband, an attractive and sometimes dangerously attractive lady; and Mr. Horne Fisher looked after her a little sardonically as she swept away with the young soldier. Then his rather dreary eye strayed to the green and prickly growths round the well, growths of that curious cactus formation in which one thick leaf grows directly out of the other without stalk or twig. It gave his fanciful mind a sinister feeling of a blind growth without shape or purpose. A flower or shrub in the West grows to the blossom which is its crown, and is content. But this was as if hands could grow out of hands or legs grow out of legs in a nightmare. "Always adding a province to the Empire," he said, with a smile, and then added, more sadly, "but I doubt if I was right, after all!"

A strong but genial voice broke in on his meditations and he looked up and smiled, seeing the face of an old friend. The voice was, indeed, rather more genial than the face, which was at the first glance decidedly grim. It was a typically legal face, with angular jaws and heavy, grizzled eyebrows; and it belonged to an eminently legal character, though he was now attached in a semimilitary capacity to the police of that wild district. Cuthbert Grayne was perhaps more of a criminologist than either a lawyer or a policeman, but in his more barbarous surroundings he had proved successful in turning himself into a practical combination of all three. The discovery of a whole series of strange Oriental crimes stood to his credit. But as few people were acquainted with, or attracted to, such a hobby or branch of knowledge, his intellectual life was somewhat solitary. Among the few exceptions was Horne Fisher, who had a curious capacity for talking to almost anybody about almost anything.

"Studying botany, or is it archaeology?" inquired Grayne. "I shall never come to the end of your interests, Fisher. I should say that what you don't know isn't worth knowing."

"You are wrong," replied Fisher, with a very unusual abruptness, and even bitterness. "It's what I do know that isn't worth knowing. All the seamy side of things, all the secret reasons and rotten motives and bribery and blackmail they call politics. I needn't be so proud of having been down all these sewers that I should brag about it to the little boys in the street."

"What do you mean? What's the matter with you?" asked his friend. "I never knew you taken like this before."

"I'm ashamed of myself," replied Fisher. "I've just been throwing cold water on the enthusiasms of a boy."

"Even that explanation is hardly exhaustive," observed the criminal expert.

"Damned newspaper nonsense the enthusiasms were, of course," continued Fisher, "but I ought to know that at that age illusions can be ideals. And they're better than the reality, anyhow. But there is one very ugly responsibility about jolting a young man out of the rut of the most rotten ideal."

"And what may that be?" inquired his friend.

"It's very apt to set him off with the same energy in a much worse direction," answered Fisher; "a pretty endless sort of direction, a bottomless pit as deep as the bottomless well."

Fisher did not see his friend until a fortnight later, when he found himself in the garden at the back of the clubhouse on the opposite side from the links, a garden heavily colored and scented with sweet semitropical plants in the glow of a desert sunset. Two other men were with him, the third being the now celebrated second in command, familiar to everybody as Tom Travers, a lean, dark man, who looked older than his years, with a furrow in his brow and something morose about the very shape of his black mustache. They had just been served with black coffee by the Arab now officiating as the temporary servant of the club, though he was a figure already familiar, and even famous, as the old servant of the general. He went by the name of Said, and was notable among other Semites for that unnatural length of his yellow face and height of his narrow forehead which is sometimes seen among them, and gave an irrational impression of something sinister, in spite of his agreeable smile.

"I never feel as if I could quite trust that fellow," said Grayne, when the man had gone away. "It's very unjust, I take it, for he was certainly devoted to Hastings, and saved his life, they say. But Arabs are often like that, loyal to one man. I can't help feeling he might cut anybody else's throat, and even do it treacherously."

"Well," said Travers, with a rather sour smile, "so long as he leaves Hastings alone the world won't mind much."

There was a rather embarrassing silence, full of memories of the great battle, and then Horne Fisher said, quietly:

"The newspapers aren't the world, Tom. Don't you worry about them. Everybody in your world knows the truth well enough."

"I think we'd better not talk about the general just now," remarked Grayne, "for he's just coming out of the club."

"He's not coming here," said Fisher. "He's only seeing his wife to the car."

As he spoke, indeed, the lady came out on the steps of the club, followed by her husband, who then went swiftly in front of her to open the garden gate. As he did so she turned back and spoke for a moment to a solitary man still sitting in a cane chair in the shadow of the doorway, the only man left in the deserted club save for the three that lingered in the garden. Fisher peered for a moment into the shadow, and saw that it was Captain Boyle.

The next moment, rather to their surprise, the general reappeared and, remounting the steps, spoke a word or two to Boyle in his turn. Then he signaled to Said, who hurried up with two cups of coffee, and the two men re-entered the club, each carrying his cup in his hand. The next moment a gleam of white light in the growing darkness showed that the electric lamps had been turned on in the library beyond.

"Coffee and scientific researches," said Travers, grimly. "All the luxuries of learning and theoretical research. Well, I must be going, for I have my work to do as well." And he got up rather stiffly, saluted his companions, and strode away into the dusk.

"I only hope Boyle is sticking to scientific researches," said Horne Fisher. "I'm not very comfortable about him myself. But let's talk about something else."

They talked about something else longer than they probably imagined, until the tropical night had come and a splendid moon painted the whole scene with silver; but before it was bright enough to see by Fisher had already noted that the lights in the library had been abruptly extinguished. He waited for the two men to come out by the garden entrance, but nobody came.

"They must have gone for a stroll on the links," he said.

"Very possibly," replied Grayne. "It's going to be a beautiful night."

A moment or two after he had spoken they heard a voice hailing them out of the shadow of the clubhouse, and were astonished to perceive Travers hurrying toward them, calling out as he came:

"I shall want your help, you fellows," he cried. "There's something pretty bad out on the links."

They found themselves plunging through the club smoking room and the library beyond, in complete darkness, mental as well as material. But Horne Fisher, in spite of his affectation of indifference, was a person of a curious and almost transcendental sensibility to atmospheres, and he already felt the presence of something more than an accident. He collided with a piece of furniture in the library, and almost shuddered with the shock, for the thing moved as he could never have fancied a piece of furniture moving. It seemed to move like a living thing, yielding and yet striking back. The next moment Grayne had turned on the lights, and he saw he had only stumbled against one of the revolving bookstands that had swung round and struck him; but his involuntary recoil had revealed to him his own subconscious sense of something mysterious and monstrous. There were several of these revolving bookcases standing here and there about the library; on one of them stood the two cups of coffee, and on another a large open book. It was Budge's book on Egyptian hieroglyphics, with colored plates of strange birds and gods, and even as he rushed past, he was conscious of something odd about the fact that this, and not any work of military science, should be open in that place at that moment. He was even conscious of the gap in the well-lined bookshelf from which it had been taken, and it seemed almost to gape at him in an ugly fashion, like a gap in the teeth of some sinister face.

A run brought them in a few minutes to the other side of the ground in front of the bottomless well, and a few yards from it, in a moonlight almost as broad as daylight, they saw what they had come to see.

The great Lord Hastings lay prone on his face, in a posture in which there was a touch of something strange and stiff, with one elbow erect above his body, the arm being doubled, and his big, bony hand clutching the rank and ragged grass. A few feet away was Boyle, almost as motionless, but supported on his hands and knees, and staring at the body. It might have been no more than shock and accident; but there was something ungainly and unnatural about the quadrupedal posture and the gaping face. It was as if his reason had fled from him. Behind, there was nothing but the clear blue southern sky, and the beginning of the desert, except for the two great broken stones in front of the well. And it was in such a light and atmosphere that men could fancy they traced in them enormous and evil faces, looking down.

Horne Fisher stooped and touched the strong hand that was still clutching the grass, and it was as cold as a stone. He knelt by the body and was busy for a moment applying other tests; then he rose again, and said, with a sort of confident despair:

"Lord Hastings is dead."

There was a stony silence, and then Travers remarked, gruffly: "This is your department, Grayne; I will leave you to question Captain Boyle. I can make no sense of what he says."

Boyle had pulled himself together and risen to his feet, but his face still wore an awful expression, making it like a new mask or the face of another man.

"I was looking at the well," he said, "and when I turned he had fallen down."

Grayne's face was very dark. "As you say, this is my affair," he said. "I must first ask you to help me carry him to the library and let me examine things thoroughly."

When they had deposited the body in the library, Grayne turned to Fisher and said, in a voice that had recovered its fullness and confidence, "I am going to lock myself in and make a thorough examination first. I look to you to keep in touch with the others and make a preliminary examination of Boyle. I will talk to him later. And just telephone to headquarters for a policeman, and let him come here at once and stand by till I want him."

Without more words the great criminal investigator went into the lighted library, shutting the door behind him, and Fisher, without replying, turned and began to talk quietly to Travers. "It is curious," he said, "that the thing should happen just in front of that place."

"It would certainly be very curious," replied Travers, "if the place played any part in it."

"I think," replied Fisher, "that the part it didn't play is more curious still."

And with these apparently meaningless words he turned to the shaken Boyle and, taking his arm, began to walk him up and down in the moonlight, talking in low tones.

Dawn had begun to break abrupt and white when Cuthbert Grayne turned out the lights in the library and came out on to the links. Fisher was lounging about alone, in his listless fashion; but the police messenger for whom he had sent was standing at attention in the background.

"I sent Boyle off with Travers," observed Fisher, carelessly; "he'll look after him, and he'd better have some sleep, anyhow."

"Did you get anything out of him?" asked Grayne. "Did he tell you what he and Hastings were doing?"

"Yes," answered Fisher, "he gave me a pretty clear account, after all. He said that after Lady Hastings went off in the car the general asked him to take coffee with him in the library and look up a point about local antiquities. He himself was beginning to look for Budge's book in one of the revolving bookstands when the general found it in one of the bookshelves on the wall. After looking at some of the plates they went out, it would seem, rather abruptly, on to the links, and walked toward the old well; and while Boyle was looking into it he heard a thud behind him, and turned round to find the general lying as we found him. He himself dropped on his knees to examine the body, and then was paralyzed with a sort of terror and could not come nearer to it or touch it. But I think very little of that; people caught in a real shock of surprise are sometimes found in the queerest postures."

Grayne wore a grim smile of attention, and said, after a short silence:

"Well, he hasn't told you many lies. It's really a creditably clear and consistent account of what happened, with everything of importance left out."

"Have you discovered anything in there?" asked Fisher.

"I have discovered everything," answered Grayne.

Fisher maintained a somewhat gloomy silence, as the other resumed his explanation in quiet and assured tones.

"You were quite right, Fisher, when you said that young fellow was in danger of going down dark ways toward the pit. Whether or no, as you fancied, the jolt you gave to his view of the general had anything to do with it, he has not been treating the general well for some time. It's an unpleasant business, and I don't want to dwell on it; but it's pretty plain that his wife was not treating him well, either. I don't know how far it went, but it went as far as concealment, anyhow; for when Lady Hastings spoke to Boyle it was to tell him she had hidden a note in the Budge book in the library. The general overheard, or came somehow to know, and he went straight to the book and found it. He confronted Boyle with it, and they had a scene, of course. And Boyle was confronted with something else; he was confronted with an awful alternative, in which the life of one old man meant ruin and his death meant triumph and even happiness."

"Well," observed Fisher, at last, "I don't blame him for not telling you the woman's part of the story. But how do you know about the letter?"

"I found it on the general's body," answered Grayne, "but I found worse things than that. The body had stiffened in the way rather peculiar to poisons of a certain Asiatic sort. Then I examined the coffee cups, and I knew enough chemistry to find poison in the dregs of one of them. Now, the General went straight to the bookcase, leaving his cup of coffee on the bookstand in the middle of the room. While his back was turned, and Boyle was pretending to examine the bookstand, he was left alone with the coffee cup. The poison takes about ten minutes to act, and ten minutes' walk would bring them to the bottomless well."

"Yes," remarked Fisher, "and what about the bottomless well?"

"What has the bottomless well got to do with it?" asked his friend.

"It has nothing to do with it," replied Fisher. "That is what I find utterly confounding and incredible."

"And why should that particular hole in the ground have anything to do with it?"

"It is a particular hole in your case," said Fisher. "But I won't insist on that just now. By the way, there is another thing I ought to tell you. I said I sent Boyle away in charge of Travers. It would be just as true to say I sent Travers in charge of Boyle."

"You don't mean to say you suspect Tom Travers?" cried the other.

"He was a deal bitterer against the general than Boyle ever was," observed Horne Fisher, with a curious indifference.

"Man, you're not saying what you mean," cried Grayne. "I tell you I found the poison in one of the coffee cups."

"There was always Said, of course," added Fisher, "either for hatred or hire. We agreed he was capable of almost anything."

"And we agreed he was incapable of hurting his master," retorted Grayne.

"Well, well," said Fisher, amiably, "I dare say you are right; but I should just like to have a look at the library and the coffee cups."

He passed inside, while Grayne turned to the policeman in attendance and handed him a scribbled note, to be telegraphed from headquarters. The man saluted and hurried off; and Grayne, following his friend into the library, found him beside the bookstand in the middle of the room, on which were the empty cups.

"This is where Boyle looked for Budge, or pretended to look for him, according to your account," he said.

As Fisher spoke he bent down in a half-crouching attitude, to look at the volumes in the low, revolving shelf, for the whole bookstand was not much higher than an ordinary table. The next moment he sprang up as if he had been stung.

"Oh, my God!" he cried.

Very few people, if any, had ever seen Mr. Horne Fisher behave as he behaved just then. He flashed a glance at the door, saw that the open window was nearer, went out of it with a flying leap, as if over a hurdle, and went racing across the turf, in the track of the disappearing policeman. Grayne, who stood staring after him, soon saw his tall, loose figure, returning, restored to all its normal limpness and air of leisure. He was fanning himself slowly with a piece of paper, the telegram he had so violently intercepted.

"Lucky I stopped that," he observed. "We must keep this affair as quiet as death. Hastings must die of apoplexy or heart disease."

"What on earth is the trouble?" demanded the other investigator.

"The trouble is," said Fisher, "that in a few days we should have had a very agreeable alternative—of hanging an innocent man or knocking the British Empire to hell."

"Do you mean to say," asked Grayne, "that this infernal crime is not to be punished?"

Fisher looked at him steadily.

"It is already punished," he said.

After a moment's pause he went on. "You reconstructed the crime with admirable skill, old chap, and nearly all you said was true. Two men with two coffee cups did go into the library and did put their cups on the bookstand and did go together to the well, and one of them was a murderer and had put poison in the other's cup. But it was not done while Boyle was looking at the revolving bookcase. He did look at it, though, searching for the Budge book with the note in it, but I fancy that Hastings had already moved it to the shelves on the wall. It was part of that grim game that he should find it first.

"Now, how does a man search a revolving bookcase? He does not generally hop all round it in a squatting attitude, like a frog. He simply gives it a touch and makes it revolve."

He was frowning at the floor as he spoke, and there was a light under his heavy lids that was not often seen there. The mysticism that was buried deep under all the cynicism of his experience was awake and moving in the depths. His voice took unexpected turns and inflections, almost as if two men were speaking.

"That was what Boyle did; he barely touched the thing, and it went round as easily as the world goes round. Yes, very much as the world goes round, for the hand that turned it was not his. God, who turns the wheel of all the stars, touched that wheel and brought it full circle, that His dreadful justice might return."

"I am beginning," said Grayne, slowly, "to have some hazy and horrible idea of what you mean."

"It is very simple," said Fisher, "when Boyle straightened himself from his stooping posture, something had happened which he had not noticed, which his enemy had not noticed, which nobody had noticed. The two coffee cups had exactly changed places."

The rocky face of Grayne seemed to have sustained a shock in silence; not a line of it altered, but his voice when it came was unexpectedly weakened.

"I see what you mean," he said, "and, as you say, the less said about it the better. It was not the lover who tried to get rid of the husband, but—the other thing. And a tale like that about a man like that would ruin us here. Had you any guess of this at the start?"

"The bottomless well, as I told you," answered Fisher, quietly; "that was what stumped me from the start. Not because it had anything to do with it, because it had nothing to do with it."

He paused a moment, as if choosing an approach, and then went on: "When a man knows his enemy will be dead in ten minutes, and takes him to the edge of an unfathomable pit, he means to throw his body into it. What else should he do? A born fool would have the sense to do it, and Boyle is not a born fool. Well, why did not Boyle do it? The more I thought of it the more I suspected there was some mistake in the murder, so to speak. Somebody had taken somebody there to throw him in, and yet he was not thrown in. I had already an ugly, unformed idea of some substitution or reversal of parts; then I stooped to turn the bookstand myself, by accident, and I instantly knew everything, for I saw the two cups revolve once more, like moons in the sky."

After a pause, Cuthbert Grayne said, "And what are we to say to the newspapers?"

"My friend, Harold March, is coming along from Cairo to-day," said Fisher. "He is a very brilliant and successful journalist. But for all that he's a thoroughly honorable man, so you must not tell him the truth."

Half an hour later Fisher was again walking to and fro in front of the clubhouse, with Captain Boyle, the latter by this time with a very buffeted and bewildered air; perhaps a sadder and a wiser man.

"What about me, then?" he was saying. "Am I cleared? Am I not going to be cleared?"

"I believe and hope," answered Fisher, "that you are not going to be suspected. But you are certainly not going to be cleared. There must be no suspicion against him, and therefore no suspicion against you. Any suspicion against him, let alone such a story against him, would knock us endways from Malta to Mandalay. He was a hero as well as a holy terror among the Moslems. Indeed, you might almost call him a Moslem hero in the English service. Of course he got on with them partly because of his own little dose of Eastern blood; he got it from his mother, the dancer from Damascus; everybody knows that."

"Oh," repeated Boyle, mechanically, staring at him with round eyes, "everybody knows that."

"I dare say there was a touch of it in his jealousy and ferocious vengeance," went on Fisher. "But, for all that, the crime would ruin us among the Arabs, all the more because it was something like a crime against hospitality. It's been hateful for you and it's pretty horrid for me. But there are some things that damned well can't be done, and while I'm alive that's one of them."

"What do you mean?" asked Boyle, glancing at him curiously. "Why should you, of all people, be so passionate about it?"

Horne Fisher looked at the young man with a baffling expression.

"I suppose," he said, "it's because I'm a Little Englander."

"I can never make out what you mean by that sort of thing," answered Boyle, doubtfully.

"Do you think England is so little as all that?" said Fisher, with a warmth in his cold voice, "that it can't hold a man across a few thousand miles. You lectured me with a lot of ideal patriotism, my young friend; but it's practical patriotism now for you and me, and with no lies to help it. You talked as if everything always went right with us all over the world, in a triumphant crescendo culminating in Hastings. I tell you everything has gone wrong with us here, except Hastings. He was the one name we had left to conjure with, and that mustn't go as well, no, by God! It's bad enough that a gang of infernal Jews should plant us here, where there's no earthly English interest to serve, and all hell beating up against us, simply because Nosey Zimmern has lent money to half the

Cabinet. It's bad enough that an old pawnbroker from Bagdad should make us fight his battles; we can't fight with our right hand cut off. Our one score was Hastings and his victory, which was really somebody else's victory. Tom Travers has to suffer, and so have you."

Then, after a moment's silence, he pointed toward the bottomless well and said, in a quieter tone:

"I told you that I didn't believe in the philosophy of the Tower of Aladdin. I don't believe in the Empire growing until it reaches the sky; I don't believe in the Union Jack going up and up eternally like the Tower. But if you think I am going to let the Union Jack go down and down eternally, like the bottomless well, down into the blackness of the bottomless pit, down in defeat and derision, amid the jeers of the very Jews who have sucked us dry—no I won't, and that's flat; not if the Chancellor were blackmailed by twenty millionaires with their gutter rags, not if the Prime Minister married twenty Yankee Jewesses, not if Woodville and Carstairs had shares in twenty swindling mines. If the thing is really tottering, God help it, it mustn't be we who tip it over."

Boyle was regarding him with a bewilderment that was almost fear, and had even a touch of distaste.

"Somehow," he said, "there seems to be something rather horrid about the things you know."

"There is," replied Horne Fisher. "I am not at all pleased with my small stock of knowledge and reflection. But as it is partly responsible for your not being hanged, I don't know that you need complain of it."

And, as if a little ashamed of his first boast, he turned and strolled away toward the bottomless well.

5

THE FAD OF THE FISHERMAN

A thing can sometimes be too extraordinary to be remembered. If it is clean out of the course of things, and has apparently no causes and no consequences, subsequent events do not recall it, and it remains only a subconscious thing, to be stirred by some accident long after. It drifts apart like a forgotten dream; and it was in the hour of many dreams, at daybreak and very soon after the end of dark, that such a strange sight was given to a man sculling a boat down a river in the West country. The man was awake; indeed, he considered himself rather wide awake, being the political journalist, Harold March, on his way to interview various political celebrities in their country seats. But the thing he saw was so inconsequent that it might have been imaginary. It simply slipped past his mind and was lost in later and utterly different events; nor did he even recover the memory till he had long afterward discovered the meaning.

Pale mists of morning lay on the fields and the rushes along one margin of the river; along the other side ran a wall of tawny brick almost overhanging the water. He had shipped his oars and was drifting for a moment with the stream, when he turned his head and saw that the monotony of the long brick wall was broken by a bridge; rather an elegant eighteenth-century sort of bridge with little columns of white stone turning gray. There had been floods and the river still stood very high, with dwarfish trees waist deep in it, and rather a narrow arc of white dawn gleamed under the curve of the bridge.

As his own boat went under the dark archway he saw another boat coming toward him, rowed by a man as solitary as himself. His posture prevented much being seen of him, but as he neared the bridge he stood up in the boat and turned round. He was already so close to the dark entry, however, that his whole figure was black against the morning light, and March could see nothing of his face except the end of two long whiskers or mustaches that gave something sinister to the silhouette, like horns in the wrong place. Even these details March would never have noticed but for what happened in the same instant. As the man came under the low bridge he made a leap at it and hung, with his legs dangling, letting the boat float away from under him. March had a momentary vision of two black kicking legs; then of one black kicking leg; and then of nothing except the eddying stream and the long perspective of the wall. But whenever he thought of it again, long afterward, when he understood the story in which it figured, it was always fixed in that one fantastic shape—as if those wild legs were a grotesque graven ornament of the bridge itself, in the manner of a gargoyle. At the moment he merely passed, staring, down the stream. He could see no flying figure on the bridge, so it must have already fled; but he was half conscious of some faint significance in the fact that among the trees round the bridgehead opposite the wall he saw a lamp-post; and, beside the lamp-post, the broad blue back of an unconscious policeman.

Even before reaching the shrine of his political pilgrimage he had many other things to think of besides the odd incident of the bridge; for the management of a boat by a solitary man was not always easy even on such a solitary stream. And indeed it was only by an unforeseen accident that he was solitary. The boat had been purchased and the whole expedition planned in conjunction with a friend, who had at the last moment been forced to alter all his arrangements. Harold March was to have traveled with his friend Horne Fisher on that inland voyage to Willowood Place, where the Prime Minister was a guest at the moment. More and more people were hearing of Harold March, for his striking political articles were opening to him the doors of larger and larger salons; but he had never met the Prime Minister yet. Scarcely anybody among the general public had ever heard of Horne Fisher; but he had known the Prime Minister all his life. For these reasons, had the two taken the projected journey together, March might have been slightly disposed to hasten it and Fisher vaguely content to lengthen it out. For Fisher was one of those people who are born knowing the Prime Minister. The knowledge seemed to have no very exhilarant effect, and in his case bore some resemblance to being born tired. But he was distinctly annoyed to receive, just as he was doing a little light packing of fishing tackle and cigars for the journey, a telegram from Willowood asking him to come down at once by train, as the Prime Minister had to leave that night. Fisher knew that his friend the journalist could not possibly start till the next day, and he liked his friend the journalist, and had looked forward to a few days on the river. He did not particularly like or dislike the Prime Minister, but he intensely disliked the alternative of a few hours in the train. Nevertheless, he accepted Prime Ministers as he accepted railway trains—as part of a system which he, at least, was not the revolutionist sent on earth to destroy. So he telephoned to March, asking him, with many apologetic curses and faint damns, to take the boat down the river as arranged, that they might meet at Willowood by the time settled; then he went outside and hailed a taxicab to take him to the railway station. There he paused at the bookstall to add to his light luggage a number of cheap murder stories, which he read with great pleasure, and without any premonition that he was about to walk into as strange a story in real life.

A little before sunset he arrived, with his light suitcase in hand, before the gate of the long riverside gardens of Willowood Place, one of the smaller seats of Sir Isaac Hook, the master of much shipping and many newspapers. He entered by the gate giving on the road, at the opposite side to the river, but there was a mixed quality in all that watery landscape which perpetually reminded a traveler that the river was near. White gleams of water would shine suddenly like swords or spears in the green thickets. And even in the garden itself, divided into courts and curtained with hedges and high garden trees, there hung everywhere in the air the music of water. The first of the green courts which he entered appeared to be a somewhat neglected croquet lawn, in which was a solitary young man playing croquet against himself. Yet he was not an enthusiast for the game, or even for the garden; and his sallow but well-featured face looked rather sullen than otherwise. He was only one of those young men who cannot support the burden of consciousness unless they are doing something, and whose conceptions of doing something are limited to a game of some kind. He was dark and well dressed in a light holiday fashion, and Fisher recognized him at once as a young man named James Bullen, called, for some unknown reason, Bunker. He was the nephew of Sir Isaac; but, what was much more important at the moment, he was also the private secretary of the Prime Minister.

"Hullo, Bunker!" observed Horne Fisher. "You're the sort of man I wanted to see. Has your chief come down yet?"

"He's only staying for dinner," replied Bullen, with his eye on the yellow ball. "He's got a great speech to-morrow at Birmingham and he's going straight through to-night. He's motoring himself there; driving the car, I mean. It's the one thing he's really proud of."

"You mean you're staying here with your uncle, like a good boy?" replied Fisher. "But what will the Chief do at Birmingham without the epigrams whispered to him by his brilliant secretary?"

"Don't you start ragging me," said the young man called Bunker. "I'm only too glad not to go trailing after him. He doesn't know a thing about maps or money or hotels or anything, and I have to dance about like a courier. As for my uncle, as I'm supposed to come into the estate, it's only decent to be here sometimes."

"Very proper," replied the other. "Well, I shall see you later on," and, crossing the lawn, he passed out through a gap in the hedge.

He was walking across the lawn toward the landing stage on the river, and still felt all around him, under the dome of golden evening, an Old World savor and reverberation in that riverhaunted garden. The next square of turf which he crossed seemed at first sight quite deserted, till he saw in the twilight of trees in one corner of it a hammock and in the hammock a man, reading a newspaper and swinging one leg over the edge of the net.

Him also he hailed by name, and the man slipped to the ground and strolled forward. It seemed fated that he should feel something of the past in the accidents of that place, for the figure might well have been an early-Victorian ghost revisiting the ghosts of the croquet hoops and mallets. It was the figure of an elderly man with long whiskers that looked almost fantastic, and a quaint and careful cut of collar and cravat. Having been a fashionable dandy forty years ago, he had managed to preserve the dandyism while ignoring the fashions. A white top-hat lay beside the Morning Post in the hammock behind him. This was the Duke of Westmoreland, the relic of a family really some centuries old; and the antiquity was not heraldry but history. Nobody knew better than Fisher how rare such noblemen are in fact, and how numerous in fiction. But whether the duke owed the general respect he enjoyed to the genuineness of his pedigree or to the fact that he owned a vast amount of very valuable property was a point about which Mr. Fisher's opinion might have been more interesting to discover.

"You were looking so comfortable," said Fisher, "that I thought you must be one of the servants. I'm looking for somebody to take this bag of mine; I haven't brought a man down, as I came away in a hurry."

"Nor have I, for that matter," replied the duke, with some pride. "I never do. If there's one animal alive I loathe it's a valet. I learned to dress myself at an early age and was supposed to do it decently. I may be in my second childhood, but I've not go so far as being dressed like a child."

"The Prime Minister hasn't brought a valet; he's brought a secretary instead," observed Fisher. "Devilish inferior job. Didn't I hear that Harker was down here?"

"He's over there on the landing stage," replied the duke, indifferently, and resumed the study of the Morning Post.

Fisher made his way beyond the last green wall of the garden on to a sort of towing path looking on the river and a wooden island opposite. There, indeed, he saw a lean, dark figure with a stoop almost like that of a vulture, a posture well known in the law courts as that of Sir John Harker, the Attorney-General. His face was lined with headwork, for alone among the three idlers in the garden he was a man who had made his own way; and round his bald brow and hollow temples clung dull red hair, quite flat, like plates of copper.

"I haven't seen my host yet," said Horne Fisher, in a slightly more serious tone than he had used to the others, "but I suppose I shall meet him at dinner."

"You can see him now; but you can't meet him," answered Harker.

He nodded his head toward one end of the island opposite, and, looking steadily in the same direction, the other guest could see the dome of a bald head and the top of a fishing rod, both equally motionless, rising out of the tall undergrowth against the background of the stream beyond. The fisherman seemed to be seated against the stump of a tree and facing toward the other bank, so that his face could not be seen, but the shape of his head was unmistakable.

"He doesn't like to be disturbed when he's fishing," continued Harker. "It's a sort of fad of his to eat nothing but fish, and he's very proud of catching his own. Of course he's all for simplicity, like so many of these millionaires. He likes to come in saying he's worked for his daily bread like a laborer."

"Does he explain how he blows all the glass and stuffs all the upholstery," asked Fisher, "and makes all the silver forks, and grows all the grapes and peaches, and designs all the patterns on the carpets? I've always heard he was a busy man."

"I don't think he mentioned it," answered the lawyer. "What is the meaning of this social satire?"

"Well, I am a trifle tired," said Fisher, "of the Simple Life and the Strenuous Life as lived by our little set. We're all really dependent in nearly everything, and we all make a fuss about being independent in something. The Prime Minister prides himself on doing without a chauffeur, but he can't do without a factotum and Jack-of-all-trades; and poor old Bunker has to play the part of a universal genius, which God knows he was never meant for. The duke prides himself on doing without a valet, but, for all that, he must give a lot of people an infernal lot of trouble to collect such extraordinary old clothes as he wears. He must have them looked up in the British Museum or excavated out of the tombs. That white hat alone must require a sort of expedition fitted out to find it, like the North Pole. And here we have old Hook pretending to produce his own fish when he couldn't produce his own fish knives or fish forks to eat it with. He may be simple about simple things like food, but you bet he's luxurious about luxurious things, especially little things. I don't include you; you've worked too hard to enjoy playing at work."

"I sometimes think," said Harker, "that you conceal a horrid secret of being useful sometimes. Haven't you come down here to see Number One before he goes on to Birmingham?"

Horne Fisher answered, in a lower voice: "Yes; and I hope to be lucky enough to catch him before dinner. He's got to see Sir Isaac about something just afterward."

"Hullo!" exclaimed Harker. "Sir Isaac's finished his fishing. I know he prides himself on getting up at sunrise and going in at sunset."

The old man on the island had indeed risen to his feet, facing round and showing a bush of gray beard with rather small, sunken features, but fierce eyebrows and keen, choleric eyes. Carefully carrying his fishing tackle, he was already making his way back to the mainland across a bridge of flat stepping-stones a little way down the shallow stream; then he veered round, coming toward his guests and civilly saluting them. There were several fish in his basket and he was in a good temper.

"Yes," he said, acknowledging Fisher's polite expression of surprise, "I get up before anybody else in the house, I think. The early bird catches the worm."

"Unfortunately," said Harker, "it is the early fish that catches the worm."

"But the early man catches the fish," replied the old man, gruffly.

"But from what I hear, Sir Isaac, you are the late man, too," interposed Fisher. "You must do with very little sleep."

"I never had much time for sleeping," answered Hook, "and I shall have to be the late man to-night, anyhow. The Prime Minister wants to have a talk, he tells me, and, all things considered, I think we'd better be dressing for dinner."

Dinner passed off that evening without a word of politics and little enough but ceremonial trifles. The Prime Minister, Lord Merivale, who was a long, slim man with curly gray hair, was gravely complimentary to his host about his success as a fisherman and the skill and patience he displayed; the conversation flowed like the shallow stream through the stepping-stones.

"It wants patience to wait for them, no doubt," said Sir Isaac, "and skill to play them, but I'm generally pretty lucky at it."

"Does a big fish ever break the line and get away?" inquired the politician, with respectful interest.

"Not the sort of line I use," answered Hook, with satisfaction. "I rather specialize in tackle, as a matter of fact. If he were strong enough to do that, he'd be strong enough to pull me into the river."

"A great loss to the community," said the Prime Minister, bowing.

Fisher had listened to all these futilities with inward impatience, waiting for his own opportunity, and when the host rose he sprang to his feet with an alertness he rarely showed. He managed to catch Lord Merivale before Sir Isaac bore him off for the final interview. He had only a few words to say, but he wanted to get them said.

He said, in a low voice as he opened the door for the Premier, "I have seen

Montmirail; he says that unless we protest immediately on behalf of Denmark, Sweden will certainly seize the ports."

Lord Merivale nodded. "I'm just going to hear what Hook has to say about it," he said.

"I imagine," said Fisher, with a faint smile, "that there is very little doubt what he will say about it."

Merivale did not answer, but lounged gracefully toward the library, whither his host had already preceded him. The rest drifted toward the billiard room, Fisher merely remarking to the lawyer: "They won't be long. We know they're practically in agreement."

"Hook entirely supports the Prime Minister," assented Harker.

"Or the Prime Minister entirely supports Hook," said Horne Fisher, and began idly to knock the balls about on the billiard table.

Horne Fisher came down next morning in a late and leisurely fashion, as was his reprehensible habit; he had evidently no appetite for catching worms. But the other guests seemed to have felt a similar indifference, and they helped themselves to breakfast from the sideboard at intervals during the hours verging upon lunch. So that it was not many hours later when the first sensation of that strange day came upon them. It came in the form of a young man with light hair and a candid expression, who came sculling down the river and disembarked at the landing stage. It was, in fact, no other than Mr. Harold March, whose journey had begun far away up the river in the earliest hours of that day. He arrived late in the afternoon, having stopped for tea in a large riverside town, and he had a pink evening paper sticking out of his pocket. He fell on the riverside garden like a quiet and well-behaved thunderbolt, but he was a thunderbolt without knowing it.

The first exchange of salutations and introductions was commonplace enough, and consisted, indeed, of the inevitable repetition of excuses for the eccentric seclusion of the host. He had gone fishing again, of course, and must not be disturbed till the appointed hour, though he sat within a stone's throw of where they stood.

"You see it's his only hobby," observed Harker, apologetically, "and, after all, it's his own house; and he's very hospitable in other ways."

"I'm rather afraid," said Fisher, in a lower voice, "that it's becoming more of a mania than a hobby. I know how it is when a man of that age begins to collect things, if it's only collecting those rotten little river fish. You remember Talbot's uncle with his toothpicks, and poor old Buzzy and the waste of cigar ashes. Hook has done a lot of big things in his time—the great deal in the Swedish timber trade and the Peace Conference at Chicago—but I doubt whether he cares now for any of those big things as he cares for those little fish."

"Oh, come, come," protested the Attorney-General. "You'll make Mr. March think he has come to call on a lunatic. Believe me, Hook only does it for fun, like any other sport, only he's of the kind that takes his fun sadly. But I bet if there were big news about timber or shipping, he would drop his fun and his fish all right."

"Well, I wonder," said Horne Fisher, looking sleepily at the island in the river.

"By the way, is there any news of anything?" asked Harker of Harold March. "I see you've got an evening paper; one of those enterprising evening papers that come out in the morning."

"The beginning of Lord Merivale's Birmingham speech," replied March, handing him the paper. "It's only a paragraph, but it seems to me rather good."

Harker took the paper, flapped and refolded it, and looked at the "Stop Press" news. It was, as March had said, only a paragraph. But it was a paragraph that had a peculiar effect on Sir John Harker. His lowering brows lifted with a flicker and his eyes blinked, and for a moment his leathery jaw was loosened. He looked in some odd fashion like a very old man. Then, hardening his voice and handing the paper to Fisher without a tremor, he simply said:

"Well, here's a chance for the bet. You've got your big news to disturb the old man's fishing."

Horne Fisher was looking at the paper, and over his more languid and less expressive features a change also seemed to pass. Even that little paragraph had two or three large headlines, and his eye encountered, "Sensational Warning to Sweden," and, "We Shall Protest."

"What the devil—" he said, and his words softened first to a whisper and then a whistle.

"We must tell old Hook at once, or he'll never forgive us," said Harker. "He'll probably want to see Number One instantly, though it may be too late now. I'm going across to him at once. I bet I'll make him forget his fish, anyhow." And, turning his back, he made his way hurriedly along the riverside to the causeway of flat stones.

March was staring at Fisher, in amazement at the effect his pink paper had produced.

"What does it all mean?" he cried. "I always supposed we should protest in defense of the Danish ports, for their sakes and our own. What is all this botheration about Sir Isaac and the rest of you? Do you think it bad news?"

"Bad news!" repeated Fisher, with a sort of soft emphasis beyond expression.

"Is it as bad as all that?" asked his friend, at last.

"As bad as all that?" repeated Fisher. "Why of course it's as good as it can be. It's great news. It's glorious news! That's where the devil of it comes in, to knock us all silly. It's admirable. It's inestimable. It is also quite incredible."

He gazed again at the gray and green colors of the island and the river, and his rather dreary eye traveled slowly round to the hedges and the lawns.

"I felt this garden was a sort of dream," he said, "and I suppose I must be dreaming. But there is grass growing and water moving; and something impossible has happened."

Even as he spoke the dark figure with a stoop like a vulture appeared in the gap of the hedge just above him.

"You have won your bet," said Harker, in a harsh and almost croaking voice. "The old fool cares for nothing but fishing. He cursed me and told me he would talk no politics."

"I thought it might be so," said Fisher, modestly. "What are you going to do next?"

"I shall use the old idiot's telephone, anyhow," replied the lawyer. "I must find out exactly what has happened. I've got to speak for the Government myself to-morrow." And he hurried away toward the house.

In the silence that followed, a very bewildering silence so far as March was concerned, they saw the quaint figure of the Duke of Westmoreland, with his white hat and whiskers, approaching them across the garden. Fisher instantly stepped toward him with the pink paper in his hand, and, with a few words, pointed out the apocalyptic paragraph. The duke, who had been walking slowly, stood quite still, and for some seconds he looked like a tailor's dummy standing and staring outside some antiquated shop. Then March heard his voice, and it was high and almost hysterical:

"But he must see it; he must be made to understand. It cannot have been put to him properly." Then, with a certain recovery of fullness and even pomposity in the voice, "I shall go and tell him myself."

Among the queer incidents of that afternoon, March always remembered something almost comical about the clear picture of the old gentleman in his wonderful white hat carefully stepping from stone to stone across the river, like a figure crossing the traffic in Piccadilly. Then he disappeared behind the trees of the island, and March and Fisher turned to meet the Attorney-General, who was coming out of the house with a visage of grim assurance.

"Everybody is saying," he said, "that the Prime Minister has made the greatest speech of his life. Peroration and loud and prolonged cheers. Corrupt financiers and heroic peasants. We will not desert Denmark again."

Fisher nodded and turned away toward the towing path, where he saw the duke returning with a rather dazed expression. In answer to questions he said, in a husky and confidential voice:

"I really think our poor friend cannot be himself. He refused to listen; he—ah—suggested that I might frighten the fish."

A keen ear might have detected a murmur from Mr. Fisher on the subject of a white hat, but Sir John Harker struck it more decisively:

"Fisher was quite right. I didn't believe it myself, but it's quite clear that the old fellow is fixed on this fishing notion by now. If the house caught fire behind him he would hardly move till sunset."

Fisher had continued his stroll toward the higher embanked ground of the towing path, and he now swept a long and searching gaze, not toward the island, but toward the distant wooded heights that were the walls of the valley. An evening sky as clear as that of the previous day was settling down all over the dim landscape, but toward the west it was now red rather than gold; there was scarcely any sound but the monotonous music of the river. Then came the sound of a half-stifled exclamation from Horne Fisher, and Harold March looked up at him in wonder.

"You spoke of bad news," said Fisher. "Well, there is really bad news now. I am afraid this is a bad business."

"What bad news do you mean?" asked his friend, conscious of something strange and sinister in his voice.

"The sun has set," answered Fisher.

He went on with the air of one conscious of having said something fatal. "We must get somebody to go across whom he will really listen to. He may be mad, but there's method in his madness. There nearly always is method in madness. It's what drives men mad, being methodical. And he never goes on sitting there after sunset, with the whole place getting dark. Where's his nephew? I believe he's really fond of his nephew."

"Look!" cried March, abruptly. "Why, he's been across already. There he is coming back."

And, looking up the river once more, they saw, dark against the sunset reflections, the figure of James Bullen stepping hastily and rather clumsily from stone to stone. Once he slipped on a stone with a slight splash. When he rejoined the group on the bank his olive face was unnaturally pale.

The other four men had already gathered on the same spot and almost simultaneously were calling out to him, "What does he say now?"

"Nothing. He says—nothing."

Fisher looked at the young man steadily for a moment; then he started from his immobility and, making a motion to March to follow him, himself strode down to the river crossing. In a few moments they were on the little beaten track that ran round the wooded island, to the other side of it where the fisherman sat. Then they stood and looked at him, without a word.

Sir Isaac Hook was still sitting propped up against the stump of the tree, and that for the best of reasons. A length of his own infallible fishing line was twisted and tightened twice round his throat and then twice round the wooden prop behind him. The leading investigator ran forward and touched the fisherman's hand, and it was as cold as a fish.

"The sun has set," said Horne Fisher, in the same terrible tones, "and he will never see it rise again."

Ten minutes afterward the five men, shaken by such a shock, were again together in the garden, looking at one another with white but watchful faces. The lawyer seemed the most alert of the group; he was articulate if somewhat abrupt.

"We must leave the body as it is and telephone for the police," he said. "I think my own authority will stretch to examining the servants and the poor fellow's papers, to see if there is anything that concerns them. Of course, none of you gentlemen must leave this place."

Perhaps there was something in his rapid and rigorous legality that suggested the closing of a net or trap. Anyhow, young Bullen suddenly broke down, or perhaps blew up, for his voice was like an explosion in the silent garden.

"I never touched him," he cried. "I swear I had nothing to do with it!"

"Who said you had?" demanded Harker, with a hard eye. "Why do you cry out before you're hurt?"

"Because you all look at me like that," cried the young man, angrily. "Do you think I don't know you're always talking about my damned debts and expectations?"

Rather to March's surprise, Fisher had drawn away from this first collision, leading the duke with him to another part of the garden. When he was out of earshot of the others he said, with a curious simplicity of manner:

"Westmoreland, I am going straight to the point."

"Well?" said the other, staring at him stolidly.

"You have a motive for killing him," said Fisher.

The duke continued to stare, but he seemed unable to speak.

"I hope you had a motive for killing him," continued Fisher, mildly. "You see, it's rather a curious situation. If you have a motive for murdering, you probably didn't murder. But if you hadn't any motive, why, then perhaps, you did."

"What on earth are you talking about?" demanded the duke, violently.

"It's quite simple," said Fisher. "When you went across he was either alive or dead. If he was alive, it might be you who killed him, or why should you have held your tongue about his death? But if he was dead, and you had a reason for killing him, you might have held your tongue for fear of being accused." Then after a silence he added, abstractedly: "Cyprus is a beautiful place, I believe. Romantic scenery and romantic people. Very intoxicating for a young man."

The duke suddenly clenched his hands and said, thickly, "Well, I had a motive."

"Then you're all right," said Fisher, holding out his hand with an air of huge relief. "I was pretty sure you wouldn't really do it; you had a fright when you saw it done, as was only natural. Like a bad dream come true, wasn't it?"

While this curious conversation was passing, Harker had gone into the house, disregarding the demonstrations of the sulky nephew, and came back presently with a new air of animation and a sheaf of papers in his hand.

"I've telephoned for the police," he said, stopping to speak to Fisher, "but I think I've done most of their work for them. I believe I've found out the truth. There's a paper here—" He stopped, for Fisher was looking at him with a singular expression; and it was Fisher who spoke next:

"Are there any papers that are not there, I wonder? I mean that are not there now?" After a pause he added: "Let us have the cards on the table. When you went through his papers in such a hurry, Harker, weren't you looking for something to—to make sure it shouldn't be found?"

Harker did not turn a red hair on his hard head, but he looked at the other out of the corners of his eyes.

"And I suppose," went on Fisher, smoothly, "that is why you, too, told us lies about having found Hook alive. You knew there was something to show that you might have killed him, and you didn't dare tell us he was killed. But, believe me, it's much better to be honest now."

Harker's haggard face suddenly lit up as if with infernal flames.

"Honest," he cried, "it's not so damned fine of you fellows to be honest. You're all born with silver spoons in your mouths, and then you swagger about with everlasting virtue because you haven't got other people's spoons in your pockets. But I was born in a Pimlico lodging house and I had to make my spoon, and there'd be plenty to say I only spoiled a horn or an honest man. And if a struggling man staggers a bit over the line in his youth, in the lower parts of the law which are pretty dingy, anyhow, there's always some old vampire to hang on to him all his life for it."

"Guatemalan Golcondas, wasn't it?" said Fisher, sympathetically.

Harker suddenly shuddered. Then he said, "I believe you must know everything, like God Almighty."

"I know too much," said Horne Fisher, "and all the wrong things."

The other three men were drawing nearer to them, but before they came too near, Harker said, in a voice that had recovered all its firmness:

"Yes, I did destroy a paper, but I really did find a paper, too; and I believe that it clears us all."

"Very well," said Fisher, in a louder and more cheerful tone; "let us all have the benefit of it."

"On the very top of Sir Isaac's papers," explained Harker, "there was a threatening letter from a man named Hugo. It threatens to kill our unfortunate friend very much in the way that he was actually killed. It is a wild letter, full of taunts; you can see it for yourselves; but it makes a particular point of poor Hook's habit of fishing from the island. Above all, the man professes to be writing from a boat. And, since we alone went across to him," and he smiled in a rather ugly fashion, "the crime must have been committed by a man passing in a boat."

"Why, dear me!" cried the duke, with something almost amounting to animation. "Why, I remember the man called Hugo quite well! He was a sort of body servant and bodyguard of Sir Isaac. You see, Sir Isaac was in some fear of assault. He was—he was not very popular with several people. Hugo was discharged after some row or other; but I remember him well. He was a great big Hungarian fellow with great mustaches that stood out on each side of his face."

A door opened in the darkness of Harold March's memory, or, rather, oblivion, and showed a shining landscape, like that of a lost dream. It was rather a waterscape than a landscape, a thing of flooded meadows and low trees and the dark archway of a bridge. And for one instant he saw again the man with mustaches like dark horns leap up on to the bridge and disappear.

"Good heavens!" he cried. "Why, I met the murderer this morning!"

Horne Fisher and Harold March had their day on the river, after all, for the little group broke up when the police arrived. They declared that the coincidence of March's evidence had cleared the whole company, and clinched the case against the flying Hugo. Whether that Hungarian fugitive would ever be caught appeared to Horne Fisher to be highly doubtful; nor can it be pretended that he displayed any very demoniac detective energy in the matter as he leaned back in the boat cushions, smoking, and watching the swaying reeds slide past.

"It was a very good notion to hop up on to the bridge," he said. "An empty boat means very little; he hasn't been seen to land on either bank, and he's walked off the bridge without walking on to it, so to speak. He's got twenty-four hours' start; his mustaches will disappear, and then he will disappear. I think there is every hope of his escape."

"Hope?" repeated March, and stopped sculling for an instant.

"Yes, hope," repeated the other. "To begin with, I'm not going to be exactly consumed with Corsican revenge because somebody has killed Hook. Perhaps you may guess by this time what Hook was. A damned blood-sucking blackmailer was that simple, strenuous, self-made captain of industry. He had secrets against nearly everybody; one against poor old Westmoreland about an early marriage in Cyprus that might have put the duchess in a queer position; and one against Harker about some flutter with his client's money when he was a young solicitor. That's why they went to pieces when they found him murdered, of course. They felt as if they'd done it in a dream. But I admit I have another reason for not wanting our Hungarian friend actually hanged for the murder."

"And what is that?" asked his friend.

"Only that he didn't commit the murder," answered Fisher.

Harold March laid down the oars and let the boat drift for a moment.

"Do you know, I was half expecting something like that," he said. "It was quite irrational, but it was hanging about in the atmosphere, like thunder in the air."

"On the contrary, it's finding Hugo guilty that's irrational," replied Fisher. "Don't you see that they're condemning him for the very reason for which they acquit everybody else? Harker and Westmoreland were silent because they found him murdered, and knew there were papers that made them look like the murderers. Well, so did Hugo find him murdered, and so did Hugo know there was a paper that would make him look like the murderer. He had written it himself the day before."

"But in that case," said March, frowning, "at what sort of unearthly hour in the morning was the murder really committed? It was barely daylight when I met him at the bridge, and that's some way above the island."

"The answer is very simple," replied Fisher. "The crime was not committed in the morning. The crime was not committed on the island."

March stared at the shining water without replying, but Fisher resumed like one who had been asked a question:

"Every intelligent murder involves taking advantage of some one uncommon feature in a common situation. The feature here was the fancy of old Hook for being the first man up every morning, his fixed routine as an angler, and his annoyance at being disturbed. The murderer strangled him in his own house after dinner on the night before, carried his corpse, with all his fishing tackle, across the stream in the dead of night, tied him to the tree, and left him there under the stars. It was a dead man who sat fishing there all day. Then the murderer went back to the house, or, rather, to the garage, and went off in his motor car. The murderer drove his own motor car."

Fisher glanced at his friend's face and went on. "You look horrified, and the thing is horrible. But other things are horrible, too. If some obscure man had been hag-ridden by a blackmailer and had his family life ruined, you wouldn't think the murder of his persecutor the most inexcusable of murders. Is it any worse when a whole great nation is set free as well as a family? By this warning to Sweden we shall probably prevent war and not precipitate it, and save many thousand lives rather more valuable than the life of that viper. Oh, I'm not talking sophistry or seriously justifying the thing, but the slavery that held him and his country was a thousand times less justifiable. If I'd really been sharp I should have guessed it from his smooth, deadly smiling at dinner that night. Do you remember that silly talk about how old Isaac could always play his fish? In a pretty hellish sense he was a fisher of men."

Harold March took the oars and began to row again.

"I remember," he said, "and about how a big fish might break the line and get away."

6

THE HOLE IN THE WALL

Two men, the one an architect and the other an archaeologist, met on the steps of the great house at Prior's Park; and their host, Lord Bulmer, in his breezy way, thought it natural to introduce them. It must be confessed that he was hazy as well as breezy, and had no very clear connection in his mind, beyond the sense that an architect and an archaeologist begin with the same series of letters. The world must remain in a reverent doubt as to whether he would, on the same principles, have presented a diplomatist to a dipsomaniac or a ratiocinator to a rat catcher. He was a big, fair, bull-necked young man, abounding in outward gestures, unconsciously flapping his gloves and flourishing his stick.

"You two ought to have something to talk about," he said, cheerfully. "Old buildings and all that sort of thing; this is rather an old building, by the way, though I say it who shouldn't. I must ask you to excuse me a moment; I've got to go and see about the cards for this Christmas romp my sister's arranging. We hope to see you all there, of course. Juliet wants it to be a fancy-dress affair—abbots and crusaders and all that. My ancestors, I suppose, after all."

"I trust the abbot was not an ancestor," said the archaeological gentleman, with a smile.

"Only a sort of great-uncle, I imagine," answered the other, laughing; then his rather rambling eye rolled round the ordered landscape in front of the house; an artificial sheet of water ornamented with an antiquated nymph in the center and surrounded by a park of tall trees now gray and black and frosty, for it was in the depth of a severe winter.

"It's getting jolly cold," his lordship continued. "My sister hopes we shall have some skating as well as dancing."

"If the crusaders come in full armor," said the other, "you must be careful not to drown your ancestors."

"Oh, there's no fear of that," answered Bulmer; "this precious lake of ours is not two feet deep anywhere." And with one of his flourishing gestures he stuck his stick into the water to demonstrate its shallowness. They could see the short end bent in the water, so that he seemed for a moment to lean his large weight on a breaking staff.

"The worst you can expect is to see an abbot sit down rather suddenly," he added, turning away. "Well, au revoir; I'll let you know about it later."

The archaeologist and the architect were left on the great stone steps smiling at each other; but whatever their common interests, they presented a considerable personal contrast, and the fanciful might even have found some contradiction in each considered individually. The former, a Mr. James Haddow, came from a drowsy den in the Inns of Court, full of leather and parchment, for the law was his profession and history only his hobby; he was indeed, among other things, the solicitor and agent of the Prior's Park estate. But he himself was far from drowsy and seemed remarkably wide awake, with shrewd and prominent blue eyes, and red hair brushed as neatly as his very neat costume. The latter, whose name was Leonard Crane, came straight from a crude and almost cockney office of builders and house agents in the neighboring suburb, sunning itself at the end of a new row of jerry-built houses with plans in very bright colors and notices in very large letters. But a serious observer, at a second glance, might have seen in his eyes something of that shining sleep that is called vision; and his yellow hair, while not affectedly long, was unaffectedly untidy. It was a manifest if melancholy truth that the architect was an artist. But the artistic temperament was far from explaining him; there was something else about him that was not definable, but which some even felt to be dangerous. Despite his dreaminess, he would sometimes surprise his friends with arts and even sports apart from his ordinary life, like memories of some previous existence. On this occasion, nevertheless, he hastened to disclaim any authority on the other man's hobby.

"I mustn't appear on false pretences," he said, with a smile. "I hardly even know what an archaeologist is, except that a rather rusty remnant of Greek suggests that he is a man who studies old things."

"Yes," replied Haddow, grimly. "An archaeologist is a man who studies old things and finds they are new."

Crane looked at him steadily for a moment and then smiled again.

"Dare one suggest," he said, "that some of the things we have been talking about are among the old things that turn out not to be old?"

His companion also was silent for a moment, and the smile on his rugged face was fainter as he replied, quietly:

"The wall round the park is really old. The one gate in it is Gothic, and I cannot find any trace of destruction or restoration. But the house and the estate generally—well the romantic ideas read into these things are often rather recent romances, things almost like fashionable novels. For instance, the very name of this place, Prior's Park, makes everybody think of it as a moonlit mediaeval abbey; I dare say the spiritualists by this time have discovered the ghost of a monk there. But, according to the only authoritative study of the matter I can find, the place was simply called Prior's as any rural place is called Podger's. It was the house of a Mr. Prior, a farmhouse, probably, that stood here at some time or other and was a local landmark. Oh, there are a great many examples of the same thing, here and everywhere else. This suburb of ours used to be a village, and because some of the people slurred the name and pronounced it Holliwell, many a minor poet indulged in fancies about a Holy Well, with spells and fairies and all the rest of it, filling the suburban drawing-rooms with the Celtic twilight. Whereas anyone acquainted with the facts knows that 'Hollinwall' simply means 'the hole in the wall,' and probably referred to some quite trivial accident. That's what I mean when I say that we don't so much find old things as we find new ones."

Crane seemed to have grown somewhat inattentive to the little lecture on antiquities and novelties, and the cause of his restlessness was soon apparent, and indeed approaching. Lord Bulmer's sister, Juliet Bray, was coming slowly across the lawn, accompanied by one gentleman and followed by two others. The young architect was in the illogical condition of mind in which he preferred three to one.

The man walking with the lady was no other than the eminent Prince Borodino, who was at least as famous as a distinguished diplomatist ought to be, in the interests of what is called secret diplomacy. He had been paying a round of visits at various English country houses, and exactly what he was doing for diplomacy at Prior's Park was as much a secret as any diplomatist could desire. The obvious thing to say of his appearance was that he would have been extremely handsome if he had not been entirely bald. But, indeed, that would itself be a rather bald way of putting it. Fantastic as it sounds, it would fit the case better to say that people would have been surprised to see hair growing on him; as surprised as if they had found hair growing on the bust of a Roman emperor. His tall figure was buttoned up in a tight-waisted fashion that rather accentuated his potential bulk, and he wore a red flower in his buttonhole. Of the two men walking behind one was also bald, but in a more partial and also a more premature fashion, for his drooping mustache was still yellow, and if his eyes were somewhat heavy it was with languor and not with age. It was Horne Fisher, and he was talking as easily and idly about everything as he always did. His companion was a more striking, and even more sinister, figure, and he had the added importance of being Lord Bulmer's oldest and most intimate friend. He was generally known with a severe simplicity as Mr. Brain; but it was understood that he had been a judge and police official in India, and that he had enemies, who had represented his measures against crime as themselves almost criminal. He was a brown skeleton of a man with dark, deep, sunken eyes and a black mustache that hid the meaning of his mouth. Though he had the look of one wasted by some tropical disease, his movements were much more alert than those of his lounging companion.

"It's all settled," announced the lady, with great animation, when they came within hailing distance. "You've all got to put on masquerade things and very likely skates as well, though the prince says they don't go with it; but we don't care about that. It's freezing already, and we don't often get such a chance in England."

"Even in India we don't exactly skate all the year round," observed Mr. Brain.

"And even Italy is not primarily associated with ice," said the Italian.

"Italy is primarily associated with ices," remarked Mr. Horne Fisher. "I mean with ice cream men. Most people in this country imagine that Italy is entirely populated with ice cream men and organ grinders. There certainly are a lot of them; perhaps they're an invading army in disguise."

"How do you know they are not the secret emissaries of our diplomacy?" asked the prince, with a slightly scornful smile. "An army of organ grinders might pick up hints, and their monkeys might pick up all sort of things."

"The organs are organized in fact," said the flippant Mr. Fisher. "Well, I've known it pretty cold before now in Italy and even in India, up on the Himalayan slopes. The ice on our own little round pond will be quite cozy by comparison."

Juliet Bray was an attractive lady with dark hair and eyebrows and dancing eyes, and there was a geniality and even generosity in her rather imperious ways. In most matters she could command her brother, though that nobleman, like many other men of vague ideas, was not without a touch of the bully when he was at bay. She could certainly command her guests, even to the extent of decking out the most respectable and reluctant of them with her mediaeval masquerade. And it really seemed as if she could command the elements also, like a witch. For the weather steadily hardened and sharpened; that night the ice of the lake, glimmering in the moonlight, was like a marble floor, and they had begun to dance and skate on it before it was dark.

Prior's Park, or, more properly, the surrounding district of Holinwall, was a country seat that had become a suburb; having once had only a dependent village at its doors, it now found outside all its doors the signals of the expansion of London. Mr. Haddow, who was engaged in historical researches both in the library and the locality, could find little assistance in the latter. He had already realized, from the documents, that Prior's Park had originally been something like Prior's Farm, named after some local figure, but the new social conditions were all against his tracing the story by its traditions. Had any of the real rustics remained, he would probably have found some lingering legend of Mr. Prior, however remote he might be. But the new nomadic population of clerks and artisans, constantly shifting their homes from one suburb to another, or their children from one school to another, could have no corporate continuity. They had all that forgetfulness of history that goes everywhere with the extension of education.

Nevertheless, when he came out of the library next morning and saw the wintry trees standing round the frozen pond like a black forest, he felt he might well have been far in the depths of the country. The old wall running round the park kept that inclosure itself still entirely rural and romantic, and one could easily imagine that the depths of that dark forest faded away indefinitely into distant vales and hills. The gray and black and silver of the wintry wood were all the more severe or somber as a contrast to the colored carnival groups that already stood on and around the frozen pool. For the house party had already flung themselves impatiently into fancy dress, and the lawyer, with his neat black suit and red hair, was the only modern figure among them.

"Aren't you going to dress up?" asked Juliet, indignantly shaking at him a horned and towering blue headdress of the fourteenth century which framed her face very becomingly, fantastic as it was. "Everybody here has to be in the Middle Ages. Even Mr. Brain has put on a sort of brown dressing gown and says he's a monk; and Mr. Fisher got hold of some old potato sacks in the kitchen and sewed them together; he's supposed to be a monk, too. As to the prince, he's perfectly glorious, in great crimson robes as a cardinal. He looks as if he could poison everybody. You simply must be something."

"I will be something later in the day," he replied. "At present I am nothing but an antiquary and an attorney. I have to see your brother presently, about some legal business and also some local investigations he asked me to make. I must look a little like a steward when I give an account of my stewardship."

"Oh, but my brother has dressed up!" cried the girl. "Very much so. No end, if I may say so. Why he's bearing down on you now in all his glory."

The noble lord was indeed marching toward them in a magnificent sixteenth-century costume of purple and gold, with a gold-hilted sword and a plumed cap, and manners to match. Indeed, there was something more than his usual expansiveness of bodily action in his appearance at that moment. It almost seemed, so to speak, that the plumes on his hat had gone to his head. He flapped his great, gold-lined cloak like the wings of a fairy king in a pantomime; he even drew his sword with a flourish and waved it about as he did his walking stick. In the light of after events there seemed to be something monstrous and ominous about that exuberance, something of the spirit that is called fey. At the time it merely crossed a few people's minds that he might possibly be drunk.

As he strode toward his sister the first figure he passed was that of Leonard Crane, clad in Lincoln green, with the horn and baldrick and sword appropriate to Robin Hood; for he was standing nearest to the lady, where, indeed, he might have been found during a disproportionate part of the time. He had displayed one of his buried talents in the matter of skating, and now that the skating was over seemed disposed to prolong the partnership. The boisterous Bulmer playfully made a pass at him with his drawn sword, going forward with the lunge in the proper fencing fashion, and making a somewhat too familiar Shakespearean quotation about a rodent and a Venetian coin.

Probably in Crane also there was a subdued excitement just then; anyhow, in one flash he had drawn his own sword and parried; and then suddenly, to the surprise of everyone, Bulmer's weapon seemed to spring out of his hand into the air and rolled away on the ringing ice.

"Well, I never!" said the lady, as if with justifiable indignation. "You never told me you could fence, too."

Bulmer put up his sword with an air rather bewildered than annoyed, which increased the impression of something irresponsible in his mood at the moment; then he turned rather abruptly to his lawyer, saying:

"We can settle up about the estate after dinner; I've missed nearly all the skating as it is, and I doubt if the ice will hold till to-morrow night. I think I shall get up early and have a spin by myself."

"You won't be disturbed with my company," said Horne Fisher, in his weary fashion. "If I have to begin the day with ice, in the American fashion, I prefer it in smaller quantities. But no early hours for me in December. The early bird catches the cold."

"Oh, I shan't die of catching a cold," answered Bulmer, and laughed.

A considerable group of the skating party had consisted of the guests staying at the house, and the rest had tailed off in twos and threes some time before most of the guests began to retire for the night. Neighbors, always invited to Prior's Park on such occasions, went back to their own houses in motors or on foot; the legal and archeological gentleman had returned to the Inns of Court by a late train, to get a paper called for during his consultation with his client; and most of the other guests were drifting and lingering at various stages on their way up to bed. Horne Fisher, as if to deprive himself of any excuse for his refusal of early rising, had been the first to retire to his room; but, sleepy as he looked, he could not sleep. He had picked up from a table the book of antiquarian topography, in which Haddow had found his first hints about the origin of the local name, and, being a man with a quiet and quaint capacity for being interested in anything, he began to read it steadily, making notes now and then of details on which his previous reading left him with a certain doubt about his present conclusions. His room was the one nearest to the lake in the center of the woods, and was therefore the quietest, and none of the last echoes of the evening's festivity could reach him. He had followed carefully the argument which established the derivation from Mr. Prior's farm and the hole in the wall, and disposed of any fashionable fancy about monks and magic wells, when he began to be conscious of a noise audible in the frozen silence of the night. It was not a particularly loud noise, but it seemed to consist of a series of thuds or heavy blows, such as might be struck on a wooden door by a man seeking to enter. They were followed by something like a faint creak or crack, as if the obstacle had either been opened or had given way. He opened his own bedroom door and listened, but as he heard talk and laughter all over the lower floors, he had no reason to fear that a summons would be neglected or the house left without protection. He went to his open window, looking out over the frozen pond and the moonlit statue in the middle of their circle of darkling woods, and listened again. But silence had returned to that silent place, and, after straining his ears for a considerable time, he could hear nothing but the solitary hoot of a distant departing train. Then he reminded himself how many nameless noises can be heard by the wakeful during the most ordinary night, and shrugging his shoulders, went wearily to bed.

He awoke suddenly and sat up in bed with his ears filled, as with thunder, with the throbbing echoes of a rending cry. He remained rigid for a moment, and then sprang out of bed, throwing on the loose gown of sacking he had worn all day. He went first to the window, which was open, but covered with a thick curtain, so that his room was still completely dark; but when he tossed the curtain aside and put his head out, he saw that a gray and silver daybreak had already appeared behind the black woods that surrounded the little lake, and that was all that he did see. Though the sound had certainly come in through the open window from this direction, the whole scene was still and empty under the morning light as under the moonlight. Then the long, rather lackadaisical hand he had laid on a window sill gripped it tighter, as if to master a tremor, and his peering blue eyes grew bleak with fear. It may seem that his emotion was exaggerated and needless, considering the effort of common sense by which he had conquered his nervousness about the noise on the previous night. But that had been a very different sort of noise. It might have been made by half a hundred things, from the chopping of wood to the breaking of bottles. There was only one thing in nature from which could come the sound that echoed through the dark house at daybreak. It was the awful articulate voice of man; and it was something worse, for he knew what man.

He knew also that it had been a shout for help. It seemed to him that he had heard the very word; but the word, short as it was, had been swallowed up, as if the man had been stifled or snatched away even as he spoke. Only the mocking reverberations of it remained even in his memory, but he had no doubt of the original voice. He had no doubt that the great bull's voice of Francis Bray, Baron Bulmer, had been heard for the last time between the darkness and the lifting dawn.

How long he stood there he never knew, but he was startled into life by the first living thing that he saw stirring in that half-frozen landscape. Along the path beside the lake, and immediately under his window, a figure was walking slowly and softly, but with great composure—a stately figure in robes of a splendid scarlet; it was the Italian prince, still in his cardinal's costume. Most of the company had indeed lived in their costumes for the last day or two, and Fisher himself had assumed his frock of sacking as a convenient dressing gown; but there seemed, nevertheless, something unusually finished and formal, in the way of an early bird, about this magnificent red cockatoo. It was as if the early bird had been up all night.

"What is the matter?" he called, sharply, leaning out of the window, and the Italian turned up his great yellow face like a mask of brass.

"We had better discuss it downstairs," said Prince Borodino.

Fisher ran downstairs, and encountered the great, red-robed figure entering the doorway and blocking the entrance with his bulk.

"Did you hear that cry?" demanded Fisher.

"I heard a noise and I came out," answered the diplomatist, and his face was too dark in the shadow for its expression to be read.

"It was Bulmer's voice," insisted Fisher. "I'll swear it was Bulmer's voice."

"Did you know him well?" asked the other.

The question seemed irrelevant, though it was not illogical, and Fisher could only answer in a random fashion that he knew Lord Bulmer only slightly.

"Nobody seems to have known him well," continued the Italian, in level tones. "Nobody except that man Brain. Brain is rather older than Bulmer, but I fancy they shared a good many secrets."

Fisher moved abruptly, as if waking from a momentary trance, and said, in a new and more vigorous voice, "But look here, hadn't we better get outside and see if anything has happened."

"The ice seems to be thawing," said the other, almost with indifference.

When they emerged from the house, dark stains and stars in the gray field of ice did indeed indicate that the frost was breaking up, as their host had prophesied the day before, and the very memory of yesterday brought back the mystery of to-day.

"He knew there would be a thaw," observed the prince. "He went out skating quite early on purpose. Did he call out because he landed in the water, do you think?"

Fisher looked puzzled. "Bulmer was the last man to bellow like that because he got his boots wet. And that's all he could do here; the water would hardly come up to the calf of a man of his size. You can see the flat weeds on the floor of the lake, as if it were through a thin pane of glass. No, if Bulmer had only broken the ice he wouldn't have said much at the moment, though possibly a good deal afterward. We should have found him stamping and damning up and down this path, and calling for clean boots."

"Let us hope we shall find him as happily employed," remarked the diplomatist. "In that case the voice must have come out of the wood."

"I'll swear it didn't come out of the house," said Fisher; and the two disappeared together into the twilight of wintry trees.

The plantation stood dark against the fiery colors of sunrise, a black fringe having that feathery appearance which makes trees when they are bare the very reverse of rugged. Hours and hours afterward, when the same dense, but delicate, margin was dark against the greenish colors opposite the sunset, the search thus begun at sunrise had not come to an end. By successive stages, and to slowly gathering groups of the company, it became apparent that the most extraordinary of all gaps had appeared in the party; the guests could find no trace of their host anywhere. The servants reported that his bed had been slept in and his skates and his fancy costume were gone, as if he had risen early for the purpose he had himself avowed. But from the top of the house to the bottom, from the walls round the park to the pond in the center, there was no trace of Lord Bulmer, dead or alive. Horne Fisher realized that a chilling premonition had already prevented him from expecting to find the man alive. But his bald brow was wrinkled over an entirely new and unnatural problem, in not finding the man at all.

He considered the possibility of Bulmer having gone off of his own accord, for some reason; but after fully weighing it he finally dismissed it. It was inconsistent with the unmistakable voice heard at daybreak, and with many other practical obstacles. There was only one gateway in the ancient and lofty wall round the small park; the lodge keeper kept it locked till late in the morning, and the lodge keeper had seen no one pass. Fisher was fairly sure that he had before him a mathematical problem in an inclosed space. His instinct had been from the first so attuned to the tragedy that it would have been almost a relief to him to find the corpse. He would have been grieved, but not horrified, to come on the nobleman's body dangling from one of his own trees as from a gibbet, or floating in his own pool like a pallid weed. What horrified him was to find nothing.

He soon become conscious that he was not alone even in his most individual and isolated experiments. He often found a figure following him like his shadow, in silent and almost secret clearings in the plantation or outlying nooks and corners of the old wall. The dark-mustached mouth was as mute as the deep eyes were mobile, darting incessantly hither and thither, but it was clear that Brain of the Indian police had taken up the trail like an old hunter after a tiger. Seeing that he was the only personal friend of the vanished man, this seemed natural enough, and Fisher resolved to deal frankly with him.

"This silence is rather a social strain," he said. "May I break the ice by talking about the weather?—which, by the way, has already broken the ice. I know that breaking the ice might be a rather melancholy metaphor in this case."

"I don't think so," replied Brain, shortly. "I don't fancy the ice had much to do with it. I don't see how it could."

"What would you propose doing?" asked Fisher.

"Well, we've sent for the authorities, of course, but I hope to find something out before they come," replied the Anglo-Indian. "I can't say I have much hope from police methods in this country. Too much red tape, habeas corpus and that sort of thing. What we want is to see that nobody bolts; the nearest we could get to it would be to collect the company and count them, so to speak. Nobody's left lately, except that lawyer who was poking about for antiquities."

"Oh, he's out of it; he left last night," answered the other. "Eight hours after Bulmer's chauffeur saw his lawyer off by the train I heard Bulmer's own voice as plain as I hear yours now."

"I suppose you don't believe in spirits?" said the man from India. After a pause he added: "There's somebody else I should like to find, before we go after a fellow with an alibi in the Inner Temple. What's become of that fellow in green—the architect dressed up as a forester? I haven't seem him about."

Mr. Brain managed to secure his assembly of all the distracted company before the arrival of the police. But when he first began to comment once more on the young architect's delay in putting in an appearance, he found himself in the presence of a minor mystery, and a psychological development of an entirely unexpected kind.

Juliet Bray had confronted the catastrophe of her brother's disappearance with a somber stoicism in which there was, perhaps, more paralysis than pain; but when the other question came to the surface she was both agitated and angry.

"We don't want to jump to any conclusions about anybody," Brain was saying in his staccato style. "But we should like to know a little more about Mr. Crane. Nobody seems to know much about him, or where he comes from. And it seems a sort of coincidence that yesterday he actually crossed swords with poor Bulmer, and could have stuck him, too, since he showed himself the better swordsman. Of course, that may be an accident and couldn't possibly be called a case against anybody; but then we haven't the means to make a real case against anybody. Till the police come we are only a pack of very amateur sleuthhounds."

"And I think you're a pack of snobs," said Juliet. "Because Mr. Crane is a genius who's made his own way, you try to suggest he's a murderer without daring to say so. Because he wore a toy sword and happened to know how to use it, you want us to believe he used it like a bloodthirsty maniac for no reason in the world. And because he could have hit my brother and didn't, you deduce that he did. That's the sort of way you argue. And as for his having disappeared, you're wrong in that as you are in everything else, for here he comes."

And, indeed, the green figure of the fictitious Robin Hood slowly detached itself from the gray background of the trees, and came toward them as she spoke.

He approached the group slowly, but with composure; but he was decidedly pale, and the eyes of Brain and Fisher had already taken in one detail of the green-clad figure more clearly than all the rest. The horn still swung from his baldrick, but the sword was gone.

Rather to the surprise of the company, Brain did not follow up the question thus suggested; but, while retaining an air of leading the inquiry, had also an appearance of changing the subject.

"Now we're all assembled," he observed, quietly, "there is a question I want to ask to begin with. Did anybody here actually see Lord Bulmer this morning?"

Leonard Crane turned his pale face round the circle of faces till he came to Juliet's; then he compressed his lips a little and said:

"Yes, I saw him."

"Was he alive and well?" asked Brain, quickly. "How was he dressed?"

"He appeared exceedingly well," replied Crane, with a curious intonation. "He was dressed as he was yesterday, in that purple costume copied from the portrait of his ancestor in the sixteenth century. He had his skates in his hand."

"And his sword at his side, I suppose," added the questioner. "Where is your own sword, Mr. Crane?"

"I threw it away."

In the singular silence that ensued, the train of thought in many minds became involuntarily a series of colored pictures.

They had grown used to their fanciful garments looking more gay and gorgeous against the dark gray and streaky silver of the forest, so that the moving figures glowed like stained-glass saints walking. The effect had been more fitting because so many of them had idly parodied pontifical or monastic dress. But the most arresting attitude that remained in their memories had been anything but merely monastic; that of the moment when the figure in bright green and the other in vivid violet had for a moment made a silver cross of their crossing swords. Even when it was a jest it had been something of a drama; and it was a strange and sinister thought that in the gray daybreak the same figures in the same posture might have been repeated as a tragedy.

"Did you quarrel with him?" asked Brain, suddenly.

"Yes," replied the immovable man in green. "Or he quarreled with me."

"Why did he quarrel with you?" asked the investigator; and Leonard Crane made no reply.

Horne Fisher, curiously enough, had only given half his attention to this crucial cross-examination. His heavy-lidded eyes had languidly followed the figure of Prince Borodino, who at this stage had strolled away toward the fringe of the wood; and, after a pause, as of meditation, had disappeared into the darkness of the trees.

He was recalled from his irrelevance by the voice of Juliet Bray, which rang out with an altogether new note of decision:

"If that is the difficulty, it had best be cleared up. I am engaged to Mr. Crane, and when we told my brother he did not approve of it; that is all."

Neither Brain nor Fisher exhibited any surprise, but the former added, quietly:

"Except, I suppose, that he and your brother went off into the wood to discuss it, where Mr. Crane mislaid his sword, not to mention his companion."

"And may I ask," inquired Crane, with a certain flicker of mockery passing over his pallid features, "what I am supposed to have done with either of them? Let us adopt the cheerful thesis that I am a murderer; it has yet to be shown that I am a magician. If I ran your unfortunate friend through the body, what did I do with the body? Did I have it carried away by seven flying dragons, or was it merely a trifling matter of turning it into a milk-white hind?"

"It is no occasion for sneering," said the Anglo-Indian judge, with abrupt authority. "It doesn't make it look better for you that you can joke about the loss."

Fisher's dreamy, and even dreary, eye was still on the edge of the wood behind, and he became conscious of masses of dark red, like a stormy sunset cloud, glowing through the gray network of the thin trees, and the prince in his cardinal's robes reemerged on to the pathway. Brain had had half a notion that the prince might have gone to look for the lost rapier. But when he reappeared he was carrying in his hand, not a sword, but an ax.

The incongruity between the masquerade and the mystery had created a curious psychological atmosphere. At first they had all felt horribly ashamed at being caught in the foolish disguises of a festival, by an event that had only too much the character of a funeral. Many of them would have already gone back and dressed in clothes that were more funereal or at least more formal. But somehow at the moment this seemed like a second masquerade, more artificial and frivolous than the first. And as they reconciled themselves to their ridiculous trappings, a curious sensation had come over some of them, notably over the more sensitive, like Crane and Fisher and Juliet, but in some degree over everybody except the practical Mr. Brain. It was almost as if they were the ghosts of their own ancestors haunting that dark wood and dismal lake, and playing some old part that they only half remembered. The movements of those colored figures seemed to mean something that had been settled long before, like a silent heraldry. Acts, attitudes, external objects, were accepted as an allegory even without the key; and they knew when a crisis had come, when they did not know what it was. And somehow they knew subconsciously that the whole tale had taken a new and terrible turn, when they saw the prince stand in the gap of the gaunt trees, in his robes of angry crimson and with his lowering face of bronze, bearing in his hand a new shape of death. They could not have named a reason, but the two swords seemed indeed to have become toy swords and the whole tale of them broken and tossed away like a toy. Borodino looked like the Old World headsman, clad in terrible red, and carrying the ax for the execution of the criminal. And the criminal was not Crane.

Mr. Brain of the Indian police was glaring at the new object, and it was a moment or two before he spoke, harshly and almost hoarsely.

"What are you doing with that?" he asked. "Seems to be a woodman's chopper."

"A natural association of ideas," observed Horne Fisher. "If you meet a cat in a wood you think it's a wildcat, though it may have just strolled from the drawing-room sofa. As a matter of fact, I happen to know that is not the woodman's chopper. It's the kitchen chopper, or meat ax, or something like that, that somebody has thrown away in the wood. I saw it in the kitchen myself when I was getting the potato sacks with which I reconstructed a mediaeval hermit."

"All the same, it is not without interest," remarked the prince, holding out the instrument to Fisher, who took it and examined it carefully. "A butcher's cleaver that has done butcher's work."

"It was certainly the instrument of the crime," assented Fisher, in a low voice.

Brain was staring at the dull blue gleam of the ax head with fierce and fascinated eyes. "I don't understand you," he said. "There is no—there are no marks on it."

"It has shed no blood," answered Fisher, "but for all that it has committed a crime. This is as near as the criminal came to the crime when he committed it."

"What do you mean?"

"He was not there when he did it," explained Fisher. "It's a poor sort of murderer who can't murder people when he isn't there."

"You seem to be talking merely for the sake of mystification," said Brain. "If you have any practical advice to give you might as well make it intelligible."

"The only practical advice I can suggest," said Fisher, thoughtfully, "is a little research into local topography and nomenclature. They say there used to be a Mr. Prior, who had a farm in this neighborhood. I think some details about the domestic life of the late Mr. Prior would throw a light on this terrible business."

"And you have nothing more immediate than your topography to offer," said Brain, with a sneer, "to help me avenge my friend?"

"Well," said Fisher, "I should find out the truth about the Hole in the Wall."

That night, at the close of a stormy twilight and under a strong west wind that followed the breaking of the frost, Leonard Crane was wending his way in a wild rotatory walk round and round the high, continuous wall that inclosed the little wood. He was driven by a desperate idea of solving for himself the riddle that had clouded his reputation and already even threatened his liberty. The police authorities, now in charge of the inquiry, had not arrested him, but he knew well enough that if he tried to move far afield he would be instantly arrested. Horne Fisher's fragmentary hints, though he had refused to expand them as yet, had stirred the artistic temperament of the architect to a sort of wild analysis, and he was resolved to read the hieroglyph upside down and every way until it made sense. If it was something connected with a hole in the wall he would find the hole in the wall; but, as a matter of fact, he was unable to find the faintest crack in the wall. His professional knowledge told him that the masonry was all of one workmanship and one date, and, except for the regular entrance, which threw no light on the mystery, he found nothing suggesting any sort of hiding place or means of escape. Walking a narrow path between the winding wall and the wild eastward bend and sweep of the gray and feathery trees, seeing shifting gleams of a lost sunset winking almost like lightning as the clouds of tempest scudded across the sky and mingling with the first faint blue light from a slowly strengthened moon behind him, he began to feel his head going round as his heels were going round and round the blind recurrent barrier. He had thoughts on the border of thought; fancies about a fourth dimension which was itself a hole to hide anything, of seeing everything from a new angle out of a new window in the senses; or of some mystical light and transparency, like the new rays of chemistry, in which he could see Bulmer's body, horrible and glaring, floating in a lurid halo over the woods and the wall. He was haunted also with the hint, which somehow seemed to be equally horrifying, that it all had something to do with Mr. Prior. There seemed even to be something creepy in the fact that he was always respectfully referred to as Mr. Prior, and that it was in the domestic life of the dead farmer that he had been bidden to seek the seed of these dreadful things. As a matter of fact, he had found that no local inquiries had revealed anything at all about the Prior family.

The moonlight had broadened and brightened, the wind had driven off the clouds and itself died fitfully away, when he came round again to the artificial lake in front of the house. For some reason it looked a very artificial lake; indeed, the whole scene was like a classical landscape with a touch of Watteau; the Palladian facade of the house pale in the moon, and the same silver touching the very pagan and naked marble nymph in the middle of the pond. Rather to his surprise, he found another figure there beside the statue, sitting almost equally motionless; and the same silver pencil traced the wrinkled brow and patient face of Horne Fisher, still dressed as a hermit and apparently practicing something of the solitude of a hermit. Nevertheless, he looked up at Leonard Crane and smiled, almost as if he had expected him.

"Look here," said Crane, planting himself in front of him, "can you tell me anything about this business?"

"I shall soon have to tell everybody everything about it," replied Fisher, "but I've no objection to telling you something first. But, to begin with, will you tell me something? What really happened when you met Bulmer this morning? You did throw away your sword, but you didn't kill him."

"I didn't kill him because I threw away my sword," said the other. "I did it on purpose—or I'm not sure what might have happened."

After a pause he went on, quietly: "The late Lord Bulmer was a very breezy gentleman, extremely breezy. He was very genial with his inferiors, and would have his lawyer and his architect staying in his house for all sorts of holidays and amusements. But there was another side to him, which they found out when they tried to be his equals. When I told him that his sister and I were engaged, something happened which I simply can't and won't describe. It seemed to me like some monstrous upheaval of madness. But I suppose the truth is painfully simple. There is such a thing as the coarseness of a gentleman. And it is the most horrible thing in humanity."

"I know," said Fisher. "The Renaissance nobles of the Tudor time were like that."

"It is odd that you should say that," Crane went on. "For while we were talking there came on me a curious feeling that we were repeating some scene of the past, and that I was really some outlaw, found in the woods like Robin Hood, and that he had really stepped in all his plumes and purple out of the picture frame of the ancestral portrait. Anyhow, he was the man in possession, and he neither feared God nor regarded man. I defied him, of course, and walked away. I might really have killed him if I had not walked away."

"Yes," said Fisher, nodding, "his ancestor was in possession and he was in possession, and this is the end of the story. It all fits in."

"Fits in with what?" cried his companion, with sudden impatience. "I can't make head or tail of it. You tell me to look for the secret in the hole in the wall, but I can't find any hole in the wall."

"There isn't any," said Fisher. "That's the secret." After reflecting a moment, he added: "Unless you call it a hole in the wall of the world. Look here; I'll tell you if you like, but I'm afraid it involves an introduction. You've got to understand one of the tricks of the modern mind, a tendency that most people obey without noticing it. In the village or suburb outside there's an inn with the sign of St. George and the Dragon. Now suppose I went about telling everybody that this was only a corruption of King George and the Dragoon. Scores of people would believe it, without any inquiry, from a vague feeling that it's probable because it's prosaic. It turns something romantic and legendary into something recent and ordinary. And that somehow makes it sound rational, though it is unsupported by reason. Of course some people would have the sense to remember having seen St. George in old Italian pictures and French romances, but a good many wouldn't think about it at all. They would just swallow the skepticism because it was skepticism. Modern intelligence won't accept anything on authority. But it will accept anything without authority. That's exactly what has happened here.

"When some critic or other chose to say that Prior's Park was not a priory, but was named after some quite modern man named Prior, nobody really tested the theory at all. It never occurred to anybody repeating the story to ask if there *was* any Mr. Prior, if anybody had ever seen him or heard of him. As a matter of fact, it was a priory, and shared the fate of most priories—that is, the Tudor gentleman with the plumes simply stole it by brute force and turned it into his own private house; he did worse things, as you shall hear. But the point here is that this is how the trick works, and the trick works in the same way in the other part of the tale. The name of this district is printed Holinwall in all the best maps produced by the scholars; and they allude lightly, not without a smile, to the fact that it was pronounced Holiwell by the most ignorant and old-fashioned of the poor. But it is spelled wrong and pronounced right."

"Do you mean to say," asked Crane, quickly, "that there really was a well?"

"There is a well," said Fisher, "and the truth lies at the bottom of it."

As he spoke he stretched out his hand and pointed toward the sheet of water in front of him.

"The well is under that water somewhere," he said, "and this is not the first tragedy connected with it. The founder of this house did something which his fellow ruffians very seldom did; something that had to be hushed up even in the anarchy of the pillage of the monasteries. The well was connected with the miracles of some saint, and the last prior that guarded it was something like a saint himself; certainly he was something very like a martyr. He defied the new owner and dared him to pollute the place, till the noble, in a fury, stabbed him and flung his body into the well, whither, after four hundred years, it has been followed by an heir of the usurper, clad in the same purple and walking the world with the same pride."

"But how did it happen," demanded Crane, "that for the first time Bulmer fell in at that particular spot?"

"Because the ice was only loosened at that particular spot, by the only man who knew it," answered Horne Fisher. "It was cracked deliberately, with the kitchen chopper, at that special place; and I myself heard the hammering and did not understand it. The place had been covered with an artificial lake, if only because the whole truth had to be covered with an artificial legend. But don't you see that it is exactly what those pagan nobles would have done, to desecrate it with a sort of heathen goddess, as the Roman Emperor built a temple to Venus on the Holy Sepulchre. But the truth could still be traced out, by any scholarly man determined to trace it. And this man was determined to trace it."

"What man?" asked the other, with a shadow of the answer in his mind.

"The only man who has an alibi," replied Fisher. "James Haddow, the antiquarian lawyer, left the night before the fatality, but he left that black star of death on the ice. He left abruptly, having previously proposed to stay; probably, I think, after an ugly scene with Bulmer, at their legal interview. As you know yourself, Bulmer could make a man feel pretty murderous, and I rather fancy the lawyer had himself irregularities to confess, and was in danger of exposure by his client. But it's my reading of human nature that a man will cheat in his trade, but not in his hobby. Haddow may have been a dishonest lawyer, but he couldn't help being an honest antiquary. When he got on the track of the truth about the Holy Well he had to follow it up; he was not to be bamboozled with newspaper anecdotes about Mr. Prior and a hole in the wall; he found out everything, even to the exact location of the well, and he was rewarded, if being a successful assassin can be regarded as a reward."

"And how did you get on the track of all this hidden history?" asked the young architect.

A cloud came across the brow of Horne Fisher. "I knew only too much about it already," he said, "and, after all, it's shameful for me to be speaking lightly of poor Bulmer, who has paid his penalty; but the rest of us haven't. I dare say every cigar I smoke and every liqueur I drink comes directly or indirectly from the harrying of the holy places and the persecution of the poor. After all, it needs very little poking about in

507

the past to find that hole in the wall, that great breach in the defenses of English history. It lies just under the surface of a thin sheet of sham information and instruction, just as the black and blood-stained well lies just under that floor of shallow water and flat weeds. Oh, the ice is thin, but it bears; it is strong enough to support us when we dress up as monks and dance on it, in mockery of the dear, quaint old Middle Ages. They told me I must put on fancy dress; so I did put on fancy dress, according to my own taste and fancy. I put on the only costume I think fit for a man who has inherited the position of a gentleman, and yet has not entirely lost the feelings of one."

In answer to a look of inquiry, he rose with a sweeping and downward gesture.

"Sackcloth," he said; "and I would wear the ashes as well if they would stay on my bald head."

7

THE TEMPLE OF SILENCE

Harold March and the few who cultivated the friendship of Horne Fisher, especially if they saw something of him in his own social setting, were conscious of a certain solitude in his very sociability. They seemed to be always meeting his relations and never meeting his family. Perhaps it would be truer to say that they saw much of his family and nothing of his home. His cousins and connections ramified like a labyrinth all over the governing class of Great Britain, and he seemed to be on good, or at least on good-humored, terms with most of them. For Horne Fisher was remarkable for a curious impersonal information and interest touching all sorts of topics, so that one could sometimes fancy that his culture, like his colorless, fair mustache and pale, drooping features, had the neutral nature of a chameleon. Anyhow, he could always get on with viceroys and Cabinet Ministers and all the great men responsible for great departments, and talk to each of them on his own subject, on the branch of study with which he was most seriously concerned. Thus he could converse with the Minister for War about silkworms, with the Minister of Education about detective stories, with the Minister of Labor about Limoges enamel, and with the Minister of Missions and Moral Progress (if that be his correct title) about the pantomime boys of the last four decades. And as the first was his first cousin, the second his second cousin, the third his brother-in-law, and the fourth his uncle by marriage, this conversational versatility certainly served in one sense to create a happy family. But March never seemed to get a glimpse of that domestic interior to which men of the middle classes are accustomed in their friendships, and which is indeed the foundation of friendship and love and everything else in any sane and stable society. He wondered whether Horne Fisher was both an orphan and an only child.

It was, therefore, with something like a start that he found that Fisher had a brother, much more prosperous and powerful than himself, though hardly, March thought, so entertaining. Sir Henry Harland Fisher, with half the alphabet after his name, was something at the Foreign Office far more tremendous than the Foreign Secretary.

Apparently, it ran in the family, after all; for it seemed there was another brother, Ashton Fisher, in India, rather more tremendous than the Viceroy. Sir Henry Fisher was a heavier, but handsomer edition of his brother, with a brow equally bald, but much more smooth. He was very courteous, but a shade patronizing, not only to March, but even, as March fancied, to Horne Fisher as well. The latter gentleman, who had many intuitions about the half-formed thoughts of others, glanced at the topic himself as they came away from the great house in Berkeley Square.

"Why, don't you know," he observed quietly, "that I am the fool of the family?"

"It must be a clever family," said Harold March, with a smile.

"Very gracefully expressed," replied Fisher; "that is the best of having a literary training. Well, perhaps it is an exaggeration to say I am the fool of the family. It's enough to say I am the failure of the family."

"It seems queer to me that you should fail especially," remarked the journalist. "As they say in the examinations, what did you fail in?"

"Politics," replied his friend. "I stood for Parliament when I was quite a young man and got in by an enormous majority, with loud cheers and chairing round the town. Since then, of course, I've been rather under a cloud."

"I'm afraid I don't quite understand the 'of course,'" answered March, laughing.

"That part of it isn't worth understanding," said Fisher. "But as a matter of fact, old chap, the other part of it was rather odd and interesting. Quite a detective story in its way, as well as the first lesson I had in what modern politics are made of. If you like, I'll tell you all about it." And the following, recast in a less allusive and conversational manner, is the story that he told.

Nobody privileged of late years to meet Sir Henry Harland Fisher would believe that he had ever been called Harry. But, indeed, he had been boyish enough when a boy, and that serenity which shone on him through life, and which now took the form of gravity, had once taken the form of gayety. His friends would have said that he was all the more ripe in his maturity for having been young in his youth. His enemies would have said that he was still light minded, but no longer light hearted. But in any case, the whole of the story Horne Fisher had to tell arose out of the accident which had made young Harry Fisher private secretary to Lord Saltoun. Hence his later connection with the Foreign Office, which had, indeed, come to him as a sort of legacy from his lordship when that great man was the power behind the throne. This is not the place to say much about Saltoun, little as was known of him and much as there was worth knowing. England has had at least three or four such secret statesmen. An aristocratic polity produces every now and then an aristocrat who is also an accident, a man of intellectual independence and insight, a Napoleon born in the purple. His vast work was mostly invisible, and very little could be got out of him in private life except a crusty and rather cynical sense of humor. But it was certainly the accident of his presence at a family dinner of the Fishers, and the unexpected opinion he expressed, which turned what might have been a dinner-table joke into a sort of small sensational novel.

Save for Lord Saltoun, it was a family party of Fishers, for the only other distinguished stranger had just departed after dinner, leaving the rest to their coffee and cigars. This had been a figure of some interest—a young Cambridge man named Eric Hughes who was the rising hope of the party of Reform, to which the Fisher family, along with their friend Saltoun, had long been at least formally attached. The personality of Hughes was substantially summed up in the fact that he talked eloquently and earnestly through the whole dinner, but left immediately after to be in time for an appointment. All his actions had something at once ambitious and conscientious; he drank no wine, but was slightly intoxicated with words. And his face and phrases were on the front page of all the newspapers just then, because he was contesting the safe seat of Sir Francis Verner in the great by-election in the west. Everybody was talking about the powerful speech against squirarchy which he had just delivered; even in the Fisher circle everybody talked about it except Horne Fisher himself who sat in a corner, lowering over the fire.

"We jolly well have to thank him for putting some new life into the old party," Ashton Fisher was saying. "This campaign against the old squires just hits the degree of democracy there is in this county. This act for extending county council control is practically his bill; so you may say he's in the government even before he's in the House."

"One's easier than the other," said Harry, carelessly. "I bet the squire's a bigger pot than the county council in that county. Verner is pretty well rooted; all these rural places are what you call reactionary. Damning aristocrats won't alter it."

"He damns them rather well," observed Ashton. "We never had a better meeting than the one in Barkington, which generally goes Constitutional. And when he said, 'Sir Francis may boast of blue blood; let us show we have red blood,' and went on to talk about manhood and liberty, the room simply rose at him."

"Speaks very well," said Lord Saltoun, gruffly, making his only contribution to the conversation so far.

Then the almost equally silent Horne Fisher suddenly spoke, without taking his brooding eyes off the fire.

"What I can't understand," he said, "is why nobody is ever slanged for the real reason."

"Hullo!" remarked Harry, humorously, "you beginning to take notice?"

"Well, take Verner," continued Horne Fisher. "If we want to attack Verner, why not attack him? Why compliment him on being a romantic reactionary aristocrat? Who is Verner? Where does he come from? His name sounds old, but I never heard of it before, as the man said of the Crucifixion. Why talk about his blue blood? His blood may be gamboge yellow with green spots, for all anybody knows. All we know is that the old squire, Hawker, somehow ran through his money (and his second wife's, I suppose, for she was rich enough), and sold the estate to a man named Verner. What did he make his money in? Oil? Army contracts?"

"I don't know," said Saltoun, looking at him thoughtfully.

"First thing I ever knew you didn't know," cried the exuberant Harry.

"And there's more, besides," went on Horne Fisher, who seemed to have suddenly found his tongue. "If we want country people to vote for us, why don't we get somebody with some notion about the country? We don't talk to people in Threadneedle Street about nothing but turnips and pigsties. Why do we talk to people in Somerset about nothing but slums and socialism? Why don't we give the squire's land to the squire's tenants, instead of dragging in the county council?"

"Three acres and a cow," cried Harry, emitting what the Parliamentary reports call an ironical cheer.

"Yes," replied his brother, stubbornly. "Don't you think agricultural laborers would rather have three acres and a cow than three acres of printed forms and a committee? Why doesn't somebody start a yeoman party in politics, appealing to the old traditions of the small landowner? And why don't they attack men like Verner for what they are, which is something about as old and traditional as an American oil trust?"

"You'd better lead the yeoman party yourself," laughed Harry. "Don't you think it would be a joke, Lord Saltoun, to see my brother and his merry men, with their bows and bills, marching down to Somerset all in Lincoln green instead of Lincoln and Bennet hats?"

"No," answered Old Saltoun, "I don't think it would be a joke. I think it would be an exceedingly serious and sensible idea."

"Well, I'm jiggered!" cried Harry Fisher, staring at him. "I said just now it was the first fact you didn't know, and I should say this is the first joke you didn't see."

"I've seen a good many things in my time," said the old man, in his rather sour fashion. "I've told a good many lies in my time, too, and perhaps I've got rather sick of them. But there are lies and lies, for all that. Gentlemen used to lie just as schoolboys lie, because they hung together and partly to help one another out. But I'm damned if I can see why we should lie for these cosmopolitan cads who only help themselves. They're not backing us up any more; they're simply crowding us out. If a man like your brother likes to go into Parliament as a yeoman or a gentleman or a Jacobite or an Ancient Briton, I should say it would be a jolly good thing."

In the rather startled silence that followed Horne Fisher sprang to his feet and all his dreary manner dropped off him.

"I'm ready to do it to-morrow," he cried. "I suppose none of you fellows would back me up."

Then Harry Fisher showed the finer side of his impetuosity. He made a sudden movement as if to shake hands.

"You're a sport," he said, "and I'll back you up, if nobody else will. But we can all back you up, can't we? I see what Lord Saltoun means, and, of course, he's right. He's always right."

"So I will go down to Somerset," said Horne Fisher.

"Yes, it is on the way to Westminster," said Lord Saltoun, with a smile.

And so it happened that Horne Fisher arrived some days later at the little station of a rather remote market town in the west, accompanied by a light suitcase and a lively brother. It must not be supposed, however, that the brother's cheerful tone consisted entirely of chaff. He supported the new candidate with hope as well as hilarity; and at the back of his boisterous partnership there was an increasing sympathy and encouragement. Harry Fisher had always had an affection for his more quiet and eccentric brother, and was now coming more and more to have a respect for him. As the campaign proceeded the respect increased to ardent admiration. For Harry was still young, and could feel the sort of enthusiasm for his captain in electioneering that a schoolboy can feel for his captain in cricket.

Nor was the admiration undeserved. As the new three-cornered contest developed it became apparent to others besides his devoted kinsman that there was more in Horne Fisher than had ever met the eye. It was clear that his outbreak by the family fireside had been but the culmination of a long course of brooding and studying on the question. The talent he retained through life for studying his subject, and even somebody else's subject, had long been concentrated on this idea of championing a new peasantry against a new plutocracy. He spoke to a crowd with eloquence and replied to an individual with humor, two political arts that seemed to come to him naturally. He certainly knew much more about rural problems than either Hughes, the Reform candidate, or Verner, the Constitutional candidate. And he probed those problems with a human curiosity, and went below the surface in a way that neither of them dreamed of doing. He soon became the voice of popular feelings that are never found in the popular press. New angles of criticism, arguments that had never before been uttered by an educated voice, tests and comparisons that had been made only in dialect by men drinking in the little local public houses, crafts half forgotten that had come down by sign of hand and tongue from remote ages when their fathers were free—all this created a curious and double excitement. It startled the well informed by being a new and fantastic idea they had never encountered. It startled the ignorant by being an old and familiar idea they never thought to have seen revived. Men saw things in a new light, and knew not even whether it was the sunset or the dawn.

Practical grievances were there to make the movement formidable. As Fisher went to and fro among the cottages and country inns, it was borne in on him without difficulty that Sir Francis Verner was a very bad landlord. Nor was the story of his acquisition of the land any more ancient and dignified than he had supposed; the story was well known in the county and in most respects was obvious enough. Hawker, the old squire, had been a loose, unsatisfactory sort of person, had been on bad terms with his first wife (who died, as some said, of neglect), and had then married a flashy South American Jewess with a fortune. But he must have worked his way through this fortune also with marvelous rapidity, for he had been compelled to sell the estate to Verner and had gone to live in South America, possibly on his wife's estates. But Fisher noticed that the laxity of the old squire was far less hated than the efficiency of the new squire. Verner's history seemed to be full of smart bargains and financial flutters that left other people short of money and temper. But though he heard a great deal about Verner, there was one thing that continually eluded him; something that nobody knew, that even Saltoun had not known. He could not find out how Verner had originally made his money.

"He must have kept it specially dark," said Horne Fisher to himself. "It must be something he's really ashamed of. Hang it all! what *is* a man ashamed of nowadays?"

And as he pondered on the possibilities they grew darker and more distorted in his mind; he thought vaguely of things remote and repulsive, strange forms of slavery or sorcery, and then of ugly things yet more unnatural but nearer home. The figure of Verner seemed to be blackened and transfigured in his imagination, and to stand against varied backgrounds and strange skies.

As he strode up a village street, brooding thus, his eyes encountered a complete contrast in the face of his other rival, the Reform candidate. Eric Hughes, with his blown blond hair and eager undergraduate face, was just getting into his motor car and saying a few final words to his agent, a sturdy, grizzled man named Gryce. Eric Hughes waved his hand in a friendly fashion; but Gryce eyed him with some hostility. Eric Hughes was a young man with genuine political enthusiasms, but he knew that political opponents are people with whom one may have to dine any day. But Mr. Gryce was a grim little local Radical, a champion of the chapel, and one of those happy people whose work is also their hobby. He turned his back as the motor car drove away, and walked briskly up the sunlit high street of the little town, whistling, with political papers sticking out of his pocket.

Fisher looked pensively after the resolute figure for a moment, and then, as if by an impulse, began to follow it. Through the busy market place, amid the baskets and barrows of market day, under the painted wooden sign of the Green Dragon, up a dark side entry, under an arch, and through a tangle of crooked cobbled streets the two threaded their way, the square, strutting figure in front and the lean, lounging figure behind him, like his shadow in the sunshine. At length they came to a brown brick house with a brass plate, on which was Mr. Gryce's name, and that individual turned and beheld his pursuer with a stare.

"Could I have a word with you, sir?" asked Horne Fisher, politely. The agent stared still more, but assented civilly, and led the other into an office littered with leaflets and hung all round with highly colored posters which linked the name of Hughes with all the higher interests of humanity.

"Mr. Horne Fisher, I believe," said Mr. Gryce. "Much honored by the call, of course. Can't pretend to congratulate you on entering the contest, I'm afraid; you won't expect that. Here we've been keeping the old flag flying for freedom and reform, and you come in and break the battle line."

For Mr. Elijah Gryce abounded in military metaphors and in denunciations of militarism. He was a square-jawed, blunt-featured man with a pugnacious cock of the eyebrow. He had been pickled in the politics of that countryside from boyhood, he knew everybody's secrets, and electioneering was the romance of his life.

"I suppose you think I'm devoured with ambition," said Horne Fisher, in his rather listless voice, "aiming at a dictatorship and all that. Well, I think I can clear myself of the charge of mere selfish ambition. I only want certain things done. I don't want to do them. I very seldom want to do anything. And I've come here to say that I'm quite willing to retire from the contest if you can convince me that we really want to do the same thing."

The agent of the Reform party looked at him with an odd and slightly puzzled expression, and before he could reply, Fisher went on in the same level tones:

"You'd hardly believe it, but I keep a conscience concealed about me; and I am in doubt about several things. For instance, we both want to turn Verner out of Parliament, but what weapon are we to use? I've heard a lot of gossip against him, but is it right to act on mere gossip? Just as I want to be fair to you, so I want to be fair to him. If some of the things I've heard are true he ought to be turned out of Parliament and every other club in London. But I don't want to turn him out of Parliament if they aren't true."

At this point the light of battle sprang into Mr. Gryce's eyes and he became voluble, not to say violent. He, at any rate, had no doubt that the stories were true; he could testify, to his own knowledge, that they were true. Verner was not only a hard landlord, but a mean landlord, a robber as well as a rackrenter; any gentleman would be justified in hounding him out. He had cheated old Wilkins out of his freehold by a trick fit for a pickpocket; he had driven old Mother Biddle to the workhouse; he had stretched the law against Long Adam, the poacher, till all the magistrates were ashamed of him.

"So if you'll serve under the old banner," concluded Mr. Gryce, more genially, "and turn out a swindling tyrant like that, I'm sure you'll never regret it."

"And if that is the truth," said Horne Fisher, "are you going to tell it?"

"What do you mean? Tell the truth?" demanded Gryce.

"I mean you are going to tell the truth as you have just told it," replied Fisher. "You are going to placard this town with the wickedness done to old Wilkins. You are going to fill the newspapers with the infamous story of Mrs. Biddle. You are going to denounce Verner from a public platform, naming him for what he did and naming the poacher he did it to. And you're going to find out by what trade this man made the money with which he bought the estate; and when you know the truth, as I said before, of course you are going to tell it. Upon those terms I come under the old flag, as you call it, and haul down my little pennon."

The agent was eying him with a curious expression, surly but not entirely unsympathetic. "Well," he said, slowly, "you have to do these things in a regular way, you know, or people don't understand. I've had a lot of experience, and I'm afraid what you say wouldn't do. People understand slanging squires in a general way, but those personalities aren't considered fair play. Looks like hitting below the belt."

"Old Wilkins hasn't got a belt, I suppose," replied Horne Fisher. "Verner can hit him anyhow, and nobody must say a word. It's evidently very important to have a belt. But apparently you have to be rather high up in society to have one. Possibly," he added, thoughtfully—"possibly the explanation of the phrase 'a belted earl,' the meaning of which has always escaped me."

"I mean those personalities won't do," returned Gryce, frowning at the table.

"And Mother Biddle and Long Adam, the poacher, are not personalities," said Fisher, "and suppose we mustn't ask how Verner made all the money that enabled him to become—a personality."

Gryce was still looking at him under lowering brows, but the singular light in his eyes had brightened. At last he said, in another and much quieter voice:

"Look here, sir. I like you, if you don't mind my saying so. I think you are really on the side of the people and I'm sure you're a brave man. A lot braver than you know, perhaps. We daren't touch what you propose with a barge pole; and so far from wanting you in the old party, we'd rather you ran your own risk by yourself. But because I like you and respect your pluck, I'll do you a good turn before we part. I don't want you to waste time barking up the wrong tree. You talk about how the new squire got the money to buy, and the ruin of the old squire, and all the rest of it. Well, I'll give you a hint about that, a hint about something precious few people know."

"I am very grateful," said Fisher, gravely. "What is it?"

"It's in two words," said the other. "The new squire was quite poor when he bought. The old squire was quite rich when he sold."

Horne Fisher looked at him thoughtfully as he turned away abruptly and busied himself with the papers on his desk. Then Fisher uttered a short phrase of thanks and farewell, and went out into the street, still very thoughtful.

His reflection seemed to end in resolution, and, falling into a more rapid stride, he passed out of the little town along a road leading toward the gate of the great park, the country seat of Sir Francis Verner. A glitter of sunlight made the early winter more like a late autumn, and the dark woods were touched here and there with red and golden leaves, like the last rays of a lost sunset. From a higher part of the road he had seen the long, classical facade of the great house with its many windows, almost immediately beneath him, but when the road ran down under the wall of the estate, topped with towering trees behind, he realized that it was half a mile round to the lodge gates. After walking for a few minutes along the lane, however, he came to a place where the wall had cracked and was in process of repair. As it was, there was a great gap in the gray masonry that looked at first as black as a cavern and only showed at a second glance the twilight of the twinkling trees. There was something fascinating about that unexpected gate, like the opening of a fairy tale.

Horne Fisher had in him something of the aristocrat, which is very near to the anarchist. It was characteristic of him that he turned into this dark and irregular entry as casually as into his own front door, merely thinking that it would be a short cut to the house. He made his way through the dim wood for some distance and with some difficulty, until there began to shine through the trees a level light, in lines of silver, which he did not at first understand. The next moment he had come out into the daylight at the top of a steep bank, at the bottom of which a path ran round the rim of a large ornamental lake. The sheet of water which he had seen shimmering through the trees was of considerable extent, but was walled in on every side with woods which were not only dark, but decidedly dismal. At one end of the path was a classical statue of some nameless nymph, and at the other end it was flanked by two classical urns; but the marble was weather-stained and streaked with green and gray. A hundred other signs, smaller but more significant, told him that he had come on some outlying corner of the grounds neglected and seldom visited. In the middle of the lake was what appeared to be an island, and on the island what appeared to be meant for a classical temple, not open like a temple of the winds, but with a blank wall between its Doric pillars. We may say it only seemed like an island, because a second glance revealed a low causeway of flat stones running up to it from the shore and turning it into a peninsula. And certainly it only seemed like a temple, for nobody knew better than Horne Fisher that no god had ever dwelt in that shrine.

"That's what makes all this classical landscape gardening so desolate," he said to himself. "More desolate than Stonehenge or the Pyramids. We don't believe in Egyptian mythology, but the Egyptians did; and I suppose even the Druids believed in Druidism. But the eighteenth-century gentleman who built these temples didn't believe in Venus or Mercury any more than we do; that's why the reflection of those pale pillars in the lake is truly only the shadow of a shade. They were men of the age of Reason; they, who filled their gardens with these stone nymphs, had less hope than any men in all history of really meeting a nymph in the forest."

His monologue stopped abruptly with a sharp noise like a thundercrack that rolled in dreary echoes round the dismal mere. He knew at once what it was—somebody had fired off a gun. But as to the meaning of it he was momentarily staggered, and strange thoughts thronged into his mind. The next moment he laughed; for he saw lying a little way along the path below him the dead bird that the shot had brought down.

At the same moment, however, he saw something else, which interested him more. A ring of dense trees ran round the back of the island temple, framing the facade of it in dark foliage, and he could have sworn he saw a stir as of something moving among the leaves. The next moment his suspicion was confirmed, for a rather ragged figure came from under the shadow of the temple and began to move along the causeway that led to the bank. Even at that distance the figure was conspicuous by its great height and Fisher could see that the man carried a gun under his arm. There came back into his memory at once the name Long Adam, the poacher.

With a rapid sense of strategy he sometimes showed, Fisher sprang from the bank and raced round the lake to the head of the little pier of stones. If once a man reached the mainland he could easily vanish into the woods. But when Fisher began to advance along the stones toward the island, the man was cornered in a blind alley and could only back toward the temple. Putting his broad shoulders against it, he stood as if at bay; he was a comparatively young man, with fine lines in his lean face and figure and a mop of ragged red hair. The look in his eyes might well have been disquieting to anyone left alone with him on an island in the middle of a lake.

"Good morning," said Horne Fisher, pleasantly. "I thought at first you were a murderer. But it seems unlikely, somehow, that the partridge rushed between us and died for love of me, like the heroines in the romances; so I suppose you are a poacher."

"I suppose you would call me a poacher," answered the man; and his voice was something of a surprise coming from such a scarecrow; it had that hard fastidiousness to be found in those who have made a fight for their own refinement among rough surroundings. "I consider I have a perfect right to shoot game in this place. But I am well aware that people of your sort take me for a thief, and I suppose you will try to land me in jail."

"There are preliminary difficulties," replied Fisher. "To begin with, the mistake is flattering, but I am not a gamekeeper. Still less am I three gamekeepers, who would be, I imagine, about your fighting weight. But I confess I have another reason for not wanting to jail you."

"And what is that?" asked the other.

"Only that I quite agree with you," answered Fisher. "I don't exactly say you have a right to poach, but I never could see that it was as wrong as being a thief. It seems to me against the whole normal notion of property that a man should own something because it flies across his garden. He might as well own the wind, or think he could write his name on a morning cloud. Besides, if we want poor people to respect property we must give them some property to respect. You ought to have land of your own; and I'm going to give you some if I can."

"Going to give me some land!" repeated Long Adam.

"I apologize for addressing you as if you were a public meeting," said Fisher, "but I am an entirely new kind of public man who says the same thing in public and in private. I've said this to a hundred huge meetings throughout the country, and I say it to you on this queer little island in this dismal pond. I would cut up a big estate like this into small estates for everybody, even for poachers. I would do in England as they did in Ireland—buy the big men out, if possible; get them out, anyhow. A man like you ought to have a little place of his own. I don't say you could keep pheasants, but you might keep chickens."

The man stiffened suddenly and he seemed at once to blanch and flame at the promise as if it were a threat.

"Chickens!" he repeated, with a passion of contempt.

"Why do you object?" asked the placid candidate. "Because keeping hens is rather a mild amusement for a poacher? What about poaching eggs?"

"Because I am not a poacher," cried Adam, in a rending voice that rang round the hollow shrines and urns like the echoes of his gun. "Because the partridge lying dead over there is my partridge. Because the land you are standing on is my land. Because my own land was only taken from me by a crime, and a worse crime than poaching. This has been a single estate for hundreds and hundreds of years, and if you or any meddlesome mountebank comes here and talks of cutting it up like a cake, if I ever hear a word more of you and your leveling lies—"

"You seem to be a rather turbulent public," observed Horne Fisher, "but do go on. What will happen if I try to divide this estate decently among decent people?"

The poacher had recovered a grim composure as he replied. "There will be no partridge to rush in between."

With that he turned his back, evidently resolved to say no more, and walked past the temple to the extreme end of the islet, where he stood staring into the water. Fisher followed him, but, when his repeated questions evoked no answer, turned back toward the shore. In doing so he took a second and closer look at the artificial temple, and noted some curious things about it. Most of these theatrical things were as thin as theatrical scenery, and he expected the classic shrine to be a shallow thing, a mere shell or mask. But there was some substantial bulk of it behind, buried in the trees, which had a gray, labyrinthian look, like serpents of stone, and lifted a load of leafy towers to the sky. But what arrested Fisher's eye was that in this bulk of gray-white stone behind there was a single door with great, rusty bolts outside; the bolts, however, were not shot across so as to secure it. Then he walked round the small building, and found no other opening except one small grating like a ventilator, high up in the wall. He retraced his steps thoughtfully along the causeway to the banks of the lake, and sat down on the stone steps between the two sculptured funeral urns. Then he lit a cigarette and smoked it in ruminant manner; eventually he took out a notebook and wrote down various phrases, numbering and renumbering them till they stood in the following order: "(1) Squire Hawker disliked his first wife. (2) He married his second wife for her money. (3) Long Adam says the estate is really his. (4) Long Adam hangs round the island temple, which looks like a prison. (5) Squire Hawker was not poor when he gave up the estate. (6) Verner was poor when he got the estate."

He gazed at these notes with a gravity which gradually turned to a hard smile, threw away his cigarette, and resumed his search for a short cut to the great house. He soon picked up the path which, winding among clipped hedges and flower beds, brought him in front of its long Palladian facade. It had the usual appearance of being, not a private house, but a sort of public building sent into exile in the provinces.

He first found himself in the presence of the butler, who really looked much older than the building, for the architecture was dated as Georgian; but the man's face, under a highly unnatural brown wig, was wrinkled with what might have been centuries. Only his prominent eyes were alive and alert, as if with protest. Fisher glanced at him, and then stopped and said:

"Excuse me. Weren't you with the late squire, Mr. Hawker?"

"Yes, sir," said the man, gravely. "Usher is my name. What can I do for you?"

"Only take me into Sir Francis Verner," replied the visitor.

Sir Francis Verner was sitting in an easy chair beside a small table in a large room hung with tapestries. On the table were a small flask and glass, with the green glimmer of a liqueur and a cup of black coffee. He was clad in a quiet gray suit with a moderately harmonious purple tie; but Fisher saw something about the turn of his fair mustache and the lie of his flat hair—it suddenly revealed that his name was Franz Werner.

"You are Mr. Horne Fisher," he said. "Won't you sit down?"

"No, thank you," replied Fisher. "I fear this is not a friendly occasion, and I shall remain standing. Possibly you know that I am already standing—standing for Parliament, in fact—"

"I am aware we are political opponents," replied Verner, raising his eyebrows. "But I think it would be better if we fought in a sporting spirit; in a spirit of English fair play."

"Much better," assented Fisher. "It would be much better if you were English and very much better if you had ever played fair. But what I've come to say can be said very shortly. I don't quite know how we stand with the law about that old Hawker story, but my chief object is to prevent England being entirely ruled by people like you. So whatever the law would say, I will say no more if you will retire from the election at once."

"You are evidently a lunatic," said Verner.

"My psychology may be a little abnormal," replied Horne Fisher, in a rather hazy manner. "I am subject to dreams, especially day-dreams. Sometimes what is happening to me grows vivid in a curious double way, as if it had happened before. Have you ever had that mystical feeling that things have happened before?"

"I hope you are a harmless lunatic," said Verner.

But Fisher was still staring in an absent fashion at the golden gigantic figures and traceries of brown and red in the tapestries on the walls; then he looked again at Verner and resumed: "I have a feeling that this interview has happened before, here in this tapestried room, and we are two ghosts revisiting a haunted chamber. But it was Squire Hawker who sat where you sit and it was you who stood where I stand." He paused a moment and then added, with simplicity, "I suppose I am a blackmailer, too."

"If you are," said Sir Francis, "I promise you you shall go to jail." But his face had a shade on it that looked like the reflection of the green wine gleaming on the table. Horne Fisher regarded him steadily and answered, quietly enough:

"Blackmailers do not always go to jail. Sometimes they go to Parliament. But, though Parliament is rotten enough already, you shall not go there if I can help it. I am not so criminal as you were in bargaining with crime. You made a squire give up his country seat. I only ask you to give up your Parliamentary seat."

Sir Francis Verner sprang to his feet and looked about for one of the bell ropes of the old-fashioned, curtained room.

"Where is Usher?" he cried, with a livid face.

"And who is Usher?" said Fisher, softly. "I wonder how much Usher knows of the truth."

Verner's hand fell from the bell rope and, after standing for a moment with rolling eyes, he strode abruptly from the room. Fisher went but by the other door, by which he had entered, and, seeing no sign of Usher, let himself out and betook himself again toward the town.

That night he put an electric torch in his pocket and set out alone in the darkness to add the last links to his argument. There was much that he did not know yet; but he thought he knew where he could find the knowledge. The night closed dark and stormy and the black gap in the wall looked blacker than ever; the wood seemed to have grown thicker and darker in a day. If the deserted lake with its black woods and gray urns and images looked desolate even by daylight, under the night and the growing storm it seemed still more like the pool of Acheron in the land of lost souls. As he stepped carefully along the jetty stones he seemed to be traveling farther and farther into the abyss of night, and to have left behind him the last points from which it would be possible to signal to the land of the living. The lake seemed to have grown larger than a sea, but a sea of black and slimy waters that slept with abominable serenity, as if they had washed out the world. There was so much of this nightmare sense of extension and expansion that he was strangely surprised to come to his desert island so soon. But he knew it for a place of inhuman silence and solitude; and he felt as if he had been walking for years.

Nerving himself to a more normal mood, he paused under one of the dark dragon trees that branched out above him, and, taking out his torch, turned in the direction of the door at the back of the temple. It was unbolted as before, and the thought stirred faintly in him that it was slightly open, though only by a crack. The more he thought of it, however, the more certain he grew that this was but one of the common illusions of light coming from a different angle. He studied in a more scientific spirit the details of the door, with its rusty bolts and hinges, when he became conscious of something very near him—indeed, nearly above his head. Something was dangling from the tree that was not a broken branch. For some seconds he stood as still as a stone, and as cold. What he saw above him were the legs of a man hanging, presumably a dead man hanged. But the next moment he knew better. The man was literally alive and kicking; and an instant after he had dropped to the ground and turned on the intruder. Simultaneously three or four other trees seemed to come to life in the same fashion. Five or six other figures had fallen on their feet from these unnatural nests. It was as if the place were an island of monkeys. But a moment after they had made a stampede toward him, and when they laid their hands on him he knew that they were men.

With the electric torch in his hand he struck the foremost of them so furiously in the face that the man stumbled and rolled over on the slimy grass; but the torch was broken and extinguished, leaving everything in a denser obscurity. He flung another man flat against the temple wall, so that he slid to the ground; but a third and fourth carried Fisher off his feet and began to bear him, struggling, toward the doorway. Even in the bewilderment of the battle he was conscious that the door was standing open. Somebody was summoning the roughs from inside.

The moment they were within they hurled him upon a sort of bench or bed with violence, but no damage; for the settee, or whatever it was, seemed to be comfortably cushioned for his reception. Their violence had in it a great element of haste, and before he could rise they had all rushed for the door to escape. Whatever bandits they were that infested this desert island, they were obviously uneasy about their job and very anxious to be quit of it. He had the flying fancy that regular criminals would hardly be in such a panic. The next moment the great door crashed to and he could hear the bolts shriek as they shot into their place, and the feet of the retreating men scampering and stumbling along the causeway. But rapidly as it happened, it did not happen before Fisher had done something that he wanted to do. Unable to rise from his sprawling attitude in that flash of time, he had shot out one of his long legs and hooked it round the ankle of the last man disappearing through the door. The man swayed and toppled over inside the prison chamber, and the door closed between him and his fleeing companions. Clearly they were in too much haste to realize that they had left one of their company behind.

The man sprang to his feet again and hammered and kicked furiously at the door. Fisher's sense of humor began to recover from the struggle and he sat up on his sofa with something of his native nonchalance. But as he listened to the captive captor beating on the door of the prison, a new and curious reflection came to him.

The natural course for a man thus wishing to attract his friends' attention would be to call out, to shout as well as kick. This man was making as much noise as he could with his feet and hands, but not a sound came from his throat. Why couldn't he speak? At first he thought the man might be gagged, which was manifestly absurd. Then his fancy fell back on the ugly idea that the man was dumb. He hardly knew why it was so ugly an idea, but it affected his imagination in a dark and disproportionate fashion. There seemed to be something creepy about the idea of being left in a dark room with a deaf mute. It was almost as if such a defect were a deformity. It was almost as if it went with other and worse deformities. It was as if the shape he could not trace in the darkness were some shape that should not see the sun.

Then he had a flash of sanity and also of insight. The explanation was very simple, but rather interesting. Obviously the man did not use his voice because he did not wish his voice to be recognized. He hoped to escape from that dark place before Fisher found out who he was. And who was he? One thing at least was clear. He was one or other of the four or five men with whom Fisher had already talked in these parts, and in the development of that strange story.

"Now I wonder who you are," he said, aloud, with all his old lazy urbanity. "I suppose it's no use trying to throttle you in order to find out; it would be displeasing to pass the night with a corpse. Besides I might be the corpse. I've got no matches and I've smashed my torch, so I can only speculate. Who could you be, now? Let us think."

The man thus genially addressed had desisted from drumming on the door and retreated sullenly into a corner as Fisher continued to address him in a flowing monologue.

"Probably you are the poacher who says he isn't a poacher. He says he's a landed proprietor; but he will permit me to inform him that, whatever he is, he's a fool. What hope can there ever be of a free peasantry in England if the peasants themselves are such snobs as to want to be gentlemen? How can we make a democracy with no democrats? As it is, you want to be a landlord and so you consent to be a criminal. And in that, you know, you are rather like somebody else. And, now I think of it, perhaps you are somebody else."

There was a silence broken by breathing from the corner and the murmur of the rising storm, that came in through the small grating above the man's head. Horne Fisher continued:

"Are you only a servant, perhaps, that rather sinister old servant who was butler to Hawker and Verner? If so, you are certainly the only link between the two periods. But if so, why do you degrade yourself to serve this dirty foreigner, when you at least saw the last of a genuine national gentry? People like you are generally at least patriotic. Doesn't England mean anything to you, Mr. Usher? All of which eloquence is possibly wasted, as perhaps you are not Mr. Usher.

"More likely you are Verner himself; and it's no good wasting eloquence to make you ashamed of yourself. Nor is it any good to curse you for corrupting England; nor are you the right person to curse. It is the English who deserve to be cursed, and are cursed, because they allowed such vermin to crawl into the high places of their heroes and their kings. I won't dwell on the idea that you're Verner, or the throttling might begin, after all. Is there anyone else you could be? Surely you're not some servant of the other rival organization. I can't believe you're Gryce, the agent; and yet Gryce had a spark of the fanatic in his eye, too; and men will do extraordinary things in these paltry feuds of politics. Or if not the servant, is it the . . . No, I can't believe it . . . not the red blood of manhood and liberty . . . not the democratic ideal . . ."

He sprang up in excitement, and at the same moment a growl of thunder came through the grating beyond. The storm had broken, and with it a new light broke on his mind. There was something else that might happen in a moment.

"Do you know what that means?" he cried. "It means that God himself may hold a candle to show me your infernal face."

Then next moment came a crash of thunder; but before the thunder a white light had filled the whole room for a single split second.

Fisher had seen two things in front of him. One was the black-and-white pattern of the iron grating against the sky; the other was the face in the corner. It was the face of his brother.

Nothing came from Horne Fisher's lips except a Christian name, which was followed by a silence more dreadful than the dark. At last the other figure stirred and sprang up, and the voice of Harry Fisher was heard for the first time in that horrible room.

"You've seen me, I suppose," he said, "and we may as well have a light now. You could have turned it on at any time, if you'd found the switch."

He pressed a button in the wall and all the details of that room sprang into something stronger than daylight. Indeed, the details were so unexpected that for a moment they turned the captive's rocking mind from the last personal revelation. The room, so far from being a dungeon cell, was more like a drawing-room, even a lady's drawing-room, except for some boxes of cigars and bottles of wine that were stacked with books and magazines on a side table. A second glance showed him that the more masculine fittings were quite recent, and that the more feminine background was quite old. His eye caught a strip of faded tapestry, which startled him into speech, to the momentary oblivion of bigger matters.

"This place was furnished from the great house," he said.

"Yes," replied the other, "and I think you know why."

"I think I do," said Horne Fisher, "and before I go on to more extraordinary things I will, say what I think. Squire Hawker played both the bigamist and the bandit. His first wife was not dead when he married the Jewess; she was imprisoned on this island. She bore him a child here, who now haunts his birthplace under the name of Long Adam. A bankruptcy company promoter named Werner discovered the secret and blackmailed the squire into surrendering the estate. That's all quite clear and very easy. And now let me go on to something more difficult. And that is for you to explain what the devil you are doing kidnaping your born brother."

After a pause Henry Fisher answered:

"I suppose you didn't expect to see me," he said. "But, after all, what could you expect?"'

"I'm afraid I don't follow," said Horne Fisher.

"I mean what else could you expect, after making such a muck of it?" said his brother, sulkily. "We all thought you were so clever. How could we know you were going to be—well, really, such a rotten failure?"

"This is rather curious," said the candidate, frowning. "Without vanity, I was not under the impression that my candidature was a failure. All the big meetings were successful and crowds of people have promised me votes."

"I should jolly well think they had," said Henry, grimly. "You've made a landslide with your confounded acres and a cow, and Verner can hardly get a vote anywhere. Oh, it's too rotten for anything!"

"What on earth do you mean?"

"Why, you lunatic," cried Henry, in tones of ringing sincerity, "you don't suppose you were meant to *win* the seat, did you? Oh, it's too childish! I tell you Verner's got to get in. Of course he's got to get in. He's to have the Exchequer next session, and there's the Egyptian loan and Lord knows what else. We only wanted you to split the Reform vote because accidents might happen after Hughes had made a score at Barkington."

"I see," said Fisher, "and you, I think, are a pillar and ornament of the Reform party. As you say, I am not clever."

The appeal to party loyalty fell on deaf ears; for the pillar of Reform was brooding on other things. At last he said, in a more troubled voice:

"I didn't want you to catch me; I knew it would be a shock. But I tell you what, you never would have caught me if I hadn't come here myself, to see they didn't ill treat you and to make sure everything was as comfortable as it could be." There was even a sort of break in his voice as he added, "I got those cigars because I knew you liked them."

Emotions are queer things, and the idiocy of this concession suddenly softened Horne Fisher like an unfathomable pathos.

"Never mind, old chap," he said; "we'll say no more about it. I'll admit that you're really as kind-hearted and affectionate a scoundrel and hypocrite as ever sold himself to ruin his country. There, I can't say handsomer than that. Thank you for the cigars, old man. I'll have one if you don't mind."

By the time that Horne Fisher had ended his telling of this story to Harold March they had come out into one of the public parks and taken a seat on a rise of ground overlooking wide green spaces under a blue and empty sky; and there was something incongruous in the words with which the narration ended.

"I have been in that room ever since," said Horne Fisher. "I am in it now. I won the election, but I never went to the House. My life has been a life in that little room on that lonely island. Plenty of books and cigars and luxuries, plenty of knowledge and interest and information, but never a voice out of that tomb to reach the world outside. I shall probably die there." And he smiled as he looked across the vast green park to the gray horizon.

❧ 8 ❧

THE VENGEANCE OF THE STATUE

It was on the sunny veranda of a seaside hotel, overlooking a pattern of flower beds and a strip of blue sea, that Horne Fisher and Harold March had their final explanation, which might be called an explosion.

Harold March had come to the little table and sat down at it with a subdued excitement smoldering in his somewhat cloudy and ˙dreamy blue eyes. In the newspapers which he tossed from him on to the table there was enough to explain some if not all of his emotion. Public affairs in every department had reached a crisis. The government which had stood so long that men were used to it, as they are used to a hereditary despotism, had begun to be accused of blunders and even of financial abuses. Some said that the experiment of attempting to establish a peasantry in the west of England, on the lines of an early fancy of Horne Fisher's, had resulted in nothing but dangerous quarrels with more industrial neighbors. There had been particular complaints of the ill treatment of harmless foreigners, chiefly Asiatics, who happened to be employed in the new scientific works constructed on the coast. Indeed, the new Power which had arisen in Siberia, backed by Japan and other powerful allies, was inclined to take the matter up in the interests of its exiled subjects; and there had been wild talk about ambassadors and ultimatums. But something much more serious, in its personal interest for March himself, seemed to fill his meeting with his friend with a mixture of embarrassment and indignation.

Perhaps it increased his annoyance that there was a certain unusual liveliness about the usually languid figure of Fisher. The ordinary image of him in March's mind was that of a pallid and bald-browed gentleman, who seemed to be prematurely old as well as prematurely bald. He was remembered as a man who expressed the opinions of a pessimist in the language of a lounger. Even now March could not be certain whether the change was merely a sort of masquerade of sunshine, or that effect of clear colors and clean-cut outlines that is always visible on the parade of a marine resort, relieved against the blue dado of the sea. But Fisher had a flower in his buttonhole, and his friend could have sworn he carried his cane with something almost like the swagger of a fighter. With such clouds gathering over England, the pessimist seemed to be the only man who carried his own sunshine.

"Look here," said Harold March, abruptly, "you've been no end of a friend to me, and I never was so proud of a friendship before; but there's something I must get off my chest. The more I found out, the less I understood how you could stand it. And I tell you I'm going to stand it no longer."

Horne Fisher gazed across at him gravely and attentively, but rather as if he were a long way off.

"You know I always liked you," said Fisher, quietly, "but I also respect you, which is not always the same thing. You may possibly guess that I like a good many people I don't respect. Perhaps it is my tragedy, perhaps it is my fault. But you are very different, and I promise you this: that I will never try to keep you as somebody to be liked, at the price of your not being respected."

"I know you are magnanimous," said March after a silence, "and yet you tolerate and perpetuate everything that is mean." Then after another silence he added: "Do you remember when we first met, when you were fishing in that brook in the affair of the target? And do you remember you said that, after all, it might do no harm if I could blow the whole tangle of this society to hell with dynamite."

"Yes, and what of that?" asked Fisher.

"Only that I'm going to blow it to hell with dynamite," said Harold March, "and I think it right to give you fair warning. For a long time I didn't believe things were as bad as you said they were. But I never felt as if I could have bottled up what you knew, supposing you really knew it. Well, the long and the short of it is that I've got a conscience; and now, at last, I've also got a chance. I've been put in charge of a big independent paper, with a free hand, and we're going to open a cannonade on corruption."

"That will be—Attwood, I suppose," said Fisher, reflectively. "Timber merchant. Knows a lot about China."

"He knows a lot about England," said March, doggedly, "and now I know it, too, we're not going to hush it up any longer. The people of this country have a right to know how they're ruled—or, rather, ruined. The Chancellor is in the pocket of the money lenders and has to do as he is told; otherwise he's bankrupt, and a bad sort of bankruptcy, too, with nothing but cards and actresses behind it. The Prime Minister was in the petrol-contract business; and deep in it, too. The Foreign Minister is a wreck of drink and drugs. When you say that plainly about a man who may send thousands of Englishmen to die for nothing, you're called personal. If a poor engine driver gets drunk and sends thirty or forty people to death, nobody complains of the exposure being personal. The engine driver is not a person."

"I quite agree with you," said Fisher, calmly. "You are perfectly right."

"If you agree with us, why the devil don't you act with us?" demanded his friend. "If you think it's right, why don't you do what's right? It's awful to think of a man of your abilities simply blocking the road to reform."

"We have often talked about that," replied Fisher, with the same composure. "The Prime Minister is my father's friend. The Foreign Minister married my sister. The Chancellor of the Exchequer is my first cousin. I mention the genealogy in some detail just now for a particular reason. The truth is I have a curious kind of cheerfulness at the moment. It isn't altogether the sun and the sea, sir. I am enjoying an emotion that is entirely new to me; a happy sensation I never remember having had before."

"What the devil do you mean?"

"I am feeling proud of my family," said Horne Fisher.

Harold March stared at him with round blue eyes, and seemed too much mystified even to ask a question. Fisher leaned back in his chair in his lazy fashion, and smiled as he continued.

"Look here, my dear fellow. Let me ask a question in turn. You imply that I have always known these things about my unfortunate kinsmen. So I have. Do you suppose that Attwood hasn't always known them? Do you suppose he hasn't always known you as an honest man who would say these things when he got a chance? Why does Attwood unmuzzle you like a dog at this moment, after all these years? I know why he does; I know a good many things, far too many things. And therefore, as I have the honor to remark, I am proud of my family at last."

"But why?" repeated March, rather feebly.

"I am proud of the Chancellor because he gambled and the Foreign Minister because he drank and the Prime Minister because he took a commission on a contract," said Fisher, firmly. "I am proud of them because they did these things, and can be denounced for them, and know they can be denounced for them, and are *standing firm for all that*. I take off my hat to them because they are defying blackmail, and refusing to smash their country to save themselves. I salute them as if they were going to die on the battlefield."

After a pause he continued: "And it will be a battlefield, too, and not a metaphorical one. We have yielded to foreign financiers so long that now it is war or ruin, Even the people, even the country people, are beginning to suspect that they are being ruined. That is the meaning of the regrettable incidents in the newspapers."

"The meaning of the outrages on Orientals?" asked March.

"The meaning of the outrages on Orientals," replied Fisher, "is that the financiers have introduced Chinese labor into this country with the deliberate intention of reducing workmen and peasants to starvation. Our unhappy politicians have made concession after concession; and now they are asking concessions which amount to our ordering a massacre of our own poor. If we do not fight now we shall never fight again. They will have put England in an economic position of starving in a week. But we are going to fight now; I shouldn't wonder if there were an ultimatum in a week and an invasion in a fortnight. All the past corruption and cowardice is hampering us, of course; the West country is pretty stormy and doubtful even in a military sense; and the Irish regiments there, that are supposed to support us by the new treaty, are pretty well in mutiny; for, of course, this infernal coolie capitalism is being pushed in Ireland, too. But it's to stop now; and if the government message of reassurance gets through to them in time, they may turn up after all by the time the enemy lands. For my poor old gang is going to stand to its guns at last. Of course it's only natural that when they have been whitewashed for half a century as paragons, their sins should come back on them at the very moment when they are behaving like men for the first time in their lives. Well, I tell you, March, I know them inside out; and I know they are behaving like heroes. Every man of them ought to have a statue, and on the pedestal words like those of the noblest ruffian of the Revolution: 'Que mon nom soit fletri; que la France soit libre.'"

"Good God!" cried March, "shall we never get to the bottom of your mines and countermines?"

After a silence Fisher answered in a lower voice, looking his friend in the eyes.

"Did you think there was nothing but evil at the bottom of them?" he asked, gently. "Did you think I had found nothing but filth in the deep seas into which fate has thrown me? Believe me, you never know the best about men till you know the worst about them. It does not dispose of their strange human souls to know that they were exhibited to the world as impossibly impeccable wax works, who never looked after a woman or knew the meaning of a bribe. Even in a palace, life can be lived well; and even in a Parliament, life can be lived with occasional efforts to live it well. I tell you it is as true of these rich fools and rascals as it is true of every poor footpad and pickpocket; that only God knows how good they have tried to be. God alone knows what the conscience can survive, or how a man who has lost his honor will still try to save his soul."

There was another silence, and March sat staring at the table and Fisher at the sea. Then Fisher suddenly sprang to his feet and caught up his hat and stick with all his new alertness and even pugnacity.

"Look here, old fellow," he cried, "let us make a bargain. Before you open your campaign for Attwood come down and stay with us for one week, to hear what we're really doing. I mean with the Faithful Few, formerly known as the Old Gang, occasionally to be described as the Low Lot. There are really only five of us that are quite fixed, and organizing the national defense; and we're living like a garrison in a sort of broken-down hotel in Kent. Come and see what we're really doing and what there is to be done, and do us justice. And after that, with unalterable love and affection for you, publish and be damned."

Thus it came about that in the last week before war, when events moved most rapidly, Harold March found himself one of a sort of small house party of the people he was proposing to denounce. They were living simply enough, for people with their tastes, in an old brown-brick inn faced with ivy and surrounded by rather dismal gardens. At the back of the building the garden ran up very steeply to a road along the ridge above; and a zigzag path scaled the slope in sharp angles, turning to and fro amid evergreens so somber that they might rather be called everblack. Here and there up the slope were statues having all the cold monstrosity of such minor ornaments of the eighteenth century; and a whole row of them ran as on a terrace along the last bank at the bottom, opposite the back door. This detail fixed itself first in March's mind merely because it figured in the first conversation he had with one of the cabinet ministers.

The cabinet ministers were rather older than he had expected to find them. The Prime Minister no longer looked like a boy, though he still looked a little like a baby. But it was one of those old and venerable babies, and the baby had soft gray hair. Everything about him was soft, to his speech and his way of walking; but over and above that his chief function seemed to be sleep. People left alone with him got so used to his eyes being closed that they were almost startled when they realized in the stillness that the eyes were wide open, and even watching. One thing at least would always make the old gentleman open his eyes. The one thing he really cared for in this world was his hobby of armored weapons, especially Eastern weapons, and he would talk for hours about Damascus blades and Arab swordmanship. Lord James Herries, the Chancellor of the Exchequer, was a short, dark, sturdy man with a very sallow face and a very sullen manner, which contrasted with the gorgeous flower in his buttonhole and his festive trick of being always slightly overdressed. It was something of a euphemism to call him a well-known man about town. There was perhaps more mystery in the question of how a man who lived for pleasure seemed to get so little pleasure out of it. Sir David Archer, the Foreign Secretary, was the only one of them who was a self-made man, and the only one of them who looked like an aristocrat. He was tall and thin and very handsome, with a grizzled beard; his gray hair was very curly, and even rose in front in two rebellious ringlets that seemed to the fanciful to tremble like the antennae of some giant insect, or to stir sympathetically with the restless tufted eyebrows over his rather haggard eyes. For the Foreign Secretary made no secret of his somewhat nervous condition, whatever might be the cause of it.

"Do you know that mood when one could scream because a mat is crooked?" he said to March, as they walked up and down in the back garden below the line of dingy statues. "Women get into it when they've worked too hard; and I've been working pretty hard lately, of course. It drives me mad when Herries will wear his hat a little crooked—habit of looking like a gay dog. Sometime I swear I'll knock it off. That statue of Britannia over there isn't quite straight; it sticks forward a bit as if the lady were going to topple over. The damned thing is that it doesn't topple over and be done with it. See, it's clamped with an iron prop. Don't be surprised if I get up in the middle of the night to hike it down."

They paced the path for a few moments in silence and then he continued. "It's odd those little things seem specially big when there are bigger things to worry about. We'd better go in and do some work."

Horne Fisher evidently allowed for all the neurotic possibilities of Archer and the dissipated habits of Herries; and whatever his faith in their present firmness, did not unduly tax their time and attention, even in the case of the Prime Minister. He had got the consent of the latter finally to the committing of the important documents, with the orders to the Western armies, to the care of a less conspicuous and more solid person— an uncle of his named Horne Hewitt, a rather colorless country squire who had been a good soldier, and was the military adviser of the committee. He was charged with expediting the government pledge, along with the concerted military plans, to the half-mutinous command in the west; and the still more urgent task of seeing that it did not fall into the hands of the enemy, who might appear at any moment from the east. Over and above this military official, the only other person present was a police official, a certain Doctor Prince, originally a police surgeon and now a distinguished detective, sent to be a bodyguard to the group. He was a square-faced man with big spectacles and a grimace that expressed the intention of keeping his mouth shut. Nobody else shared their captivity except the hotel proprietor, a crusty Kentish man with a crab-apple face, one or two of his servants, and another servant privately attached to Lord James Herries. He was a young Scotchman named Campbell, who looked much more distinguished than his bilious-looking master, having chestnut hair and a long saturnine face with large but fine features. He was probably the one really efficient person in the house.

After about four days of the informal council, March had come to feel a sort of grotesque sublimity about these dubious figures, defiant in the twilight of danger, as if they were hunchbacks and cripples left alone to defend a town. All were working hard; and he himself looked up from writing a page of memoranda in a private room to see Horne Fisher standing in the doorway, accoutered as if for travel. He fancied that Fisher looked a little pale; and after a moment that gentleman shut the door behind him and said, quietly:

"Well, the worst has happened. Or nearly the worst."

"The enemy has landed," cried March, and sprang erect out of his chair.

"Oh, I knew the enemy would land," said Fisher, with composure. "Yes, he's landed; but that's not the worst that could happen. The worst is that there's a leak of some sort, even from this fortress of ours. It's been a bit of a shock to me, I can tell you; though I suppose it's illogical. After all, I was full of admiration at finding three honest men in politics. I ought not to be full of astonishment if I find only two."

He ruminated a moment and then said, in such a fashion that March could hardly tell if he were changing the subject or no:

"It's hard at first to believe that a fellow like Herries, who had pickled himself in vice like vinegar, can have any scruple left. But about that I've noticed a curious thing. Patriotism is not the first virtue. Patriotism rots into Prussianism when you pretend it is the first virtue. But patriotism is sometimes the last virtue. A man will swindle or seduce who will not sell his country. But who knows?"

"But what is to be done?" cried March, indignantly.

"My uncle has the papers safe enough," replied Fisher, "and is sending them west to-night; but somebody is trying to get at them from outside, I fear with the assistance of somebody inside. All I can do at present is to try to head off the man outside; and I must get away now and do it. I shall be back in about twenty-four hours. While I'm away I want you to keep an eye on these people and find out what you can. Au revoir."

He vanished down the stairs; and from the window March could see him mount a motor cycle and trail away toward the neighboring town.

On the following morning, March was sitting in the window seat of the old inn parlor, which was oak-paneled and ordinarily rather dark; but on that occasion it was full of the white light of a curiously clear morning—the moon had shone brilliantly for the last two or three nights. He was himself somewhat in shadow in the corner of the window seat; and Lord James Herries, coming in hastily from the garden behind, did not see him. Lord James clutched the back of a chair, as if to steady himself, and, sitting down abruptly at the table, littered with the last meal, poured himself out a tumbler of brandy and drank it. He sat with his back to March, but his yellow face appeared in a round mirror beyond and the tinge of it was like that of some horrible malady. As March moved he started violently and faced round.

"My God!" he cried, "have you seen what's outside?"

"Outside?" repeated the other, glancing over his shoulder at the garden.

"Oh, go and look for yourself," cried Herries in a sort of fury. "Hewitt's murdered and his papers stolen, that's all."

He turned his back again and sat down with a thud; his square shoulders were shaking. Harold March darted out of the doorway into the back garden with its steep slope of statues.

The first thing he saw was Doctor Prince, the detective, peering through his spectacles at something on the ground; the second was the thing he was peering at. Even after the sensational news he had heard inside, the sight was something of a sensation.

The monstrous stone image of Britannia was lying prone and face downward on the garden path; and there stuck out at random from underneath it, like the legs of a smashed fly, an arm clad in a white shirt sleeve and a leg clad in a khaki trouser, and hair of the unmistakable sandy gray that belonged to Horne Fisher's unfortunate uncle. There were pools of blood and the limbs were quite stiff in death.

"Couldn't this have been an accident?" said March, finding words at last.

"Look for yourself, I say," repeated the harsh voice of Herries, who had followed him with restless movements out of the door. "The papers are gone, I tell you. The fellow tore the coat off the corpse and cut the papers out of the inner pocket. There's the coat over there on the bank, with the great slash in it."

"But wait a minute," said the detective, Prince, quietly. "In that case there seems to be something of a mystery. A murderer might somehow have managed to throw the statue down on him, as he seems to have done. But I bet he couldn't easily have lifted it up again. I've tried; and I'm sure it would want three men at least. Yet we must suppose, on that theory, that the murderer first knocked him down as he walked past, using the statue as a stone club, then lifted it up again, took him out and deprived him of his coat, then put him back again in the posture of death and neatly replaced the statue. I tell you it's physically impossible. And how else could he have unclothed a man covered with that stone monument? It's worse than the conjurer's trick, when a man shuffles a coat off with his wrists tied."

"Could he have thrown down the statue after he'd stripped the corpse?" asked March.

"And why?" asked Prince, sharply. "If he'd killed his man and got his papers, he'd be away like the wind. He wouldn't potter about in a garden excavating the pedestals of statues. Besides—Hullo, who's that up there?"

High on the ridge above them, drawn in dark thin lines against the sky, was a figure looking so long and lean as to be almost spidery. The dark silhouette of the head showed two small tufts like horns; and they could almost have sworn that the horns moved.

"Archer!" shouted Herries, with sudden passion, and called to him with curses to come down. The figure drew back at the first cry, with an agitated movement so abrupt as almost to be called an antic. The next moment the man seemed to reconsider and collect himself, and began to come down the zigzag garden path, but with obvious reluctance, his feet falling in slower and slower rhythm. Through March's mind were throbbing the phrases that this man himself had used, about going mad in the middle of the night and wrecking the stone figure. Just so, he could fancy, the maniac who had done such a thing might climb the crest of the hill, in that feverish dancing fashion, and look down on the wreck he had made. But the wreck he had made here was not only a wreck of stone.

When the man emerged at last on to the garden path, with the full light on his face and figure, he was walking slowly indeed, but easily, and with no appearance of fear.

"This is a terrible thing," he said. "I saw it from above; I was taking a stroll along the ridge."

"Do you mean that you saw the murder?" demanded March, "or the accident? I mean did you see the statue fall?"

"No," said Archer, "I mean I saw the statue fallen."

Prince seemed to be paying but little attention; his eye was riveted on an object lying on the path a yard or two from the corpse. It seemed to be a rusty iron bar bent crooked at one end.

"One thing I don't understand," he said, "is all this blood. The poor fellow's skull isn't smashed; most likely his neck is broken; but blood seems to have spouted as if all his arteries were severed. I was wondering if some other instrument . . . that iron thing, for instance; but I don't see that even that is sharp enough. I suppose nobody knows what it is."

"I know what it is," said Archer in his deep but somewhat shaky voice. "I've seen it in my nightmares. It was the iron clamp or prop on the pedestal, stuck on to keep the wretched image upright when it began to wobble, I suppose. Anyhow, it was always stuck in the stonework there; and I suppose it came out when the thing collapsed."

Doctor Prince nodded, but he continued to look down at the pools of blood and the bar of iron.

"I'm certain there's something more underneath all this," he said at last. "Perhaps something more underneath the statue. I have a huge sort of hunch that there is. We are four men now and between us we can lift that great tombstone there."

They all bent their strength to the business; there was a silence save for heavy breathing; and then, after an instant of the tottering and staggering of eight legs, the great carven column of rock was rolled away, and the body lying in its shirt and trousers was fully revealed. The spectacles of Doctor Prince seemed almost to enlarge with a restrained radiance like great eyes; for other things were revealed also. One was that the unfortunate Hewitt had a deep gash across the jugular, which the triumphant doctor instantly identified as having been made with a sharp steel edge like a razor. The other was that immediately under the bank lay littered three shining scraps of steel, each nearly a foot long, one pointed and another fitted into a gorgeously jeweled hilt or handle. It was evidently a sort of long Oriental knife, long enough to be called a sword, but with a curious wavy edge; and there was a touch or two of blood on the point.

"I should have expected more blood, hardly on the point," observed Doctor Prince, thoughtfully, "but this is certainly the instrument. The slash was certainly made with a weapon shaped like this, and probably the slashing of the pocket as well. I suppose the brute threw in the statue, by way of giving him a public funeral."

March did not answer; he was mesmerized by the strange stones that glittered on the strange sword hilt; and their possible significance was broadening upon him like a dreadful dawn. It was a curious Asiatic weapon. He knew what name was connected in his memory with curious Asiatic weapons. Lord James spoke his secret thought for him, and yet it startled him like an irrelevance.

"Where is the Prime Minister?" Herries had cried, suddenly, and somehow like the bark of a dog at some discovery.

Doctor Prince turned on him his goggles and his grim face; and it was grimmer than ever.

531

"I cannot find him anywhere," he said. "I looked for him at once, as soon as I found the papers were gone. That servant of yours, Campbell, made a most efficient search, but there are no traces."

There was a long silence, at the end of which Herries uttered another cry, but upon an entirely new note.

"Well, you needn't look for him any longer," he said, "for here he comes, along with your friend Fisher. They look as if they'd been for a little walking tour."

The two figures approaching up the path were indeed those of Fisher, splashed with the mire of travel and carrying a scratch like that of a bramble across one side of his bald forehead, and of the great and gray-haired statesman who looked like a baby and was interested in Eastern swords and swordmanship. But beyond this bodily recognition, March could make neither head nor tail of their presence or demeanor, which seemed to give a final touch of nonsense to the whole nightmare. The more closely he watched them, as they stood listening to the revelations of the detective, the more puzzled he was by their attitude—Fisher seemed grieved by the death of his uncle, but hardly shocked at it; the older man seemed almost openly thinking about something else, and neither had anything to suggest about a further pursuit of the fugitive spy and murderer, in spite of the prodigious importance of the documents he had stolen. When the detective had gone off to busy himself with that department of the business, to telephone and write his report, when Herries had gone back, probably to the brandy bottle, and the Prime Minister had blandly sauntered away toward a comfortable armchair in another part of the garden, Horne Fisher spoke directly to Harold March.

"My friend," he said, "I want you to come with me at once; there is no one else I can trust so much as that. The journey will take us most of the day, and the chief business cannot be done till nightfall. So we can talk things over thoroughly on the way. But I want you to be with me; for I rather think it is my hour."

March and Fisher both had motor bicycles; and the first half of their day's journey consisted in coasting eastward amid the unconversational noise of those uncomfortable engines. But when they came out beyond Canterbury into the flats of eastern Kent, Fisher stopped at a pleasant little public house beside a sleepy stream; and they sat down to eat and to drink and to speak almost for the first time. It was a brilliant afternoon, birds were singing in the wood behind, and the sun shone full on their ale bench and table; but the face of Fisher in the strong sunlight had a gravity never seen on it before.

"Before we go any farther," he said, "there is something you ought to know. You and I have seen some mysterious things and got to the bottom of them before now; and it's only right that you should get to the bottom of this one. But in dealing with the death of my uncle I must begin at the other end from where our old detective yarns began. I will give you the steps of deduction presently, if you want to listen to them; but I did not reach the truth of this by steps of deduction. I will first of all tell you the truth itself, because I knew the truth from the first. The other cases I approached from the outside, but in this case I was inside. I myself was the very core and center of everything."

Something in the speaker's pendent eyelids and grave gray eyes suddenly shook March to his foundations; and he cried, distractedly, "I don't understand!" as men do when they fear that they do understand. There was no sound for a space but the happy chatter of the birds, and then Horne Fisher said, calmly:

"It was I who killed my uncle. If you particularly want more, it was I who stole the state papers from him."

"Fisher!" cried his friend in a strangled voice.

"Let me tell you the whole thing before we part," continued the other, "and let me put it, for the sake of clearness, as we used to put our old problems. Now there are two things that are puzzling people about that problem, aren't there? The first is how the murderer managed to slip off the dead man's coat, when he was already pinned to the ground with that stone incubus. The other, which is much smaller and less puzzling, is the fact of the sword that cut his throat being slightly stained at the point, instead of a good deal more stained at the edge. Well, I can dispose of the first question easily. Horne Hewitt took off his own coat before he was killed. I might say he took off his coat to be killed."

"Do you call that an explanation?" exclaimed March. "The words seem more meaningless, than the facts."

"Well, let us go on to the other facts," continued Fisher, equably. "The reason that particular sword is not stained at the edge with Hewitt's blood is that it was not used to kill Hewitt."

"But the doctor," protested March, "declared distinctly that the wound was made by that particular sword."

"I beg your pardon," replied Fisher. "He did not declare that it was made by that particular sword. He declared it was made by a sword of that particular pattern."

"But it was quite a queer and exceptional pattern," argued March; "surely it is far too fantastic a coincidence to imagine—"

"It was a fantastic coincidence," reflected Horne Fisher. "It's extraordinary what coincidences do sometimes occur. By the oddest chance in the world, by one chance in a million, it so happened that another sword of exactly the same shape was in the same garden at the same time. It may be partly explained, by the fact that I brought them both into the garden myself . . . come, my dear fellow; surely you can see now what it means. Put those two things together; there were two duplicate swords and he took off his coat for himself. It may assist your speculations to recall the fact that I am not exactly an assassin."

"A duel!" exclaimed March, recovering himself. "Of course I ought to have thought of that. But who was the spy who stole the papers?"

"My uncle was the spy who stole the papers," replied Fisher, "or who tried to steal the papers when I stopped him—in the only way I could. The papers, that should have gone west to reassure our friends and give them the plans for repelling the invasion, would in a few hours have been in the hands of the invader. What could I do? To have denounced one of our friends at this moment would have been to play into the hands of your friend Attwood, and all the party of panic and slavery. Besides, it may be that a man over forty has a subconscious desire to die as he has lived, and that I wanted, in a sense, to carry my secrets to the grave. Perhaps a hobby hardens with age; and my hobby has been silence. Perhaps I feel that I have killed my mother's brother, but I have saved my mother's name. Anyhow, I chose a time when I knew you were all asleep, and he was walking alone in the garden. I saw all the stone statues standing in the moonlight; and I myself was like one of those stone statues walking. In a voice that was not my own, I told him of his treason and demanded the papers; and when he refused, I forced him to take one of the two swords. The swords were among some specimens sent down here for the Prime Minister's inspection; he is a collector, you know; they were the only equal weapons I could find. To cut an ugly tale short, we fought there on the path in front of the Britannia statue; he was a man of great strength, but I had somewhat the advantage in skill. His sword grazed my forehead almost at the moment when mine sank into the joint in his neck. He fell against the statue, like Caesar against Pompey's, hanging on to the iron rail; his sword was already broken. When I saw the blood from that deadly wound, everything else went from me; I dropped my sword and ran as if to lift him up. As I bent toward him something happened too quick for me to follow. I do not know whether the iron bar was rotted with rust and came away in his hand, or whether he rent it out of the rock with his apelike strength; but the thing was in his hand, and with his dying energies he swung it over my head, as I knelt there unarmed beside him. I looked up wildly to avoid the blow, and saw above us the great bulk of Britannia leaning outward like the figurehead of a ship. The next instant I saw it was leaning an inch or two more than usual, and all the skies with their outstanding stars seemed to be leaning with it. For the third second it was as if the skies fell; and in the fourth I was standing in the quiet garden, looking down on that flat ruin of stone and bone at which you were looking to-day. He had plucked out the last prop that held up the British goddess, and she had fallen and crushed the traitor in her fall. I turned and darted for the coat which I knew to contain the package, ripped it up with my sword, and raced away up the garden path to where my motor bike was waiting on the road above. I had every reason for haste; but I fled without looking back at the statue and the body; and I think the thing I fled from was the sight of that appalling allegory.

"Then I did the rest of what I had to do. All through the night and into the daybreak and the daylight I went humming through the villages and markets of South England like a traveling bullet, till I came to the headquarters in the West where the trouble was. I was just in time. I was able to placard the place, so to speak, with the news that the government had not betrayed them, and that they would find supports if they would push eastward against the enemy. There's no time to tell you all that happened; but I tell you it was the day of my life. A triumph like a torchlight procession, with torchlights that might have been firebrands. The mutinies simmered down; the men of Somerset and the western counties came pouring into the market places; the men who died with Arthur and stood firm with Alfred. The Irish regiments rallied to them, after a scene like a riot, and marched eastward out of the town singing Fenian songs. There was all that is not understood, about the dark laughter of that people, in the delight with which, even when marching with the English to the defense of England, they shouted at the top of their voices, 'High upon the gallows tree stood the noble-hearted three . . . With England's cruel cord about them cast.' However, the chorus was 'God save Ireland,' and we could all have sung that just then, in one sense or another.

"But there was another side to my mission. I carried the plans of the defense; and to a great extent, luckily, the plans of the invasion also. I won't worry you with strategics; but we knew where the enemy had pushed forward the great battery that covered all his movements; and though our friends from the West could hardly arrive in time to intercept the main movement, they might get within long artillery range of the battery and shell it, if they only knew exactly where it was. They could hardly tell that unless somebody round about here sent up some sort of signal. But, somehow, I rather fancy that somebody will."

With that he got up from the table, and they remounted their machines and went eastward into the advancing twilight of evening. The levels of the landscape were repeated in flat strips of floating cloud and the last colors of day clung to the circle of the horizon. Receding farther and farther behind them was the semicircle of the last hills; and it was quite suddenly that they saw afar off the dim line of the sea. It was not a strip of bright blue as they had seen it from the sunny veranda, but of a sinister and smoky violet, a tint that seemed ominous and dark. Here Horne Fisher dismounted once more.

"We must walk the rest of the way," he said, "and the last bit of all I must walk alone."

He bent down and began to unstrap something from his bicycle. It was something that had puzzled his companion all the way in spite of what held him to more interesting riddles; it appeared to be several lengths of pole strapped together and wrapped up in paper. Fisher took it under his arm and began to pick his way across the turf. The ground was growing more tumbled and irregular and he was walking toward a mass of thickets and small woods; night grew darker every moment. "We must not talk any more," said Fisher. "I shall whisper to you when you are to halt. Don't try to follow me then, for it will only spoil the show; one man can barely crawl safely to the spot, and two would certainly be caught."

"I would follow you anywhere," replied March, "but I would halt, too, if that is better."

"I know you would," said his friend in a low voice. "Perhaps you're the only man I ever quite trusted in this world."

A few paces farther on they came to the end of a great ridge or mound looking monstrous against the dim sky; and Fisher stopped with a gesture. He caught his companion's hand and wrung it with a violent tenderness, and then darted forward into the darkness. March could faintly see his figure crawling along under the shadow of the ridge, then he lost sight of it, and then he saw it again standing on another mound two hundred yards away. Beside him stood a singular erection made apparently of two rods. He bent over it and there was the flare of a light; all March's schoolboy memories woke in him, and he knew what it was. It was the stand of a rocket. The confused, incongruous memories still possessed him up to the very moment of a fierce but familiar sound; and an instant after the rocket left its perch and went up into endless space like a starry arrow aimed at the stars. March thought suddenly of the signs of the last days and knew he was looking at the apocalyptic meteor of something like a Day of judgment.

Far up in the infinite heavens the rocket drooped and sprang into scarlet stars. For a moment the whole landscape out to the sea and back to the crescent of the wooded hills was like a lake of ruby light, of a red strangely rich and glorious, as if the world were steeped in wine rather than blood, or the earth were an earthly paradise, over which paused forever the sanguine moment of morning.

"God save England!" cried Fisher, with a tongue like the peal of a trumpet. "And now it is for God to save."

As darkness sank again over land and sea, there came another sound; far away in the passes of the hills behind them the guns spoke like the baying of great hounds. Something that was not a rocket, that came not hissing but screaming, went over Harold March's head and expanded beyond the mound into light and deafening din, staggering the brain with unbearable brutalities of noise. Another came, and then another, and the world was full of uproar and volcanic vapor and chaotic light. The artillery of the West country and the Irish had located the great enemy battery, and were pounding it to pieces.

In the mad excitement of that moment March peered through the storm, looking again for the long lean figure that stood beside the stand of the rocket. Then another flash lit up the whole ridge. The figure was not there.

Before the fires of the rocket had faded from the sky, long before the first gun had sounded from the distant hills, a splutter of rifle fire had flashed and flickered all around from the hidden trenches of the enemy. Something lay in the shadow at the foot of the ridge, as stiff as the stick of the fallen rocket; and the man who knew too much knew what is worth knowing.

Made in the USA
Columbia, SC
24 March 2021

34945623R00324